FINDING OUT

An Introduction to LGBT Studies

Deborah T. Meem
University of Cincinnati

Michelle A. Gibson
University of Cincinnati

Jonathan F. Alexander
University of California, Irvine

⑤SAGE

Los Angeles • London • New Delhi • Singapore • Washington DC

For information:

SAGE Publications, Inc.
2455 Teller Road
Thousand Oaks, California 91320
E-mail: order@sagepub.com

SAGE Publications Ltd.
1 Oliver's Yard
55 City Road
London EC1Y 1SP
United Kingdom

SAGE Publications India Pvt. Ltd.
B 1/I 1 Mohan Cooperative Industrial Area
Mathura Road, New Delhi 110 044
India

SAGE Publications Asia-Pacific Pte. Ltd.
33 Pekin Street #02-01
Far East Square
Singapore 048763

Printed in the United States of America

Library of Congress Cataloging-in-Publication Data

Meem, Deborah T. (Deborah Townsend), 1949–
Finding out : an introduction to LGBT studies / Deborah T. Meem, Michelle A. Gibson, Jonathan F. Alexander.
    p. cm.
Includes bibliographical references and index.
ISBN 978-1-4129-3864-8 (cloth)
ISBN 978-1-4129-3865-5 (pbk.)
    1. Homosexuality—History. 2. Gays—History. 3. Bisexuals—History. 4. Transgender people—History. I. Gibson, Michelle. II. Alexander, Jonathan. III. Title.

HQ76.25.M45 2009
306.76′609—dc22   2008027577

This book is printed on acid-free paper.

09 10 11 12 13   10 9 8 7 6 5 4 3 2 1

Acquisitions Editor:	Todd R. Armstrong
Editorial Assistant:	Aja Baker
Production Editor:	Astrid Virding
Copy Editor:	Gillian Dickens
Typesetter:	C&M Digitals (P) Ltd.
Proofreader:	Scott Oney
Indexer:	Molly Hall
Cover Designer:	Gail Buschman
Marketing Manager:	Carmel Schrire
Cover Art:	Court manicurists Niankhkhnum and Khnumhotep, from necropolis at Saqqara, Egypt. Illustration (c) Greg Reeder, 2008.

Contents

Preface: To the Instructor

Why do we teach introductory sexuality studies courses? For us, the motivation for developing these courses is our own sense that this curriculum has value, that it is important in and of itself, and that the kinds of fundamental knowledge and theoretical "practice" students learn can be applied in other academic and intellectual locations. In our experience, students come to these courses for similar reasons—they want to learn about issues that touch their lives in one way or another, and they want to do that learning in an academic setting that challenges them with new ways of knowing.

This book originated in our own classroom experiences. In teaching an Introduction to LGBT Studies course, we found that students ranged in background from advanced undergraduate women's studies majors well versed in the rudiments of queer history and basic interdisciplinary methodology to first-year students who enrolled in the course after having met the first person they knew to be lesbian, gay, bisexual, or transgender (LGBT). Before writing *Finding Out,* we noticed that much of what was available for use in sexuality studies courses was either too simplistic (celebratory texts that did little to engage students in theoretical analyses of issues related to sexuality) or too advanced (anthologies of theoretical articles that assumed a basic knowledge of the theories themselves and of general LGBT history and culture). Our students encountered the first type of text with enthusiasm, but as instructors, we felt frustrated by the absence in the texts themselves of tools for teaching analysis and encouraging more sophisticated thinking. The latter type of text had students feeling frustrated; we spent much of our time in our courses helping students understand what they had read, a reality that left us wishing for more time to engage students in discussions that critiqued and connected those texts.

As far as we knew, no book existed that offered a general introduction to this subject matter grounded in an accessible theoretical framework. So, we created *Finding Out* principally out of our own need to bring together texts and materials to facilitate the teaching of LGBT studies at the introductory level. In other words, we designed *Finding Out* to lie between what we might call the "oversimplification" extreme and the "undersimplification" extreme. This has meant offering in each chapter discussion and analyses that penetrate below the surface to underlying ideas and ideologies, while at the same time presenting the material clearly and accessibly enough to be interesting to a reader new to the subject matter. It has also meant foregrounding primary sources in the end-of-chapter readings, on the assumption that students will encounter critical and theoretical material in more advanced courses.

We recognize that LGBT studies is a fairly new area of academic endeavor, and these courses still elicit strong negative reactions in certain places. It is not uncommon to make attempts at mitigating these reactions by approaching courses with LGBT content as attempts to educate "toward tolerance," thereby garnering support for LGBT people. We begin with the assumption that teaching about diversity, including sexual and affectional diversity, needs no justification. Thus, as you will see, our language is not about "tolerating" diversity but about honoring it. In the United States, one of the best-known organizations designed to promote multicultural education is Teaching Tolerance, which "provides educators with free educational materials that promote respect for differences and appreciation of diversity in the classroom and beyond" ("About"). Supported by the Southern Poverty Law Center, this organization maintains a website that is accessed by educators whose desire is to help their students learn about difference—including some nonnormative sexualities—as a way of becoming more "tolerant" citizens. We support such an endeavor. We do believe that the culture and society benefit from education, and as queer scholars, we are particularly interested in education about sexuality. We are concerned, though, that the notion of "tolerance" presupposes certain assumptions that we hope *Finding Out* challenges. The very idea of tolerance, for instance (to borrow Wendy Brown's words) "is necessitated by something one would prefer did not exist. It involves managing the presence of the undesirable" (25). The very act of tolerating, then, is an act of subordination that places one group in the position of power—the power to confer tolerance— and another in the position of subordination—the desire to be tolerated.

We recognize that learning tolerance may be a good starting place for many students, particularly those coming to a study of LGBT people and culture for the first time. But we also hope for much more. In writing *Finding Out,* we have sought an intellectual approach that analyzes how sexuality has become a central component in contemporary self-understanding—individually, culturally, and politically. We also desire a recognition of how many queer cultures bring substantive, potentially transformative insights to bear on mainstream and dominant modes of being. Put simply, we value how our queer visions help us see the world in intellectually, politically, and personally capacious ways. We have tried to create an accessible introductory text—and doing so has entailed its own particular risks.

In aiming this book at a general audience, including academic beginners, we have risked the criticism of being *too* introductory. It is true that we intend *Finding Out* to be used in introductory-level college classes (in sexuality studies, of course, but also possibly in English composition, sociology, or other areas). But we have taken pains not to condescend to our readers; we have sought to include considerable detail as well as in-depth discussion and theoretical grounding to maintain the intellectual challenge throughout. You may regret that many of the readings are excerpted rather than reproduced in their entirety. We have had to bow to the economic reality of word count requirements. These requirements may also mean that readers will not see everything they hope for in the text. We have tried to choose topics that allow us to discuss issues through selected examples rather than exhaustive lists. *Finding Out* is, after all, a textbook, not an encyclopedia, and we have attempted to elucidate principles and ideas, knowing that much will be left out.

Through our weaving together of primary documents, secondary sources, and our own commentary, we hope not only to illuminate events and ideas but also to raise the vexed issue of who is empowered to tell the stories of LGBT lives. To be sure, from the time of Plato and Sappho through Walt Whitman and Gertrude Stein and James Baldwin to Sarah Schulman and Manuel Muñoz, homosexed individuals have written their stories. But the "queer" aspect of these stories has often been denied in a bid for safety and respect, or coded to avoid general understanding, or subsumed under the culture's dominant narratives, or produced in a location far from home and friends. Only in the past few decades have LGBT people—in a few particular places in the world—had the luxury of expressing their queerness publicly. In writing *Finding Out*, we claim the privilege of writing about our own people, in our own language, from our own point of view.

Acknowledgments

From the very beginning, *Finding Out* has been a collaborative effort. Not only were we writing the book collaboratively (no mean feat!), but we have relied on the help of many colleagues, students, and friends in bringing this project to fruition. We would like particularly to thank the following:

- Kimberly Campanello, the Queen of Permissions, without whom we might not have finished this project;
- Kai Kohlsdorf, the Knave of Permissions, who got the permissions ball rolling before passing it on to Kimberly;
- Matthew Conley, LaNaya Freeman, Nicole Karr, Emily Schweppe, Emma Southard, and Tracie Williams, undergraduate students in Deb's LGBT

studies class at the University of Cincinnati in winter 2008, who produced the first version of the glossary that appears at the end of this book;

- Maika Arnold, David Bailey, Hannah Bare, Scott Cahall, Sarah Charlesworth, Kersha Deibel-Trotter, Jessica Elliott, Lucas Hartman, Eric Holtel, Tara King, Jane Meek, Keyra Miller, Lura Miller, Emma Plikerd, Jennifer Poon, Jamie Royce, Sarah Szekeresh, and Angelina Venti, the remainder of the winter 2008 LGBT studies class, who offered helpful suggestions and put up with small inconveniences as we field-tested *Finding Out*;
- Mary Bucklin and her Introduction to LGBT Studies class at Northern Kentucky University, who field-tested *Finding Out* during fall semester 2007;
- Anne Runyan and the Department of Women's Studies at the University of Cincinnati, for general practical and moral support;
- The Friends of Women's Studies, University of Cincinnati, for a grant to help with permissions;
- John Bryan, former Dean of University College at the University of Cincinnati, for supporting our intention to offer sexuality studies courses;
- Janet Reed, former Head of the Language Arts Department in University College at the University of Cincinnati, for making sure LGBT Studies was consistently scheduled;
- Dorothy Smith, archivist extraordinaire, for teaching us how to produce hi-res photos;
- Stuart Blersch, Professor Emeritus of English at the University of Cincinnati, for information on gays and lesbians under the Nazi regime;
- Jana Braziel, Associate Professor of English, University of Cincinnati, for references concerning diaspora;
- Liz Roccoforte (Women's Studies MA, 2005) for the insight that *Shrek 2* is at root a "home-to-meet-the-folks" coming-out story;
- Todd Armstrong, our editor at Sage Publications, and also Aja Baker, Katie Grim, Sarah Quesenberry, and Camille Herrera, editorial assistants at Sage; and
- reviewers of the text, who provided insightful and helpful comments throughout this project:

    Mary A. Armstrong (Department of Women's Studies, California Polytechnic State University, San Luis Obispo)

    John C. Beynon (Department of English, California State University, Fresno)

    Stephanie Brzuzy (Department of Social Work, Xavier University)

    Dane S. Claussen (Department of Journalism and Mass Communication, Point Park University)

    Stefanie K. Dunning (Department of English, Miami University)

Bradley Gangnon (Department of Communication and Theatre Arts, College of St. Scholastica)

Carol Guess (Department of English and American Cultural Studies, Western Washington University)

David M. Halperin (Department of English, University of Michigan)

Laura A. Harris (Department of English, World Literature, and Black Studies, Pitzer College)

Keguro Macharia (Department of Rhetoric, University of Illinois, Urbana-Champaign)

Sarah-Hope Parmeter (Department of Writing, University of California, Santa Cruz)

David A. Powell (LGBT Studies Program, Hofstra University)

Meredith Raimondo (Department of Comparative American Studies, Oberlin College)

Joyleen Valero Sapinoso (Women's Studies and LGBT Studies, University of Maryland)

Cole Woodcox (Department of English, Truman State University)

Gust A. Yep (Department of Speech & Communication Studies, San Francisco State University)

Naida Zukic (Department of Speech Communication, Southern Illinois University, Carbondale)

Finally, we wish to thank the people in our lives who have supported us while we have worked on this multiyear project: Deb thanks her mother, Barbara T. Meem, for reading and commenting on a draft of the manuscript; Michelle thanks her sister Julie Edwards, whose courage and strength inspire; and Jonathan thanks his partner, Mack McCoy, for living with this project for three years.

REFERENCES

"About Teaching Tolerance." Tolerance.org: A Web Project of the Southern Poverty Law Center. <http://www.tolerance.org/teach/about/index.jsp>.

Brown, Wendy. *Regulating Aversion: Tolerance in the Age of Identity and Empire.* Princeton, NJ: Princeton UP, 2006.

Introduction:
To the Reader

I n the Middle Ages, the Catholic Church prescribed the death penalty for same-sex erotic behavior but also created liturgies for same-sex marriages. In the late nineteenth century, European sexologist Richard von Krafft-Ebing argued for same-sex desire as an illness to be "cured" at the same time that his contemporary, Havelock Ellis, saw it as a variation of human typology. In 1977, Anita Bryant's Save Our Children organization successfully defeated a gay-positive human rights ordinance in Dade County, Florida; at the same time, Harvey Milk was elected as the first openly gay member of the San Francisco Board of Supervisors. And in the first decade of the twenty-first century, U.S. president George W. Bush supported a constitutional amendment banning gay marriage; his counterparts in other nations—such as Spain, South Africa, and Canada—enacted constitutional protections for lesbian and gay people.

So much of what we know to be "fact" about lesbian, gay, bisexual, and transgender (LGBT) life and culture is given to us as story, as narratives that transmit ideas, information, and values about who queer people are. But who tells those stories, and what do they tell us?

Finding Out is a book about these and many other similar questions. It narrates and analyzes some of the ways in which LGBT and queer people have been represented—and have come to represent themselves—in a variety of fields: literature, history, the arts, the sciences, media, and politics. But if *Finding Out* is, as its subtitle indicates, an *introduction* to LGBT studies, then what does that mean, exactly? The very act of introducing a topic is often about the telling of stories. One common assignment given by instructors who want students to see the connections between what they are studying in the classroom and the world outside the classroom is the interview assignment. The storytelling involved in the interview process creates connection between teller and listener, and often between past and present. We hope that the stories we tell in *Finding Out* will help to create (or, in the case of readers who are already somewhat familiar with LGBT culture and history, capitalize upon) a similar kind of connection.

But we also recognize that the process of telling and retelling these stories is challenging. As you can see in the examples above, narratives of LGBT experience have often embodied a push-me/pull-you simultaneity of coexisting yet conflicting forces. Given this, we have written *Finding Out* to enact a kind of theorized storytelling, a simultaneous offering and critique of narratives that contribute to our understanding of terms such as *lesbian, gay, bisexual,* and *transgender.* As you read, you will see this theorized storytelling consistently at work. On one hand, we have the opportunity to highlight the many ways same-sex desires and gender nonconformity have existed throughout history. On the other hand, the stories told about those desires and about that nonconformity are often very complex. At different times and in different locations, people tell very different stories about their desires, even if, on the surface, the similarities tempt us to understand their stories as like our own. Paying attention to critical differences, however, is an important part of understanding not only how same-sex desires and gender variance were experienced in the past but also how they have come to exist today.

Some Theoretical Starting Places

As you can see, our approach to LGBT history, culture, and politics is not simply to record facts. History is never as simple as the recorded facts. Like most students and all scholars, we begin with theories about what forces have affected the evolution of LGBT history and the emergence of LGBT culture. We assume first that any historical survey must be undertaken with great care and caution. In writing about the history of same-sex desires and the formation of LGBT identities, we acknowledge a lineage of queer thinking. We attempt to attend carefully to Judith Halberstam's notion of "perverse presentism." Halberstam warns that anyone writing about the past needs to consider responsibly how contemporary notions and constructions of desire and identity can easily be imposed on past persons, incidents, or issues. She argues instead for a "perversely presentist model of historical analysis, a model, in other words, that avoids the trap of simply projecting contemporary understandings back in time, but one that can apply insights from the present to conundrums of the past" (52–53). When we write about the past, we do not assume that contemporary labels are necessarily useful to describe past desires. What looks like a gay, lesbian, bi, or trans identity from our current perspective may have meant something very different to people in earlier times.

Second, we have attempted to highlight the diversity of same-sex desire and gender variance. Understanding that the "queer" experience is complex, we honor the varieties and diversities of that experience by looking not only at gay and lesbian lives but also at bisexual and trans lives. Terminology takes on particular importance in this context, for the attempt to avoid constructing the past in contemporary terms often means taking great care with the way we choose to name. *Lesbian,* for instance, shifts in meaning over time from a geographical term to a poetic style to an identity marker. *Gay* as a slang term originally referred to a (female) prostitute. The meaning has since slipped to delineate a sexually transgressive subculture, a black lesbian, and a homosexual man. *Bisexual* originally functioned as a synonym for what we now call *heterosexual,* a term that was itself originally coined to describe nonprocreative sexuality between men and women. Today, the term *bisexual* refers to a person who experiences sexual desire for both men and women. The terms *transgender, transsexual, transman, tranny boi, FtM, MtF,* and so forth describe varieties of role nonconformism based on either biological sex or gender, assuming that these are not only socially constructed but also fluid. *Queer* is perhaps the most elusive of such terms. Once a taunt used against homosexuals, queer has recently been reclaimed by a variety of activists and theorists—as an "umbrella" term to signify the diversity of LGBT identities and to assert positively the value of *difference.* However, many object to the term, arguing that it erases important differences among the L, the G, the B, and the T.

Third, we believe that the same awareness needs also to be applied when we think cross-culturally; while same-sex desires might imply gay, lesbian, or bisexual identity in the United States, this is not necessarily true in other cultures, particularly outside of the Global North. We reject the notion of a global gay identity, and we believe that it is imperative to understand sexual and gendered experiences in the contexts—the time and the place—in which they occur. We refuse, for instance,

> to fix the term "gay" . . . as a prerequisite for global interaction and coalition. For it is in the permutations of this term and its legacies, as they circulate around the globe, in queer organizations and gatherings, from Mexico City's Semana Cultural Lésbico-Gay to New Delhi's Campaign for Lesbian Rights and Beijing's International Women's Conference, from Buenos Aires's Marcha de Orgullo Gay to the diasporic South Asian and Latino Lesbian and Gay Pride Parade in Queens, New York, that the future of the human and civil rights of queers also lies. (Cruz-Malavé and Manalansan 4)

We hope, in other words, to examine same-sex and nonnormative desires in various locations worldwide not with the purpose of fitting them into a grand teleological narrative linking globalization with sexual freedom. Rather, we identify connections and similarities among movements and experiences as we observe them, and where possible, we allow agents to tell their own stories. We intend these stories to trouble monolithic social narratives, believing with Gayatri Gopinath that "essentialized concepts of national and diasporic identity are most fruitfully contested from a 'queer diasporic' positionality" (150). However, while we attempt to offer a sense of the global experience of LGBT people, same-sex practices, and gender variance, we must acknowledge that our strengths as scholars lie in the history and culture of LGBT people in the Global North in general and in the United States in particular. Still, *Finding Out* ranges widely across major events, issues, and ideas pertaining to nonnormative sexualities and gender variance around the world.

Fourth, we believe that the experiences of race, social class, and sexuality are intertwined in compelling ways, and we have attempted throughout *Finding Out* to represent those intersections. Too often, LGBT and sexuality studies have been dominated by scholars who have paid scant attention to issues of race and social class. Failing to pay such attention, however, robs our understanding of same-sex histories, identities, and issues of important dimensions. Our experiences are multiply inflected—not just by sexuality but also by race, ethnicity, and social class. For instance, to understand gays and lesbians participating as artists in the Harlem Renaissance of the 1920s is to see those artists not just as gays and lesbians but also as African American gays and lesbians living in a racist and homophobic culture. In terms of social class, it is important to understand that the primary participants in the Stonewall riots of 1969 were working-class drag queens; the riots occurred in a specifically working-class context. However, since 1969, gay and lesbian rights organizations in the United States have come to be dominated by middle-class people and middle-class concerns. How did this happen? Answering that question involves looking critically not only at issues of sexuality but also at issues of social class. Doing so, however, can be intellectually—and personally—challenging.

In *Disidentifications: Queers of Color and the Performance of Politics*, José Esteban Muñoz writes, "Subjects who are outside the purview of dominant public spheres encounter obstacles in enacting identifications. Minority identifications are often neglectful or antagonistic to other minoritarian positionalities" (8). In the United States, for instance, we generally see identity in binary terms—of color or white, gay or straight. A person occupying multiple "nonnormative" categories may be met with incomprehension and even hostility, both from the normative culture and from the minority groups with which one identifies. A working-class Asian American lesbian, for instance, may have her queer identification overlooked by a dominant culture that sees her first and foremost as "not white," while some in her ethnic community may find her queerness disgraceful, to herself, to her family, and to Asian Americans in general. Examining such complexities is crucial if we are to honor the varieties of LGBT and queer experience as well as understand some of the difficulties that people face, individually and collectively, in their search for equality, freedom, and community. To enrich our understanding of these dimensions of experience, *Finding Out* actively marks class, race, and ethnicity, both in general discussion and separated out for deeper analysis.

Finally, because of the complexities we have discussed, we assume that the study of LGBT sexualities, same-sex desires, and gender variance is necessarily an interdisciplinary enterprise, and *Finding Out* borrows extensively from scholarship in fields including history and the social sciences, the arts and humanities, popular culture and media studies, and politics and law. We have attempted to represent as carefully as possible both the methodologies and the findings generated by scholars in these various fields—and we have learned much ourselves from thinking about queer lives and cultures from an interdisciplinary perspective. When we talk about "identity" and "culture," we are talking about constructs that are simultaneously personal, aesthetic, social, cultural, and political. Stated in political terms, what individual LGBT people experience is important—but not just to the individual; it is important for the way it speaks to and interacts with the experiences of others.

About This Book

We initially envisioned *Finding Out* as a textbook for use in a wide variety of college courses that focus on lesbian, gay, bisexual, and transgender identities, communities, and sexualities. To that end, we have included in the text a number of features designed to advance your thinking—whether you are reading this book for a class, as part of a reading group, or on your own—as you find out more about LGBT/queer lives and cultures. For instance, throughout the chapters, Lambda Links—indicated by lambda [λ] signs—alert readers that an issue under discussion is related to a similar topic in another chapter. You can use these like "hot links" on a website to follow threads of content throughout the book. Then, at the end of each chapter, you will find sets of questions and suggestions for further reading. These are designed as teaching tools for use by students in classroom environments or by individual readers who wish to think or read more deeply about issues addressed in the chapter. They are not intended to be comprehensive; they will not address all of the issues in a given chapter. We urge you to use the discussion questions to continue your own exploration of the many contexts in which same-sex desires and gender variance exist. Finally, **boldfaced** terms in each chapter are defined in the glossary at the end of *Finding Out*.

Part of the challenge of writing *Finding Out* has been recognizing the interdisciplinary nature of LGBT studies. To address this interdisciplinarity, *Finding Out* has four large sections: History, Politics, Literature and the Arts, and Media. These four sections are subdivided into chapters. The first section, History, introduces you to and surveys the various ways sexuality has been configured in a variety of cultural, scientific, and psychological arenas from ancient Greek and Roman culture to the contemporary world. Chapter 1, "Before Identity: The Ancient World through the Nineteenth Century," focuses on same-sex relationships, gender bending, and other aspects of queerness from antiquity to the nineteenth century, specifically elucidating the preidentity history of queerness that either helped shape or stood in opposition to later, more formal claims to queer identity. Picking up the historical thread in the late nineteenth century, Chapter 2, "Sexology: Constructing the Modern Homosexual," describes how medical and sexological models at the fin de siècle pathologized a wide variety of sexual "deviances." This chapter explores some of the pressures that led to the development of this model. In the context of the pathologization of homosexuality by the psychological establishment in the early twentieth century, Chapter 3, "Toward Liberation," examines the rise of queer liberation movements. We end this chapter with the removal of homosexuality from the *Diagnostic and Statistical Manual of Mental Disorders.* Then, recognizing that many LGBT people in the English-speaking world view the Stonewall riots in New York City as a kind of turning point in LGBT history, Chapter 4, "Stonewall and Beyond," focuses on queer Americans as we integrated the lessons learned from other liberation movements into our own struggles for human and civil rights.

The second section, Politics, explores how sex and sexuality—particularly queer sexualities—remain a hot topic in contemporary political arenas. Chapters in this section challenge you to think deeply and critically about the political dimensions of LGBT life and culture, with discussions ranging from LGBT identity politics to a consideration of the challenges queer theory issues to such a politics. These chapters also provide an examination of the uses (and abuses) of strategies of assimilation, as well as exploration of intersections among LGBT and other marginalized identities and communities. Chapter 5, "Nature, Nurture, and Identity," focuses on one of the central ongoing debates about queerness: whether homosexuality is a biological essence or a social construction. Chapter 6, "Inclusion and Equality," examines a related set of debates regarding the integration or exclusion of queers in society, focusing particularly on the complex and sometimes conflicting attitudes that create the tensions within the discussion. Such debates about inclusion and exclusion also occur *within* queer communities, and Chapter 7, "Queer Diversities," details the parameters of some of those debates.

Finally, Chapter 8, "Intersectionalities," looks specifically at how race, social class, gender, and sex are aspects of identity that intersect with queerness. This chapter highlights common struggles across aspects of identities as well as divergences in how multiply-identified individuals and groups understand and represent their experiences.

In the third section, Literature and the Arts, we consider how the arts have long been a space in which homo-, bi-, and trans-erotic desires and identities have been explored and interrogated. Chapters in this section include a number of primary texts—both literary and graphical—that highlight how many artists, working in a variety of forms and genres, have grappled with the meaning of queer sexualities. Our critical introductions and discussions frame each literary or artistic text. Chapter 9, "Homosexed Art and Literature," ranges from Walt Whitman to Audre Lorde, Michelangelo to Frida Kahlo. Our focus is on art and literature that is well known in LGBT communities, and we include examples of political and activist art in addition to purely aesthetic work. Moving away from the realm of "high" art, Chapter 10, "Lesbian Pulp Novels and Gay Physique Pictorials," focuses on the two main forms of popular homosexed entertainment during the middle of the twentieth century in the United States; this chapter illustrates how popular culture helps solidify a sense of queer identity. Chapter 11, "Queer Transgressive Aesthetics," notes how some works of art and literature intentionally challenge our understanding of sexuality with highly provocative images and rhetoric. This chapter presents material that encourages analysis of sexuality that runs deeper than traditional distinctions among sexual preferences; such work questions normalizing assumptions. Chapter 12, "Censorship and Moral Panic," considers controversies about homosexed art and documents particular cases of censorship motivated by homophobia.

Chapters in the final section, Media, discuss mass media, including television, movies, the Internet, and alternative publications. Chapter 13, "Film and Television," examines how images of queers in film and TV have had a long and complicated history in the twentieth century. The explosion of lesbian and gay images beginning in the 1990s represents a turning point in queer visibility. In this chapter, we see how visibility can operate as a double-edged sword, diluting the power of underground community while ostensibly promoting mainstream acceptance. We also know that contemporary LGBT people find representation and community through the Internet, which can provide queer community in a virtual world. Chapter 14, "Queers and the Internet," discusses myths about the Internet, as well as social networking and activist sites and their uses. And Chapter 15, "The Politics of Location: Alternative Media and the Search for Queer Space," describes how a variety of nonmainstream media have assisted LGBT people in developing both identity and community. We situate our discussion of such media in terms of how a variety of queer people use them to foster and develop a livable space in which to encounter, explore, and build a queer culture.

We hope that you will find *Finding Out* a lively, provocative, and challenging experience. You will not agree with everything you read, and at times you will probably feel that there is much we have left out—and you will be right. But we believe that *Finding Out* offers you a substantive and critical approach to thinking about the history of sexuality, the emergence of LGBT identities, and the development of a queer culture. If it prompts you to find out more about queerness, then it will have accomplished its primary goal. So, with that in mind, we invite you to start finding out. . . .

References

Cruz-Malavé, Arnaldo, and Martin F. Manalansan IV. "Introduction: Dissident Sexualities/Alternative Globalisms." *Queer Globalizations: Citizenship and the Afterlife of Colonialism*. Ed. Arnaldo Cruz-Malavé and Martin F. Manalansan IV. New York: NYU P, 2002. 1–10.

Gopinath, Gayatri. "Local Sites/Global Contexts: The Transnational Trajectories of Deepa Mehta's *Fire*." *Queer Globalizations: Citizenship and the Afterlife of Colonialism*. Ed. Arnaldo Cruz- Malavé and Martin F. Manalansan IV. New York: NYU P, 2002. 149–61.

Halberstam, Judith. *In a Queer Time and Place: Transgender Bodies, Subcultural Lives*. New York: NYU P, 2005.

Muñoz, José Esteban. *Disidentifications: Queers of Color and the Performance of Politics*. Minneapolis: U of Minnesota P, 1999.

SECTION I

History

CHAPTER 1

Before Identity

The Ancient World through the Nineteenth Century

Homosexuality has been conceived of as an innate or acquired identity only in the past century and a half, but same-sex practices, desires, and intimacies, as well as gender variance, can be found in nearly every culture in recorded history. Until the "invention" of homosexual identity, these practices and desires typically were not described in written records; instead, their existence is revealed in words in national lexicons (such as *skesana* or boy-wife in South Africa or *kojobesia* in Ghana) or in laws against same-sex sexual practices (such as the "ignorance" forbidden in Qur'an 27:55). In some communities, including many in the pre-Columbian Americas and in India, males who adopted female gender had special shamanic or ceremonial places in cultural practice. In ancient Egypt, two men who served as

Figure 1.1 Court manicurists Niankhkhnum and Khnumhotep, from the necropolis at Saqqara, Egypt.

manicurists to the king were buried together, pictured in the same stylized embrace that characterized the depiction of husband-wife pairs in formal funerary art.

In Greece, the social and sexual relationship between an older man and a youth represented the ideal form of love. A 2,000-year-old rock painting in Zimbabwe shows male-male sex. This chapter presents a brief glimpse into historical records that imply the existence of same-sex intimacies in various cultures prior to the nineteenth-century conceptualization of homosexual identity.

We do not claim that these historical records attest to the presence of "homosexuality" or "gay identity" across cultures and time. Contemporary scholars debate whether such is the case. Some thinkers—Charley Shively and Blanche Wiesen Cook, to name two—have operated on the assumption that the sexual categories observable in the Global North today are "universal, static, and permanent, suitable for the analysis of all human beings and all societies" (Padgug 56). Others argue that sexuality has a history and has evolved over time. Robert Padgug, for instance, observes that "[s]exuality is relational" (58)—in other words, how any given social group or culture thinks of sexuality relates to historical time and place. Historian Stephen Garton argues that "sexuality has emerged as a major field of historical inquiry" over the past half century; thus, "instead of being something natural, [sexuality] came to be seen by historians as subject to historical change" (28–29). One major consequence of this shift in our understanding about sexuality is that most historians are careful not to read historical records of same-sex desire as "gay" or "homosexual" in the contemporary sense.

We should keep in mind that casting an eye to the past to find evidence of "gay," "lesbian," or "trans" identity is to assume that history can and should be read through contemporary lenses. It is also to assume that people and groups of the past understood their sexual intimacies in the same way we do. These are problematic assumptions. This is one moment when it might be useful to refer back to the theory of "perverse presentism" discussed in the introduction to this book [λ Introduction]. It highlights the need to avoid imposing current ideas about and constructions of sexuality on the past at the same time that it acknowledges the historical expression of sexual intimacies and practices that seem connected to current LGBT identifications and practices. To understand past sexual practices—and to honor them—we, like many contemporary historians of sexuality, refrain from identifying historical representations of same-sex desires as specifically "gay," "lesbian," or "homosexual." Likewise, regarding past instances of apparent gender variance, we avoid the terms *transgender* and *transsexual*.

At the same time, while the Egyptian manicurists who were buried together may not be "gay" in contemporary parlance, we acknowledge that it has been very important and empowering for many contemporary lesbian, gay, bisexual, and transgender (LGBT) people to discover and identify what looks like same-sex intimacy and gender variance in the annals of history. Such identification has been a crucial part of "finding out" about ourselves as contemporary queers and LGBT folk. It has at times provided a sense of history to those who have found themselves left out of world histories that stigmatize or simply ignore **gender** and sexual "outlaws" or nonconformists.

Greek *Paiderastia*

Gay men and lesbians often cite the ancient Greeks as their historical forbears—and for good reason. The ancient Greeks developed ways of recognizing and even honoring same-sex desires. Probably the principal source for ancient Greek *paiderastia* (or **pederasty**: love between a man and a boy) is Homer's *Iliad.* In that epic, likely composed in the eighth or ninth century BCE, the Greek hero Achilles, feeling slighted by the king, withdraws from the fighting outside Troy. His youthful lover Patroclus, fearing that Achilles is losing honor, puts on Achilles's armor and goes out to fight in his place. The less powerful Patroclus is killed; his death spurs Achilles to return to the battlefield and defeat the Trojan Hector.

This model of heroic love was absorbed into Greek cultural life in the centuries following the *Iliad.* In Plato's *Symposium,* written in 360 BCE, Phaedrus declares, "I know not any greater blessing to a young man who is beginning life than a virtuous lover or to the lover than a beloved youth" (5). A Greek same-sex pair included the *erastes* or older man and an *eromenos* or youth. The eromenos was typically a postadolescent between the ages of about twelve and eighteen; once a young man's beard sprouted, he was considered past the age of eromenos. The Greeks did not favor same-sex relationships between men of similar age; the erastes-eromenos pairing was designed to provide pleasure and friendship for the older erastes in exchange for protection, training, and social advantage for the younger eromenos. Same-sex attachments did not preclude heterosexual marriage, but the pederastic combination of spiritual and physical connection represented a higher kind of love, more conducive to the military, political, and educational responsibilities of the (male) citizen of the Greek state.

Nearly all literary production was accomplished by men, and women in the classical world were generally depicted as "goddesses, whores, wives, and slaves" (Pomeroy). Ancient Greek women were certainly not invisible in their lives, but they might as well have been, if all we knew of them was what the literature contained. A notable exception was the poet Sappho, who lived in the seventh century BCE on the island of Lesbos (thus the word *Lesbian*). Sappho was known in her day as an unparalleled

Find Out More in the Sappho poems at the end of this chapter.

lyric poet, meaning that her poems were written to be accompanied by a lyre. Her refinements upon common lyric meter led poets after her time to attempt writing in "Sapphic meter." Little of Sappho's work has survived, and that which has is mostly in fragments, yet she is still known for her sensuous and personal poetic voice. Many young wealthy Greek women were sent to Lesbos to study the arts with Sappho. Much of Sappho's surviving poetry is love lyrics to these young women.

Pederasty in Other Early Cultures: The Middle East and Far East

Find Out More in the Abu Nuwas poem at the end of this chapter.

The Qur'an sends a mixed message concerning same-sex desires. On one hand, it specifically forbids same-sex intercourse on earth; on the other, the virtuous man will be surrounded by beautiful boys in Paradise. Indeed, historically, a long tradition of man-boy love exists in the Arab world. The practice of *liwat* (pederasty) involved a relationship between a *luti* (a man with a predilection for beardless boys) and an *amrad* (unpaid beardless boy) or a *murd mu'ajirin* (paid boy).

Abu Nuwas, well-known Iraqi poet of the eighth to ninth century CE, began his career as amrad to the older poet Walibah ibn al-Hubab. By the time of Sultan Mahmud of Ghazni (in present-day Afghanistan) around 1000 CE, liwat had come to represent a type of ideal love. Sultan Mahmud and his slave Ayaz were devoted partners; Mahmud later appointed Ayaz ruler of Lahore (in present-day Pakistan). Like Greek pederasty, liwat signified passion and pleasure for the luti, as well as affection and social advancement for the amrad.

In Japan, endorsed courtly same-sex desire was known as *wakashu-do,* or the way of the boy. It first appears in written records beginning in the Heian (Peace and Tranquility) period (794–1185 CE). Its rise in popularity in the twelfth century seems to have coincided with that of the *No* and *Kabuki* theater traditions, which featured boy actors. Wakashu-do, like Greek and Islamic pederasty, was built around the pedagogic relationship between an adult man

Figure 1.2 Sultan Mahmud and his slave Ayaz.

and a youth. Like the others, it also flourished in the upper classes of society; it was specifically valued among the samurai in the sixteenth and seventeenth centuries. Beginning around 1600, as Japan began to be influenced by Western Christianity, wakashu-do gradually lost favor; when the Americans arrived, armed and wealthy, in 1854, Japanese same-sex desires sank into invisibility.

In China, a powerful male-male culture surrounding opera performers lasted throughout the Qing dynasty (1644–1911). Upper-class opera patrons saw the attractive adolescents playing female roles as models of feminine beauty; these young men were also trained as catamites, or boys for hire. In postimperial twentieth-century China, the opera (and, by extension, its connection with male-male love) was scorned as a throwback to the time of feudal excesses.

> **Find Out More** in the selection from "Bamboo Clappers Strike the Hateful Number" at the end of this chapter.

> **Find Out More** in the "Song of Beau Wang" at the end of this chapter.

Gender Variance in Pre-Columbian America and India

In many Native American tribes before first contact with white missionaries or settlers, a person who possessed characteristics of both genders was thought of as a "two-spirit," one who understands male and female. This border knowledge carried with it spiritual and physical power; thus, "two-spirit" individuals were particularly suited to function as shamans or healers and were valued in some tribal groups accordingly. In the centuries before contact with Europeans, tribal languages developed various words for the two-spirit person: *nadle* (Navajo), *lhamana* (Zuñi), *winkte* (Lakota), and so on. European explorers brought with them the term *berdache*, now often used to describe Native American postcontact gender nonconformists. A berdache typically switched gender entirely. We-wha (c. 1849–1896), a Zuñi, dressed as a woman and did women's work exclusively. We-wha was highly skilled in weaving and pottery making and was also a central figure in the pueblo's spiritual life. In 1886, she accompanied her white friend, anthropologist Matilda Coxe Stevenson, to Washington, D.C.; no one, including Stevenson, knew at the time that We-wha was born

Figure 1.3 We-wha, c. 1886.

male. While some recorded instances exist of females appropriating male roles as berdaches, this seems to have been rare and less demarcated (Roscoe).

Like berdaches, *hijras* in India and Pakistan are biological males who live as women. Hijras trace their existence to the eunuchs who served as guards to nobility during the Mughal Empire (1526–1858). Some hijras are intersexed, some are transsexual, and some are castrated; many have been rejected by their families of origin and form communities with other hijras, earning their livings by prostitution. They often live in communal settings in households comprising several *chelas* (disciples) and supervised by a "guru." Hijras play a cultural role in the larger community, frequently appearing uninvited to dance and sing at weddings and births of male children. Their role is to entreat the deities to bestow fertility on the husband or male child (Thadani).

Same-Sex Relationships and Desires in Judeo-Christian Cultures

The Torah includes 613 laws (365 prohibitions and 248 positive commandments), which are known as the Mosaic code. Two of these, Leviticus 18:22 and 20:13, prohibit a man from lying "with mankind as with womankind," calling this practice "abomination" and stating the penalty as death. In addition, the story of Sodom and Gomorrah (Genesis 19) is often read as describing God's punishment on Sodom for homosexuality (thus gay men have been called "sodomites"), although some commentators, notably John Boswell *(Christianity)*, have pointed out that the men of Sodom appear to sin more through failure of hospitality than sexual depravity. In the New Testament, Jesus is silent on the subject, but Paul in his epistles (Romans 1:25-27, I Corinthians 6:9) castigates both men and women who engage in same-sex sexual acts. Some scholars cast doubt on Paul's intention, saying that the Greek words he uses for those engaging in same-sex sexual behaviors (*malakoi* and *arsenokoitai* rather than the more common term *paideraste*) are ambiguous in meaning. Moreover, some biblical stories seem to honor same-sex affection and intimacy. The friendship between David and Jonathan, as well as the close relationship between Ruth and Naomi, frequently have been cited by lesbian and gay people as instances of same-sex intimacy that are depicted in the Bible as idealized and worthy of respect. Still, it is clear that Judeo-Christian tradition generally forbids same-sex sexual practices for both men and women.

During the first centuries of the Roman Empire, the Lex Scantinia (or Scantinian Law) governed sexual practices. It seems to have stipulated that most forms of same-sexual activity were illegal and punishable by a fine. After the "Constantinian change," whereby the emperor Constantine Christianized the Roman Empire in the fourth century CE, the punishment for same-sex sexual behavior (then classified as a "crime against nature" following Paul's charge in Romans 1:26) was upgraded to death. In the Middle Ages, such behavior, particularly **sodomy**, was reclassified as heresy, and during the fifteenth century, a number of men were beheaded or burned at the stake for having committed the "crime of Sodom." This period also saw sodomy referred to as the *peccatum mutum* or "silent sin," that is, a transgression that could not be spoken of. Most of what was written on this subject focused on men exclusively, although as early as the fifth century, St. Augustine warned his sister not to indulge in carnal or immodest love in the convent where she was a nun (Betteridge). In general, female-female sexuality was regarded as a lesser offense than male-male sexuality, for various reasons: lacking a penis, a woman could not commit the sin of "spilling the seed." Lesbian sex was widely considered to be merely a preliminary activity preparing a woman for marriage; a sexually aggressive woman was thought to be emulating men—in other words, aspiring to a more perfect state of nature. Still, proto-lesbian sexuality was not condoned, especially when it appeared to function as a throwback to pre-Christian Wiccan or pagan religions. For example, early Church fathers (third and fourth centuries CE) disapproved of and ridiculed "binding spells" used by Upper Egyptian women to attract other women (Brooten). Later, a woman could be severely punished for **cross-dressing,** and it is now believed that during the so-called burning times (the prosecution and killing of witches in Europe between the fourteenth and eighteenth centuries CE), many of the female victims were women who violated accepted gender practice.

> **Find Out More** in Sophia's spell at the end of this chapter.

At the same time as the Church excoriated same-sex "heresy" and executed some of its practitioners, certain liturgical elements within it acknowledged, even celebrated, same-sex relationships. Saints Serge and Bacchus, Roman soldiers of the third century CE and also Christian converts and martyrs, are said to have been "joined in life." A document from the tenth century describes Serge as the "sweet companion and lover" of Bacchus; their image is depicted on an icon found in the monastery of St. Catherine on Mt. Sinai, with Jesus appearing as *pronubus* or best man between them.

Figure 1.4   Icon of Sts. Serge and Bacchus, seventh century CE.

> **Find Out More** in the "Hymn to Saints Serge and Bacchus" at the end of this chapter.

Find Out More in the "Order for Solemnization of Same-Sex Union" at the end of this chapter.

In fact, a number of Offices of Same-Sex Union exist, dating from the seventh to the sixteenth centuries CE; most of these were written in Greek or Serbian Slavonic (and thus originate in Eastern Orthodox Christianity), although a very few are in Latin. It is not clear exactly what kind of partnership was envisioned by the authors of these rituals, but certainly they indicate an ecclesiastical acceptance of binding same-sex relationships as part of Church history (Boswell, *Same-Sex Unions*).

Desires for Identity

In the year 1101 CE, Anselm, Archbishop of Canterbury, issued a decree against clerical marriage. Commentators immediately observed an increase in sodomy among priests; offenders were excommunicated, and their crimes and sentences were published weekly in churches throughout England. Instead of eliminating sodomy by shaming the perpetrators, publishing the crimes seems to have caused heightened interest among male parishioners, who spent considerable time discussing who did what to whom. As a result, the publication ceased, but not before revealing the existence of a subculture of men who would be glad for an excuse to gather (Betteridge).

Most intriguing about this story is the persistence of the unspoken community, even in an atmosphere of condemnation and harsh punishment. Extremely severe consequences were the norm in cases of sodomy. The 1598 case of Ludwig Boudin serves as a dramatic example. Boudin, a married pastry baker from Frankfurt, Germany, was accused of sodomy by a jealous competitor. The witnesses mostly recalled events from years in the past, speaking of Boudin as propositioning them when he was drunk; none of them described any activity more serious than an unwelcome advance on Boudin's part. Unable to prove the charge but inclined to find the defendant guilty, the city council subjected Boudin to extensive torture, hoping to force a confession. Repeated applications of the leg screw and the rack failed to achieve the desired result, although they did weaken Boudin to the point where the council decided that further torture would be counterproductive. Boudin was ultimately sentenced to time in the pillory, followed by banishment for life from Frankfurt (Hergemöller).

The Italian Renaissance (fifteenth century) led to a somewhat more open attitude toward male-male sexuality, as the revival of classical standards for art and literature rekindled ancient Greek and Roman ideas about, for instance, male beauty and pederasty. Despite the Inquisition breathing down his throat, the Franciscan friar Antonio Rocco wrote *Alcibiades the Schoolboy* in about 1631. This book is the story of the attempted (and finally successful) seduction of a youth by his teacher Filotimo; it is a type of extended Socratic argument in which the two parties engage in prolonged intellectual and flirtatious give-and-take before the teacher's inevitable victory. Alcibiades of Rocco's novel is named after Socrates's young lover in Plato's *Symposium*, and Filotimo argues for a return to socially sanctioned pederasty as practiced by the Greeks. Various modern writers have called *Alcibiades the Schoolboy* the first "gay" novel because Filotimo describes himself as a man who loves other men rather than women. Filotimo, then, does more than perform homosexual acts; he identifies himself as a homosexual, an early example of a man whom we in the contemporary world might understand as "gay."

In the Middle Ages—and through the nineteenth century, in fact—women had little access to either schools or public establishments, and their general disenfranchisement from church or government tended to isolate them in their homes. Church doctrine pictured women as sexually insatiable and accordingly created rules confining them to the "natural" purpose of sex—that is, procreation. A woman who wished to move freely in the world and initiate sexual activity with another woman would of necessity have to pass as a man, and indeed passing women were most frequently punished for the sin of *mulier cum muliere fornicatio* (woman-with-woman fornication). For example, in 1477, a German woman named Katherina Hetzeldorfer was drowned in the Rhine River after being convicted of an unnamed crime, which involved dressing as a man and "abducting" and seducing at least two women using a leather **dildo.** So skillful was Hetzeldorfer in the use of this device that both her female partners testified in court that they believed her to be a man; of course, had they admitted they knew she was female, they might have shared her fate (Puff). Hetzeldorfer was an early example of a passing woman unlucky enough to get caught; her case and others like it illustrate the difficulties facing women who sought either freedom of movement or sex with other women. Though they could operate in the world as men, they lacked a community of women with similar desires.

If Professor Filotimo in Antonio Rocco's *Alcibiades the Schoolboy* represented the first modern (i.e., self-conscious) gay man, then Anne Lister (1791–1840) was the first modern lesbian. Lister was a wealthy Yorkshire landowner whose social class provided her not only with the freedom to dress as she pleased and to court women, but also with the education she needed to write down her exploits in elaborate coded journals. Like Filotimo, Lister describes her predilection for same-sex desire as part of her nature: "I love and only love the fairer sex and thus beloved by them in turn, my heart revolts from any love but theirs" (145).

Romantic Friendships and Boston Marriages

Contemporary historians of sexuality have recorded and discussed a variety of same-sex sexual and romantic arrangements between women. While a passing working-class "**Tommy**" or a wealthy Anne Lister possessed the ability to move around fairly freely in the world, most women before the twentieth century did

Figure 1.5 Eleanor Butler and Sarah Ponsonby, *The Ladies of Llangollen.*

not. Yet middle- and upper-class women had long participated in socially sanctioned romantic friendships, characterized by love letters and poetry, emotional intimacy, and even physical affection. In *Surpassing the Love of Men,* Lillian Faderman gives examples of both French and British women of the seventeenth century—Mme. de La Fayette, Katherine Philips, and others—who openly expressed their love for another woman. She also cites Michel de Montaigne as an example of a man who declared that his romantic love for his friend Éstienne de la Boëtie constituted a "sacred bond" between them. By the eighteenth century, such romantic friendships had become the fashion, especially among women. Probably the most well-known pair was Sarah Ponsonby and Eleanor Butler, Irish gentlewomen who eloped to Wales in 1778 and lived there together for fifty-three years. Their cozy idyllic retreat became a fashionable destination for travelers who were anxious to meet the "Ladies of Llangollen."

Although the Ladies themselves wrote that their relationship had nothing to do with sex (which they euphemistically called "Vulgar Eros"), it is nevertheless true that such literary proto-lesbians as Anna Seward and Anne Lister visited them and wrote admiringly of their Welsh ménage, and the writer Hester Thrale Piozzi called them "damned sapphists" (Stanley 163). Ponsonby and Butler represent a success story for early female romantic couples, in contrast to, for instance, Marianne Woods and Jane Pirie, Scottish schoolmistresses whose livelihood was entirely undermined when they were accused by a student of having engaged in "improper and criminal conduct" with each other. They went to court in 1811 to claim the charge was libelous and won, but their school for girls nonetheless closed because of the scandal.

Woods and Pirie won their libel case in part because Lord Gillies, the judge, believed that "the crime here alleged has no existence" (Faderman, *Scotch Verdict* 282). In the nineteenth century, romantic friendship was seen as benign, even salutary. In contrast to the Middle Ages, people now regarded middle- and upper-class women as asexual, and even if they were not, without a penis present, sex "has no existence." Given this view of privileged women, it is not surprising that Queen Victoria, when asked if she thought the 1885 Criminal Law Amendment Act outlawing same-sex acts between men should also apply to women, expressed her disbelief that such acts between women were physically possible (Castle). This attitude allowed some women to express their love for other women without being suspected of sexual deviance. The poet Emily Dickinson, for example, wrote to her friend and future sister-in-law Sue Gilbert, "If you were here—and Oh that you were, my Susie, we need not talk at all, our eyes would whisper for us, and your hand fast in mine, we would not ask for language" (Faderman, *Surpassing* 175). Interestingly, Dickinson's niece Martha Dickinson Bianchi cut this passage from her 1924 edition of Emily Dickinson's letters; by that time, the popularization of Freud had put an end to the assumption of female innocence [λ Chapter 3].

In the second half of the nineteenth century, as a few fortunate (white, upper-class) women gained the opportunity to attend college and embark on careers outside the home, a new phenomenon arose: the Boston marriage. Lillian Faderman defines a Boston marriage as "a long-term monogamous relationship between two otherwise unmarried women" (Faderman, *Surpassing* 190). The reference to Boston resulted from the many women's colleges in that area. At a time when marriage to a man always meant retirement from the public sphere and exclusive focus on home and family, many educated professional women chose to remain unmarried. They formed intense loving relationships with other women, often combining their work and home lives. Katharine Lee Bates, professor of English at Wellesley College and author of "America the Beautiful," lived with economics professor Katharine Coman for twenty-five years. Jane Addams, founder of Hull House in Chicago, lived with coworker Mary Rozet Smith for over thirty years. These women and others in similar circumstances could form same-sex "marriages" precisely because they lived during the romantic friendship era, when such relationships were assumed to be beneficial and asexual.

Molly-Houses: Early Homoerotic Subculture in England

The first **Buggery** Act outlawing male sodomy was passed in England in 1533, and during the sixteenth century, some prosecutions took place. Popular sentiment held, however, that Rome, not London, was the "cistern full of sodomy," and there was little evidence of a cohesive subculture. Rictor Norton claims that in the early seventeenth century, the court of James I was "very nearly a gay subculture unto itself" for the first fifteen years of his reign (21). James's most notorious favorite was George Villiers, Duke of Buckingham. So marked were his attentions to Buckingham that the Privy Council held an acrimonious debate in 1617 concerning the moral nature of James's affections. James responded openly, "I love the Earl of Buckingham more than anyone else" and compared their relationship to that of Jesus and St. John. "Christ had his son John," wrote the king, "and I have my George" (qtd. Norton 21). At the same time, we should remember that James I was married and had very cordial relations with his wife, with whom he fathered children.

Find Out More in the Wadham limericks at the end of this chapter.

The open male-male intimacy at court waned in the last years of James's reign, and during the Puritan years, there is little evidence of the growth of urban subcultures. By the turn of the eighteenth century, however, much had changed. In 1700, the Royal Exchange was the prime cruising ground in London, where so-called Swarthy Buggerantoes ogled handsome young men. By 1720, the negative publicity against same-sex behavior originating from the Society for Reformation of Manners had sent some men to trial but also advertised places and practices for others. In 1726, the police raided an establishment known as Mother Clap's Molly House and took forty men to Newgate prison. The resulting trial led to three executions, one death in prison, one acquittal, one reprieve, and many gone into hiding. More than this, the British press was full of the subject for months, and enterprising reporters located and revealed dozens of molly-houses and cruising areas. As the Reformation Society became increasingly accused of officious meddling in the years that followed the Mother Clap raid, cruising for sex and meeting in particular public houses became safer and relatively routine (Norton ch. 3). An active molly subculture developed in England during the eighteenth century, whereby effeminate men ("mollies") engaged in transgressive gender play. Male-male sexuality was thought to run rampant in boys' schools and universities as well. In *The Construction of Homosexuality,* David Greenberg mentions that this phenomenon occurred throughout Europe at that time: there were transvestite balls in Portugal, men in ribbons and powder in France, men with female nicknames in Holland, and cross-dressers in Italy.

Lest it seem as if these men gained meaningful acceptance in London in the 1700s, it is important to consider that homophobia grew along with awareness of homoeroticism. Public hangings, confinement to the pillory, imprisonment, and heavy fines were common. Men were convicted and punished for sodomy at a far higher rate than for other crimes. For example, in 1811, the first year criminal statistics were compiled by the Home Office, 80% of convicted sodomists were executed, as compared with 13% of other capital offenders (Norton 132). Mob violence against pilloried "sods" (sodomites) was common.

The gradual urbanizing trend of the nineteenth century led to sufficient growth of many cities in Europe and the United States to provide the anonymity needed for more modern homosexual cultures to develop. Cabarets and clubs in Berlin, specialized houses of prostitution in Amsterdam, molly taverns in New York and London—these and many other places catered to men looking for contact with others. By the last decades of the 1800s, nearly every big city in the Western world had its cruising areas and entertainment houses, and the word *gay* had slipped from its mid-century meaning of prostitute to include men interested in sex with other men and "gay girls," or lesbians. Mollies developed elaborate codes to signal their availability to other men.

Tommies, that is, boyish or passing women, might also be found in "gay" establishments. In many ways, what we would recognize as a gay subculture was coming into being. Contemporary historians interpret such cultures as signaling the beginning of a recognizably modern "gay" culture or identity. How such identities solidified into the forms we actually recognize today—both in the eyes of those invested in homoerotic love and in the eyes of larger societies—is the subject of the next chapter.

QUESTIONS FOR DISCUSSION

1. Thinking seriously about the theory of perverse presentism, recall some of the conversations you have had with friends about the issue of homosexuality in history. What historical figures have you heard are homosexual? What are their birth and death dates? Knowing what you know after reading this chapter, how accurate do you think it is to claim these historical figures as homosexual? Do some Internet research about these figures and then try to come up with ways of talking about their sexual identities or performances that are accurate to their lives.

2. Throughout this chapter, we have mentioned a number of historical figures who have become important in tracing the history of same-sex desires and non-normative gender identities and performances. Pick one figure who interests you and find out more about that individual's biography. Pay particular attention to that person's importance in the history of same-sex sexuality. As you browse through a variety of biographical and critical materials—on the Web, in histories, in journal articles—keep track of how the individual is labeled. Is he or she or ze referred to as "gay"? Homosexual? Queer? What do the labels suggest not only about the individual in question but about the assumptions of the author of the biographical or critical materials you are reading?

3. In this chapter, we have tried to acknowledge the different terms used at different points in history and in different cultures to refer to people practicing same-sex desires or engaging in gender variant performances. What are *contemporary* terms for such desires, identities, and performances? Research some of the historical and contemporary terms to find out more about the contexts in which they were—and are—used.

REFERENCES AND FURTHER READING

Abelove, Henry, Michèle Aina Barale, and David M. Halperin, eds. *The Lesbian and Gay Studies Reader.* New York: Routledge, 1993.

Betteridge, Tom. *Sodomy in Early Modern Europe.* Manchester, UK: Manchester UP, 2002.

Boswell, John. *Christianity, Social Tolerance, and Homosexuality.* Chicago: U of Chicago P, 1980.

———. *Same-Sex Unions in Premodern Europe.* New York: Vintage, 1994.

Brooten, Bernadette J. *Love between Women: Early Christian Responses to Female Homoeroticism.* Chicago: U of Chicago P, 1996.

Castle, Terry. *The Apparitional Lesbian.* New York: Columbia UP, 1995.

Cook, Blanche Wiesen. "'Women Alone Stir My Imagination': Lesbianism and the Cultural Tradition." *Signs* 4.4 (Summer 1979): 718–39.

Dover, K. J. *Greek Homosexuality.* Cambridge, MA: Harvard UP, 1989 [1978].

Downing, Christine. *Myths and Mysteries of Same-Sex Love.* New York: Continuum, 1989.

Duberman, Martin Bauml, Martha Vicinus, and George Chauncey Jr., eds. *Hidden from History: Reclaiming the Gay and Lesbian Past.* New York: New American Library, 1989.

Epprecht, Marc. *Hungochani: The History of a Dissident Sexuality in Southern Africa.* Montreal: McGill-Queen's UP, 2004.

Faderman, Lillian. *Scotch Verdict.* New York: Columbia UP, 1993.

———. *Surpassing the Love of Men: Romantic Friendship and Love between Women from the Renaissance to the Present.* New York: William Morrow, 1981.

Fone, Byrne R. S., ed. *Hidden Heritage: History and the Gay Imagination.* New York: Avocation, 1980.

Garton, Stephen. *Histories of Sexuality: Antiquity to Sexual Revolution.* New York: Routledge, 2004.

Greenberg, David E. *The Construction of Homosexuality.* Chicago: U of Chicago P, 1988.

Hergemöller, Berndt-Ulrich. *Sodom and Gomorrah: On the Everyday Reality and Persecution of Homosexuals in the Middle Ages.* Trans. John Phillips. London: Free Association Books, 2001.

Kugle, Scott. "Sultan Mahmud's Makeover: Colonial Homophobia and the Persian-Urdu Literary Tradition." *Queering India: Same-Sex Love and Eroticism in Indian Culture and Society.* Ed. Ruth Vanita. New York: Routledge, 2002. 30–46.

Lister, Anne. *I Know My Own Heart: The Diaries of Anne Lister (1791–1840).* Ed. Helena Whitbread. London: Virago, 1988.

Murray, Stephen O., and Will Roscoe. *Boy-Wives and Female Husbands: Studies of African Homosexualities.* New York: St. Martin's, 1998.

———. *Islamic Homosexualities: Culture, History, and Literature.* New York: NYU P, 1997.

Norton, Rictor. *Mother Clap's Molly House: The Gay Subculture in England 1700–1830.* London: GMP, 1992.

Padgug, Robert. "Sexual Matters: Rethinking Sexuality in History." *Hidden from History: Reclaiming the Gay and Lesbian Past.* Ed. Martin Duberman, Martha Vicinus, and George Chauncey Jr. New York: Penguin, 1989. 54–64.

Plato. *Symposium.* Trans. Benjamin Jowett. 19 July 2008 <http://www.lyon.edu/webdata/users/mbeck/Plato/Symposium,%201.doc>.

Pomeroy, Sarah. *Goddesses, Whores, Wives, and Slaves: Women in Classical Antiquity.* New York: Shocken, 1975.

Puff, Helmut. *Sodomy in Reformation Germany and Switzerland 1400–1600.* Chicago: U of Chicago P, 2003.

Reeder, Greg. "Same-Sex Desire, Conjugal Constructs, and the Tomb of Niankhkhnum and Khnumhotep." *World Archaeology* 32.2 (Oct. 2000): 193–208.

Rocco, Antonio. *Alcibiades the Schoolboy.* Trans. J. C. Rawnsley. Amsterdam: Entimos, 2000.

Roscoe, Will. *The Zuñi Man-Woman.* Albuquerque: UNM P, 1992.

Shively, Charley. *Drum Beats: Walt Whitman's Civil War Boy Lovers.* San Francisco: Gay Sunshine, 1989.

Stanley, Liz. "Epistemological Issues in Researching Lesbian History: The Case of 'Romantic Friendship.'" *Working Out: New Directions for Women's Studies.* Ed. Hilary Hinds, Ann Phoenix, and Jackie Stacey. London: Falmer, 1992. 161–72.

Thadani, Giti. *Sakhiyani: Desire in Ancient and Modern India.* London: Cassell, 1996.

Vanita, Ruth, ed. *Queering India: Same-Sex Love and Eroticism in Indian Culture and Society.* New York: Routledge, 2002.

Watanabe, Tsuneo, and Jun'ichi Iwata. *The Love of the Samurai: A Thousand Years of Japanese Homosexuality.* Trans. D. R. Roberts. London: GMP, 1989.

Wu, Cuncun. *Homoerotic Sensibilities in Late Imperial China.* London: RoutledgeCurzon, 2004.

READINGS

➢ **Sappho**

(c. Seventh Century BCE), Ancient Greece

"To a Maiden"

Peer of gods he seemeth to me, the blissful

Man who sits and gazes at thee before him,

Close beside thee sits, and in silence hears thee
     Silverly speaking,

Laughing love's low laughter. Oh this, this only

Stirs the troubled heart in my breast to tremble!

For should I but see thee a little moment,
     Straight is my voice hushed;

Yea, my tongue is broken, and through and through me

'Neath the flesh impalpable fire runs tingling;

Nothing see mine eyes, and a noise of roaring
     Waves in my ear sounds;

Sweat runs down in rivers, a tremor seizes

All my limbs, and paler than grass in autumn,

Caught by pains of menacing death, I falter,
     Lost in the love-trance.

Translated by John Addington Symonds (1840–1893), 1885 Rictor Norton, "The John Addington Symonds Pages" © 1997 <http://www.infopt.demon.co.uk/translat.htm>.

"Hymn to Aphrodite"

Glittering-throned, undying Aphrodite,

Wile-weaving daughter of high Zeus, I pray thee,

Tame not my soul with heavy woe, dread mistress,
     Nay, nor with anguish!

But hither come, if ever erst of old time

Thou didst incline, and listenedst to my crying,

And from thy father's palace down descending,
     Camest with golden

Chariot yoked: thee fair swift-flying sparrows
Over dark earth with multitudinous fluttering,
Pinion on pinion, through middle ether
    Down from heaven hurried.

Quickly they came like light, and thou, blest lady,
Smiling with clear undying eyes didst ask me
What was the woe that troubled me, and wherefore
    I had cried to thee:

What thing I longed for to appease my frantic
Soul: and Whom now must I persuade, thou askedst,
Whom must entangle to thy love, and who now,
    Sappho, hath wronged thee?

Yea, for if now he shun, he soon shall chase thee;
Yea, if he take not gifts, he soon shall give them;
Yea, if he love not, soon shall he begin to
    Love thee, unwilling.

Come to me now too, and from tyrannous sorrow
Free me, and all things that my soul desires to
Have done, do for me, queen, and let thyself too
    Be my great ally!

Selection copyright © 1997 by Rictor Norton.

➤ Abu Nuwas
(756–c. 815 CE), Persia

"In the Bath-house"

In the bath-house, the mysteries hidden by trousers
    Are revealed to you.

All becomes radiantly manifest.
    Feast your eyes without restraint!

You see handsome buttocks, shapely trim torsos,
    You hear the guys whispering pious formulas
        to one another
    ("God is Great!" "Praise be to God!")

Ah, what a palace of pleasure is the bath-house!
    Even when the towel-bearers come in
        And spoil the fun a bit.

Nuwas, Abu. *Carousing with Gazelles: Homoerotic Songs of Old Baghdad.* Trans. Jaafar Abu Tarab. New York: iUniverse, Inc., 2005.

"My Lover Has Started to Shave"

Jealous people and slanderers overwhelm me with sarcasm

because my lover has started to shave.

I answer them: friends, how wrong you are!

Since when has fuzz been a flaw?

It enhances the splendor of his lips and his teeth,

like silk cloth which is brightened by pearls.

And I consider myself fortunate that his sprouting beard

preserves his beauty from indiscreet glances:

it gives his kisses a different flavor

and makes a reflection glisten on the silver of his cheeks.

Quoted in Greenberg, *The Construction of Homosexuality* (174). Greenberg's source: Daniel, Marc. "Arab Civilization and Male Love." Trans. Winston Leyland. *Gay Sunshine* 32 (1977): 1–11, 27.

➢ Zulali Khwansari

(d. 1615 CE), Iran

From the Epic Poem *Masnavi*

Mahmud, Sultan of Ghazna, has purchased young Ayaz as a slave.

Mahmud set a cup beside him and a decanter before him
Full of burgundy wine, as if distilled from his own heart

He filled the cup with wine like his love's ruby lips
Entangled in the curls of Ayaz, Mahmud began to lose control

He filled the cup with wine from the clouds of forgetfulness
The glow of Ayaz set the glass aflame with scintillating colors

He lifted the cup to Ayaz and bade him drink
His heart melted as he held the cup to his lips

Mahmud urged him to drink wine from his own hand
Yet a complaint showed in the eyes of Ayaz, a fear of intoxication

But as a servant, Ayaz drank from the cup
As a ruby droplet rolled from his lip to his shirt

His words lay in jumbles as the drop rolled to his foot
And the wine sent him spinning in drunkenness

Hard of breath, Mahmud said, "In this intimacy one can pursue desire
But I can only utter sighs while watching you delicately drink!

Tonight, I'm in the mood to finally reach you
How long has my only wish from God been delayed

Your lips have become ruby red, as intense as the wine
Such a ruby spells the death of better discretion

Your mouth is a wine bottle overflowing
Since the color of wine flows over your lips

Those are not black curls nestled against your cheeks
Since your glance is aflame they must be wisps of smoke

Gazing at you, they seem not like musk-scented curls
For where there is burning desire there must be smoke

Come to me now, bare all, that I may kiss your lips
Those very rose petals that make a beard tender and soft

Your lip is a single drop of wine distilled
My heart's desire is only to taste it unconstrained

Against the black lashes, how bright are your eyes
Am I fated to glimpse them only from a distance?

You never look at me directly in the eye
Though with one glance you will rob me of my heart

This is the last breath I will release from my soul
Without your beauty open before me, I will surely die

If you let me embrace your full form
From my grave stately box-trees will grow tall like you

That idol of Kashmir, like a rose blooming in a graceful cypress

From head to toe your elegant form has set me boiling!"

Ayaz's sweet mouth drawing close, closer

His smile fully prepared, his lip set for the charge

Then from his smile, sweetness boiled over

He took the wine-cup from the Sultan's hand

From that moment, Ayaz was the cupbearer of Mahmud

Whose whole world became drunk with his playful grace.

Translated by Scott Kugle. Kugle, Scott. "Sultan Mahmud's Makeover: Colonial Homophobia and the Persian-Urdu Literary Tradition." *Queering India: Same-Sex Love and Eroticism in Indian Culture and Society.* Ed. Ruth Vanita. New York: Routledge, 2002. 30–46. [Selection pp. 33–34]

➢ Ihara Saikaku

(1642–1693), Japan

"Bamboo Clappers Strike the Hateful Number"

A monk's hermitage papered with love letters.

Boy actors hide their age.

A pushy samurai loses his whiskers.

When being entertained by a kabuki boy actor, one must be careful never to ask his age.

It was late in autumn, and rain just light enough not to be unpleasant had been falling since early morning. It now lifted and the afternoon sun appeared below the clouds in the west, forming a rainbow over Higashiyama. Just then a group of boy actors appeared wearing wide-striped rainbow robes of satin. The most handsome among them was an actor in the Murayama theater troupe, a jewel that sparkled without need of polishing, named Tamamura Kichiya.[1] He was in the full flower of youth, and every person in the capital was in love with him.

On that particular day, a well-known lover of boys called Ko-romo-notana Shiroku had invited him to go mushroom picking at Mt. Shiroyama in Fushimi, so a large group of actors and their spirited companions left Shijo-gawara and soon arrived at Hitsu-kawa. Leaves of the birch cherries, the subject of a long-ago poem,[2] had turned bright red, a sight more beautiful even than spring blossoms. After spending some time gazing at the scene, the group continued past the woods at Fuji-no-mori, where the tips of the leaves were just beginning to turn brown, and moved south up the mountain.

They parked their palanquins at the base and alighted, heads covered with colorful purple kerchiefs. Since pine trees were their only observers, they removed their sedge hats and revealed their lovely faces. Parting the tangled pampas grass, they walked on with sighs of admiration. The scene was reminiscent of the poem, "My sleeves grow damp since first entering the mountain of your love,"[3] for these were boys at the peak of physical beauty. An outsider looking at them could not but have felt envious of their gentleman companions. A certain man well acquainted with the ways of love once said, "In general, courtesans are a pleasure once in bed; with boys, the pleasure begins on the way there."

It was already close to dusk by the time they began hunting for mushrooms. They found only a few, which they carried like treasures back to an isolated thatched hut far from any village. Inside, the walls were papered at the base with letters from actors. Their signatures had been torn off and discarded. Curious, the boys looked more closely and discovered that each letter concerned matters of love. Each was written in a different hand, the parting messages of kabuki boy actors. The monk who lived there must once have been a man of some means, they thought. He apparently belonged to the Shingon sect, for when they opened the Buddhist altar they found a figure of Kaba Daishi adorned with chrysanthemums and bush clover, and next to it a picture of a lovely young actor, the object no doubt of this monk's fervent devotion.

When they questioned him, the monk told them about his past. As they suspected, he was devoted body and soul to the way of boy love.

"I was unhappy with my strict father and decided to seclude myself in this mountain hermitage. More than two years have passed, but I have not been able to forget about boy love even in my dreams." The tears of grief he wept were enough to fade the black dye of his priestly robes. Those who heard it were filled with pity for him.

"How old are you?" someone asked.

"I am no longer a child," he said. "I just turned 22."

"Why then, you are still in the flower of youth!" they exclaimed.

All of the actors in the room dutifully wrung the tears from their sleeves, but their expressions seemed strangely reticent. Not one of them was under 22 years of age! Among them was one boy actor who, judging from the time he worked the streets, must have been quite old. In the course of the conversation, someone asked him his age.

"I don't remember," he said, causing quite some amusement among the men.

Then, the monk who lived in the cottage spoke up.

"By good fortune, I have here a bamboo clapper that has the ability to tell exactly how old you are."

He gave the clapper to the boy actor and had him stand there while the monk himself gravely folded his hands in prayer. Shortly, the bamboo clappers began to sound. Everyone counted aloud with each strike.

At first, the actor stood there innocently as it struck seventeen, eighteen, nineteen, but beyond that he started to feel embarrassed. He tried with all his strength to separate his right hand from his left and stop the clappers from striking, but, strangely, they kept right on going. Only after striking 38 did the bamboo clappers separate. The boy actor's face was red with embarrassment.

"These bamboo clappers lie!" he said, throwing them down.

The monk was outraged.

"The Buddhas will attest that there is no deceit in them. If you still have doubts, try it again as many times as you like."

The other actors in the room were all afraid of being exposed, so no one was willing to try them out. They were beginning to lose their party mood.

When sake had been brought out and the mushrooms toasted and salted, they all lay back and began to entertain their patrons. One of the boy actors took the opportunity to request a new jacket, another was promised a house with an entrance six ken wide, and still another was presented right there with a short sword (It was amusing to see how nimbly he took the sword and put it away!).

Into the midst of this merry-making came a rough samurai of the type rarely seen in the capital. He announced his arrival with the words,

"Part, clouds, for here I am!" as if to boast of his bad reputation. He forced his way through the twig fence and into the garden, handed his long sword to an attendant, and went up to the bamboo veranda.

"Bring me the sake cup that Tamamura Kichiya is using," he demanded.

Kichiya at first pretended he had not heard, but finally he said, "There is already a gentleman here to share my cup."

The samurai would not tolerate such an answer.

"I will have it at once," he said angrily, "and you will be my snack!"

He took up his long sword mentioned earlier and waved it menacingly at the boy's companion. The poor man was terrified and apologized profusely, but the samurai refused to listen.

"What an awful fellow," Kichiya laughed.

"I won't let him get away with this."

"Leave him to me," he told the others and sent them back home.

When they had gone, Kichiya snuggled up to the foolish samurai.

"Today was so uninteresting," he said.

"I was just having a drink with those boring merchants because I had to. It would be a real pleasure to drink with a lord like yourself."

Kichiya poured cup after cup of sake for the man and flattered and charmed him expertly. Soon, the fool was in a state of waking sleep, unaware of anything but the boy. The man was ready to make love, but Kichiya told him: "I can't go any further because of your scratchy whiskers. It hurts when you kiss me."

"I wouldn't dream of keeping anything on my face not to your liking, boy. Call my servant and have him shave it off," the samurai said.

"If you don't mind, please allow me to improve my lord's good looks with my own hands." Kichiya picked up a razor and quickly shaved off the whiskers on the left side of the samurai's face, leaving the mustache intact on his upper lip. He also left the right side as it was. The samurai just snored loudly, completely oblivious to what was going on.

Kichiya saw his opportunity and escaped from the place as quickly as possible. He took the man's whiskers with him as a memento. Everyone laughed uproariously when he showed them the hair.

"How in the world did you get hold of that! This deserves a celebration!" they said. Akita Hikosabura[4] invented an impromptu "whisker dance" and had the men holding their sides with laughter.

Later, when the samurai awoke, he was furious at the loss of his whiskers. Without his beard he had no choice but to quit living by intimidation. Rather than seek revenge, he decided to act as if the whole thing had never happened.

When they saw him some time later, he was making his living as a marksman with his bow. Recalling how he had lost his beard, they could not help but laugh at the man.

Notes

1. Tamamura Kichiya was an actor of female roles from 1658 to 1660 in the Kyoto Ebisuya Theater, where he scored a great success as Yang Kuei Fei in the play *Hanaikusa* (Yang Kuei Fei: legendary beauty and consort of the Chinese T'ang emperor T'ai Tzung). In 1661, he moved to the Inishie Theater in Edo, but nothing is known of him after 1673.
2. Fubokusho poem 11307 by Fujiwara no Ieyoshi: "Fragrant on the banks of the Hitsukawa, the late-blooming birch cherries drop their petals, signaling the blossoms' final end."
3. Shinchokusen poem 657 by Minamoto no Tamenaka: "Since first parting the luxuriant growth of dew-covered grass on the mountain of your love, how damp my sleeves have grown."
4. Founder of the Akita dynasty of actors, Hikosabura played jester roles in Kyoto and Osaka in the years 1661 to 1680. Yakusha hyaban gejigeji (1674) describes him as a master of mime, acrobatics, and humorous monologues.

Translated by Paul Gordon Schalow, *Nanshoku Okagami* (*The Great Mirror of Male Love*), by Ihara Saikaku (1642–1693). Copyright © 1990 by the Board of Trustees of the Leland Stanford Jr. University.

➤ Wu Meicun

(1609–1671 CE), China

"Song of Beau Wang"[1]

Beau Wang reappears on the capital's stage in his thirties,

He has grown up and sings sentimental tunes for the former dynasty.

Oh, his face is even more endearing than in the old days,

Dark pupils darting from his white jade eyes.

All the young dandies from the great families of Wuling

Vie to give their life for Beau Wang.

Calmly missing appointments with the imperial ministers,

How they suffer over missing Beau Wang.

Unhurried by the approach of evening curfews,

How they all rush to be on time for Beau Wang.

None before succeeded in calming an audience's cheers and waves,

But just a peep from Beau Wang brings the whole theatre to a hush.

Everybody jostles and leans to gaze upon Beau Wang

Like looking over someone never seen before.

The old capital was fascinated with Little Song

Who entertained in the household of Duke Tian.

Hearing once more the strains of Beau Wang's song,

We no longer grieve for the emperor of yore.

Note

1. Wang Zijia (c. 1622–54), a famous boy actor during the late Ming dynasty, whom the poet met again in Beijing in 1651, the eighth year of the Qing dynasty.

Translated by Wu Cuncun. Wu Cuncun. *Homoerotic Sensibilities in Late Imperial China*. London: RoutledgeCurzon, 2004.

➢ Ancient Egyptian Binding Spell

(c. Third/Fourth-Century CE)

"An oval-shaped lead tablet from Hermoupolis Magna (known today as el-Ashmunen) in Upper Egypt contains a sixty-two-line spell inscribed in a third- or fourth-century CE script. . . . The ten lines at the beginning and the ten lines at the end taper off to form an oval-shaped inscription.

A woman named Sophia used this tablet to attract another woman, Gorgonia."

Fundament of the gloomy darkness, jagged-tooth dog, covered with coiling snakes, turning three heads, traveler in the recesses of the underworld, come, spirit-driver, with the Erinyes, savage with their stinging whips; holy serpents, maenads, frightful maidens, come to my wroth incantations. Before I persuade by force this one and you, render him immediately a fire-breathing daemon. Listen and do everything quickly, in no way opposing me in the performance of this action; for you are the governors of the earth.

By means of this corpse-daemon inflame the heart, the liver, the spirit of Gorgonia, whom Nilogenia bore, with love and affection for Sophia, whom Isara bore. Constrain Gorgonia, whom Nilogenia bore, to cast herself into the bath-house for the sake of Sophia, whom Isara bore; and you, become a bath-woman. Burn, set on fire, inflame her soul, heart, liver, spirit with love for Sophia, whom Isara bore. Drive Gorgonia, whom Nilogenia bore, drive her, torment her body night and day, force her to rush forth from every place and every house, loving Sophia, whom Isara bore, she, surrendered like a slave, giving herself and all her possessions to her, because this is the will and command of the great god, Blessed lord of the immortals, holding the scepters of Tartaros and of terrible, fearful Styx and of life-robbing Lethe, the hair of Kerberos trembles in fear of you, you crack the loud whips of the Erinyes; the couch of Persephone delights you, when you go to the longed bed, whether you be the immortal Sarapis, whom the universe fears, whether you be Osiris, star of the land of Egypt; your messenger is the all-wise boy; yours is Anoubis, the pious herald of the dead. Come hither, fulfill my wishes, because I summon you by these secret symbols, swallowing the tip of the tail.

Constrain Gorgonia, whom Nilogenia bore, to cast herself into the bath-house for the sake of Sophia, whom Isara bore, for her. Aye, lord, king of the chthonic gods, burn, set on fire, inflame the soul, the heart, the liver, the spirit of Gorgonia, whom Nilogenia bore, with love and affection for Sophia, whom Isara bore; drive Gorgonia herself, torment her body night and day; force her to rush forth from every place and every house, loving Sophia, whom Isara bore, she, Gorgonia surrendered like a slave, giving herself and all her possessions. Aye, lord, king of the chthonic gods, carry out what is inscribed on this tablet, for I adjure you who divided the entire universe, a single realm.

So, do not disobey my request, but cause Gorgonia, whom Nilogenia bore, force her to cast herself into the bath-house for the sake of Sophia, whom Isara bore, for her. Burn, set on fire, inflame the heart, the liver, the spirit of Gorgonia, whom Nilogenia bore, with love and affection for Sophia, whom Isara bore, for a good end.

Burn, set on fire the soul, the heart, the liver, the spirit of Gorgonia, whom Nilogenia bore, with love and affection for Sophia, whom Isara bore, because this is the will of the great god.

Force Gorgonia, whom Nilogenia bore, to cast herself into the bath-house for the sake of Sophia, whom Isara bore, for her, so that she love her with passion.

Burn, set on fire the soul, the heart, the liver, the spirit of Gorgonia, whom Nilogenia bore, with love and affection for Sophia, whom Isara bore, with passion, longing, love.

Drive, Sun, honey-holder, honey-cutter, honey-producer, drive Gorgonia, whom Nilogenia bore, to love Sophia, whom Isara bore; burn, set on fire the soul, the heart, the liver, the spirit of burned, inflamed, tortured Gorgonia, whom Nilogenia bore, until she casts herself into the bath-house for the sake of Sophia, whom Isara bore; and you, become a bath-woman.

Brooten, Bernadette J. *Love between Women: Early Christian Responses to Female Homoeroticism.* Chicago: U of Chicago P, 1996. 81–82.

➤ Hymn to Saints Serge and Bacchus

(Sixth Century), Ancient Greece

---

i.

Of Serge and Bacchus,

the pair

filled with grace,

let us sing, O ye faithful!

Glory to Him who worketh

through his saints

amazing and wonderful deeds!

ii.

Let thy grace overshadow

thy servant, beyond what words can say,

O Christ, creator of all,

cleanser of all my sins

of word and deed,

that I may appear before you

pleasing and humbled,

for I am full of weakness,

[lacuna]

But do thou accept me as thy servant,

that I may call on thee in purity.

Glory to Him who worketh

through his saints

amazing and wonderful deeds!

iii.

Be ye brightened, O people,

by the noble

memory of these warriors!

By God Himself,

as the prophet foretold, were they consumed

in torture:

divine coals,

lighting the world,

verily, in the bright splendor of their miracles,

dazzling their enemies.

Come, let us share

in their virtues as in their joining together,

proclaiming again

to the creator,

Glory to Him who worketh

through his saints

amazing and wonderful deeds!

iv.

Strengthen me now,

in imitation of Christ, o ye warriors;

for I am sickened in fear

at the serpent's assault on my soul;

drive ye away

vain thought

as with a mallet;

force ye my steps in the direction

of the good,

as the healing benefactors ye are

to all

them that call on you in joy:

Glory to Him who worketh

through his saints

amazing and wonderful deeds!

> Enjoying fame and wealth
> forasmuch as the beautiful pair had been found pleasing
> in the sight of the earthly king,
> possessing wisdom and courage,
> prudence and love for all,
> and for Christ,
> planted within their hearts.
> In Him alone they placed their hopes,
> counting as dross the things of the earth,
> and eagerly hastening to heaven,
> singing out loudly,
> Behold, how good and how pleasant it is for brethren to dwell
> together in unity.

When, therefore, the evil ones realized that

these two worshipped the Son of God,

and would not sacrifice to idols,

they came privately to denounce them,

and barked such things as,

"Majesty, those who eat thy bread

have dared the worst,

to raise their heels against Thee.

If they do not die,

they will not stop proclaiming

as if they had a single soul,

Behold, how good and how pleasant it is for brethren to dwell

together in unity."

v.

It was not desire for this world

that captivated Serge for Christ,

nor the empty life of worldly affairs

[that captivated] Bacchus;

rather, made one

as brethren

in the bond of love

they called out valiantly to the tyrant,

"See in two bodies

one soul and heart,

one will and virtue.

Take those that

Yearn to please God."

Glory to Him who worketh

through his saints

amazing and wonderful deeds!

vi.

The haughty judge

wickedly denieth

any return for their kindnesses [to him],

and repayeth them with the cloak of dishonor.

O madness!

O thoughtless,

unjust man!

In return for the good done to him

he rusheth into oblivion,

showing himself an enemy unto his friends

as Judas [was] to the creator.

So the athletes

cry out,

Glory to Him who worketh

through his saints

amazing and wonderful deeds!

Hymn to Saints Serge and Bacchus from *Same-Sex Unions in Premodern Europe* by John Boswell, copyright ©
1994 by John Boswell. Used by permission of Villard Books, a division of Random House, Inc.

➤ Order for Solemnization of Same-Sex Union

(Thirteenth Century), Medieval Europe (Greek) Translation

i.

*Those intending to be united shall come before the priest, who shall place the Gospel
on the center of the altar, and the first of them that are to be joined together shall place
his hand on the Gospel, and the second on the hand of the first. And thus sealing them,
the priest sayeth the litany.*

ii.
In peace we beseech Thee, O Lord.
For heavenly peace we beseech Thee, O Lord.
For the peace of all the world, [we beseech Thee, O Lord].
For these servants of God, N. and N., and their love in Christ, we beseech Thee, O Lord.
That they be granted love in the spirit and honor each other, we beseech Thee, O Lord.
That the Lord our God grant them blameless life and pleasing conduct.
That they and we be saved from all [danger, need, and tribulation].

iii.
Receive us. Save us. Have mercy upon us.
Mindful of our lady, the all-holy, undefiled, most blessed and glorious ever-virgin Mary,
mother of God, and all the saints, we commend ourselves and one another and all that
liveth unto Christ our God.

iv.

Let us pray.

Lord our God and ruler, who madest humankind after thine image and likeness and didst bestow upon us power of life eternal, whom it pleased that thine holy apostles Philip and Bartholomew be joined together, not bound by the law of nature, but in the mode of faith, who didst commend the union of thy holy martyrs Serge and Bacchus, not bound by the law of nature, but in a holy spirit and the mode of faith, do Thou vouchsafe unto these thy servants grace to love one another and to abide unhated and not a cause of scandal all the days of their lives, with the help of the Holy Mother of God and all thy saints. Forasmuch as Thou art our unity and certainty and the bond of peace, and thine is endless glory, Father, Son, and Holy Spirit.

v.

Peace be with you.

<Bow> your heads.

O Lord our God, who hast favored us with all those things necessary for salvation and hast commanded us to love one another and to forgive one another our failings, [bless], kind Lord and lover of good, these thy servants who love each other and are come unto this thy holy church to receive thy benediction. Grant unto them unashamed faithfulness, true love, and as Thou didst bestow upon thy holy disciples and apostles thy peace and love, grant also unto these, O Christ our God, all those things necessary for salvation and eternal life.

For Thou art the light, the truth, and life eternal, and thine is the glory.

vi.

O Lord our God, who in thine ineffable providence didst deem it fit to call brothers the holy apostles and heirs of thy kingdom, accept now these thy servants, N. and N., to be united in spirit and faith, and find them meet to abide unscathed by the wiles of the devil and of his evil spirits, to prosper in virtue and justice and sincere love, that through them and through us may be glorified thine all-holy name, the Father, the Son, and the Holy Spirit, now and forever.

vii.

Lord our God, magnified in the congregation of the saints, great and awesome ruler over all that is round about Thee, bless these thy servants <N. and N.>, grant unto them knowledge of thy Holy Spirit. Guide them in thy holy fear, bestow upon them joy in thy power, that they be joined together more in spirit than in flesh. Forasmuch as it is Thou who dost bless and sanctify all things, and <thine> is the glory.

viii.

O Lord our God, who dwellest in the heavens and dost look down upon those things below, who for the salvation of the human race didst send thine only-begotten son, our Lord, Jesus Christ, and didst choose Peter and Paul (Peter from Caesarea of Philippi, Paul from Tarsus of Cilicia), joining them together in holy spirit, make these thy servants like unto those two apostles. Keep them blameless all the days of their lives, for the sake of thy most venerable and honored name, Father, Son and Holy Spirit, which is <thus> sanctified and glorified, now and forever.

ix.
And they shall kiss the holy Gospel and each other, and it shall be concluded.

Order for Solemnization of Same-Sex Union from *Same-Sex Unions in Premodern Europe* by John Boswell, copyright © 1994 by John Boswell. Used by permission of Villard Books, a division of Random House, Inc.

➢ Wadham Limericks

There once was a warden of Wadham
Who approved of the folkways of Sodom,
     For a man might, he said,
     Have a very poor head
But be a fine fellow, at bottom.

When they said to a Fellow of Wadham
Who had asked for a ticket to Sodom,
     "Oh, sir, we don't care
     To send people there,"
He said, "Don't call me Sir, call me Modom."

Well did the amorous sons of Wadham
Their house secure from future flame;
They knew their crime, the crime of Sodom
And judg'd their punishment the same.

CHAPTER 2

Sexology

Constructing the Modern Homosexual

I n 1894, twenty-four-year-old Lord Alfred Douglas (lover of poet and playwright Oscar Wilde) published a poem titled "Two Loves." It depicts an idyllic scene, into which a beautiful young man enters. The poet's persona asks him,

> . . . Sweet youth,
> Tell me why, sad and sighing, thou dost rove
> These pleasant realms?

The young man answers that he is not the "true Love" that fills "the hearts of boy and girl with mutual flame." He is instead, he sighs, "the Love that dare not speak its name" (Douglas). The homoeroticism that saturates the poem suggests that this "Love that dare not speak its name" is love between men or between women. But at the end of the nineteenth century, that love was nameless in a number of important ways [λ "silent sin" Chapter 1]. First, such love "dare[d] not speak its name" because many same-sex sexual practices were criminalized. For instance, Britain's Criminal Law Amendment Act, passed in 1885, criminalized sexual touching between men. Anal intercourse (known as buggery) was already considered a reprehensible criminal act, once punishable by death; at the time of Douglas's writing, it was punishable by imprisonment from ten years to life ("Timeline"). Second, little public discourse about homoeroticism and homosexuality existed. In the contemporary world, Western media frequently offer news reports, movies, or conversation about a variety of lesbian, gay, bisexual, and transgender (LGBT) issues. This was not the case in nineteenth-century Europe, where "sexual inversion" was considered an illness and discussed in journals aimed primarily at medical professionals. Finally, Douglas's same-sex "Love" not only "dare not" but *could* not "speak its name." The term *homosexual* had just been coined and had not gained much public circulation when Douglas composed his poem and committed acts of "gross indecency" with Wilde [λ Chapter 12]. At the time, then, few terms existed that described same-sex relations or acts in any way except as "sinful" or criminal.

In many ways, our contemporary Western understanding of sexuality was constructed at the turn of the twentieth century by practitioners of the emerging disciplines of psychiatry, psychology, and sociology. Members of the legal profession, as well as early homosexual rights activists in Europe, also helped disseminate a way of talking about sex and sexuality that prefigured how we talk about sexuality today. Perhaps most important, the work of late nineteenth-century **sexologists** was crucial in constructing a discourse about sexuality that was scientific rather than laden with religious condemnation or criminal accusation. Such work was not without its own set of judgments and valuations, but our contemporary understanding of homosexuality as an *identity* begins with the sexologists.

Victorian Sex: Some Background

In the late nineteenth century, there was widespread disagreement about sex and its benefits—or potential hazards—physically, morally, and socially. On one hand, according to Jonathan Margolis in *O: The Intimate History of the Orgasm*, "Most Victorian doctors considered sexual desire in women to be pathological and warned that female sexual excitement and indulgence could damage their reproductive organs and urinary system" (282). Similarly, Richard von Krafft-Ebing, in *Psychopathia Sexualis* ([1886] 1965), "linked masturbation to criminality" and described women "who exhibited 'excessive' sexual desire" as "nymphomaniacs" (Margolis 287). On the other hand, Margolis points out that Havelock Ellis argued that in marriage, "one should ascertain not just the sexual needs of the husband but of the wife too" (293). What's more, in Europe and the United States, Victorian-era doctors believed that inducing **paroxysm** (or orgasm) was an effective treatment for **hysteria**.

These divergent views are not surprising when we consider the numerous social, cultural, and political upheavals that characterize the turn of the twentieth century. Change was in the air. The era was marked by increased urbanization, a growing middle class with greater earning power, continued industrialization, the further development of overseas empires, and, along with this, growing colonial unrest. Perhaps most significantly, the rise of scientific thought challenged reliance on biblical or religious modes of understanding the human condition. Scientific upheavals, such as Darwin's theory of evolution or the geological discovery of ancient fossils, suggested that the world was far older than the six thousand years of recorded biblical history; many people found that scientific discovery could provide a deeper understanding of humanity than scriptural accounts, which were beginning to seem unreliable as sources of knowledge.

These changes affected the way individuals organized and understood their personal lives. As people moved into cities to find jobs and make money, family structures changed. Just a century before, most families consisted of complex and extended kinship networks in mostly rural areas; by the late nineteenth century, many people were living in smaller familial units, on their own, or in other pairings or groupings. In *Surpassing the Love of Men* (1981), Lillian Faderman describes the emergence of "romantic friendships" among women at that time, such as so-called Boston marriages, in which two professional women set up housekeeping together [λ Chapter 1]. Concomitant with such "alternative" familial groupings were calls for women's rights, particularly the vote, as women entered the paid workforce in greater numbers. The move to cities also brought individuals into closer contact with prostitution and the "sexual underground." Urban centers were (and still are, to a large extent) areas in which people could explore and construct a variety of intimate and erotic arrangements. Historian George Chauncey notes that "[i]n the half-century between 1890 and the beginning of the Second World War, a highly visible, remarkably complex, and continually changing gay male world took shape in New York City" (1). Jonathan Margolis points out that this era also saw an increase in the availability of contraceptives, such as condoms and diaphragms. People were not necessarily having more sex than before, but the available evidence suggests that sex, sexual diversity, and alternative intimate arrangements were more visible and becoming subjects of discussion—and concern.

In fact, a variety of Europeans—ranging from medical professionals and politicians to religious leaders and laypeople—were deeply troubled by the rapid changes they were seeing in family structures and sexual practices. Out of this concern, and motivated by an interest in understanding what people were doing and why, the field of **sexology** was born. It is also important to note that sexology arose in the context of the professionalization of the sciences in the West, as part of the grand nineteenth-century project of discovery and taxonomy. The sexologists' early documentation, theoretical musings, and scientific debates were crucial in providing a language with which to talk about sexuality in general and homosexuality in particular.

Sexology: Defining a Field of Study

In 1869, the German physician Karl Westphal (1833–1890) noted in the *Archive for Psychiatry and Nervous Diseases* a new abnormality or mental disorder, which he called "contrary sexual feeling," meant to describe men whose sexual feelings were largely for other men and women whose sexual feelings were largely for other women. According to Westphal, such men were generally effeminate and the women "mannish" in behavior and appearance. Westphal and later sexologists called these men and women *inverts* because their gender presentation and, to some degree, their sexual desires seemed to these researchers inverse to the expected norms for their sex ("Invert"). Also in 1869, the writer Karl Maria Kertbeny invented the term *homosexual* to describe similar behaviors ("Karl Maria Kertbeny"). This term was then used by a variety of others in the developing field of sexology to describe same-sex sexual interest.

One of the key characteristics of much sexological thinking about **inversion** was the belief that male inverts were in some way more feminine than "normal" men and that female inverts were more masculine than "normal" women. Iwan Bloch's (1872–1922) *The Sexual Life of Our Times* (1907) offers a striking description of inversion, highlighting this gender "confusion":

> More especially after removing any beard or mustache that be present, we sometimes see much more clearly the feminine expression of face in a male homosexual, whilst before the hair was removed they appeared quite man-like. Still more important for the determination of a feminine habitus are direct physical characteristics. Among these there must be mentioned a *considerable deposit of fat,* by which the resemblance to the feminine type is produced, the contours of the body being more rounded than in the case of the normal male. In correspondence with this the *muscular system* is less powerfully developed than it is in heterosexual men, the skin is delicate and soft, and the complexion is much clearer than is usual in men. (qtd. in Bristow 36)

This kind of thinking about homosexuality was to remain influential, permeating the popular consciousness and seemingly supported by scientific research. The supposed link between deviation from sex and gender norms and homosexuality has continued to function as a fundamental assumption underlying many studies throughout the twentieth century and into the twenty-first [λ Chapter 5].

Find Out More about "Nature, Nurture, and Identity" in Chapter 5.

In 1886, German psychiatrist Dr. Richard von Krafft-Ebing (1840–1902) published *Psychopathia Sexualis,* in which he catalogued, described, and discussed a number of sexual "perversions." According to Krafft-Ebing, "Homosexuals . . . had feelings that represented an 'abnormal congenital manifestation,' and 'the essential feature of this strange manifestation of the sexual life is the want of sexual sensibility for the opposite sex, even to the extent of horror, while sexual inclination and impulse toward the same sex are present'" (Fout 274–75). Krafft-Ebing based his conclusions in large part on numerous case histories of those claiming to have same-sex sexual attractions. His goal in reviewing and analyzing these case histories was in line with much sexological practice: to categorize and provide a taxonomy for the variety of sexual interests and expressions. Krafft-Ebing also studied those whose sexual interests involved **masochism, fetishism,** and **sadism**—all terms that he invented.

Krafft-Ebing generally believed that homosexuality was **congenital,** a condition with which an individual was unfortunately born. At the same time, homosexuality could arise from other **etiologies:** "a hypochondriacal fear of infection during sexual intercourse," fear of pregnancy, and "mental or moral weakness," for instance (qtd. in Bristow 32). Homosexuality was seen as a "perversion"— something to be avoided or at best pitied. Krafft-Ebing's language suggested that homosexuality was a mental illness, a belief many psychologists and psychiatrists supported well into the twentieth century [λ Chapter 3]. As a point of clarification, Krafft-Ebing used the term *heterosexual* to describe what he saw as the perverse practice of engaging in sexual relations with a member of the opposite sex without the aim of reproduction. Interestingly, Krafft-Ebing's views on homosexuality as a perversion shifted toward the end of his life; his final edition of *Psychopathia Sexualis* asserted that homosexuality was one manifestation of sexual desire and not necessarily a mental disease ("Krafft-Ebing").

Krafft-Ebing's view may have shifted in part due to the work of other sexologists and writers who were interested in homosexuality and who felt that homosexuals were neither perverse nor mentally ill. Karl Heinrich Ulrichs (1825–1895), a German student of law and theology, believed that homosexuals comprised a "third sex," which he called **Urnings,** a sexological category he described at some length in *The Riddle of "Man-Manly" Love,* a series of pamphlets published from 1864 to 1880. According to Ulrichs's theory, Urnings were the product of heredity and displayed visible physical differences from heterosexuals. For Ulrichs, the innateness of the Urning condition was the most significant reason that it should not be considered abnormal—hence his insistence that we recognize Urnings as a third sex beyond men and women (Bristow 20–26).

Given the enormous influence of the sexologists in creating a language to discuss homosexuality (and other sexual diversities), some contemporary thinkers

Figure 2.1 Magnus Hirschfeld's sexual types: masculine (top), Urning (center), and feminine (bottom).

Find Out More in D'Emilio's "Capitalism and Gay Identity" at the end of this chapter.

have credited the turn of the twentieth century with "giving birth" to the modern homosexual. Most notably, French philosopher Michel Foucault (1926–1984) famously asserted in his *History of Sexuality* ([1976] 1978) that the sexological categorization of sexual diversities in the late nineteenth century served to create not only new categories of mental illness but also new *identities* based on sexuality. As Foucault points out, those (e.g., sodomites) who had earlier engaged in homoerotic behavior were frequently condemned for their *acts;* now, with the rise of medical classifications and the science of psychology, such people were diagnosed as suffering from mental disorders—and thus "the homosexual was now a species" (43). As David Halperin puts it, "although there are persons who seek sexual contact with other persons of the same sex in many different societies, only recently and only in some sectors of our society have such persons—or some portion of them— been homosexuals" (qtd. in Jagose 46). Hence, categorization worked not just to pathologize a new species of humans but also to allow those "afflicted" with homosexuality to consider themselves a "species" of people who could describe and talk about their lives beyond the often negative judgments of the medical establishment. Ulrichs, himself an Urning, used the medical classification of inversion and homosexuality to create a "reverse discourse" that attempted to speak positively about his sexual experiences and insist on the naturalness of the Urning condition as a "third sex" [λ Chapter 7].

It is important to keep in mind, as Foucault does, that the identity-creating process was enormously complex, involving not only the circulation of discourses in a variety of professional fields (medicine, law, psychiatry) but also the shifting economic circumstances of many European nations at the time. As noted earlier, increased urbanization allowed for greater contact among people with divergent sexual interests, and some scholars—John D'Emilio, for instance—have pointed to such economic shifts as just as important as sexological research in the formation of a modern homosexual identity. As we shall see throughout the rest of this book, complex forces and phenomena always play crucial roles in the development of personal identities, as well as social and political organizations based on those identities.

A Sexologist in Depth: Havelock Ellis

To understand how sexologists worked, one should look at one famous sexologist in more depth. Havelock Ellis (1859–1939) was a British physician who wrote prolifically about sex and sexuality at the turn of the twentieth century. One of his most important works, *Sexual Inversion,* coauthored with the writer John Addington Symonds in 1897, was an important early and relatively sympathetic discussion of homosexual men. Indeed, Ellis wanted to present a fair—and scientific—representation of homosexuality. His *Studies in the Psychology of Sex,* a two-volume work collecting a sampling of his writing on sex (published in 1937, but including work copyrighted as early as 1905), reveals Ellis's interest in a variety of sexual practices, not just homosexuality.

Figure 2.2   Havelock Ellis

In this book, Ellis attempts to differentiate between "inversion" and other kinds of homosexuality. For Ellis, inverts are *primarily* disposed to sexual attraction to members of the same sex, whereas other forms of homosexual attraction may be due to "accidental absences." For instance, when boys or girls are separated from one another in boarding schools, the "natural" object of sexual attraction (a member of the opposite sex) is absent; hence, sexual attraction "between persons of the same sex" may occur.

Ellis's language is intriguing. He characterizes heterosexual attraction as "natural" while at the same time suggesting that homoerotic attraction is "a phenomenon of wide occurrence among all human races and among most of the higher animals" (1). This curious split—naturalizing heterosexuality but not wanting to condemn homosexuality—appears throughout Ellis's writing. For example, he writes that "[p]rison life develops and fosters the homosexual tendency of criminals; but there can be little doubt that that tendency, or else a tendency to sexual indifference or bisexuality, is a radical character of a very large number of criminals" (26). He goes on to note that "[t]he fact that homosexuality is especially common among men of exceptional intellect was long since noted by Dante" (26). Ellis then spends several pages listing and discussing "famous inverts," such as the writers Oscar Wilde and Edward Fitzgerald. He also reports on some "near misses": "While Shakespeare . . . narrowly escapes inclusion in the list of distinguished inverts, there is much better ground for the inclusion of his great contemporary, Francis Bacon" (44). Ellis then reviews the work of some of the major sexologists of his time; he also presents several "cases" in which inverts describe their lives in narrative form, offering detailed sexual histories. It is clear that this listing of famous inverts and examples of inversion is designed to somewhat normalize (if not necessarily naturalize) homosexuality. In other words, given its presence among various human (and "higher animal") populations, Ellis believed that homosexuality should probably be treated as another variation in human sexual behavior.

Ellis's treatment of female inverts is similar. He notes that "[h]omosexuality is not less common in women than in men" (195) and that "[i]t has been noted of distinguished women in all ages and in all fields of activity that they have frequently displayed some masculine traits" (196). Ellis holds to the theory of inversion—that homosexual women are more often than not more masculine in presentation. At the same time, Ellis admits that relatively little is known about sexual inversion in women and that the topic needs further study. But he is willing to share some of his initial insights and findings. Most notably, he argues that "[w]hile the use of the clitoris is rare in homosexuality, the use of an artificial penis is by no means uncommon and very widespread" (258). Ellis maintains that "[a]n enlarged clitoris is but rarely found in inversion and displays a very small part in the gratification of feminine homosexuality" (258). Here he repudiates the myth that "mannish" female inverts are endowed by nature with abnormally large sexual organs that can, by themselves, produce "paroxysm" in a female partner.

Despite Ellis's sensible rejection of some ridiculous myths about inverts, one doubts the validity of his scientific method when reading his characterization of some of their more pronounced physical attributes. For instance, he writes that "[a] marked characteristic of many inverts, though one not easy of precise definition, is their youthfulness of appearance, and frequently child-like faces, equally in both sexes" (290). Granted, Ellis qualifies his comments ("one not easy of precise definition"), but many of his other findings are outrageous, such as his belief that female inverts are "very good whistlers" (256) and that male inverts prefer "green garments" (299). At the same time, Ellis maintains, sympathetically, that "[a]ll avocations are represented among inverts" (293). Despite his often quirky conclusions, Ellis wanted to portray inverts in particular and homosexuality in general in a positive light.

A significant issue facing sexologists was the cause of inversion and homosexuality, and Ellis has much to say on this subject, even if he will not commit to one particular or necessary cause. As noted earlier, he believed that lack of a "natural" object of sexual attraction can induce homoerotic attractions. He says that, in the case of women, for instance, "[h]omosexuality is specially fostered by those employments which keep women in constant association, not only by day, but often at night also, without the company of men" (212). Such employments may include the work of nuns in convents or leaders of the "woman movement" (262). Ellis also felt, in line with the received wisdom of his day, that masturbation had deleterious side effects: "I am certainly inclined to believe that an early and excessive indulgence in mastur- bation, though not an adequate cause, is a favoring condition for the development of inversion, and that this is especially so in women" (277). This would be true because masturbation presupposes sexual desire, which was considered by Ellis and his contemporaries to be exclusively a masculine characteristic. Hence, a masturbating woman would be considered sexually "mannish," and thus, an invert.

In general, Ellis subscribed to three principal causes of homoerotic sexual attrac- tion: (1) the absence of more "natural" objects of affection, (2) significant dis- appointment in romantic relationships with the opposite sex, or (3) seduction by a member of the same sex. Presumably, a combination of these factors could also induce inversion. At the same time, Ellis did not want to preclude the strong possi- bility of congenital predisposition to inversion or homosexual attraction. He wrote,

> These three influences, therefore . . . example at school, seduction, disap- pointment in normal love,—all of them drawing the subject away from the opposite sex and concentrating him on his own sex, are exciting causes of inversion; but they require a favourable organic predisposition to act on, while there are a large number of cases in which no exciting cause at all can be found, but in which, from earliest childhood, the subject's interest seems to be turned on his own sex, and continues to be so turned through- out life. (324)

Interestingly, this passage prefigures the "nature versus nurture" debates that would become so important in academic circles throughout the twentieth century: are complex behaviors and feelings, such as sexual attraction, biologically innate or the product of social influences or forces? [λ Chapter 5]

For Ellis, discussions of sexual inversion and homosexuality consisted not only of scientific explorations and theories but also of an awareness of the social dimen- sion of the objects under study. He believed he viewed the topic of homosexuality from an unbiased perspective. But Ellis's aim was more than just avoiding an "attitude of moral superiority" (356). He felt that bias against inverts and homo- sexuals was legally unfounded and untenable. He wrote that "legislation against

Find Out More in the Ellis case histories at the end of this chapter.

homosexuality has no clear effect either in diminishing or increasing its prevalence" (350). This view is clearly related to his sense that there is no real "cure" for inversion or homosexuality: "The question of the treatment of homosexuality must be approached with discrimination, caution, and scepticism. Nowadays we can have but little sympathy with those who, at all costs, are prepared to 'cure' the invert. There is no sound method of cure in radical cases" (327). Given its congenital nature and apparent incurability, legislating against homosexuality seemed to Ellis nonsensical.

Paving the Way for Freud

In many significant ways, the sexologists paved the way for Sigmund Freud (1856–1939), Austrian neurologist and founder of psychoanalysis. While Freud was not a sexologist per se, his theories of sexuality became guiding principles for many twentieth-century approaches to the study of sex, sexuality, identity, and personality. His influence has been tremendous, but it is worth keeping in mind that Freud was working in the same cultural and intellectual milieu that gave rise to the study of sexology. Freud certainly knew the work of the sexologists and was acquainted with many of them personally. He also took very seriously the importance of sex and sexual feeling in the development of the individual. Much of his work focused on tracing "healthy" psychosexual development through various stages (such as oral, anal, genital), and Freud suggested that the failure to navigate a particular stage successfully ("arrested development") might result in homosexuality. But for Freud, this was not necessarily serious cause for alarm since the successful resolution of each stage and the consequent development of a fully adjusted heterosexual personality and identity is, he felt, a rare achievement. We all get stuck somewhere.

Much of Freud's central thinking about sexuality and its relationship to identity is found in *Three Essays on the Theory of Sexuality*, published in 1905. Freud believed in an innate "polymorphous perversity" that had to be shaped by social forces to achieve reproductive heterosexuality. This theory sharply differentiates Freud's work from that of the sexologists. As Steven Seidman writes, "[w]hereas sexologists defined the sexual instinct as reproductive and naturally heterosexual, Freud argued that the sexual instinct is oriented to pleasure. [. . .] Freud argued that the body has many erotic areas and that there are many ways of experiencing sexual satisfaction" (7). According to this view, possibilities for sexual excitation were multiple, and the path of one's desire could not be reduced to particular physiological characteristics. British theorist Alan Sinfield notes as well that "[i]n

Three Essays on the Theory of Sexuality . . . , Freud dismisses the sexologists' theories of innate inversion as crude, and disputes the anatomical basis they had been claiming. Even a change-over of 'mental qualities, instincts and character traits' cannot be demonstrated, let alone a physiological cross-over" (164).

Despite these differences, Freud and the sexologists shared some common insights into and beliefs about sexuality. According to Seidman, "Freud opened the way to thinking about sex as a fundamentally psychosocial reality; however, Freud never abandoned the sexological view that sex is natural" (12). David Halperin sees Havelock Ellis's and Freud's theories "separating sexual practices from gender" as representing "a key stage in the development of the possibility of gay identity" (Sinfield 163).

Sexology and Early Sexual Rights Movements

As Foucault points out, the intense medical, psychiatric, and sexological scrutiny of inversion and homosexuality allowed some of those pathologized as homosexuals to create "reverse discourses" in which they recast their "illness" as positive identification. Ulrichs is a powerful example of this, leading some contemporary theorists to look favorably on the sexological enterprise. Steven Seidman, for instance, argues that "[s]exology has always had a social purpose." He notes that "[s]ome sexologists saw their work as contributing to the creation of a healthy, fit population. [. . .] Some policies even discouraged active sexual behavior by so-called inferior races and the sexual intermingling of races" (5). Such eugenic implications clearly complicate any "positive" intentions on behalf of sexologists to promote sex as a "natural" and "normal" practice, but we should not overlook the early sexual rights activists who used sexological research to fight laws designed to criminalize homoerotic behavior [λ Chapter 4].

Such laws were coming into existence at roughly the same time that sexologists were describing and categorizing homosexual behavior. While practices such as anal sex had previously been punishable in several European nations, a number of homoerotic practices were now coming under legal scrutiny and being not only pathologized but criminalized as well. For instance, the newly formed German state adopted Paragraph 175 in 1871, which banned all sexual activity between men (as well as **bestiality**) ("Germany") [λ Chapter 3]. Paragraph 175 spurred Ulrichs and others to become pro-homosexual activists, essentially creating the first relatively visible homosexual rights groups in Western history. Another prominent activist, the physician Magnus Hirschfeld (1868–1935), wrote pamphlets, books, and even a movie script (*Different from the Others,* 1919) to advocate on behalf of the "third sex" [λ Chapter 13]. John C. Fout details events of the early sexual rights movements in Germany, noting that "[i]n 1897 Magnus Hirschfeld and his newly created *Wissenschaftlich-humanitares Komittee* (Scientific humanitarian committee, or WhK) petitioned the Reichstag to reform [¶] 175 of the German penal code, which criminalized sexual acts between males" (265). Fout argues that governments enacted anti-homosexual legislation to calm the sociopolitical chaos that seemed to characterize the era.

Other important early sexual rights activists included the British writers Edward Carpenter (1844–1929) and Radclyffe Hall (1880–1943). Carpenter's poetry, pamphlets, and nonfiction works argued forcefully for thinking of sexual freedom for all as a basic right and privilege to be protected by democratic institutions as they slowly moved toward communist-style utopias. Hall is credited with writing the first novel recognizably about a lesbian, *The Well of Loneliness* (1928), which was subsequently banned in Britain and the subject of a censorship trial in the United States. *The Well of Loneliness* is an important document in that it borrows from sexological views circulating at the time; Havelock Ellis himself wrote a preface for the book in which he praised it for its "notable psychological and sociological significance [as] a completely faithful and uncompromising [depiction of] one particular aspect of sexual life as it exists among us to-day" (Hall, preface). Its hero, Stephen Gordon, is clearly a congenital invert in the sense that she is depicted (as Hall described herself) as a woman born with a man's soul. The end of the novel is a passionate and moving plea for tolerance: "Acknowledge us, oh God, before the whole world. Give us also the right to our existence!" (437) [λ Chapters 7 and 12].

Such pleas fell on deaf ears as the European continent drifted toward war spurred by imperial ambitions, economic collapse, the rise of National Socialism and other fascist movements, and yet more global war. Amid this increasing social and political chaos, many politicians sought stability by imposing order based on clear class divides and gender roles. In their view, we should all know our place in the social scheme of things. Unfortunately, the maintenance of the status quo and the attendant social control that such maintenance entailed would keep further Western movements for sexual rights and freedom below the political radar until the 1950s and 1960s.

Sexology's Legacy

As we think back on the development of sexology as a science, we quickly dismiss some of its practitioners' more audacious claims, such as the predilection of male homosexuals for the color green. In many other ways, though, the sexologists helped shape our contemporary understanding of sex and sexuality. Their classifications of sexuality and the development of the categories "homosexual" and "heterosexual" survive today as "gay" and "straight," two of the most significant identity markers in contemporary Western culture, society, and politics. Furthermore, Dennis Altman suggests that turn-of-the-century categorizations of sexuality in the West have not only survived into the twenty-first century but have proliferated across the globe:

> Globalization has helped create an international gay/lesbian identity, which is by no means confined to the western world: there are many signs of what we think of as "modern" homosexuality in countries such as Brazil, Costa Rica, Poland, and Taiwan. Indeed, the gay world—less obviously the lesbian, largely due to marked differences in women's social and economic status— is a key example of emerging global "subcultures," where members of particular groups have more in common across national and continental boundaries than they do with others in their own geographically defined societies. (87)

We will see examples of this commonality, as well as some striking challenges to it, throughout the remainder of this book, particularly as we look at examples of queerness in countries across the globe.

QUESTIONS FOR DISCUSSION

1. Sexologists at the turn of the century considered themselves scientists. Whatever the merits of their scientific practices (and those practices are obviously not without their faults), a scientific understanding of homosexuality has continued to be important to this day. In what ways? Do you think a scientific understanding of homosexuality is beneficial to contemporary LGBT people? Why or why not?

2. If you were to write your own "case history" for a sexologist, what would it look like? Try your hand at such a case history, whatever your sexual orientation, and then compare it with one collected by Ellis. What are the similarities and differences? Look closely at particular ways in which you phrase your experience. Do you find any resemblances between what you have written and what others wrote a century ago?

3. Although we in the contemporary world often think of the Stonewall riots in 1969 as inaugurating the contemporary fight for gay and lesbian civil rights, we have seen in this chapter some much earlier manifestations of sexual rights advocacy. Using the Internet, a local library, or a local LGBT community center, research other late nineteenth- and early twentieth-century homosexual or sexual rights movements.

What do those earlier movements have in common with contemporary organizations and movements? What are some of the more striking differences? Consider how the sociopolitical situation today differs from that of a century ago.

REFERENCES AND FURTHER READING

Altman, Dennis. *Global Sex.* Chicago: U of Chicago P, 2001.

Bristow, David. *Sexuality.* London: Routledge, 1997.

Carpenter, Edward. *The Intermediate Sex: A Study of Some Transitional Types of Men and Women.* New York: Kennerley, 1921 [c. 1912].

Chauncey, George. *Gay New York: Gender, Urban Culture, and the Making of the Gay Male World, 1890–1940.* New York: Basic Books, 1994.

Douglas, Lord Alfred. "Two Loves." 19 July 2008 <http://www.law.umkc.edu/faculty/projects/ftrials/wilde/poemsofdouglas.htm>.

Duberman, Martin Bauml, Martha Vicinus, and George Chauncey Jr., eds. *Hidden from History: Reclaiming the Gay and Lesbian Past.* New York: New American Library, 1989.

Ellis, Havelock. *Studies in the Psychology of Sex.* New York: Random House, 1937.

Faderman, Lillian. *Surpassing the Love of Men: Romantic Friendship and Love between Women from the Renaissance to the Present.* New York: Morrow, 1981.

Foucault, Michel. *The History of Sexuality, Volume 1.* Trans. Robert Hurley. New York: Vintage, 1978 [1976].

Fout, John C., ed. *Forbidden History: The State, Society, and the Regulation of Sexuality in Modern Europe.* Chicago: U of Chicago P, 1992.

Freud, Sigmund. *Three Essays on the Theory of Sexuality.* Trans. James Strachey. New York: Basic Books, 1975 [1905].

"Germany Adopts Paragraph 175." *Timeline: Nations and Laws.* 19 July 2008 <http://www.gayhistory.com/rev2/factfiles/ff1871.htm>.

GLBTQ: An Encyclopedia of Gay, Lesbian, Bisexual, Transgender, & Queer Culture. 19 July 2008 <http://www.glbtq.com/>.

Greenberg, David F. *The Construction of Homosexuality.* Chicago: U of Chicago P, 1988.

Hall, Radclyffe. *The Well of Loneliness.* New York: Avon, 1981 [1928].

"Invert." *Words: A Glossary of Words Unique to Modern Gay History.* 19 July 2008 <http://www.gayhistory.com/rev2/words/invert.htm>.

Jagose, Annamarie. *Queer Theory: An Introduction.* New York: NYU P, 1996.

"Karl Maria Kertbeny." *Timeline: Culture and Identity.* 19 July 2008 <http://www.gayhistory.com/rev2/factfiles/ffkertbeny.htm>.

Katz, Jonathan Ned. *The Invention of Heterosexuality.* New York: Dutton, 1995.

"Krafft-Ebing, Richard von (1840–1902)." *GLBTQ: An Encyclopedia of Gay, Lesbian, Bisexual, Transgender, and Queer Culture.* 19 July 2008 <http://www.glbtq.com/social sciences/krafft_ebing_r.html>.

Krafft-Ebing, Richard von. *Psychopathia Sexualis: A Medico-forensic Study.* Trans. Harry E. Wedeck. New York: Putnam, 1965 [1886].

Margolis, Jonathan. *O: The Intimate History of the Orgasm.* London: Century, 2004.

Oosterhuis, Harry. *Stepchildren of Nature: Krafft-Ebing, Psychiatry, and the Making of Sexual Identity.* Chicago: U of Chicago P, 2000.

Seidman, Steven. *The Social Construction of Sexuality.* New York: Norton, 2003.

Sinfield, Alan. *The Wilde Century: Effeminacy, Oscar Wilde and the Queer Moment.* New York: Columbia UP, 1994.

"Timeline: Nations and Laws." *Timeline: The People and the Stories of Modern Gay History.* 19 July 2008 <http://www.gayhistory.com/rev2/factfiles/ff1861.htm>.

Weeks, Jeffrey. *Sexuality and Its Discontents: Meanings, Myths, and Modern Sexualities.* London: Routledge, 1985.

READINGS

➤ **Havelock Ellis**

Studies in the Psychology of Sex

(1937), United Kingdom

From "History II"

My parentage is very sound and healthy. Both my parents (who belong to the professional middle class) have good general health; nor can I trace any marked abnormal or diseased tendency, of mind or body, in any records of the family.

Though of a strongly nervous temperament myself, and sensitive, my health is good. I am not aware of any tendency to physical disease. In early manhood, however, owing, I believe, to the great emotional tension under which I lived, my nervous system was a good deal shattered and exhausted. Mentally and morally my nature is pretty well balanced, and I have never had any serious perturbations in these departments.

At the age of 8 or 9, and long before distinct sexual feelings declared themselves, I felt a friendly attraction toward my own sex, and this developed after the age of puberty into a passionate sense of love, which, however, never found any expression for itself till I was fully 20 years of age. I was a day-boarder at school and heard little of school-talk on sex subjects, was very reserved and modest besides; no elder person or parent ever spoke to me on such matters; and the passion for my own sex developed gradually, utterly uninfluenced from the outside. I never even, during all this period, and till a good deal later, learned the practice of masturbation. My own sexual nature was a mystery to me. I found myself cut off from the understanding of others, felt myself an outcast, and, with a highly loving and clinging temperament, was intensely miserable. I thought about my male friends—sometimes boys of my own age, sometimes elder boys, and once even a master—during the day and dreamed about them at night, but was too convinced that I was a hopeless monstrosity ever to make any effectual advances. Later on it was much the same, but gradually, though slowly, I came to find that there were others like myself. I made a few special friends, and at last it came to me occasionally to sleep with them and to satisfy my imperious need by mutual embraces and emissions. Before this happened, however, I was once or twice on the brink of despair and madness with repressed passion and torment. Meanwhile, from the first, my feeling, physically, toward the female sex was one of indifference, and later on, with the more special development of sex desires, one of positive repulsion. Though having several female friends, whose society I like and to whom I am sincerely attached, the thought of marriage or cohabitation with any such has always been odious to me.

As a boy I was attracted in general by boys rather older than myself; after leaving school I still fell in love, in a romantic vein, with comrades of my own standing. Now,—at the age of 37,—my ideal of love is a powerful, strongly built man, of my own age or rather younger—preferably of the working class. Though having solid sense and character, he need not be specially intellectual. If endowed in the latter way, he must not be too glib or refined. Anything effeminate in a man, or anything of the cheap intellectual style, repels me very decisively.

[. . .]

I cannot regard my sexual feelings as unnatural or abnormal, since they have disclosed themselves so perfectly naturally and spontaneously within me. All that I have read in books or heard spoken about the ordinary sexual love, its intensity and passion, lifelong devotion, love at first sight, etc., seems to me to be easily matched by my own experiences in the homosexual form; and, with regard to the morality of this complex subject, my feeling is that it is the same as should prevail in love between man and woman, namely: that no bodily satisfaction should be sought at the cost of another person's distress or degradation. I am sure that this kind of love is, notwithstanding the physical difficulties that attend it, as deeply stirring and ennobling as the other kind, if not more so; and I think that for a perfect relationship the actual sex gratifications (whatever they may be) probably hold a less important place in this love than in the other.

From "History XXXVI.—Miss H., aged 30"

Among her paternal relatives there is a tendency to eccentricity and to nervous disease. Her grandfather drank; her father was eccentric and hypochondriacal, and suffered from obsessions. Her mother and mother's relatives are entirely healthy, and normal in disposition.

At the age of 4 she liked to see the nates of a little girl who lived near. When she was about 6, the nurse-maid, sitting in the fields, used to play with her own parts, and told her to do likewise, saying it would make a baby come; she occasionally touched herself in consequence, but without producing any effect of any kind. When she was about 8 she used to see various nurse-maids uncover their children's sexual parts and show them to each other. She used to think about this when alone, and also about whipping. She never cared to play with dolls, and in her games always took the part of a man. Her first rudimentary sex-feelings appeared at the age of 8 or 9, and were associated with dreams of whipping and being whipped, which were most vivid between the ages of 11 and 14, when they died away on the appearance of affection for girls. She menstruated at 12.

Her earliest affection, at the age of 13, was for a schoolfellow, a graceful, coquettish girl with long golden hair and blue eyes. Her affection displayed itself in performing all sorts of small services for this girl, in constantly thinking about her, and in feeling deliciously grateful for the smallest return. At the age of 14 she had a similar passion for a girl cousin; she used to look forward with ecstasy to her visits, and especially to the rare occasions when the cousin slept with her; her excitement was then so great that she could not sleep, but there was no conscious sexual excitement. At the age of 15 or 16 she fell in love with another cousin; her experiences with this girl were full of delicious sensations; if the cousin only touched her neck, a thrill went through her body which she now regards as sexual. Again, at 17, she had an overwhelming, passionate fascination for another schoolfellow, a pretty, commonplace girl, whom she idealized and etherealized to an extravagant extent. The passion was so violent that her health was, to some extent, impaired; but it was purely unselfish, and there was nothing sexual in it. On leaving school at the age of 19 she met a girl of about the same age as herself, very womanly, but not much attracted to men. This girl became very much attached to her, and sought to gain her love. After some time Miss H. was attracted by this love, partly from the sense of power it gave her, and an intimate relation grew up. This relation became vaguely physical, Miss H. taking the initiative, but her friend desiring such relations and taking extreme pleasure in them; they used to touch and kiss each other tenderly (especially on the *mons veneris*), with equal ardour. They each experienced a strong pleasurable feeling in doing this, and sexual erethism, but no orgasm, and it does not appear that this ever occurred. Their general behavior to each other was that of lovers, but they endeavoured, as far as possible, to hide this fact from the world. This relation lasted for several years, and would have continued, had not Miss H.'s friend, from religious and moral scruples, put an end to the physical relationship. Miss H. had been very well and happy during this relationship; the interference with it seems to have exerted a disturbing influence, and also to have aroused her sexual desires, though she was still scarcely conscious of their real nature.

[. . .]

She has never masturbated. Occasionally, but very rarely, she has had dreams of riding accompanied by pleasurable sexual emotions (she cannot recall any actual experience to suggest this, though fond of riding). She has never had any kind of sexual dreams about a man; of late years she has occasionally had erotic dreams about women. Her feeling toward men is friendly, but she has never had sexual attraction toward a man. She likes them as good comrades, as men like each other. She enjoys the society of men on account of their intellectual attraction.

[. . .]

She is attracted to womanly women, sincere, reserved, pure, but courageous in character. She is not attracted to intellectual women, but at the same time cannot endure silly women. The physical qualities that attract her most are not so much beauty of face as a graceful, but not too slender, body with beautiful curves. The women she is drawn to are usually somewhat younger than herself. Women are much attracted to her, and without any effort on her part. She likes to take the active part and protecting role with them. She is herself energetic in character, and with a somewhat neurotic temperament. She finds sexual satisfaction in tenderly touching, caressing, and kissing the loved one's body. (There is no *cunnilinctus*, which she regards with abhorrence.) She feels more tenderness than passion.

[. . .]

She believes that homosexual love is morally right when it is really part of a person's nature, and providing that the nature of homosexual love is always made plain to the object of such affection. She does not approve of it as a mere makeshift, or expression of sensuality, in normal women. She has sometimes resisted the sexual expression of her feelings, once for years at a time, but always in vain. The effect on her of loving women is distinctly good, she asserts, both spiritually and physically, while repression leads to morbidity and hysteria. She has suffered much from neurasthenia at various periods, but under appropriate treatment it has slowly diminished. The inverted instinct is too deeply rooted to eradicate, but it is well under control.

Ellis, Havelock. *Studies in the Psychology of Sex*. New York: Random House, 1937.

➤ **John D'Emilio**

"Capitalism and Gay Identity"
(1993), United States

[. . .]

I believe that a new, more accurate theory of gay history must be part of [the gay and lesbian] political enterprise. When the gay liberation movement began at the end of the 1960s, gay men and lesbians had no history that we could use to fashion our goals and strategy. In the ensuing years, in building a movement without a knowledge of our history, we instead invented a mythology. This mythical history drew on personal experience, which we read backward in time. For instance, most lesbians and gay men in the 1960s first discovered their homosexual desires in isolation, unaware of others, and without resources for naming and understanding what they felt. From this experience, we constructed a myth of silence, invisibility, and isolation as the essential characteristics of gay life in the past as well as the present. Moreover, because we faced so many oppressive laws, public policies, and cultural beliefs, we projected this onto an image of the abysmal past: until gay liberation, lesbians and gay men were always the victims of systematic, undifferentiated, terrible oppression.

These myths have limited our political perspective. They have contributed, for instance, to an overreliance on a strategy of coming out—if every gay man and lesbian in America came out, gay oppression would end—and have allowed us to ignore the institutionalized ways in which homophobia and heterosexism are reproduced. They have encouraged, at times, an incapacitating despair, especially at moments like the present: How can we unravel a gay oppression so pervasive and unchanging?

There is another historical myth that enjoys nearly universal acceptance in the gay movement, the myth of the "eternal homosexual." The argument runs something like this: gay men and lesbians always were and always will be. We are everywhere; not just now, but throughout history, in all societies and all periods. This myth served a positive political function in the first years of gay liberation. In the early 1970s, when we battled an ideology that either denied our existence or defined us as psychopathic individuals or freaks of nature, it was empowering to assert that "we are everywhere." But in recent years it has confined us as surely as the most homophobic medical theories, and locked our movement in place.

Here I wish to challenge this myth. I want to argue that gay men and lesbians have *not* always existed. Instead, they are a product of history, and have come into existence in a specific historical era. Their emergence is associated with the relations of capitalism; it has been the historical development of capitalism—more specifically, its free labor system— that has allowed large numbers of men and women in the late twentieth century to call themselves gay, to see themselves as part of a community of similar men and women, and to organize politically on the basis of that identity. Finally, I want to suggest some political lessons we can draw from this view of history.

What, then, are the relationships between the free labor system of capitalism and homosexuality? First, let me review some features of capitalism. Under capitalism, workers are "free" laborers in two ways. We have the freedom to look for a job. We own our ability to work and have the freedom to sell our labor power for wages to anyone willing to buy it. We are also freed from the ownership of anything except our labor power. Most of us do not own the land or the tools that produce what we need, but rather have to work for a living in order to survive. So, if we are free to sell our labor power in the positive sense, we are also freed, in the negative sense, from any other alternative. This dialectic—the constant interplay between exploitation and some measure of autonomy— informs all of the history of those who have lived under capitalism.

As capital—money used to make more money—expands, so does this system of free labor. Capital expands in several ways. Usually it expands in the same place, transforming small firms into larger ones, but it also expands by taking over new areas of production: the weaving of cloth, for instance, or the baking of bread. Finally, capital expands geographically. In the United States, capitalism initially took root in the Northeast, at a time when slavery was the dominant system in the South and when noncapitalist Native American societies occupied the western half of the continent. During the nineteenth century, capital spread from the Atlantic to the Pacific, and in the twentieth, U.S. capital has penetrated almost every part of the world.

The expansion of capital and the spread of wage labor have effected a profound transformation in the structure and functions of the nuclear family, the ideology of family life, and the meaning of heterosexual relations. It is these changes in the family that are most directly linked to the appearance of a collective gay life.

The white colonists in seventeenth-century New England established villages structured around a household economy, composed of family units that were basically self-sufficient, independent, and patriarchal. Men, women, and children farmed land owned by the male head of household. Although there was a division of labor between men and women, the family was truly an interdependent unit of production: the survival of each member depended on the cooperation of all. The home was a workplace where women processed raw farm products into food for daily consumption, where they made clothing, soap, and candles, and where husbands, wives, and children worked together to produce the goods they consumed.

By the nineteenth century, this system of household production was in decline. In the Northeast, as merchant capitalists invested the money accumulated through trade in the production of goods, wage labor became more common. Men and women were drawn out of the largely self-sufficient household economy of the colonial era into a capitalist system of free labor. For women in the nineteenth century, working for wages rarely lasted beyond marriage; for men, it became a permanent condition.

The family was thus no longer an independent unit of production. But although no longer independent, the family was still interdependent. Because capitalism had not expanded very far, because it had not yet taken over—or socialized—the production of consumer goods, women still performed necessary productive labor in the home. Many families no longer produced grain, but wives still baked into bread the flour they bought with their husbands' wages; or, when they purchased yarn or cloth, they still made clothing for their families. By the mid-1800s, capitalism had destroyed the economic self-sufficiency of many families, but not the mutual dependence of the members.

This transition away from the household family-based economy to a fully developed capitalist free labor economy occurred very slowly, over almost two centuries. As late as 1920, 50 percent of the U.S. population lived in communities of fewer than 2,500 people. The vast majority of blacks in the early twentieth century lived outside the free labor economy, in a system of sharecropping and tenancy that rested on the family. Not only did independent farming as a way of life still exist for millions of Americans, but even in towns and small cities women continued to grow and process food, make clothing, and engage in other kinds of domestic production.

But for those people who felt the brunt of these changes, the family took on new significance as an affective unit, an institution that produced not goods but emotional satisfaction and happiness. By the 1920s, among the white middle class, the ideology surrounding the family described it as the means through which men and women formed satisfying, mutually enhancing relationships and created an environment that nurtured children. The family became the setting for "personal life," sharply distinguished and disconnected from the public world of work and production.

The meaning of heterosexual relations also changed. In colonial New England, the birthrate averaged over seven children per woman of childbearing age. Men and women needed the labor of children. Producing offspring was as necessary for survival as producing grain. Sex was harnessed to procreation. The Puritans did not celebrate *hetero*sexuality but rather marriage; they condemned *all* sexual expression outside the marriage bond and did not differentiate sharply between sodomy and heterosexual fornication.

[. . .]

As wage labor spread and production became socialized, then, it became possible to release sexuality from the "imperative" to procreate. Ideologically, heterosexual expression came to be a means of establishing intimacy, promoting happiness, and experiencing pleasure. In divesting the household of its economic independence and fostering the separation of sexuality from procreation, capitalism has created conditions that allow some men and women to organize a personal life around their erotic/emotional attraction to their own sex. It has made possible the formation of urban communities of lesbians and gay men and, more recently, of a politics based on a sexual identity.

Evidence from colonial New England court records and church sermons indicates that male and female homosexual behavior existed in the seventeenth century. Homosexual *behavior*, however, is different from homosexual *identity*. There was, quite simply, no "social space" in the colonial system of production that allowed men and women to be gay. Survival was structured around participation in a nuclear family. There were certain homosexual acts—sodomy among men, "lewdness" among women—in which individuals engaged, but family was so pervasive that colonial society lacked even the category of homosexual or lesbian to describe a person. It is quite possible that some men and women experienced a stronger attraction to their own sex than to the opposite sex—in fact, some colonial court cases refer to men who persisted in their "unnatural" attractions—but one could not fashion out of that preference a way of life. Colonial Massachusetts even had laws prohibiting unmarried adults from living outside family units.

By the second half of the nineteenth century, this situation was noticeably changing as the capitalist system of free labor took hold. Only when *individuals* began to make their living through wage labor, instead of as parts of an interdependent family unit, was it possible for homosexual desire to coalesce into a personal identity—an identity based on the ability to remain outside the heterosexual family and to construct a personal life based on attraction to one's own sex. By the end of the century, a class of men and women existed who recognized their erotic interest in their own sex, saw it as a trait that set them apart from the majority, and sought others like themselves. These early gay lives came from a wide social spectrum: civil servants and business executives, department store clerks and college professors, factory operatives, ministers, lawyers, cooks, domestics, hoboes, and the idle rich: men and women, black and white, immigrant and native born.

In this period, gay men and lesbians began to invent ways of meeting each other and sustaining a group life. Already, in the early twentieth century, large cities contained male homosexual bars. Gay men staked out cruising areas, such as Riverside Drive in New York City and Lafayette Park in Washington. In St. Louis and the nation's capital, annual drag balls brought together large numbers of black gay men. Public bathhouses and YMCAs became gathering spots for male homosexuals. Lesbians formed literary societies and private social clubs. Some working-class women "passed" as men to obtain better paying jobs and lived with other women—lesbian couples who appeared to the world as husband and wife. Among the faculties of women's colleges, in the settlement houses, and in the professional associations and clubs that women formed one could find lifelong intimate relationships supported by a web of lesbian friends. By the 1920s and 1930s, large cities such as New York and Chicago contained lesbian bars. These patterns of living could evolve because capitalism allowed individuals to survive beyond the confines of the family.

Simultaneously, ideological definitions of homosexual behavior changed. Doctors developed theories about homosexuality, describing it as a condition, something that was inherent in a person, a part of his or her "nature." These theories did not represent scientific breakthroughs, elucidations of previously undiscovered areas of knowledge; rather, they were an ideological response to a new way of organizing one's personal life. The popularization of the medical model, in turn, affected the consciousness of the women and men who experienced homosexual desire, so that they came to define themselves through their erotic life. [. . .]

CHAPTER 3

Toward Liberation

The turn of the twentieth century in the United States and in Europe was marked by a continuation of the process of women gaining increasing access to education and autonomy from the interdependency of family life and its many obligations. In the last half of the nineteenth century, many women's colleges were established in the United States—Mills in 1865, Smith and Wellesley in 1875, Spelman (the first black women's college) in 1881, and Bryn Mawr in 1888, which is also the year that Mount Holyoke Seminary became Mount Holyoke College. For many women, choosing college was tantamount to refusing heterosexual marriage. Between 1889 and 1908, 53% of women educated at Bryn Mawr were unmarried, and more generally, between 1877 and 1924, 75% of women earning doctorates did not marry (McGarry 52). The eugenicists of their day were alarmed at this development. As early as 1838 (that is, pre-Darwin), Henry F. Harrington had warned that educated women were no more than "mental hermaphrodites" (293). A generation later, Dr. Edward Clarke castigated educated middle-class young women in the United States for developing their brains at the expense of their reproductive capacities. By 1900, Dr. William Lee Howard could refer to independent women as "disgusting anti-social being[s] . . .—degenerates" (687). The reaction set in even as progress was taking place. Educated, independent, unmarried women were figured as representing evolutionary decay, and the benign Boston marriage could then be seen as a "degenerate" lesbian sexual relationship.

As we saw in the last chapter, however, some turn-of-the-century psychologists offered more moderate opinions regarding lesbianism in particular and homosexuality in general. For example, Sigmund Freud believed that homosexuality resulted from arrested sexual development, though he refused to go so far as to characterize it as an illness and did not believe that homosexual behavior should be criminalized. In fact, in a letter written to a mother who asked Freud for advice about her son's homosexuality, he wrote,

> Homosexuality is assuredly no advantage, but it is nothing to be ashamed of, no vice, no degradation, it cannot be classified as an illness; we consider it to be a variation of the sexual function produced by a certain arrest of sexual development. Many highly respectable individuals of ancient and modern times have been homosexuals, several of the greatest among them (Plato, Michelangelo, Leonardo da Vinci, etc.). It is a great injustice to persecute homosexuality as a crime, and cruelty too. ("Letter to an American Mother")

British physician Havelock Ellis, whose work Freud suggests that this mother read, countered popular opinion by writing in *Sexual Inversion* that homosexuality was neither a crime nor a disease, considering it instead an alternative sexual preference probably resulting from a combination of factors related to upbringing and the physical makeup of the individual. German sexologist Magnus Hirschfeld was among the first to argue that homosexuality is not necessarily linked to gender variance: "One thing that often causes a wrong assumption that someone is homosexual is masculine behavior in women and feminine behavior in men. . . . For a long time in many circles it was almost the rule to assume without further ado that women with short hair or men who appeared as female impersonators were homosexual. The matter is just not that simple" (77) [λ Chapter 2].

Freud, Ellis, and Hirschfeld stood in opposition to Howard in seeing homosexuality as neither a sin nor a sign of degeneracy but simply as a natural variation of the human species. Others have argued that in part because it is a variation and not the norm—and also because of the long history of persecution and punishment of those engaging in same-sex (and other nonsanctioned) sexual acts—homosexuality should continue to be restricted or outlawed by the state. Such thinking persists in the contemporary world. For example, when Supreme Court Justice Antonin Scalia wrote a dissenting opinion to the Court's *Lawrence v. Texas* ruling (2003) [λ Chapter 6] that laws prohibiting sodomy are a violation of "personal dignity and autonomy," he noted that in the United States, sodomy laws date back to the colonial era and that there are "records of 20 sodomy prosecutions and 4 executions during the colonial period" (Scalia dissent). Scalia, in short, was arguing that society needs sodomy laws because society has always had sodomy laws—in other words, that a law's prior existence is sufficient reason for it to continue to exist, whether or not the norms of society have evolved in a different direction. Many countries in the world either presently have or have had laws that prohibit homosexual behavior, mostly based on religious beliefs that homosexuality is both abnormal and immoral. In the Western world, these laws have been under continuous scrutiny and discussion, but there are still places in the world—India and Singapore, for instance—where homosexual acts can bring the offender a sentence of life in prison. In Afghanistan and Iran, homosexuality is punishable by execution. However, many countries in the world have either overturned their sodomy statutes or never imposed them at all.

Medical Models of Homosexuality

In support of arguments that homosexuality is a deviation from the norm, much of the scientific work related to homosexuality is based on a medical model designed to discover the reasons for individuals' homosexual tendencies. Often, this work was couched in phraseology that made it seem as if the goal of such research was to identify homosexuality early to develop "cures" for those who "suffer" from it. Because human behavior is seen as closely linked to the brain, many of the medical studies of homosexuals have focused on explaining how the brain of a homosexual works [λ Chapter 5]. This notion that homosexuals are somehow physically different from heterosexuals and that homosexuality is a psychological deviation has been adopted not only by the medical establishment but also by gay men and lesbians themselves throughout the twentieth century. We see it, for instance, in Radclyffe Hall's 1928 novel *The Well of Loneliness* [λ Chapters 2 and 12], and the theme runs back into the nineteenth century and forward into the late twentieth century. For Hall and other lesbian and gay people in the early twentieth century, it was important to embrace the medical model despite its emphasis on deviance because this model provided (1) a language with which homosexuals could describe their lives and (2) lists of characteristics homosexuals could use to recognize each other in the world. The notion that homosexuality results from biological factors out of the control of individuals is called **essentialism**, and its impact has been useful to a gay rights movement that needed to assert the innocence of homosexuals and the naturalness of homosexuality. Most recently, with advances in genetic science, Dean Hamer and others have tried to isolate a "gay gene," but this attempt to discover a biological reason for homosexuality is not new [λ Chapter 5]. To date, no irrefutable evidence exists that homosexuals are biologically different from heterosexuals. Still, gay activists employ **strategic essentialism** as a method whereby homosexuals' presumably fixed identity is deployed as an argument against discrimination. Despite the political usefulness of essentialism, many activists have wondered whether focusing so much on the notion of innate sexuality might fuel a desire among antigay elements to "catch" and perhaps even

Figure 3.1 *Time* magazine cover, 31 October 1969.

"cure" homosexuality, and such suspicions are borne out by the existence of programs all over the Western world that promise to make homosexual teens and adults into "ex-gays."

During much of the twentieth century, psychiatrists in the United States and throughout the world treated homosexuality as an illness primarily caused by poor parenting—domineering mothers and passive or inadequate fathers. Many prominent psychiatrists— Sandor Rado, Irving Bieber, and Charles Socarides, for example—argued vehemently that homosexuality should be treated as a pathology in need of treatment and cure. In fact, in a 1969 *Time* magazine article that brought "the homosexual lifestyle" to the fore of American public consciousness, Socarides espoused this view in a very public forum.

Around the same time, Cornelia Wilbur, the psychiatrist whose work with "Sybil" (Shirley Ardell Mason) popularized the multiple personality disorder (MPD) diagnosis, also studied lesbian sexuality. Her article "Clinical Aspects of Female Homosexuality" (1965) argued that, like gay men, lesbians typically grew up in families with passive fathers and domineering mothers. The Wilbur study is one of the few analyses of lesbians done by the group of mid-twentieth-century psychiatrists that scholar Neil Miller calls the "'Gay Is Sick' Shrinks"; most of the studies focused on male sexuality, portraying homosexual men as predatory, effeminate, and emotionally unstable. This notion that "gay is sick" has had enormous negative personal implications for lesbian, gay, bisexual, and transgender (LGBT) men and women; as well, the idea has served as justification for laws against "deviant" (nonheterosexual) sexuality. Because of widespread social acceptance of this idea, gay men and lesbians have been subjected to many invasive and traumatic medical interventions, including electroshock convulsive therapy (shock treatments), lobotomies, castration, hormone therapy, aversion therapy, and forced incarceration in mental hospitals.

Transsexual individuals have also been frequently under the scrutiny of the medical community. The first male-to-female surgical transformation took place in Germany in the 1930s, and the first radical mastectomy for a female-to-male **transgender** person occurred in the United States in 1917; in 1946, New Zealand surgeon Harold Gillies performed the first sex reassignment surgery from female to male, a more complex surgery than from male to female. But access to surgery has been limited by the fact that, despite the medical profession's insistence that a diagnosis of **gender identity disorder** be required before surgery is performed, insurance companies do not generally provide coverage for sex reassignment surgery. Harry Benjamin, influenced by the work of Magnus Hirschfeld, was the best-known physician for patients diagnosed with gender identity disorder, or what he called **gender dysphoria**. Benjamin developed a set of Standards of Care (1979) for transsexual individuals; these standards require extensive psychotherapy and a letter of support from a psychiatrist before a person seeking sex reassignment can be approved for surgery (Meyerowitz). Transpeople are particularly at the mercy of the medical communities in their countries if they desire any level of sex reassignment—from hormonal therapy to surgery. Even after physical reassignment, transsexuals face a daunting array of legal and social problems as they attempt to adjust to their new lives [λ Chapters 5 and 7].

Urban Life and Sexual Expression

Despite the uneasy relationship between LGBT people and the medical establishment throughout much of the twentieth century, that time also saw the rise of many prominent and visible queer communities. In the United States, the era known as the Harlem Renaissance, which lasted from the "Roaring Twenties" until the Depression in the 1930s, helped provide meeting places and creative and sexual outlets for many African American artists and writers [λ Chapter 9]. Known primarily as an era during which African American art, literature, music, dance, and social commentary flourished in the Harlem section of New York City, the Harlem Renaissance was also marked by an accepting attitude that viewed homosexuality as a personal matter. As a result, artists, actors, musicians, and literati who earned respect for their artistic and scholarly work could be fairly open about their sexuality. Lesbian and gay performers and artists such as Ma Rainey, Mabel Hampton, Alain Locke, and Claude McKay were significant figures in the Harlem Renaissance. Though it is important to understand that the "closet door" was somewhat open for these individuals, their ability to be "out" should not be read in contemporary terms. There was, for these gay men and lesbians, a significant threat should their sexuality become too much of a focus. Discrimination in housing and employment, as well as the threat of institutionalization or imprisonment, was a danger—and for African American homosexuals, the intertwining of racial discrimination and homophobia intensified these threats.

Communities where expressions of nonnormative sexuality were somewhat accepted were also emerging in Europe. In Berlin in 1904, for example, Anna Rüling urged

Find Out More in Anna Rüling's speech at the end of this chapter.

the fledgling women's movement to attend to "Uranian" concerns. In Parisian salons, artists and intellectuals gathered in relative safety to find both intellectual and emotional community, and sexual openness was welcomed. Famous lesbians and **bisexuals** such as Natalie Barney, Gertrude Stein and her partner Alice B. Toklas, Djuna Barnes, and Colette developed a community in which nonjudgmental attitudes and emotional and creative support were offered freely [λ Chapter 9]. The Bloomsbury group in London, which included bisexual and homosexual individuals such as Dora Carrington, Vita Sackville-West, Virginia Woolf, and E. M. Forster, was known for its plain sex talk, and many of its members openly supported Radclyffe Hall's *The Well of Loneliness,* which had been taken to court on obscenity charges [λ Chapter 12]. While it is true that many LGBT people today see *The Well of Loneliness* as afflicted by self-loathing and internalized homophobia, it was the first novel to present a portrayal of lesbian life, and backing it clearly indicated support of a sexual lifestyle alternative to heterosexuality.

As we can see, popular attitudes about sexuality evolve inconsistently based on the realities of particular moments in time. Contemporary Americans who identify as lesbian, gay, bisexual, transgendered, or even queer might be tempted to look back at the history of their predecessors' treatment and see the past as "the bad old days" and the present as marked by openness and liberation. Such a view of history, though, does not take into account the tendency of attitudes toward sexuality to loosen and then tighten again. There have been many historical moments when fairly accepting societies' attitudes toward sexuality became more restrictive as a result of a particular social crisis. In the United States, the social openness of the 1920s and early 1930s was interrupted by the Depression. Many believed that the Depression was a kind of "retribution" for a generation of American decadence, and one response to a growing scarcity of resources and access to the necessities for living was an increasing conservatism in social attitudes. In Germany, the rise to power of the Nazis—also related indirectly to the worldwide Depression—led not only to more conservative attitudes toward homosexuals but also to their outright persecution.

World War II and Homosexuality

Due in part to the work of scholars such as Erwin Haeberle, we can see that before World War II, Germany was perhaps the leader in research and activist reform work around the acceptance of homosexuality as a reasonable sexual alternative to heterosexuality. Much of the early sexological research was done by German Jews—Magnus Hirschfeld, for example. During the turbulence of the 1930s, however, much of the sexologists' work was lost when the Nazis destroyed all German sexological research and began their persecution of Jews, homosexuals, and others. Figure 3.2 shows the different badges used to identify groups who were persecuted by the Nazis.

Using Paragraph 175, the sodomy provision of the German penal code that dates back to 1871, the Nazis, between 1933 and 1945, arrested approximately 100,000 men they had identified as homosexual (*Paragraph 175*). Before the Nazis came to power, there had been concerted efforts made in Germany to reform the law against sodomy, but the Nazis actually extended the law. One result of this extension was that at the end of World War II, when the remaining prisoners in concentration camps were set free, only the homosexuals were still classified as criminals. Interestingly, Paragraph 175 criminalized sexual activity among men but not among women. It is noteworthy that the pink triangle used to identify homosexuals so that they could be singled out for persecution in the Nazi concentration camps has now become an international symbol for gay liberation.

Before World War II, there was no formal policy against homosexuals serving in the U.S. military. During the war, American women were called upon to serve in the military and to work outside their homes in ways they never had before; furthermore, since World War I, the armed services had had the reputation of being an "ideal breeding ground" for lesbianism. In the 1940s, the military began to use psychiatrists to keep homosexuals from enlisting and to issue what were called "blue discharges" (because they were often printed on blue paper) to military personnel identified as homosexuals. After the war was over, and when the armed services could afford to remove their homosexual recruits, a *Newsweek* article from 9 June 1947 reported that the United States military now considered the blue discharges "vague and protective" and would no longer use them; from this point on, even homosexuals who had not been "guilty of a definite offense would receive an 'undesirable' discharge" (Miller 241). The article also stated that case histories in Army files revealed, among other things, that homosexual soldiers "topped the average soldier in intelligence, education, and rating," with 10% holding college degrees and only "a handful" being illiterate, and on the "whole [homosexual] army personnel were law-abiding and hard-working"

Figure 3.2 This is a chart of the different badges prisoners of Nazi concentration camps were forced to wear.

(240). Despite these realities, official policy of the U.S. military was to ferret out homosexuals attempting to enlist by identifying and refusing those men whose looks or behavior seemed effeminate or by testing potential enlistees for knowledge of homosexual customs or vocabulary. Their rationale was that the morale of heterosexual servicemen would be compromised if they were required to live and work with homosexuals, whose supposed uncontrollable and inappropriate sexual desire made them inherently untrustworthy. As Kathleen Parker writes, the prohibition of gay servicemen was based solely on "military objectives: unit cohesion, military discipline, order and morale. It [was] not about the rights of gays to serve, but about the rights of non-gays to be protected from forced intimacy with people who may be sexually attracted to them" (B7).

A number of lesbians who served in the Women's Army Corps (WAC) reported that their direct supervisors were unwilling to push the sexuality issue since their services were so desperately needed. Among these was Johnnie Phelps, whose story is recounted by Elizabeth Lapovsky Kennedy and Madeline D. Davis, Randy Shilts, and several film documentaries. According to Phelps, she was summoned by the general-in-command of her battalion (Dwight D. Eisenhower), who told her that he wanted to rid the battalion of lesbians and commanded that she draw up a list of women who fit that description. Phelps claims she told Eisenhower that she would be willing to draw up such a list as long as he understood that her name would be at its top and that the list would include at least "95%" of the women in the battalion; Eisenhower quickly rescinded the order.

We should remember that World War II was not the first moment when gay men and lesbians visibly served the war effort. World War I was an important turning point for women who wanted to serve in the military. Britain, the United States, Russia, and Germany all allowed women to officially enlist in the military for the first time. Though Britain, the United States, and Germany did not allow women to serve in combat, the Russian military included about 2,000 women soldiers who fought in what was called the "Women's Battalion of Death," formed and commanded by Maria Bochkareva. There are, of course, no data on the number of lesbians serving in the Battalion of Death, and Bochkareva herself was twice married to men. Among women identifying as lesbian who served in some capacity during World War I were Gertrude Stein, Alice B. Toklas, and Radclyffe Hall, all of whom served as ambulance drivers. Stein and Toklas had a Ford shipped to Paris from the United States and outfitted it as an ambulance. Radclyffe Hall's *The Well of Loneliness* and her short story "Miss Ogilvy Finds Herself" tell of lesbians serving in the British military during World War I; both works describe women experiencing for the first time (1) the self-validation involved in serving one's country as a uniformed citizen and (2) the exhilaration of being recognized as a lesbian in a world of women.

McCarthy and the Purge of the "Perverts"

The now-infamous Joseph McCarthy was, during the early part of his career, a fairly unknown member of the U.S. Senate. In 1950, he and other political leaders led an attempt to ferret out and purge the country of Communists; they also charged that homosexuals were a threat to national security, publicly referring to them as "perverts" and claiming that they had infiltrated the government and were "perhaps as dangerous as the actual Communists" (McGarry 37). The fear that homosexuals were both emotionally unstable and particularly susceptible to blackmail lay at the core of the argument made by McCarthy and his aide, Roy Cohn [λ Chapter 9], a closeted gay man and the actual architect of the campaign to purge the government of homosexuals. In 1953, President Dwight D. Eisenhower signed Executive Order 10450. This order made "sexual perversion" sufficient reason for exclusion from federal employment; as a result, homosexuals were fired from federal jobs eight times more frequently than before 1950 (McGarry 37).

From the very beginning, the notion that the government was overrun with Communist sympathizers was closely linked to the idea that the Communist threat was related to homosexuality. At about the same time that McCarthy announced to an audience in Wheeling, West Virginia, that he had in his hand a list of 205 members of the Communist Party who were working in the State Department (he later admitted that what he actually waved before that audience was a laundry list), Undersecretary of State John Peurifoy testified before a Senate committee that there were 91 "persons in the shady category" working in the government. He added that "[m]ost of these were homosexuals." Guy George Gabrielson, chairman of the Republican National Committee from 1949 to 1952, warned that "perhaps as dangerous as the actual Communists are the sexual perverts [homosexuals] who have infiltrated the Government in recent years." The connection of Communism to homosexuality became embedded in the popular imagination when a *New York Daily News* political commentator reported that an "all-powerful, super-secret inner circle of highly educated, socially highly placed sexual misfits" had "infiltrated" the State Department and warned that these people were "all easy to blackmail, all susceptible to blandishments by homosexuals in foreign nations" (Miller 258–59).

Ironically, the period of the McCarthy witch hunts was also the time when much of the work took place that finally led to the declassification of homosexuality as a mental illness. Before that time, most American studies of homosexuality had focused on mental patients or prisoners. In the 1950s, Evelyn Hooker did the first extensive study of homosexuals not incarcerated in mental hospitals or prisons. Hooker found that there were few if any clear psychological differences between homosexuals and heterosexuals besides those related to the burdens of oppression and the necessity for hiding one's sexual preferences from family, friends, and coworkers. She also found the psychological diversity of homosexuals to be similar to that of heterosexuals. The psychological community responded to this work with surprise and sometimes skepticism. Other scholars also began to question long-held assumptions about sexuality.

Alfred Kinsey's *Sexual Behavior in the Human Male* (1948) and *Sexual Behavior in the Human Female* (1953), coauthored with Wardell B. Pomeroy and Clyde E. Martin, elicited great interest from the average American. In these books, Kinsey characterized homosexuality as a normally occurring sexual alternative. Because Kinsey was so well known, Americans often see him as the "father of sexology" [λ Chapters 2 and 5]. Kinsey's books popularized the idea of homosexuality as a normal variation of human sexuality. He proposed that all people exist on a heterosexual-homosexual continuum and that approximately 10% of the population is homosexual. Picking up on this work, "Donald Webster Cory" (a pseudonym for Edward Sagarin) wrote *The Homosexual in America* in 1951. This widely read book was among the first to describe homosexual life, focusing on both emerging gay culture and discrimination.

Kinsey and Cory were liberalizing voices in the repressive postwar years. Such thinking occurred in a cultural context of growing critique, particularly in the United States. Some artists, writers, and social nonconformists were gathering around the term *beat* to describe both a sense of being "beaten down" by conservative views and forces and a desire to "march to the beat of a different drummer," to paraphrase Thoreau. The "Beats" gained much notoriety in the 1950s, and they were often very sympathetic to the plight of homosexuals. Some among them, such as poet Allen Ginsberg, became outspoken homosexual artists [λ Chapter 9].

Still, the McCarthyite prejudices lingered. Even as countercultural movements arose in the 1960s, some social critics who seemed very different from figures such as McCarthy and Cohn felt free to speak out against homosexuals. Feminist leader Betty Friedan, for instance, lamented "the homosexuality that is spreading like a murky smog over the American scene." Friedan picked up on the "gay is sick" theme by saying that homosexuality was created by the "parasitical motherlove" of women confined to the home by social pressures designed to keep women out of the workforce (Wolfe). Friedan also coined the phrase "The Lavender Menace" to describe lesbians in the feminist movement; this phrase eventually became a rallying call for lesbians who left mainstream organizations such as the National Organization for Women (NOW) to form more welcoming communities around political activism on behalf of lesbians.

The Homophile Movement

At the close of World War II, some lesbians and gay men began to understand themselves as a social minority oppressed and made invisible by a larger, unfeeling, and wrongheaded heterosexual majority. This new way of seeing homosexuality helped create an environment in which the notion that homosexuality was a sickness or a perversion could be effectively challenged not only by physicians and psychotherapists but also by homosexuals themselves. In a 1948 issue of her self-published newsletter *Vice Versa,* "Lisa Ben" (an anagram for lesbian) proclaimed, "I for one consider myself neither an error of nature nor some sort of psychological freak. Friends of similar tendencies . . . also refuse to regard themselves in this light. . . . Is it not possible that we are just as natural and normal by our standards as so-called 'normals' are by theirs?" (McGarry 142).

In the United States, this kind of resistant thinking gave rise to what is known as the **homophile movement.** The primary goal of homophile organizations was to gain acceptance for gay men and lesbians by heterosexuals. In the early 1950s, Harry Hay founded the Mattachine Society, and Del Martin and Phyllis Lyon founded the Daughters of Bilitis (DOB) [λ Chapter 6]. These and other organizations made some advances in gaining acceptance and rights for lesbians and gay men, and they were successful in increasing visibility. The mainstream media, by contrast, continued to present gay life as seedy, sordid, and dangerous. Consider, for instance, the *Time* article mentioned earlier in this chapter, which presents homosexuals as part of a dark "underground" and features a debate among "experts" about whether homosexuality is an illness. Although it did bring news of the existence of other homosexuals to many nonurban heterosexuals and homosexuals, still it generally supported the notion that homosexuals were sad, sick, and even sexually predatory.

At this time, police frequently harassed gay men and lesbians—especially those they saw as resisting traditional gender roles—in gay bars and on the streets. Landlords could evict gay men and lesbians without cause. In response, the Veterans' Benevolent Association, founded in New York City in 1945, focused its efforts on helping homosexuals who were arrested or who were discriminated against in employment or housing because of their homosexuality. The Knights of the Clock, founded in Los Angeles in 1950, served as a social group for interracial gay couples who were not comfortable with the "bar scene" (McGarry 142). The Mattachine Society, founded by Harry Hay in 1950, was perhaps the best-known homophile organization in the country. Hay, a longtime member of the Communist Party, founded the group in response to the anti-Communist/ anti-homosexual environment created by McCarthy and his cronies. The group had a complex administrative structure that was developed to maintain the anonymity of its founders and to give it the impenetrable structure Hay thought would protect it against outside assault. The organization adopted the name "Mattachine" in reference to a group of medieval French townsmen who "conducted dances and rituals in the countryside during the Feast of Fools at the vernal equinox" (Miller 334). Generally, the Mattachine Society and the DOB worked toward assimilation of gays and lesbians and argued their similarity to the heterosexual mainstream. In keeping with this philosophy, homophile organizations often asked men participating in gay rights marches to wear business suits complete with ties and women to wear skirts that fell to the knee or below. Some members of the homophile movement did not fully embrace the **assimilationist** goals of Mattachine and DOB. For instance, one subgroup of Mattachine began publishing *One*, a magazine that eventually had a national circulation of five thousand. *One* was less assimilationist in its tone than the official rhetoric of the Mattachine Society. Similarly, the DOB was not a monolithic organization; as the middle-class lesbians in the group began to become more and more political, many working-class lesbians broke away from the DOB to form localized social groups.

The early and mid-twentieth century saw dramatic challenges that directly affected both popular and political perceptions of LGBT people and the evolving self-perception of gays and lesbians, many of whom were searching for a way to articulate their emerging sense of identity in an often hostile sociocultural and political climate. Americans tend to understand the late 1960s and early 1970s as a time when attitudes about alternative sexualities changed dramatically, fueled in part by the Stonewall riots in 1969 [λ Chapter 4] and the removal of homosexuality from the American Psychiatric Association's *Diagnostic and Statistical Manual* in 1973—two major events we will talk about in depth in Chapter 4. We see similar changes in other countries. In the United Kingdom, although the 1957 Wolfenden Act decriminalized homosexuality, it was classified as a disease there until 1994. In 1992, the World Health Organization stopped classifying homosexuality as a disease. In 2001, the Chinese government did the same ("China"). In short, the efforts of activists working for sexual freedom in the 1950s, 1960s, and early 1970s led to important changes in medical opinion and criminal statutes, many of which have paved the way for later activists to challenge long-held negative opinions about lesbians and gay men. In the next chapter, we will see the profound impact of such activism on more recent history.

QUESTIONS FOR DISCUSSION

1. The Harlem Renaissance offers us a rich glimpse into a talented, creative, and often politically astute group of writers, musicians, and artists who examined how race works in American society. Several artists who participated in the Harlem Renaissance were also gay, lesbian, or bisexual. Research one artist—a writer, singer, or graphic artist—and find out more about how this person examined both racial *and sexual* issues in his or her work.

2. View the film *Paragraph 175*. Immediately after you have finished the film, summarize its main factual points in a freely written paragraph or in a list. Mark those facts that you have heard before with a star; then mark the facts that are new to you with an asterisk. Before viewing the film, did you know that homosexuals were persecuted by the Nazis? How does knowing that affect you? What do you feel that you still need to know about this issue? What does it mean to you that the pink triangle, which we now identify as an international symbol of gay power and community, was first used by the Nazis as a way of marking homosexuals for persecution?

3. Read the majority opinion (written by Kennedy) and the concurrence (by O'Connor), as well as the dissenting opinions by Scalia and Thomas, in the case of *Lawrence v. Texas*. Compose a letter to one or more of the Supreme Court justices in the case supporting her or his written opinion on the case. Make sure to refer to aspects of LGBT history and culture that you have learned as you have read chapters from this book. The opinions can be found at the Cornell Law School website (http://www.law.cornell.edu/supct/html/02-102.ZS.html).

REFERENCES AND FURTHER READING

"China Decides Homosexuality No Longer Mental Illness." *The South China Morning Post* 8 March 2001. 24 March 2008 <http://www.hartford-hwp.com/archives/55/325.html>.

Clarke, Edward H. *Sex in Education; or, A Fair Chance for the Girls.* Boston: Osgood, 1873.

Cory, Donald Webster. *The Homosexual in America: A Subjective Approach.* New York: Greenberg, 1951.

Duberman, Martin Bauml, Martha Vicinus, and George Chauncey Jr., eds. *Hidden from History: Reclaiming the Gay and Lesbian Past.* New York: New American Library, 1990.

Faderman, Lillian. *Odd Girls and Twilight Lovers: A History of Lesbian Life in Twentieth-Century America*. New York: Columbia UP, 1991.

Freud, Sigmund. "Letter to an American Mother." 19 July 2008 <http://www.psychpage.com/gay/library/freudsletter.html>.

Harrington, Henry F. "Female Education." *Ladies' Companion* 9 (1838): 293.

Hirschfeld, Magnus. *The Homosexuality of Men and Women*. Trans. Michael A. Lombardi-Nash. Amherst, NY: Prometheus, 2000.

Hooker, Evelyn. "The Adjustment of the Male Overt Homosexual." *Journal of Projective Techniques* 21 (1957): 18–31.

Howard, William Lee. "Effeminate Men, Masculine Women." *New York Medical Journal* 71 (1900): 686–87.

Kennedy, Elizabeth Lapovsky, and Madeline D. Davis. *Boots of Leather, Slippers of Gold: The History of a Lesbian Community*. New York: Routledge, 1993.

Kinsey, Alfred and the staff of the Institute for Sex Research, Indiana University. *Sexual Behavior in the Human Female*. Philadelphia: Saunders, 1953.

Kinsey, Alfred, Wardell B. Pomeroy, and Clyde E. Martin. *Sexual Behavior in the Human Male*. Philadelphia: Saunders, 1948.

McGarry, Molly. *Becoming Visible: An Illustrated History of Lesbian and Gay Life in Twentieth-Century America*. New York: Penguin Studio, 1998.

Meyerowitz, Joanne. *How Sex Changed: A History of Transsexuality in the United States*. Cambridge, MA: Harvard UP, 2004.

Miller, Neil. *Out of the Past: Gay and Lesbian History from 1869 to the Present*. New York: Vintage, 1995.

Paragraph 175. Dir. Epstein, Rob, and Jeffrey Friedman. Rupert Everett, Klaus Müller (III), Karl Gorath, and Pierre Seel. New Yorker Video, 2001. DVD. 2004.

Parker, Kathleen. "Clinton, Gays-in-Military Issue Likely behind Change of Joint Chiefs." Cincinnati *Enquirer* 14 June 2007: B7.

Scalia, Antonin. Dissent. *Lawrence v. Texas* (02-102) 539 U.S. 558 (2003).

Shilts, Randy. *Conduct Unbecoming: Gays and Lesbians in the US Military*. New York: Ballantine, 1994.

Wilbur, Cornelia. "Clinical Aspects of Female Homosexuality." *Sexual Inversion: Multiple Roots of Homosexuality*. Ed. J. Marmor. New York: Basic Books, 1965. 268–301.

Wolfe, Alan. "The Mystique of Betty Friedan." *Atlantic Monthly* 284.3 (September 1999). 19 July 2008 <http://www.theatlantic.com/issues/99sep/9909friedan.htm>.

READINGS

➤ **Anna Rüling**

Excerpt from "What Interest Does the Women's Movement Have in Solving the Homosexual Problem?"

(1904), Berlin, Germany

Ladies and Gentlemen, The Women's Movement is a historical and cultural necessity. Homosexuality is a historical and cultural necessity, and homosexuality is an obvious and natural bridge between man and woman.

Today this is an undisputed scientific fact which the ignorant and impatient cannot dispute. Many people have asked how I came to this conclusion and could utter the truth about historical and cultural and natural and historical concepts in one breath, two things which on the surface seem to be opposites.

The interest to research the reason for this extended viewpoint is that people in general, when the matter concerns homosexuals, think only of male Urnings and overlook how many female homosexuals there are. They are, of course, less discussed because they—I was just about to say "unfortunately"—have had no unjust cause to fight against, such as penal code paragraphs which arise out of having false moral views.

No cruel justice menaces women nor does the penitentiary if they follow their natural instincts. But the mental pressure which Urninds suffer is just as great, indeed even greater than the yoke which their male fellow-sufferers must bear.

To the world which judges by outward appearances they are even more obvious than the female Urning. Only too often they are overwhelmed by people's moralized misunderstandings. In our total social life, however, Uranian women are at least just as important as their male counterparts because they influence our lives in many ways, even if they are not discussed.

If people would just observe, they would soon come to the conclusion that homosexuality and the Women's Movement do not stand opposed to each other, but rather they aid each other reciprocally to gain rights and recognition, and to eliminate the injustice which condemns them on this earth.

The Homosexual Movement fights for the right of all homosexuals, for men as for women.

The Scientific Humanitarian Committee has distinguished itself by taking an interest in the women's fight, which is more than any other movement which should have struggled with women has done, and has also participated in the interest of Urninds with such lively dedication.

The Women's Movement strives to have its long-despised rights recognized. It fights, namely, for as much independence as possible and for a just and equal standing of women with men, married or unmarried.

These latter strivings are especially important because firstly, of the condition of our present economical state, and secondly, because a great number of women will remain unmarried due to a statistical nominal surplus of women in the population of our fatherland.

These women are forced, when a sufficient means of earning money is not at their disposal away from the home—which is only the case for approximately 10%—to take up the fight for life and to win their bread by any means available.

The homosexual women's position and participation in the Women's Movement in its all-important problem is of the greatest and the most decisive importance and deserves the most basic and extensive analysis. One must differentiate between the homosexual woman's personality as well as her sexual instinct.

Most important, of course, is her personality in general. In the second place is the tendency of her sexual drive, which, without the exact knowledge of her tendency, no unbiased evaluation could be rendered, because of the incapability to make full and just considerations of the same, because the physical sex drive is almost always just an overflow, naturally following psychical characteristics; i.e., in persons with dominant masculine characteristics it is directed toward women and vice versa, without always taking into account the outer bodily structure.

Homosexual women have many characteristics, inclinations, and abilities which we usually consider as valid for men. They take much less interest in the emotional life than the average women.

While for the expressly heterosexual woman, feeling is almost always—even here exceptions prove the rule—dominant and decisive, while mostly a sharp clarity and reason predominate in the Urnind.

She is, as in the average, normal man, more objective, more energetic and goal oriented than the feminine woman; she thinks and feels like a man; she does not imitate men; she is conditioned as he; this is the all-decisive point which haters and calumniators of so-called "men-women" always ignore, because they do not even take the time to do basic research on the homosexual.

It is easy to judge what one does not understand, and it is just as easy, even if it only seems to be difficult to correct pre-established and false opinions, to correct them by reasoning.

I would like to note that there is an absolute and a separate psychic homosexuality, that, therefore, masculine characteristics do not necessarily and unconditionally result in the sexual drive being forced toward one's own sex; because each Urnind naturally possesses numerous feminine characteristics to a certain degree, which may be expressed in one of the numerous intermediate stages in the transitional stages between the sexes, even by being sexually attracted to a man.

Of course, the drive in these cases is in most cases directed to a very effeminate man, as a natural completion of the woman who has a strong masculine soul. I recall, for example, George Sand and Daniel Stern, who both loved men, those of the side of the feminine, Friedrich Chopin and Franz Liszt. Klara Schumann, the great artist, also, was married to a man who had strong feminine characteristics—Robert Schumann.

It seems, moreover, as if in the women whom I have characterized as psychic homosexuals, the sex drive was never especially strongly developed; even George Sand and Daniel Stern loved their artists much more with their souls than with their senses; therefore, I am inclined to speak of psychic homogenic women somewhat as "sexless" natures.

Since a woman who has a masculine nature and masculine traits would never satisfactorily fulfill a full-fledged man, without further ado, it is clear that the Urnind is not suitable for marriage. Even Uranian women know this is true or feel this way.

Unconsciously and naturally they voluntarily refuse to walk up the aisle to the justice of the peace.

But how often had they to deal with parents, cousins, aunts, and other dear friends and relatives who, day in and day out, tried to talk them into the necessity of marriage and make life a misery with their wise advice.

Girls Often Marry without
Understanding Sexuality and Sexual Life

Often, as young girls, they had to blindly fall into marriage, and thanks to our stunted education, without having had a clear view and understanding of sexuality and sexual life.

As long as it remains the opinion of so-called society that late spinsterhood, namely, unmarried women, experience unpleasantness, indeed, that it is something demeaning, then it will occur only too often that the Urnind will allow herself to be driven to marry by exterior conditions, where she will find no happiness and be incapable of creating happiness.

Such a marriage is far more immoral than the love which ties two persons when a powerful nature attracts them forcefully together.

The Women's Movement wants to reform marriage. It wishes to change many rights so that the inconsolable conditions of the present cease, so that discontent and injustice, arbitrary, and slavish subjugation disappear out of the home of the family, so that a healthier and powerful race blossoms.

While striving for these reforms, the Women's Movement should not forget the amount of guilt it bears in the false, unfriendly evaluation of homosexual women. I say expressly, "how much guilt."

Obviously far from it that I would want to burden the Women's Movement with full responsibility for this false evaluation. But for the sake of this portion of the guilt it is a simple and inescapable duty of the Women's Movement to explain to as many persons as possible by speaking and by writing how very destructive it is for homosexuals to enter into marriage.

First of all, naturally, for both partners' sake. The man is simply duped, because aside from its ideal meaning, entering into marriage is a two-sided contract in which both partners undertake duties and assume rights.

A homosexual woman, however, can only fulfill her duties to the man with disinclination, in the best case, with indifference.

A forced sexual communion is, without a doubt, a misery, and no conventional man could see anything to strive for or find happiness with a Uranian woman whom he wanted to marry.

It happens very often, that such a man will avoid sexual intercourse with her out of friendly sympathy and searches for sexual satisfaction of his drives in the arms of a mistress or with a prostitute.

True morality and the health of our people concern the Women's Movement, which must do everything in its power to prevent homosexual marriages. And the Women's Movement can do much in the work of explaining to all circles that the marriage of Urninds creates a three-fold injustice: to the state, society, and an unborn race.

Because experience teaches that the successors of Uranian persons are only seldom healthy. The unfortunate, unloved creatures are received unwanted and make up a great percentage of the number of weak-minded, idiotic, epileptic, chest-diseased degenerates of all sorts.

Even unhealthy sexual drives as sadism and masochism are often inherited by Uranian persons who have children against their nature. State and society should show an urgent interest to prevent Uranians from marrying, because later they must bear not such a small portion of the care for such unhealthy and weak beings, from whom they may hardly expect a profit.

A substantially more practical point for heterosexual women, it seems to me, is that if Urninds could remain unmarried without ruining [their] social reputation, they would find it much easier, as is their nature, to find the great satisfaction they do in the circle of the wife, housekeeper, and mother.

Still lacking, unfortunately, is an exact statistical survey of the number of homosexual women, but, taking into consideration my immense experience and thorough studies in this field, the result yielded by the statistical survey by Dr. Hirschfeld on the extensiveness of male homosexuality may also be applied to women. According to this survey, there are as many Urninds as there are unmarried women. This should not be misunderstood. For example, I mean that there may be as many as two million unmarried women and as many as two million homosexual women.

Among the two million unmarried women there is a greater percentage of Urninds, let's say 50%, thus one million; among the homosexuals, however, there are again as many, approximately 50% who, because of external circumstances, are married, therefore, you may calculate that 50% of normal unmarried women have lost the opportunity to marry.

The consequences are easy to deduce according to these figures. When Urninds are free of having to marry, the possibility of marriages for the heterosexual women would increase enormously.

But I do not mean to say that I present here a universal means to prevent late spinsterhood, because increasing animosity from men toward marriage has its roots more in social relationships.

But this is not the place to speak about that. If, however, the Women's Movement forcefully takes the side of the homosexual in the marriage question, then it takes a step forward toward reaching beautiful and lofty goals, the original idea of marriage, and the love ties between men and women would then be allowed to attain their rightful place.

Many Important Women Have Been Homosexual

There are men who, like Weininger, believe that all great historical literary, scientific or otherwise known, important or famous women have been homosexuals.

According to my past statements, I do not have to especially accentuate that this highly one-sided view is unproved, because not only history, but also our own eyes daily show us the weakness in this theory. On the other hand, I would not deny that many important women have been homosexual, just to mention Sappho, Christine of Sweden, Sonja Kowalewska, [and] Rosa Bonheur. However, it would seem strange if one wanted to classify Elizabeth of England and Catharine the Great of Russia as Uranian persons; the latter was perhaps bisexual—her many male and female "friendships" seem to imply this—a pure homosexual, however, she was not.

In opposition to the anti-feminists who claim that the female sex is inferior and who acknowledge only those women who exhibit strong masculine characteristics, I accept both as equals, but I am convinced that a homosexual woman is especially best suited to play a leading role in the enormous movement for the rights of women which is worldwide.

And, in fact, from the very beginning of the Women's Movement to the present day it has been more often than not homogenic women who took over the leadership in numerous battle[s]. . . . [O]nly by means of their energy [is] the average woman, indifferent to her nature and easily subjugating herself, brought to the awareness of her worth as a person and of her inalienable rights.

I cannot and will not name anyone, because as long as homosexuality remains something criminal and is considered to be against nature, as in many circles, as something unhealthy, some women may be offended whom I would like to indicate as being homosexual. We must always be proper and dutiful and not be indiscreet, and the noble feelings of the Uranian love of a female Women's-Rights-Fighter, as heterosexual sentimentality, do not belong before a public forum.

One who has only just superficially followed the development of the Women's Movement, one who is acquainted with a few or many leading women, one who has a spark of understanding for homosexuals would soon pick out those female Women's-Rights-Fighters and would recognize that not the worst is among them.

If we weigh all the contributions which homosexual women have made to the Women's Movement, one would be astounded that its large and influential organizations have not lifted a finger to obtain justice in the state and in society for the not so small number of its Uranian members, and that they have done absolutely nothing to this very day to protect so many of its most well-known and most worthy female predecessors in this battle from ridicule and scorn when they explain to the greater public about the true essence of Uranism.

One should never have found it so difficult to point out how the characteristics of the homosexual tendency express themselves more involuntarily and without the slightest personal, intentional assistance of appearance, speech, behavior, gesture, clothing, etc.

And the Urninds concerned are most unjustly given up to the ridicule of unknowing persons. Also, notice that many homosexual women naturally do not always appear masculine, which would be in harmony with her nature.

There are also numerous Urninds who appear completely feminine, who go through all the motions to hide their homosexuality, a comedy which makes them uncomfortable and under which they suffer.

I am well acquainted with the reason why this doubly exceptional hesitation exists, because the Women's Movement has handled even general sexual matters with an odd frankness and matter-of-factness.

It is the fear that the movement would suffer because of the broach of the homosexual question by becoming active by flashing the human rights of homosexuals in the blind eyes of the ignorant masses.

I cannot deny that having this fear so early in the movement is justified, and it should be avoided in order to not lose friends again, and there should be a fully unconditional apology made for the total ignorance of the homosexual problem in earlier times.

Today, however, when the movement is moving incessantly forward, when no bureaucratic wisdom, no bourgeois ignorance can be victorious over it any longer, today I must point out that a total rejection of the doubtless very important question is unjust, is an injustice which is brought upon the Women's Movement by itself in many cases.

The so-called "moderate" tendency will not help homosexuals one bit for the simple reason that deeds of this kind have no tendency at all. Victory will come as a sign of radicalism, and we expect that the radicals will change the direction and for once make it honestly and openly recognized: indeed, there is a great number of Urninds among us, and we owe them a word of thanks for their efforts and their work and for many a fine success.

I do not mean to say that all questions of the Women's Movement will be handled from the homosexual viewpoint, just as I do not ascribe all this success to the Urninds or even a greater portion of it—that would be just as insane as it is wrong to take no notice at all of the homosexual problem.

Translated by Michael Lombardi-Nash, Ph.D. <http://lesbianalliance.com/content.cfm?cat=legal&sub=legal&file=annaspeech>. Source of the translation: *Jahrbuch für sexuelle Zwischenstufen unter besonderer Berücksichtigung der Homosexualität* (*Annual for Sexual Intermediaries with Special Emphasis on Homosexuality*), ed. Magnus Hirschfeld, vol. 7 (1905), pp. 131–51.

➤ "Donald Webster Cory" (Edward Sagarin) and John P. LeRoy

"Should Homosexuality Be Eliminated?"

(1963), United States

The large majority of the population, in America and abroad, being themselves heterosexual and being antagonistic for various reasons to homosexuals and to their activities, would like to see this aspect of human life eliminated. They may learn, in time, to tolerate it, but it is tolerance in the literal meaning of the word; that is, something that one is able to stand, but of which one does not approve. But, by and large, their aim is the elimination of all sex activities between members of the same sex.

Unfortunately, although the ends sought by such people may, if placed within a realistic contemporary context, seem commendable, the motivations that lead them to these ends are frequently less so. For they condemn homosexual activity, not because the people involved in it are disturbed or unhappy—in fact, just the opposite, because the activities of the hostile community make *them* more disturbed, more unhappy. They condemn it because it is immoral, or decadent, or ungodly, or for some other equally subjective and entirely unverifiable reason.

Actually, a great deal of the discussion that has been taking place on the question of homosexuality has been centered around the viewpoint that it is a problem, a sign of cultural **decadence** on a societal level and of immaturity on a personal level; that it is a disease, a maladjustment, or a disturbance. Though some of these descriptive words may be fitting, and others less so, it is entirely possible that it may well be as much of a disturbance in this culture *not* to accept sexuality—homo-, hetero-, or any other that is voluntarily engaged in among adults.

Upon close observation of the relationship between society and the homosexual, one finds that many people have focused on the neurotic character of individual inverts, while minimizing the social oppression which they must silently bear, while others have ignored the former and emphasized only the latter. Neither should be neglected.

[. . .]

By means of a variety of legal, social, and moral pressures, society makes clear its strong disapproval of homosexuality. But disapproval and punishment do not imply effective diminution. What, if anything, is being done to deter the desire for this activity; to prevent it; to cure it; or to eliminate it? Very little, and for complex reasons that psychologists are beginning to grapple with. The hostile measures of an antagonistic society may even serve to foster the homosexual way of life.

Homosexuality is not deliberately and perversely chosen. A man (or woman) discovers that his psychosexual development has progressed in a different direction from that which is regarded as normal and, for better or worse, must adjust his erotic life accordingly, if he is to have any erotic life at all. All the legal and social sanctions are usually discovered after the person has realized that he is homosexual and, of course, by then it is too late.

The hostility that society directs toward the invert drives him underground, where he must conceal his erotic preferences, rather than bring those desires out into the open, where they can be dealt with objectively. For some, the existence of a twilight world attracts the adventurous rebel for whom living in immediate proximity to danger serves as a source of excitement in an otherwise drab existence. Aside from forcing many homosexuals into a sub-society, which they frequently abhor and in which they function only with anxiety, the hostility also serves to help some homosexuals hate themselves so thoroughly that they unconsciously get themselves into trouble in order to be punished, thereby convincing themselves that the self-hatred was justified. Those inverts whose self-hatred is bound up with a more general type of paranoia would have to find other ways of getting rejected if society were not so antagonistic, but since the hostility is ready-made, the conditions are there on which the pathology can thrive.

The rejection that homosexuals must endure forces them to pretend to be something they are not. Under such conditions, they have difficulty functioning well, either as humans or as homosexuals. Their self-image is undermined, they must lead a double life. None of these difficulties help to eliminate homosexuality, nor do they keep it from spreading, nor do they deter it, nor do they help people find a cure for it. Hostility serves *only* to add anxieties to life, not to overcome them. It creates wide chasms between those who would otherwise be close, such as members of the same family. It makes the gathering of accurate information about homosexuality difficult, because homosexuals fear an open avowal of their lives and hence few are available as subjects for research. Worst of all, it makes people hate themselves who do nobody any harm and who might otherwise have led happier, healthier, and more useful lives.

The reasons for the officially expressed hatred of homosexuality are many and varied. In ancient and medieval times, semen was looked upon as a precious substance, for in it was contained the seed for a new human being to be sown in the woman. Sexual activities and activities that were not procreative in aim were seen as deliberate waste of seed, and in societies riddled by war, famine, disease, and tyranny, a high value was placed on procreation and hence on the seminal fluid. The same antagonisms affected masturbation and promiscuity, which aroused the disapproval of the moralists of the time, but (probably because the lawmakers were themselves involved) did not incite the same social condemnation as did male homosexuality.

In relations between two males, one of whom is a receptor and the other the insertor, the receptor was thought to be allowing his body to be used as a substitute for a woman's, while the insertor was lowering or corrupting another man to the level of a woman, hence bringing shame upon the institution of manhood. Because men usually have stronger muscles than women, Western societies have placed man in a superior position to women, and man would not tolerate having that position undermined. Lesbian relationships were seen as trivial by comparison, for there could be no analogy so far as lowering or demeaning the status of one or both participants.

[. . .]

Toward the latter part of the nineteenth century, it was popular to think of homosexuality as an inborn biological phenomenon, linked with genetic imbalance, endocrinological disorder, or intermediate sexuality. The work of [Edward] Carpenter, Havelock Ellis, and [Richard von] Krafft-Ebing [λ Chapter 2] seemed to point up these conclusions.

Twentieth-century psychology and psychoanalysis laid bare certain psychodynamic aspects of the origins of homosexuality, and proliferated elaborate theories, case histories, and emphasis upon the assumption that homosexuality is a learned tendency and, theoretically at least, should be able to be unlearned. Since homosexuality is a form of human behavior, and since all human behavior has as its root cause a combination of heredity and environment, the etiology of homosexuality must be explained in terms of both, which does not imply a return, even in part, to the discarded concept of inborn inversion. Everyone has a biological capacity for sexual expression, an undirected energy that has been termed the libido. Past the age of puberty, this capacity will manifest itself in a heterosexual fashion in the majority of cases if society effectively and intelligently uses its power to promote such relationships. For the undirected sexual drive can, under favorable social conditions, go toward the other sex, if only because men and women are more biologically compatible than persons of the same sex.

In the cases where homosexuality develops, it is seen as a reaction to some form of frustration, the acting out of some defense mechanism, or an attempt to adjust to a difficult situation in which the other sex is viewed with fearfulness or suspicion, or cannot be obtained for gratification at a certain period, or an inability to obtain such gratification is feared.

However, these psychological factors may only be precipitating ones, since it is possible for two different people to respond to the same environment in different ways.

Can heredity explain the reaction to a given environment peculiar to any given individual? For the fact is that certain conditions may precipitate homosexuality for some, but very similar (although never identical) circumstances may not for others. For still others, a similar set of circumstances may make for other types of adjustments, living patterns, or anxieties, sexual or otherwise.

Until more is known, we can only say, in terms that are unfortunately vague, that exclusive homosexuality is a result of reacting to certain types of environmental conditions, usually centering around some traumatic childhood episode, or through continual unhealthful relationships with parents or siblings, usually in which a distorted concept of sexuality is involved. Sometimes these relationships appear to have been the causes for homosexuality, but at other times a different form of maladjustment has resulted.

To define homosexuality as a disease because it is considered socially deviant, with all the consequences of this social attitude, is purely tautological. It is saying that if society considers a phenomenon a disease, it is a disease. But to reduce this to the individual level, one should first determine the prevalence of undefined anxiety, a person's conception of himself, his ability to function realistically and to have positive relationships with other people, in deciding whether or not a given homosexual is to be regarded as neurotic, psychotic, or emotionally disabled. No doubt many of them are, but this is not a good reason to increase their anxieties and disturbances by condemnation.

The problem is made even more confusing by the fact that many of our social conventions and our hectic way of life tend to precipitate neuroses and psychoses to such an extent that, in a recent study conducted in midtown New York, some eighty percent of the population was judged by a competent team of psychiatrists to be suffering from some form of neurosis, and one-quarter of the population was diagnosed as being emotionally or mentally so disabled as to be nonfunctioning.

So a question has been raging: Are homosexuals always, necessarily, and invariably disturbed? And if they are, is such disturbance a symptom of their general personality disorder—or is it inspired by the hostile society and by life in an environment that fosters not only hate but self-hate?

There are many corollaries and side-issues to this question. Are heterosexuals also disturbed? It would seem that they are, but that their sex orientation is not, in and of itself, a symptom or a cause of such anxieties as they harbor. The same cannot be said of the homosexuals. On the other hand, are we still, despite the advances, despite the Mattachine Society and research grants, obtaining a distorted sample, consisting of those who have, because of their compulsive and self-defeating actions, gotten into trouble, or because of their self-rejection sought therapeutic aid?

One knows so little about the homosexuals who do not come for therapy, and objective comparisons with this type of homosexual along with their heterosexual counterparts have been few and far between. It is probable that, within limits, homosexuals vary in their state of mental health. Some function better than the average; others are similar to most people so far as mental health is concerned, but in all likelihood, the average person is disturbed and anxiety-ridden. If significant differences can be shown between the amount of mental illness present in the homosexual and the heterosexual, one would have to conclude that this difference is not due exclusively to social hostility, nor to faulty personality development, but to a combination of both.

To claim that homosexuality is immature is likewise tautological, for it is a refined way of saying that one is biased against homosexuals. The criteria for maturity are always arbitrary, set up differently for each age and for each society. In our society, one cannot be mature unless one marries and raises a family. Not to do so is regarded as being biologically irresponsible. Freudianism and theories of regression, infantile fixation, and arrested development are glibly mentioned in support of this, as well as the opposition to using sex for something other than procreation. It does not occur to many people who argue that homosexuality is immature that one can have sexual preferences different from their own and still conduct one's life in a positive, dedicated, and enlightened manner and meet all other criteria for maturity.

This is sometimes taken to mean that although homosexuals may be mature in other respects they are sexually immature because their form of sexuality does not lead to further offspring. By this line of reasoning, the spinster virgin, the celibate priest, the devout nun, and the responsible, contraceptive-using married pair who cannot afford, and hence do not want, children, are all to be grouped into one category of immature people, where they will join the homosexual. The standards for maturity often reflect the biases of those who adopt them.

Our society is preoccupied with family life, and anyone who is not so preoccupied is seen as a lesser person. Single men and women are looked upon with disfavor, while the family man and the loyal wife are seen as pure, wholesome, and virtuous. We are not trying to disparage the advantages of being married and raising a happy, healthy family, nor are we trying to minimize the gratifications that can be obtained thereby. Are we, therefore, to inflict punishment on one who does not fulfill this function? If so, then society should impartially punish all the unmarried, all the childless, lest one suspect that some are being singled out for reasons entirely extraneous to their non-family statuses.

Most homosexuals do not get married, and do not raise families. This, in and of itself, in a society already suffering from *over*population, is not a sufficiently good reason for wanting to eliminate homosexuality, but it is a good reason why *most* people should be heterosexual. But heterosexuality having been the primary form of sexuality since time immemorial, and likely to remain so, there seems to be little danger of the family's dying out as an institution. In fact, there would be no problem of continuing the human species, even if half the population were bisexual half the time! Since we now have a problem of too many people in the world, and with the issue of birth control making headlines, it is untenable that homosexuality should be condemned on the grounds that it is non-procreative. A good deal of time, money, and effort is now going toward making heterosexuality less procreative so that future generations will have enough space on this planet.

Thus, the answer to the question "Should homosexuality be eliminated?" can be made only by clarifying the query itself. A wide variety of sexual experiences, all in non-coercive form, is always desirable, if it helps the individual to explore the many ways of making love and relating to other human beings. Unfortunately, by definition, the homosexuals are not enjoying such a variety, but then, neither are the exclusive heterosexuals. The benefits, if any, accruing to society from such variation are of little help to one who is personally distressed. So the real task should be to eliminate the personal and social unhappiness that is a part of homosexuality in contemporary society, rather than try to do away with the phenomenon itself as an alternative kind of behavior.

Furthermore, all effort should be made to prevent and cure compulsive homosexuality and heterosexuality, so that it will be possible for human beings to function better with either sex. That most people, under most conditions, would choose the other sex, would be inevitable, but this would not make pariahs out of those who choose their own, or both.

American society can begin by examining the totality of its attitudes on all sexual matters. Not bound by outmoded traditions, laws, and customs when they are at variance with scientific tenets, and not hampered by moral codes that are irrelevant and tautological, great progress can be made. With more enlightened attitudes, less hostility, and greater objectivity, we can seek to bring up our children so that they know all that they need to know about sex *and its variations,* with no shame or guilt associated with them.

America must begin to accept homosexuals as people, and give them whatever prestige, social acceptance, and rewards that are due them on their own merits as individuals, instead of viewing them as curious outcasts. If this is done, perhaps the homosexual will be better able to accept himself, thus alleviating great human distress, but perhaps also laying a foundation for diminished neurotic homosexual activity.

We can encourage therapists to work with their homosexual patients, with the goal of making better people out of them, better suited to lead a happier, healthier existence, less burdened with anxiety, and more capable of dealing with life on its own terms in a positive, realistic fashion. If partial or complete change in sexual orientation is involved in this, then so be it. If it is not, then helping the patient to overcome whatever problems are confronting him and to function in a more psychologically healthy way with himself and the people around him are sufficiently important therapeutic goals, far more important than merely making a heterosexual of him without removing the neuroses and anxieties.

Finally, we can use what resources we have to further enlightened research, so that knowledge about the unknown areas will be forthcoming. If the world powers can afford to spend billions of dollars on armaments, which only serve to destroy people when used, can we not afford to make a worthwhile investment to find out more about the things that may help make life happier for all of us? We can further explore the means for increasing the sexual well-being of the nation, rather than add to our too-high rate of mental illness.

To summarize, should homosexuality be eliminated? We believe:

1. Society should seek to eliminate the personal distress and anxieties that arise as a result of social hostility.

2. Society should cease to define homosexuality per se as immoral, lecherous, or anti-social.

3. Society should aim to isolate those patterns in the contemporary world that are encouraging the development of neurotic and compulsive sexuality.

4. Society should simultaneously seek to make life more pleasurable for those who are homosexual and yet encourage all its growing members to follow the less difficult, more normative path of heterosexuality.

It is a program that is not only, in our opinion, free of contradictions, but it is one that in a practical sense is achievable.

When all is said and done, the important thing is not whether a person is homosexual or heterosexual. The important thing is that he is sexual, that society accepts him as such, and that he accepts himself as such.

"Donald Webster Cory" (Edward Sagarin) and John P. LeRoy. *The Homosexual and His Society: A View from Within.* New York: Citadel, 1963.

CHAPTER 4

Stonewall and Beyond

On 27 November 1978, former city supervisor Dan White sneaked into San Francisco City Hall through a basement window, avoiding metal detectors. He entered the office of Mayor George Moscone and shot him dead. White then walked down the hall to Supervisor Harvey Milk's office and killed him too. That night a huge crowd gathered outside City Hall to mourn Milk, the first openly gay member of the San Francisco Board of Supervisors. The candlelight vigil was seen on newscasts around the country and not only elicited sympathy from millions of Americans but also produced a strong outcry against antigay rhetoric and violence.

Milk had been elected to the Board of Supervisors eleven months earlier. He and White had served together on the board, though their relationship was strained. As a supervisor, White had vowed to rid the city of "radicals, social deviates, and incorrigibles" and represented the only actively antigay voice on the board (Sinclair 221). White resigned from the board after serving less than a year because he could not support his family on the low salary.

Figure 4.1   Harvey Milk and George Moscone

Figure 4.2   Dan White (directly beneath 'Fraud' sign) suspect in the killing of San Francisco Mayor George Moscone and Supervisor Harvey Milk is led by police officers towards jail elevator at Hall of Justice.

Figure 4.3   Anita Bryant after activist threw a pie in her face.

After the murders, White's lawyers blamed his actions on "diminished capacity" due to depression and convinced a nearly all-white, largely working-class and conservative jury to find the defendant guilty of voluntary manslaughter, not first-degree murder, with a sentence of seven years in prison (Miller 407). After the verdict, the public mood shifted from grief to fury. Angry and disillusioned gays and lesbians took to the streets, burning police cars and vandalizing property in what became known as the "White Night Riots." In response, the San Francisco police virtually invaded the Castro gay district.

In 1977, the same year Milk was elected to the San Francisco Board of Supervisors, Dade County, Florida, passed a Human Rights Ordinance including lesbians and gays among those protected from discrimination. In response, former Miss America and Florida orange juice pitchwoman Anita Bryant led a "Save Our Children" campaign seeking to repeal the ordinance. Bryant's group marched under the catchphrase, "Homosexuals cannot reproduce, so they must recruit," to which Milk's campaign responded, "My name is Harvey Milk and I'm here to recruit you." Forging alliances with fundamentalist Christian ministers and mobilizing antigay voters throughout Florida, the Save Our Children campaign won a resounding victory in June 1977, overturning the Human Rights Ordinance with nearly 70% of the vote (Miller 403). Save Our Children was a response to the growing gay and lesbian liberation movement, which saw visibility as an avenue to increased political power. Bryant's organization folded in 1979, but during its brief existence, it came to represent the new tactics of a resurgent religious right.

Milk's election and the furor after his assassination on one hand, and Bryant's antigay campaign on the other, characterize the tumultuous history of increasing lesbian, gay, bisexual, and transgender (LGBT) visibility in the United States during the second half of the twentieth century. As LGBT people moved into mainstream institutions and claimed both greater visibility and political power, reactionaries and social conservatives redoubled efforts to promote traditional values. Reactions among LGBT people and progressive allies have been varied, with numerous positions and stances, sometimes conflicting, evolving as the debate over "gay rights" has taken shape. In this chapter, we look at the social and political events that have shaped queer visibility and activism since the late 1960s. In many ways, this period has seen some of the most significant gains in civil rights, protections, and enfranchisement for LGBT people; in other ways, it has seen significant social and political challenges that continue to face queer people today.

Emerging Visibility and Activism

Many LGBT people identify the beginning of a highly visible gay rights movement in the United States with the Stonewall riots, which occurred on 27–28 June 1969, in New York City. The riots erupted in response to police harassment of patrons of the Stonewall Inn, a popular gay bar. Having experienced decades of consistent raids on gay bars by police, customers who had been in the Stonewall Inn when the police shut it down that night gathered outside the building, cheering whenever another person was released by the police and emerged. Most of the bar patrons were eventually released, but the bar staff, three drag queens, and two male-to-female transgendered people were held and eventually escorted outside to be loaded into a paddy wagon. The crowd's jovial irreverence quickly gave way to anger and protest as others swarmed around the Stonewall Inn, throwing bricks and trash cans and initiating several days of riots in the area (Duberman). The Stonewall riots immediately took on a significance disproportionate to the actual events, and within a month, the Gay Liberation Front had formed and begun organizing for gay rights and liberation, calling specifically for job protection for gay employees, an end to police harassment, and the decriminalization of sodomy.

Find Out More: *Screaming Queens* (2005), a film by Victor Silverman and Susan Stryker, argues that the Compton Cafeteria riot in 1966 was the "first known act of collective, violent resistance to the social oppression of queer people in the United States" ("Screaming"). The riots involved a number of transpeople.

As we saw in the preceding chapter, organizing for lesbian and gay visibility and rights was not new; the Mattachine Society and the Daughters of Bilitis (DOB), among others, made important attempts during the 1950s to organize gays and lesbians politically and to educate American society about discrimination against queer people. Mattachine and DOB frequently argued that gays and lesbians were "normal" Americans, and these groups encouraged members to dress and behave in ways that conformed to middle-class gender norms. In contrast, the Stonewall riots represented a more spontaneous form of direct action and civil unrest, carried out primarily by working-class people. Hence, the Stonewall rioters in some ways resembled many youth, antiwar, and civil rights movements engaging in political activism at that time. Furthermore, coming at the end of the 1960s, the Stonewall riots occurred at a time when a variety of American citizens were questioning sexual mores and traditional values. The time seemed ripe for gays, lesbians, and gender nonconformists to articulate their political desires in more direct and even confrontational ways. Many of these countercultural movements began in grassroots working-class rebellion and subsequently morphed into rights organizations with middle-class leadership and gradually less radical goals. In many ways, the Stonewall riots have served as an important symbol of the fight for greater queer visibility and political power. LGBT social and political organizations around the world use *Stonewall* in their names, and annual pride parades in June across the globe celebrate the uprisings (Manalansan). But what kind of political action did the riots suggest was emerging in the late 1960s and early 1970s?

The Gay Liberation Front (GLF) took its activist energy from other left-leaning movements, specifically socialist organizations and those protesting the Vietnam War. The name of the organization derived from North Vietnam's National Liberation Front and thus served to mark the group as confrontationally countercultural. Among their positions, the GLF sought to raise consciousness about the capitalist systems that they felt oppressed gays, lesbians, and others. In their view, the "GAY LIBERATION FRONT is a revolutionary group of homosexual women and men formed with the realization that complete sexual liberation for all people cannot come about unless existing social institutions are abolished" (McGarry 163). In publications such as *COME OUT!* and Carl Wittman's "Refugees from Amerika: A Gay Manifesto," the GLF strongly encouraged gays and lesbians to assert their visibility and claim political power. More specifically, they felt that social institutions such as the heteronormative nuclear family and persistent sexism were responsible for the oppression of gays and lesbians and that these institutions should be actively challenged and overthrown. Making common cause with blacks, workers, and the Vietnamese, among others, the GLF figured itself as fighting American imperialism in addition to the homophobia that seemed so much a part of it (D'Emilio). In 1970, meetings of a London-based GLF, soon followed by similar meetings in France, signaled the spread of gay activism in Europe. Front Homosexuel d'Action Revolutionnaire, following on the heels of widespread student riots across France in 1968, fought for both homosexual rights and access to free abortion and contraception (Miller).

The rise of lesbian feminism suggested that some activists and thinkers at this time agreed in part with the GLF's aims but wanted to critique social structures and institutions from more specific and challenging perspectives. The women's movement had already introduced feminism and feminist concerns to the popular consciousness, and lesbian feminism highlighted the connection between feminist theory and lesbian practice. A rallying call of lesbian feminism, commonly attributed to Ti-Grace Atkinson, was, "Feminism is the theory; lesbianism is the practice." In 1969, activist/author Rita Mae Brown and two of her colleagues resigned from the National Organization of Women (NOW) because Betty

Figure 4.4   Original album cover, Alix Dobkin's *Lavender Jane Loves Women.*

Friedan, one of NOW's founders, warned of a "lavender menace" of lesbians who might co-opt the organization for their own ends and, worse, undermine potential public sympathy [λ Chapter 3]. Emerging lesbian feminist collectives, such as The Furies and Radicalesbians, argued specifically for a separate "Lesbian Nation" (Johnston). In a manifesto titled "The Woman-Identified Woman," Radicalesbians praised the "primacy of women relating to women" as a way of achieving unity. In 1973, the message was "Lesbian, lesbian, any woman can be a lesbian" (from the album *Lavender Jane Loves Women,* Alix Dobkin, 1973). After all, they reasoned, if the term *woman-identified woman* was substituted for the troublesome term *lesbian,* more women could be gathered under their radical umbrella.

Find Out More in "The Woman-Identified Woman" at the end of this chapter.

Lesbian feminists believed that the antiwar movement was sexist and the women's movement homophobic, so they advocated for social and political separatism. Believing that all men, including gay men, were sexist, they argued that "working with men only takes away valuable time that should be spent working with lesbians" (McGarry 179). In significant ways, a vibrant and varied women's culture emerged out of such activist work; women-only music festivals, such as the National Women's Music Festival and the Michigan Womyn's Music Festival [λ Chapter 15], as well as women-centered publishers such as Naiad, Crossing, Kitchen Table, and Aunt Lute, promoted lesbian feminist thinking and activism. Clearly, lesbian feminism highlighted many lesbians' feeling that an enormous political and social divide existed between their worlds and goals for liberation movements, and those of their male

Find Out More in "The Combahee River Collective Statement" at the end of this chapter.

counterparts. Not all lesbians were separatists, however, and not all gay men were misogynists. The Combahee River Collective specifically rejected separatism for black lesbians.

Liberation politics gave progressive lesbians and gay men a sense of belonging to a community that was both political and social, and activism had a positive impact on the day-in-and-day-out treatment of bar owners and their patrons. The gay bar—including the newly popular discotheque—became a safer meeting place than it had been during the 1950s and 1960s. Nonetheless, a sense at the time was that there was a clear and strongly policed divide between "the bar" and the more political LGBT work being done outside the bar. It was not uncommon for LGBT activists to critique those they believed "wasted time" on the bar scene as being unconcerned about larger political issues; as well, it was not uncommon for disco queens and bar dykes to see the earnest activists as outsiders and "downers." The reality is, though, that both the bars and the political organizations served different, but equally important, purposes: the bar tended to be a source of information about local clinics, a place for gay candidates to distribute campaign brochures, and a venue in which people could share advertisements and addresses for gay-friendly businesses. Outside the bar, activists began to organize campaigns to gain visibility for LGBT people and to help further national and international political goals.

In October 1979, 75,000 to 100,000 people converged on Washington, D.C., to hold the first National March on Washington for Lesbian and Gay Rights, which featured speakers such as "Allen Ginsberg and Audre Lorde, feminist activist and writer Kate Millett, D.C. Mayor Marion Barry, San Francisco Supervisor Harry Britt, ousted gay U.S. Army Sgt. Leonard Matlovich, and U.S. Rep. Ted Weiss, the chief sponsor of a House gay rights bill" (Chibbaro). After much contentious debate, organizers decided to invite radical black writer and activist Angela Davis as a speaker, a move that indicated that issues of race and social class were on the minds of at least some of the leaders at the time. Davis declined to speak at the march because the Communist Party, of which she was a member, did not want to lend tacit support to homosexual rights. The 1979 march had been a pet project of the late Harvey Milk, part of his vision of a truly national LGBT movement.

AIDS Activism

In the early 1980s, doctors in some large urban centers in the United States began reporting a syndrome affecting an individual's ability to fight disease. The syndrome, which seemed viral in nature, was appearing predominantly among gay men, prompting doctors and health officials to call it "gay related immune deficiency" (GRID) or "gay cancer." Eventually, reports spread about other affected groups, mostly prostitutes and intravenous drug users, and the syndrome was relabeled AIDS—acquired immune deficiency syndrome. Initial reports about the disease were largely confined to gay or large urban news sources, but AIDS reached national awareness when actor Rock Hudson, looking emaciated and frail, held a press conference in 1985 to announce that he had AIDS—and was gay. In addition, some early cases of the disease resulting from blood transfusions, such as the illness of teenager Ryan White, helped to spread publicity; the Ryan White CARE Act, which provided services for people living with HIV (human immunodeficiency virus, which can lead to AIDS) and AIDS, was signed on 18 August 1990.

Panic spread first among gay men and then among the larger public, prompting some officials to close bathhouses. Some politicians argued for quarantining gay men, or at least those diagnosed with AIDS. HIV is passed from person to person through semen, blood, or breast milk, and the virus can lie dormant for several years before compromising an individual's immune system, resulting in the syndrome itself, AIDS. Because the disease is primarily transmitted through anal sex and intravenous drug use, government officials during the 1980s, particularly in the Reagan-controlled White House, were reluctant to identify it as a public health concern. In fact, President Reagan himself never mentioned the term *AIDS* until after the death of Rock Hudson, and even then his administration never supported meaningful funding for AIDS research (Shilts).

In the face of government apathy, a variety of gay and lesbian activists began organizing politically both to protest the government's inaction and to assist those with AIDS. They were aided in the popular consciousness by revelations that certain well-known, presumably straight figures, such as athletes Arthur Ashe and Magic Johnson, had contracted AIDS as "innocent victims" (Ashe from a blood transfusion, Johnson from heterosexual sex). The AIDS epidemic galvanized gay and lesbian people in ways that more abstract political issues such as repeal of sodomy laws had not (Miller). Organizations such as Gay Men's Health Crisis (GMHC) responded directly to both health concerns and political necessities around AIDS. ACT UP—the AIDS Coalition to Unleash Power—was formed in 1987. Using direct action techniques, ACT UP employed tactics that were often confrontational and

Figure 4.5 ACT UP activists hanging a banner on the White House gates.

Find Out More in Douglas Crimp's book, *AIDS: Cultural Analysis, Cultural Activism* (Cambridge: MIT Press, 1988).

controversial. For instance, ACT UP activists yelled slogans and threw condoms during a 1989 mass held by Cardinal John Henry O'Connor, a New York priest who outspokenly opposed gay and lesbian rights. Spin-off groups from ACT UP, such as Queer Nation and Lesbian Avengers, continued this work into the 1990s, holding kiss-ins and zaps and popularizing one of the major slogans protesting the government's reluctance to deal with AIDS: "Silence = Death." At this time, many gay activists started using the term queer to describe their politics and identities; the term suggested an unwillingness to conform and a desire to oppose the norms that called for silence around gay and lesbian sexualities [λ Chapter 7].

Randy Shilts estimates that "[o]n the day the world learned that Rock Hudson was stricken [1985], some 12,000 Americans were already dead or dying of AIDS and hundreds of thousands more were infected with the virus that caused the disease" (xxii). Twenty years later, in December 2005, the World Health Organization reported that the number of people living with HIV worldwide was 33.2 million (with 2.5 million being children younger than 15 years of age) and that 2.1 million people worldwide died of AIDS in 2007 alone ("AIDS Epidemic Update"). Over half a million people have died in the United States since the beginning of the epidemic ("United States AIDS Cases"). In the United States, new drugs have greatly improved the quality of life for people living with HIV/AIDS. But in parts of sub-Saharan Africa, the disease continues to spread to the point where it can paralyze national economies. In Zambia, for example, one in six adults lives with HIV. The life expectancy at birth has fallen below forty-five years, and in 2005 there were 710,000 AIDS orphans ("HIV and AIDS in Zambia").

U.S. AIDS advocacy groups were astonishingly successful at promoting public awareness of the epidemic and at raising money for patient services and research. Nonetheless, widespread publicity and increased visibility led to a backlash against gay men in particular, who were seen as the cause of AIDS, despite the fact that the disease had been identified as a health problem in Africa in the 1970s. In 1982, for instance, a Georgia man named Michael Hardwick was arrested for sodomy; his lawyers argued the case during the same years as AIDS was causing national panic in the United States, and in 1986, the Supreme Court, by a 5–4 vote, upheld Georgia's sodomy statute and, by extension, the right of states to outlaw sodomy. In the years following the *Bowers v. Hardwick* decision, a number of states, mostly in the South, refined their laws to criminalize only homosexual, not heterosexual, sodomy. Fear of AIDS was clearly leading to a polarization of national opinion, for which homosexuality served as a fulcrum.

Antigay Backlash

In many ways, the election of conservative governments throughout the West, as well as the fall of communist states in Eastern Europe and the former Soviet Union at the end of the 1980s, signaled a mass cultural shift toward more conservative values and ideas. As early as the late 1960s, the phrase "family values" began to be used to describe ideals related to a valuing of the "traditional" heterosexual, intact family unit. The phrase came to function as a euphemism for various anti-abortion, anti–sex education, antifeminist, and anti-LGBT ideologies. Most notable for LGBT people are movements such as the above-mentioned "Save Our Children" campaign, Abstinence-Only Education, and the "ex-gay" movement, which has given rise to a rhetoric of healing through programs designed to convince gay and lesbian youth and adults to pursue a heterosexual lifestyle. Avoiding the essentialist argument about whether LGBT people are born with their sexualities, these programs have been successful in employing a "gay is a choice" ideology to connect homosexuality to sin and to assert the righteousness of allowing active discrimination against LGBT people. In 1991, the Colorado for Family Values organization wrote the following proposed amendment to the state constitution:

> No Protected Status Based on Homosexual, Lesbian, or Bisexual Orientation. Neither the State of Colorado, through any of its branches or departments, nor any of its agencies, political subdivisions, municipalities or school districts, shall enact, adopt or enforce any statute, regulation, ordinance or policy whereby homosexual, lesbian or bisexual orientation, conduct, practices or relationships shall constitute or otherwise be the basis of or entitle any person or class of persons to have or claim any minority status, quota preferences, protected status or claim of discrimination.

Colorado voters passed this amendment in 1992 by a 54% to 47% margin. However, after a protracted legal battle, the Supreme Court overturned the amendment in 1996, stating that Colorado could not pass laws making homosexuals "unequal to everyone else. [. . .] A State cannot so deem a class of persons a stranger to its laws" (Robinson). A similar ordinance passed in Cincinnati, Ohio, in 1993, but the Supreme Court refused to hear an appeal against the discriminatory Article XII of that city's charter. Eventually, voters in Cincinnati overturned Article XII in 2004, swayed more by economic arguments (a boycott against bringing convention business to town, for example) than by fairness arguments. Clearly, battles over gay rights are very much a part of the current political landscape in the United States.

The recent spate of Defense of Marriage Acts (DOMA) outlawing gay marriage (11 U.S. states passed versions of these in 2004 and three more in 2008) have led some legislators to talk about a national constitutional amendment restricting marriage to a man and a woman. As of September 2007, 45 states have either an amendment or a law against same-sex marriage; as of 2008, only Massachusetts and Connecticut specifically allow same-sex marriage, and six states (Vermont, Connecticut, New Jersey, New Hampshire, California, and Oregon) have either "civil union" or "domestic partnership" laws that offer "the equivalent of state-level spousal rights to same-sex couples within the state" (Human Rights Campaign). The drive to restrict marriage to heterosexual participants has reached its zenith in the first decade of the twenty-first century. In this same period, the U.S. Supreme Court overturned sodomy laws (*Lawrence v. Texas*, 2003). Interestingly, the language in most DOMA legislation closely mirrors the proposed anti-miscegenation constitutional amendment proposed in 1912 by Rep. Seaborn Roddenberry of Georgia.

Debates about gay marriage elicit strong reactions. What can get lost in discussions of ideals and values is the personal cost to individual lives when rhetoric touches reality. For instance, who pays when Jerry Falwell calls AIDS "God's punishment for homosexuality"? Who pays when legislation or policy insists on drawing a connection between sex education and immorality? Since HIV disease is still spread primarily through sexual contact, the disease has sparked calls for greater and more comprehensive sex education, both in the West and throughout the world. In the United States, such calls have prompted heated debates among politicians and their constituents about promoting alternative lifestyles. At the beginning of the twenty-first century, the Republican-dominated government in the United States aggressively promoted abstinence-only sex education, which essentially eliminates discussion about young gay, lesbian, and bisexual sex lives and has been implicated in the rise of unprotected sex among young people ("Dangers").

Battles over gay rights, particularly marriage rights, have occurred in a global context that has witnessed the spread of religious fundamentalism, which is notoriously hostile to gays, lesbians, and bisexuals. These belief systems work against progressive impulses to enhance freedoms and life choices. In Iran, a conservative Muslim government arrests and at times executes those convicted of sodomy. In 2005, two Iranian teens were hanged, the government claiming that they were guilty of raping a thirteen-year-old boy; gay rights organizations around the world claimed that the "crime" they were "guilty" of was really consensual sodomy. In an article about the hanging, Homan, a Los Angeles–based Iranian LGBT group, quotes *OutRage!*, which asserts that "according to Iranian human rights campaigners, over 4000 lesbians and gay men have been executed since the Ayatollahs seized power in 1979" (Homan).

At the same time, other countries have adopted progressive legislation promoting recognition of LGBT lives. The Netherlands and Belgium were among the first European nations to legalize gay marriage. In 1996, the new constitution of South Africa was the first in the world to specifically prohibit discrimination on the grounds of sexual preference. And on 1 July 2005, shortly after its conservative government was ousted in a general election, Spain legalized same-sex marriage. The context in which same-sex marriage was legalized in Spain underscores the tensions between progressive and conservative impulses— a tension found in many countries across the globe.

Figure 4.6   Iranian teens hanged.

Gays in the Military and Hate Crimes Legislation

Two cases that show the difficulty faced when a progressive political agenda in favor of LGBT rights meets political opposition can be seen in the efforts of President Bill Clinton to end the ban on gays in the military and to add lesbian and gay people to proposed hate crimes legislation. A frequent flashpoint for debates about LGBT rights has been the issue of gays in the military. A number of nations—Israel, Canada, Denmark, Great Britain, and others—allow LGBT people to serve openly in the armed forces. The United States, however, implements a "Don't Ask, Don't Tell" policy, which neither progay nor antigay groups much like. In 1993, public opinion seemed primed for a reversal of the policy instituted during World War II stipulating that homosexuals be discharged from the armed forces [λ Chapter 3]. During the 1992 presidential campaign, candidate Bill Clinton promised to lift the ban on gays in the military, but after his election, he encountered stiff opposition from the Pentagon and Republican leadership. To the intense disappointment of many LGBT activists, Clinton instituted a compromise policy officially named "Don't Ask, Don't Tell, Don't Pursue, Don't Harass," which is still in force today. This policy has not succeeded in integrating homosexual people into the military; what it has done is mandate punishment for those who come out while serving. Today, a member of the armed services must not "make a statement that they are lesbian, gay or bisexual; engage in physical contact with someone of the same sex for the purposes of sexual gratification; or marry, or attempt to marry, someone of the same sex" (Human Rights Campaign). Ironically, this policy, which was supposed to be a **progressive** move designed to end the U.S. military's practice of ferreting out or actively pursuing LGBT people, actually extends the "offenses" that can result in expulsion from the military to include fairly contemporary concepts related to "coming out" and "marriage." Since the "Don't Ask, Don't Tell" policy has been in force, more than 9,000 LGBT people have been discharged from the military; the estimated cost of these proceedings is more than a quarter billion dollars (Human Rights Campaign).

President Clinton's attempt to end the ban on gays in the U.S. military met much the same fate as did his later attempt to add gays and lesbians to federal hate crime legislation that protects racial minorities. During Clinton's presidency, several particularly gruesome cases of gay bashing received wide publicity, and the nation saw the devastating results of homophobic violence. In December 1993, Brandon Teena, a twenty-one-year-old transman, was killed—along with his friends Lisa Lambert and Philip DeVine—in Lambert's home in Humboldt, Nebraska. Teena was killed by John Lotter and Tom Nissen in an attempt to keep him from testifying against them for raping him during an attack motivated by their discovery of Teena's biological sex. After the brutal murder of Matthew Shepard, a University of Wyoming student, in October 1998, Clinton's attempt to push the addition of lesbians and gays to the hate crimes bill was defeated in Congress. A year later, in 1999, Wyoming also tried to add lesbians and gays to its hate crimes statute; that measure was defeated after a 30–30 tie in the Wyoming House of Representatives. That same year, Billy Jack Gaither, an Alabama man, was killed by two men after Gaither allegedly showed sexual interest in them. The murderers attempted what has come to be known as the "gay panic" legal defense, claiming that Gaither's "talking queer stuff" caused them to respond with uncontrollable violence (*Frontline*). The two men were sentenced to life in prison without possibility of parole. President Clinton compared Gaither's killing to Shepard's and also to that of James Byrd, an

African American man dragged to death in a racially motivated attack in Texas the year before. As recently as 2002, lesbians Carla Grayson and Adrienne Neff, along with their twenty-two-month-old son, barely escaped after arsonists set fire to their Montana home. The fire was apparently set in retaliation for a lawsuit filed against the University of Montana by Grayson and other employees that called for the extension of domestic partner benefits to same-sex couples [λ Chapter 6]. These attacks and many others like them have been cited as examples of how antigay rhetoric seems to condone, or even encourage, violence against sexual minorities.

In many ways, the treatment of gays, lesbians, bisexuals, and the transgendered has come to mark how progressive a particular country is—or is not. In his book *The Rise of the Creative Class,* Richard Florida notes that the presence of an open, vibrant gay subculture is one of the markers of intellectual and creative stimulation in U.S. cities. In *Maneuvers,* Cynthia Enloe proposes a connection between LGBT rights and a progressive national image on the global stage. While some cultures have begun to recognize LGBT/queer lives through progressive laws and attitudes, the battle over what rights to extend to LGBT people continues around the world.

QUESTIONS FOR DISCUSSION

1. Earlier in this chapter, we pointed out how different organizations across the world have used the name *Stonewall* in the titles of a variety of LGBT social and political organizations. Research one of these organizations on the Web and examine how exactly the term *Stonewall* is used. Is reference made to the Stonewall riots of 1969? What other markers of LGBT identity are used that are familiar to you? What markers are new to you?

2. The manifestos of the early gay rights and lesbian feminist activists make for provocative and challenging reading, even today. If you had to write your own contemporary manifesto about LGBT, queer, or sexual issues, what would you put in it? What form would it take? To whom would you address it? Try your hand at writing such a manifesto and compare your writing with the manifestos of early gay and lesbian feminist thinkers.

3. Take a look at the AIDS Memorial Quilt website at www.AIDSQuilt.org and think about how people who have died of AIDS have been memorialized in this creative and emotionally evocative way. Thinking about the LGBT people and issues we have discussed in the past four chapters, choose either one person or one event to memorialize in a creative way. What form will your memorial take? How will you creatively talk about the past in ways that will be educational, relevant, and meaningful for contemporary audiences?

REFERENCES AND FURTHER READING

"AIDS Epidemic Update 2007." World Health Organization/UNAIDS. 19 July 2008 <http://data.unaids.org/pub/EPISlides/2007/2007_epiupdate_en.pdf>.

Chibbaro, Lou. "Gay Movement Boosted by '79 March on Washington." *The Washington Blade* 5 November 2004. 2 February 2008 <http://www.washblade.com/2004/11-5/news/national/movement.cfm>.

Crimp, Douglas. *AIDS: Cultural Analysis, Cultural Activism.* Cambridge, MA: MIT Press, 1988.

"The Dangers of Abstinence-Only Education." Planned Parenthood Fact Sheet. 25 March 2008 <http://www.ppacca.org/site/pp.asp?c=kuJYJeO4F&b=139536>.

D'Emilio, John. "After Stonewall." *Making Trouble: Essays on Gay History, Politics, and the University.* New York: Routledge, 1992. 234–74.

Duberman, Martin Bauml. *Stonewall.* New York: Plume, 1994.

Enloe, Cynthia. *Maneuvers: The International Politics of Militarizing Women's Lives.* Berkeley: U of California Press, 2000.

Florida, Richard L. *The Rise of the Creative Class.* New York: Basic Books, 2004.

Frontline. "Assault on Gay America: The Life and Death of Billy Jack Gaither." *Frontline.* 2 February 2008 <http://www.pbs.org/wgbh/pages/frontline/shows/assault/>.

"HIV and AIDS in Zambia." 19 July 2008 <http://www.avert.org/aids-zambia.htm>.

Homan. *Execution of Two Teenagers Accused of Homosexual Acts.* Los Angeles: Homan: The Iranian Gay, Lesbian, Bisexual, & Transgendered Organization, Incorporated, 2005.

———. 31 January 2008 <http://www.homanla.org/New/executions.htm>.

Human Rights Campaign. 2 February 2008 <http://www.hrc.org/>.

———. 2 February 2008 <http://www.hrc.org/Content/NavigationMenu/HRC/Get_Informed/Issues/Military2/Fact_Sheets>.

Johnston, Jill. *Lesbian Nation: The Feminist Solution.* New York: Touchstone, 1973.

Kennedy, Elizabeth Lapovsky, and Madeline D. Davis. *Boots of Leather, Slippers of Gold: The History of a Lesbian Community.* New York: Penguin, 1994.

Lawrence v. Texas. 539 U.S. 558 (2003).

Manalansan, Martin. "In the Shadows of Stonewall: Examining Gay Transnational Politics and the Diasporic Dilemma." *GLQ: A Journal of Lesbian and Gay Studies* 2.4 (1995): 425–38.

McGarry, Molly. *Becoming Visible: An Illustrated History of Lesbian and Gay Life in Twentieth-Century America.* New York: Penguin Studio, 1998.

Miller, Neil. *Out of the Past: Gay and Lesbian History from 1869 to the Present.* New York: Vintage, 1995.

Patton, Cindy. *Sex and Germs: The Politics of AIDS.* Boston: South End, 1985.

Reese, R. "The Socio-political Context of the Integration of Sport in America." *Journal of African American Men* 4.3 (1999). 2 February 2008 <http://www.csupomona.edu/~rrreese/INTEGRATION.HTML>.

Robinson, B. A. "Targeting Gays and Lesbians: Ruling by the U.S. Supreme Court in *Romer v. Evans.*" Religious Tolerance.org. 16 September 2004, 2 February 2008 <http://www.religioustolerance.org/hom_laws7.htm>.

"Screaming Queens: The Riot at Compton's Cafeteria." Frameline. 25 March 2008 <http://cart.frameline.org/ProductDetails.asp?ProductCode=T636>.

Shilts, Randy. *And the Band Played On: Politics, People and the AIDS Epidemic.* New York: St. Martin's, 1987.

Sinclair, Mick. *San Francisco: A Cultural and Literary History.* Northampton, MA: Interlink, 2004.

Smith, Barbara, ed. *Home Girls: A Black Feminist Anthology.* New York: Kitchen Table Women of Color Press, 1983.

Smith, R. R., and R. R. Windes. *Progay/Antigay: The Rhetorical War over Sexuality.* Thousand Oaks, CA: Sage, 2000.

"United States AIDS Cases and Deaths by Year." 19 July 2008 <http://www.avert.org/usastaty.htm>.

READINGS

➤ **Radicalesbians**

"The Woman-Identified Woman" (1970)

(c. late 1960s–early 1970s), United States

What is a lesbian? A lesbian is the rage of all women condensed to the point of explosion. She is the woman who, often beginning at an extremely early age, acts in accordance with her inner compulsion to be a more complete and freer human being than her society—perhaps then, but certainly later—cares to allow her. These needs and actions, over a period of years, bring her into painful conflict with people, situations, the accepted ways of thinking, feeling and behaving, until she is in a state of continual war with everything around her, and usually with her self. She may not be fully conscious of the political implications of what for her began as personal necessity, but on some level she has not been able to accept the limitations and oppression laid on her by the most basic role of her society—the female role. The turmoil she experiences tends to induce guilt proportional to the degree to which she feels she is not meeting social expectations, and/or eventually drives her to question and analyze what the rest of her society more or less accepts. She is forced to evolve her own life pattern, often living much of her life alone, learning usually much earlier than her "straight" (heterosexual) sisters about the essential aloneness of life (which the myth of marriage obscures) and about the reality of illusions. To the extent that she cannot expel the heavy socialization that goes with being female, she can never truly find peace with herself. For she is caught somewhere between accepting society's view of her—in which case she cannot accept herself—and coming to understand what this sexist society has done to her and why it is functional and necessary for it to do so. Those of us who work that through find ourselves on the other side of a tortuous journey through a night that may have been decades long. The perspective gained from that journey, the liberation of self, the inner peace, the real love of self and of all women, is something to be shared with all women—because we are all women.

It should first be understood that lesbianism, like male homosexuality, is a category of behavior possible only in a sexist society characterized by rigid sex roles and dominated by male supremacy. Those sex roles dehumanize women by defining us as a supportive/serving caste *in relation to* the master caste of men, and emotionally cripple men by demanding that they be alienated from their own bodies and emotions in order to perform their economic/political/military functions effectively. Homosexuality is a by-product of a particular way of setting up roles (or approved patterns of behavior) on the basis of sex; as such it is an inauthentic (not consonant with "reality") category. In a society in which men do not oppress women, and sexual expression is allowed to follow feelings, the categories of homosexuality and heterosexuality would disappear.

But lesbianism is also different from male homosexuality, and serves a different function in the society. "Dyke" is a different kind of put-down from "faggot," although both imply you are not playing your socially assigned sex role . . . are not therefore a "real woman" or a "real man." The grudging admiration felt for the tomboy, and the queasiness felt around a sissy boy point to the same thing: the contempt in which women—or those who play a female role—are held. And the investment in keeping women in that contemptuous role is very great. Lesbian is a word, the label, the condition that holds women in line. When a woman hears this word tossed her way, she knows she is stepping out of line. She knows that she has crossed the terrible boundary of her sex role. She recoils, she protests, she reshapes her actions to gain approval. Lesbian is a label invented by the Man to throw at any woman who dares to be his equal, who dares to challenge his prerogatives (including that of all women as part of the exchange medium among men), who dares to assert the primacy of her own needs. To have the label applied to people active in women's liberation is just the most recent instance of a long history; older women will recall that not so long ago, any woman who was successful, independent, not orienting her whole life about a man, would hear this word. For in this sexist society, for a woman to be independent means she *can't be* a woman—she must be a dyke. That in itself should tell us where women are at. It says as clearly as can be said: women and person are contradictory terms. For a lesbian is not considered a "real woman." And yet, in popular thinking, there is really only one essential difference between a lesbian and other women: that of sexual orientation—which is to say, when you strip off all the packaging, you must finally realize that the essence of being a "woman" is to get fucked by men.

"Lesbian" is one of the sexual categories by which men have divided up humanity. While all women are dehumanized as sex objects, as the objects of men they are given certain compensations: identification with his power, his ego, his status, his protection (from other males), feeling like a "real woman," finding social acceptance by adhering to her role, etc. Should a woman confront herself by confronting another woman, there are fewer rationalizations, fewer buffers by which to avoid the stark horror of her dehumanized condition. Herein we find the overriding fear of many women toward being used as a sexual object by a woman, which not only will bring her no male-connected compensations, but also will reveal the void which is woman's real situation. This dehumanization is expressed when a straight woman learns that a sister is a lesbian; she begins to relate to her lesbian sister as her potential sex object, laying a surrogate male role on the lesbian. This reveals her heterosexual conditioning to make herself into an object when sex is potentially involved in a relationship, and it denies the lesbian her full humanity. For women, especially those in the movement, to perceive their lesbian sisters through this male grid of role definitions is to accept this male cultural conditioning and to oppress their sisters much as they themselves have been oppressed by men. Are we going to continue the male classification system of defining all females in sexual relation to some other category of people? Affixing the label lesbian not only to a woman who aspires to be a person, but also to any situation of real love, real solidarity, real primacy among women, is a primary form of divisiveness among women: it is the condition which keeps women within the confines of the feminine role, and it is the debunking/scare term that keeps women from forming any primary attachments, groups, or associations among ourselves.

Women in the movement have in most cases gone to great lengths to avoid discussion and confrontation with the issue of lesbianism. It puts people up-tight. They are hostile, evasive, or try to incorporate it into some "broader issue." They would rather not talk about it. If they have to, they try to dismiss it as a "lavender herring." But it is no side issue. It is absolutely essential to the success and fulfillment of the women's liberation movement that this issue be dealt with. As long as the label "dyke" can be used to frighten women into a less militant stand, keep her separate from her sisters, keep her from giving primacy to anything other than men and family—then to that extent she is controlled by the male culture. Until women see in each other the possibility of a primal commitment which includes sexual love, they will be denying themselves the love and value they readily accord to men, thus affirming their second-class status. As long as male acceptability is primary—both to individual women and to the movement as a whole— the term lesbian will be used effectively against women. Insofar as women want only more privileges within the system, they do not want to antagonize male power. They instead seek acceptability for women's liberation, and the most crucial aspect of the acceptability is to deny lesbianism—i.e., to deny any fundamental challenge to the basis of the female. It should also be said that some younger, more radical women have honestly begun to discuss lesbianism, but so far it has been primarily as a sexual "alternative" to men. This, however, is still giving primacy to men, both because the idea of relating more completely to women occurs as a negative reaction to men, and because the lesbian relationship is being characterized simply by sex, which is divisive and sexist. On one level, which is both personal and political, women may withdraw emotional and sexual energies from men, and work out various alternatives for those energies in their own lives. On a different political/psychological level, it must be understood that what is crucial is that women begin disengaging from male-defined response patterns. In the privacy of our own psyches, we must cut those cords to the core. For irrespective of where our love and sexual energies flow, if we are male-identified in our heads, we cannot realize our autonomy as human beings.

But why is it that women have related to and through men? By virtue of having been brought up in a male society, we have internalized the male culture's definition of ourselves. That definition consigns us to sexual and family functions, and excludes us from defining and shaping the terms of our lives. In exchange for our psychic servicing and for performing society's non-profit-making functions, the man confers on us just one thing: the slave status which makes us legitimate in the eyes of the society in which we live. This is called "femininity" or "being a real woman" in our cultural lingo. We are authentic, legitimate, real to the extent that we are the property of some man whose name we bear. To be a woman who belongs to no man is to be invisible, pathetic, inauthentic, unreal. He confirms his image of us—of what we have to be in order to be acceptable by him—but not our real selves; he confirms our womanhood—as he defines it, in relation to him—but cannot confirm our personhood, our own selves as absolutes. As long as we are dependent on the male culture for this definition, for this approval, we cannot be free.

The consequence of internalizing this role is an enormous reservoir of self-hate. This is not to say that the self-hate is recognized or accepted as such; indeed most women would deny it. It may be experienced as discomfort with her role, as feeling empty, as numbness, as restlessness, as a paralyzing anxiety at the center. Alternatively, it may be expressed in shrill defensiveness of the glory and destiny of her role. But it does exist, often beneath the edge of her consciousness, poisoning her existence, keeping her alienated from herself, her own needs, and rendering her a stranger to other women. They try to escape by identifying with the oppressor, living through him, gaining status and identity from his ego, his power, his accomplishments—and by not identifying with other "empty vessels" like themselves. Women resist relating on all levels to other women who will reflect their own oppression, their own secondary status, their own self-hate. For to confront another woman is finally to confront one's self—the self we have gone to such lengths to avoid. And in that mirror we know we cannot really respect and love that which we have been made to be.

As the source of self-hate and the lack of real self are rooted in our male-given identity, we must create a new sense of self. As long as we cling to the idea of "being a woman," we will sense some conflict with that incipient self, that sense of I, that sense of a whole person. It is very difficult to realize and accept that being "feminine" and being a whole person are irreconcilable. Only women can give to each other a new sense of self. That identity we have to develop with reference to ourselves, and not in relation to men. This consciousness is the revolutionary force from which all else will follow, for ours is an organic revolution. For this we must be available and supportive to one another, give our commitment and our love, give the emotional support necessary to sustain this movement. Our energies must flow toward our sisters, not backward toward our oppressors. As long as woman's liberation tries to free women without facing the basic heterosexual structure that binds us in one-to-one relationship with our oppressors, tremendous energies will continue to flow into trying to straighten up each particular relationship with a man, into finding how to get better sex, how to turn his head around—into trying to make the "new man" out of him, in the delusion that this will allow us to be the "new woman." This obviously splits our energies and commitments, leaving us unable to be committed to the construction of the new patterns which will liberate us.

It is the primacy of women relating to women, of women creating a new consciousness of and with each other, which is at the heart of women's liberation, and the basis for the cultural revolution. Together we must find, reinforce, and validate our authentic selves. As we do this, we confirm in each other that struggling, incipient sense of pride and strength, the divisive barriers begin to melt, we feel this growing solidarity with our sisters. We see ourselves as prime, find our centers inside of ourselves. We find receding the sense of alienation, of being cut off, of being behind a locked window, of being unable to get out what we know is inside. We feel a realness, feel at last we are coinciding with ourselves. With that real self, with that consciousness, we begin a revolution to end the imposition of all coercive identifications, and to achieve maximum autonomy in human expression.

From *Out of the Closets: Voices of Gay Liberation,* edited by Karla Jay and Allen Young, © 1972, 1977, and 1992 by Karla Jay and Allen Young. Reprinted with permission of the editors.

➤ Combahee River Collective

"The Combahee River Collective Statement"* (1977)

(1974–1980), United States

We are a collective of Black feminists who have been meeting together since 1974.[i] During that time we have been involved in the process of defining and clarifying our politics, while at the same time doing political work within our own group and in coalition with other progressive organizations and movements. The most general statement of our politics at the present time would be that we are actively committed to struggling against racial, sexual, heterosexual, and class oppression, and see as our particular task the development of integrated analysis and practice based upon the fact that the major systems of oppression are interlocking. The synthesis of these oppressions creates the conditions of our lives. As Black women we see Black feminism as the logical political movement to combat the manifold and simultaneous oppressions that all women of color face.

We will discuss four major topics in the paper that follows: (1) the genesis of contemporary Black feminism; (2) what we believe, i.e., the specific province of our politics; (3) the problems in organizing Black feminists, including a brief herstory of our collective; and (4) Black feminist issues and practice.

1. The Genesis of Contemporary Black Feminism

Before looking at the recent development of Black feminism we would like to affirm that we find our origins in the historical reality of Afro-American women's continuous life-and-death struggle for survival and liberation. Black women's extremely negative relationship to the American political system (a system of white male rule) has always been determined by our membership in two oppressed racial and sexual castes. As Angela Davis points out in "Reflections on the Black Woman's Role in the Community of Slaves," Black women have always embodied, if only in their physical manifestation, an adversary stance to white male rule and have actively resisted its inroads upon them and their communities in both dramatic and subtle ways. There have always been Black women activists—some known, like Sojourner Truth, Harriet Tubman, Frances E.W. Harper, Ida B. Wells Barnett, and Mary Church Terrell, and thousands upon thousands unknown—who have had a shared awareness of how their sexual identity combined with their racial identity to make their whole life situation and the focus of their political struggles unique. Contemporary Black feminism is the outgrowth of countless generations of personal sacrifice, militancy, and work by our mothers and sisters.

A Black feminist presence has evolved most obviously in connection with the second wave of the American women's movement beginning in the late 1960s. Black, other Third World, and working women have been involved in the feminist movement from its start, but both outside reactionary forces and racism and elitism within the movement itself have served to obscure our participation. In 1973, Black feminists, primarily located in New York, felt the necessity of forming a separate Black feminist group. This became the National Black Feminist Organization (NBFO).

Black feminist politics also have an obvious connection to movements for Black liberation, particularly those of the 1960s and 1970s. Many of us were active in those movements (Civil Rights, Black Nationalism, the **Black Panthers**), and all of our lives were greatly affected and changed by their ideologies, their goals, and the tactics used to achieve their goals. It was our experience and disillusionment within these liberation movements, as well as experience on the periphery of the white male left, that led to the need to develop a politics that was anti-racist, unlike those of white women, and anti-sexist, unlike those of Black and white men.

There is also undeniably a personal genesis for Black feminism, that is, the political realization that comes from the seemingly personal experiences of individual Black women's lives. Black feminists and many more Black women who do not define themselves as feminists have all experienced sexual oppression as a constant factor in our day-to-day existence. As children we realized that we were different from boys and that we were treated differently. For example, we were told in the same breath to be quiet both for the sake of being "ladylike" and to make us less objectionable in the eyes of white people. As we grew older we became aware of the threat of physical and sexual abuse by men. However, we had no way of conceptualizing what was so apparent to us, what we *knew* was really happening.

Black feminists often talk about their feelings of craziness before becoming conscious of the concepts of sexual politics, patriarchal rule, and most importantly, feminism, the political analysis and practice that we women use to struggle against our oppression. The fact that racial politics and indeed racism are pervasive factors in our lives did not allow us, and still does not allow most Black women, to look more deeply into our own experiences and, from that sharing and growing consciousness, to build a politics that will change our lives and inevitably end our oppression. Our development must also be tied to the contemporary economic and political position of Black people. The post World War II generation of Black youth was the first to be able to minimally partake of certain educational and employment options, previously closed completely to Black people. Although our economic position is still at the very bottom of the American capitalistic economy, a handful of us have been able to gain certain tools as a result of tokenism in education and employment which potentially enable us to more effectively fight our oppression.

A combined anti-racist and anti-sexist position drew us together initially, and as we developed politically we addressed ourselves to heterosexism and economic oppression under capitalism.

2. What We Believe

Above all else, our politics initially sprang from the shared belief that Black women are inherently valuable, that our liberation is a necessity not as an adjunct to somebody else's but because of our need as human persons for autonomy. This may seem so obvious as to sound simplistic, but it is apparent that no other ostensibly progressive movement has ever considered our specific oppression as a priority or worked seriously for the ending of that oppression. Merely naming the pejorative stereotypes attributed to Black women (e.g., mammy, matriarch, Sapphire, whore, bulldagger), let alone cataloguing the cruel, often murderous, treatment we receive, indicates how little value has been placed upon our lives during four centuries of bondage in the western hemisphere. We realize that the only people who care enough about us to work consistently for our liberation are us. Our politics evolve from a healthy love for ourselves, our sisters and our community which allows us to continue our struggle and work.

This focusing upon our own oppression is embodied in the concept of identity politics. We believe that the most profound and potentially most radical politics come directly out of our own identity, as opposed to working to end somebody else's oppression. In the case of Black women this is a particularly repugnant, dangerous, threatening, and therefore revolutionary concept because it is obvious from looking at all the political movements that have preceded us that anyone is more worthy of liberation than ourselves. We reject pedestals, queenhood, and walking ten paces behind. To be recognized as human, levelly human, is enough.

We believe that sexual politics under patriarchy is as pervasive in Black women's lives as are the politics of class and race. We also find it difficult to separate race from class from sex oppression because in our lives they are most often experienced simultaneously. We know that there is such a thing as racial-sexual oppression which is neither solely racial nor solely sexual, e.g., the history of rape of Black women by white men as a weapon of political repression.

Although we are feminists and Lesbians, we feel solidarity with progressive Black men and do not advocate the fractionalization that white women who are separatists demand. Our situation as Black people necessitates that we have solidarity around the fact of race, which white women of course do not need to have with white men, unless it is their negative solidarity as racial oppressors. We struggle together with black men against racism, while we also struggle with black men about sexism.

We realize that the liberation of all oppressed peoples necessitates the destruction of the political-economic systems of capitalism and imperialism as well as patriarchy. We are socialists because we believe that work must be organized for the collective benefit of those who do the work and create the products, and not for the profit of the bosses. Material resources must be equally distributed among those who create these resources.

We are not convinced, however, that a socialist revolution that is not also a feminist and anti-racist revolution will guarantee our liberation. We have arrived at the necessity for developing an understanding of class relationships that takes into account the specific class position of Black women who are generally marginal in the labor force, while at this particular time some of us are temporarily viewed as doubly desirable tokens at white-collar and professional levels. We need to articulate the real class situation of persons who are not merely raceless, sexless workers, but for whom racial and sexual oppression are significant determinants in their working/economic lives. Although we are in essential agreement with Marx's theory as it applied to the very specific economic relationships he analyzed, we know that his analysis must be extended further in order for us to understand our specific economic situation as Black women.

A political contribution which we feel we have already made is the expansion of the feminist principle that the personal is political. In our consciousness-raising sessions, for example, we have in many ways gone beyond white women's revelations because we are dealing with the implications of race and class as well as sex. Even our Black women's style of talking/testifying in Black language about what we have experienced has a resonance that is both cultural and political. We have spent a great deal of energy delving into the cultural and experiential nature of our oppression out of necessity because none of these matters has ever been looked at before. No one before us has ever examined the multilayered texture of Black women's lives. An example of this kind of revelation/conceptualization occurred at a meeting as we discussed the ways in which our early intellectual interests had been attacked by our peers, particularly Black males. We discovered that all of us, because we were "smart" had also been considered "ugly," i.e., "smart-ugly." "Smart-ugly" crystallized the way in which most of us had been forced to develop our intellects at great cost to our "social" lives. The sanctions in the Black and white communities against Black women thinkers is comparatively much higher than for white women, particularly ones from the educated middle and upper classes.

As we have already stated, we reject the stance of Lesbian separatism because it is not a viable political analysis or strategy for us. It leaves out far too much and far too many people, particularly Black men, women, and children. We have a great deal of criticism and loathing for what men have been socialized to be in this society: what they support, how they act, and how they oppress. But we do not have the misguided notion that it is their maleness, per se—i.e., their biological maleness—that makes them what they are. As Black women we find any type of **biological determinism** a particularly dangerous and reactionary basis upon which to build a politic. We must also question whether Lesbian separatism is an adequate and progressive political analysis and strategy, even for those who practice it, since it so completely denies any but the sexual sources of women's oppression, negating the facts of class and race.

3. Problems in Organizing Black Feminists

During our years together as a Black feminist collective we have experienced success and defeat, joy and pain, victory and failure. We have found that it is very difficult to organize around Black feminist issues, difficult even to announce in certain contexts that we *are* Black feminists. We have tried to think about the reasons for our difficulties, particularly since the white women's movement continues to be strong and to grow in many directions. In this section we will discuss some of the general reasons for the organizing problems we face and also talk specifically about the stages in organizing our own collective.

The major source of difficulty in our political work is that we are not just trying to fight oppression on one front or even two, but instead to address a whole range of oppressions. We do not have racial, sexual, heterosexual, or class privilege to rely upon, nor do we have even the minimal access to resources and power that groups who possess any one of these types of privilege have.

The psychological toll of being a Black woman and the difficulties this presents in reaching political consciousness and doing political work can never be underestimated. There is a very low value placed upon Black women's psyches in this society, which is both racist and sexist. As an early group member once said, "We are all damaged people merely by virtue of being Black women." We are dispossessed psychologically and on every other level, and yet we feel the necessity to struggle to change the condition of all Black women. In "A Black Feminist's Search for Sisterhood," Michele Wallace arrives at this conclusion:

> We exist as women who are Black who are feminists, each stranded for the moment, working independently because there is not yet an environment in this society remotely congenial to our struggle—because, being on the bottom, we would have to do what no one else has done: we would have to fight the world.[ii]

Wallace is pessimistic but realistic in her assessment of Black feminists' position, particularly in her allusion to the nearly classic isolation most of us face. We might use our position at the bottom, however, to make a clear leap into revolutionary action. If Black women were free, it would mean that everyone else would have to be free since our freedom would necessitate the destruction of all the systems of oppression.

Feminism is, nevertheless, very threatening to the majority of Black people because it calls into question some of the most basic assumptions about our existence, i.e., that sex should be a determinant of power relationships. Here is the way male and female roles were defined in a Black nationalist pamphlet from the early 1970s:

> We understand that it is and has been traditional that the man is the head of the house. He is the leader of the house/nation because his knowledge of the world is broader, his awareness is greater, his understanding is fuller and his application of this information is wiser . . . After all, it is only reasonable that the man be the head of the house because he is able to defend and protect the development of his home . . . Women cannot do the same things as

men—they are made by nature to function differently. Equality of men and women is something that cannot happen even in the abstract world. Men are not equal to other men, i.e. ability, experience or even understanding. The value of men and women can be seen as in the value of gold and silver—they are not equal but both have great value. We must realize that men and women are a complement to each other because there is no house/family without a man and his wife. Both are essential to the development of any life.[iii]

The material conditions of most Black women would hardly lead them to upset both economic and sexual arrangements that seem to represent some stability in their lives. Many Black women have a good understanding of both sexism and racism, but because of the everyday constrictions of their lives, cannot risk struggling against them both.

The reaction of Black men to feminism has been notoriously negative. They are, of course, even more threatened than Black women by the possibility that Black feminists might organize around our own needs. They realize that they might not only lose valuable and hardworking allies in their struggles, but that they might also be forced to change their habitually sexist ways of interacting with and oppressing Black women. Accusations that Black feminism divides the black struggle are powerful deterrents to the growth of an autonomous Black women's movement.

Still, hundreds of women have been active at different times during the three-year existence of our group. And every Black woman who came, came out of a strongly-felt need for some level of possibility that did not previously exist in her life.

When we first started meeting early in 1974 after the NBFO first eastern regional conference, we did not have a strategy for organizing, or even a focus. We just wanted to see what we had. After a period of months of not meeting, we began to meet again late in the year and started doing an intense variety of consciousness-raising. The overwhelming feeling that we had is that after years and years we had finally found each other. Although we were not doing political work as a group, individuals continued their involvement in Lesbian politics, sterilization abuse and abortion rights work, Third World Women's International Women's Day activities, and support activity for the trials of Dr. Kenneth Edelin, Joan Little, and Inéz García. During our first summer, when membership had dropped off considerably, those of us remaining devoted serious discussion to the possibility of opening a refuge for battered women in a Black community. (There was no refuge in Boston at that time.) We also decided around that time to become an independent collective since we had serious disagreements with NBFO's bourgeois-feminist stance and their lack of a clear political focus.

We also were contacted at that time by socialist feminists, with whom we had worked on abortion rights activities, who wanted to encourage us to attend the National Socialist Feminist Conference in Yellow Springs. One of our members did attend and despite the narrowness of the ideology that was promoted at that particular conference, we became more aware of the need for us to understand our own economic situation and to make our own economic analysis.

In the fall, when some members returned, we experienced several months of comparative inactivity and internal disagreements which were first conceptualized as a Lesbian-straight split but which were also the result of class and political differences. During the summer those of us who were still meeting had determined the need to do political work and to move beyond consciousness-raising and serving exclusively as an emotional support group. At the beginning of 1976, when some of the women who had not wanted to do political work and who also had voiced disagreements stopped attending of their own accord, we again looked for a focus. We decided at that time, with the addition of new members, to become a study group. We had always shared our reading with each other, and some of us had written papers on Black feminism for group discussion a few months before this decision was made. We began functioning as a study group and also began discussing the possibility of starting a Black feminist publication. We had a retreat in the late spring which provided a time for both political discussion and working out interpersonal issues. Currently we are planning to gather together a collection of Black feminist writing. We feel that it is absolutely essential to demonstrate the reality of our politics to other Black women and believe that we can do this through writing and distributing our work. The fact that individual Black feminists are living in isolation all over the country, that our own numbers are small, and that we have some skills in writing, printing, and publishing makes us want to carry out these kinds of projects as a means of organizing Black feminists as we continue to do political work in coalition with other groups.

4. Black Feminist Issues and Projects

During our time together we have identified and worked on many issues of particular relevance to Black women. The inclusiveness of our politics makes us concerned with any situation that impinges upon the lives of women, Third World and working people. We are of course particularly committed to working on those struggles in which race, sex and class are simultaneous factors in oppression. We might, for example, become involved in workplace organizing at a factory that employs Third World women or picket a hospital that is cutting back on already inadequate health care to a Third World community, or set up a rape crisis center in a Black neighborhood. Organizing around welfare and daycare concerns might also be a focus. The work to be done and the countless issues that this work represents merely reflect the pervasiveness of our oppression.

Issues and projects that collective members have actually worked on are sterilization abuse, abortion rights, battered women, rape and health care. We have also done many workshops and educationals on black feminism on college campuses, at women's conferences, and more recently for high school women.

One issue that is of major concern to us and that we have begun to publicly address is racism in the white women's movement. As Black feminists we are made constantly and painfully aware of how little effort white women have made to understand and combat their racism, which requires among other things that they have a more than superficial comprehension of race, color, and Black history and culture. Eliminating racism in the white women's movement is by definition work for white women to do, but we will continue to speak to and demand accountability on this issue.

In the practice of our politics we do not believe that the end always justifies the means. Many reactionary and destructive acts have been done in the name of achieving "correct" political goals. As feminists we do not want to mess over people in the name of politics. We believe in collective process and a nonhierarchical distribution of power within our own group and in our vision of a revolutionary society. We are committed to a continual examination of our politics as they develop through criticism and self-criticism as an essential aspect of our practice. In her introduction to *Sisterhood Is Powerful* Robin Morgan writes:

> I haven't the faintest notion what possible revolutionary role white heterosexual men could fulfill, since they are the very embodiment of reactionary-vested-interest-power.

As Black feminists and Lesbians we know that we have a very definite revolutionary task to perform and we are ready for the lifetime of work and struggle before us.

Notes

*The Combahee River Collective was a black feminist group in Boston whose name came from the guerilla action conceptualized and led by Harriet Tubman on 2 June 1863, in the Port Royal region of South Carolina. This action freed more than 750 slaves and is the only military campaign in American history planned and led by a woman.

i. This statement is dated April 1977.
ii. Wallace, Michele. "A Black Feminist's Search for Sisterhood," *The Village Voice,* 28 July 1975, pp. 6–7.
iii. Mumininas of Committee for Unified Newark, Mwanamke Mwananchi (The Nationalist Woman), Newark, N.J., © 1971, pp. 4–5.

The "Combahee River Collective Statement" appeared originally in *Capitalist Patriarchy and the Case for Socialist Feminism,* edited by Zillah R. Eisenstein, published by Monthly Review Press.

SECTION II

Politics

CHAPTER 5

Nature, Nurture, and Identity

For more than a century, scientists and scholars have sought to identify the combination of factors that makes a person feel sexual desire for someone of the same sex. This quest began in the nineteenth century, as Western medicine claimed status as a profession, with standardized training academies, curricula, and practices. The professionalization of medicine evolved through a number of developments in science at that time, including (1) refinement of scientific methods, (2) significant advances in technology, (3) a mania for taxonomy, and (4) a new understanding of human behavior as pathology. Chapters 2 and 3 of this text focused on the early sexologists and their often gender-stereotypical ideas about homosexuality, culminating in discussion of the popularization of Freudian terms and ideas in Europe and the United States. This chapter discusses more recent biological and psychological theories purporting to explain the etiology of same-sex desire, gender nonconformity, or both, as well as the impact of these theories on the contemporary social and political arenas. We will also see how science and other seemingly "objective" sexual research can be motivated by social and political interests.

Kinsey

Before turning his attention to human sexuality in the 1940s, zoologist Alfred Kinsey was best known for his meticulously researched study of the gall wasp. In 1940, he and his research team at Indiana University began the massive undertaking that culminated in publication of *Sexual Behavior in the Human Male* in 1948 and *Sexual Behavior in the Human Female* in 1953. The group interviewed thousands of men and women, taking detailed sexual histories. When the 1948 volume appeared, public reaction was intense. Many were shocked and displeased by Kinsey's frank and unapologetic discussion of sexual matters ("Kinsey in the News"). Others were glad to see puritan America exposed as a "nation of sexual hypocrites" (Reisman). Still others were simply titillated. In any case, the country echoed Kinsey's name. Two hundred thousand copies of *Sexual Behavior in the Human Male* sold in the first two months after it appeared in January 1948. Popular magazines featured articles and cartoons about Kinsey's book. Singer and comedienne Martha Raye had a hit tune in 1949 titled "Ooh, Dr. Kinsey!" Archie "Stomp" Gordon recorded a blues number, "What's Her Whimsy, Dr. Kinsey," after *Sexual Behavior in the Human Female* appeared in 1953:

> I had a gal named Mabel, she used to call me her Hon,
>
> But since your book came out, old Mabel always carries a gun.
>
> What is her whimsy, Dr. Kinsey? Won't you tell me if you could,
>
> Why she ain't behavin' the way your book says she would.

In fact, the rage for Kinsey has continued nearly unabated for sixty years. As Bob Kanefsky's 1988 parody "Kinsey Scale" and Momus's 2001 song "Psychopathia Sexualis" attest, Kinsey's reputation for opening the Pandora's box of sex has not diminished (Kanefsky, Currie). In 2004, the feature film *Kinsey* met with reasonable popular success, and Kinsey was profiled in 2005 as part of PBS's *American Experience* series.

One element of Kinsey's work on sexuality that distinguished it from that of his sexologist predecessors was his absolute refusal to allow moral or medical concerns to enter into his examination. Kinsey insisted that human sexuality in all its variations was simply a matter of stimulus and response—given sufficient stimulus, human beings experience

"Is there a <u>Mrs.</u> Kinsey?"

Figure 5.1 "Is there a *Mrs.* Kinsey?"

sexual arousal. Kinsey took the same approach to men and women as he had taken to gall wasps a decade earlier: gather an extraordinary amount of raw data, keep careful records, and draw no conclusions not directly supported by the data. Another element that distinguished Kinsey's work was that his goal was primarily descriptive; he sought to chronicle American men's and women's sexual histories and practices, but he was far less interested in *why* they behaved as they did. He included almost no discussion of the etiology of homosexuality in the *Human Male* volume and, in the *Human Female* follow-up, relegated the topic to a single footnote reviewing previous published work proposing causes of lesbianism.

Kinsey's stimulus-and-response approach to sexuality in general and homosexuality in particular flew in the face of the "congenital sexual inversion" theories of Richard von Krafft-Ebing and Havelock Ellis [λ Chapter 2]. Kinsey rejected the idea of a fixed, inborn (homo-)sexual identity. "Only the human mind," he wrote, "invents categories and tries to force facts into separate pigeon-holes" (*Male* 639). But because "nature rarely deals with discrete categories," and because he believed that "the capacity of an individual to respond erotically to any sort of stimulus, whether it is provided by another person of the same or of the opposite sex, is basic in the species" (*Male* 660), Kinsey devised a seven-point scale upon which people could chart their degree of homo- or heterosexual inclination and experience.

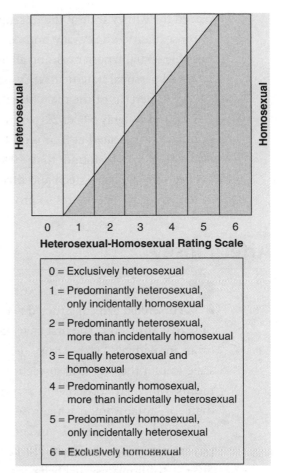

Figure 5.2 Kinsey scale

Kinsey Scale

Since the appearance of *Human Male*, the Kinsey scale has become a common measure for psychologists and others to gauge an individual's tendency toward same-sex or different-sex attraction; the scale seemed to provide a flexible way of understanding the diversity of human sexual expression. More than this, however, the enormous popularity of Kinsey's sexual behavior books among laypeople has placed the Kinsey scale at the fulcrum of contemporary debates about the nature of homosexuality. Kinsey saw homosexuality as a fluid position on a continuum of possible sexual experiences, and all his conclusions were reached on the basis of self-reported personal statements. His sexual history interviews led him to conclude that "40 to 50 percent of the male population" (*Male* 660) has some homosexual experience, and roughly 5% to 22% of the male population and 2% to 6% of the female population is located at 5 or 6 on the Kinsey scale, or "± exclusively homosexual" (*Female* 488). He found that 10% of males were predominantly homosexual between the ages of sixteen and fifty-five (*Male* 651). This is the source of the "one in ten" concept that figures so prominently in gay rights discussions today.

After Kinsey

Kinsey did not invent his sexuality scale out of thin air. As early as 1896, Magnus Hirschfeld had constructed two elaborate schemata for measuring the intensity of sexual attraction. The first chart laid out a ten-point scale indicating the strength of an individual's "Love Drive," irrespective of object. The second chart used that scale to plot the degree of attraction to the same sex or a different sex. Hirschfeld's results, which are conveniently symmetrical, identify three sexual "types": the "total man" or "total woman" (heterosexual), the "psychological hermaphrodite" (what we would call "bisexual" today), and the "complete Uranian" (homosexual) [λ Chapter 2]. Kinsey adapted this continuum format to demonstrate the range and diversity of human sexual behavior. As a *scientist*, studying observable behaviors, he sought to move the topic of homosexuality out of the realm of the "soft" sciences (e.g., psychology) and into the "hard" sciences (e.g., biology). Some scientists have taken issue with Kinsey's research methods, pointing out that his interviewees were not truly randomly chosen and thus may not have reflected a reliable cross section of the population.

Still, many researchers in a variety of fields have found a "continuum" approach to sexuality and gender useful in theorizing varieties of human experience, behavior, and identification. A decade after Kinsey's death (1956), Dr. Harry Benjamin's book *The Transsexual Phenomenon* (1966) introduced the Gender Disorientation Scale. Benjamin's scale has six stages:

Figure 5.3 An expression of gay pride, this button shows the way Kinsey's scale has become part of the popular consciousness.

- Type One: Transvestite (Pseudo)
- Type Two: Transvestism (Fetishistic)
- Type Three: Transvestism (True)
- Type Four: Transsexual (nonsurgical)
- Type Five: True Transsexual (moderate intensity)
- Type Six: True Transsexual (high intensity)

Benjamin breaks each of these six classifications down into eight subcategories: gender feeling, dressing habits and social life, sex object and sex life, Kinsey scale, conversion operation, estrogen medication, psychotherapy, and remarks. For example, he discusses the Type Six "True Transsexual" as follows:

Gender Feeling: Feminine. Total psycho-sexual inversion.

Dressing Habits and Social Life: May live and work as a woman. Dressing gives insufficient relief. Gender discomfort intense.

Sex Object Choice and Sex Life: Intensely desires relations with normal male as female if young. May have been married and have children, by using fantasies in intercourse.

Kinsey Scale: 6

Conversion Operation: Urgently requested and usually attained. Indicated.

Estrogen Medication: Required for partial relief.

Psychotherapy: Psychological guidance or psychotherapy for symptomatic relief only.

Remarks: Despises his male sex organs. Danger of suicide or self-mutilation, if too long frustrated.

Benjamin's classification system was specifically designed to serve as a diagnostic tool for gender dysphoric men, and not until later did anyone seriously consider the situation of gender dysphoric women. Such sexism—a lack of attention to born women undergoing sexual-reassignment therapies and procedures—is all too common in both scientific research and medical practice. Still, the Benjamin standards, as they are known, have come to represent threshold requirements for approval of sex reassignment surgery. The Gender Disorientation Scale references the Kinsey scale; thus the Benjamin Type Six, or True Transsexual, measures Kinsey 6 (exclusively homosexual). Benjamin assumes that male homosexuality involves effeminacy; in so doing, he maintains the inversion model of homosexuality favored by the nineteenth-century sexologists. According to Benjamin's interpretation of this model, gender—that is, learned behaviors and attitudes supposed to correspond with biological sex—serves as an indicator of sexuality and transsexuality. Benjamin also assumes that all appropriate sexual desire is heterosexual. Therefore, a man whose gender is "feminine" and who desires other men exclusively possesses one of the indicators for sex reassignment surgery, which would "correct" his sexual attractions by making him into a woman who desires a man. The original Benjamin standards required that a candidate for the "conversion operation" score high on the Kinsey scale because this would indicate that the individual's gender was already feminine. So even though transsexuals often do not consider themselves to be homosexual, many lied to their therapists knowing they needed to present as close to "total psycho-sexual inversion" as possible to be eligible for surgery. Erwin Haeberle criticizes the early sexologists for making an "arbitrary linkage of erotic inclination and gender role." The Benjamin standards, though applied somewhat less stringently today than in the past, are characterized by this same "arbitrary linkage."

Klein's Sexual Orientation Grid

In the years following the 1969 Stonewall uprising [λ Chapter 4] and the 1973 removal of homosexuality from the *Diagnostic and Statistical Manual* of mental illnesses [λ Chapter 3], psychologists attempted to devise more complex schemata

Klein Sexual Orientation Grid			
Variable	**Past**	**Present**	**Ideal**
A. Sexual Attraction			
B. Sexual Behavior			
C. Sexual Fantasies			
D. Emotional Preference			
E. Social Preference			
F. Self-Identification			
G. Straight/Gay Lifestyle			

1	2	3	4	5	6	7
Other sex only	Other sex mostly	Other sex somewhat more	Both sexes equally	Same sex somewhat more	Same sex mostly	Same sex only

Figure 5.4 Klein Sexual Orientation Grid

for charting sexuality, in part due to calls from lesbian, gay, bisexual, and transgender (LGBT) activists for more gay-positive approaches. In 1978, psychiatrist Fritz Klein introduced the Klein Sexual Orientation Grid (KSOG), which was based on the Kinsey scale but with the addition of multiple dimensions (such as sexual fantasies and perception of lifestyle) designed to produce unique results for each person. The KSOG builds upon the Kinsey scale (bottom row) but operates by plugging those numbers into a chart built from sexual/emotional categories and three time scales. The user is asked to average her or his responses on the twenty-one items to arrive at a single "Kinsey" number. It has become common over the years, however, to dispense with the final average and use the chart to emphasize the multifaceted nature of sexual identity.

The Storms Sexuality Axis

The Kinsey scale, the Benjamin standards, and the Klein grid have been criticized for their assumption of an inevitable homosexual-heterosexual binary. Contemporary sexuality researchers have faced considerable difficulty thinking about sexuality in a way that truly challenges that binary. In 1981, psychologist Michael Storms positioned bisexuality as the area between homosexuality and heterosexuality, rather than encompassing all sexuality (as implied by Kinsey). The Storms Sexuality Axis (SSA) positions homosexuality and heterosexuality on x- and y-axes, with bisexuality representing points in between. The SSA also accounts for **asexuality** in its attempt to offer a more individualized set of identifiers. In 1990, a group of University of Dayton psychologists offered still another variation on the Kinsey scale, the Multidimensional Scale of Sexuality (MSS). The MSS asks forty-five true-false questions, then proposes a scoring scheme based on a combination of Kinsey 0–6 and the SSA. It was designed to produce ratings of both the behavioral and the cognitive/affective components of sexuality (Berkey). A recent attempt at a post-Kinsey

Figure 5.5 The Storms Sexuality Axis

explication of gradations in sexuality comes from psychiatrist Michael Kauth, whose 2006 article in the *Journal of Bisexuality* aims "to unmask implicit social beliefs about same-sex attraction and attraction to both sexes and to promote reliable, testable models of sexual orientation" with an ultimate goal "to expand and standardize the concept of sexual orientation" (79). Like Benjamin, Klein, Storms, and Berkey before him, Kauth begins with Kinsey's (experience-based, not psychological) continuum, applies it to the psychological study of sexuality, and tweaks it to achieve a more wide-ranging and descriptive method of identifying sexual orientations.

Recognizing the sociopolitical dimensions affecting and in some cases shaping desire, Vivian Cass and Adrienne Rich adapted the continuum format to overtly political purposes, and they thus may be thought of as "distant cousins" to Kinsey. In 1979, Australian psychiatrist Cass introduced a six-stage model of sexual identity integration:

- Stage I: Identity Confusion
- Stage II: Identity Comparison
- Stage III: Identity Tolerance
- Stage IV: Identity Acceptance
- Stage V: Identity Pride
- Stage VI: Identity Synthesis

Cass's model is restricted to mapping the identity development of lesbian and gay people, not those who are transgender or bisexual. Because the focus is on internal self-recognition and growth, this model is assumed to be particularly useful for college students and other young people, although the basic progression is supposed to be more or less the same for all ages. A notable feature of Cass's model is Stage VI, "Identity Synthesis," in which the fully adapted homosexual transcends a primarily gay consciousness to reach a stage in which she or he recognizes that various aspects of identity are equally important and should be blended. Other homosexual identity models have occasionally omitted this last stage, assuming that "Identity Pride" is a sufficient goal in itself, but Cass argues that a person must transcend anger and rebelliousness (characteristics of Stage V) to achieve healthy **self-actualization.** Another notable feature of this model is Cass's recognition of LGBT culture and community. In 1979, when she published "Homosexual Identity Formation," few resources were available to assist LGBT people as they came out. Still, Cass understood (especially in Stages III–V) that an LGBT community existed and represented a key part of the coming-out process. Later models, such as Susan Meyer and Alan Schwitzer's continuum that appeared in 1999, keep Cass's six stages but refer to more established community institutions.

Meyer and Schwitzer's Stage 6 (Networking and Connecting) differs from Cass's Stage VI (Identity Synthesis) in that the final identity is validated through connection with other subcultural individuals and institutions. The other primary difference between Cass and Meyer/Schwitzer is that the former focused only on lesbian and gay people, proposing that the model could apply to any age-group; Meyer and Schwitzer, by contrast, refer to "college students with gay, lesbian, bisexual, and other minority sexual orientations" (41). As sensitive as these thinkers are to the importance of "queer" culture, none of them really address the issues of transgendered people, whose struggle for acceptance or at least toleration is sometimes complicated by the fact that they are often shunned both by the larger, heterosexist culture *and* by many in the lesbian and gay community with whom they supposedly share common cause as sexual and gender "outsiders."

While many researchers have approached the nature-nurture question through biological and psychological research, others approached the question from a more theoretical or philosophical angle. Adrienne Rich, award-winning poet and long-time lesbian activist, introduced the concept of a lesbian continuum in her important essay "Compulsory Heterosexuality and Lesbian Existence" in 1980. Rich hoped to find a way to lessen the conflict between heterosexual and lesbian feminists in the women's movement [λ Chapter 4]. She also hoped to unearth lesbian existence from the centuries of neglect in which it had been buried. Her primary strategy for accomplishing these goals was the concept of the lesbian continuum: "I mean the term *lesbian continuum* to include a range—through each woman's life and throughout history—of woman-identified experience, not simply the fact that a woman has had or consciously desired genital sexual experience with another woman" (239). Rich's continuum bears some resemblance to the "Woman-Identified Woman" (WIW) [λ Chapter 4] but differs in one significant respect: the WIW idea was designed to expand the definition of *lesbian* by including women who experienced primary relationships with other women. The lesbian continuum posited a deep and abiding connection among women across time and geography, such that a woman might recognize herself as occupying a position on a preexisting and ongoing timeline. "If we consider the possibility," wrote Rich, "that all women . . . exist on a lesbian continuum, we can see ourselves as moving in and out of this continuum, whether we identify ourselves as lesbian or not" (240). Rich hoped that this recognition would have the power to unify women across superficial differences that divide them and to empower women to rebel against the compulsory heterosexuality imposed upon them by every culture in the world: "We begin to observe behavior, both in history and in individual biography, that has hitherto been invisible or misnamed, behavior which often constitutes . . . radical rebellion. And we can connect these rebellions and the necessity for them with the physical passion of woman for woman which is central to lesbian existence: the erotic sensuality which has been, precisely, the most violently erased fact of female experience" (241). Rich's lesbian continuum has been criticized—she even attaches a letter challenging it to later editions of the essay—for indulging a privileged white woman's vision of the unity of "all women" when all women do not enjoy the same benefits or acknowledge the same needs. Still, it represented a stunning indictment of the phenomenon of compulsory heterosexuality, and by removing the concept *lesbian* from an exclusively sexual definition, it created a vision of a politically viable movement based on femaleness. Rich's vision is far from Kinsey's scale, since its examples come from neither the "hard" nor the "soft" sciences but rather from philosophy and literature, but it nonetheless reveals the power of the continuum format in conceptualizing sexual connection.

The Quest for the Gay Gene

In *Human Male,* Kinsey warned future researchers that discovering "Factors Accounting for the Homosexual" (660) was going to be a daunting task. Psychologists, he wrote, must be aware that "it is one thing to account for an all-or-none proposition, as heterosexuality and homosexuality have ordinarily been taken to be. But it is a totally different matter to recognize factors which will account for the continuum which we find existing between the exclusively heterosexual and the exclusively homosexual history" (661). Scientists seeking to locate a biological basis for homosexuality must show that "the fluctuations in preferences for female or male partners are related to fluctuations in the hormones, the genes, or the other biologic factors which are assumed to be operating" (661). Kinsey went on to lay out a detailed set of conditions that would need to be met in order to prove that homosexuality is an inherited condition in humans:

1. It would be necessary to define strictly what is meant in the study by the term homosexual. [. . .]
2. There should be a determination of the incidence of the phenomenon in groups of siblings in which the complete sexual history of every individual in each family is known. [. . .]
3. Especial attention should be paid to the balance between the homosexual and the heterosexual behavior in the histories of each of the siblings in such a study.
4. The recognition of homosexuality in any individual should not be considered sufficient unless a complete sexual history is available. [. . .]
5. Similarly, the heterosexuality of any individual who enters into the calculations should be determined through complete sex histories. In

nearly all studies to date, heterosexuality has been assumed . . . when there was no public knowledge of homosexuality. These are, of course, untrustworthy sources of information. [. . .]

6. There should be data on enough cases of siblings to be statistically significant. [. . .]

7. The incidence of the homosexual, as it is defined in the study, should be shown to be higher among siblings than it is in the histories of the nonsiblings in the study. Inasmuch as our present data indicate that more than a third (37%) of the white males in any population (or probably, for that matter, among anyone's ancestors) have had at least some homosexual experience, and inasmuch as the data indicate that a quarter of the males in the population (and a quarter of the males in anyone's ancestry) may have more than incidental homosexual experience in the course of their lives, it would be necessary to show that the incidence of the homosexual in groups of siblings is higher than that. This, of course, has never been shown in any study on the inheritance of the homosexual.

8. Whatever the hereditary mechanisms which are proposed, they must allow for the fact that some individuals change from exclusively heterosexual to exclusively homosexual patterns in the course of their lives, or vice versa, and they must allow for frequent changes in ratings of individuals on the heterosexual-homosexual scale. (662–63)

Kinsey's layout of the requirements scientists would need to fulfill in order to ascertain a link between biology and homosexuality has structured much of the biological research in the sixty years since the appearance of *Human Male*. This is interesting because Kinsey's conditions, especially those dealing with sibling samples, make a point of alerting researchers to issues that he believes will make it close to impossible to gather valid data. Nevertheless, a host of studies both before and after Kinsey have attempted to identify genetic, hormonal, or anatomical factors linked to homosexuality in humans.

A number of these studies have used animals; one of the earliest seems to have been Richard Goldschmidt's 1917 study of what he called "intersexuality" in insects. Goldschmidt's observations of the gypsy moth *Lymantria* identified a number of intermediate types between male and female; he reasoned that these types demonstrated a hereditary basis for homosexuality in humans. Kinsey, among others, dismissed Goldschmidt's findings because "he identified homosexual males and females in the human species as intersexes" (*Male* 661) rather than simply as people engaging in a spectrum of sexual experiences. Still, scientists have continued to attempt to extrapolate from animals to people.

I. L. Ward's work with rats, C. E. Roselli and colleagues' work with rams, and Ebru Demir and Barry Dickson's work with fruit flies all suggest genetic explanations for homosexuality in humans. The Demir and Dickson study of *Drosophila* (2005) identifies one gene, named *fruitless* or *fru,* that they believe appears to control sexual orientation. It is true that when a female fruit fly is engineered to splice *fru* in a male-specific fashion, she approaches and attempts to copulate with other females. It has not been demonstrated, however, that any similar gene operates in humans.

Sibling studies—particularly of twins—were seen by Kinsey as promising in terms of establishing a hereditary pattern of homosexuality. Indeed, an early study from Kinsey's era reported a concordance rate (the likelihood that if one monozygotic—or "identical"—twin is gay, the other will be too) near 100% (Kallmann). More recent studies make much less extravagant claims: J. Michael Bailey and Richard C. Pillard's research, for instance, shows concordance rates of 52% and 48% for male and female monozygotic twins, respectively, and 22% and 16% for male and female dizygotic ("fraternal") twins, respectively. Since the concordance results for monozygotic twins are less than 100%, it is impossible to conclude that genes absolutely determine sexual orientation; but these studies seem to indicate the possibility of a genetic *influence* on sexuality. Using pairs of gay brothers, a research group led by Dean Hamer attempted to locate a "gay gene" that controls sexual orientation. They reported finding a promising site in an area called Xq28 on the X chromosome, but a later group failed to confirm the discovery. A 2005 study by Brian Mustanski et al. found possible sites on chromosomes 7, 8, and 10 but did not present firm evidence of an actual connection between the gene and homosexuality. Simon LeVay asserts that "sexual orientation is . . . partly inherited, at least in men" ("Biology" 6); however, no irrefutable genetic evidence has surfaced.

A number of studies have focused on hormones as a cause of homosexuality in men and women. German neuroendocrinologist Günter Dörner's prenatal hormonal theory of homosexuality proposed that the brains of prehomosexual fetuses develop in a sex-atypical way, due either to unusual amounts of hormones or to specific brain responses to hormones. Another set of hormone studies claims that the ring finger (D4) in lesbians is significantly longer than the index finger (D2), whereas in most women, D2 is nearly the same length as D4. The relatively low D2:D4 ratio in lesbians is similar to most men; the theory postulates that these individuals were exposed prenatally to high androgen, or male hormone, levels.

Find Out More in "Differences in Finger Length Ratios between Self-Identified 'Butch' and 'Femme' Lesbians" at the end of this chapter.

One of the most important and controversial hormone studies was undertaken by LeVay in 1991. In an autopsy study of gay men, LeVay found that the third interstitial nucleus of the anterior hypothalamus (INAH3) was smaller than in straight men—in fact, similar in size to women's. The hypothalamus is a part of the brain that serves a number of functions, among which is hormonal/neurotransmitter regulation. Therefore, a man with a smaller than usual INAH3 might be expected to have developed in a sex-atypical way. LeVay's study was verified in 2001 and is probably the most plausible of the biological studies of homosexuality. Nevertheless, LeVay's sample of gay men, most of whom had died from AIDS, points to two problems with his study. First, it is not clear what effect AIDS may have on the human hypothalamus, and therefore the possibility exists that its unusual size in these men results from disease and has no relationship to sexual orientation. Second, the sample itself is suspect. LeVay's own definition of homosexuality—"a dissociation between anatomical sex and sex-typical sexual orientation" ("Biology" 4)—presupposes subjects who self-identify as gay since, unlike skin color, for example, homosexuality is not visibly marked on the human body. The sample problem is not unique to LeVay, of course. Kinsey anticipated it in 1948 by urging future researchers in this area to undertake detailed sexual histories and to resist the assumption that "homosexuals" and "heterosexuals" are somehow distinct and opposite. Many have ignored his warning, and it is common practice to assemble a research sample of sexual minority individuals through suspect means, such as "snowballing"—beginning with people the researcher knows personally, then asking them to recruit their friends into the study—or using LGBT political or social groups. These methods produce samples that tend to be skewed with respect to (1) race, (2) social class, (3) "outness," and (4) attitude toward gayness and gay rights issues.

A third problem with LeVay's study that is not related to the AIDS sample—and that is common to virtually all sexual orientation research—is the assumption that what he calls "sex-typical" orientation is based on traditional ideas of what constitutes maleness and femaleness. The androgen receptor gene, for instance, "plays the key role in mediating testosterone's influence on the body and brain" (LeVay, "Biology" 6). Testosterone increases behaviors identified in many cultures as "male" (e.g., sexual aggressiveness and propensity toward violence). Therefore, researchers reason, if a woman is sexually aggressive or a man is gentle, they are sex atypical and might be lesbian or gay. In other words, much of the research on sexual orientation seems tied to the gender inversion models that were in fashion over a century ago but that are today seen as limiting to both men and women. It should also be noted that these researchers have focused on homosexuality as it is constructed in the United States and the Global North. Attention

Find Out More in "Essentialism" at the end of this chapter.

to non-Western constructions of sexuality will surely problematize the assumptions upon which these scientific studies are based. For instance, how might researchers collect interviews in a culture in which *homosexual* and *heterosexual* are not common terms of identity? It may be tempting for Western-trained researchers to apply sexual orientation identity terms to people who do not self-identify as "gay" or "straight," but would such terms adequately reflect the interviewees' experiences and desires?

Nature-Nurture: What's at Stake?

Let us conclude this chapter by considering what is at stake in the nature-nurture debate. Simon LeVay argues that "the continued search for the responsible genes [for sexual orientation] and their mechanism of action is certainly warranted" ("Biology" 6), and many LGBT activists have employed a kind of "strategic essentialism" [λ Chapter 3] in their ongoing quest for civil rights; this has meant adopting the position that homosexuality is inherited in the same way that race or brown eyes are inherited. If one is simply born a homosexual, then discrimination is not morally justifiable. Proving that sexual orientation is a genetic trait thus seems to support the rights movement. One might expect that LGBT activists would unhesitatingly embrace the genetic explanation. Indeed, strategic essentialism has proven useful, and some still support it. But many LGBT people distrust the biological approach. For one thing, some prefer a liberationist politics (supporting sexual freedom) to one that emphasizes biological determinism. Interviewees throughout Vera Whisman's *Queer by Choice: Lesbians, Gay Men, and the Politics of Identity* assert that a central component of their sense of identity is not so much "gay" identity as sexual self-determination, the right to choose how, when, and why they engage with other people intimately. Some also fear that the genetic explanation leads back to the "gay is sick" [λ Chapter 3] philosophy, where the medical establishment made draconian attempts to "cure" LGBT people. Some imagine fetuses genetically marked as homosexual being aborted or otherwise eliminated in families that prefer heterosexual children. Some critique the science as flawed due to the elision of racial diversity from virtually all research studies. Still others simply reject the sexist ideas of "gender confusion" and the pathologization of the "masculine female or the non-masculine male" (Pickering and Saunders 7).

Those who do not support gay rights use combinations of both "nature" and "nurture" arguments to oppose queer activists. The Concerned Women for

America (CWA) charge, for instance, that "LeVay is an open homosexual, and . . . he had an agenda from the outset" (Chun). CWA criticizes LeVay's work as bogus science undertaken to support the "gay agenda." Probe Ministries traces the biology argument back to Kinsey's 10% estimate, which was used by "Harry Hay, the father of the homosexual 'civil rights' movement, urging that homosexuality be seen no longer as an act of sodomy but as a 10% minority class" [λ Chapter 3] (Bohlin 1).

Find Out More in "Is Your Baby Gay?" at the end of this chapter.

Probe counters by including homosexuality among "sexual sins" that may be genetically influenced but must be resisted because they are immoral; they use Leviticus 18 and 20 [λ Chapter 1] to link homosexuality to incest, adultery, bestiality, and child sacrifice. So, from Probe's standpoint, the nature argument is irrelevant; homosexuality, even if "natural," should still be resisted, much as one might resist other socially "unacceptable" impulses. Arguing from a nurture position, Dr. Paul Cameron of the Family Research Institute maintains that "homosexual behavior is learned" (1) and therefore can be unlearned, through psychotherapy and "ex-gay ministries" (6). The argument that homosexuality is a chosen set of behaviors has been deployed frequently in the fight *against* LGBT civil rights.

Whatever side one may occupy in the nature-nurture debate, it is clear that, even in the realm of science, political investments often influence the type and nature of research projects undertaken, as well as the way those projects are understood, interpreted, and used by a variety of activists—both pro- and anti-queer. Both Kinsey and LeVay, for instance, pursued their research not just to understand human sexuality but to make room for a more capacious appreciation for sexual diversity. The fact that scientists such as LeVay, among many others, have argued for a *biological* basis for homosexuality suggests the power and cultural capital of science in Western societies. Such research is pursued in an effort to cash in on that capital, demonstrating the seeming naturalness of sexual behaviors found in all cultures throughout history. Still, as persuasive as some of the biological research seems to be in arguing for a genetic basis for homosexuality, and despite the fact that "five decades of psychiatric evidence demonstrate that homosexuality is immutable, and nonpathological" (Burr 65), no one appears to regard the issue as definitively settled. Methodological weaknesses have been perceived in both biological and psychological research, not the least of which is that both still assume heterosexuality as the default position. We can see heteronormativity at work in scientific inquiry; researchers look for a "gay gene," but why do they not attempt to isolate a "straight gene"? Presumably, only the nonnormative—the queer—needs to be explained, while the normative goes unremarked as obviously and unquestionably natural. In addition, both the "gay agenda" and the "antigay agenda" weigh in on the debate, typically ignoring what the scientists are saying entirely (Mucciaroni and Killian).

QUESTIONS FOR DISCUSSION

1. This chapter has included a number of instruments designed to measure a person's homosexuality (the Kinsey scale, the Benjamin Gender Disorientation Scale, the Klein Sexual Orientation Grid, and so forth). Take several of these tests yourself. What are your results? Is one instrument more accurate than another in expressing how you feel about your own sexual identity? What questions or measurements seem most effective to you? What might be missing from these instruments? If you were to design your own scale, what would it look like?

2. In this chapter, we have asserted that a number of biological and psychological studies about homosexuality rest on some typically dualistic assumptions about gender: men normally act a certain way and women another. Such assumptions are founded on cultural beliefs about what "normal men" and "normal women" are supposed to be like. As you read the "Find Out More" article by Brown et al. analyzing the D2:D4 finger length ratio in butch and femme lesbians, attempt your own gender critique. What unstated assumptions about gender underlie the authors' argument?

3. There are those who argue that some scientists pursuing work that examines the relationship of nature and nurture to sexuality are supporting what they call "the gay agenda," and it cannot be denied that much scientific research is done with an eye toward answering questions related to larger social issues. Can it not be argued that groups who accuse scientists such as Simon LeVay of having a "gay agenda" might have agendas of their own? Do some investigative work to find out more about organizations such as the Concerned Women of America, Probe Ministries, and the Family Research Institute. Do they have agendas? If so, describe them.

REFERENCES AND FURTHER READING

Bailey, J. M., and R. C. Pillard. "Genetics of Human Sexual Orientation." *Annual Review of Sex Research* 6 (1995): 126–50.

Bailey, J. M., R. C. Pillard, M. C. Neale, and Y. Agyei. "Heritable Factors Influence Sexual Orientation in Women." *Archives of General Psychiatry* 50 (1993): 217–23.

Benjamin, Harry. *The Transsexual Phenomenon*. 1966. 19 July 2008 <http://www.transgenderzone.com/downloads/tphenom.htm>.

Berkey, B. R., T. Perelman-Hall, and L. A. Kurdek. "The Multidimensional Scale of Sexuality." *Journal of Homosexuality* 19 (1990): 67–87. To take the MSS: <http://www.psych.wright.edu/Kurdek01/MSS.htm>.

Bohlin, Sue. "Homosexual Myths." Probe Ministries. 19 July 2008 <http://www.probe.org/content/view/699/72/>.

Brown, Windy M., Christopher J. Finn, Bradley M. Cooke, and S. Marc Breedlove. "Differences in Finger Length Ratios between Self-Identified 'Butch' and 'Femme' Lesbians." *Archives of Sexual Behavior* 31.1 (2002): 123–27.

Burr, Chandler. "Homosexuality and Biology." *The Atlantic Monthly* 271.3 (1993): 47–65.

Cameron, Paul. "What Causes Homosexual Desire and Can It Be Changed?" 19 July 2008 <http://www.biblebelievers.com/Cameron3.html>.

Cass, Vivian C. "Homosexual Identity Formation: A Theoretical Model." *Journal of Homosexuality* 4.3 (1979): 219–35.

Chun, Trudy. "Born or Bred? The Debate over the Cause of Homosexuality." Concerned Women for America, 1 June 2000. 19 July 2008 <http://www.cwfa.org/articledisplay.asp?id=1097&department=CWA&categoryid=family>.

Currie, Nick (Momus). "Psychopathia Sexualis." 2001. 19 July 2008 <http://www.phespirit.info/momus/20010112.htm>.

Demir, E., and B. J. Dickson. "*fruitless* Splicing Specifies Male Courtship Behavior in *Drosophila.*" *Cell* 121 (2005): 785–94.

Dörner, Günter. "Hormone Dependent Differentiation, Maturation and Function of the Brain and Sexual Behavior." *Endokrinologie* 69 (1977): 306–20.

Goldschmidt, Richard. "Intersexuality and the Endocrine Aspect of Sex." *Endocrinology* 1 (1917): 433–56.

Gordon, Archie "Stomp." "What's Her Whimsey, Dr. Kinsey?" 19 July 2008 <http://www.theonlineblues.com/archie-stomp-gordon-what-s-her-whimsey-dr-kinsey-lyrics.html>.

Haeberle, Erwin J. "Bisexuality: History and Dimensions of a Modern Scientific Problem." 1998. 19 July 2008 <http://www2.hu-berlin.de/sexology/GESUND/ARCHIV/SEXOR4.HTM>.

Hamer, D. H., S. Hu, V. L. Magnuson, N. Hu, and A. M. L. Pattatucci. "A Linkage between DNA Markers on the X Chromosome and Male Sexual Orientation." *Science* 261 (1993): 320–26.

Hirschfeld, Magnus. *Sappho und Sokrates: Wie erklärt sich die Liebe der Männer und Frauen zu Personen des eigenen Geschlechts?* 2nd ed. Leipzig: Max Spohr, 1902.

Kallmann, E. J. "Comparative Twin Studies on the Genetic Aspects of Male Homosexuality." *Journal of Nervous and Mental Disease* 115 (1952): 283–98.

Kanefsky, Bob. "Kinsey Scale." 1988. 19 July 2008 <http://www.songworm.com/lyrics/songworm-parody/KinseyScale.html>.

Kauth, Michael R. "Revealing Assumptions: Explicating Sexual Orientation and Promoting Conceptual Integrity." *Journal of Bisexuality* 5.4 (2006): 79–105.

Kinsey, Alfred, and the staff of the Institute for Sex Research, Indiana University. *Sexual Behavior in the Human Female.* Philadelphia: W. B. Saunders, 1953.

Kinsey, Alfred, Wardell B. Pomeroy, and Clyde E. Martin. *Sexual Behavior in the Human Male.* Philadelphia: W. B. Saunders, 1948.

"Kinsey in the News." 19 July 2008 <http://www.pbs.org/wgbh/amex/kinsey/sfeature/sf_response_male.html>.

Klein, Fritz. *The Bisexual Option: A Concept of One Hundred Percent Intimacy.* New York: Arbor House, 1978.

LeVay, Simon. "The Biology of Sexual Orientation." 2003. Latest update February 2006. 19 July 2008 <http://members.aol.com/slevay/page22.html>.

———. "A Difference in Hypothalamic Structure between Heterosexual and Homosexual Men." *Science* 253 (1991): 1034–37.

Meyer, Susan, and Alan M. Schwitzer. "Stages of Identity Development among College Students with Minority Sexual Orientations." *Journal of College Student Psychotherapy* 13.4 (1999): 41–66.

Mohler, R. Albert, Jr. "Is Your Baby Gay? What If You Could Know? What If You Could Do Something About It?" Blog posting. 19 July 2008 <http://www.albertmohler.com/blog_print.php?id=891>.

Mucciaroni, Gary, and Mary Lou Killian. "Immutability, Science and Legislative Debate over Gay, Lesbian and Bisexual Rights." *Journal of Homosexuality* 47.1 (2004): 53–77.

Munsey, David. "The Love That Need Not Name Its Speaker." *National Journal of Sexual Orientation Law* 2.1 (1996). <http://www.ibiblio.org/gaylaw/issue3/issue3.html>.

Mustanski, B. S., M. G. Dupree, C. M. Nievergelt, S. Bockland, N. J. Schork, and D. H. Hamer. "A Genomewide Scan of Male Sexual Orientation." *Human Genetics* 116 (2005): 272–78.

Norton, Rictor. "Essentialism." 19 July 2008 <http://www.rictornorton.co.uk/social03.htm>.

Pickering, Rachael, and Peter Saunders. "What Causes Homosexuality?" *Nucleus* (October 1997). <http://www.cmf.org.uk/literature/content.asp?context=article&id=630>.

Reisman, Judith. "Kinsey and the Homosexual Revolution." 19 July 2008 <http://www.leaderu.com/jhs/reisman.html>.

Rich, Adrienne. "Compulsory Heterosexuality and Lesbian Existence." *The Lesbian and Gay Studies Reader.* Eds. H. Abelove, M. Aina Barale, and D. Halperin. New York: Routledge, 1993. 227–54 [1980].

Roselli, C. E., K. Larkin, J. A. Resko, J. N. Stellflug, and F. Stormshak. "The Volume of a Sexually Dimorphic Nucleus in the Ovine Medial Preoptic Area/Anterior Hypothalamus Varies with Sexual Partner Preference." *Endocrinology* 145.2 (2004): 478–83.

Storms, Michael. "A Theory of Erotic Orientation Development." *Psychological Review* 88.4 (1981): 340–53.

Ward, I. L. "Prenatal Stress Feminizes and Demasculinizes the Behavior of Males." *Science* 175.17 (1972): 82–84.

Whisman, Vera. *Queer by Choice: Lesbians, Gay Men, and the Politics of Identity.* New York: Routledge, 1996.

READINGS

➤ **Windy M. Brown, Christopher J. Finn, Bradley M. Cooke, and S. Marc Breedlove**

"Differences in Finger Length Ratios between Self-Identified 'Butch' and 'Femme' Lesbians"

(2002), United States

In nonhuman mammals, sexual differentiation of behavior seems largely driven by exposure to steroid hormones during the perinatal period (Breedlove, Cooke, & Jordan, 1998). The Y chromosome in males causes the undifferentiated gonads to develop as testes, and the testes to secrete androgen, which masculinizes the structure of the brain, permanently molding the animal's behavior to a male-like form (Phoenix, Goy, Gerall, & Young, 1959). Whether early androgen exposure also directly alters the structure of the developing human brain, and thereby adult behavior, remains undetermined.

In the study of sexual orientation, there is little direct evidence that individual differences in early androgen exposure affect the sexual preferences of men. In women, however, there have been several reports of a difference between heterosexual and homosexual women in purported markers of prenatal or neonatal androgen exposure. McFadden and Champlin (2000) found that auditory evoked potentials (AEP) are more masculine in lesbians than in heterosexual women. Because the sex difference in AEP is present in newborn humans, and because other somatic sex differences in newborns appear to be due to the masculinizing influence of androgen in males, presumably AEP are influenced by, and can therefore serve as markers for, fetal androgen exposure. Thus the AEP results suggest that homosexual women were exposed to more fetal androgen than were heterosexual women. McFadden and Champlin also found that the AEP of homosexual men suggested that they, if anything, had experienced significantly higher levels of perinatal androgen than did heterosexual men. McFadden and Pasanen (1998) also found that otoacoustic emissions, which are also sexually dimorphic at birth (and therefore may also serve as markers for fetal androgen), are significantly more male-like in homosexual women than in heterosexual women. This result is a further indication that lesbians may have been exposed to higher fetal androgen levels than heterosexual women (for an overview, see McFadden, 2002).

Another purported somatic marker of fetal androgen is the ratio of the length of the index finger (2D) to the ring finger (4D). This ratio, 2D:4D, is smaller in men than in women (Ecker, 1875), a sex difference that is stable from 2 years of age to adulthood (Manning, Scott, Wilson, & Lewis-Jones, 1998). As most somatic differences between young boys and girls have been attributed to differences in exposure to androgen before and just after birth (George & Wilson, 1994), the sex difference in 2D:4D was presumed to reflect sex differences in early androgen.

We have tested this hypothesis by examining the 2D:4D of people with congenital adrenal hyperplasia (CAH). CAH is a disorder that causes the adrenals to produce excessive androgens beginning prenatally and extending to treatment, which usually begins shortly after birth following an accurate diagnosis. We found that the ratios were indeed smaller in CAH females than in control females, and were also smaller in CAH males than in control males (Brown, Hines, Fane, & Breedlove, 2001). The difference between CAH males and control males was especially prominent when comparing relatives, suggesting that genetic background can affect the finger length ratios but that, within a particular genetic background, greater early androgen exposure reduces the finger ratios. We have also found a similar sex difference in the digit length ratios of mice: rear paw 2D:4D is smaller in males than in females at weaning and in adulthood (Brown, Finn, & Breedlove, 2001), which suggests that adult digit length ratios may provide a retrospective indication of perinatal androgens in many mammalian species.

Accordingly, the report of Williams et al. (2000) that the 2D:4D of homosexual women was more masculine (smaller) than that of heterosexual women indicates again that lesbians are, on average, exposed to more prenatal androgen than are heterosexual women. If so, then increased exposure to fetal androgen may increase the probability of homosexuality in human females. This study found no differences in the 2D:4D of heterosexual versus homosexual men.

If early hormone levels affect human sexual orientation in the same manner as they do other sex dimorphic behaviors in other animals, this influence would be expected to be organizational in nature such that the behavior pattern affected is set from a young age and remains constant throughout the life span. There is some evidence, however, that some women have a heterosexual orientation during certain periods of their lives and a homosexual orientation at other periods (Diamond, 1998). This suggests that other factors, including social influences, can also affect sexual orientation in women. Therefore, presumably some of the lesbians studied in the previously cited reports were exposed to low levels of androgen in development, i.e., perinatal androgens played no role in the development of their sexual orientation. Because other, nonandrogenic factors influence female sexual orientation, the experimental detection of effects of early androgen, especially via indirect measures, requires large sample sizes. We therefore wondered whether it would be possible to subdivide lesbian participants into groups in which perinatal androgen exposure might be more or less likely to have played a role in the development of a homosexual orientation. Because some lesbians consider themselves to be more masculine ("butch") than other women, we tested whether the finger length ratios of "butch" lesbians would show evidence of greater perinatal androgen exposure than those of "femme" lesbians.

Methods

A booth was rented for the August 2000 Gay Pride Mardi Gras in Oakland, CA. All adult participants were offered a California Lottery "scratcher" ticket in return for answering an anonymous survey that asked their age, sex at birth, and number of older brothers and sisters.

Participants and Measures. Participants identified themselves as "exclusively heterosexual," "predominantly heterosexual," "bisexual," "predominantly homosexual," or "exclusively homosexual." They were also asked the gender of their sexual partners ("exclusively males," "predominantly males," "males and females equally," "predominantly females," or "exclusively females") and the gender of sexual partners in their fantasies. These latter two questions were asked to confirm self-reports of orientation and, in this study, all participants gave answers that were consistent with their reported sexual orientation. They were also asked to answer the following question: "If I had to describe myself as one of the two types below, I would consider my overall outlook to be (circle one)": with the choices butch and femme on the line beneath. The questionnaire informed them that answering any question was voluntary and would not affect their receipt of a ticket. Participants were not asked to report their ethnicity.

The participants then had their hands copied on a portable photocopier. A clear Plexiglas form was placed on the glass platen. This form had two posts, 6 mm in diameter, 147 mm apart. Participants were asked to place their hands flat, palm-down, thumbs near each other, fingers on each hand together, on the form with the posts between the index and middle fingers of each hand, snug against the junction of the two fingers. A millimeter scale was present 12 mm lateral to the posts and the participants' middle fingers were aligned on this scale. A white plastic bag, filled with rice for ballast, was placed over the hands before photocopying. Matching numbered stickers were affixed to the back of each questionnaire and photocopy to discern which answers were associated with each photocopy.

Finger lengths were measured by an experimenter, without knowledge of any participant's group membership. If the tip of either finger was obscured in the photocopy, then no ratio was available for that hand for that participant. Measures were taken for each finger to the nearest 0.5 mm, based on their alignment to the photocopied ruler running along the middle finger. This method of measuring finger length differs slightly from other recent reports, but is much more efficient than the method we used previously (Williams et al., 2000). It also more closely matches the measurement method reported by George (1930), confirming Ecker's report (Ecker, 1875). Two mixed-design ANOVAs, with an independent factor of either male/female (to evaluate sex differences) or butch/femme (to evaluate lesbian subgroups), and right and left hand finger ratios as repeated measures, were conducted. Further analysis of differences between groups were evaluated by Student's *t* tests, with all reported *p* values two-tailed.

Results

The present measurement method detected the previously reported sex difference in 2D:4D between the 267 female and 168 male participants. ANOVA revealed a sex difference in which ratios were greater in females than in males, $F(1, 432) = 28.3$, $p < .001$, a laterality effect in which the ratios were greater on the right than on the left, $F(1, 432) = 6.0$, $p < .02$, and a significant interaction of the two factors, $F(1, 432) = 18.6$, $p < .001$. Student's *t* tests indicated that the interaction was due to a greater sex difference on the right than on the left. For the right hand, the ratio was 0.994 ± 0.003 (*SEM*) for women, 0.958 ± 0.004 for men, $t(431) = 6.6$; $p < 10^{-10}$; for the left hand, the ratio was 0.967 ± 0.003 for women and 0.938 ± 0.004 for men, $t(431) = 5.9$, $p < 10^{-8}$. Our previous report (Williams et al., 2000) also found the sex difference in 2D:4D to be greater on the right hand than on the left hand.

Of the 267 women, 29 identified themselves as heterosexual (either "predominantly heterosexual" or "exclusively heterosexual"), 28 as bisexual, 207 as homosexual (either "predominantly homosexual" or "exclusively homosexual"), and one declined to answer the questions about sexual orientation. The data from bisexuals were not examined. Among the homosexual women, 89 identified themselves as femme, 87 as butch, whereas 31 declined to answer the question. Self-identified butch versus femme lesbians were not significantly different in age (femme: mean of 39.41 ± .98 years, range, 22–58; butch: 41.12 ± .90 years, range, 24–66). [. . .]

Discussion

We found that it was possible to classify homosexual women into two self-reported categories: those who regard themselves as having a "butch" outlook and those who regard themselves as having a "femme" outlook. Although there is debate over the validity of segregating homosexual women into these categories (Laner & Laner, 1980), most participants in this study appeared to intuitively understand what we were referring to by these classifications and most of them, when asked, appeared to readily identify more with one than the other. These two groups differed significantly in the 2D:4D ratio of the right hand, suggesting that the femme group had been exposed to less prenatal androgen than had the butch group. Nevertheless, the overlap between the two groups for this measure was considerable. The data thus indicate that there are more factors influencing sexual orientation than simply early androgen exposure.

The finding that women who identify themselves as either butch or femme lesbians differ in this biological marker for androgen suggests that it may be worthwhile to try to more rigorously define subgroups of individuals regarded as either heterosexual or homosexual. The present classification was simple (an answer to a single, rather amorphous question) and therefore surely crude. It should be possible, with more extensive probing of personality traits, to more accurately classify homosexual women. Such refined classifications might reveal a greater difference in 2D:4D, or might reveal personality traits that co-vary with finger ratios, which might shed light on the butch-femme distinction. For example, after conducting the study we learned of the report by Wilson (1983) regarding women who answered a newspaper survey. Those who reported that their index finger was shorter than their ring finger were more likely to describe themselves as "assertive and competitive" than those whose index finger was longer than the ring finger. Again, the sample size was large (985 women), so it is not a question of whether early androgens determine this personality style, only whether they increase the probability of such a personality developing. It is possible that the present differences in 2D:4D reflect a difference in assertiveness between butch and femme lesbians.

The 2D:4D difference between butch and femme lesbians is consistent with the idea that early androgens have some influence on later sexual orientation, at least in females. The present findings also conform to the report from Singh, Vidaurri, Zambarano, and Dabbs (1999) that butch lesbians had a higher waist-to-hip ratio, higher salivary testosterone levels, and more reports of childhood gender-atypical behavior than did femme lesbians. These results and the previously discussed auditory system measures suggest that early exposure to androgen can increase the probability of a homosexual orientation in human females.

We have so far detected no difference between heterosexual and homosexual men in 2D:4D, suggesting that early androgens do not differ between the two groups and may not play a role in the development of male sexual orientation. But the present findings suggest that it might be possible to classify homosexual men into categories that might reveal a difference in early androgen exposure. For example, some homosexual men report a history of gender nonconformity as children, whereas others do not. It is possible that a relative lack of early androgen exposure might contribute to the development of homosexuality in the former, and/or that a relative surplus of early androgen might contribute to homosexuality in the latter. Robinson and Manning (2000) in fact report that the finger ratios of gay men differ according their score on the Kinsey sexual orientation scale.

We have several times found the sex difference in 2D:4D to be greater on the right hand than on the left (Williams et al., 2000, the present study, and unpublished observations), as have other groups (Manning et al., 1998). We also found that the difference between CAH and control women was greater on the right hand than on the left (Brown, Hines, et al., 2001). These data suggest that the right hand finger ratios are more sensitive to prenatal androgen than are those on the left. We can offer no explanation for why androgen would affect the developing right hand more than the left.

While reviewing the proofs for this article, we learned that Tortorice (2001) recently reported 2D:4D to be smaller in self-rated butch lesbians than in femme lesbians.

References

Breedlove, S. M., Cooke, B., & Jordan, C. L. (1998). The orthodox view of sexual differentiation of the brain. *Brain, Behavior and Evolution, 54,* 8–14.

Brown, W. M., Finn, C., & Breedlove, S. M. (2001). A sex difference in the digit length ratio in mice [Abstract]. *Hormones and Behavior, 39,* 325.

Brown, W. M., Hines, M., Fane, B., & Breedlove, S. M. (2001). Masculinized finger length ratios in humans with congenital adrenal hyperplasia (CAH) [Abstract]. *Hormones and Behavior, 39,* 325–326.

Diamond, L. M. (1998). Development of sexual orientation among adolescent and young adult women. *Developmental Psychology, 34,* 1085–1095.

Ecker, A. (1875). Einige bemerkungen über einen schwankenden character in der hand des menschen. [Some remarks about a varying character in the hand of humans.] *Archiv für Anthropologie, 8,* 68–74.

George, F. W., & Wilson, J. D. (1994). Sex determination and differentiation. In E. Knobil & J. D. Neil (Eds.), *The physiology of reproduction* (pp. 3–28). New York: Raven Press.

George, R. (1930). Human finger types. *Anatomical Record, 46,* 199–204.

Laner, M. R., & Laner, R. H. (1980). Sexual preference or personal style? Why lesbians are disliked. *Journal of Homosexuality, 5,* 339–356.

Manning, J. T., Scott, D., Wilson, J., & Lewis-Jones, D. I. (1998). The ratio of 2nd to 4th digit length: A predictor of sperm numbers and concentrations of testosterone, luteinizing hormone and oestrogen. *Human Reproduction, 13,* 3000–3004.

McFadden, D. (2002). Masculinization effects in the auditory system. *Archives of Sexual Behavior, 31,* 93–105.

McFadden, D., & Champlin, C. A. (2000). Comparison of auditory evoked potentials in heterosexual, homosexual, and bisexual males and females. *Journal of the Association of Research in Otolaryngology, 1,* 89–99.

McFadden, D., & Pasanen, E. G. (1998). Comparison of the auditory systems of heterosexuals and homosexuals: Click-evoked otoacoustic emissions. *Proceedings of the National Academy of Sciences of the United States of America, 95,* 2709–2713.

Phoenix, C. H., Goy, R. W., Gerall, A. A., & Young, W. C. (1959). Organizing action of prenatally administered testosterone propionate on the tissues mediating mating behavior in the female guinea pig. *Endocrinology, 65,* 369–382.

Robinson, S. J., & Manning, J. T. (2000). The ratio of 2nd to 4th digit length and male homosexuality. *Evolution and Human Behavior, 21,* 333–345.

Singh, D.,Vidaurri, M., Zambarano, R. J., & Dabbs, J. M. (1999). Lesbian erotic role identification: Behavioral, morphological, and hormonal correlates. *Journal of Personality and Social Psychology, 76,* 1035–1049.

Tortorice, J. (2001). Gender identity, sexual orientation, and second-to-fourth-digit ratio in females [Abstract]. *Human Behavior and Evolution Society Abstracts, 13,* 35.

Williams, T. J., Pepitone, M. E., Christensen, S. E., Cooke, B. M., Huberman, A. D., Breedlove, T. J., Jordan, C. L., et al. (2000). Finger length patterns indicate an influence of fetal androgens on human sexual orientation. *Nature, 404,* 455–456.

Wilson, G. D. (1983). Finger-length as an index of assertiveness in women. *Personality and Individual Differences, 4,* 111–112.

Brown, Windy M., Christopher J. Finn, Bradley M. Cooke, and S. Marc Breedlove. "Differences in Finger Length Ratios between Self-Identified 'Butch' and 'Femme' Lesbians." *Archives of Sexual Behavior* 31 (February 2002): 123–27.

➤ Albert Mohler Jr.

"Is Your Baby Gay? What If You Could Know? What If You Could Do Something about It?"

(2 March 2007), United States

What if you could know that your unborn baby boy is likely to be sexually attracted to other boys? Beyond that, what if hormonal treatments could change the baby's orientation to heterosexual? Would you do it? Some scientists believe that such developments are just around the corner.

For some time now, scientists have been looking for a genetic or hormonal cause of sexual orientation. Thus far, no "gay gene" has been found—at least not in terms of incontrovertible and accepted science. Yet, it is now claimed that a growing body of evidence indicates that biological factors may at least contribute to sexual orientation.

The most interesting research along these lines relates to the study of sheep. Scientists at the U.S. Sheep Experiment Station are conducting research into the sexual orientation of sheep through "sexual partner preference testing." As William Saletan at *Slate.com* explains:

> A bare majority of rams turn out to be heterosexual. One in five swings both ways. About 15 percent are asexual, and 7 percent to 10 percent are gay.
>
> Why so many gay rams? Is it too much socializing with ewes? Same-sex play with other lambs? Domestication? Nope. Those theories have been debunked. Gay rams don't act girly. They're just as gay in the wild. And a crucial part of their brains—the "sexually dimorphic nucleus"—looks more like a ewe's than like a straight ram's. Gay men have a similar brain resemblance to women. Charles Roselli, the project's lead scientist, says such research "strongly suggests that sexual preference is biologically determined in animals, and possibly in humans."

What makes the sheep "sexual partner preference testing" research so interesting is that the same scientists who are documenting the rather surprising sexual behaviors of male sheep think they can also change the sexual orientation of the animals. In other words, finding a biological causation for homosexuality may also lead to the discovery of a "cure" for the same phenomenon.

That's where the issue gets really interesting. People for the Ethical Treatment of Animals [PETA] has called for an end to the research, while tennis star Martina Navratilova called the research "homophobic and cruel" and argued that gay sheep have a "right" to be homosexual. No kidding.

Homosexual activists were among the first to call for (and fund) research into a biological cause of homosexuality. After all, they argued, the discovery of a biological cause would lead to the normalization of homosexuality simply because it would then be seen to be natural, and thus moral.

But now the picture is quite different. Many homosexual activists recognize that the discovery of a biological marker or cause for homosexual orientation could lead to efforts to eliminate the trait, or change the orientation through genetic or hormonal treatments.

Tyler Gray addresses these issues in the current issue of *Radar* magazine. In "Is Your Baby Gay?," Gray sets out a fascinating scenario. A woman is told that her unborn baby boy is gay. This woman and her husband consider themselves to be liberal and tolerant of homosexuality. But this is not about homosexuality now; it is about their baby boy. The woman is then told that a hormone patch on her abdomen will "reverse the sexual orientation inscribed in his chromosomes." The *Sunday Times* [London] predicts that such a patch should be available for use on humans within the decade. Will she use it?

This question stands at the intersection of so many competing interests. Feminists and political liberals have argued for decades now that a woman should have an unrestricted right to an abortion, for any cause or for no stated cause at all. How can they now complain if women decide to abort fetuses identified as homosexual? This question involves both abortion and gay rights—the perfect moral storm of our times.

Homosexual activists have claimed that sexual orientation cannot be changed. What if a hormone patch during pregnancy will do the job?

As Gray suggests:

> In a culture that encourages us to customize everything from our Nikes to our venti skinny lattes, perhaps it is only a matter of time before baby-making becomes just another consumer transaction. Already have a girl? Make this one a boy! Want to impress your boho friends? Make a real statement with lesbian twins!

More to the point, Gray understands that such a development would reshape the abortion and gay-rights debates in America:

> Conservatives opposed to both abortion and homosexuality will have to ask themselves whether the public shame of having a gay child outweighs the private sin of terminating a pregnancy (assuming the stigma on homosexuality survives the scientific refutation of the Right's treasured belief that it is a "lifestyle choice.)" Pro-choice activists won't be spared either. Will liberal moms who love their hairdressers be as tolerant when faced with the prospect of raising a little stylist of their own? And exactly how pro-choice will liberal abortion-rights activists be when thousands of potential parents are choosing to filter homosexuality right out of the gene pool?

The development of Preimplantation Genetic Diagnosis [PGD] is one of the greatest threats to human dignity in our times. These tests are already leading to the abortion of fetuses identified as carrying unwanted genetic markers. The tests can now check for more than 1,300 different chromosomal abnormalities or patterns. With DNA analysis, the genetic factors could be identified right down to hair and eye color and other traits. The logic is all too simple. If you don't like what you see on the PGD report . . . just abort and start over. Soon, genetic treatments may allow for changing the profile. Welcome to the world of designer babies.

If that happens, how many parents—even among those who consider themselves most liberal—would choose a gay child? How many parents, armed with this diagnosis, would use the patch and change the orientation?

Christians who are committed to think in genuinely Christian terms should think carefully about these points:

1. There is, as of now, no incontrovertible or widely accepted proof that any biological basis for sexual orientation exists.

2. Nevertheless, the direction of the research points in this direction. Research into the sexual orientation of sheep and other animals, as well as human studies, points to some level of biological causation for sexual orientation in at least some individuals.

3. Given the consequences of the Fall and the effects of human sin, we should not be surprised that such a causation or link is found. After all, the human genetic structure, along with every other aspect of creation, shows the pernicious effects of the Fall and of God's judgment.

4. The biblical condemnation of all homosexual behaviors would not be compromised or mitigated in the least by such a discovery. The discovery of a biological factor would not change the Bible's moral verdict on homosexual behavior.

5. The discovery of a biological basis for homosexuality would be of great pastoral significance, allowing for a greater understanding of why certain persons struggle with these particular sexual temptations.

6. The biblical basis for establishing the dignity of all persons—the fact that all humans are made in God's image—reminds us that this means *all* persons, including those who may be marked by a predisposition toward homosexuality. For the sake of clarity, we must insist at all times that all persons—whether identified as heterosexual, homosexual, lesbian, transsexual, transgendered, bisexual, or whatever—are equally made in the image of God.

7. Thus, we will gladly contend for the right to life of all persons, born and unborn, whatever their sexual orientation. We must fight against the idea of aborting fetuses or human embryos identified as homosexual in orientation.

8. If a biological basis is found, and if a prenatal test is then developed, and if a successful treatment to reverse the sexual orientation to heterosexual is ever developed, we would support its use as we should unapologetically support the use of any appropriate means to avoid sexual temptation and the inevitable effects of sin.

9. We must stop confusing the issues of moral responsibility and moral choice. We are all *responsible* for our sexual orientation, but that does not mean that we freely and consciously *choose* that orientation. We sin against homosexuals by insisting that sexual temptation and attraction are predominately chosen. We do not always (or even

generally) choose our temptations. Nevertheless, we are absolutely responsible for what we *do* with sinful temptations, whatever our so-called sexual orientation.

10. Christians must be very careful not to claim that science can never prove a biological basis for sexual orientation. We can and must insist that no scientific finding can change the basic sinfulness of all homosexual behavior. The general trend of the research points to at least some biological factors behind sexual attraction, gender identity, and sexual orientation. This does not alter God's moral verdict on homosexual sin (or heterosexual sin, for that matter), but it does hold some promise that a deeper knowledge of homosexuality and its cause will allow for more effective ministries to those who struggle with this particular pattern of temptation. If such knowledge should ever be discovered, we should embrace it and use it for the greater good of humanity and for the greater glory of God.

➢ Rictor Norton

Selection from "Essentialism"

(1997), United States

My traditionalist historical position is termed "essentialism" by postmodern theorists, which they regard with contempt, in the same way that I regard social constructionist theory as the main impediment to the understanding of queer history. The history of ideas (and ideologies) can be interesting and valuable, but it is tragic that homosexuals have been subsumed *totally* within the idea of the 'homosexual construct'. The result is little better than intellectual ethnic cleansing.

In the social constructionist view, knowledge is constructed, deconstructed, and reconstructed through ideological discourse. In my traditionalist or essentialist view, knowledge is discovered, repressed, suppressed, and recovered through history and experience. **Social constructionism** emphasizes revolutionary development (the dialectic); I emphasize evolutionary development, cultural growth and permutation, and sometimes mere change in fashion. Rather than the word 'construct', which implies building from scratch according to an arbitrarily chosen blueprint, I prefer the words 'consolidate' or 'forge', implying that the basic material already exists but can be subjected to shaping and polishing.

'Cultural constructs' are sometimes set up in opposition to 'universal truths' in an effort to force traditionalists/essentialists into an impossibly idealistic corner, but 'culture' is a concept that can be claimed by essentialists as well as by social constructionists. The essentialist position is that queer culture is organic rather than artificial. Social constructionists see culture as a construct whose arbitrary foundation is determined by the builder; I see culture as the cultivation of a root, and I shall be developing the ethnic view that queer culture grows naturally from personal queer identity and experience and is self-cultivated by queers rather than by the ideology and labels of straight society.

I cannot reasonably object if critics wish to label me an 'essentialist' pure and simple, because I believe that homosexuals are born and not made, and that homosexuality is hard-wired. However, I also believe that queers fashion their own culture (using their own resources rather than being imposed upon by society), and this is a significant focus of my own version of essentialism, which might be called 'queer cultural essentialism'. I take the view that there is a core of queer desire that is transcultural, transnational, and transhistorical, a queer essence that is innate, congenital, constitutional, stable or fixed in its basic pattern. However, I distinguish between queer persons, queer sexual acts and behaviour, and queer social interactions, and try not to confuse the constancy of the desire with the variability of its expression. Personal queer identity arises from within, and is then consolidated along lines suggested by the collective identity of the queer (sub)culture.

In the theoretical literature it is generally assumed that essentialism is the same as uniformism/conformism (often made explicit in lesbian-feminist theory). But the view that homosexuality is a monolith is not at all an essential feature of essentialism. The essentialist does not say there is only *one* gay root: in fact a *diversity of roots* has been a key feature of essentialism since the early 1970s—witness the plural title of the two-volume collection of essays from *Gay Sunshine: Gay Roots*. It is really social constructionist theorists who have forced traditionalism into this straightjacket, just as they have forced gay experience into the political straitjacket.

I have no problem in reconciling the view that queer desire is innate but that it expresses itself in sexual or social actions and (sub)cultures that may reflect to a greater or lesser degree the time and place in which they occur. Self-presentation can be carefully constructed even though it is founded upon an innate self-conception.

Rictor Norton <http://www.rictornorton.co.uk/social03.htm>, adapted from material in Norton, Rictor. *The Myth of the Modern Homosexual.* London: Cassell, 1997.

CHAPTER 6

Inclusion and Equality

Acrucial distinction to make when talking about notions related to inclusion and equality is between civil rights (the rights of citizenship) and human rights (the rights many assume that we should have *because we are human*). Lesbian, gay, bisexual, and transgender (LGBT) activists in the Global North are sometimes criticized because, in our efforts to garner civil rights for sexual and gender nonconformists, we can become blinded to the needs of people (including LGBT people) who lack access to food, shelter, and health care. This critique assumes that human rights are more basic than civil rights, in that they focus on the bedrock conditions of existence rather than on legislative mechanisms. And granted, the fight for civil rights only occurs in contexts where many or most citizens generally enjoy freedom of association, speech, and religion—freedoms that many consider fundamental but are not necessarily respected as civil rights by some governments.

But as we shall see, a focus internationally on human rights has also been helpful as LGBT people have fought for inclusion and equality in their respective countries. Just after World War II (1948), as the post-Holocaust world attempted to come to grips with what had just occurred, the United Nations announced the Universal Declaration of Human Rights, which writer Donn Mitchell interprets as establishing "a right to be free from discrimination of *any kind*." The Universal Declaration states that "everyone is entitled to all the rights and freedoms set forth in this Declaration, without distinction of any kind, such as race, colour, sex, origin, property, birth or other status" (qtd. in Mitchell 13). Mitchell argues that the use of the phrase "such as" allows for expansion of the protections offered by the Declaration. It seems reasonable to assume that the Declaration applies to gender nonconformists and sexual minorities, particularly because it was a response to the Holocaust, and homosexuals were among the groups persecuted by the Nazis. Richard Schneider, editor of the *Harvard Gay and Lesbian Review,* points out that "[a]t a time when our enemies are able to score points by charging 'special rights,' perhaps a shift toward a broader definition of human rights, one that encompasses the rights of all oppressed groups in society, would make sense" (4) [λ Chapter 8]. One of the great challenges in creating a movement that works for LGBT people around the world has been to articulate the connections between local organizations and priorities and the concept of universal human rights. Schneider's advocacy of "a broader definition of human rights" implies an insistence on others viewing LGBT people as fully human, working with other fully human individuals for the benefit of "all oppressed groups in society."

Civil and Human Rights in a Global Context

One way to understand our local work for inclusion and equality in a global context is to think seriously about the mythology that has grown up around the U.S. LGBT civil rights struggle. The common assumption is that the United States is a leader in the quest for LGBT inclusion and equality; in reality, however, our efforts have occurred in a global context of similar and related struggles. Much is made in this country of the dangers faced by lesbian and gay people before and during the 1960s. The story is that the Stonewall riots occurred partly in response to systematic police harassment of lesbian and gay people who met in bars and other social spaces. While this is true, that harassment was not unique to the United States. For instance, as Joe Knowles points out, in the 1960s, Cuban homosexuals "were rounded up and put to work in military camps. This was also the time when the Cuban government passed Resolución Número 3, which mandated that homosexuals working in the arts be fired and reassigned jobs in hard labor" (19). *Lawrence v. Texas* [λ Chapter 4], the 2003 case in which the U.S. Supreme Court ruled that state laws against sodomy were unconstitutional, followed two decades after the 1981 European Court of Human Rights decision that bans on homosexual sex violated the European Convention on Human Rights. Dian Killian argues that while the "Republic of Ireland is still perceived by many Americans as a bog island of thatched cottages and donkey carts, and the United States as the gay-mythologized land of Stonewall," stringent hate crimes laws in Ireland "make it an offense even to incite violence against lesbians or gay men." Ireland has amended its Unfair Dismissals Act to protect gays in the workplace, and Ireland's national gay paper is "partially funded" by the state (24–25). Denmark also has national hate crimes legislation and other protections against discrimination on the basis of sexual orientation, although that country still denies LGBT people the right to adopt children, except for the biological children of partners (Jensen). In 2006, however, Danish legislators ruled that lesbians and single women were entitled to the same access to artificial insemination in public hospitals as heterosexual women (Wockner, "International News").

African struggles for LGBT inclusion and equality are perhaps the best illustration of the mixed attitudes toward LGBT people internationally. South Africa is the first country in the world to write LGBT equality into its constitution. Under the leadership of Nelson Mandela [λ Chapter 8] and others attempting to create a post-Apartheid liberal government, South Africa adopted a constitution that protects its people from discrimination based on "race, gender, sex, pregnancy, marital status, ethnic or social origin, colour, sexual orientation, age, disability, religion, conscience, belief, culture, language and birth." What's more, South Africa's sodomy laws have been struck down. In stark contrast, across the border in neighboring Zimbabwe, President Robert Mugabe has referred to homosexuals as "dogs and pigs" and said, "Animals in the jungle are better than these people because at least they know how to distinguish between a male and a female" (Monifa 41). Similarly, the prime minister of nearby Swaziland, Sibusiso Dlamini, called homosexuality an "abnormality and sickness," and one of his predecessors, Princh Bhekimpi, proclaimed that "homosexuality is regarded as satanic in Swaziland. Therefore, I am forced to evict all gays and lesbians in my area" (Monifa 41). The official position in Zambia is that gays are to be arrested. Many of these African countries have organizations that work to address the needs of and provide some protections for LGBT people, but in national climates where homosexuality is officially demonized, protections are limited and providers of such services place themselves in physical danger. These widely varying situations in southern Africa exemplify the inconsistent practice of governments around the world toward their LGBT citizens and highlight the difficulty of crafting policy for positive change.

Find Out More in the excerpt from the Constitution of the Republic of South Africa at the end of this chapter.

Inclusion versus Assimilation: Two Approaches to Securing Rights

In the United States, one way the problem of public policy fairness plays out is in questions about the approach rights-based organizations take to securing civil rights for LGBT people [λ Chapter 4]. The Human Rights Campaign (HRC), the largest and best-funded American civil rights organization, describes its mission in this way:

> By inspiring and engaging all Americans, HRC strives to end discrimination against GLBT citizens and realize a nation that achieves fundamental fairness and equality for all. HRC seeks to improve the lives of GLBT Americans by advocating for equal rights and benefits in the workplace, ensuring families are treated equally under the law and increasing public support among all Americans through innovative advocacy, education and outreach programs. HRC works to secure equal rights for GLBT individuals and families at the federal and state levels by lobbying elected officials, mobilizing grassroots supporters, educating Americans, investing strategically to elect fair-minded officials and partnering with other GLBT organizations. ("About HRC")

Recently, HRC has focused much of its energy and financial resources on advocating the rights of gays and lesbians to marry, to serve openly in the military, and to feel secure and free from discrimination in the workplace. HRC has also initiated dialogues with religious leaders in an effort to address homophobia in church communities. In general, despite the words *human rights* in its name, HRC is a civil rights organization, which works to obtain for LGBT people the same rights that are enjoyed by heterosexual citizens of the United States.

Some U.S. gay organizations take a more in-your-face approach, even though their work shares the HRC's focus on civil rights. A leaflet distributed in 1990 at a New York pride march by an organization called Queers announced, "I Hate Straights." The authors advocated a forceful approach marked by pride in sexuality and "sexualness." While the pamphlet is not as "anti-straight" as the title might suggest, the tone is aggressive:

> The next time some straight person comes down on you for being angry, tell them that until things change, you don't need any more evidence that the world turns at your expense. You don't need to see only hetero couples grocery shopping on your TV. . . . You don't want any more baby pictures shoved in your face until you can have or keep your own. No more weddings, showers, anniversaries, please, unless they are our own brothers and sisters celebrating. And tell them not to dismiss you by saying, "You have rights," "You have privileges," "You are overreacting," or "You have a victim's mentality." Tell them "Go away from me, until you change." Go away and try on a world without the brave, strong queers that are its backbone, that are its guts and brains and souls. Go tell them go away until they have spent a month walking hand in hand in

public with someone of the same sex. After they survive that, then you'll hear what they have to say about queer anger. (Anonymous Queers 148)

The HRC and Queers strategies couldn't be more different. HRC's approach has consistently emphasized the need for equality with straights because anything less is unfair and unjust. Queers, in contrast, provocatively asks straights to examine their own privilege, their lives, and their behavior. HRC wants to ensure that queers are treated as well as heterosexuals. Queers suggests LGBT people have much to teach heterosexuals about sexuality and gender.

An example of how these different philosophies approach a specific issue may be useful. Many queer activists and theorists have criticized the push among some Western gays and lesbians for the right to marry and thus to assimilate into the mainstream of society; they feel that strategizing for marriage rights, while laudable in many ways, distracts us from more fundamentally questioning the institution of marriage itself. Marriage, they argue, honors commitments between two people who are not of the same sex, but what about intimate arrangements that don't fit those parameters? Is marriage an institution designed specifically to channel sexual expression into monogamous, sexist, and hetero-sexist forms? Marital rights extended to gays and lesbians, as the HRC imagines them, might honor some relationships but would most likely still be limited in significant ways. Thus, it is important to look beyond the civil rights paradigm and critique institutional systems, asking who is served by them and who is excluded.

Exclusion, Inequality, and Physical Violence

Inevitably, the battle over inclusion and equality is fought not only at the state level but also at the local or personal level. In the United States, for example, there are myriad stories of violence perpetrated against individuals who work for—or sometimes just assume the "rightness" of—inclusion and equality for LGBT people. The stories of Barry Winchell and Fred C. Martinez are fairly representa-tive. These two stories demonstrate the local/personal impact of a national climate of exclusion and inequality in which official policy at the local and federal levels denies LGBT people the right to protection from discrimination—in housing, employment, family matters such as marriage and adoption, and other areas.

The 1999 death of Pfc. Barry Winchell focused attention on the military policy popularly referred to as "Don't Ask, Don't Tell" [λ Chapter 4]. While stationed at Ft. Campbell, Kentucky, Winchell began going to a Nashville club that featured transgendered performers. There Winchell met Calpernia Addams, a male-to-female transsexual performer (who prefers to be called a "transgendered woman"),

Figure 6.1 Calpernia Addams

Figure 6.2 Pfc. Barry Winchell

with whom he later became romantically involved (France). The relationship between Winchell and Addams eventually became known to Winchell's peers, and many began to think of him as a homosexual, though he seems not to have self-identified as such. On 4 July 1999, after hours of drinking on the base, Winchell and Calvin Glover began to argue; as the argument escalated, the two men became engaged in a physical altercation, which culminated in Winchell punching Glover. According to Glover, over the next few hours, Justin Fisher (Winchell's roommate) taunted him, saying that he had been bested by a gay man. In the early morning hours of 5 July, after hours of harassment by Fisher, Glover used a baseball bat to beat Winchell into unconsciousness (Sciolino). Eventually, Winchell died.

After the killing, many gay rights activists claimed Winchell as a kind of gay martyr whose death symbolized all that was wrong with the "Don't Ask, Don't Tell" policy in the military. In 2000, Addams told David France of the *New York Times,* "I'm disappointed in a lot of ways with almost every organization that I thought would help me with this. A lot of things I don't want to go in print—speaking out against these major national gay and lesbian organizations—but a lot of them I thought would come and help me or say something, or do a press release or give me some advice. And they just didn't." The tone of France's article, titled "An Inconvenient Woman," indicates his concern that gay rights activists ignored Addams because she was transsexual, in effect sacrificing her in their quest to overturn "Don't Ask, Don't Tell." This critique exemplifies the difficulties faced by organizations such as the National Gay and

Lesbian Task Force presently working to secure rights for LGBT people. Many argue that a more complex view of sexuality—moving beyond gay and lesbian to other less well understood sexual minorities—is necessary to significantly lessen gender and sexual oppression.

The Barry Winchell case highlights a military climate in which violence based on sexuality and gender is not only tolerated but also rewarded and encouraged. A twenty-one-month Army investigation of the Winchell murder resulted in the exoneration of all officers involved and a finding that "no climate of homophobia existed at the base" in Ft. Campbell, Kentucky (Sciolino). Nonetheless, in 2002, the *New York Times* reported the following: "The number of military discharges of gays has risen to its highest level in 14 years, and reported incidents of anti-gay harassment have climbed by 23 percent in a year" (Marquis). On 15 August 2006, the Associated Press reported that in 2005, Ft. Campbell had the second highest "Don't Ask, Don't Tell" dismissal rate of all bases in the country, with more than twice the number of dismissals as in 2004 ("Missouri"). If we assume a correlation between higher "Don't Ask, Don't Tell" dismissal rates and an increasing frequency of bias incidents toward LGBT people on U.S. military bases, then it becomes clear that "official" policing of sexuality and gender creates a sense that "unofficial policing" through intimidation and other types of violence is not only acceptable but also desirable. What's more, it is hard to imagine how military officials could deny that this kind of environment is not only homophobic but also transphobic.

> **Find Out More** in "Military Discharges of Gays Rise, and So Do Bias Incidents" at the end of this chapter.

Fred C. Martinez, who was sixteen years old at the time of his murder, identified as gay, transgender, and "two-spirited." A Native American living in the town of Cortez, Colorado, Martinez was a gender nonconformist. He was sent home from school on several occasions for carrying a purse and wearing makeup and fingernail polish. In addition, he was consistently harassed by peers. In 2001, Martinez was murdered by eighteen-year-old Shaun Murphy, who claimed to have acted in self-defense but, in the days after the murder, bragged to friends that he had "bug-smashed a fag" (Rostow). An *Advocate* article about the murder quotes Denise de Percin, executive director of the Colorado Anti-Violence Project, as saying, "Everything so far leads us to believe [Martinez] was targeted for transgressing gender. . . . People who transgress gender and whose expression is not considered normal are the ones who are most often targeted for bias-motivated violence" (Quittner 2). Federal hate crimes legislation in the United States does not include protections for LGBT people, so it would have been outside the purview of the Department of Justice and the Federal Bureau of Investigation (FBI) to become involved in a case where sexual orientation or gender nonconformity were the motivations for murder; hence, Murphy was charged with (and pled guilty to) second-degree murder, not with the commission of a hate crime. Even after his sentencing, Murphy told officials that he was acting in self-defense when he murdered Martinez, whom he said attacked him first; this claim, as well as his mother's that Murphy was not homophobic, both seem spurious in light of the "bug-smashed a fag" comment.

In both the Martinez and Winchell murder cases, official policies of exclusion and unequal treatment must be seen as complicit in the crimes committed by individuals. The lack of hate crimes legislation, including provisions explicitly addressing gender and sexual orientation, sends a strong message to citizens that violence against certain individuals is, if not condoned, at least less serious than other crimes motivated by prejudice. Social systems that impose standards of gender conformity—as administrators at Martinez's high school did when they sent him home for wearing makeup and carrying a purse—create a circumstance in which gender nonconformists are seen as deserving harassment and in which peers consider it their right (and perhaps subconsciously their responsibility) to police one another's gender behaviors. Social restrictions on behavior related to gender and sexuality, as well as a perception that LGBT people are predatory outsiders, contribute to exclusionary attitudes based on a sense of the inherent inferiority of LGBT people as compared with gender conformists and heterosexuals; those restrictions also encourage perpetrators of violence to claim self-defense when their victims are lesbian, gay, bisexual, or transgendered. Of course, these three elements of the Martinez case are interrelated, for they arise from a social structure that assumes that sexual and gender difference are threatening.

Exclusion and Inequality— Both "Outside" and "Inside"

The preceding cases give us a sense of the difficulties facing queer people seeking inclusion and equality—difficulties that many LGBT people experience as a mixture of exclusion and inequality both from "mainstream" culture and, at times, from "queer" culture or communities. Consider the following examples:

- In 1990, the Manhattan chapter of the Ancient Order of Hibernians denied the Irish Lesbian and Gay Organization (ILGO) the right to march in New York City's St. Patrick's Day parade. In 2006, the ban was still in effect, and the organizer of the event, John Dunleavy, commented, "If we let the ILGO in, is it the Irish Prostitute Association next?" During the parade, protesters pointed out the uniqueness of the ban on their participation with the following chant: "We can march in Dublin, we can march in Cork, why can't we march in New York?" (Dobnik).

- "Avowed homosexuals" are banned from participation in the Boy Scouts of America (BSA) at any level. According to a BSA spokesman, "An avowed homosexual wouldn't be a role model for [traditional family] values" (Snyder A2).

- In the 1990s and early 2000s, gay men were not explicitly excluded from the Million Man March or the Millions More Movement march, but the executive director of the latter event, the Reverend Willie Wilson, delivered a blisteringly antigay sermon just three months before the Millions More event. The sermon resulted in the resignation of Reverend Dr. Amina Binta, co-chair of the local organizing committee for the march. Binta said, "They're not serious about allowing us to sit at the table. . . . And if they are, I don't care to eat their fare, because they're serving up a steady diet of homophobia that is very venomous" (Volin and Chibbaro).

> **Find Out More** in the excerpt from Rev. Wilson's speech in the readings at the end of this chapter.

These successful efforts to exclude take on enormous import when we consider their connections to violence perpetrated against LGBT people. Exclusionary practices such as these send the clear message to a society that the policing of gender and adult sexuality is both necessary and desirable.

We can see such policing at work in responses to the AIDS pandemic. Historically, discussions around AIDS—in the United States and in the rest of the world—have focused on the notion that homosexual sex spreads disease. As we mentioned in Chapter 4, the disease was initially called gay-related immune deficiency (GRID), and through-out most of the 1980s, it was assumed that only gay people got AIDS. In fact, in the late 1980s, Sebastian Bach of the band Skid Row appeared on stage wearing a T-shirt that read, "AIDS: Kills Fags Dead," a parody of the popular slogan for the spray insecticide Raid, which was, "RAID: Kills Bugs Dead."

Though Bach issued a public apology for the incident and claimed he had no idea what was written on the T-shirt, the slogan was then popularized—to the point where the Westboro Baptist Church in Topeka, Kansas (infamous for its "God Hates Fags" campaign), adopted it as a slogan when they protested at the

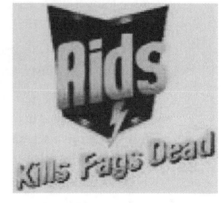

Figure 6.3 Logo displayed on Sebastian Bach's T-shirt.

funeral of Matthew Shepard (Rosen) [λ Chapter 4]. Even today, some people still believe that HIV and AIDS are "gay diseases." The American Red Cross is among the many organizations that have attempted to correct this flawed assumption. According to the Red Cross fact sheet on HIV/AIDS,[1]

As of July 2002, the Joint United Nations Programme on HIV/AIDS (UNAIDS) estimated that about 18 million women were living with HIV/AIDS worldwide, accounting for 47 percent of the 37.2 million adults living with HIV/AIDS. In many countries, HIV spreads mostly through sex between men and women. And in the United States, the number of people with HIV/AIDS who became infected through sex between men and women continues to grow. ("This Month's")

Nonetheless, antigay activists continue to equate HIV and AIDS with homosexuality. As an extreme example, Fred Phelps, who leads the "God Hates Fags" crusade, claims that those who die from complications related to HIV/AIDS, as well as American casualties of war, are being punished by a higher power to make the United States suffer for becoming a "fag nation" (Westboro).

The issue of sexual freedom is not as simple as it might seem on the surface. LGBT activist groups, even as they fight for inclusion in society, have historically disputed issues of inclusion and equality within their own ranks. Consider the following examples:

• Transgender and transsexual individuals have argued for at least a generation that lesbian and gay organizations do not recognize and respond to their struggle for inclusion and equality.

• In the late twentieth century, many lesbian feminists believed butch and femme lesbians were replicating "the heterosexual institution with its role playing dualities" (Johnston 155).

• LGBT people who also identify as sadomasochist have historically been seen as "outside the mainstream" in the larger LGBT movement.

• In many ways and over many years, white-led LGBT political and social groups have engaged in overtly and covertly racist behavior. Bars, for example, have refused to admit black patrons ("Director's Finding"). Even online chat room participants describe eliciting more responses if they claim to be white rather than of color (Gosine).

• In the 1970s, some radical lesbian groups articulated negative feelings toward bisexual women, who, they claimed, "take energy from women and give it to men" (Moore).

The debates around these issues and others have consistently arisen within organizations whose work it is to fight for inclusion and equality. In "Messages of Exclusion: Gender, Movements, and Symbolic Boundaries," Joshua Gamson describes and theorizes controversies surrounding two groups, the Michigan Womyn's Music

Festival (MWMF) and the International Lesbian and Gay Association (ILGA) as they attempt to police the boundaries of their own communities.

One highly visible debate among lesbians grew up around what many saw as the exclusionary practices of the MWMF [λ Chapters 4 and 15]. The MWMF was founded by Lisa and Kristie Vogel and Mary Kindig in 1976. Conceived as a space for female performers to showcase their work in a supportive and nurturing environment, the festival draws thousands of women each year and has become a legendary cultural event for lesbian feminists throughout the United States. Throughout its history, the MWMF has undergone repeated critiques from women who challenged the festival to be more inclusive. Some claimed the MWMF needed to respond more fully to the specific needs of women of color, women with disabilities, poor women, and others. And, in many cases, organizers made significant changes to the festival in order to address those concerns. The most heated debate concerning MWMF, however, began in 1991 when a "festie-goer" (as attendees are called) was removed from the land after revealing that she was transsexual. Nancy Burkholder, who by all reports had attended the festival the year before without difficulties, came to represent what many believe is the inappropriately exclusionary MWMF policy that only "women-born-women" (WBW) be allowed to attend the festival. After the Burkholder incident, a group of women within the festival began protesting the WBW policy. In 1993, some women who practiced S&M approached the protesters and offered their services as security. In 1999, under the leadership of trans activist Riki Wilchins, a group of transwomen established Camp Trans, an annual protest outside the festival grounds. Of the controversy, Lisa Vogel says, "It's our right and it's our responsibility to say who we want the event to be for and . . . who we're organizing it for; it's not making a judgment or a statement . . . about anybody else. It wasn't back in 1976 when we said it was women only, and it's not in 2005 when we want it to be for women-born-women. Our queer community is diverse, and I support separate and whole space for anybody who wants it" (Lo). Vogel clearly does not see exclusionary practices as problematic in this instance. Her argument seems to be that this process of exclusion highlights the complexities that arise when groups are oppressed on a number of different levels. In this case, Vogel argues that "women-born-women," as a result of living a lifetime of oppression related to their sex, experience femaleness very differently than do transwomen, who bring with them to women-only environments the experience of privilege born of living as males in a sexist society. Trans activists counter this argument by pointing out that many male-to-female transgendered and transsexual individuals face a type of sexist discrimination similar to that faced by girls and women. Choosing to live as women in a sexist world, they argue, neutralizes any previous male privilege they may have enjoyed earlier in their lives. Moreover, they claim the right to define their womanness outside of exclusionary terms such as "women-born-men." This ongoing controversy foregrounds the complexities of identity and identity politics.

A very different debate concerning inclusion and equality in organizations fighting for sexual freedom has to do with the distinction between the freedoms adults should enjoy with other consenting adults and the freedoms adults should enjoy in their relationships with children. The North American Man/Boy Love Association (NAMBLA), for example, has argued for decades that its members are treated as outsiders in the LGBT movement, and debates about whether NAMBLA's concerns fall within or outside the parameters of the larger fight for sexual freedom are intense, emotional, and politically significant. In 1993, the ILGA became the first LGBT group to receive consultative status in the United Nations (UN) Economic and Social Council; a year later, the ILGA lost its consultative status because UN members complained about its connections to **pedophile** groups such as NAMBLA and the Dutch group Vereniging Martijn. ILGA responded by expelling NAMBLA, Vereniging Martijn, and a group called Project Truth from its ranks and began the work of regaining its consultative status; still, as of 2008, the ILGA had not been reinstated (Gamson). Partly in response to the ILGA situation, Gregory King of the Human Rights Campaign Fund declared, "NAMBLA is not a gay organization. They are not part of our community and we thoroughly reject their efforts to insinuate that pedophilia is an issue related to gay and lesbian civil rights" (qtd. in Gamson 179). Some would argue that ILGA's expulsion of NAMBLA is tantamount to retreating from a liberationist view of sexuality that would question long-held attitudes that create sexually repressive environments. Others counterargue that supporting pedophiles who want to legalize sexual relationships between children and adults means supporting the oppression of children who are not prepared to make sexual decisions that serve their own best interests.

As Gamson points out, there is an odd relationship between the MWMF and the ILGA/NAMBLA controversies. The situations are, of course, extremely different, for it is impossible to equate the desire of male-to-female transsexual and transgendered people to be accepted as women with the efforts of a group whose goal is to secure the right for adult men to engage in sexual activity with boys. But in both cases, important questions are being asked about the issue of inclusion and exclusion. Gamson articulates these questions in this way: "Who is calling the question of public exclusion and for what political purposes? Who are the audiences being targeted and how do they (or the perception of them by those attacking and defending versions of collective identity) shape the outcome?" (192). In the case of MWMF, the question was called by participants in the festival, women who believed strongly that in a sexist culture, women-born-men would bring with them to women's space the sexist values and attitudes that women in such a space were attempting to resist. In the case of the ILGA, the question was called by the American religious right in the person of Jesse Helms, who proposed a bill (signed into law by Bill Clinton) that would withhold $119 million in donations to the UN until the U.S. president could determine that no organizations supporting pedophilia were granted any "official status, accreditation, or recognition" within the UN (Gamson 185).

For as long as there has been a gay rights movement, gay rights opponents have asserted a connection between homosexuality and pedophilia; despite consistent refutation of such correlation by the psychiatric community, the notion has persisted that gay men are sexual predators who pose a danger to children. The power of this myth showed up in the popular support for Anita Bryant's "Save Our Children Campaign"; in the argument made by many in the Catholic Church that the problem of child sexual abuse by priests would be solved by purging the priesthood of all homosexuals; in the argument by the Boy Scouts of America that gay scout leaders pose a threat to scouts; in the efforts across the United States and throughout the Global North to keep LGBT people from teaching, adopting, and raising children; and in the myriad other circumstances in which pedophilia and homosexuality are conflated. These attempts to link LGBT people with pedophiles are based in the notion that all sexual difference is equivalent—and dangerous.

Amnesty International's statement on the oppression of LGBT people includes the following:

> In virtually every part of the globe, LGBT lives are constrained by a web of laws and social practices which deny them an equal right to life, liberty and physical security, as well as other fundamental rights such as freedom of association, freedom of expression and rights to private life, employment, education and health care. While the degree to which discrimination is institutionalized varies from country to country, almost nowhere are LGBT people treated as fully equal before the law. ("Crimes")

In many cases, the struggle of LGBT people for inclusion and equality focuses on eliminating discrimination in the most basic areas of human life. We struggle for the fundamental freedoms granted to our heterosexual counterparts—to raise our families, to enjoy the civil liberties our governments provide for their citizens, and to have our basic human rights protected. But issues related to inclusion and equality have as much to do with the way people treat one another on a daily basis as they have to do with "rights." Governments and other institutions—LGBT organizations included—that engage in exclusionary practices and treat groups of citizens unequally establish and maintain an environment that sharply delineates between insiders and outsiders.

Note

1. Despite its sensible statement on the spread of HIV/AIDS, the American Red Cross still refuses to accept blood donations from any "male who has had sexual contact with another male, even once, since 1977" ("Blood").

QUESTIONS FOR DISCUSSION

1. The *New York Times* article "Military Discharges of Gays Rise, and So Do Bias Incidents," included among the readings at the end of this chapter, implies a connection between discharges for sexual orientation and bias within the ranks of the military. Are there local policies—in your community, at your school, in social organizations to which you belong—that send the message to members that sexuality should be policed? What are those policies? How do you see them playing themselves out in the organization? Remember to look carefully at the way the policies are officially enforced and at the way members of the organization take it upon themselves to enforce them unofficially.

2. In most of the American popular culture, the discussion of "gay marriage" is framed as a debate about whether lesbian and gay people should have the right to the social, political, and material benefits that heterosexual married people already enjoy. This pro/con framing, though, tends to beg deeper questions about the institution of marriage—its efficacy in the contemporary world, its use as a social control, and the materialism and conspicuous consumption promoted by the "wedding industry" in the United States. Choose an article or other media representation (television or radio, for instance) of the "gay marriage debate" from the popular culture and identify several questions that the piece does *not* ask. How is *not* asking these questions an implicit endorsement of certain values and ideas?

3. Do some research on gays and lesbians serving openly in the armed forces of countries other than the United States. What problems have they encountered, if any? Has their presence changed the cultures of the armed forces in any way? What is the rhetoric in those countries around the issue of gays serving in the military—if there is any?

REFERENCES AND FURTHER READING

"About HRC." *Human Rights Campaign.* 13 October 2007 <http://www.hrc.org/about_us/>.
Anonymous Queers. "Queers Read This: I Hate Straights." *Queer Cultures.* Eds. Deborah Carlin and Jennifer DiGrazia. Upper Saddle River, NJ: Prentice Hall, 2004. 138–48.

"Blood Donation Eligibility Guidelines." American Red Cross. 25 March 2008 <http://www.redcross.org/services/biomed/0,1082,0_557_,00.html>.

"Crimes of Hate, Conspiracy of Silence: Torture and Ill-Treatment Based on Sexual Identity." Amnesty International. 25 March 2008 <http://www.ai-lgbt.org/ai_report_torture.htm#impunity>.

"Director's Finding." San Francisco Human Rights Commission, 26 April 2005. 25 March 2008 <http://www.sflnc.com/binary.php/528/Badlands%20Finding%20.pdf>.

Dobnik, Verena. "NYC Parade Protested for Antigay Stance." *The Boston Globe* 18 March 2006. 25 March 2008 <http://www.boston.com/news/nation/articles/2006/03/18/nyc_parade_protested_for_antigay_stance/>.

France, David. "An Inconvenient Woman." *New York Times* 28 May 2000. 25 March 2008 <http://query.nytimes.com/gst/fullpage.html?res=9902E5DB1E3AF93BA15756C0A9669C8B63&scp=2&sq=barry+winchell&st=nyt>.

Gamson, Joshua. "Messages of Exclusion: Gender, Movements, and Symbolic Boundaries." *Gender & Society* 11.2 (1997): 178–99.

Gosine, Andil. "Brown to Blonde at Gay.com: Passing White in Queer Cyberspace." *Queer Online: Media Technology and Sexuality*. Eds. Kate O'Riordan and David J. Phillips. New York: Peter Lang, 2007.

Jensen, Steffen. "Denmark: The Nordic Model." *Harvard Gay and Lesbian Review* 6.1 (1999): 36–37.

Johnston, Jill. *Lesbian Nation: The Feminist Solution*. New York: Touchstone, 1973.

Killian, D(ian). "Ireland's Fast Track to Equality." *Harvard Gay and Lesbian Review* 6.1 (1999): 24–26.

Knowles, Joe. "The Boys in Havana." *Harvard Gay and Lesbian Review* 6.1 (1999): 19–20.

Koyema, Emi. "Michigan/Trans Controversy Archive." 2000–2008. 29 March 2008 <http://eminism.org/michigan/documents.html>.

Lawrence v. Texas. 539 U.S. 558 (2003).

Lo, Malinda. "Behind the Scenes at the Michigan Womyn's Music Festival." *AfterEllen* 20 April 2005. 25 March 2008 <http://www.afterellen.com/archive/ellen/Music/2005/4/michigan3.html>.

Marquis, Christopher. "Military Discharges of Gays Rise, and So Do Bias Incidents." *New York Times* 14 March 2002. 25 March 2008 <http://query.nytimes.com/gst/fullpage.html?res=9C00E2DC1039F937A25750C0A9649C8B63>.

"Missouri Army Base Leads 'Don't Ask, Don't Tell' Dismissal Rate." Associated Press 14 August 2006. 25 March 2008 <http://www.foxnews.com/story/0,2933,208247,00.html>.

Mitchell, Donn. "Get to Know the Universal Declaration." *Harvard Gay and Lesbian Review* 6.1 (1999): 13–14.

Monifa, Akilah. "Sub-Saharan Africa and South Africa." *Harvard Gay and Lesbian Review* 6.1 (1999): 41–42.

Moore, Jennifer. "A Few Key Political Issues for Bi People." 25 March 2008 <http://www.uncharted-worlds.org/bi/bipol.htm>.

"Queers Read This." June 1990. 25 March 2008 <http://www.qrd.org/qrd/misc/text/queers.read.this>.

Quittner, Jeremy. "Death of a Two Spirit." *The Advocate* 28 August 2001. 25 March 2008 <http://findarticles.com/p/articles/mi_m1589/is_2001_August_28/ai_77660063/>.

Rosen, Craig. "How Do You Spell Hate?" 31 July 2003. 25 March 2008 <http://www.lacitybeat.com/cms/story/detail/?id=148&IssueNum=8>.

Rostow, Ann. "Martinez's Killer Gets 40 Years," 3 June 2002. 29 March 2008 <http://www.tgcrossroads.org/news/?AID=221&IID=31&type=Headlines>.

Schneider, Richard. "Human Rights around the World." *Harvard Gay and Lesbian Review* 6.1 (1999): 4.

Sciolino, Elaine. "Army Exonerates Officers in Slaying of Gay Private." *New York Times.* 19 July 2000 <http://query.nytimes.com/gst/fullpage.html?res=9D0DE3DC113BF93AA25754C0A9669C8B63&sec=&spon=&pagewanted=all>.

Snyder, David. "Court Ruling Spurs Protest of Boy Scouts in Baltimore." *Washington Post* 6 July 2000: A2.

"This Month's HIV/AIDS Facts." American Red Cross, July 2002. 19 July 2008 <http://www.redcross.org/services/hss/tips/gaydisease.html>.

Volin, Katherine, and Lou Chibbaro Jr. "Minister's Fiery Anti-gay Sermon Riles Activists." *The Washington Blade.* 15 July 2005 <http://www.washblade.com/print.cfm?content_id=6077>.

Westboro Baptist Church. "God Hates America." 25 March 2008 <http://www.godhatesamerica.com/>.

Wilets, James D. "The Human Rights of Sexual Minorities: A Comparative and International Law Perspective." *Human Rights: Journal of the Section of Individual Rights & Responsibilities* 22.4 (1995): 22–27.

Wockner, Rex. "Gay Sex Legal across Europe." *Bay Windows* 21.34: 11.

———. "International News." *San Francisco Bay Times* 14 September 2006. 18 September 2006 <http://www.sfbaytimes.com>.

READINGS

➤ South African Constitution

Excerpts

(1996), South Africa

Preamble

We, the people of South Africa,

Recognise the injustices of our past;

Honour those who suffered for justice and freedom in our land;

Respect those who have worked to build and develop our country; and

Believe that South Africa belongs to all who live in it, united in our diversity.

We therefore, through our freely elected representatives, adopt this Constitution as the supreme law of the Republic so as to

> Heal the divisions of the past and establish a society based on democratic values, social justice and fundamental human rights;
>
> Lay the foundations for a democratic and open society in which government is based on the will of the people and every citizen is equally protected by law;
>
> Improve the quality of life of all citizens and free the potential of each person; and
>
> Build a united and democratic South Africa able to take its rightful place as a sovereign state in the family of nations.

May God protect our people.

Nkosi Sikelel' iAfrika. Morena boloka setjhaba sa heso.

God seën Suid-Afrika. God bless South Africa.

Mudzimu fhatutshedza Afurika. Hosi katekisa Afrika.

Section on Equality From the Bill of Rights

Equality

9. (1) Everyone is equal before the law and has the right to equal protection and benefit of the law.

(2) Equality includes the full and equal enjoyment of all rights and freedoms. To promote the achievement of equality, legislative and other measures designed to protect or advance persons, or categories of persons, disadvantaged by unfair discrimination may be taken.

(3) The state may not unfairly discriminate directly or indirectly against anyone on one or more grounds, including race, gender, sex, pregnancy, marital status, ethnic or social origin, colour, sexual orientation, age, disability, religion, conscience, belief, culture, language and birth.

(4) No person may unfairly discriminate directly or indirectly against anyone on one or more grounds in terms of subsection (3). National legislation must be enacted to prevent or prohibit unfair discrimination.

(5) Discrimination on one or more of the grounds listed in subsection (3) is unfair unless it is established that the discrimination is fair.

➢ Christopher Marquis

"Military Discharges of Gays Rise, and So Do Bias Incidents"

(14 March 2002), United States

WASHINGTON, March 13—The number of military discharges of gays has risen to its highest level in 14 years, and reported incidents of anti-gay harassment have climbed by 23 percent in a year, a legal aid group said today.

The rise in gay-related incidents comes despite a Pentagon strategy to clarify its "don't ask, don't tell" policy throughout the armed services and to make work conditions hospitable for gays who keep their sexuality private.

The Defense Department discharged 1,250 men and women last year for declaring themselves gay or engaging in homosexual conduct, a slight increase over the 1,212 ousted in 2000, according to the legal aid group, the Servicemembers Legal Defense Network, which opposes the "don't ask, don't tell" policy.

Citing Pentagon statistics released under Freedom of Information Act requests, the group said the number of cases of anti-gay harassment in the four services rose to 1,075 incidents last year from 871 in 2000.

C. Dixon Osburn, the group's executive director, called the statistics "an affront to liberty, unity and military readiness."

"As lesbian, gay and bisexual service members are fighting to protect our country from terrorism, they should not be denied their freedom at home," Mr. Osburn said.

The increase in gay-related incidents comes as Pentagon officials say they are applying new guidelines for handling such cases and providing materials and training at all levels of the services.

"We definitely don't condone harassment," said Lt. Col. James Cassella, a Pentagon spokesman. "When it comes to enforcing the policy, we balance readiness and unit cohesion with an individual's right to privacy and the expectation of a safe and harassment-free work environment."

In recent years, the Pentagon has acknowledged difficulties in carrying out the "don't ask, don't tell" policy, which was codified by Congress. The 1993 law ended screening against gays in the application process, but said that gay activity while in the military was grounds for discharge.

The 1999 murder of Pfc. Barry Winchell by two fellow soldiers who thought he was gay prompted a Pentagon review.

In a survey of 75,000 service members, the department's inspector general found that 37 percent of service members had witnessed hostile words or actions against gays in the previous year.

William S. Cohen, who was then the defense secretary, approved a 13-point plan to curb anti-gay harassment in 2000. Colonel Cassella said he had personally witnessed training and the distribution of manuals to help troops comply with the plan.

"This is generally followed," he said. "I've seen it carried out at the unit level."

Mr. Cohen did not respond to telephone calls seeking comment.

But Mr. Osburn said the training was "sporadic at best" in the Army, which he said was the most diligent of the services. He said the fault lay in a lack of political leadership.

"There's been no political will in the Bush administration in their first year to carry through on the promises that the Pentagon made," he said.

Mr. Osburn's group found that women were disproportionately affected by current policy. Women accounted for 30 percent of all discharges of gays last year, it found, even though they made up about 14 percent of the population of the forces.

Discharges of gays continued to be especially high in certain bases, most notably at Fort Campbell, Ky., the site of Private Winchell's murder. Last year, 222 soldiers at the base were discharged for being gay, accounting for 36 percent of all such discharges in the Army.

The service members' group said that the base's new commander, Maj. Gen. Richard Cody, had improved the overall climate at the base, but that his subordinates continued to tolerate hostility toward suspected gays.

➤ **Larry Rohter**

"Lesbian Judge Fights Chilean Court for Taking Her Children"

(July 20, 2006), United States, Chile

SANTIAGO, Chile, July 17—As a young judge, inspired by the democratic glow that followed the ouster of Gen. Augusto Pinochet and his dictatorship in 1990, Karen Atala had an unwavering faith in justice and the rule of law. But that was all before Chile's Supreme Court stripped her of custody of her three daughters two years ago because she had publicly identified herself as a lesbian.

Now Judge Atala, 42, has become a symbol of what she and gay rights groups that have emerged here in recent years, at first tentatively but now with growing assertiveness, describe as a different kind of human rights violation.

Rather than accept the ruling and the beliefs underlying it, she is fighting to have the decision overturned and for the rights of homosexuals to be recognized in what is often described as Latin America's most socially conservative country.

The Atala case, as it is known here, has thrust homosexuality, considered a marginal issue just a few years ago, onto the national political agenda. During last year's presidential campaign, candidates were asked how they would have ruled if they had been judges, and newspapers regularly publish polls on the case. They show the country nearly evenly divided between those who support and those who disagree with the ruling.

"What happened to Karen Atala has opened the doors to a debate," said Anatolia Hernández, president of the Unified Movement of Sexual Minorities, an advocacy group. "Homosexuals are still being killed, and you can go to jail for kissing in the street, but at least we are no longer invisible."

Citing norms that prevent Chilean judges from talking about pending cases, Judge Atala declined a request for an interview on the record. But she was present at an interview at the apartment she shares with her domestic partner, Emma de Ramón, a historian, and she often nodded in agreement as Ms. de Ramón spoke of their situation.

"The dictatorship may be long gone, but there is still a lot of obscurantism in this country," Ms. de Ramón said. "We recognize that we could still lose this case, but we both believe this needs to be a different country, one that is respectful of differences."

Divorce did not exist in Chile until 2004, and even now, there is no provision for joint custody of children. In a manifestation of traditional roles that normally works in favor of women, custody is almost automatically awarded to the mother—unless she is proved to be a prostitute, drug addict, alcoholic or, in Judge Atala's case, lesbian. The children now live with their father.

Two appellate courts ruled in Judge Atala's favor, finding that her sexual orientation did not affect her ability to be a good mother. But the Supreme Court intervened in the case, improperly according to some legal analysts, and ruled in May 2004 that by living with their mother, the girls were in "a situation of risk" whose "pernicious consequences" would "damage their psychic development" and make them "objects of social discrimination."

"It seems to us inappropriate for two people of the same sex to attempt to form a matrimonial union," the Rev. Ignacio Fernández, vicar of the family ministry of the archdiocese of Santiago, said in announcing the support of the politically influential Roman Catholic Church for the decision. "All of us were born in families, and we know that the contributions of men and women are different."

Ordinarily, that would have been the end of the matter, but late in 2004, Judge Atala and her supporters decided to take the case to the Inter-American Commission on Human Rights. After the commission, based in Washington, agreed to review the case at a hearing in March, the Chilean government and Judge Atala's lawyer agreed to suspend the proceeding at the commission while they sought a negotiated solution.

"Various types of rights were violated when Karen Atala lost custody of her children," said Macarena Sáez, a Chilean lawyer at American University in Washington who is handling the case. "Due process was not respected, her right to privacy was violated when courts had her computers searched looking for evidence of strange behavior, and the right of her children to be heard, which is binding in Chile, was completely set aside."

The proceeding at the commission, a branch of the Organization of American States, is being closely watched throughout Latin America. Several countries in the region have constitutions that place a ruling by the Inter-American system above those of their own courts, meaning that a ruling in Judge Atala's favor would benefit gay couples throughout the hemisphere.

Jorge Contesse, another of Judge Atala's lawyers, said that "first and foremost we are demanding that the civil code be amended so that sexual orientation cannot be grounds for a judge to withhold custody of the children." In addition, he said, the lawyers are seeking congressional approval of an anti-discrimination bill and "some sort of economic compensation" for Judge Atala.

Recent changes here have led Judge Atala's supporters to believe those objectives are now achievable. The new president, Michelle Bachelet, is a single mother, feminist and physician who as health minister in the previous government was in charge of AIDS programs.

But Ms. Bachelet's governing coalition includes both her Socialist Party and the more socially conservative Christian Democrats. Within the alliance, there are divisions on issues like euthanasia, the morning-after pill and, above all, abortion that, if allowed to fester, could threaten her ability to build majorities for the changes in economic regulations, taxation and social security legislation she has pledged.

"Everyone expects Michelle to have a more progressive social agenda," said María Antonieta Saa, a congressional deputy and ally of Ms. Bachelet's who was one of the sponsors of the divorce law. "But the pressure from the other side is just as intense."

Divisions among gay groups also cloud the picture. Some favor new laws that would specifically authorize civil unions for gay couples, for instance, while others say they want no special legislation, just legal language that would grant them the same status as religious and racial minorities.

"The ruling in the Atala case showed the gap between the Supreme Court and the rest of society, and we need to take advantage of that," said Rolando Jiménez, leader of the Movement for the Integration and Liberation of Homosexuals. "We are living through a profound transition of ethics, values and morals, one that is occurring more rapidly among common people than elite institutions, including political parties that are supposedly progressive."

➤ **Reverend Willie Wilson**

Excerpt from "You've Got to Fight to Be Free"

(3 July 2005), United States

We live in a time when our brothers have been so put down, can't get a job, lot of the sisters making more money than brothers. And it's creating problems in families. That's one of the reasons our families' breaking up. And that's one of the reasons many of our women are becoming lesbians. You got to be careful when you say you don't need no man. I can make it by myself. Well, if you don't need a man, what's left? Lesbianism is about to take over our community. I'm talking about young girls. My son in high school last year, trying to go to the prom, he said, "Dad, I ain't got nobody to take to the prom because all the girls in my class are gay. There ain't but two of them straight and both of them are ugly. I ain't got nobody to take to the prom." Now, can I talk here? I ain't homophobic, because everybody in here got something wrong with him. Whoever you point at, you can point at your own self. You got something wrong with your life. But when you get down to this thing, women falling down on another woman, strapping yourself up with something, it ain't real. That thing ain't got no feeling in it. It ain't natural. Any time somebody got to slap some grease on your behind, and stick something in you, it's something wrong with that. Your butt ain't made for that. [Audience shouts and yells its approval in the background.] You got blood vessels and membranes in your behind. And if you put something unnatural in there, it breaks them all up. No wonder your behind is bleeding. It's destroying us. Can't make no connection with a screw and another screw. The Bible says God made them male and female. The Hebrew word "neged," which means complementary nature—there is something unique to man and unique to woman and it takes those two things to complement each other. You can't make a connection with two screws. It takes a screw and a nut! (shouting).

Excerpt from a sermon, delivered at Union Temple Baptist Church in Washington, D.C. Reprinted with permission of the *Washington Blade*.

➤ **Katherine Volin and Lou Chibbaro Jr.**

"Minister's Fiery Anti-gay Sermon Riles Activists"

(15 July 2005), United States

An influential D.C. minister is under fire by local gay activists following an anti-gay sermon in which he claimed that "lesbianism is about to take over our community."

Rev. Willie Wilson delivered the remarks at Union Temple Baptist Church in Southeast D.C., where he is pastor. Wilson is a former mayoral candidate and serves as executive director of the Millions More Movement march, an effort to commemorate the 10th anniversary of the Million Man March.

Efforts by gay civil rights advocates to secure a visible role at the march stalled again this week when excerpts from Wilson's anti-gay sermon came to light. One lesbian march organizer quickly resigned in protest.

"Sisters making more money than brothers and it's creating problems in families . . . that's one of the reasons many of our women are becoming lesbians," Wilson said.

The Blade obtained a copy of the sermon, titled "You've Got to Fight to Be Free," which Wilson delivered at Union Temple on July 3.

"Lesbianism is about to take over our community. . . . I ain't homophobic because everybody here got something wrong with him," he said. "But . . . women falling down on another woman, strapping yourself up with something, it ain't real. That thing ain't got no feeling in it. It ain't natural. Anytime somebody got to slap some grease on your behind and stick something in you, it's something wrong with that. Your butt ain't made for that.

"No wonder your behind is bleeding," he said. "You can't make no connection with a screw and another screw. The Bible says God made them male and female."

The congregation can be heard shouting its approval in the background during Wilson's sermon.

Wilson declined to comment for this story.

Reaction was swift from gay civil rights advocates, several of whom have been organizing monthly community meetings related to being included in the Millions More Movement march, which is to take place in D.C., Oct. 14–16.

Longtime gay rights activist Phil Pannell, one of the most visible and vocal advocates in favor of gay participation in the upcoming event, said he was disappointed when he learned of Wilson's sermon.

"It's very difficult to go forth in the community to even try to have a meeting with Rev. Wilson because, with views expressed like that, particularly in the pulpit of the church, it makes it very difficult for the GLBT community to think that any conversation or dialogue regarding inclusion . . . would be constructive and fruitful," he said. "I'm quite distressed."

At a planning meeting held earlier this year at D.C.'s Union Temple Baptist Church, Louis Farrakhan, the Nation of Islam leader who organized the Million Man March in 1995, told Pannell that black gay people were welcome to take part in all aspects of the event, Pannell said. He also said Wilson invited him to that planning meeting and told him that a gay speaker at the October event might be possible.

But black gays were absent on May 2 when a group of African-American leaders held a news conference in D.C. to announce the Millions More Movement march.

Carlene Cheatam, another longtime gay civil rights advocate who has been spearheading efforts to organize gay participation at the anniversary event in October, agreed with Pannell.

"I'm terribly upset. It is sickening that he said it," she said. "I'm surprised that that's how he feels, but it truly shows his colors.

"The reaction in the community has been very dramatic and dynamic. People are very angry," Cheatam said. "I'm not sure how we will move forward, because there are people who say, 'I don't want to have anything to do with that because of him.' But the movement is bigger than he is."

The next "GLBT Dinner Meeting about the Millions More Movement" is scheduled to be held from 6 to 9 p.m., Sunday, July 17, at Freedom Fellowship Church, 400 H St., NE. A citywide meeting of the Millions More Movement organizers and supporters is to take place at 6 p.m., Saturday, July 16, at Scripture Cathedral, 810 O St., NW.

Wilson has been pastor at Union Temple for 22 years.

Rick Rosendall, vice president of the Gay & Lesbian Activists Alliance, said he also was disappointed with Wilson's anti-gay sermon.

"It is certainly appalling, if not surprising, to hear a self-professed minister of God spewing such hatred from the pulpit of a church," he said.

Political observers consider Wilson one of the city's most politically influential ministers. Many of the city's leaders, including Mayor Anthony Williams, and D.C. Congressional Del. Eleanor Holmes Norton, have sought Wilson's advice on matters related to sections of the city east of the Anacostia River, where Union Temple is located.

In 2000, Williams appointed Wilson to the Board of Trustees of the University of the District of Columbia, and the D.C. Council confirmed the appointment. Two years later, Wilson ran against Williams in the Democratic mayoral primary.

"You would think that such a divisive figure would be treated as persona non grata by the city's leaders, but this has not been the case," Rosendall said.

Rev. Dr. Amina Binta, co-chair of one of the Millions More Movement march's local organizing committees, resigned her post this week, based on Wilson's comments.

"They're not serious about allowing us to sit at the table," she said. "And if they are, I don't care to eat their fare, because they're serving up a steady diet of homophobia that is very venomous."

Rhonda Smith contributed to this report.

Reprinted with permission of the *Washington Blade*.

CHAPTER 7

Queer Diversities

I magine a gay pride day parade. A sunny weekend in mid-June, crowds bustling, veneeeeedors hawking their rainbow goods. The parade starts with its floats, marching bands, and costumed characters filing past. There go the leaders of the local gay rights organization. Then proud parents from Parents and Friends of Lesbians and Gays (PFLAG). A growling rumble ushers in the Dykcs on Bikes, followed by a leathermen troop. A gaggle of drag queens, bringing up the rear, draws the largest number of shouts, catcalls, and whistles as the parade draws to a close.

Of course, numerous other folks, organizations, and groups may march past you in such a parade—all attesting to the *diversity* of those who identify with or as the lesbian, gay, bisexual, and transgender (LGBT) community. But the good cheer and festivities of a pride

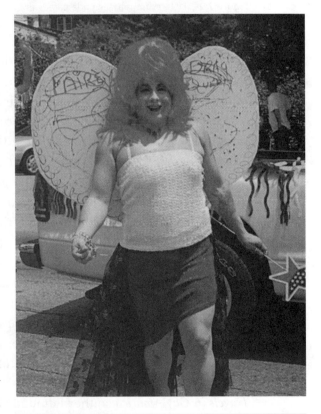

Figure 7.1 Pictures from a gay pride parade in Cincinnati, Ohio.

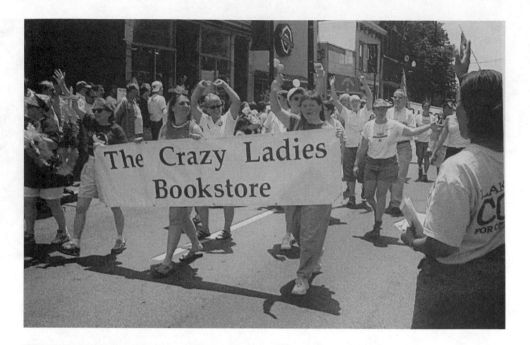

Figure 7.2 Pictures from a gay pride parade in Cincinnati, Ohio.

day parade conceal tensions within that diversity, the kind of strain that accompanies any large "family" who has gathered together to make—and *define*—a community. In the process of defining community, the place or even desirability of some is called into question. For instance, the equality and rights activists at the front of the parade might frown a bit at the presence of the leathermen and drag queens; after all, the more flamboyant members of our community might strike an unsettling chord with sympathetic straight voters and dispel the sense that we queers are "normal folk," just like everyone else. Conversely, that woman, marching with the drag queens, the one transitioning from being a man who likes men to a straight-identified woman, may be wondering if she is marching in the right parade. Will her queer community accept her once she has completed her transition and married her sweetheart? Will she still be *queer*?

In many ways, we can trace the expansion of the LGBT community by looking at some work that has attempted to capture the richness of who we are as a people. It is remarkably easy to leave out, either by accidental oversight or unexamined prejudice, potential allies or others who could make common cause with us. When attempting to chronicle gay life in America in his 1980 book, *States of Desire: Travels in Gay America,* author Edmund White had to admit, "I criticize my book for concentrating on gay men in big cities and for ignoring lesbians as well as small-town or rural life" (336). In 400 pages, he could only cover so much of our diversity, our wealth—and ended up leaving out any significant discussion of women! Over a decade later, anthropologist Gilbert Herdt's collection, *Gay Culture in America: Essays from the Field* (1992), attempted a more comprehensive view of what it means to be "gay" in the United States; his book contains essays on black men, "nonghetto" or suburban gays, and gay Mexican Americans. Still, bisexuals and the transgendered were largely ignored by the authors in Herdt's collection.

Diversity enriches our communities, our sense of what it means to be a member of the LGBT family. It also complicates matters. Just as feminists have debated whether pornography has a place in feminism, many queers have debated at different times whether "challenging" or "controversial" aspects of our community deserve a place. Within queer communities, intense debates have raged over who is really queer, who belongs under the queer umbrella. Of course, what is called "challenging" or "controversial" and decisions about who "belongs" often change over time and as context changes. This chapter details the parameters of some of the most visible debates about diversity and what it means for queer communities.

In some societies, homosexuality and queerness are assumed to be nonexistent; in others, complex social roles have grown up around expressions of nonnormative sexuality and gender. It is important, then, to realize that diversity—and even the notion that diversity is important and desirable—is socially constructed. This means that the very decision to present a chapter on queer diversity in a text such as this is dependent on (1) the existence of a social setting in which diversity is acknowledged, (2) the existence of persistent attention to differences among those who identify as queer, and (3) a resistance to monolithic thinking about queerness. Hence, this chapter focuses on some of the visible points of contestation in the emergence of self-consciously queer communities. One way we can develop a sense of how diversity problematizes—and enriches—a queer community is by examining the common label—LGBT—used to describe who we are and whom we include. Some commentators and comedians quip that the alphabetic shorthand of "LGBT" itself is insufficient to encompass the diversity of queers seeking community, shelter, or acknowledgment. Some have suggested, for instance, that we are LGBTQ (Q for queer . . . or is it Q for questioning?), LGBTQA (A for allies), LGBTQIA (I for intersexuals), and so forth. With this in mind, let us consider how diversity complicates the sense of community—in some challenging but perhaps ultimately productive ways.

L . . . G . . . T . . . : A Story of Push and Pull

As we have noted in previous chapters, some lesbian feminists have promoted lesbian *separatism* [λ Chapter 4], understanding that sexism is as significant an issue to lesbians as is homophobia. For some, the idea of separatism has sparked debates about definitions of woman and womanhood itself. Monique Wittig, a French philosopher and feminist, is famous for arguing that "lesbians are not women." Following Simone De Beauvoir, the French existentialist who argued that "one is not born a woman" but learns the cultural expectations of womanhood and femininity as part of her lived experience, Wittig argues that in heterosexist patriarchal systems, the category "woman" only makes sense in relation to men. Lesbians invested in woman-to-woman relationships thus abandon significant relations to men and are therefore not women. As Wittig explains, "[I]t would be incorrect to say that lesbians associate, make love, live with women, for 'woman' has meaning only in heterosexual systems of thought and heterosexual economic systems. Lesbians are not women" (32). Of course, many other women and lesbian thinkers, such as Adrienne Rich, disagree, stating that lesbians are women who must confront both homophobia and sexism in a patriarchal and male-dominated society [λ Chapter 5].

Find Out More in the readings at the end of Chapter 6.

Other lesbians have made stark distinctions between different kinds of lesbians. In the introduction to her dystopian novel, *Doc and Fluff,* Pat Califia, writing as a lesbian, says that *Doc and Fluff* is "about dykes, not lesbians" (xiv). Califia characterizes lesbians as assimilationists: "To affiliate with lesbians is to select a strategy of mainstreaming, emphasizing what one has in common with straight people, working for the recognition of domestic partnership, and basically accepting a heterosexual and capitalist model for the good life"; "uncritically adopting those standards and those ideals"; and a failure to focus on the "real enemy—the institution of heterosexuality." "Dykes," on the other hand, "have no choice about being visible," and "Dyke culture is about confrontation, acquiring and protecting territory, and taking care of your own" (xv–xvi).

As you can see, definitional debates about identity—who we are and what our identities mean—can create provocative positions and disagreements. Recognition and discussion of transgenderism and transsexualism, for instance, have resulted in significant challenges to the parameters of the identity *woman.* Are male-born male-to-female (MtF or M2F) transsexuals actually *women*? [λ Chapter 6] Since they once lived as men, can they truly understand the sexism that many women find to be a key experience of women in patriarchal societies? What about those who become involved intimately with transsexuals? A lesbian activist friend of ours recently married a female-to-male (FtM or F2M) transsexual activist. Is the lesbian still a lesbian? Her husband was once a woman but is now a man; how does such a change affect the way our friend feels about her own identity—and about how *others* perceive her identity?

Debates about lesbian-identified women undergoing transition to become *men* have raged within the lesbian community. Some feel that these men should be excluded from lesbian communities, even if FtMs began their lives as lesbian-identified women. Alix Dobkin, writing in "The Emperor's New Gender," suggests that the rise and appeal of transgenderism is tempting some women to reject their womanhood and embrace gender ambiguity (at best) or male identification (at worst); she sees such changes as ongoing symptoms of sexism and misogyny:

> Gays and lesbians have struggled for decades to be able to name ourselves and to BE ourselves. But now, in our own community we are expected to applaud Dykes rejecting womanhood and embrace men taking it over. In our smart, brave and compassionate community, being "different" is the unifying thread holding us together in a diverse crazy quilt of which queers are justifiably proud.
>
> But while we're at it, let's also honour our identity and history. And our women. Then maybe our girls won't be so eager to run. So let's put away the knives. Can we talk?

Pat Califia herself was one such woman who transitioned from (lesbian) female to male; he lives with another FtM transsexual and now goes by the name Patrick Califia Rice.

Speaking Sex to Power: The Politics of Queer Sex, written by Califia-Rice post-transition, includes a chapter in which he considers the Michigan Womyn's Music Festival, Alix Dobkin, and the challenges that transpeople sometimes pose to lesbians. The chapter titled "Sexual Politics, FtMs, and Dykes: Who Will Leap out of Bed First?" poignantly details Califia-Rice's own personal struggles to maintain connections with the lesbian communities that nurtured her and were her first home:

> I think lesbians have a right to ask why FTM's who pass fully as male want to be given the right to participate in all-women events. It's legitimate to ask if this is simple opportunism. Yes, it can be difficult to clarify one's identity; sometimes simply saying you are a man or a woman is not entirely accurate. [. . .] Since the FTM community is much smaller than the lesbian community, and many of us maintain friendship ties or erotic connections there, it can be painful and frightening to have to give up these resources. (117)

Califia-Rice also points out that FtMs have a difficult time fitting into *gay male* communities, if they identify as gay or bi men. He writes in the chapter "Trannyfags Unzipped" that "[g]ay/bisexual female-to-male transsexuals (FTMs) are just starting to become more visible. This can be pretty jarring for gay men who base their common identity on having a dick" (132). Even other FtMs balked at Califia-Rice and his partner's decision to interrupt the partner's transition so he could give birth, since "real men" aren't really "supposed" to want to bear children. Califia-Rice, writing in an article titled "Family Values," says that he and his partner received verbal taunts from "a handful of straight-identified homophobic FtMs online who started calling Matt by his girl name, because real men don't get pregnant. One of these bigots even said it would be better for our baby to be born dead than be raised by two people who are 'confused about their gender.'"

In an attempt to bridge the gap between his various communities, Califia-Rice has suggested that female-to-male transsexuals and butch dykes may have much in common, such as having to grapple with what typically "masculine" interests or presentation might mean for their lives. Vik Savage, self-described as a "Butch Dyke not FTM," sharply disagrees, saying that past lesbians "had good boundaries around men and oppression. We don't. We're all freakin' wishy-washy with our B***SH*T about 'oh but they're SO like us!'. Fuck that! They're MEN, dudes! MEN, MEN, MEN, MEN. Hello!!!!!." Despite Califia-Rice's eloquence and his insistence that he has not "renounced" his history as a dyke, questions of community still haunt his discussions about transmen, transwomen, lesbianism, and feminism. Diverse experiences of sexuality and gender have complicated intimacies and identities within and among these communities.

Bisexual Erasure in the LGBT Community

Bisexuality has been among the most vexed internal issues facing Western queer communities. For years, the letter *B* has been tacked onto the *L* and the *G*, with *T* coming a bit more recently; but many *B*s have never found themselves particularly welcome in or a part of their lesbian and gay communities. Many gays and lesbians have suggested that bisexuals are just "going through a phase" on their way to "true" gayness or lesbianism or that they are trying to hold on to straight privileges while fooling around with people of their own sex. And, in fact, a controversial article published in 2005 in the *New York Times* pointedly asked, "Gay, Straight, or Lying? Bisexuality Revisited." The article's author, Benedict Carey, reported on some studies suggesting that "[p]eople who claim bisexuality . . . are usually homosexual, but are ambivalent about their homosexuality or simply closeted." Despite such negativity and bad press, bisexual activists have formed groups locally, nationally, and even throughout the world to educate others about bisexuality and bisexual identity. In the United States, BiNet USA (http://www.binetusa.org/) is perhaps the largest and most politically active of organizations for bisexual people.

Bi-eroticism is a trans-historical and trans-cultural phenomenon, as evidenced by scholarly works such as Marjorie Garber's influential 1995 book, *Vice Versa: Bisexuality and the Eroticism of Everyday Life,* which traces the representation of bi-erotic intimacies in over two millennia of Western art, texts, and media. Garber carefully avoids labeling bi-eroticism as "bisexual identity," and she thus avoids the fallacy of perverse presentism. Rather, Garber carefully and exhaustively documents how numerous major artists, actors, thinkers, and philosophers—from Shakespeare to Wilde, from Sappho to Frida Kahlo—explored in their works attraction and intimate affection that are neither exclusively "straight" nor "gay." Shakespeare's acclaimed sonnet sequence, for instance, contains sets of love poems written about and to a woman (the "dark lady" of the sonnets) as well as to a young male friend (the actual subject of the famous sonnet often used in weddings, "Let me not to the marriage of true minds"). Garber's work ultimately asks that we question our assumptions about the sexual identities of past figures. Oscar Wilde, for instance, has long been thought of as a gay icon, but he was also a loving father who deeply cared for his children and his wife. Is Wilde then "gay"? What do his bi-erotic investments say about his sexuality and his identity? Along the same lines, other scholars and writers, such as Wayne Bryant and his 1997 book *Bisexual Characters in Film: From Anaïs to Zee,* as well as Lorraine Hutchins and Lani Ka'ahumanu and their 1991 collection of bisexual coming-out stories, *Bi Any Other Name,* document the presence of bi-eroticism in a variety of media products and nonfiction narratives. *Bi Any Other Name* in particular shows the difficulties faced by those attempting to assert an identity as bisexuals; such individuals often face hostility from both gays and straights who deny their existence as bisexuals and question their right to name themselves and their attractions.

Some scholars note that the seemingly persistent unwillingness to acknowledge or discuss bisexuality and bi-eroticism throughout the West has roots in both a general fear of sexuality and an attempt to delineate clear distinctions between gays and straights. Bisexuals, existing somewhere between the two, pose a threat to the binary construct that gives both homosexuality and heterosexuality their meaningfulness in relation to one another. Along these lines, Yale law professor Kenji Yoshino has argued provocatively in "The Epistemic Contract of Bisexual Erasure" that bisexuality should be contrasted to monosexuality, or the erotic and affectional investment in loving either people of the same sex or the opposite sex—but not both. For Yoshino, monosexuals have much to gain not just by ignoring bisexuality but by actively denying its existence:

> The first investment monosexuals have in bisexual erasure is an interest in stabilizing sexual orientation. The component of that interest shared by both straights and gays is an interest in knowing one's place in the social order: both straights and gays value this knowledge because it relieves them of the anxiety of identity interrogation. Straights have a more specific interest in ensuring the stability of heterosexuality because that identity is privileged. Less intuitively,

gays also have a specific interest in guarding the stability of homosexuality, insofar as they view that stability as the predicate for the "immutability defense" or for effective political mobilization. [. . .] Bisexuality is thus threatening to all monosexuals because it makes it impossible to prove a monosexual identity.

Yoshino also suggests that "monosexuals" are troubled by the specter of bisexual "nonmonogamy," which many gays, lesbians, and straights assume to be a key aspect of bisexuality. Gays and lesbians seeking to be accepted by mainstream Western society, which figures intimate relationships as ideally monogamous, fear that bisexual nonmonogamy threatens gays' ability to pass as "normal." The truth, of course, is much more complicated. Many bisexually identified people are indeed monogamous, just as many gays, lesbians, and straights are most decidedly *not* monogamous. Furthermore, many gays and lesbians fear bisexuality because it seems to suggest that one can *choose* one's sexuality. In contrast, many gays and lesbians (as well as some straights) want to argue that their sexuality is not chosen and is thus natural—a powerful argument in some people's eyes for extending civil rights and protections to gays and lesbians [λ Chapter 5]. Bisexuality, then, is an intolerable position in the eyes of many gays, lesbians, and straights.

We can see the extent of "bisexual erasure" in reactions to Ang Lee's controversial film about an erotic relationship between two male cowboys, *Brokeback Mountain* (2005). Both cowboys are married and have intimate relations with women in addition to their stormy and complex decades-long affair with one another. Amy Andre, in an article for *American Sexuality Magazine,* proposes that

> *Brokeback Mountain* is not a movie about gay people, and there are no gay people in it. There. I said it. Despite what you may have read in the many reviews that have come out about this new cowboy feature film, *Brokeback Mountain* is a bisexual picture. Why can't film reviewers say the word "bisexual" when they see lead characters with sexual and romantic relationships with both men and women?

Andre's assertion that the film is actually about two bisexual men, not just two closeted gay men, may be debatable. But her point that discussion about the film largely avoided any consideration of the potential bisexuality of the characters speaks to the extent to which bisexuality and bi-eroticism are seldom taken seriously or even acknowledged in the larger culture. When bisexuality is noticed by the media, it is often depicted in damaging and noxious ways. In the introduction to their edited collection, *Bisexual Men in Culture and Society* (2002), Brett Beemyn and Erich Steinman assert that "[n]ot only are there relatively few cultural images of men who are attracted to more than one gender, but the representations that do exist often focus on how behaviorally bisexual men supposedly pose a hidden HIV threat to heterosexual women" (3) [λ Chapter 8]. According to the myth, then, bisexual men are on the "down low," sneaking off for secret liaisons with other men and potentially bringing home to their wives sexually transmitted diseases. Such representations, as well as the persistent attempts to erase bisexuality from the culture, are frequent targets of bisexual activists. The American Institute of Bisexuality, for instance, has pledged to raise awareness of not only the existence of bisexuality but also the many contributions that bisexuals make to culture, society, the arts, and the numerous communities to which they belong (http://www.bisexual.org).

Intersexuality

Intersexuals may be the newest to find voice in the LGBT community. Intersexuals are individuals who in the past would have been labeled hermaphrodites; they are typically born with both male and female genitalia or sex organs or with indeterminate genitalia—that is, genitals that are not clearly male or female sex organs, such as large clitorises that resemble small penises. Many intersexuals in the West are subject to surgery as infants to "correct" their gender indeterminacy and to "fix" them as either clearly male or clearly female. While some intersexuals are not aware that their hermaphroditism was corrected, others report being shocked to discover that they were subjected to such surgical procedures as infants.

The Intersex Society of North America (ISNA) advocates for an end to these surgeries and, in their words, "is devoted to systemic change to end *shame, secrecy, and unwanted genital surgeries* for people born with an anatomy that someone decided *is not standard for male or female.*" ISNA believes firmly that "[i]ntersexuality is primarily a problem of *stigma and trauma,* not *gender,*" and that "[p]arents' *distress* must not be treated by surgery on the child." Many intersexed activists argue that their fight is comparable to that of queers who advocate for the rights of individuals to self-determine and to pursue freedom from normative gender constructions. We can hear the connections between intersexed and queer activists in the following quotation from Morgan Holmes's essay, "Queer Cut Bodies": "Intersexed adults are first intersexed minors who have been subjected to the wills of their families and doctors. Avoidance of surgeries serving no purpose except to make the intersexed child more appealing to parents and to their culture is a fine place to start reconceptualizing the intersexed body" (106). Many queers can identify with Holmes's characterization of children "subjected to the wills of their families" and to being forced to become "more appealing" (i.e., less queer). But more than such similarities, the intersexed and many queers collectively fight the imposition of heteronormative values and ideas—not only on the way we choose to love and to be intimate but on our very bodies as well.

Q: Beyond Sexual Identity

The letter *Q* is sometimes added to the LGBT grouping to signify either those who are "questioning" or those who prefer the term *queer* to describe their sexual identities or affinities. Some use the word *queer* as a catch-all for the LGBT conglomerate, but many others prefer *queer* as a political term. Specifically, *queer* is used to mark those whose sexualities, sexual practices, or erotic and affectional investments lie outside the mainstream of normative heterosexuality. Some activists in the 1990s (and to this day) use the term *queer* aggressively, signaling that they have taken a term once used to stigmatize homosexuals and other "perverts" and are now using it proudly, even defiantly. We are queer—so what? The reclamation of the word *queer,* then, serves to defy normative, conventional society and its bigoted exclusions. As David Halperin puts it in *Saint Foucault,* "Queer is by definition whatever is at odds with the normal, the legitimate, the dominant" (62).

Some writers have explored the usefulness of *queer* as a marker of the transgressive margins, while others have developed different terms to promote a queer ethos—the celebration of sexual difference and nonnormative eroticism. For instance, Carol Queen and Lawrence Schimel use the term *pomosexual* to describe a postmodern sexuality that is free, exploratory, and unwilling to confine itself to specific labels. In their edited collection, *Pomosexuals: Challenging Assumptions about Gender and Sexuality,* they note the similarity between the terms *pomosexual* and *queer:*

> the "pomosexual," who, like the queer s/he closely resembles, may not be tied
> to a single sexual identity, may not be content to reside within a category mea-
> surable by social scientists or acknowledged by either rainbow-festooned gays
> or by Ward and June Cleaver. (23)

For many writers such as Queen, a well-known sex activist, *queer* foregrounds not only difference but also pleasure, an aspect of sexual politics that many pomosexuals feel is often overlooked or underconsidered in public discussions of sex and sexuality.

Along similar lines, others in the LGBTQ community have attempted to emphasize the diversity of sexual interests and erotic styles by forming subcultural groups focused on particular identifications. For instance, some gay men identify strongly with "bear culture" and call themselves "bears" (men a bit larger or hairier than the norm) or "bear cubs" (men who love men who are a bit larger or hairier than the norm). Bears break out of the consumerist stereotype, fostered by shows such as *Queer Eye for the Straight Guy,* which figures gay men as slim, super health-conscious, interior-decorating gurus; bears, in contrast, are large men whose interests tend to be typically (even stereotypically) masculine, such as sports, camping, and rough-housing. In *The Bear Book II,* Les Wright notes that bears challenge any sense of normative gayness or queerness: "All of these Ur-springs of the bearstream trickled along because in the invention of 'gaymen' and 'gay culture,' ideas and concepts required the invention of a new vocabulary to describe categories and subcategories inside the love that so long had dared not speak its name" (xlii).

While groups such as the bears highlight the diversity of erotic interest and lifestyling within the LGBT community, many queers do not necessarily experience queer communities as stylistic free-for-alls. For some, the challenge of diversity is finding a comfortable place *within* the diversity, and some critics and scholars worry about the establishment of hierarchies that oppress people who do not fit into particular groups. For instance, in some gay male communities, men who are "straight-acting" are more valued and sought after as sexual partners than others. Wayne Martino argues that discriminating hierarchies may be evolving within gay male communities around the notion of "straight-acting," particularly "[w]ithin a socio-cultural context in which specific discourses about straight-acting masculinities gain a particular authoritative status or ascendancy—for example, from 'Bears' who claim that they don't engage in 'faggoty sex' to 'gainers' who deliberately put on weight to adopt a particular way of being masculine that challenges the idealization of the gay male body" (Kendall and Martino 58). In general, the seeming freedom implied in terms such as *queer* or *pomosexual* needs to be considered against the often restrictive, even oppressive social and sexual practices in which people actually engage.

Conforming to certain styles, fashions, or self-presentations may be one way to deal with the diversity within LGBTQ communities, but the pressure to conform has created a fair amount of backlash. For example, Christy Calame and Robbie Scott Phillips capture some of the frustration with conformity. In their provocative manifesto, "Fuck Your Healthy Gay Lifestyle (The FRINGE Manifesto—Freaks, Radicals, and Inverts Nail Gay Elite!)," they argue that "[g]ays and lesbians do not exist—there are only queers and straights. Those known as 'gay and lesbian people' are essentially straight assholes who sleep with members of their same sex and have nothing to do with queerness except their fear and rape of it. Queers are twisted and disgusting, beautiful and glamorous, extreme and alive. We live outside the margin and move to keep working edges, surviving co-optations, decimation, and attack by those so-called gay and lesbian people" (233). Scholars such as Michael Warner have taken such critiques seriously; his book, *The Trouble with Normal,* analyzes how some gays and lesbians seek political favor by attempting to demonstrate that little difference exists between gays and straights; they argue that rights should be equitably distributed because we are all, essentially, the same. For instance, the Log Cabin Republicans, a national group of U.S. lesbian and gay Republicans, advocate primarily for legalizing gay marriage and open military service since extending these rights will bring gays into the American mainstream—thus promoting a sense of queers as "normal" citizens. Many other queers, such as Calame and Phillips, argue strongly that access to rights should not hinge on sameness but should be available to all irrespective of difference.

Historian John D'Emilio, writing in "Gay Politics, Gay Community," notes that the "[g]rowth [of the lesbian and gay community] has also meant differentiation, diversity, and divisions. Gay communities around the country are coming to mirror the society at large with all of the conflicting interests that stem from differences of gender, race, and class" (94). This recognition prompts many questions. In particular, when we attempt to capture the diversity of the LGBT/queer community, we still need to ask, "Who is *not* represented by the LGBTQ label?" Is the experience, for instance, of African American gays and lesbians in the United States the same as their white counterparts? What about Latinos and Asian Americans? What about queers in different national contexts? We will have much more to say about the *intersections* among different identity categories (queerness, race, ethnicity, social class, and gender) in the following chapter.

For now, we can consider briefly how the experience of social class often intersects with and complicates the experience of queerness. Some critics have—with no small justification—claimed that LGBT communities and rights organizations have been dominated by white, middle-class interests, values, and participants. Social class has long been overlooked as an important consideration when understanding and representing oneself as queer. Amber Hollibaugh writes eloquently about the enforced silences imposed on working-class LGBT people. A recent documentary film, *Small Town Gay Bar,* poignantly demonstrates Hollibaugh's point: the film depicts queer life in rural Mississippi where LGBT people only feel safe identifying themselves in bars, many of which are not visibly marked as queer and are found by word of mouth. Nicola Field, in her book *Over the Rainbow: Money, Class and Homophobia,* summarizes the importance of considering social class as a significant dimension of one's experience of queerness:

> **Find Out More** in Amber Hollibaugh's article "Queers without Money" at the end of this chapter.

> Demonstrating as lesbians and gay men, many of us would not dare to wear our working clothes. We may be afraid of being recognised, of facing repercussions at work where we are isolated and alone. [. . .] We are visible in a crowd but we remain largely invisible in our daily lives. The sense of solidarity that comes

> with marching and mingling as part of a mass of gay people is therefore a wel-
> come relief from the isolation of everyday life. When we march we say that this
> is the one day of the year that belongs to "us." However, it is impossible to sus-
> tain this sense of political power once the carnival is over. (152)

Indeed, the "invisibility" experienced by many working-class queers is at times a
necessary component of moving out of the working class. Many working-class
queers, for instance, consider service in the armed forces a way to obtain money for
a college education. The U.S. military's "Don't Ask, Don't Tell" [λ Chapters 4 and 6]
policy makes being queer in the military much more challenging, complicating
class mobility for many queers.

A for Allies

The queer community has also had complex, productive, and at times troubled
relationships with those who might be potential "allies." These allies have
much to offer the queer community in terms of support and insight, but alliances
have not always been easy. For instance, people throughout the "kink" community,
including a wide variety of fetishists and sadomasochists interested in alternative
forms of sexual expression, may not necessarily be interested in homo- or bi-erotic
behavior, but their nonnormative sexualities make them likely allies with queers.
Many of them consider themselves queer in the broadest sense of the word.
Sadomasochists (S/M), in particular, face social stigmas comparable to those of
many in the LGBT community; in "The Joy of S/M," Susan Wright suggests that
"[t]he biggest burden for s/m practitioners is the social stigma. I've come to expect
that the Christian Right will attack us for our sexual choices, deriding us and labeling our behavior as wrong because it is not what they would choose to do." While
such discrimination might make practitioners of S/M seemingly natural allies with
queers, Wright notes that many in the LGBT community actively discriminate
against those who are vocal about their kink interests. She cites a 1994 survey that
"found that 56% of the 539 s/m women surveyed had been the victim of violence—
harassment, discrimination, or assault—by fellow lesbians because of their s/m orientation. Clearly s/m practitioners have a long fight ahead for equal protection and
our civil rights." Of course, some queers are themselves actively invested in S/M, both
as an erotic practice and as a vehicle for forming community with other like-minded
individuals. Califia-Rice has long been a strong advocate for S/M, and queer authors
such as Dennis Cooper have written extensively—and provocatively—about fringe,
fetish, and sadomasochistic sexual practices [λ Chapter 11]. Still, many in the LGBT
community find such interests repugnant, particularly as they seem "abnormal," and

give the lie to arguments that queers are much like straights. What is ironic about such objections is the reality that many in S/M communities are themselves straight!

Another group that has both supporters and detractors within the larger LGBT community is sex workers. The International Union of Sex Workers has identified a number of demands that would benefit sex workers throughout the world. These include the following:

- Clean and safe places to work.
- The right to choose whether to work on our own or co-operatively with other sex workers.
- The absolute right to say no.
- Access to training—our jobs require very special skills and professional standards.
- Access to health clinics where we do not feel stigmatised.
- Re-training programmes for sex workers who want to leave the industry.
- An end to social attitudes which stigmatise those who are or have been sex workers. (http://www.iusw.org/start/index.html)

Certainly, many queers have also argued for access to health services, the right to feel safe at work, and freedom from stigmatization. Amber Hollibaugh asks why it has taken so long for the needs of sex workers to attract the attention of feminist thinkers and activists—those who are invested in protecting the rights of women. Her answer underscores the social class division that frequently exists between middle- and upper-class feminists and many female sex workers: "Maybe because it's hard to listen—I mean really pay attention to—a woman who, without other options, could easily be cleaning your toilet? Maybe because it's intolerable to listen to the point of view of a woman who makes her living sucking off your husband?" (181). Hollibaugh suggests that ignorance about *queer* sex workers is even more acute: "If the world of sex work is usually concealed, the world of lesbian sex workers is completely invisible. Throughout every part of the sex-trade business there are lesbians working as hookers and dancers, as dykes who function in massage parlors and as the lesbian madams of brothels and escort services—and as prostitutes' rights organizers around the world" (183).

As you can see, the issue of diversity within the LGBT/queer community is complex and often vexed. In significant ways, we are queer because of that diversity, because of our difference from normative cultural conceptions of appropriate gender behavior and accepted sexual practice. Still, many queers, when encountering sexual diversity, act much as many straights do when encountering queerness— with hesitation, skepticism, and sometimes hostility. Whether such skepticism and hostility are warranted varies from issue to issue, identity to identity, and community to community. In his apologia for homosexuality titled *Corydon,*

French author André Gide requests that we do not "understand" him too quickly—that we do not assume that what seems different can be honored by viewing it as less complex than it actually is. The diversity within the LGBT/queer community ensures that any understanding of queerness that jumps to quick conclusions is likely to be foiled upon closer examination. This diversity—this complexity—makes our experiences in many ways all the richer, particularly as we are prompted to think more deeply and critically about what queer is—and could be.

QUESTIONS FOR DISCUSSION

1. One myth of American culture suggests that we in the United States comprise a "melting pot" of different nationalities, identities, and communities. In what ways is the queer or LGBT community in this country a melting pot? Is the metaphor of the melting pot appropriate or even accurate? Try to generate a list of other or better metaphors. Consider your experiences or those of queers you might know. Record your own and others' reflections on queerness and the melting pot metaphor.

2. Certainly, issues of diversity complicate unified and collective political action, particularly in that different identity groups may want to promote different agendas addressing their own particular issues or experiences. At the same time, a variety of different queers—ranging from gay men and intersexuals to FtM transsexuals and lesbian separatists—might have commonalities around which to organize politically. What are they? Are there "queer values" that many diverse members of LGBT/queer communities might be able to advance as a political agenda?

3. Early in this chapter, we raised the "alphabet issue"—the expanding string of letters used to identify the diversity within queer communities. As we noted, some people prefer to use the term *queer* as a "catch-all" for this diversity, while others, particularly some feminists, feel that the word *queer* erases or elides women's interests and focuses on men. Can you think of another word or phrase to replace *queer* or *LGBT* to represent the LGBT/queer community? What are the advantages of your chosen word or phrase? What are its potential disadvantages? Who is likely to support it? Who not? Why?

REFERENCES AND FURTHER READING

Andre, Amy. "Bisexual Cowboys in Love." *American Sexuality Magazine* (Winter 2006). <http://nsrc.sfsu.edu/MagArticle.cfm?Article=554>.

Beemyn, Brett, and Erich Steinman, eds. *Bisexual Men in Culture and Society.* New York: Harrington Park Press, 2002.

Bisexual Foundation. <http://www.bisexual.org>.

Bryant, Wayne M. *Bisexual Characters in Film: From Anaïs to Zee.* New York: Haworth Press, 1997.

Calame, Christy, and Robbie Scott Phillips. "Fuck Your Healthy Gay Lifestyle (The FRINGE Manifesto—Freaks, Radicals, and Inverts Nail Gay Elite!)." *Generation Q: Gays, Lesbians, and Bisexuals Born around 1969's Stonewall Riots Tell Their Stories of Growing Up in the Age of Information.* Eds. Robin Bernstein and Seth Clark Silberman. Los Angeles: Alyson Publications, 1996. 233–36.

Califia, Pat. *Doc and Fluff.* Boston: Alyson Publications, 1990.

Califia-Rice, Patrick. "Family Values." *The Village Voice* 20 June 2000. 19 July 2008 <http://villagevoice.com/2000-06-20/news/family-values/>.

———. *Speaking Sex to Power: The Politics of Queer Sex.* San Francisco: Cleis Press, 2002.

Carey, Benedict. "Gay, Straight, or Lying? Bisexuality Revisited." *New York Times* 5 July 2005. 19 July 2008 <http://select.nytimes.com/gst/abstract.html?res=F20714FB3B550C768 CDDAE0894DD404482>.

D'Emilio, John. "Gay Politics, Gay Community: San Francisco's Experience." *Making Trouble: Essays on Gay History, Politics, and the University.* New York: Routledge, 1992.

Dobkin, Alix. "The Emperor's New Gender." *Off Our Backs.* April 2000. 19 July 2008 <http://www.rapereliefshelter.bc.ca/issues/newgender.html>.

Eulenspiegel Society. 19 July 2008 <http://www.tes.org/>.

Field, Nicola. *Over the Rainbow: Money, Class and Homophobia.* East Haven, CT: Pluto Press, 1995.

Garber, Marjorie. *Vice Versa: Bisexuality and the Eroticism of Everyday Life.* New York: Simon & Schuster, 1995.

Gide, André. *Corydon.* New York: Farrar, Straus, Giroux, 1983.

Halperin, David M. *Saint Foucault: Towards a Gay Hagiography.* New York: Oxford University Press, 1995.

Herdt, Gilbert, ed. *Gay Culture in America: Essays from the Field.* Boston: Beacon, 1992.

Hollibaugh, Amber L. *My Dangerous Desires: A Queer Girl Dreaming Her Way Home.* Durham, NC: Duke University Press, 2000.

Holmes, Morgan. "Queer Cut Bodies." *Queer Frontiers: Millennial Geographies, Genders, and Generations.* Ed. *Queer Frontiers* Editorial Collective (Joseph A. Boone, Martin Dupuis, Martin Meeker, Karin Quimby, Cindy Sarver, Debra Silverman, and Rosemary Weatherston). Madison: University of Wisconsin Press, 2000. 84–110.

Hutchins, Lorraine, and Lani Ka'ahumanu, eds. *Bi Any Other Name: Bisexual People Speak Out.* Boston: Alyson Publications, 1991.

International Union of Sex Workers. <http://www.iusw.org/start/index.html>.

Intersex Society of North America. <http://www.isna.org/>.

Kendall, Christopher, and Wayne Martino, eds. *Gendered Outcasts and Sexual Outlaws: Sexual Oppression and Gender Hierarchies in Queer Men's Lives.* New York: Harrington Park Press, 2006.

Martino, Wayne. "Straight-Acting Masculinities: Normalization and Gender Hierarchies in Gay Men's Lives." *Gendered Outcasts and Sexual Outlaws: Sexual Oppression and*

Gender Hierarchies in Queer Men's Lives. Eds. Christopher Kendall and Wayne Martino. New York: Harrington Park Press, 2006. 35–60.

Ochs, Robyn. *Getting Bi: Voices of Bisexuals around the World.* Boston: Bisexual Resource Center, 2005.

Queen, Carol, and Lawrence Schimel, eds. *Pomosexuals: Challenging Assumptions about Gender and Sexuality.* San Francisco: Cleis Press, 1997.

Savage, Vik. "Point/Counterpoint: Reactions to Pat Califia." Technodyke.com. 19 July 2008 <http://www.technodyke.com/features/point_cp_pat.asp>.

Warner, Michael. *The Trouble with Normal: Sex, Politics, and the Ethics of Queer Life.* New York: The Free Press, 1999.

White, Edmund. *States of Desire: Travels in Gay America.* New York: Dutton, 1980.

Wittig, Monique. *The Straight Mind.* Boston: Beacon, 1992.

Wright, Les K., ed. *The Bear Book II: Further Readings in the History and Evolution of a Gay Male Subculture.* New York: Harrington Park Press, 2001.

Wright, Susan. "The Joy of S/M." Fetish Information Exchange, 10 September 1999. 19 July 2008 <http://www.fetishexchange.org/joyofsm.shtml>.

Yoshino, Kenji. "The Epistemic Contract of Bisexual Erasure." *Stanford Law Review* 1 January 2000. 19 July 2008 <http://www.kenjiyoshino.com/articles/epistemiccontract.pdf>.

READINGS

➢ **Amber Hollibaugh**

"Queers without Money: They Are Everywhere. But We Refuse to See Them."

(2001), United States

> I mean, homosexuals have high incomes, they have high levels of education; they're owners of major credit cards. There was a survey done. So you're not talking about poor people, homeless people living under a bridge.
>
> —Reverend Lou Sheldon, a conservative Christian leader

I lived the first year of my life in a converted chicken coop in back of my grandmother's trailer. The coop was hardly tall enough for my 6'4" father and 5'8" mother to stand up in. My dad, a carpenter, tore out the chickens' egg-laying ledges and rebuilt the tiny inside space to fit a bed, a table, two chairs, a basin they used as a sink (there was no running water), a shelf with a hot plate for cooking, and a small dresser. They used the hose outside to wash with, and ran extension cords in from my grandmother's trailer for light and heat. My bed, a dresser drawer, sat on top of the table during the day. At night it was placed next to where they slept.

I was sick the entire first year of my life. So was my mother, recovering from a nasty C-section and a series of ensuing medical crises. By the time she and I were discharged, three months later, whatever money my parents had managed to save was used up, and they were deeply in debt. They had been poor before my birth, and poor all of their lives growing up, but this was the sinker.

After my first year, we moved from the chicken coop into a trailer. My father worked three jobs simultaneously, rarely sleeping. My mother took whatever work she could find: mending, washing, and ironing other people's clothes. But we never really recovered. We were impoverished. Growing up, I was always poor. I am also a lesbian.

This, then, is my queer identity: I am a high-femme, mixed-race, white-trash lesbian. And even after all these years of living in a middle-class gay community, I often feel left outside when people speak about their backgrounds, their families. And if you listen to the current telling of "our" queer tale, people like me would seem an anomaly. Because, we are told—and we tell ourselves—queerness can't be poor.

Yet this seeming anomaly is the tip of the proverbial iceberg. It represents hundreds of thousands of us who come from poor backgrounds, or are living them still—and are very, very queer.

That would seem obvious when you combine the proportion of the population reputed to be queer (between 4 and 10 percent) with the 37 million poor people in America. Yet the early surveys done on gay and lesbian economic status in this country told a different tale: that queers had more disposable income than straights, lived more luxurious lives, and were all DINKs (Dual Income No Kids). "My book begins as a critique of those early surveys, which were done largely to serve the interests of gay and lesbian publications and a few marketing companies," says economist M. V. Lee Badgett in her new book, *Money, Myths, and Change: The Economic Lives of Lesbians and Gay Men.* "Those surveys are deeply flawed."

Badgett notes that "opposition to gay people is often based on the perception that queers are better off than everybody else; that we're really asking for 'special rights'—and that breeds resentment." Badgett's research shows something else. It constitutes the first true picture of queer economic reality. Among other things, Badgett found that:

• Gays, lesbians, and bisexuals do *not* earn more than heterosexuals, or live in more affluent households.

• Gay men earn 13 to 32 percent less than similarly qualified straight men (depending on the study).

• Though lesbians and bisexual women have incomes comparable to straight women—earning 21 percent less than men—lesbian couples earn significantly less than heterosexual ones.

But . . . try finding representations of poor or working-class gay people on *Will & Grace.* See how hard you have to search for media images of queers who are part of the vast working poor in this country. Find the homeless transgendered folks. Find stories of gay immigrants, lesbian moms working three jobs, bisexual truckers falling asleep from too many hours on the road, gay men in the unemployment line. Try finding an image of queer people who are balancing on the edge—or have fallen off.

The myth of our wealth goes deep, so deep that even other gay people seem to believe it. We have tried to protect ourselves from the hard truths of our economic diversity by perpetuating the illusion of material wealth, within the confines of male/female whiteness. This is a critical aspect of how we present ourselves in this country at this point in time. We treat the poverty that exists among us—as well as the differences of class—as a dirty secret to be hidden, denied, repelled. We treat economic struggle as something that functions outside the pull of queer desires, removed from our queerly lived lives.

As Badgett notes, by celebrating the myth of queer affluence, we have "drawn attention to exactly the kind of picture that Lou Sheldon is drawing of gay and lesbian people." There is a richer—and ultimately more sympathetic—queer reality: "We are everywhere—but we're all different."

Why is it so hard to acknowledge this? Why is poverty treated as a queer secret? And why does it produce a particular kind of homosexual shame? Bear with me. Imagine what you've never allowed yourself to see before.

When I directed the Lesbian AIDS Project at Gay Men's Health Crisis, stories of the hundreds of HIV-positive lesbians who were a part of that project literally came roaring out of those women's mouths. These were lesbians who had almost never participated in queer politics or visited any of New York City's queer institutions. On those rare occasions when they had tried, they quickly departed, unseen and unwelcomed.

Andrew Spieldenner, a young gay organizer of color who has worked for years with men who have sex with men, has a name for this phenomenon. He calls it "a queer and invisible body count." It is made up of poor lesbians and gay men, queer people of color, the transgendered, people with HIV and AIDS and—always and in large numbers—the queer young and the queer elderly.

The Metropolitan Community Church, a largely gay denomination, reports that the demand for food at its New York pantry has doubled since the beginning of welfare reform in 1996. The Lesbian & Gay Community Services Center says that homeless people in their addiction programs have tripled since then. The Hetrick-Martin Institute, which serves "gay and questioning youth," estimates that 50 percent of homeless kids in New York City are queer.

"We are entering a time when the economy is going into a slump," says Joseph De Filippis, who coordinates the Queer Economic Justice Network. "This isn't going to be like the '90s, when it was easy for employers to give things like domestic-partner benefits. There are going to be more and more of us who are affected by joblessness and economic crisis. And the welfare reform law expires in 2002. It's our issue, damn it. It has always been our issue."

Ingrid Rivera, director of the Racial & Economic Justice Initiative of the National Gay and Lesbian Task Force, has lived this issue. "I was on welfare, I was homeless, I thought I'd be lucky if I finished high school. I am a woman of color, I am a mother, and I am queer. I've worked and lived in a poor world and I've worked in queer organizations that are primarily white. I've seen it from both perspectives, and there's a kind of disconnect. In the gay, mostly white world, race and economic justice isn't talked about as a queer issue. And because of that split, queerness becomes a white thing."

Poverty and outright destitution can happen to anyone—and the queerer you are, the fewer safety nets exist to hold you up or bounce you back from the abyss. Queerness intensifies poverty and compounds the difficulty of dealing with the social service system. The nightmares—even in this city, with its gay rights law—include:

• Being separated from your partner if you go into the shelter system. Straight couples can remain together by qualifying for the family system.

• Being mandated into homophobic treatment programs for drug or drinking problems and having the program decide to treat your queerness instead of your addiction. If you leave the program, you lose any right to benefits—including Medicaid.

• Being unable to apply as a family for public housing.

• Ending up a queer couple in the only old-age home you can afford and being separated when you try to share a room.

Barbara Cassis came from a wealthy Long Island family. But when he began to understand and acknowledge his transgendered nature, his parents kicked him out. He was homeless, young, and broke. "Thank God for drag queens," she says, looking back. "A drag queen found me crying in Times Square and took me home. She talked to me about what I was going through, let me stay with her in her apartment, taught me how to support myself, how to get clients as a prostitute or in the gay bars where I could work as I transitioned. But then she died of AIDS and I was homeless again."

The homeless shelters were the worst experience of all for Barbara as a transwoman. Often, it felt easier to just stay on the streets. If you're homeless, and you haven't transitioned—which costs a fortune—you're forced to go to a shelter based on birth gender. The risk of violence and danger is always high for everyone; the shelters are crowded, short of staff, and the staff that is there has no training in how to deal with trans or gay issues. So if you are a transperson, just taking a shower means that you're taking your life in your hands.

"It took me years to get on my feet," says Cassis, now an administrative assistant at the Positive Health Project, "to start dealing with being HIV-positive, and get the training and education I needed to find a decent job. It has also taken years for me to reconcile with my family, which I have. If it hadn't been for the kind of people the gay community often discounts and despises, I wouldn't be here today."

Like my mother said, the only difference between a poor drunk and a rich one is which drunk can hide it. The shame of being poor is an acutely public shame, difficult to hide. And *queer* homosexuality—the kind of queerness that makes gender differences and radical sexual desires crystal clear—this queerness triggers similar ruinous social perils.

We punish people in this country for being poor and we punish homosexuality. When both are combined, it does more than double the effect: It twists and deepens it, gives it sharper edges, and heightens our inability to duck and cover or slide through to a safer place. It forces you to live more permanently outside than either condition dictates.

The problem intensifies when you realize what queers are in the mind of America. We stand for the culture's obsession with the erotic. It is we who are portrayed as always doing it or trying to, we who quickly become the sexual criminals at the heart of any story. We are the ones who are dangerous; our sexuality is more explosive, more explicit, more demanding, more predatory.

And so it goes for poor people: part stereotype (read trailer trash or welfare queen), part object of blame for being too stupid not to have done better. The underlying assumption is that the only appropriate desires are those that rest comfortably atop plenty of money. The desires and needs afforded by wealth—and plenty of it, earned or not—are appropriate, acceptable, good. But messy desires? Desires that combine with class and color? Desires and needs that ricochet around the erotic? These needs are not acceptable. They are condemned.

No wonder the gay movement can't see the poverty in its midst. The one thing this culture longs for and seems to value in queer life is the image of wealth. It appears to be the only thing we do right. And it is the only piece of our queerness that we can use when our citizenship is at stake. We learned this at the beginning of the AIDS crisis, when we activated that wealth to do what the government wouldn't: We built institutions to care and protect and serve our own. It is a riveting example of how we have claimed our own and valued what the mainstream culture despised about our lives. We could do the same with queer poverty.

"If the community got involved in the issues of being queer and poor," says Jay Toole, a lesbian in the LGBT caucus of the Coalition for the Homeless, "it would be like the community saying, 'I'm here, and here's my hand. You can go further, I'm here.'"

Toole is finishing school now. She plans to work as a substance abuse counselor, to go back into the shelters and bring gay people into the community, "so that they don't have to be so alone as I was. Because when Ann Duggan [from the Coalition] brought me back down to the Lesbian & Gay Center from the shelter, it was finally like coming home."

"Queers without Money: They Are Everywhere. But We Refuse to See Them" by Amber Hollibaugh.

➤ John Aravosis

"How Did the T Get in LGBT?"

(2007), United States

Like an ever-expanding mushroom cloud of diversity, every few years America's gay leaders and activists welcome a new category of member to the community. Wikipedia walks us through our complicated family history:

"LGBT [lesbian, gay, bisexual and transgendered] or GLBT are the most common terms [to describe the gay community]. . . . When not inclusive of transgender people it is shortened to LGB. It may also include two additional Qs for queer and questioning (sometimes abbreviated with a question mark) (LGBTQ, LGBTQQ, GLBTQ2); a variant being LGBU, where U stands for 'unsure', an I for intersex (LGBTI), another T for transsexual (LGBTT), another T (or TS or the numeral 2) for two-spirited people, and an A for straight allies or asexual (LGBTA). At its fullest, then, it is some permutation of LGBTTTIQQA."

In simpler times we were all gay. But then the word "gay" started to mean "gay men" more than women, so we switched to the more inclusive "gay and lesbian." Bisexuals, who were only part-time gays, insisted that we add them too, so we did (not without some protest), and by the early 1990s we were the lesbian, gay and bisexual, or LGB community. Sometime in the late '90s, a few gay rights groups and activists started using a new acronym, LGBT—adding T for transgender/transsexual. And that's when today's trouble started.

America's gay community, or rather, its leadership, is apoplectic over the imminent passage of the first federal gay civil rights legislation, the Employment Non-Discrimination Act, or ENDA. ENDA would make it illegal for an employer to fire, or refuse to hire or promote, an otherwise qualified candidate simply because of their sexual orientation (gay, straight, lesbian or bisexual). (Contrary to popular belief, it is legal to fire someone for being gay under federal law and in 31 states.) You'd think this would be cause for celebration, but not so much.

ENDA was first introduced 30 years ago. In all that time, it only protected sexual orientation and never included gender identity. This year, that changed, and gender identity was added to the bill. Coincidentally, this year is also the first time that ENDA actually has a real chance of passing both the House and Senate—but only if gender identity isn't in the bill. So the bill's author, openly gay Rep. Barney Frank, D-Mass., dropped the transgendered from the bill, and all hell broke loose. Gay activists and 220 national and local gay rights groups angrily demanded that gender identity be put back in the bill, guaranteeing its defeat for years to come. Many of them, suddenly and conveniently, found all sorts of "flaws" with legislation that they had embraced the previous 29 years. They convinced House Democratic leaders to delay action on ENDA till later in October. They'd rather have no bill at all than pass one that didn't include the transgendered.

Then an odd thing happened. I started asking friends and colleagues, ranging from senior members of the gay political/journalistic establishment to apolitical friends around the country to the tens of thousands of daily readers of my blog, if they thought we should pass ENDA this year even without gender identity. Everyone felt bad about taking gender identity out of ENDA, everyone supported transgender rights, and everyone told me "pass it anyway."

Their main argument, which I support: practical politics. Civil rights legislation—hell, all legislation—is a series of compromises. You rarely get everything you want, nor do you get it all at once. Blacks, for example, won the right to vote in 1870. Women didn't get that same right until 1920. The Civil Rights Act of 1964 provided a large umbrella of rights based on race, religion, sex and national origin, but failed to mention gays or people with disabilities. People with disabilities were finally given specific rights under the Americans with Disabilities Act of 1990, but gays as a class have still to be granted a single civil right at the federal level. If we waited until society was ready to accept each and every member of the civil rights community before passing any civil rights legislation, we'd have no civil rights laws at all. Someone is always left behind, at least temporarily. It stinks, but it's the way it's always worked, and it's the way you win.

[. . .]

I have a sense that over the past decade the trans revolution was imposed on the gay community from outside, or at least above, and thus it never stuck with a large number of gays who weren't running national organizations, weren't activists, or weren't living in liberal gay enclaves like San Francisco and New York. Sure, many of the rest of us accepted de facto that transgendered people were members of the community, but only because our leaders kept telling us it was so. A lot of gays have been scratching their heads for 10 years trying to figure out what they have in common with transsexuals, or at the very least why transgendered people qualify as our siblings rather than our cousins. It's a fair question, but one we know we dare not ask. It is simply not p.c. in the gay community to question how and why the T got added on to the LGB, let alone ask what I as a gay man have in common with a man who wants to cut off his penis, surgically construct a vagina, and become a woman. I'm not passing judgment, I respect transgendered people and sympathize with their cause, but I simply don't get how I am just as closely related to a transsexual (who is often not gay) as I am to a lesbian (who is). Is it wrong for me to simply ask why?

[. . .]

I know firsthand that it's not safe in the gay community to ask questions about how the transgendered fit in. I also know that I am not alone in my questions, or my fear of asking them. While I've been taking abuse for my position, I've also been amazed by the number of phone calls, e-mails and people stopping me on the street here in Washington, both straight and gay, thanking me for asking the questions I did, for voicing the doubts that they share. (Not surprisingly, many of these expressions of solidarity have been off-the-record.)

[. . .]

Conservatives understand that cultural change is a long, gradual process of small but cumulatively deadly victories. Liberals want it all now. And that's why, in the **culture wars,** conservatives often win and we often lose. While conservatives spend years, if not decades, trying to convince Americans that certain judges are "activists," that gays "recruit" children, and that Democrats never saw an abortion they didn't like, we often come up with last-minute ideas and expect everyone to vote for them simply because we're right. Conservatives are happy with piecemeal victory, liberals with noble failure. We rarely make the necessary investment in convincing people that we're right because we consider it offensive to have to explain an obvious truth. When it comes time to pass legislation, too many liberals just expect good and virtuous bills to become law by magic, without the years of legwork necessary to secure a majority of the votes in Congress and the majority support of the people. We expect our congressional allies to fall on their swords for us when we've failed to create a culture in which it's safe for politicians to support our agenda and do the right thing. ENDA, introduced for the first time 30 years ago, is an exception to that rule. It took 30 years to get to the point where the Congress and the public are in favor of legislation banning job discrimination against gays.

[. . .]

That's why James Dobson, Tony Perkins and the men at the Concerned Women for America are so hell-bent on defeating ENDA. To the religious right, ENDA without gender identity isn't a weak, meaningless bill fraught with loopholes. Our enemies know that passage of any federal gay civil rights legislation is a legislative and cultural milestone that would make it that much easier for all of us—gays and lesbians, bisexuals and eventually even the transgendered—to realize all of our civil rights in our lifetime.

I'll take that half-a-loaf any day.

"How Did the T Get in LGBT?" by John Aravosis, 8 October 2007.

> ## Susan Stryker

"Why the T in LGBT Is Here to Stay"

(2007), United States

Pity poor John Aravosis, the gay rights crusader from AmericaBlog whose "How Did the T Get in LGBT?" essay, in reference to the controversy over gender identity protections in the pending Employment Non-Discrimination Act, was published on Salon a few days ago.

To hear Aravosis tell it, he and multitudes of like-minded gay souls have been sitting at the civil rights table for more than 30 years, waiting to be served. Now, after many years of blood, sweat, toil and tears, a feast in the form of federal protection against sexual orientation discrimination in the workplace has finally been prepared. Lips are being licked, chops smacked, saliva salivated, when—WTF!?!—a gaunt figure lurches through the door.

It is a transgender person, cupped hands extended, begging for food. Seems some-body on the guest list—maybe a lot of somebodies—let this stranger in off the streets without consulting everyone else beforehand, claiming he-she-it-or-whatever was a rela-tive of some sort. Suddenly, what was supposed to be a fabulous dinner party starts sur-really morphing into one of those OxFam fundraisers dramatizing third-world hunger whose sole function is to make the "haves" feel guilty for the plight of the "have-nots."

Maitre d' Barney Frank offers an elegant pretext for throwing the bum out. The estab-lishment's new management, Speaker Nancy Pelosi, is caught off-guard by the awkward turn of events, but deftly shuffles the hubbub into the wings and starts working the room, all smiles, to reassure the assembled guests that a somber and long-sought civil rights victory will be celebrated in short order.

Aravosis and those who share his me-first perspective are not so sure. Seeing half a loaf of civil rights protection on the table before them, and sensing that the soirée might come to a premature and unexpected denouement, they make a grab, elbows akimbo, for said truncated loaf. This is, after all, their party.

In my line of work—teaching history and theory of sexuality and gender—we've invented a polysyllabic technical term applicable to Aravosis & Co., which is homocentric, whose definition Aravosis supplies when he asserts, as he did in his recent essay, that gay is the term around which the GLBT universe revolves. By gay he means gay men like him-self, to which is added (in descending order of importance), lesbian, bisexual and trans-gender, beyond which lies an even more obscure region of poorly understood and infrequently observed identities.

Aravosis isn't questioning the place of the T in the GLBT batting order; he's just concerned with properly marking the distinction between "enough like me" and "too different from me" to merit inclusion in the categories with which he identifies.

[. . .]

Aravosis, not being one to mince words when it comes to mincing meat, wants to know what he, as a gay man, has "in common with a man who wants to cut off his penis, surgically construct a vagina, and become a woman." The answer is "gender." The last time I checked my dictionary, homosexuality had something to do with people of one gender tending to fall in love with people of the same gender. The meaning of homo-sexuality thus depends on the definition of gender. However much Aravosis might wish to cut the trannies away from the rest of his herd, thereby preserving a place free of gen-der trouble for just plain gay guys such as himself, that operation isn't conceptually pos-sible. Gender and sexuality are like two lines intersecting on a graph, and trying to make them parallel undoes the very notion of homo-, hetero- or bisexuality.

[. . .]

Without solid theoretical ground to stand on, Aravosis resorts to flights of rhetorical fancy in lieu of an argument against gender protections. He characterizes the more than 300 GLBT organizations nationwide now on record as supporting a gender-inclusive ENDA, which collectively speak on behalf of hundreds of thousands if not millions of people, as plotting something of a palace coup. They attempt, he claims, to force the gay movement—along with the country that is poised to embrace them—to crawl unwillingly into bed with a big bunch of tranny whatevers. Aravosis positions himself as a man giving voice to an oppressed silent majority, a majority too cowed by their fear of appearing "politically incorrect" to express their true feelings, in order to proclaim "that over the past decade the trans revolution was imposed on the gay community from outside, or at least above."

[. . .]

Transgender people have their own history of civil rights activism in the United States, one that is in fact older, though smaller and less consequential, than the gay civil rights movement. In 1895, a group of self-described "androgynes" in New York organized a "little club" called the Cercle Hermaphroditos, based on their self-perceived need "to unite for defense against the world's bitter persecution." Half a century later, at the same time some gay and lesbian people were forming the Mattachine Society and the Daughters of Bilitis, transgender people were forming the Society for Equality in Dress. When gay and lesbian people were fighting for social justice in the militant heyday of the 1960s, transgender people were conducting sit-in protests at Dewey's lunch counter in Philadelphia, fighting in the streets with cops from hell outside Compton's Cafeteria in San Francisco's Tenderloin, and mixing it up at Stonewall along with lots of other folks.

There was a vibrant history of transgender activism and movement building through the 1970s, when it suddenly became fashionable on the left to think of transgender people as antigay and antifeminist. Gay people were seen as freeing themselves from the straitjacket of psychopathology, while transgender people were clamoring to get into the Diagnostic and Statistical Manual of the American Psychiatric Association; feminists were seen as freeing themselves from the oppressiveness of patriarchal gender, while transgender people were perpetuating worn-out stereotypes of men and women. It's a familiar refrain, even now. Transgender arguments for access to appropriate healthcare, or observations that no one is ever free from being gendered, fell on deaf ears.

Until the early 1990s, that is, when a new generation of queer kids, the post–baby boomers whose political sensibilities had been forged in the context of the AIDS crisis, started coming into adulthood. They were receptive to transgender issues in a new way—and that more-inclusive understanding has been steadily building for nearly two decades.

Aravosis and those who agree with him think that the "trans revolution" has come from outside, or from above, the rank-and-file gay movement. No—it comes from below, and from within. The outrage that many people in the queer, trans, LGBT or whatever-you-want-to-call-it community feel over how a gender-inclusive ENDA has been torpedoed from within is directed at so-called leaders who are out of touch with social reality. It has to do with a generation of effort directed toward building an inclusive movement being pissed away by the clueless and the phobic. That's why every single GLBT organization of any size at the national and state levels—with the sole exception of the spineless Human Rights Campaign—has unequivocally come out in support of gender protections within ENDA, and has opposed the effort to pass legislation protecting only sexual orientation.

What happens in Congress in the weeks ahead on this historic issue is anybody's guess. I urge all of you who support the vision of an inclusive ENDA to contact your representatives in government and let your views be known.

"Why the T in LGBT Is Here to Stay," by Susan Stryker, 11 October 2007.

CHAPTER 8

Intersectionalities

Audre Lorde is known for describing herself as "Black, lesbian, feminist, mother, warrior, poet." For Lorde, these markers interacted and affected her life simultaneously.

Today, feminists, other activists, and those involved in the professions of law and social work use the term **intersectionality** to describe our complex awareness that we inhabit—and are inhabited by—multiple categories of identity and that our experience of several identities taken together may be emotionally, culturally, and materially different than the experience of any one particular identity category by itself. A white gay man, for instance, might feel oppressed by society's negative attitudes toward lesbian, gay, bisexual, and transgender (LGBT) people at the same time that he enjoys privilege connected to being a white man. Conversely, a black gay man may experience his queerness not only as a gay man but as a black man; that is, he negotiates two minoritized categories in U.S. culture. His experience, however, is not necessarily one of just "doubled" oppression; rather, he may experience both a dominant culture and an African American culture that code "gayness" as a white phenomenon, so his queerness may be invisible to many in his different communities. His experience of himself as a "black gay man" assumes complexities and nuances that are intrinsic to how this culture understands and constructs both race and sexuality. At the same time, intersectionality also allows us to see not only how multiple identities complicate our lives but also how the very aspects of our identity that are sources of oppression in one environment serve as sources of privilege in another. A butch lesbian, for example, may experience sexist and heterosexist oppression associated with her femaleness and her homosexuality; that same sexism may also transform her

Find Out More about Marlon Riggs's view of his documentary, *Tongues Untied,* in Chapter 12 of this text.

perceived masculinity into a kind of power (Gibson, Marinara, and Meem). And intersectionality is inescapable; we are all, as Lorde points out, influenced by a number of different (and sometimes even oppositional) aspects of our identities—whether we are conscious of it or not.

Let us consider a more specific example of how this may work. A New York court case known as *In the Matter of the Adoption of Evan* ruled that a nonbiological lesbian parent (Diane F.) could adopt the artificially inseminated child of her partner (Valerie C.). In reaching this ruling, the court found the adoption to be in the best interest of the child Evan and also cited other lesbian adoption decisions. The highest rationale seemed to be the validation of the nuclear family: "While noting financial and emotional reasons favoring the adoption, the court clearly viewed the legitimization of Evan's family as primary" (Rosenblum 98). The court officer made it clear that the class position of Evan's mothers was a strong supporting factor in his ruling: "Diane, age 39, is an Assistant Professor of Pediatrics and an attending physician at a respected teaching hospital. Valerie, age 40, holds a Ph.D. in psychology and teaches at a highly regarded private school" (Rosenblum 104). We may note the subjective inclusion of value judgments here: the hospital is "respected" and the school is "highly regarded." In contrast, let us consider the Mississippi case *White v. Thompson.* In this case, lesbian mother White lost custody of her children to her ex-husband's parents. Part of the stated reason for this ruling was that the court found White and her partner to be "unfit, morally and otherwise" to raise children because they were lesbians (Rosenblum 105). But a strong corroborating factor was social class. White worked in a convenience store, occasionally leaving the children unsupervised while they slept because she could not afford a babysitter. In addition, wrote the court, "[s]he and her lover . . . lived together in a trailer with their children" (qtd. in Rosenblum 105). Did Valerie and Diane win their adoption petition partly because of their class privilege? Did White and her partner lose custody partly because they were poor? Certainly the cases raise questions about the way social class affects individuals' ability to show what in our culture is considered to be a "stable family environment" and to marshal the resources necessary to wage a protracted legal battle. The intersection of lesbianism and social class—and geographical location—had strong bearing on the legal outcomes of both of these cases.

Feminist scholars Gwyn Kirk and Margo Okazawa-Rey define intersectionality as "an integrative perspective that emphasizes the intersection of several attributes, for example, gender, race, class, and nation" (G-3). This definition seems straightforward, but as the two cases described above indicate, the impact on the personal lives of individuals can be quite complicated and varied since the complex of attributes differs from person to person. Within the intersectional paradigm, a lesbian is never just a lesbian, a gay man is never just a gay man, and so forth. The focus on intersectionality as a tool for conceptualizing the nature of interlocking oppressions arose in the late 1980s, when legal scholar Kimberlé Crenshaw used the idea specifically "to articulate the intersection of racism and patriarchy" and "to describe the location of women of color both within overlapping systems of subordination and at the margins of feminism and anti-racism" ("Mapping" 1265). Crenshaw pointed out that these "problems of exclusion cannot be solved simply by including Black women within an already established analytical structure. Because the intersectional experience is greater than the sum of racism and sexism, any analysis that does not take intersectionality into account cannot sufficiently address the particular manner in which Black women are subordinated" ("Demarginalizing" 140). Here she seems to be rejecting then-popular "inclusion" theories, such as multiculturalism. She implies that thinking in terms of intersectionality means doing important critical work that thinking in terms of inclusion does not. In an inclusive environment, individuals are encouraged to represent categories (a black man speaks for black men, or a lesbian speaks for lesbians, for example); inclusivity, in other words, involves the habitual use of essentializing, even stereotypical, attributes.

> **Find Out More** in "The Friday Night Bunch" in the readings at the end of this chapter.

> **Find Out More:** For more on queer theory and identity, see Chapter 11.

Intersectional analyses, on the other hand, attempt to de-essentialize identity by assuming multiple and shifting identifications; they also pick up on queer theory's postmodern notion of strategic identity performance. We recall that the women of the Combahee River Collective articulated their experience of multiple oppressions and general invisibility as black lesbians in the 1970s [λ Chapter 4]. Crenshaw's work builds upon theirs, highlighting how the experience of sexuality must be understood as it intersects other identity experiences and positions. In that spirit, using examples from the law, literature, domestic violence discourse, and sensational public debate (the Anita Hill testimony at Clarence Thomas's confirmation hearing, for example), Crenshaw challenges antiracism and antisexism groups to rethink "the entire framework that has been used as a basis for translating 'women's experience' or 'the Black experience' into concrete policy demands" ("Demarginalizing" 140).

The introduction of intersectionality as a schema for approaching the study of queer oppression has developed as LGBT people have become increasingly aware of the ways in which attributes other than sexuality create intellectual, emotional, and material diversity. In the previous chapter on "Queer Diversities," we discussed specific instances of how LGBT people are tolerated or discriminated against for their specific "queerness" [λ Chapter 7]. Intersectionality allows us to see an even more complex picture of how individuals are included or excluded by considering their queerness in its relationship to other identity categories, such as race, class, age, and nationality. In fact, we have come to see that the very notion of LGBT community is problematic since every member of the groups represented by those letters has had experiences that might not be shared or experienced similarly by the others based on their complex and multiple identities.

Keeping in mind these rich sociocultural contexts is crucial if we are to understand what sexual behavior means to individuals and to groups and if we are to avoid the trap of "perverse presentism" [λ Introduction]. When collecting data about sexual behaviors in the 1940s and 1950s, Alfred Kinsey interviewed whites and blacks, rich and poor, but his analysis never focused on how sexuality is experienced differently across race and social class [λ Chapter 5]. Why are such omissions problematic? We know, for instance, that historically and contemporaneously, some people engage in homoerotic behavior without adopting gay or lesbian identities. It is also the case that, in some African American and Latino cultures, a man can penetrate another man in a sexual encounter and not consider himself—or be considered by others—gay. In those cultures, men are figured as *penetrators* and women or gay men as the *penetrated*. Such examples clearly demonstrate that how one understands his or her sexuality is deeply rooted in other social and cultural contexts. Understanding the intersection of those contexts provides us a richer sense of how sexuality, race, class, gender, nationality, and other identity markers function simultaneously. We need to develop this sense if we are to understand better how sex and sexuality function in people's lives.

The "Down Low" and
Applied Intersectional Theory

Near the beginning of his article "Some Queer Notions about Race," Samuel R. Delany admits that he has "always felt a difficulty in discussing the problems [of race and sexuality] together." Specifically, he feels that "[t]o speak of gay oppression in the context of racial oppression always seemed an embarrassment. Somehow it was to speak of the personal and the mechanics of desire in the face of material deprivation and vast political and imperialist and nationalist systemics" (201). While we respect Delany's point of view and observe that he complicates the argument as the article goes on, we believe that our discussion of the importance of intersectional analyses demonstrates that issues such as race and sexuality cannot easily be separated. Claiming that one issue (such as race) is about "material deprivation" whereas another (sexuality) is about the "mechanics of desire" fails to account for the many ways in which sexuality issues are entangled in economic issues, as well as the many ways in which racial issues are entangled in cultural notions about sex. Moreover, Delany's statement ignores the core feminist insight that "the personal is political" and that separating them elides the experiences of women and other "muted groups" (Ardener).

We can see the intersection of the personal and the political, and of race and sexuality, in representations of the phenomenon of the *down low,* a slang term describing what many (J. L. King, for instance) identify as a sexual phenomenon among some black men. The popular media tell us that these men form secretive groups whose purpose is providing opportunities to have clandestine sexual encounters with one another. The idea has been so intriguing to the American public that it became a topic on *The Oprah Winfrey Show* and *Law and Order: Special Victims Unit.* Between February and December 2001, the down low was the subject of feature stories in newspapers all over the country and in magazines such as *VIBE, Essence,* and *Jet.* Most of these stories portrayed black women as the unknowing victims of black men engaging in sexual behavior with one another and connected the down low

Figure 8.1 Keith Boykin (left)

with the spread of HIV/AIDS to these straight black women. Gay author and activist Keith Boykin, who doubts the truth of much "down low" mythology, writes, "The down low fit perfectly into larger cultural dynamics because it confirmed stereotypical values that many of us already believed. For some whites, it confirmed their hypersexualized perception of black people, and for some blacks it confirmed their hypersexualized perception of gay men. Given society's stereotypical view of black men combined with societal beliefs about homosexuality, the story became more believable because it vilified a group of people we did not understand and many of us did not want to know" (151).

Boykin's discussion is intersectional in that it deploys an analysis of race, sexuality, social class, and gender dynamics to help us understand why a phenomenon such as the down low so fully captured the American imagination. The enormous interest in the idea of black men meeting regularly to engage in sexual acts—and the idea that such behavior was somehow predatory and that it threatened the precarious hold many believed the United States had on the spread of HIV/AIDS—confirmed myths about black men that have been part of the public consciousness in this country since slavery. It also helped confirm what many people believed about gay men—namely, that sexually insatiable homosexual men spread disease through their behavior, which constitutes a sin punishable by painful death. What's more, stories about families affected by men on the down low confirmed what many have come to believe about heterosexual relationships by portraying women as the unwitting victims of men's sexual promiscuity. A single-issue analysis of media hype around the down low might have encouraged LGBT people to "adopt" the men portrayed in the coverage as gay men oppressed by a society that provides few outlets for the more open expression of their sexuality and pushes them into heterosexual relationships. And the statistics delivered by the Centers for Disease Control and Prevention (CDC), which seemed to indicate that more black women were getting AIDS than at any other point in the history of the disease, appeared to confirm the existence of a covert down low. However, Boykin points out that the CDC reported 4,000 *fewer* new cases of AIDS among blacks in 2001 than in 1991, while the *percentage* of AIDS cases among black women rose because the number of AIDS cases among white women decreased sharply during that same period (167). A misreading of the statistics, particularly the percentages, seemed to indicate a widespread "down low" phenomenon, while a closer look at the numbers challenged this assumption.

J. L. King, who is a primary focus of Boykin's criticism, as well as other men interviewed for stories on the down low, disagree with Boykin's claim that "America's recent obsession with the down low is not about the truth" (5), but it seems obvious that whether or not the cultural phenomenon exists, Boykin's point about the reasons for its prominence in the collective American psyche makes some sense. After all, as the discussion of Kinsey in Chapter 5 illustrates, thinking about the private sexual lives of our neighbors titillates many Americans. What's more, on a very real level, confirmation of our stereotypes is comforting. When we examine the issue intersectionally—that is, when we consider how not only queerness but also race are understood and constructed in American society—we can easily see how panic about the "down low" arises. Many in the United States fear not only queer sexualities but also people of color; the combination of queerness and blackness, coupled with basic assumptions of male aggressiveness, led to a scenario in which it was easy to imagine covert black gay male predators infecting women at an alarming rate. The reality, of course, is not nearly so simple.

Women, Class, and Internationality

Other important sexuality issues, particularly those involving the locations of women and lesbians, are best understood through intersectional analyses. In "Spirit and Passion," Carmen Vazquez argues that many gay rights strategies do not sufficiently or critically take into account "those of us who happen to be female, of color, working-class, or poor" (697). For Vazquez, political strategies that argue that gays and lesbians should be "mainstreamed" and given exactly the same rights as heterosexuals fail to recognize the economic injustices that many women throughout the world already face. Put another way, she asks us to reconsider the "mainstream" and whether or not it is worth joining. Gays, for instance, may seek the right to marry, but if the right to marry occurs in a context in which women are at a persistent economic disadvantage to men, then how do lesbians materially benefit from the right to marry? Marriage, too,

Figure 8.2   Vazquez (right)

is a double-edged sword since in many countries, it is *the* vehicle of women's social and economic disempowerment.

The importance of considering such issues intersectionally becomes clear when examining marriage in an international context. In Bulgaria, for example, marriage is an economic imperative for women. A young woman typically goes directly from her parents' house to her husband's, never living on her own. This life trajectory militates against the development of lesbian relationships and cultures. Monika Pisankaneva writes that Bulgarian women "encounter more difficulties than men in starting a career; they are driven to low-rank professions like teachers, secretaries, nurses or shop-assistants; these 'female' professions are so poorly paid that no one could live independently earning so little" (139). Pisankaneva acknowledges that "young lesbians are more motivated than heterosexual women to leave their homes" but may be hampered in finding work if they appear too masculine. Thus, "[i]n long-term lesbian relationships it is usually the more feminine partner who becomes the breadwinner" while "[m]asculine-looking

Find Out More in Kathy Y. Wilson's "Just a Closer Walk with Thee" in the readings at the end of this chapter.

women usually find low-paid jobs such as shop assistants, construction or service workers" (139). This pattern resembles some typical butch-femme relationships in the United States in the 1950s, where the femme (because she enacted gender-normative female behavior) often functioned as the primary family wage earner (Kennedy and Davis). In both cases, the "employable" woman was invisible *as* a lesbian and merely put up with the economic deprivations associated with femaleness in her culture.

Find Out More in Seo Dong-Jin's "Mapping the Vicissitudes of Homosexual Identities in South Korea" in the readings at the end of this chapter.

Both Pisankaneva and Kennedy and Davis link butch-femme gender presentation to nonelite class positioning. Alison Murray's analysis of Indonesian lesbian life points out that "[t]here is no lesbian 'community' in Jakarta, since class overdetermines both gender and sexuality" (166). At the same time, "lower class lesbians" are associated with "butch-femme roles, promiscuity, and insalubrious nightlife" (175). Murray interprets the correlation of lower social class with more rigid gender roles as an indicator of "outness": "For the lower class without privileges to lose, overt signifiers of 'deviance' within a subcultural street milieu suggest a source of resistance to power" (166). Here again, we see that it is impossible to understand what it means to be lesbian in Indonesia without an intersectional analysis that includes gender and class in addition to sexuality.

We must not assume, however, that only women are restricted by cultural norms and economic placement from easy access to a queer life. Shivananda Khan describes the relationship between "high levels of sexual repression" and "urgent sexual release" for men in India. Sexual expression, writes Khan, must take place in a context of absolute lack of privacy. A man in New Delhi commented, "Privacy? What privacy? I share a room with my three older brothers, and I have had sex with all of them. The other room is where my parents and grandparents sleep. There is no lock on the door. In the hallway, my uncle and aunt sleep. It's like this everywhere in India" (Khan 110). Similarly, Tomás Almaguer writes that "[t]he constraints of family life often prevent homosexual Mexican men from securing unrestricted freedom to stay out late at night, to move out of their family's home before marriage, or to take an apartment with a male lover. Thus their opportunities to make homosexual contacts in other than anonymous locations, such as the balconies of movie theaters or certain parks, are severely constrained" (260). These examples highlight customs that work against male independence in ways that parallel the traditional cloistering of women within family space. In some cultures, familial identifications override other identity categories. In China, as Wah-Shan Chou argues, the traditional culture "simply refuses to classify people into homo or hetero because individuals (both women and men, homo or heterosexually inclined ones) are first and foremost members of the family and wider society"

(34). Both parents and children internalize this way of being in the world. Thus, if a child "comes out" as a *tongzhi* (homosexual), parents feel "the shame of losing face for having a deviant child who does not get married." The young person, too, feels pain because "[i]n a society where filial piety is given the utmost importance in defining a person, hurting one's parents can be the most terrible thing for a *tongzhi* to experience" (34). Here the intersection of nonendorsed sexuality and a powerful family-centric social organization works against individual agency. This pattern may obtain even in a space of relative freedom such as the United States, where individualism is a central value. Ann Allen Shockley, for instance, writes of the fictional Roz, a black woman who brings her white lover Marge "Home to Meet the Folks." Roz's mother is surprised and disappointed, but her brother and his wife are overtly hostile; they castigate Roz not only for being a lesbian but for being a race traitor.

The idea of homosexuality making one a traitor to one's race or nation is not new. In Russia after the 1917 revolution, the Bolshevik state considered homosexuality a "degenerate disease of the terminally bourgeois" and urged prominent gay men to marry women or leave the country. According to Laurie Essig, "Under the Soviets, . . . [h]omosexuality was a crime not just against 'nature' but against society. Homosexual acts were treasonous in the (dis)utopia of the Workers' State" (5). Similarly, in Cuba during the 1960s (and to some extent still today), homosexuals were defined as second-class citizens. They were excluded from membership in the Communist Party, which in itself guaranteed an inability to rise in the social order. Fidel Castro reportedly refused to believe that any homosexual could be "a true Revolutionary, a true Communist militant" (Lockwood 124). Ian Lumsden feels that the real sin was never homosexuality per se but rather male resistance to the powerful cult of *machismo*, or hypermasculinity. The Cuban state seems to have worried less about bourgeois corruption than about effeminacy. In Cuba, Lumsden writes, "[s]exual orientation is inferred from gender identity rather than vice versa, as tends to be the case in North America" (132). Therefore, a man who exhibits even the slightest "effeminate" behavior (crossing one leg at the knee or gesturing expressively while talking) is assumed to be homosexual. Here again, we see how an intersectional analysis reveals linkages among sexuality, gender, cultural and social organization, and citizenship.

Tools for Intersectional Analysis

The concept of intersectionality is often difficult to grasp until we think simultaneously—and critically—about *our own* multiple identities. When we consider our personal traits and characteristics in relation to one another, in relation to varying cultural contexts in which those identities occur, and in relation to changes in those identities over time, we can understand how the concept of intersectionality applies to our own lives. Scholars have invented several different diagrams and exercises designed to enhance our understanding of intersectionality. These diagrams offer us a picture of how identities, socio-cultural contexts, and political realities intersect.

A popular self-classification tool from the feminist consciousness-raising movement of the 1970s (with some modifications by us) asks its users to position themselves within a hierarchical model according to their multiple identifications and their experience of privilege or oppression associated with each (see Figure 8.3).

Most Relative Privilege	Male	Middle class	Heterosexual	White	Young	Able-bodied	Thin	Christian	Butch
Less Relative Privilege	Female	Working class	Lesbian, gay	Of color	Middle-aged	Differently abled	Larger	Religion other than Christian	Femme
Least Relative Privilege	Gender not easily pegged as female or male	Poor	Bisexual, transgender		Old	Disabled	Fat		

Figure 8.3   Relative privilege and oppression

Users of this tool mark characteristics of their own identities, then think about them in terms of the privilege or oppression they experience in relation to those identifications. As you may notice, when you try this exercise for yourself, the outcome is more complicated than you might expect. For instance, someone who performs the intersectional identification female, lesbian, of color, and butch might find that the butch identification, when combined with other factors, does not necessarily translate into a greater degree of privilege than the femme, as the table indicates it should.

In "Thinking Sex: Notes for a Radical Theory of the Politics of Sexuality," Gayle Rubin observes that "the realm of sexuality . . . has its own internal politics, inequities, and modes of oppression" (4). Rubin describes a "sex hierarchy" composed of an inner "charmed circle" and the "outer limits." She characterizes the charmed circle as comprising "normal, natural, healthy, holy" sex and the outer circle as "abnormal, unnatural, sick, sinful" sex (14) (see Figure 8.4).

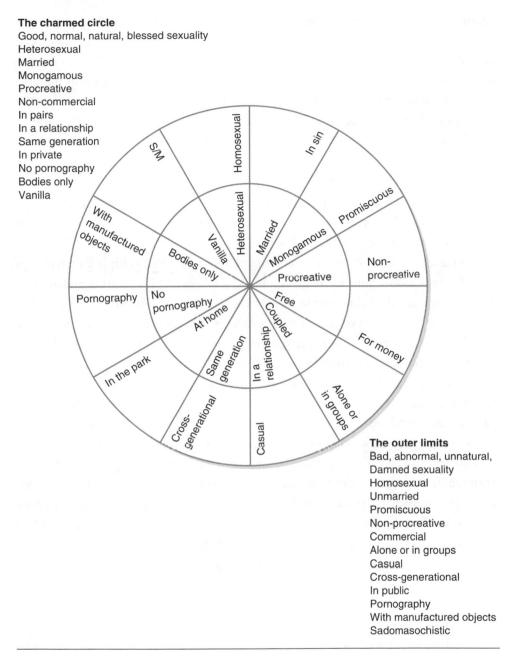

The charmed circle
Good, normal, natural, blessed sexuality
Heterosexual
Married
Monogamous
Procreative
Non-commercial
In pairs
In a relationship
Same generation
In private
No pornography
Bodies only
Vanilla

The outer limits
Bad, abnormal, unnatural,
Damned sexuality
Homosexual
Unmarried
Promiscuous
Non-procreative
Commercial
Alone or in groups
Casual
Cross-generational
In public
Pornography
With manufactured objects
Sadomasochistic

Figure 8.4   Gayle Rubin's charmed circle

Rubin observes that "[t]his kind of sexual morality . . . grants virtue to the dominant groups, and relegates vice to the underprivileged." This particular way of doing intersectionality simultaneously analyzes political/legal and moral usage; we may recall the value judgments that lay behind the New York and Mississippi adoption/custody decisions discussed earlier in this chapter. Rubin makes the point that this way of figuring sexuality resembles what she calls "ideologies of racism" (15), and if you examine Rubin's "Charmed Circle" carefully, you will see how it recognizes also ideologies of classism in our society. Monogamous married heterosexual sex at home is far closer to the center of the circle as opposed to sex "for money" or in public. What assumptions are made here? Certainly, the economic stability of married home life is privileged over alternative forms of sexual expression, and the close connection of sexuality with economic stability (you should have sex in the privacy of your own home) stigmatizes those who cannot afford such a luxury as privacy or who need to supplement low incomes through sex work. As such, sexuality and class intersect to promote certain kinds of lives and intimacies and to disparage others.

Intersectional analyses provide a valuable sense of how multiple constructs of identity, community, and ideology combine to reinforce social norms and squelch dissent. Patricia Hill Collins, writing in *Black Sexual Politics,* argues that "[r]acism and heterosexism . . . share a common set of practices that are designed to discipline the population into accepting the status quo" (96). For example, both racism and heterosexism draw boundaries around whom it is appropriate to love and be intimate with, and they reinforce the norm (at least in the West) as predominantly white and heterosexual. Indeed, crossing racial lines in love is still culturally discouraged in many parts of the world—whether those relationships are hetero- or homoerotic. And so too is crossing generational boundaries. Age intersects sexuality in powerful ways, as we demonstrated with the example of ancient Greek pederasty and the contrasting example of the contemporary North American Man/Boy Love Association (NAMBLA). But in many other ways, we draw boundaries around age and sexuality; we are often disturbed by older men pursuing younger adult women, while an older woman/younger man coupling doesn't seem as challenging or odd. Why is this so? At the same time, in many queer communities, pairings of older and younger people are not uncommon, particularly as an older individual can assist a younger individual financially and in "getting a start" in adulthood. Examining such dynamics offers us a richer sense of how people organize—and are allowed to imagine—their lives.

Thinking about race, gender, class, age, and sexuality simultaneously shows us how ideologies based on them serve particular political interests and agendas. Understanding these matrices provides us a way to analyze—and critique—interlocking oppressions. In the following chapters, we will continue to represent queerness as it intersects a variety of other significant markers of identity, community, and ideology. Doing so not only will allow us to represent queerness with the complexity it deserves but will also show us how many different members of LGBT communities throughout the world construct their identities, form communities, and critique the sociocultural pressures that frequently oppress them.

QUESTIONS FOR DISCUSSION

1. Intersectional analyses offer us ways to understand queerness in particular and sexuality in general as they are embedded in other sociocultural and political contexts. Look back at some of the ways in which we, the authors of this textbook, have represented queerness in earlier chapters. Where might some of our representations, in specific cases, have become all the richer with additional intersectional analysis? Try your hand at rewriting some of our examples with that added emphasis.

2. Some critics have argued that intersectional analyses provide such complex understandings of particular experiences and situations that it is difficult to know, in the face of such specificity, how to proceed politically. That is, if situations are so complex, then how can we argue for and achieve broad political change? How might you address such a criticism? What are the ways in which intersectional analyses might actually support political change?

3. Consider the three readings included at the end of this chapter: Wilson's "Just a Closer Walk with Thee," Nichols's "The Friday Night Bunch," and Seo's "Mapping the Vicissitudes of Homosexual Identities in South Korea." On the surface, they may seem to be so different from each other that they have nothing in common. When you look at them together, what connections do you perceive among them? How does each accomplish an intersectional analysis?

REFERENCES AND FURTHER READING

"About Audre Lorde." *The Audre Lorde Project Inc.* 19 July 2008 <http://www.alp.org/about/audre>.

Almaguer, Tomás. "Chicano Men: A Cartography of Homosexual Identity and Behavior." *The Lesbian and Gay Studies Reader.* Eds. H. Abelove, M. Barale, and D. Halperin. New York: Routledge, 1993. 255–73.

Ardener, Shirley, ed. *Perceiving Women.* London: Malaby Press, 1975.

Boykin, Keith. *Beyond the Down Low.* New York: Carroll & Graf, 2005.

Chou, Wah-Shan. "Homosexuality and the Cultural Politics of *Tongzhi* in Chinese Societies." *Gay and Lesbian Asia: Culture, Identity, Community.* Eds. G. Sullivan and P. Jackson. Binghamton, NY: Harrington Park Press, 2001. 27–46.

Collins, Patricia Hill. *Black Sexual Politics: African Americans, Gender, and the New Racism.* New York: Routledge, 2005.

Crenshaw, Kimberlé. "Demarginalizing the Intersection of Race and Sex: A Black Feminist Critique of Antidiscrimination Doctrine, Feminist Theory and Antiracist Politics." *The University of Chicago Legal Forum* (1989): 139–67.

———. "Mapping the Margins: Intersectionality, Identity Politics, and Violence against Women of Color." *Stanford Law Review* 43 (July 1991): 1241–99.

Delany, Samuel R. "Some Queer Notions about Race." *Queer Cultures.* Eds. D. Carlin and J. DiGrazia. Upper Saddle River, NJ: Pearson/Prentice Hall, 2004. 199–219.

Essig, Laurie. *Queer in Russia: A Story of Sex, Self, and the Other.* Durham, NC: Duke UP, 1999.

Fellows, Will. *Farm Boys: Lives of Gay Men from the Rural Midwest.* Madison: U of Wisconsin P, 1998.

Gibson, Michelle, Martha Marinara, and Deborah T. Meem. "Bi, Butch, and Bar Dyke: Pedagogical Performances of Class, Gender, and Sexuality." *College Composition and Communication* 52.1 (2000): 69–95.

Kennedy, Elizabeth Lapovsky, and Madeline Davis. "Living Arrangements and the Organization of Domestic Life." *Boots of Leather, Slippers of Gold: The History of a Lesbian Community.* New York: Routledge, 1993. 283–93.

Khan, Shivananda. "Culture, Sexualities, and Identities: Men Who Have Sex with Men in India." *Gay and Lesbian Asia: Culture, Identity, Community.* Eds. G. Sullivan and P. Jackson. Binghamton, NY: Harrington Park Press, 2001. 99–115.

King, J. L. *On the Down Low: A Journey into the Lives of "Straight" Black Men Who Sleep with Men.* New York: Broadway, 2004.

Kirk, Gwyn, and Margo Okazawa-Rey. *Women's Lives: Multicultural Perspectives.* New York: McGraw-Hill, 2000.

Lockwood, Lee. *Castro's Cuba, Cuba's Fidel.* New York: Macmillan, 1967.

Lumsden, Ian. *Machos, Maricones, and Gays: Cuba and Homosexuality.* Philadelphia: Temple UP, 1996.

Murray, Alison J. "Let Them Take Ecstasy: Class and Jakarta Lesbians." *Gay and Lesbian Asia: Culture, Identity, Community.* Eds. G. Sullivan and P. Jackson. Binghamton, NY: Harrington Park Press, 2001. 165–84.

Nichols, Jean Brashear. "The Friday Night Bunch: A Lesbian Community in West Texas." *Journal of Lesbian Studies* 9 (2005): 73–80.

Pisankaneva, Monika. "Reflections on Butch-Femme and the Emerging Lesbian Community in Bulgaria." *Femme/Butch: New Considerations of the Way We Want to Go.* Eds. M. Gibson and D. Meem. Binghamton, NY: Harrington Park Press, 2002. 135–44.

Rosenblum, Darren. "Queer Intersectionality and the Failure of Recent Lesbian and Gay 'Victories.'" *Law & Sexuality* 4 (1994): 83–122.

Rubin, Gayle. "Thinking Sex: Notes for a Radical Theory of the Politics of Sexuality." *The Lesbian and Gay Studies Reader.* Eds. H. Abelove, M. Barale, and D. Halperin. New York: Routledge, 1993. 3–44.

Seo, Dong-Jin. "Mapping the Vicissitudes of Homosexual Identities in South Korea." *Gay and Lesbian Asia: Culture, Identity, Community.* Eds. G. Sullivan and P. Jackson. Binghamton, NY: Harrington Park Press, 2001. 65–79.

Shockley, Ann Allen. "Home to Meet the Folks." *The Black and White of It.* Weatherby Lake, MO: Naiad, 1980. 51–59.

Vazquez, Carmen. "Spirit and Passion." *Queer Cultures.* Eds. D. Carlin and J. DiGrazia. Upper Saddle River, NJ: Pearson/Prentice Hall, 2004. 689–98.

Wilson, Kathy Y. "Just a Closer Walk with Thee." *Cincinnati Magazine* (July 2008). 21 November 2008. <http://www.cincinnatimagazine.com/article.aspx?id=54522>.

READINGS

➢ **Kathy Y. Wilson**
"Just a Closer Walk with Thee"
(2008), United States

Call her a radical. Call her an upstart. Call her a lesbian BaptiMethoCostal. Just don't call Pastor Lesley E. Jones's Truth & Destiny Covenant Ministries a gay church.

The chrome-studded motorcycle should be a dead giveaway. So should the lovers' casual touch during service. But at first blush, little about Truth & Destiny Covenant Ministries in Northside is easily reconcilable or recognizable if yours is a—let's get this out of the way right now—homophobic, fire-and-brimstone church experience.

Not the motorcycle out front on warm Sundays driven there by a black lesbian; not the same-gender couples who share Bibles and blithely brush against one another like intimates; not the teenagers who run the aisles with abandon, dancing and shouting in Pentecostal fits of Holy Spirit calisthenics. And certainly not the Rev. Lesley E. Jones, the lesbian pastor who cofounded Truth & Destiny Covenant Ministries (TDCM) in 2003. Adorned in a cassock and square-toed patent leather loafers, Jones sings, sweats, prays, shouts, and leads her congregation of 100-plus members through to salvation.

Worship at TDCM is different from worship at mainline white churches; different from worship at many black churches, too. Rest assured, at Truth & Destiny, no one will ever use the lame analogy about God creating "Adam and Eve, not Adam and Steve." If you're gay or lesbian, you will not be preached about in the third person; you won't be told to change your ways or risk eternal damnation. All gender identities, races, sexual orientations, and even faiths are embraced at TDCM. Jones's business card states the mission clearly: "Preaching the Radically Inclusive Gospel." The banner hanging outside above the door trumpets a similar message: "Boldly Proclaiming God's Love For All People."

TDCM exists despite, and maybe even because of, the homophobia and misogyny ensconced in some segments of the black church, whether Baptist, Pentecostal, Episcopal, or Methodist, and it's on its way to being a groundbreaking model of "radically inclusive" worship for congregations struggling to adopt more progressive practices. This small church is gearing up for nothing short of a revolution. And Reverend Jones, a 41-year-old lesbian mother who dedicated her life to Christ during childbirth—*she shall lead them.*

"You wanna know how to stay on the battlefield?" Reverend Jones asks rhetorically, surveying her congregation. "Listen to a good soldier. Don't just study the Bible, study the people of God."

Her robe is cinched at the waist by a wide purple sash. She's skulking across the pulpit, wiping her brow and gripping the microphone. Directly behind her, seven small glass block windows form a cross in the wall. To the left, there's a full drum kit. A center aisle leads directly to the pulpit. The church is casual, with worshipers wearing jeans, shorts, and sneakers and walking around during songs, sermons, and passages of personal testimony. They call out "Pastor Lesley" while she's preaching or making announcements. In turn, she is relaxed, confident, straightforward. Of average height and build, she is a brown-skinned woman with thick, shoulder-length black hair that she wears tied back until, in a moment of particular fire and fervor, she unleashes it for effect.

It's the first Sunday in April and the small, spare church is nearly full. There are teenagers, elderly women from the neighborhood, lesbian couples, and several single men all sitting on straight-back chairs. The congregants are rapt and responsive. Some fidget with Holy Spirit tics—rocking, pushing to the edges of their seats, hands flapping mid-air. They are filled with religious energy waiting to be uncorked by the right scripture, the perfect intonation, the well-placed hymn.

"I can tell who's saved and who's carnal-minded," she says.

"C'mooon, pastor," someone pleads.

"And just because you're carnal-minded doesn't mean you're not saved. It means you're nominal . . ."

"*Huh!*" someone hiccups in a James Brown punctuation.

". . . you're doing just enough," Jones finishes.

Then Jones mixes the sin of Saturday night with the redemption of Sunday morning. "Some of y'all need to git *loooow*!" she exhorts, dramatically stomping back to the corner of the pulpit and squatting low to the ground. It's the lyric from a strip club anthem, the song directed at strippers dancing for cash, but she's flipped it into an admonition for the heaven-bound: *Get low to avoid being beaten down by life.*

Then Jones redirects the sermon. She's responding to the way some people—Christian folks—gossip about TDCM. She's talking about the way the community-at-large whispers that her church is "The Gay Church."

"I keep telling you this ain't a *gay* thing. It's a *God* thing," Jones says. Therein lies the mission and founding tenet of Truth & Destiny Covenant Ministries: Everyone is welcome here. The fact that outsiders translate that as "gay church" is a testament to how unwelcome gay and lesbian Christians feel in other churches.

"Some churches make you fill out applications," Jones points out to her congregation. "They want to know your income and they make you show a W-2, ask you about your roommate," she says, pantomiming air quotes when she says *roommate*. "'Well, how many bedrooms you got?'"

This mockery of other, less tolerant congregations draws titters. "God is creating a movement of the radically inclusive," she tells them. "When we go out into the world we need to be careful that we're teaching people not what we *think* is right, but what we *know* is right. And that is that God has always been radically inclusive."

Jones's proclamation is the antidote to long-held beliefs among some Christians about what constitutes abomination (homosexuality); who goes to hell for it (homosexuals); and even who is welcome in the church (homosexuals generally aren't, unless they are choir members or musicians). Reconciling faith and sexuality for blacks is no more difficult than it is for white believers. However, blackness can cloud and confound that reconciliation. Some black Christians believe homosexuality is an "attack" on the black family; some feel the fight for gay rights distracts from racial equality; others believe homosexuality is just plain wrong, or it's "the white man's problem." Conversely, progressive black theologians say all discriminatory thought and practice is wrong, and they call for the black church to return to its role as the center of unbiased social and faith works.

Meeting Jones and visiting her church blurs all the right/wrong/heaven/hell absolutes, the judgment, theory, and theology. A conversation with her could be subtitled "How To Reconcile Faith and Sexuality For Bigoted Dummies." That's what her church is about.

But don't call it "the Gay Church."

"Pastoring can take a toll on your relationship, especially if you're pastoring alone," says Jones. We're sitting in the cold and cramped supply room that doubles as the church office. She's dressed casually in a gray T-shirt, loafers, and slacks with a faint pinstripe. In person she is warm and forthcoming, even-keeled and funny. But her pulpit and her personal life have commingled with difficulty. She explains that she and her partner of nine years, Rosa Jones, the woman with whom she founded TDCM, separated in December. (They are now in the process of reconciling.)

"Planning a church is like any other business," Jones says. "The first five years you work to build." And in building her church, she says, "one of the things I failed at was publicly acknowledging my spouse."

In that way, Jones isn't so different from many mainline pastors who struggle to balance their public and private lives. Except that most pastors don't have to put so much energy into explaining that what they do is, indeed, the Lord's work. "Everybody here is not lesbian, gay, bisexual, trans, questioning, or queer," she says. "There are straight folks who are here because the gospel is taught and they believe in inclusion. They also believe in the social justice [work] we do here. We take care of the poor, the sick—and that attracts a lot of people. We purposely don't wave a [gay] pride flag."

Further, in the sanctuary there's no picture of Christ—He of the flowing dark hair, sandals, and robes who could double as a Grateful Dead fan. Why? "We can't put Jesus up on the wall until we can find a rainbow Jesus of every hue, image, and nationality," Jones says. "That white male dogma? That's not the Jesus I know."

Searching for that Jesus, six years ago Jones and Rosa gathered 20 friends for dinner at their home. "What would your church look like?" the two women asked. Then they scribbled notes on newsprint they hung around the room.

"They wanted a place where their family could be celebrated," Jones says. "A place where youth and children were valued, a variety in the worship style—a blend of liturgical and freestyle. They wanted a multi-ethnic and multi-racial [church] . . . a place where people valued people. I remember this one," she recalls. "They said, 'If I'm not at church, I want someone to miss me.'"

Despite the passion and specificity of those worship wishes, after dinner the pages were rolled up and slid beneath the bed. Jones attended several racially diverse, gay-friendly congregations in Cincinnati, but never felt satisfied. She hungered for something more deeply rooted in the black church tradition of bombast and pageantry. After three years and deep consultation with the Rev. Darlene Franklin, pastor of Full Truth Ministries in Detroit, Michigan's oldest predominantly black radically inclusive congregation, and with the Rev. Bonnie Daniel, now retired from New Spirit Metropolitan Community Church in Northside, Jones took the next step. She and Rosa started TDCM in 2003 as "a place to worship in the full truth of our life that also met our spiritual needs."

"I didn't one day plant myself and just say, 'I'm gonna pastor me a church,'" Jones jokes. She started her career as a teacher—first in Cincinnati Public Schools and then at Marva Collins Preparatory School in Silverton. Fans of 1320 AM WCVG, a now-defunct gospel station, may remember her; she was the station's morning show announcer and sales manager from 1995 to 2000. She also worked as a program director at the YMCA. In 2000 she joined the Hamilton County Human Relations Commission, ultimately ascending to director, a post she held until 2006. Jones has a bachelor's degree in social sciences from Miami University and certificates in ministry and pastoral counseling from Light University, an online pastoral program, but she is also working on a certificate of ministry from New York Theological Seminary, from which she intends to ultimately receive a master's degree in divinity. When people ask about her credentials, she likes to say, "I got a SBG degree—Sent By God!"

A self-described "BaptiMethoCostal," Jones was born in North Carolina but raised off and on in Middletown, where she graduated from Middletown High School. Her father is Baptist, her mother Methodist, and one of her grandmothers was a Pentecostal evangelist. She's the only child of her parents' marriage, but has two teenaged adopted stepbrothers. Coming out to her family was "a challenge," she says; she didn't do it until she was 33. She knew she was gay as a teenager. But she was also sexually curious, and she got pregnant at 19 as a freshman at Kentucky State University. The birth of her son Blake, now a student at Cincinnati State, was her "coming to know Jesus experience," as she calls it.

"I really prayed for a son," she says. "I was reading the story of Hannah and she prayed for a son [Samuel], so I prayed that prayer. It was during a time when I was really being beaten down in the church."

The judgment leveled at her by church members made Jones more spiritually determined. In 1988, when she turned 21, she rededicated her life to Jesus Christ. However, revealing her sexuality to her family didn't come so easily. When she did finally come out to her mother, she did it in a letter. With a letter, she says, "I could say what I needed to say without being interrupted." Her mother's initial reaction was to declare that she was going to have her daughter "kidnapped and deprogrammed." Jones accepted it as an emotional and visceral response to life-altering news. "Although my mother has struggled with who I am, she's come to church, she's participated," she says. Her mother's way of letting Jones know that she was OK with her daughter's sexuality was by bringing Jones's brothers to church, too. "We have to realize our parents are grieving," she says. "They're coming out, too."

Jones, however, has less patience for the myopia of some black ministers and their churches. "They're so comfortable in their chauvinism, [and] in their homophobia," she says. "Misogyny and homophobia [are] prevalent in ministry across the board. They're comfortable with the 'Don't ask/Don't tell' policy."

Jones wants to be part of changing that. She wants her church to make people stand up and take notice. "We're a revolutionary concept," she says. "I believe it's in process."

The chasm between traditional black churches and their gay and lesbian brethren is part of the complicated history of black Christianity in America.

Theologian and author Kelly Brown Douglas, the Elizabeth Connolly Todd Distinguished Professor of Religion at Goucher College in Baltimore, Maryland, knows the subject well. In 1985, Douglas was the first black woman—and only the fifth nationwide—ordained an Episcopal priest in the Southern Ohio Diocese. She is straight, but the Dayton native's path was sometimes made arduous by a black male bishop who "stopped my ordination a few times for no other reason than that I was a woman," she says. She notes that, paradoxically, early black Christians incorporated the oppression, repression, and bigotry they saw in white churches into their own.

"Most black people became Christian during the Great Awakenings, the Evangelical revivals of the late 1700s and the early 1800s," Douglas says. In the Evangelical view, "You had to overcome the passion of the body. Paul's edict in Corinthians—it's better to marry than to burn with passion—speaks to that."

In 1999, Douglas published *Sexuality and the Black Church: A Womanist Perspective,* a seminal text outlining the far-reaching roots of homophobia and sexism throughout the black faith community. "We must take into account how black people have been caricatured in this country and that is sexualized," she says. "To be 'normal sexually' is to abide by the norms and standards of white patriarchal narratives—however they do it." And that includes using religion as a weapon of oppression.

"The black church's own history is ironic," she says. "They weren't allowed to be who they are and now they're not allowing [gay and lesbian] people to be who they are."

However, the black church clearly is not a monolith. "The 'capital C' black Church is made up of multitudinous, disparate churches, diverse by congregational size," she explains. "You can have megachurches and storefronts; you can have very sedate and very rapturous. It is rural, suburban, urban, AME, CME. What makes black churches part of the black Church is what roots them to history."

The Rev. Damon Lynch Jr., the brazenly progressive 69-year-old pastor of New Jerusalem Baptist Church in Carthage, a 2,200-member "megachurch," is one such minister rooted to history. He says that he was galvanized to support and protect gay rights by the historical events that unfolded during his lifetime. "I was fortunate to come along when the country was on fire," he says. "When the Kings and the Andy Youngs and the Abernathys came to town, I was the one who went to the airport to go get them."

Lynch sits back in his spacious church office, its walls crammed with images: Nelson Mandela, Malcolm X, the Rev. Martin Luther King Jr., framed clips of Lynch marching, several city proclamations, and a strange photo of Lynch and the Rev. Donald Jordan stiffly flanking George W. Bush. "I've been a proponent for gay rights for years—during the days when this city was intolerant," says Lynch. "Me coming up in Cincinnati and Georgia before that, I know what that was about. Discrimination of any kind isn't right."

From 1996 to 1999, Lynch was president of the Baptist Ministers' Conference of Greater Cincinnati and Vicinity. Lynch would intermittently come to public loggerheads with the Rev. Fred Shuttlesworth, the proudly conservative civil rights stalwart who has opposed gay rights. The disagreement reached its apex in the battle over Cincinnati's human rights ordinance, which culminated in 2004 with the repeal of Article XII, the city's so-called "anti-gay amendment."

"I became the bad guy within the black ministers," Lynch recalls. "'Reverend—you go out there for those homosexuals and those sissies!'" he adds, mocking black preachers who questioned his loyalties. "Shuttlesworth was saying, 'If Martin was alive, he'd be siding with us.' Miss Coretta King came here and said, 'That's not true, Fred,'" his voice affecting that of a genteel southern woman's.

Despite some public grilling for his beliefs, Lynch doesn't mince words about the homophobia still rampant in some black churches. "I think we're the most homophobic going," he says. "We can be as liberal as we wanna be on social issues but when it comes to sexuality issues, we're hypocrites."

Lynch says Jones has visited his church; he also knows her because of her involvement with the Human Relations Commission. Her work is "exemplary," he says. "It's impeccable."

In Lynch's view, there are black preachers who are simply stultified by their own homophobia. Scripture in their hands is a tactic. "The Bible says 'unequally yoked' and it has nothing to do with sexuality, it has to do with unbelievers," he says. "But they will take it and make it any other thing."

Like Brown-Douglas, Lynch weaves the ugly dangling threads between black homophobia and white supremacy. "White folks used [religion] against black and white," he says. "When people are working out of emotion and don't know the Bible, you've got a helluva problem on your hands."

For her own support and continued growth, Jones attends a Bible study every Monday along with eight theologians—all female. She says being a woman in the black church is as groundbreaking as being a lesbian, but it's those inherent differences that make women (gay or straight) effective church leaders.

"Women bring balance to the church when they're in leadership roles. Pastoring among men is mainly competitive. In the black church you're not considered a great preacher unless you can tune"—an old-school, singsong-y practice that blends preaching with singing. "Women tend to be more theologically sound because they have something to prove. Men compete: 'How big is your church?' That size thing is for real," she says. "Being women in the church allows us to be more sensitive. Women bring a balance to that hard, direct kind of way and we balance men in their competitiveness."

Jones feels that women have historically been "unwelcome" in the pulpit. She cites Isaiah 54, an account of "the future glory of Zion," which begins: "Sing, O barren woman, you who never bore a child."

"[There] we'll get into the unwelcome, the unclean, the unproven," she says, paraphrasing Isaiah 56: 3–5. "God speaks to the eunuch and says, *Because of your faithfulness I will make your home greater than my sons and daughters in Israel*. When I read that, God obviously was looking for something different in the heart of man. That's where my faith journey toward God really speaks to me. As a woman I've been relegated to second-class citizen in the church."

TDCM is part of The Fellowship, a 100-member trans-denominational network of congregations practicing radical inclusion. It's led by Bishop Yvette Flunder, pastor of San Francisco's City of Refuge Church. Terry Hocker, TDCM's associate pastor, sees Jones taking a leadership role in an organization like The Fellowship, perhaps even becoming a bishop herself. "When I look at it from the outside, yes, I believe [TDCM] is revolutionary," Hocker says. "It is the stuff denominations are made of."

For Jones, a woman whose church started in her heart and then her living room, it's a noteworthy progression. The historical ramifications of being in the vanguard of a fledgling movement with such personal investments at stake aren't lost on her. "We're forerunners in this," she says. "I don't think the congregation has gotten it yet, but we're on the cusp."

She believes that ultimately other people of faith will open the doors of their sanctuaries to this new idea and to the brothers and sisters they've cast aside. "I can still go to a Baptist church and meet Jesus in my heart," she says. "But if my heart doesn't change about people, I'll never see the people for who they are."

Originally published in the July 2008 issue of *Cincinnati Magazine*.

➢ Jean Brashear Nichols

"The Friday Night Bunch: A Lesbian Community in West Texas"

(2005), United States

I have always lived on the Llano Estacado ("the Staked Plains"), where the West Texas prairie stretches in all directions as far as I can see. In fact, I still live in the house my parents built in 1952. The farthest I have lived from home is 40 miles, and that was while I was teaching in the sixties. I've never thought of leaving. I'm secure here. I have the farm, the community I've always belonged to, and, close enough, a city and its university, where the cultural gifts of a diverse population are easily available. Why leave? Why start over? I could. I have three degrees from the university—a Big 12 school, after all—where the women's basketball team and Sheryl Swoopes put us on the national map by winning the NCAA National Championship in '93. Now Bobby Knight has been hired, without much controversy, to make the men's team as competitive. "Texas Tech: Where Men are Men and Women are National Champions" is a bumper sticker seen often in Lubbock. I'm comfortable with the immense horizon the prairie provides. The social horizons here are not as broad or encompassing, and limits on what is "permissible" are rigid. Back in 1964, the lesbian/gay "community" was neither visible nor political, a condition that prevails in the rural United States still. We are easy targets. In the mid-1960s there was a large-scale purge of lesbians and gay men who lived here; they were told to leave because the sheriff's department could no longer "guarantee their safety." Many left, but

I stayed and, with them, entered my own closet and locked the door behind me. Since 1967 I have had security and civic respect as a married, presumed heterosexual, woman. Because of my choice, I have enjoyed heterosexual privilege, and paid dearly for it. I have spent the better part of my life trying to be someone I wasn't.

The women's movement that swept the rest of the United States in the 1960s and 1970s, like the rains off the Rockies, never reached Lubbock. Those who own Lubbock and the media that serve them locked Women's Liberation out, keeping its "ladies" in their "place," including me. "Them women libbers," we were told, "is just a bunch of dyke bra-burners. What they need is a good f__k." Feminism challenged the foundations of Lubbock culture, and my own ways of thinking. Yet I secretly joined the National Organization of Women.

If you want to understand the United States, you must understand West Texas. If you want to understand West Texas, take a look at G. W. Bush, the president-select decreed for us by the Supremes: He is our most exemplary product (out of Midland, where he was a perfect failure), embodying all our hypocrisies and contradictions. He doesn't make sense; W. Texas doesn't make sense. He is know-nothingism personified and blatantly, obnoxiously proud of it. There is no logic to life here. Logic is poof! Banished. What is real here is the surreal. Nothing is what it seems: It just is. For example, you cannot assume that, because a woman is married, she is heterosexual. I am married. I am not heterosexual and never have been. [. . .] Contradictions are our way of life.

Change. It was not my choice, but in order to have an original topic accepted for my dissertation my dissertation adviser brushed aside my objections and convinced me to research a "women's issue." In the male-dominated setting of Texas Tech, I was a housewife, and so incapable of writing a "serious" dissertation: A "women's issue" it had to be. My research leading to the dissertation, "The Role of Women in Production Agriculture in a Nine-County Region of West Texas," combined with personal and marital issues, turned my world upside down. The rusty hinges of my closet door slowly began to move and the door began to open. I had to face, name, and deal with the anger that engulfed me as I emerged from my closet to struggle with the isolation of living as a lesbian in a fundamentalist rural setting. And I was menopausal.

The Baptist Church and my parents collaborated to teach me what I have, in retrospect, come to call "The Dance," oppression embraced as social "necessity," a masquerade in which, my heterosexual mask secure, I followed the "steps" outlined before me. My Friday night bunch defines The Dance as a compulsory ritualistic performance. I had worn that mask for 29 years and gone through all the motions, but my dissertation research included interviewing 40 farmwomen so much like myself that I had to admit that I was a feminist. (I discovered, after I learned the theories and language, that I am a very radical feminist.) Then, as if I needed any more complications, I was diagnosed with Attention Deficit Hyperactivity Disorder (ADHD). Still, and even so, I finally acknowledged that I am a lesbian. To be more exact, I am a radical lesbian feminist with ADHD living in the rural United States. At least menopause has ended.

My anger, like that of the women I interviewed, stemmed from an isolation coupled with an oppression that dictated we have no power unless governed by our husbands. The real problem was that, in many cases, we were unwilling to use our power or exert the power we had. When one is trying to get the cows back in the barn or the hay picked up before it rains, it doesn't matter who has the power. The job must be done and some way must be found to work together or the farmer/husband might find he has no help. Find the hidden agent in that sentence.

Life on the farm is not easy, but it is my choice. When we have not been able to hire extra help, I have driven the tractors, worked in the fields, and ignored the housework (gladly). Being a mother limited some of what I had time to do so I changed my focus. Now, having finished my PhD, I have more opportunities available, but the farm and the land may still be my future. Like other women who have chosen to stay on the farm, I thought I knew my value. In the past, it was trying not to be a feminist and proving I was just doing what had to be done. Today, I am angry because I have realized I did not know my value: I felt guilty if I assumed any power and, like so many other farmwomen, I did not exist. By any name (agrarian women, farmwomen, farm wives, farmers who are women, or planters' wives), we are the invisible people who have through the years done a job, received little or no recognition or support, but have "made things work." Our anger then has to be respected and acknowledged. But does anyone care? Are we still so invisible?

What could explain the sources of our shared anger? There was nothing but dry data for the population in my study. I tried not to become part of my research, but my conclusions were meaningless: I had to tell my story in order to tell their stories. None of it made sense until I realized that the only way the intense, suppressed (and denied) anger of farmwomen makes any sense is within the context of feminist thought. Women are the backbone of the small communities near Lubbock, but few seek elected positions or visible leadership roles. I had not been content within the narrow restraints of my wifely role so I did serve on a school board and was a leader in most organizations I belong to. But even after receiving a PhD I am not content.

Yes, we are invisible and the status of women in West Texas is, well, ambiguous. Until 1968, in Texas, married women could not own property or have a bank account in their name without the husband's consent. Until 1991, married women were not recognized as entities distinct from their husbands by the United States Department of Agriculture! Texas Tech University does have a women's studies program with a director, even a coordinator, and finally this year, after 21 years, its own office space. There are the usual elite women's groups, like the Junior League, the usual country club groups and auxiliaries found in every U.S. city and town, and churches on almost every street corner. In 1998, a woman was elected mayor.

Four activities are important to women here: the community, the church they attend, the school their children attend, and Lady Raider basketball.

My Friday Night Bunch. I was given hope and have allowed myself a chance to grow by meeting some well-traveled and wonderful women these past seven years:

my Friday night bunch. One, JP, a radical feminist and separatist lesbian, has lived all over the United States and known many leaders of the women's movement. She was an activist and is a published author, but burned out. Another, MA, brings her African American cultural heritage to feminism. Born here, she has also traveled widely, and taught in Kansas and Chicago during the seventies and eighties. She is an early childhood teacher specializing in English as a Second Language, a woman with a generous heart and deep spirit. She was in Chicago when the Black Panthers were strong and also shares common experiences with separatist feminists such as Chicago's Mountain Moving Coffeehouse. MA and I attend the same church, Metropolitan Community Church.

The group began almost accidentally. Because I wanted company on Friday nights, my buddy, MA, was willing to join me for supper. Then the linguist, JP, wanted to join us because she was lonely and isolated here without other feminists to talk to. She and my buddy from MCC could share and remember the seventies in Chicago. The three of us were the core of the group but Miz insisted she could not be left out and joined us. She is an aspiring theologian who taught high school English and is an administrator at a community college. She is forever going on and on about important women in the Bible and preaches about how each one of them has great value. She's also excited about **Lilith,** expunged from the patriarchal "official" world, but only talks to us about her. Recently she has had to admit to being a radical lesbian feminist. So now there are four; at times out-of-town friends join us.

I'd never thought much about how women's communities are organized because they were already there when I arrived, like the group of networking community women I was invited to join in 2001. They have eaten lunch together since the late 1970s. The Friday night bunch is mine. Now I know what it takes for a women's and lesbian community to become. It is important that each member feel important and have a recognized place. My role is to facilitate and make sure everyone knows where we're going to eat. Checking out different restaurants and deciding whether we want to return is fun, but eating together in one of our homes is better because we can spread out and linger to talk.

We talk! All of us, not always at once or on the same night. It depends. Politics is a frequent subject, as is feminist theory; not religion so much as spirituality; the important events of the past week: international, national, regional, who is killing whom or planning to; our jobs, starting new classes, even things that seem insignificant on a large scale may be very important to one of us. One week last year it was the 40,000 black-tailed prairie dogs the city planned to exterminate in brutal ways (and they're back at it again, with poison this time). The past few weeks it has been women's basketball and the loss of the Lady Raiders' high scorer for "medical reasons." Everyone in Lubbock knows she's pregnant. Around here, we learn how to read through such deliberate obfuscations. If it were an injury or disease we'd have gotten all the details.

"The Friday Night Bunch: A Lesbian Community in West Texas," Jean Brashear Nichols, *Journal of Lesbian Studies,* 2005, reprinted by permission of Taylor and Francis.

➢ **Seo Dong-Jin**

"Mapping the Vicissitudes of Homosexual Identities in South Korea"

(2001), South Korea

In the past few years, many have received a shock as homosexuality has been, for the first time, discussed openly in Korea. Now, or one might say, at last, discussions of homosexuality can be held regularly. Indeed, Korean society has, in the past few years, become accustomed to discussions concerning homosexuality or homosexuals. It is as if the intellectual climate concerning homosexuals has turned to spring, and, with the thawing forces of spring, a torrent of discussions concerning homosexuals has appeared. In colleges, among intellectual organizations, and in the mass media, homosexual issues are being brought up.

[. . .]

Korean homosexuals have continuously worked to organize themselves. In many of the other metropolitan areas besides Seoul, i.e., Pusan, Kwangju and Taegu, lesbian and gay groups have gradually begun to form, and lesbian and gay student groups have also been created in universities. Among these, the lesbian organizations are noteworthy as being very active. Although *Kkirikkiri* is the only lesbian group with a relatively stable organization, lesbians have begun to make their presence known on the Internet and other places. In Korea, opportunities to make sexual contacts are distinctly different for females and males. Even when menstruation and pregnancy are disregarded, it is very difficult for women to have a spontaneous attitude towards their own sexuality. Women could more accurately be called non-sexual entities, since, in Korean society, women are caught up in the double standard of a conservative sexual ideology that stresses motherhood, chastity, and virginity. In these circumstances, it is extremely difficult for lesbians to actively come to terms with their own sexuality. Even so, at least the lesbian identity of relatively refined, middle-class university students and unmarried graduates has begun to be understood. Although there is only one place so far, a lesbian bar (Lesbos) has now opened in Seoul, and *Kkirikkiri* membership is rapidly expanding. Even though the distinction between transvestite and exclusive lesbians in Korea must still be seen as various shades on a continuum, it has become possible to recognize the existence of lesbians as distinct from heterosexuals. In particular, terms such as butch, femme and dyke have come into use as an indication of the structuring of the community.

Yet it must be pointed out that these lesbian and gay communities are still centered around people in their twenties and early thirties, and most of these are middle-class people who have at least a four-year college degree. As a social group that can readily access the press, written works, or mass media, these people have the particularly free attitudes characteristic of the middle class. In other words, these people identify with cultural ideals related to personal choice, individual preference, and freedom. In addition, as a result of being sensitive to ideological changes concerning cultural habits of the middle class, this group has been open to a diverse range of cultural information. As a result, these people have found it easy to obtain information concerning the latest lesbian and gay groups and have consequently formed associations with relative ease.

Lesbians and gays of other ages and social classes, on the other hand, have not found it easy to make contact with the homosexual community. In particular, those homosexuals past their mid-thirties, most of whom are married, are quite often completely unaware of the existence of lesbian and gay communities. Even if they are aware of these new groups, they tend to reject and avoid them. Instead of looking at their own homosexual identity as an "identity," these people have seen it as a shameful desire that constantly hounds them. In particular, homosexual fathers with children have found it difficult to go against expectations concerning their own social position. Especially in Korean society, one's economic livelihood is completely determined by family-based social structures, independent of one's particular social class. It follows that the livelihood of one's wife and children is almost totally determined by the man's economic ability. This dependence on the male breadwinner is seen clearly when we look at Korean society's economic structure, and, of course, is clearly evident in cultural patterns of behavior. In these circumstances, there will inevitably be clear differences between the homosexual identities of older lesbians and gays from a blue-collar background and [those] of the newly formed community of educated lesbian[s] and gays from the middle class. Moreover, although it is still only a minor issue within the small homosexual groups now forming, this gap in identities is creating discord concerning cultural and social issues and matters of hegemony.

Of course, even lesbians and gays from middle-class backgrounds are not completely free in Korea's family-based society. They also dread coming out whether it be forced or of their own accord. (In Korea, only myself and several other lesbians and gays have publicly come out.) Although these homosexuals may find it relatively easy to come out among their peers, at school or work, etc., they would never think of coming out in front of their families. This can be credited to the strong psychological bonds that exist between parents and children and the fact that these bonds are reinforced in Korea's family-based society. In these circumstances, Korea's lesbian and gay movement inevitably finds it difficult to follow the example of Western lesbian and gay movements, which encourage liberation from heterosexual prejudices and pride in oneself. In other words, it is not easy for Koreans to view themselves as autonomous individuals and, on this basis, advocate their own freedom and dignity outside of the context of communities such as their family and relatives. Indeed, most Korean homosexuals consistently see family as the biggest problem troubling them. Moreover, they see the discovery of their homosexual identity by their family as the greatest possible calamity threatening their future. More than society's hatred and prejudice, these homosexuals fear the anxiety and stress that would result from the breaking of their familial bond. As a result of this psychological barrier, the Korean homosexual movement, unable to demand specific public activities from its members, must limit itself to private activities within the lesbian and gay communities.

However, it seems to me that too much can be made of this point. It would be foolish to reduce Korea's strong family values to "oriental," Korea's specific form of Confucianism and patriarchy. Not only Westerners, but even the majority of Koreans would support this stereotype. I see this attitude as a mere ideological fix for Korea, which has once more become aware of itself as non-Western after its recent confused race to Westernize. In a sense, this view could be called reversed orientalism. Unlike Western orientalism, this is a reproduced orientalism coming from the orient itself. Of course, sexuality and the family, the extended family system, and the Confucian ideology surrounding marriage cannot be ignored; yet, these concerns have developed into a mythology which seeks to explain the complex conflicts and changes that Korean society has undergone in trans-historical, abstract, and absolute terms.

The social reverberations that came in the wake of the founding of Come Together [a homosexual student organization at Yongsei University] have nearly ceased to be felt. As a result of the group's efforts, many people have come to recognize the existence of homosexuals, and the term homosexual has definitely become part of the vocabulary of this generation. As the social turmoil surrounding homosexual issues has subsided, lesbians and gays have been busy searching for a life and a future within their communities. It seems to me that these trends will continue for a long time. As long as no major transformations take place, the extreme social reactions and debates surrounding homosexuals in Korean society will not reoccur.

Needless to say, in light of the recently changing circumstances, people have come to recognize the existence of homosexuals, that is to say, the existence of a type of person called a homosexual. Even so, when I look back on the quelled commotion surrounding homosexuality, I have a hard time looking at this as a firm victory or the beginning of positive changes that will guarantee a rosy future.

Personally, I do not like to think of homosexual identity as a biological result, i.e., a physical and psychological constitution or an inborn condition. At the same time, I oppose the view that homosexuality is simply the result of nurture or ideas acquired during the process of socialization. When one reflects on the changes regarding homosexual identity in Korean society, it is clear that homosexual subjectivity is a socially constructed complex process.

Yet, Korean society also has access to a half-century of discourse by Western homosexuals who sought to define homosexual identity. From the last century's attempts to understand homosexuality from a medical or scientific standpoint to the present "queer discourse" based on the fragmented point of view of postmodern capitalism, there has been a plethora of competing views aimed at defining homosexuality in Korean society. One could say that in the West there has been a historical progression of views related to homosexual identity, whereas these views have appeared in Korea all at once. Thus, in Korea, there hasn't been a predominant view of homosexual identity. To the contrary, the various views on the matter have become little whirlpools, each with [its] own centripetal force. In these circumstances, no hegemonic discourse or master narrative has been able to develop. In Korean society, homosexual identity is merely the sketchy descriptions resulting from skimming through the various discourses on the subject.

"Mapping the Vicissitudes of Homosexual Identities in South Korea," by Seo Dong-Jin, *Journal of Homosexuality,* 2001.

SECTION III

Literature and the Arts

CHAPTER 9

Homosexed Art and Literature

Lesbian, gay, bisexual, and transgender (LGBT) supporters and activists have claimed many great artists, musicians, and writers of the past as gay despite the fact that they lived before, to use Foucault's phrase, "the homosexual was . . . a species" (43). During the Renaissance in Europe, for example, one aspect of classical Greek and Roman culture that was "reborn" was homoerotic art. Italian artists Donatello (1386–1466), Leonardo da Vinci (1452–1519), and Michelangelo (1475–1564) created sculptures of young men that were clearly designed to showcase the male body. There is in fact evidence indicating that all three men were what we would today call "gay": Donatello, it was claimed, had love affairs with his male apprentices; da Vinci was arrested for sodomy in 1476; and Michelangelo's great-nephew carefully changed all the pronouns in the love

Figure 9.1 "Il Sodoma," St. Sebastian, 1525.

sonnets from male to female as he was editing the artist's poetry in 1623. There was even an artist popularly known as "Il Sodoma" (the sodomite: Giovanni Antonio Bazzi, 1477–1549).

Still, it is important to remember that although these men, like many others in their time, engaged in homosexual *acts,* they lived prior to consciousness of a homosexual *identity* [λ Chapter 1]. Thus, we risk slipping into the practice of "presentism" if we insist upon interpreting their art as expressing something essentially gay [λ Introduction]. Nonetheless, these artists are just a few of the well-known figures—including Shakespeare, Emily Dickinson, and countless others—who regularly appear on Internet lists of "Famous Lesbians and Gay Men in History." Clearly, there has been no lack of encomiums—both popular and scholarly—praising the influence of queers (especially gay men) on Western culture. With tongue in cheek, Cathy Crimmins, playing on this idea, titled her book about gay male aesthetic culture *How the Homosexuals Saved Civilization: The True and Heroic Story of How Gay Men Shaped the Modern World.*

This chapter makes no attempt to re-hike that well-trodden path. Instead, we focus here on art, literature, and public performance that have contributed directly to building queer culture. We must warn you, however: no single chapter can do justice to the range, diversity, and depth of "queer art." We can only provide a sampling, "highlights," of LGBT artistic production. (Given their immense impact on contemporary culture, television and movies will be discussed separately in Chapters 13–15.) Since a self-consciously homosexed art came into existence with the emergence of sexological terms for sexual identity, our initial focus will be on the work of nineteenth-century artists in the West, who exerted a great influence on artistic production by a variety of queer artists throughout the twentieth century. Proceeding chronologically, we also turn our attention to the development of a self-conscious queer art in a variety of national contexts, particularly as notions of LGBT identity have spread around the world, meeting both acceptance and resistance as diverse people attempt to represent their lives, intimacies, and experiences.

Whitman and His Descendants

Walt Whitman (1819–1892) is generally acknowledged to be among the very finest of nineteenth-century American poets. To some, Whitman was the "good grey poet" singing an epic of America and placing himself at the center of its national life. To others, he was the notorious Mr. Whitman, whose unabashed descriptions of the human "body electric" shocked buttoned-up Victorian-era Americans, who virtuously forbade their innocent daughters from reading him. To still others, his long free-verse lines and philosophy of personal liberation positioned him as a harbinger of literary modernism. And finally, to a small but growing cadre of late nineteenth-century men, Whitman was the prophet of homosexuality, openly celebrating love between men. From his own time through today, gay advocates have pointed to Whitman's life and work as important expressions of early gay consciousness.

Whitman's principal life work was *Leaves of Grass,* a collection of poems first published in 1855 and subsequently revised, enhanced, and expanded to the point that at the poet's death in 1892, it had appeared in at least seven different versions. The 1860 edition of *Leaves of Grass* introduced a group of poems under the title "Calamus," referring to the phallus-shaped calamus plant, which in turn is associated with the ancient Greek god Kalamos, who was transformed through grief at the death of his male lover ("Walt Whitman"). The Calamus poems openly celebrate what Whitman called "adhesiveness," the "love that fuses, ties and aggregates, making the races comrades, and fraternizing all," as distinguished from "individualism, which isolates" (*Poetry and Prose* 973). In Calamus 1, "In Paths Untrodden," the poet describes himself as

> Resolved to sing no songs to-day but those of manly attachment,
>
> . . . To tell the secret of my nights and days,
>
> To celebrate the needs of comrades. (268)

Throughout *Leaves of Grass,* Whitman proclaims his "adhesive" love for men and refers to God in the same terms:

> My rendezvous is appointed, it is certain.
>
> The Lord will be there and wait till I come on perfect terms,
>
> The great Camerado, the lover true for whom I pine will be there. (241)

Within the context of nineteenth-century Western culture, intimate expressions between men (and women, for that matter) were not uncommon, even if not explicitly sexual in nature. The idea of "romantic" (nonsexual) friendship can be traced through much writing of the period. But Whitman's gestures move beyond the platonically "romantic"; in fact, the poet suggests that the uncensored language of sexuality, particularly in the "Calamus" poems, will doubtless shock and offend some potential readers:

> Through me forbidden voices,
>
> Voices of sexes and lusts . . . voices veiled, and I remove the veil,
>
> Voices indecent by me clarified and transfigured. (50)
>
> "Who but I," wrote Whitman in "Starting from Paumanok" in 1860, "should be the poet of comrades?" (179).

The open secret of his homoerotic interests, plainly articulated from the first appearance of *Leaves of Grass,* revolted many contemporary critics and reviewers.

Figure 9.2 Thomas Eakins, *The Swimming Hole*

Rufus Griswold, for example, reviewing *Leaves of Grass* for the New York *Criterion* in 1855, excoriated Whitman for indulging in a "degrading, beastly sensuality that is fast rotting the healthy core of all the social virtues" (24). Still, Whitman and his poetry fascinated people far and near. John Addington Symonds, an Englishman a generation younger than Whitman, declared himself a "Whitmanian" and initiated in 1871 a correspondence with the older poet that was to last until Whitman's death in 1892. In his biography of Symonds, Rictor Norton sees the writer's obsession with Whitman as part of a lifelong effort to make sense of his own homosexuality. It took Symonds twenty years to work up the courage to ask Whitman directly whether, since the "Calamus" poems clearly "prais[ed] and propagat[ed] a passionate affection between men," the "delicate difficulties" surrounding physical sex might properly be left to "the persons' own sense of what is right and fit" (Norton). In other words, Symonds hoped that Whitman was making a place for physical sex between men. Imagine Symonds's disappointment when Whitman wrote back that his "morbid inferences" concerning homosexuality "are disavow'd by me & seem damnable" (Katz 349). Despite Whitman's refusal during his lifetime to advocate publicly for the new "sexual inversion" identity named by the sexologists [λ Chapter 2], his practice of "adhesive" love combined with his vast fame to humanize homosexuality.

We can see Whitman's influence on the beginnings of "gay" art in the last part of the nineteenth century. Two significant figures from this period are Americans Winslow Homer (1836–1910) and Thomas Eakins (1844–1916). Homer typically portrayed the camaraderie of men doing "masculine" things: hunting, laboring, boxing, and so on. This can also be said of Eakins, who specifically intended much of his art of the 1890s to convey the ideas of Whitman. Richard Mann writes that "Eakins' carefully composed images of naked youths in arcadian landscape settings (such as *The Swimming Hole*, 1885) constitute visual equivalents of Whitman's poems, celebrating male beauty and comradeship." While Homer and Eakins expressed Whitman's "adhesiveness," they, like the poet, never self-consciously identified with the new homosexual identity described by the sexologists. Whitman's influence continued into the twentieth century. English painter David Hockney (b. 1937) openly referenced Whitman throughout his early career. He titled a 1960 painting *Adhesiveness* and included lines from Whitman's poetry in other works (e.g., "We Two Boys Together Clinging" [1961]).

Among the many twentieth-century poets who identified with Whitman was Portuguese Modernist Fernando Pessoa (1888–1935). Actually, it is misleading to attribute the poem "Saudação a Walt Whitman" ("Greetings to Walt Whitman," 1915) to Pessoa since, like most of his work, "Saudação" appeared under the name of one of Pessoa's "heteronyms" or aliases—in this case, Álvaro de Campos. (Even Pessoa's core identity is suspect since *pessoa* means "person" or "persona" in Portuguese.)

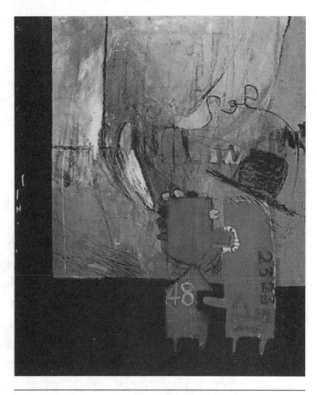

Figure 9.3   David Hockney's *Adhesiveness*

The Álvaro de Campos who composed "Saudação" was a Whitmanesque *pessoa* who could write in "Tabacaria" (Tobacco Shop), "*tenho em mim todos os sonhos do mundo*" ("I hold in myself all the dreams of the world"). In "Saudação," Campos addresses Whitman as a "*grande pederasta*" and exclaims, "*Quantas vezes eu beijo o teu retrato!*" ("How many times I kiss thy portrait!"). Here we see Campos insisting upon a connection to his "*grande herói . . . Cantor da fraternidade*" ("great hero . . . singer of brotherhood").

Just as Symonds and Pessoa/Campos imagined a link with Whitman, gay literary critic Newton Arvin (1900–1963) unmasked the poet's "abnormal sexuality" (273) to depathologize and empower it. In 1938, when Arvin wrote *Whitman,* the phenomenon of sexual inversion had emerged from sexological obscurity into the popular consciousness and was considered an illness [λ Chapter 3]. The first four chapters of Arvin's book argue for a view of Whitman as a social progressive, even a radical; then, in the fifth chapter, Arvin switches gears and takes up the issue of Whitman's homosexuality, a daring move at that time. He points to the preface to the 1876 edition of *Leaves of Grass,* where Whitman announces that "the special meaning of the *Calamus* cluster . . . mainly resides in its Political significance" (*Selected Poems* 359). Arvin concludes that although Whitman was "unmistakably homosexual" (274), he was no "mere invert" (277) but rather a transcendent "poet of fraternity" (280) in whose hands sexual inversion became "as strong and normal an emotion in men as love between the sexes" (272). Arvin, in short, pleads for a critical interpretation of Whitman that rehabilitates homosexuality. Sadly, in 1960, Arvin was arrested for possession of pornographic material (most of which consisted of physique pictorial magazines such as those discussed in Chapter 10) and fired from his teaching position at Smith College.

The combination of Whitman's proto-gay "adhesiveness" and his unmistakable poetic style exerted a powerful influence on generations of twentieth-century queer poets. Langston Hughes (1902–1967), arguably the finest of the Harlem Renaissance poets, wrote with a decidedly Whitmanesque sensibility, especially in his early poems, which adopt Whitman's use of colloquial language and his concern with democratic inclusiveness to address the position of blacks in a racist society. The Beat poets of the 1950s, particularly Allen Ginsberg (1926–1997), praised and emulated Whitman's expansive vision of a humanistic America [λ Chapter 11]. Ginsberg's "A Supermarket in California" (1955) specifically addresses Whitman the lover of boys, and his epic "Howl" (written in 1955) echoes Whitman's self-styled "barbaric yawp" (Whitman, *Poetry and Prose* 247). Judy Grahn's (b. 1940) *Common Woman* poems (1969) and *A Woman Is Talking to Death* (1974) embody some of the same Whitmanian content and style. June Jordan (1936–2002), activist poet, writer, and teacher, praised the "politicizing significance of bisexual affirmation . . . to insist upon the equal validity of all the components of social/sexual complexity" ("June Jordan"). Jordan's poetry also references Whitman's style; we see this clearly in "Poem for South African Women" (1980). We can see it as well in Audre Lorde's poem "A Woman Speaks" and her "biomythography" *Zami,* through their relentless expansiveness and their reimagining of the outside world with respect to the inner reality of the same-sex-loving person. We also see it in the use to which later writers, such as Charley Shively, put Whitman's life and work. Shively, fiery gay activist and scholar, known for burning a Bible during his keynote speech at the 1977 Boston Gay Pride rally and for serving as founding editor of the early gay publication *Fag Rag,* edited two collections of Whitman's letters to young men. In these volumes, *Calamus Lovers* (1987) and *Drum Beats* (1989), Shively insists upon Whitman's overt homosexuality, not hesitating to use late twentieth-century terms (such as *butch, basket, gay, boyfriend, queen, queer,* and the like) anachronistically to argue for an essentialist reading of Whitman. While Shively may be committing the presentist fallacy, Lorde's and Jordan's

Find Out More about Whitman and his influence on contemporary queer poets by reading the poetry in the readings at the end of this chapter.

uses of Whitman speak to their desire to expand a powerful poetic tradition, particularly in their case by directly addressing issues of race and gender that Whitman did not.

The Expatriates

For nineteenth-century women and men seeking to develop same-sex relationships and an artistic life, Rome, Paris, and other European capitals seemed to represent freedom from sex, gender, and racial constraints that inhibited them at home. Homosexual British and American men often traveled to Italy seeking the lost tradition of classical Greek and Roman homoeroticism [λ Chapter 1]. Women, who were for the first time testing the waters of personal and artistic freedom, had no such ready-made models and had to invent new ways of being. The community of artistic proto-lesbians that coalesced around actress Charlotte Cushman (1816–1876) in Rome in the 1850s was one such significant experiment in same-sex living. Cushman and writer Matilda Hays (1823–1908) migrated together to Rome in 1852, where Elizabeth Barrett Browning described their relationship as "a female marriage" (qtd. in Browning 27). They were soon followed by sculptor Harriet Hosmer (1830–1908) and other expatriate women artists: sculptors Emma Stebbins (1815–1882), Edmonia Lewis (1845–c. 1911), and Mary Lloyd (1819–1896); actress Fanny Kemble (1809–1893) and her sister, singer Adelaide Kemble Sartoris (c. 1814–1879); and others. Both Cushman and Hosmer possessed confident and powerful personalities, and

Figure 9.4   Edmonia Lewis

both had been described (by Barrett Browning and Nathaniel Hawthorne, among others) as decidedly mannish in behavior and dress. Henry James raised the spectre of deviant sexuality when he called the group a "strange sisterhood"; he also implied that they were cold and celibate by referring to them as "a white, marmoreal flock" (1: 257). The intense and shifting relationships within the group gave the lie to

Figure 9.5   Tamara de Lempicka (1898–1982). *Portrait of the Duchess de la Salle, 1925.*

James's assumption of female frigidity. Their consistent production of fine and marketable art bespoke the power of freedom for women artists from the shackles imposed by family and mid-Victorian social mores.

By the beginning of the twentieth century, the prime locale for expatriate homosexual artists was no longer Rome but Paris. Led by wealthy American writer Natalie Barney (1876–1972) and British poet Renée Vivien (1877–1909), an intense, prolific, and decidedly non-monogamous coterie of lesbian expatriates took up residence there during the *Belle Époque.* Among these were American writer Gertrude Stein (1874–1946) and her partner Alice B. Toklas (1877–1967). Both Stein and Barney were as well known for the salons at which they entertained other (usually poorer) artists of their day as for their own published work. Journalist Solita Solano (1888–1975) wrote of Barney's entertainments, "Natalie did not collect modern art, she collected people, and you could be sure of being dazzled any Friday (her day) you dropped in for tea" (Solano). Stein, by contrast, did collect modern art—by Picasso, Renoir, Gauguin, and others—but she also felt that her European home and expatriate artist friends fueled a kind of artistic genius in her. "I have lived half my life in Paris," she wrote, "not the half that made me but the half in which I made what I made" (62). Other notable lesbian or bisexual expatriate women who turned up at Barney's gatherings at 20 Rue Jacob included American painter Romaine Brooks (1874–1970); Radclyffe Hall (1880–1943), British author of the enormously influential novel *The Well of Loneliness* [λ Chapters 2 and 12]; American journalist Janet Flanner (1892–1978); American author Djuna Barnes (1892–1982); and Polish Art Deco painter Tamara de Lempicka (1898–1980).

Many African American artists emigrated to Paris during the twentieth century to escape American racism. Those who were gay, lesbian, or bisexual had even more reason to leave, as France was far more accepting of homosexuality than the United States. Gay poet Claude McKay (1889–1948) wrote acidly about New York while in "European self-exile" (Lewis xxvii). Bisexual performer Josephine Baker (1906–1975) was far more popular in Paris than she ever was at home. After being called a "Negro wench" by the

New York Times during an American tour in the 1930s (CMG), she returned to France, saying bitterly, "[The Eiffel Tower] looked very different from the Statue of Liberty, but what did that matter? What was the good of having the statue without the liberty?" (Vorotova). The best known of the black expatriates was James Baldwin (1924–1987), who moved to Europe in 1948 for a combination of reasons: "strained relations with his stepfather, problems over sexual identity, suicide of a friend, and racism" (Liukkonen). While in Paris, Baldwin wrote what Henry Louis Gates Jr. calls "his most successfully crafted and fully realized novel" (xxvi), *Giovanni's Room* (1956), which describes a young white man's struggle with his homosexuality. After his initial exploration of homosexuality, Baldwin turned in later novels, such as *Another Country* (1962) and *Tell Me How Long the Train's Been Gone* (1968), to complex examinations of both sexuality and race. In *Another Country,* for instance, Baldwin takes on some of the sociocultural difficulties of men loving across racial lines.

> **Find Out More** about James Baldwin and his views on homosexuality by reading "Preservation of Innocence" in the readings at the end of this chapter.

Performing Queer: Theater

The limp-wristed aesthete, swishing into a drawing room or contemplating a lily, was a figure of fun before Oscar Wilde came to be his ideal embodiment. William S. Gilbert and Arthur Sullivan's operetta *Patience* (1881), for instance, tells the love story of Reginald Bunthorne, who admits to being an "aesthetic sham." Bunthorne instructs the audience precisely how to affect the persona of a "fleshly poet" by walking

> . . . down Piccadilly with a poppy
> or a lily in your medieval hand.
> And ev'ryone will say,
> As you walk your flow'ry way,
> "If he's content with a vegetable love
> which would certainly not suit me,
> Why, what a most particularly pure
> young man
> this pure young man must be!"
> (*Patience* No. 6)

Figure 9.6   George Grossmith as Bunthorne, 1881

Bunthorne was a satirical rendering of the poet and noted aesthete Algernon Swinburne (1837–1909).

But it was through the witty and epigrammatical Wilde that the figure of the aesthete solidified into the popular image of the homosexual man. Early in 1895, just weeks before the trials that were to end Wilde's successful career as a dramatist—and that led directly to his death five years later—his satirical comedy of manners, *The Importance of Being Earnest,* opened at the St. James Theatre in London [λ Chapter 12]. The play's two male leads, Algernon and Jack, are both clever young men who seek wives, believing all the while that "[d]ivorces are made in Heaven." Both men engage in the practice of "Bunburying," which permits them to escape from tedious obligations. As Algernon remarks,

> I have invented an invaluable permanent invalid called Bunbury, in order that I may be able to go down into the country whenever I choose. Bunbury is perfectly invaluable. If it wasn't for Bunbury's extraordinary bad health, for instance, I wouldn't be able to dine with you at Willis's to-night.

Figure 9.7 Aubrey Beardsley's *Woman in the Moon*

While not an explicitly sexual term, Bunburying seems to serve as a metaphor for living a double life, as Wilde himself (married and carrying on homosexual affairs) certainly needed to do.

The British artist Aubrey Beardsley (1872–1898) was part of Wilde's circle of aesthetes and illustrated Wilde's play *Salome* in 1893. Beardsley's distorted pen-and-ink erotic drawings earned him notoriety during his short life. As he wrote, "I have one aim—the grotesque. If I am not grotesque I am nothing" ("Aubrey Beardsley"). The *Salome* illustrations included "naked figures, hermaphroditic men, ugly, deformed dwarfs and sinister women" (Cooper 80). Like Beardsley, the Russian Léon Bakst (1866–1924) received his first boost to fame through connection to a circle of artists and writers—in this case, one led by impresario Sergei Diaghilev (1872–1929). This group founded a journal, *Mir iskusstva* (*World of Art*), which promoted the principles of Art Nouveau. Through Diaghilev, Bakst became associated with the Ballet Russes, which formed in Paris in 1909. As artistic director of the ballet, Bakst designed sets and costumes; his famous painting of dancer Vaslav Nijinsky (1890–1950) in costume for Debussy's *L'après-midi d'un faune* (*Afternoon of a Faun*) reveals at once his homoerotic gaze and the Beardsley-like grotesquerie of the costume. We should note that all of these artistic endeavors, from Wilde's plays to Diaghilev's ballet, were generally part of a privileged "high art" cultural scene that was somewhat tolerant of homoerotic gestures—provided that they could be passed off as "artistic" (as in Beardsley's case) or laughable (as in Wilde's).

Figure 9.8   Bakst Nijinsky

In contrast, the American stage at the time was more conservative than its European counterparts. *The God of Vengeance* (1907), by Yiddish playwright Sholem Asch (1880–1957), enjoyed a successful run in Berlin in 1910, before Asch emigrated from Germany to the United States in 1914. But when the play (in English translation) opened in New York in 1922, its lesbian theme, combined with its setting in a brothel, so offended local censors that the producer, director, and twelve actors were arrested and later found guilty of presenting an indecent play. British writer Ronald Firbank's (1886–1926) three-act comedy *The Princess Zoubaroff* (1920), which deals with a lesbian convent, avoided the censors by having no major public performances in Europe and no performances at all in the United States. When *The Captive*, by French author Edouard Bourdet (1887–1945), opened on Broadway in 1926, Mayor Jimmy Walker signed the now-infamous "Padlock law," whereby city authorities would literally padlock the doors and arrest the cast of any theater that dared to present homosexuality, sex outside of marriage, or prostitution (Whittaker 278). From this time through the next four decades, censorship kept most LGBT-themed drama off the stage in American cities [λ Chapter 12]. To be sure, Lillian Hellman's 1934 play, *The Children's Hour,* had a long run at New York's Maxine Elliot Theatre, but the play might well have won the Pulitzer Prize had not the selection committee refused to see it. Furthermore, its core plot involving a teacher accused of lesbian-ism by a student [λ Chapter 1, the 1811 Pirie and Woods case] simply vanished in the 1936 film version, replaced by a heterosexual love triangle. The Breen Office, charged with enforcing adherence to the Motion Picture Production Code, excised the homosexual references from Tennessee Williams's *A Streetcar Named Desire* (1947) when it was made into a film in 1951. In London, however, despite state censorship that officially continued into the 1960s, gay-themed plays such as Noel Coward's *Design for Living* (1934) and Robert Anderson's *Tea and Sympathy* (1953) escaped prosecution for obscenity, probably because they took a low-key approach, not directly tackling homophobia, as had Hellman's play (Morley).

By the late twentieth century, especially in the United States, the concerns and attitudes of a newly empowered gay movement were beginning to be reflected onstage. Such plays as *Boys in the Band* (1968), *Bent* (1979), and *Torch Song Trilogy* (1981) brought gay men to center stage as never before. The devastation of AIDS, ironically, seems to have contributed to the success of dramas such as Larry Kramer's *The Normal Heart* (1984), Tony Kushner's *Angels in America* (1991), and Jonathan Larson's *Rent* (1996). The change over a decade from the searing accusatory tone of Kramer's play to the slick mainstream appeal of *Rent* reflected the way AIDS had positioned gay men as protagonists in a great national tragedy; moreover, organizing against the scourge provided gay male artists with access to media and entertainment power brokers.

Not surprisingly, lesbian drama was absent from high-visibility venues, reflecting the ongoing exclusion of women in public per-formance generally. Carolyn Gage (b. 1952) attributes lesbian invisibility in theater to les-bian playwrights' tendency to focus on socially threatening "uncolonized women." Gage's one-woman play, *The Second Coming of Joan of Arc* (1986), is one such threatening play: "We watch," says Gage, "as [Joan] decolonizes herself—from the church, from the military, from the state—and at the end names and separates herself from her internalized misogyny" (interview). This play, Gage's best known, was performed in church basements and at festivals for years before receiving any wide attention.

Figure 9.9   Carolyn Gage as Joan of Arc

A similar erasure is Sarah Dreher's (b. 1937) award-winning play *8 × 10 Glossy* (1985), which is seldom performed—in fact, has never been performed by anyone outside the author's own drama circle. Like Gage, Dreher focuses on sexual abuse, which wreaks lifelong damage upon women and enforces oppressive silence. Both these plays, and many others by lesbians, are overtly political, even polemical, and this appears to have stood in the way of their gaining wide crossover recognition. It is important to note, however, that these and other lesbian plays never aimed for such recognition but focused instead on reaching lesbians oppressed by homophobic culture. As Gage says, "Telling the truth is always disruptive. And theatre, of all the art forms, is a particularly powerful medium for truth-telling. Playwrights historically have ended up in hot water, because the nature of live theatre is inherently political" (Cramer 7).

Homosexed Literature: Global Disruptions

Given that gay identity is largely a construct of American and European civilization, the treatment of the homoerotic outside the West and the Global North reveals tensions and issues surrounding sex and sexuality that are particular to their contexts. At times, we may note some similarities between Western and non-Western understandings of queerness. Japanese ultra-traditionalist author Yukio Mishima (1925–1970), for example, staked out new territory with his 1948 *Bildungsroman Confessions of a Mask,* which is assumed to be at least semi-autobiographical. We might compare this book with American Rita Mae Brown's (b. 1944) *Rubyfruit Jungle* (1973) or with Sri Lankan Shyam Selvadurai's (b. 1965) *Funny Boy* (1994); all three novels offer unapologetic reality-based accounts of young people recognizing their homo- or bisexuality, coming out, and growing into adulthood. Still, their cultural specificity must be noted. Mishima's and Selvadurai's protagonists face cultural and familial pressures that may *seem* similar to those of comparable gay characters in the West but are not necessarily equivalent. Mishima's Japanese characters, for instance, face cultural pressures not just to conform to certain gendered and sexual roles but to rebuild a country that has lost a world war. The account of the "closet" in *Confessions of a Mask* is nuanced not just by family politics but by national politics at a time when Japan's international reputation had been devastated by military defeat; in this context, homosexuals seemed not only like sexual deviants but national deviants by not engaging in the kinds of relationships that would help to restore and repopulate the country.

Although some Latin countries tolerate fairly open expressions of homosexuality, many do not. Hostile cultural environments have produced three characteristic types of LGBT literature in the Latin world. One response to such hostility is a highly coded literature; the Spanish Majorcan author Carme Riera (b. 1948), for instance, uses a prison cell to symbolize the closeted lesbian life in her story *I Leave You the Sea* (1975). A second type of Latin LGBT literature reflects the forced exile of many gay men to more accepting locations. Here we think of gay "Uncle Sergio" in Puerto Rican Magali García Ramis's (b. 1946) novel *Felices Días, Tío Sergio* (*Happy Days, Uncle Sergio*, 1986) or Eduardo in Brazilian Silviano Santiago's (b. 1936) *Stella Manhattan* (1994). Perhaps most notably, Cuban author Reinaldo Arenas (1943–1990) recounts in his memoir *Before Night Falls* the widespread oppression of homosexuals in Castro's Cuba and the author's eventual immigration to the United States as a refugee. In Arenas's account of communist Cuba, homosexuality is cast as a Western decadence, a self-indulgence contrary to the spirit of working collectively to build a strong nation. Finally, some Latin authors have chosen an intersectional approach, burying LGBT plotlines within discussions of social or political struggles. Sara Levi Calderón (b. 1942), for example, writes about a lesbian relationship between two Jewish women in Mexico in her 1990 novel *Dos Mujeres* (*Two Women*). This book, set in the context of the North American Free Trade Agreement (NAFTA) and Mexico's efforts to become a "first-world" nation, raises issues of diaspora—Jewish and lesbian. Chilean author Pedro Lemebel (b. about 1955) uses the 1986 anti-Pinochet tensions in Santiago to contextualize the gay relationship in his novel *Tengo Miedo Torero* (*My Tender Matador*, 2001). And Antonio José Ponte's (b. 1964) *Contrabando de Sombras* (*Smuggled Shadows*, 2002) envisions the Spanish Inquisition and the Cuban Revolution as parallel events that encouraged the persecution of homosexual men.

In South Africa, a mostly white LGBT community has developed a visible subculture on the Euro-American model. But elsewhere in sub-Saharan Africa, LGBT literature is almost unknown. Works such as Nigerian Wole Soyinka's (b. 1934) novel *The Interpreters* (1965) and Senegalese Mariama Bâ's (1929–1981) *Scarlet Song* (1981) mention same-sex love but only negatively and among minor characters. A notable exception to LGBT invisibility in African literature is *No Past, No Present, No Future* (1973) by Sierra Leonean Yulisa Amadu Maddy (b. 1936). In this novel, one of the three main characters is a gay man who leaves Africa for Europe; this is a case of racial and homosexual expatriation that recalls Baldwin's work.

Fine Art: From the Beautiful to the Political

American Charles Demuth (1883–1935) was best known during his lifetime as a Precisionist. That is, as Robert Hughes writes, he was "painting a functional American landscape refracted through a deadpan modernist lingo." But among his images of "grain elevators, water towers, and factory chimneys" are brightly colored paintings of Greenwich Village bathhouses. His *Turkish Bath with Self-Portrait* (1918) reveals the existence—and the allure—of the thriving gay subculture in New York City.

Bright colors also characterize the art of Mexican Frida Kahlo (1907–1954). Kahlo lived in pain after a gruesome bus accident in 1925; many of her paintings combine visions of her physical agony with the cheerful reds and golds and yellows associated with much Mexican folk art and culture. In fact, over a third of her works are self-portraits, often emphasizing the disfigurements of her body. Kahlo was bisexual, and in her well-known painting *Two Nudes in the Jungle* (1939), she presents same-sex intimacy as a comfortable release from pain and tension.

French Surrealist photographer Claude Cahun (1894–1954), like Kahlo,

Figure 9.10   Charles Demuth's *Turkish Bath with Self-Portrait*

executed many self-portraits. These elaborately staged photographs memorialized Cahun's flamboyant transvestism; along with her open lesbianism and her Stein-like salon, they created for Cahun a reputation as a transgressive and theatrical figure.

Beginning roughly at the time of the Stonewall riots in 1969, LGBT art in the United States took on an overtly political purpose. Harmony Hammond, for instance, defines "lesbian art" as "art that comes out of a feminist consciousness and reflects the experience of having lesbian relationships or being lesbian in patriarchal culture" (8). Unlike art by men, claims Arlene Raven, "None of it was developed exclusively in the rarefied world of art" (6). Photographers such as Ann Meredith, Bettye Lane, and

Figure 9.11   Claude Cahun portrait, 1928

Joan E. Biren (b. 1944) used the camera to freeze and celebrate moments in the development of Lesbian Nation [λ Chapter 4]. Kate Millett's (b. 1934) monumental papier mâché *Naked Ladies* (1977) spoke to the necessity for women to take up physical space in a world controlled by men. Louise Fishman's (b. 1939) *Angry Painting* (1973) embodied an attitude common to many lesbians of that era. And of course, even in that period when representations of sex were seen as problematic, Tee A. Corinne (b. 1943) and others produced images of female genitalia. In Australia, the galvanizing event for lesbian art was police violence at the 1978 Sydney Mardi Gras parade. Over the following decade, homosexuals in Australia gradually obtained rights and freedom from most harassment; visibility in the art world grew as well. Artists such as Maree Azzopardi, Fiona Lawry, and Jane Becker came into their own in the 1990s.

Some artists, such as Andy Warhol, became as famous for their lifestyles as for their art. One of the principal proponents of Pop Art in the 1960s, Warhol's famous canvases, many silk-screened, took items from popular culture—such as Campbell's soup cans or pictures of Marilyn Monroe—and recast them as art objects intended for contemplation in museums. While such work was not explicitly "queer" or even homoerotic, it quickly became associated with a "gay aesthetic," perhaps in that it valued the typically undervalued or cast a sympathetic light on objects normally cast off or ignored. Warhol's portraits of Monroe, Liza Minelli, Elizabeth Taylor, and Judy Garland seemed "gay" in the sense that they idolized figures popular among gay male subcultures. Such work seemed to validate for many gay men the value of their cultural icons. But Warhol's lesser known work, such as the film *Blow Job* (1964), is frankly homoerotic. *Blow Job* focuses our attention on the face of a handsome young man as he supposedly receives fellatio from another man. Blurring the boundary between pornography and art, Warhol challenged viewers to consider the beauty in the homoerotic.

Beginning in the 1980s, the AIDS epidemic led to a rush of new political art. The powerful image "Silence = Death" [λ Chapter 4] was the most widely recognized but by no means the only production by political graphics collectives such as Gran Fury and Visual AIDS in New York and General Idea in Toronto. Their immediate goal was to raise money for AIDS research since their governments were slow in responding to the crisis. Simultaneously, activist Cleve Jones (b. 1954) conceived of the NAMES Project Quilt, which has "ballooned into the largest gay art project in history" (Saslow 279). Keith Haring (1958–1990) drew cartoonlike figures that came to stand for AIDS activism. The photographer Robert Mapplethorpe (1946–1989) created deliberately provocative images that raised right-wing hackles and led to calls for censorship and elimination of funding for the National Endowment for the Arts [λ Chapter 12]. These powerful images elicited sympathy for AIDS victims while often refusing to soften the confrontational queer effect.

In the early twenty-first century, at least in some parts of the United States and the Global North, queer art links aesthetic production to cultural and political concerns. An art project titled "Hey Hetero!" performs an educational function on buses and billboards in Australia. The artist created large posters featuring straight couples with captions like, "Hey Hetero! Get married because you can!" (Kelly and Fiveash). Pulitzer Prize–winning cartoonist Jim Borgman (b. 1954) used the bully pulpit of his syndicated newspaper connection to argue for an end to gay bashing in the wake of the murder of Matthew Shepard in 1998, with a cartoon featuring a religious figure standing next to a grave and the caption, "Gay Rites" (Borgman). And Chicana artist Ester Hernández (b. 1944) overlays the iconic figure of the Virgin of Guadalupe upon a lesbian figure (*La Ofrenda*, 1990). In short, queer artists producing queer-themed art and literature have made a significant impact on cultures worldwide.

QUESTIONS FOR DISCUSSION

1. In her 1998 book *Stagestruck*, Sarah Schulman describes recognizing plot and characters from her novel *People in Trouble* (1987) in the smash Broadway hit *Rent*. More than the issue of plagiarism, Schulman raises other questions: "How is AIDS going to be represented in this society? What is the result of the cultural appropriation of gay and lesbian work? What happens when an individual artist is dominated by a corporate product?" (2). Read *People in Trouble* and see *Rent* (film version 2005). How might you answer Schulman's questions?

2. This chapter offered you a broad overview of homosexed art and literature, and inevitably, we had to leave out discussion of much worthy and important art. Several online resources readily provide useful introductions to queer art and literature. Locate one, perhaps starting with a search on Google, glbtq.com, or Wikipedia, and find an artist whom we have not covered in this chapter. Investigate his, her, or ze's life and art, paying particular attention to the social and historical contexts in which that person worked. Write a proposal in which you explain why the artist you have researched should be included in a new edition of this book.

3. In this chapter, we identified Whitman as a poet who has "descendants"— that is, artists and writers coming after him who were influenced by his work enough either to imitate him (Ginsberg) or to expand on issues, such as race and gender, that he didn't explore in great depth (Hughes and Lorde). Consider why it has been important for some LGBT and queer artists to engage previous queer (or queer-seeming) artists—aesthetically, culturally, and politically. What do they gain by doing so? What do their readers or viewers gain? How might such "conversations" among artists across time create a sense of "tradition," and how can such a

sense be important for LGBT and queer people? At the same time, keep in mind the risk of "presentism" we have discussed at earlier points in this book. What are the dangers in contemporary LGBT artists "claiming" past artists as queer?

REFERENCES AND FURTHER READING

Anderson, Nancy Fix. *Woman against Women in Victorian England: A Life of Eliza Lynn Linton.* Bloomington: Indiana UP, 1987.

Arvin, Newton. *Whitman.* New York: Macmillan, 1938.

"Aubrey Beardsley." 23 July 2008. 8 August 2008 <http://en.wikipedia.org/wiki/Aubrey_Beardsley>.

Baldwin, James. "Preservation of Innocence." Reprinted in *Collected Essays.* Ed. Toni Morrison. New York: Library of America, 1998 [1949].

Borgman, Jim. "Gay Rites." *The Cincinnati Enquirer* 16 October 1998. 26 March 2008 <http://borgman.enquirer.com/>.

Browning, Robert. *Dearest Isa: Robert Browning's Letters to Isabella Blagden.* Ed. Edward C. McAleer. Austin: U of Texas P, 1951.

CMG Worldwide. *The Official Josephine Baker Website.* N.d. 8 August 2008 <http://www.cmgww.com/stars/baker/index.php>.

Cooper, Emmanuel. *The Sexual Perspective: Homosexuality and Art in the Last 100 Years in the West.* London: Routledge & Kegan Paul, 1986.

Cramer, Pat. Interview with Carolyn Gage. *Off Our Backs* (Jan.–Feb. 2002). 8 August 2008 <http://findarticles.com/p/articles/mi_qa3693/is_200201/ai_n9067922>.

Crimmins, Cathy. *How the Homosexuals Saved Civilization: The True and Heroic Story of How Gay Men Shaped the Modern World.* New York: Tarcher, 2004.

Foucault, Michel. *The History of Sexuality, Volume 1: An Introduction.* Trans. Robert Hurley. New York: Vintage, 1990.

Gage, Carolyn. Telephone interview with D. Meem. 23 April 2007.

Gates, Henry Louis, Jr. "Introduction." *The Annotated Uncle Tom's Cabin.* New York: W. W. Norton, 2007.

Gilbert, William S. (libretto). *Patience, or, Bunthorne's Bride.* N.d. 8 August 2008 <http://www.karadar.com/Librettos/sullivan_PATIENCE.html>.

Griswold, Rufus. Review of *Leaves of Grass. Criterion* 1 (10 November 1855): 24.

Hammond, Harmony. *Lesbian Art in America: A Contemporary History.* New York: Rizzoli, 2000.

Henderson, Mae. "James Baldwin: Expatriation, Homosexual Panic, and Man's Estate." *Callaloo* 23.1 (2000): 313–27.

Hughes, Robert. *American Visions: The Epic History of Art in America.* Quoted on *Artchive.* N.d. 8 August 2008 <http://www.artchive.com/artchive/D/demuth.html>.

James, Henry. *William Wetmore Story and His Friends: From Letters, Diaries, and Recollections.* 2 vols. Boston: Houghton Mifflin, 1903.

"June Jordan." 2002. 8 August 2008 <http://sunsite.berkeley.edu/gaybears/jordan/>.

Katz, Jonathan Ned. *Gay American History: Lesbians & Gay Men in the U.S.A.* Rev. ed. New York: Meridian, 1992.

Kelly, Deborah, and Tina Fiveash. "Hey, Hetero!" 2003. 26 March 2008 <http://www.abc.net .au/arts/design/stories/s455304.htm>.

Lewis, David Levering. *The Portable Harlem Renaissance Reader.* New York: Penguin, 1995.

Liukkonen, Petri. "James (Arthur) Baldwin." 2002. 8 August 2008 <http://www.kirjasto .sci.fi/jbaldwin.htm>.

Mann, Richard G. "American Art: Gay Male, Nineteenth Century." *glbtq: An Encyclopedia of Gay, Lesbian, Bisexual, Transgender, and Queer Culture.* 2002. 8 August 2008 <www .glbtq.com/arts/am_art_gay_19c.html>.

Morley, Sheridan. "Minimalist View of a Gay Scene." *International Herald Tribune.* 10 February 1999. 8 August 2008 <http://www.iht.com/articles/1999/02/10/lon.t_0.php>.

Norton, Rictor. *The John Addington Symonds Pages.* 1997. 8 August 2008 <http://rictornorton .co.uk/symonds/index.htm>.

Pessoa, Fernando. "Saudação a Walt Whitman." *Poesias de Álvaro de Campos.* N.d. 8 August 2008 <http://www.secrel.com.br/jpoesia/facam05.html>.

———. "Tabacaria." In *Poesias de Álvaro de Campos.* N.d. 8 August 2008 <http:// www.insite.com.br/art/pessoa/ficcoes/acampos/456.html>.

Raven, Arlene. "Los Angeles Lesbian Arts." *Art Paper* 18.6 (Nov.–Dec. 1994): 6.

Saslow, James M. *Pictures and Passions: A History of Homosexuality in the Visual Arts.* Harmondsworth, UK: Penguin, 1999.

Schulman, Sarah. *Stagestruck: Theater, AIDS, and the Marketing of Gay America.* Durham, NC: Duke UP, 1998.

Solano, Solita. "1920s Expats on Natalie's Salon." *The World of Natalie Clifford Barney.* N.d. 8 August 2008 <http://www.natalie-barney.com/1920swriters.htm>.

Stein, Gertrude. "An American and France." *What Are Masterpieces.* Ed. Robert Bartlett Haas. New York: Pitman, 1970. 59–70.

Vorotova, Katerina. "Josephine Baker." 2008–2012. 8 August 2008 <http://www.harlemlive .org/shethang/profiles/josephinebaker/jbaker.html>.

"Walt Whitman." 5 August 2008. 8 August 2008 <http://en.wikipedia.org/wiki/Walt_ Whitman#_note-4>.

Whitman, Walt. *Poetry and Prose.* Ed. Justin Kaplan. New York: Library of America, 1996.

———. *Selected Poems 1855–1892: A New Edition.* Ed. Gary Schmidgall. New York: St. Martin's, 1999.

Whittaker, Donald E., III. *Subversive Aspects of American Musical Theatre.* Diss. Louisiana State University, 2002. <http://etd.lsu.edu/docs/available/etd-0418102173116/unrestricted/ Whittaker_III_dis.pdf>.

Wilde, Oscar. "The Importance of Being Earnest: A Trivial Comedy for Serious People." Project Gutenberg eBook. N.d. 8 August 2008 <http://www.gutenberg.org/files/ 844/844-h/844-h.htm>.

READINGS

➤ **Walt Whitman**

From Leaves of Grass, *"We Two Boys Together Clinging"*

(1860, 1867), United States

We two boys together clinging,

One the other never leaving,

Up and down the roads going—North and South excursions making,

Power enjoying—elbows stretching—fingers clutching,

Arm'd and fearless—eating, drinking, sleeping, loving,

No law less than ourselves owning—sailing, soldiering, thieving, threatening,

Misers, menials, priests alarming—air breathing, water drinking, on the turf or the sea-beach dancing,

Cities wrenching, ease scorning, statutes mocking, feebleness chasing,

Fulfilling our foray.

➤ **Langston Hughes**

"I, Too, Sing America"

(1902–1967), United States

I, too, sing America.

I am the darker brother.

They send me to eat in the kitchen

When company comes,

But I laugh,

And eat well,

And grow strong.

Tomorrow,

I'll be at the table

When company comes.

Nobody'll dare

Say to me,

"Eat in the kitchen,"

Then.

Besides,

They'll see how beautiful I am

And be ashamed—

I, too, am America.

➤ James Baldwin

"Preservation of Innocence"

(1924–1987), United States

The problem of the homosexual, so vociferously involved with good and evil, the unnatural as opposed to the natural, has its roots in the nature of man and woman and their relationship to one another. [. . .]

We arrive at the oldest, the most insistent and the most vehement charge faced by the homosexual: he is unnatural because he has turned from his life-giving function to a union which is sterile. This may, in itself, be considered a heavy, even an unforgivable crime, but since it is not so considered when involving other people, the unmarried or the poverty-stricken or the feeble, and since his existence did not always invoke that hysteria with which he now contends, we are safe in suggesting that his present untouchability owes its motive power to several other sources. Let me suggest that his present debasement and our obsession with him corresponds to the debasement of the relationship between the sexes; and that his ambiguous and terrible position in our society reflects the ambiguities and terrors which time has deposited on that relationship as the sea piles seaweed and wreckage along the shore.

For, after all, I take it that no one can be seriously disturbed about the birth-rate: when the race commits suicide it will not be in Sodom. Nor can we continue to shout unnatural whenever we are confronted by a phenomenon as old as mankind, a phenomenon, moreover, which nature has maliciously repeated in all of her domain. If we are going to be natural then this is part of nature; if we refuse to accept this, then we have rejected nature and must find another criterion.

[. . .] As one may close [Laura Z. Hobson's] *Gentlemen's Agreement,* which is about Gentiles and Jews, having gained no insight into the mind of either; as [Mary Jane Ward's] *The Snake Pit* reveals nothing of madness and James M. Cain tells us nothing of men and women, so one may read any current novel concerned with homosexual love and encounter merely a procession of platitudes the ancestry of which again may be traced to The Rover Boys and their golden ideal of chastity. It is quite impossible to write a worthwhile novel about a Jew or a Gentile or a Homosexual, for people refuse, unhappily, to function in so neat and one-dimensional a fashion. If the novelist considers that they are no more complex than their labels he must, of necessity, produce a catalogue, in which we will find, neatly listed, all those attributes with which the label is associated; and this can only operate to reinforce the brutal and dangerous anonymity of our culture.

A novel insistently demands the presence and passion of human beings, who cannot ever be labeled. Once the novelist has created a human being he has shattered the label and, in transcending the subject matter, is able, for the first time, to tell us something about it and to reveal how profoundly all things involving human beings interlock.

"Preservation of Innocence" was originally published in *Zero*. © 1949 by James Baldwin. Copyright renewed. Reprinted by arrangement with the James Baldwin Estate.

➢ Allen Ginsberg

"A Supermarket in California"

(1926–1997), United States

What thoughts I have of you tonight, Walt Whitman, for I walked down the sidestreets under the trees with a headache self-conscious looking at the full moon.

In my hungry fatigue, and shopping for images, I went into the neon fruit supermarket, dreaming of your enumerations!

What peaches and what penumbras! Whole families shopping at night! Aisles full of husbands! Wives in the avocados, babies in the tomatoes!

—and you, García Lorca, what were you doing down by the watermelons?

I saw you, Walt Whitman, childless, lonely old grubber, poking among the meats in the refrigerator and eyeing the grocery boys.

I heard you asking questions of each: Who killed the pork chops? What price bananas? Are you my Angel?

I wandered in and out of the brilliant stacks of cans following you, and followed in my imagination by the store detective.

We strode down the open corridors together in our solitary fancy tasting artichokes, possessing every frozen delicacy, and never passing the cashier.

Where are we going, Walt Whitman? The doors close in a hour. Which way does your beard point tonight?

(I touch your book and dream of our odyssey in the supermarket and feel absurd.)

Will we walk all night through solitary streets? The trees add shade to shade, lights out in the houses, we'll both be lonely.

Will we stroll dreaming of the lost America of love past blue automobiles in driveways, home to our silent cottage?

Ah, dear father, graybeard, lonely old courage-teacher, what America did you have when Charon quit poling his ferry and you got out on a smoking bank and stood watching the boat disappear on the black waters of Lethe?

➤ Frank O'Hara

"Ode: Salute to the French Negro Poets" (1958)

(1926–1966), United States

from near the sea, like Whitman my great predecessor, I call
To the spirits of other lands to make fecund my existence

do not spare your wrath upon our shores, that trees may grow
upon the sea, mirror of our total mankind in the weather

one who no longer remembers dancing in the heat of the moon may call
across the shifting sands, trying to live in the terrible western world

here where to love at all's to be a politician, as to love a poem
is pretentious, this may tendentious but it's lyrical

which shows what lyricism has been brought to by our fables times
where cowards are shibboleths and one specific love's traduced

by shame for what you love more generally and never would avoid
where reticence is paid for by a poet in his blood or ceasing to be

blood! Blood that we have mountains in our veins to stand off jackals
in the pillaging of our desires and allegiances, Aimé Césaire

for if there is fortuity it's in the love we bear each other's differences
in race which is the poetic ground on which we rear our smiles

standing in the sun of marshes as we wade slowly toward the culmination
of a gift which is categorically the most difficult relationship

and should be sought as such because it is our nature, nothing
inspires us but the love we want upon the frozen face of earth

and utter disparagement turns into praise as generations read the message

of our hearts in adolescent closets who once shot at us in doorways

or kept us from living freely because they were too young then to know what they would

ultimately need from a barren and heart-sore life

the beauty of America, neither cool jazz nor devoured Egyptian heroes, lies in

lives in the darkness I inhabit in the midst of sterile millions

the only truth is face to face, the poem whose words become your mouth

and dying in black and white we fight for what we love, not are.

"Ode: Salute to the French Negro Poets," edited by Donald Allen, copyright © 1971 by Maureen Granville-Smith, Administratrix of the Estate of Frank O'Hara. Used by permission of Alfred A. Knopf, a division of Random House, Inc.

➢ **Judy Grahn**

"A History of Lesbianism"

(1940–), United States

How they came into the world,
the women-loving-women
came in three by three
and four by four
the women-loving women
came in ten by ten
and ten by ten again
until there were more
than you could count

> they took care of each other
> the best they knew how
> and of each other's children,
> if they had any.

How they lived in the world,
the women-loving-women
learned as much as they were allowed

and walked and wore their clothes

the way they liked

whenever they could. They did whatever

they knew to be happy or free

and worked and worked and worked.

The women-loving-women

in America were called dykes

and some liked it

and some did not.

>they made love to each other
>
>the best they knew how
>
>and for the best reasons

How they went out of the world,

the women-loving-women

went out one by one

having withstood greater and lesser

trials, and much hatred

from other people, they went out

one by one, each having tried

in her own way to overthrow

the rule of men over women,

they tried it one by one

and hundred by hundred,

until each came in her own way

to the end of her life

and died:

>The subject of lesbianism
>
>is very ordinary; it's the question
>
>of male domination that makes everybody
>
>angry.

"A History of Lesbianism" from *The Work of a Common Woman* by Judy Grahn.

➤ June Jordan

"Poem about My Rights"

(1936–2002), United States

Even tonight and I need to take a walk and clear
my head about this poem about why I can't
go out without changing my clothes my shoes
my body posture my gender identity my age
my status as a woman alone in the evening/
alone on the streets/alone not being the point/
the point being that I can't do what I want
to do with my own body because I am the wrong
sex the wrong age the wrong skin and
suppose it was not here in the city but down on the beach/
or far into the woods and I wanted to go
there by myself thinking about God/or thinking
about children or thinking about the world/all of it
disclosed by the stars and the silence:
I could not go and I could not think and I could not
stay there
alone
as I need to be
alone because I can't do what I want to do with my own
body and
who in the hell set things up
like this
and in France they say if the guy penetrates
but does not ejaculate then he did not rape me
and if after stabbing him if after screams if
after begging the bastard and if even after smashing
a hammer to his head if even after that if he
and his buddies fuck me after that
then I consented and there was
no rape because finally you understand finally

they fucked me over because I was wrong I was

wrong again to be me being me where I was/wrong

to be who I am

which is exactly like South Africa

penetrating into Namibia penetrating into

Angola and does that mean I mean how do you know if

Pretoria ejaculates what will the evidence look like the

proof of the monster jackboot ejaculation on Blackland

and if

after Namibia and if after Angola and if after Zimbabwe

and if after all of my kinsmen and women resist even to

self-immolation of the villages and if after that

we lose nevertheless what will the big boys say will they

claim my consent:

Do You Follow Me: We are the wrong people of

the wrong skin on the wrong continent and what

in the hell is everybody being reasonable about

and according to the Times this week

back in 1966 the C.I.A. decided that they had this problem

and the problem was a man named Nkrumah so they

killed him and before that it was Patrice Lumumba

and before that it was my father on the campus

of my Ivy League school and my father afraid

to walk into the cafeteria because he said he

was wrong the wrong age the wrong skin the wrong

gender identity and he was paying my tuition and

before that

it was my father saying I was wrong saying that

I should have been a boy because he wanted one/a

boy and that I should have been lighter skinned and

that I should have had straighter hair and that

I should not be so boy crazy but instead I should

just be one/a boy and before that

it was my mother pleading plastic surgery for

my nose and braces for my teeth and telling me
to let the books loose to let them loose in other
words
I am very familiar with the problems of the C.I.A.
and the problems of South Africa and the problems
of Exxon Corporation and the problems of white
America in general and the problems of the teachers
and the preachers and the F.B.I. and the social
workers and my particular Mom and Dad/I am very
familiar with the problems because the problems
turn out to be
me

I am the history of rape
I am the history of the rejection of who I am
I am the history of the terrorized incarceration of
myself

I am the history of battery assault and limitless
armies against whatever I want to do with my mind
and my body and my soul and
whether it's about walking out at night
or whether it's about the love that I feel or
whether it's about the sanctity of my vagina or
the sanctity of my national boundaries
or the sanctity of my leaders or the sanctity
of each and every desire
that I know from my personal and idiosyncratic
and indisputably single and singular heart
I have been raped
be-
cause I have been wrong the wrong sex the wrong age
the wrong skin the wrong nose the wrong hair the
wrong need the wrong dream the wrong geographic
the wrong sartorial I

I have been the meaning of rape
I have been the problem everyone seeks to
eliminate by forced
penetration with or without the evidence of slime and/
but let this be unmistakable this poem
is not consent I do not consent
to my mother to my father to the teachers to
the F.B.I. to South Africa to Bedford-Stuy
to Park Avenue to American Airlines to the hardon
idlers on the corners to the sneaky creeps in
cars
I am not wrong: Wrong is not my name
My name is my own my own my own
and I can't tell you who the hell set things up like this
but I can tell you that from now on my resistance
my simple and daily and nightly self-determination
may very well cost you your life

➤ Audre Lorde

"A Woman Speaks"

(1934–1992), United States

Moon marked and touched by sun
my magic is unwritten
but when the sea turns back
it will leave my shape behind.
I seek no favor
untouched by blood
unrelenting as the curse of love
permanent as my errors
or my pride
I do not mix
love with pity
nor hate with scorn
and if you would know me

look into the entrails of Uranus

where the restless oceans pound.

I do not dwell within my

birth nor my divinities

who am ageless and half-grown

and still seeking

my sisters

witches in Dahomey

wear me inside their coiled cloths

as our mother did

mourning.

I have been woman

for a long time

beware my smile

I am treacherous with old magic

and the noon's new fury

with all your wide futures

promised

I am

woman

and not white.

"A Woman Speaks," from *The Collected Poems of Audre Lorde* by Audre Lorde. Copyright © 1997 by the Audre Lorde Estate. Used by permission of W. W. Norton & Company, Inc.

➤ **Dorothy Allison**

"The Women Who Hate Me"

(1949–), United States

1

The women who do not know me.

The women who, not knowing me, hate me
mark my life, rise in my dreams and shake their loose hair
throw out their thin wrists, narrow their already sharp eyes
say "Who do you think you are?"

"Lazy, useless, cuntsucking, scared, stupid
What you scared of anyway?"
Their eyes, their hands, their voices
Terrifying.

The women who hate me cut me
as men can't. Men don't count.
I can handle men. Never expected better
of any man anyway.
But the women,
shallow-cheeked young girls the world was made for
safe little girls who think nothing of bravado
who never got over by playing it tough.

What do they know of my fear?

What do they know of the women in my body?
My weakening hips, sharp good teeth
angry nightmares, scarred cheeks
fat thighs, fat everything.

"Don't smile too wide, You look like a fool."
"Don't want too much, You an't gonna get it."
An't gonna get it.
Goddamn.

Say Goddamn and kick somebody's ass
that I am not even half what I should be,
full of terrified angry bravado
BRAVADO.

The women who hate me
don't know
can't imagine
life-saving, precious bravado.

2

God on their right shoulder
righteousness on their left,

the women who hate me never use words
like hate, speak instead of nature
of the spirit not housed in the flesh
as if my body, a temple of sin,
didn't mirror their own.

Their measured careful words echo
earlier coarser stuff, say

"What do you think you're doing?"
"Who do you think you are?"

"Whitetrash

no-count

bastard

mean-eyed

garbage-mouth

cuntsucker

cuntsucker

no good to anybody, never did diddlyshit anyway."

"You figure out yet who you an't gonna be?"

The women who hate me hate
their insistent desires, their fat lusts
swallowed and hidden, disciplined to nothing
narrowed to bone and dry hot dreams.
The women who hate me deny
hunger and appetite,

the cream delight

of a scream

that arches the thighs and fills

the mouth with singing.

3

Something hides here
a secret thing shameful and complicated.
Something hides in a tight mouth a life too easily rendered
a childhood of inappropriate longing
a girl's desire to grow into a man
a boyish desire to stretch and sweat.

Every three years I discover again
that No I knew nothing before.
Everything must be dragged out,
looked over again, The unexamined life
is the lie, but still
must I every time deny
everything I knew before?

4

My older sister tells me flatly
she don't care who I take to my bed
what I do there. Tells me finally
she sees no difference between
her husbands, my lovers. Behind it all
we are too much the same to deny.

My little sister thinks my older crazy
thinks me sick
more shameful to be queer than crazy
as if her years hustling ass,
her pitful junky whiteboy
saved through methadone and marriage, all that
asslicking interspersed with asskicking
all those pragmatic family skills we share mean nothing

measured against the little difference
of who and what I am.

My little sister too
is one of the women who hate me.

5

I measure it differently, what's shared,
what's denied, what no one wants recognized.
My first lover's skill at mystery,
how one day she was there, the next gone;
the woman with whom I lived for eight years
but slept with less than one;
the lover who tied me to the foot of her bed
when I didn't really want that
but didn't really know
what else I could get.

What else can I get?
Must I rewrite my life
edit it down to a parable where everything
turns out for the best?

But then what would I do with the lovers
too powerful to disappear, the women
too hard to melt to soft stuff?
Now that I know that soft stuff
was never where I wanted to put my hand.

6

The women who hate me
hate too my older sister
with her many children, her weakness for
good whiskey, country music, bad men.
She says the thing "women's lib" has given her

is a sense she don't have to stay too long
though she does
still she does
much too long.

7

I am not sure anymore of the difference.
I do not believe anymore in the natural superiority
of the lesbian, the difference between my sisters and me.

Fact is, for all I tell my sisters
I turned out terrific at it myself:
sucking cunt, stroking ego, provoking
manipulating, comforting and keeping.
Plotting my life around mothering
other women's desperation
the way my sisters
build their lives
around their men.
Til I found myself sitting at the kitchen table
shattered glass, blood in my lap and her
the good one with her stern insistence
just standing there wanting me
to explain it to her, save her from being
alone with herself.

Or the other one
another baby-butch wounded girl.
How can any of us forget how wounded
any of us have to be to get that hard?
Never to forget that working class says nothing
does not say who she was how she was
fucking me helpless. Her hand on my arm
raising lust to my throat, that lust
everyone says does not happen

though it goes on happening
all the time.

How can I speak of her, us together?
Her touch drawing heat from my crotch to my face
her face, terrifying, wonderful.
My saying, *"Yeah, goddamn it, yeah,*
put it to me, ease me, fuck me, anything . . ."
til the one thing I refused
then back up against a wall
her rage ugly in the muscles of her neck
her fist swinging up to make a wind,
a wind blowing back to my mama's cheek
past my stepfather's arm.

I ask myself over and over how I
came to be standing in such a wind?
How I came to be held up like my mama
with my jeans, my shoes locked in a drawer
and the woman I loved breathing on me
"You bitch. You damned fool."

"You want to try it?"
"You want to walk to Brooklyn
barefooted?"
"You want to try it
mothernaked?"

Which meant, of course, I had to decide
how naked I was willing to go where.

Do I forget all that?
Deny all that?
Pretend I am not
my mama's daughter
my sisters' mirror.

Pretend I have not

at least as much lust

in my life as pain?

Where then will I find the country

where women never wrong women

where we will sit knee to knee

finally listening

to the whole

naked truth

of our lives?

CHAPTER 10

Lesbian Pulp Novels and Gay Physique Pictorials

I n Chapter 1, we discussed the attempts of Anselm, Archbishop of Canterbury in England, to shame priests found guilty of sodomy by excommunicating them and publishing their crimes and sentences. As we noted, these publications eventually ceased because they drew extraordinary attention from male parishioners who showed great interest in discussing who did what to whom [λ Chapter1]. Clearly, one of the unintended consequences of making sodomy public was that a community of "interested parties" formed around a practice meant to punish men who engaged in sodomy. Nearly 900 years later, in the mid-twentieth century, a similar phenomenon began to emerge in the United States with the publication of physique pictorials and lesbian and gay male pulp novels. In the case of physique pictorials, magazines chock-full of photos of nearly nude male bodybuilders and ostensibly intended for a heterosexual, health-conscious readership soon became favorites of a largely gay male audience. In the case of lesbian pulp novels and exposé texts written to titillate heterosexual males with innuendo of lesbian sex and that purported to warn of the dangers of lesbians and lesbianism, the books were so widely read by lesbians that very early on, lesbian authors began writing them, knowing full well that they were reaching out to readers very much like themselves. Gay male pulp novels, even those published as "literary" texts and in cloth before their publication as cheap paperbacks, served a similar function for gay men.

The 1950s and early 1960s in the United States were marked by a number of important cultural contradictions. On one hand, the popular culture was focused on encouraging strict gender roles; women were encouraged to refocus their creative energies and labor on the home and (heterosexual) family because men had returned from World War II and needed employment in the factories that had used women's labor during the war. On the other hand, many women had learned during the war that they were capable of doing the high-paying industrial work hitherto reserved for men, and many wanted to continue in that work and contribute to the support of their families or to support themselves outside the constraints of the heterosexual family. The McCarthy era was in full swing, and much attention was paid to ferreting out Communists and "perverts" in the government, to which end Executive Order 10450 was signed by President Eisenhower in 1953. At the same time, the Mattachine Society and the Daughters of Bilitis were formed, and both Alfred Kinsey and Evelyn Hooker were studying human sexuality in more objective ways than ever before [λ Chapter 3]. The physique pictorials and lesbian and gay pulp novels straddled these oppositional cultural forces and became conduits through which lesbian, gay male, and transgender culture passed.

Physique Magazines

Figure 10.1   Eugen Sandow Getty caption: "British muscle man Eugen Sandow in pose of The Farnese Hercules" (front view).

Physique magazines began in the late nineteenth century when Prussian bodybuilder Eugen Sandow (1867–1925) established *Physical Culture Magazine* in London to help publicize his Institute for Physical Culture. According to writer Jim Webber, Sandow's magazine, "along with the Boy Scouts and the Olympics, which were founded at about the same time, became part of the 'muscular Christian' movement, which promoted nationalism, racial purity, and brazen heterosexuality."

Bernarr Macfadden began publishing the U.S. version of *Physical Culture* at the beginning of the twentieth century for a heterosexual male audience interested in diet, exercise, and overall physical fitness. By the end of World War II, physique magazines had gained a significant audience among physical fitness buffs. These magazines, and the fitness craze of which they were a part, met the demands of a culture in which more and more working men were employed in fairly sedentary office jobs and in which technological advances—particularly in domestic appliances—were reducing the physical requirements of maintaining a home. Charles Atlas, whom *Physical Culture* called "The World's Most Handsome Man," had by the mid-twentieth century posed for thirty years in scanty clothing; Atlas, an Italian whose real name was Angelino Siciliano, turned sixty-two in 1955, and advertisements for his exercise method, Dynamic Tension, were commonplace at that time in the United States (Waldron).

In 1956, the issue of fitness became a public concern when a study was released showing that American children were less physically fit than their European counterparts; accordingly, the President's Council on Physical Fitness and Sports was formed. In fact, the bodybuilding, diet, and fitness boom so generally permeated American culture that Alan Miller (writing for the gay magazine *Body Politic*) remembers being initiated to the pleasures of beefcake magazines in a barbershop:

Figure 10.2 Charles Atlas, strongman

I first encountered *Physique Pictorial* in 1960. Several issues were thrown among the magazine collection of Top's Barber Shop hidden behind a variety store on Queen Mary Road in Montreal. The six barbers were—or so I vaguely remember—not the least bit embarrassed at having these things about, let alone that a young boy would be flipping through them. . . . Even when blatantly erotic, physique magazines were excused (one is not sure how successfully) as works for those interested in bodybuilding, art or nudism—anything to avoid labels being applied to the purchasers.

As Miller's experience indicates, bodybuilding and beefcake magazines soon became popular homoerotica.

According to David Bianco, though, Bernarr Macfadden "didn't intend his magazine for sexual titillation. When he became aware of its homosexual following, he publicly denounced his gay readers as 'painted, perfumed, kohl-eyed, lisping, mincing youths,' whom he encouraged other men to "beat up." Nonetheless, the popularity of bodybuilding magazines helped create a climate that allowed photographer Bob Mizer to begin publishing gay-oriented *Physique Pictorial* in 1951. As early as 1948, Mizer distributed a catalogue of photographs he advertised as "invaluable for artists, inspirational for bodybuilders" (McGarry and Wasserman 117). Mizer and others capitalized on bodybuilding magazines' underground gay male following. James M. Saslow says, "Under cover of the venerable physical culture movement, monthlies like *Tomorrow's Man* and *Adonis* printed reams of bodybuilders and sportsmen in the scantiest G-strings that would pass censorship. Bob Mizer . . . set up [the] Athletic Model Guild . . . to connect would-be poster-boys with artists and photographers" (252–53). U.S. postal codes, though vague, were generally interpreted as prohibiting full-frontal nudity, so models in Mizer's original brochure/catalogues and in *Physique Pictorial* wore posing straps and showed no body hair below the neck (McGarry and Wasserman 121). Bianco points out that the number of physique magazines aimed at a gay male readership grew until, by 1958, there were "several dozen" with as many as 70,000 readers.

Tom of Finland, whose given name was Touko Laaksonen, was probably the best-known illustrator to contribute work to physique magazines. He began publishing in *Physique Pictorial* when Mizer used one of his drawings for the cover of the spring 1957 issue. Micah Ramakers claims that Bob Mizer invented Laaksonen's pseudonym, though other sources claim that Laaksonen chose the name "Tom" himself because he worried that Touko would be difficult for the American tongue. Tom of Finland would eventually publish over 100 images in Mizer's publication and in other physique magazines, and many of those appeared on the covers (Ramakers 4).

Figure 10.3 Tom of Finland drawing
(www.Tomsparties.com/Galleries/ToF/index.html)

Highly stylized pieces featuring muscled men with enlarged penises and torsos, Tom's work often portrayed men engaged in sexual acts with one another. Many of his subjects wore uniforms—law enforcement, military, athletic—signaling a masculinity at odds with some sexologists' assertions that homosexual men had the souls of women trapped in male bodies [λ Chapter 2]. The drawings were often inspired by the photos appearing in the very magazines for which Tom was working and, as Ramakers points out, were "intended to complement the photos of desirable young men, which were the basis of the physique magazines' success" (48).

Clearly, beefcake magazines served a particular function for white gay men. However, they also reflected the pervasive racism that has so plagued U.S. constructions of maleness and, by extension, male homosexuality. Tracy Morgan points out that when the Mattachine Society and the Daughters of Bilitis were protesting the McCarthy purges of white homosexuals from government jobs, "few Black people were federally employed" at all (284). Morgan notes that the kind of racism that excluded blacks from government employment was reflected as well in the pages of physique magazines, where the portrait of masculinity was "patriotic, strong, and white" (284) and that gay men who found these images sexually arousing might enjoy the magazines less if the images were more racially diverse. This does not mean, however, that no men of color appeared as models in physiques. Of the three main types of magazines Morgan found—those using a Grecian metaphor, the "all-American" style directed at fitness buffs, and those that served as "early homophile publications" (287)—the second type was the most (though not significantly) racially integrated. Morgan says,

> Black men were generally underrepresented in physique publications in relation to their actual numbers in U.S. society during the years 1955–60. . . . The "all-American"-style physique magazines I surveyed included more than four times as many images of Black men as did the Grecian publications. In the latter category, in approximately twenty-six volumes published over a five-year period (1955–60), a paltry four images of Black men made it into print. . . . In contrast, the magazines oriented toward bodybuilding . . . included an average of one Black male image per issue, and often more. (289)

To understand the presence of black men in some physique magazines as indicative of any kind of effort to resist the racism in the larger culture would be a mistake. As Morgan notes, black men were often photographed with "props" like heavy chains and cargo crates, and the few Latino men who appeared in the pages of physiques, though "generally represented with fewer accouterments, occasionally don straw hats while surrounded by rum bottles" (290). As is clear, the racial stereotypes of the mid-century United States and the tendency to exoticize the racial other were reflected in these magazines, and as we will see in a later chapter, Robert Mapplethorpe's homoerotic photographs of black men in the 1980s may represent a later version of this practice [λ Chapter 12].

Lesbian Pulp Novels

The first modern paperbacks appeared in 1939 but did not proliferate until World War II when the military distributed them to soldiers on the front as entertainment. These books, known as "pulps" because of the cheap paper used in their production, were designed to appeal to mainstream (as opposed to "literary") readers, so they tended to focus on topics and use storylines that would enrapture a reader from the very first page. This meant that they were generally formulaic westerns, detective fiction, romance, and "ripped from the headlines" sensational texts that tended to reinforce ideas popularly held in the culture. Pulp novels had their heyday between 1950 and 1965, and they were sold on newsstands, as well as in drugstores and bus terminals, usually for about 25 cents. Their low price and pocket-sized format meant that most people considered them disposable in the same way that their predecessors, pulp magazines, had been. Scholar Yvonne Keller describes lesbian pulps as "typically lurid, voyeuristic and frequently homophobic, easily the opposite of 'high literature.' At the time, they were called 'trashy,' or 'dirty books'; they are somewhat like *National Enquirer* in book form" ("Ab/Normal" 177–78). Initially, lesbian pulps were written with a heterosexual male audience in mind, an audience that would find their contents titillating and would read them with a voyeuristic gaze. Hence, many of the early authors of lesbian-themed pulps were men.

The covers of lesbian pulp novels, as Jaye Zimet shows in *Strange Sisters: The Art of Lesbian Pulp Fiction, 1949–1969*, often featured illustrations of busty, scantily clad, traditionally beautiful, almost always white women, and most often there were two women on the cover—one kneeling or lying on the floor or a bed and the other standing above her or sitting nearby, either looking at the first woman or gazing out at the viewer/reader. With titles like *Women's Barracks* (1950), *Female Convict* (1952), *Women in Prison* (1953), *Women without Men* (1957), and *Reformatory Girls* (1960), these books promised to reveal the sultry underside of environments where nontraditional women—soldiers, prisoners, and wayward teens—lived together as emotional and sexual companions. Of the women portrayed on pulp covers, Ann Bannon says,

> Who were these "girls"? Gazing at the pulp-art covers of lesbian fiction published half a century ago is like reconnecting with old acquaintances; I hesitate to call them friends, since I never really recognized them as such. In fact, over the years as my own books [the Beebo Brinker series] were published, I looked in astonishment at the choices the editors and art directors had made. The books arrived in brown packets, for the very good reason that they were deliberately evocative of shady sex. With only small adjustments, and sometimes

none at all, the young women I was looking at could easily have walked off those pulp covers and onto the pages of *Harper's Bazaar* to sell the "New Look." Many could have graced the ladies' undies section of the Sears, Roebuck catalog just as they were. (qtd. in Zimet 9)

The covers of lesbian-themed pulps, then, were not the lesbians with whom most women—those who knew they knew lesbians, that is—were familiar, especially early on; these were the lesbians of heterosexual male fantasies.

Women's Barracks, by Tereska Torres, was the book that started "the golden age of paperback originals" (Stryker 49). The novel is based at least partially on Torres's experiences serving in Charles de Gaulle's Free French army during World War II. Though *Women's Barracks* deals openly with the sexual dalliances among the military women who are its characters, that is not its primary focus.

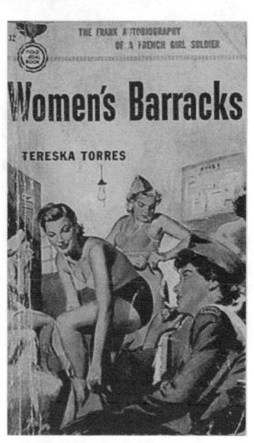

The book sold over a million copies in 1950, and eventually it gained such notoriety that it became the focus of obscenity trials in Canada and the United States. Noting that after World War II, Canadian newsstands "were opened to a huge range of mass market publications from the United States," Mary Louise Adams explains that Crown Attorney Raoul Mercier showed no interest in "the parts where heterosexual women find themselves pregnant, or where they discuss their plans to sleep with married men or where they attempt suicide. The definition of immorality was too narrow to include them. For Mercier, what made this

Figure 10.4   *Women's Barracks* cover

book obscene was its discussion of lesbianism" (111). In 1952, *Women's Barracks* was brought before a U.S. House of Representatives committee led by Congressman Ezekiel Candler Gathings; the committee "refused to quote it in their *Report of the Select Committee into Current Pornographic Materials,* claiming that its lesbian passages—which were restrained by contemporary standards—were too graphic to be included in a government document" (Stryker 51). According to Stryker, the report from the Gathings Committee resulted in publishers attempting to tone down the sexual content of their books and placing "greater emphasis on stories that drove home

A story once told in whispers now frankly, honestly written

SPRING FIRE

Vin Packer

AN ORIGINAL NOVEL—NOT A REPRINT ©

Figure 10.5 *Spring Fire* cover

the generally tragic consequences of straying from the straight and narrow path" (51).

Some lesbians, most writing under pseudonyms, began to author lesbian-themed pulp novels specifically for a lesbian audience. Vin Packer, whose given name is Marijane Meaker and whose other pennames were Ann Aldrich and M. E. Kerr, wrote what was probably the first of these novels, *Spring Fire.* The novel is about Leda and Mitch, two sorority sisters who become involved in a dramatic, sexually charged romance marked by overwrought drama and betrayal. The story ends tragically with Leda lapsing into psychosis and Mitch clearly "scared straight" by the entire sordid affair.

Meaker is quick to point out that previous to the publication of *Spring Fire,* a lesbian market was not evident to anyone at Fawcett (the book's publisher), which was merely spurred on to publish more lesbian-themed paperbacks by the economic success of *Women's Barracks:*

> [*Spring Fire*] was not aimed at any lesbian market, because there wasn't any that we knew about. I was just out of college. I was gay . . . it wasn't a prurient book . . . Tereska Torres wasn't aiming [*Women's Barracks*] at any market either—just telling her experiences the best she could, as I was. We were amazed, *floored,* by the mail that poured in. That was the first time that anyone was aware of the gay audience out there. (qtd. in Keller, "Was It Right" 390)

Stryker echoes Meaker's characterization of the impact of *Spring Fire,* claiming that it "called attention to an enthusiastic lesbian readership whose extent had not been appreciated previously but one to which Fawcett and other mainstream paperback publishers would cater for the next fifteen years" (57). Perhaps for the first time, and clearly by accident, a lesbian market had emerged.

Roberta Yusba notes that "perhaps 40 or 50 lesbian novels were written by women and were also good enough to become underground classics. Dog-eared copies of books by Ann Bannon, Valerie Taylor, Artemis Smith, and Paula Christian were passed among friends in lesbian communities . . . and also reached isolated, small-town lesbians who could read them and see that they were not the only lesbians in the world" (qtd. in Nealon 748). Though the publishers still had ultimate control over the covers of the books, the stories between the covers tended to act as "tour books" of places where lesbians seemed to congregate and interact with one another—places such as Greenwich Village, the scene of Bannon's Beebo Brinker series.

Figure 10.6   Ann Bannon

They also functioned as what Joan Nestle has called "survival literature" in that they helped provide a sense of what romantic relationships between women might look like. In her anthology of excerpts from lesbian-themed pulp novels, Katherine V. Forrest explains that very little biographical information exists for the novelists who produced these books because many of "the pulp fiction lesbian writers were deeply closeted, and some have dissolved into the mists like Cheshire cats, leaving only their printed words behind" (xi).

Two authors who did not exactly dissolve into the mists were Patricia Highsmith (Mary Patricia Plangman) and Ann Bannon (Ann Weldy). Highsmith, writing as Claire Morgan, produced what many claim to be the first lesbian novel to end "happily"—that is, with the possibility that the two main characters, Therese and Carol, might enjoy an ongoing lesbian relationship with one another. *The Price of Salt* was not a paperback original, but

Figure 10.7   Patricia Highsmith

it reached the height of its popularity after it appeared in paperback in 1952. Because it was published first by a mainstream publisher, Highsmith's novel had less of the

Find Out More about lesbian pulps by reading a selection from Ann Bannon's *I Am a Woman*, the reading at the end of this chapter.

potboiler character of paperback originals and more of the relative complexity of mainstream literature. Although popular novelist Highsmith (author of *Strangers on a Train, The Talented Mr. Ripley,* and other books) did not acknowledge until 1984 that she was indeed the Claire Morgan who wrote *The Price of Salt,* the fact that it sold a million copies indicates that it met a need for a lesbian readership hungry for representation.

By contrast, Ann Bannon's Beebo Brinker novels were published as paperback originals; they tended to have more fully developed, less stereotypical lesbian characters and plots, as well as slightly more hopeful endings than many of the pulps. Bannon's novels were rereleased in the 1980s and 1990s by well-known lesbian publishing house Naiad Press and in the 2000s by Cleis Press, and all of Highsmith's novels were recently rereleased by W. W. Norton.

Gay Male Pulp Novels

Like their lesbian-themed counterparts, which were much "more numerous and popular than those that dealt with male homosexuality," gay male-themed pulps "represent, beneath a veneer of enticing exploitation, a compendium of the not-so-hidden preoccupations and fears of the tempestuous and socially unstable postwar years" (Bronski, *Pulp Friction* 3). Michael Bronski notes, though, that the "trajectory for gay male pulps is very different [from that of lesbian-themed pulps]. There was no burgeoning market for gay male novels in the 1950s because they apparently had little crossover appeal for a substantial heterosexual readership" (4). Although some gay male-themed pulp novels were published as paperback originals, many were republications of earlier novels originally published in hardback by mainstream houses.

A few gay male books written and published in hardback during the 1930s and republished in paperback format after World War II were André Tellier's *Twilight Men,* which was originally published in 1931 and republished in paperback by Greenberg in 1948 and by Pyramid Books in 1957; Blair Niles's (a woman

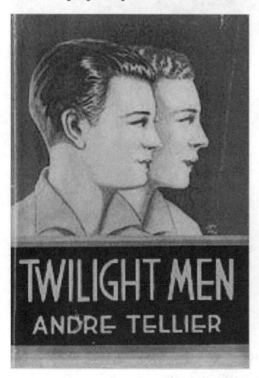

Figure 10.8   *Twilight Men* cover

best known at the time for the travel and nature writing she wrote collaboratively with her husband) *Strange Brother,* also originally published in 1931, then republished in 1952; and Forman Brown's *Better Angel,* published in 1933 and republished in 1951 as *Torment* under the pseudonym Richard Meeker. Novels by mainstream authors such as Gore Vidal (*The City and the Pillar,* 1948) and Truman Capote (*Other Voices, Other Rooms,* 1948) received critical attention and notoriety because of their gay male content—explicit in the case of Vidal and implicit in the case of Capote.

We should not assume, however, that Vidal's fame and connections granted his gay-themed novel immunity from homophobia in the publishing business. *The City and the Pillar* "so unnerved *The New York Times* it refused even to print the publisher's ads" (Young). This rejection was surely a factor in how Vidal composed the original ending of his novel. The original edition of *The City and the Pillar* ends with the main character, Jim, murdering Bob, the childhood friend with whom he has

Figure 10.9   Truman Capote's jacket photo for *Other Voices, Other Rooms*

been in love ever since their sexual encounters in the woods when both boys were teens. The murder occurs in the context of Jim's realization of Bob's homophobia. The 1965 version of *The City and the Pillar* was revised by Vidal and ends with Jim raping rather than murdering Bob, ostensibly because Vidal no longer needed to conform to publisher mandates that the book end in the death of one of the main characters. Capote's *Other Voices, Other Rooms* focuses on Joel Knox, who is sent to live in a rural Alabama mansion with his estranged father and a cast of other characters, including Randolph, who is a transvestite. Near the end of the novel, the reader is led to believe that Randolph is also the character described by Joel earlier as the "queer lady" who appears in one of the mansion's windows. *Other Voices, Other Rooms* did not enjoy great critical success because reviewers

Figure 10.10   James Baldwin

saw it as contrived and lacking in narrative structure. However, the implicit homosexual themes in the novel, combined with the provocative jacket photo—Capote lounging on a sofa and giving the camera a "come hither" look—caused a controversy that helped make Capote a literary star. Vidal's novel was republished in paperback in 1950 and Capote's in 1949, making theirs among the first gay-themed novels to appear in paperback format.

Like *The City and the Pillar* and *Other Voices, Other Rooms,* James Baldwin's *Giovanni's Room* (1956) [λ Chapter 9] appeared in paperback after experiencing little success in its initial hardback printing. *Giovanni's Room* is a book Michael Bronski characterizes as among those gay "self-hating novels . . . which end in either murder or self-destruction" ("Queer Eye"). As a Signet pulp, however, featuring a sexy Giovanni on the cover and a pseudo-journalistic subscript ("A daring novel that treats a controversial subject with honesty and compassion"), *Giovanni's Room* sold much better than before—signaling, perhaps, a growing mainstream interest in frank treatments of homosexual lives.

We should also note that some of the women writing lesbian pulps were also writing books with gay male themes. "Vin Packer" (Marijane Meaker), for example, published *Whisper His Sin* in 1954. Stryker says of this novel, "Prior to the mid-1960s there were simply no mass-market books that dealt with male-male desire that did not somehow couch it in terms of bisexual conflict, illustrate it with misleading cover art containing both men and women, or hide it behind pathologizing marketing blurbs. This was certainly the case with *Whisper his Sin . . .* which did a little of all three" (107).

Transgender Novels

At mid-century, North American and Western European ideas about the nature of homosexuality—which deeply affected the packaging of pulp novels—still reflected the influence of the German sexologists' ideas about gender inversion [λ Chapter 2]. As a result, post–World War II pulp novels often portrayed lesbians and gay men as possessing the qualities commonly associated with "the other" gender. What's more, U.S. popular media and culture, profoundly affected by advances in technology, were asking ethical questions often associated with technological progress—How far is too far for science to go in altering nature? What is the relationship between science and nature? In previous generations, these questions had manifested themselves in fascination with the human potential to create monsters in the name of science—as in, for instance, Mary Shelley's *Frankenstein.* In 1952, this type of fascination focused on transsexuality when the news broke that Christine Jorgensen, formerly George, had received successful sex reassignment surgery in Denmark. According to Stryker, though Jorgensen's autobiography (with an introduction by Harry Benjamin) [λ Chapter 5] would not be published until 1967, the "journalism trade publication *Editor and Publisher* announced in the spring of 1954 that more newsprint had been generated about Jorgensen during the previous year than about any other individual—over a million and a half words" (73).

As is evidenced in the work of B-movie director Edward D. Wood Jr. (featured in the 1994 bio-pic *Ed Wood*, by Tim Burton), in 1950s U.S. popular culture, almost no distinction was made among transvestitism, transsexuality, and intersexuality. Capitalizing on the Jorgensen media frenzy, Wood directed *Glen or Glenda* based on Jorgensen's sex change operation. Humorously dubbed the "Worst Director of All Time," Wood supplemented his income as a producer by writing pulp novels, most of which contained transvestite characters or focused exclusively on transvestitism. Among the titles are *Black Lace Drag* (1963), featuring a transvestite hit man named Glen and his drag persona, Glenda, and its sequel, *Death of a Transvestite* (1967). Wood's quickly composed, sensationalist work—both in film and in print—has gained such a following in recent years that there is currently an Internet religion called The Church of Ed Wood, which boasts a membership of over 3,000.

Stryker points out that some "novels written in the late 1940s, well before the Jorgensen media blitz, suggest that transgender issues were actually quite central to postwar American anxieties about sexuality, and to the paperback phenomenon itself" (77). One example of how these anxieties were expressed is Stuart Engstrand's *The Sling and the Arrow*. Engstrand's sensational novel is about a man who not only cross-dresses but asks his wife to do the same; he eventually becomes psychotic, imagines that he has transformed into a woman, kills his wife, and "drives off into the night where he takes his place near the head of a long line of gender-bent pop culture killers" (Stryker 78).

Lesbian pulp novels were seen for at least a decade following the advent of feminism as having very little positive to say to women wishing to build identities not constricted by stereotypes and sexist constructions of gender. However, queer pulps and, more recently, pulp cover art have reemerged as popular artifacts. The current use of pulp covers as refrigerator magnets, postcards, and T-shirt transfers celebrates campy images that recall, if not a more difficult time, then at least a more closeted time. The celebration of pulp reveals a sense of connection to a past today's LGBT people both eschew and embrace. Many critics focus on the unhappy endings and bizarre characterizations in these books, but Katherine Forrest proclaims, "Their words reached us, they touched us in different and deeply personal ways, and they helped us all" (xix). Though it is clear that most pulp texts were meant to teach readers that queers were . . . well, queer, and therefore doomed to difficult lives filled with sleaze and shame, our predecessors found in them important connections to one another.

QUESTIONS FOR DISCUSSION

1. Works of pulp fiction, despite their often tragic endings, can be great fun to read, particularly as they offer an insight into what gay, lesbian, bisexual, and transgendered lives might have been like in mid-century America. Read a few pulp fiction stories from Katherine V. Forrest's anthology of lesbian pulps or Michael Bronski's anthology of gay male pulps. What characterizes the representation of gay and lesbian lives or homoerotic desire in these novels and stories? For instance, what bisexual plots do you see? Are there any similarities between these pulp representations and contemporary figurings of queer life in mainstream media?

2. The art of Tom of Finland typically eroticizes uniformed, jackbooted, muscular men in scenarios where they dominate other men. What do you believe the artist intended viewers to experience? Is there any political or social meaning to Tom's art?

3. The selection from Ann Bannon's pulp novel *I Am a Woman* included in the readings for this chapter focuses on the coming-out conversation between Laura and her controlling and abusive father. During the course of this conversation, Laura accuses her father of having caused her to become a lesbian. Consider this idea in light of the discussion of 1950s pop Freudianism in Chapter 3. What are some of the major narratives purporting to explain why people are L, G, B, or T?

REFERENCES AND FURTHER READING

Adams, Mary Louise. "Youth, Corruptibility, and the English-Canadian Postwar Campaigns against Indecency, 1948–1955." *Journal of History of Sexuality* 6.1 (1995): 89–117.

Barale, Michéle Aina. "When Jack Blinks: Si(gh)ting Gay Desire in Ann Banno's *Beebo Brinker.*" *Feminist Studies* 18.1 (1992): 533–49.

Bianco, David. "Physique Magazines." *PlanetOut History.* 2007. 8 August 2008 <www.planetout .com/news/history/archive/09271999.html>.

Brandt, Kate. *Happy Endings: Lesbian Writers Talk about Their Lives and Work.* Tallahassee, FL: Naiad, 1993.

Bronski, Michael. *Pulp Friction: Uncovering the Golden Age of Gay Male Pulps.* New York: St. Martin's Griffin, 2003.

———. "Queer Eye for the 50s Guy." *Utne Reader.* January/February 2004. 8 August 2008 <http://www.utne.com/2004-01-01/Queer-Eye-for-the-50s-Guy.aspx>.

Cruikshank, Margaret. *Lesbian Studies: Present and Future.* New York: Feminist Press, 1982.

Duberman, Martin, Martha Vicinus, and George Chauncey, eds. *Hidden from History: Reclaiming the Gay and Lesbian Past.* New York: Meridian, 1990.

Foote, Stephanie. "Deviant Classics: Pulps and the Making of Lesbian Print Culture." *Signs: Journal of Women in Culture and Society* 31.1 (2005): 169–90.

Forrest, Katherine V. *Lesbian Pulp Fiction: The Sexually Intrepid World of Lesbian Paperback Novels, 1950–1965.* San Francisco: Cleis, 2005.

Foster, Jeannette H. *Sex Variant Women in Literature.* Tallahassee, FL: Naiad, 1985.

Goldman, Jason. "The Golden Age of Gay Porn: Nostalgia and the Photography of Wilhelm von Gloeden." *Gay and Lesbian Quarterly* 12.2 (2006): 237–58.

Grier, Barbara. *The Lesbian in Literature.* Tallahassee, FL: Naiad, 1981.

Hooven, Valentine. "Tom of Finland: A Short Biography." *Tom of Finland.* 2003–2006. Tom of Finland Foundation. 7 April 2007 <www.tomoffinlandfoundation.org/foundation/touko.html>.

Keller, Yvonne. "Ab/Normal Looking: Voyeurism and Surveillance in Lesbian Pulp Novels and US Cold War Culture." *Feminist Media Studies* 5.2 (2005): 177–95.

———. "Was It Right to Love Her Brother's Wife So Passionately? Lesbian Pulp Novels and U.S. Lesbian Identity, 1950–1965." *American Quarterly* 57.2 (2005): 385–410.

McGarry, Molly, and Fred Wasserman. *Becoming Visible: An Illustrated History of Lesbian and Gay Life in Twentieth-Century America.* New York: Penguin, 1998.

Miller, Alan. "Beefcake before Blueboy." *The Body Politic* 90 (Jan.–Feb. 1983). 8 August 2008 <http://www.clga.ca/Material/PeriodicalsLGBT/docs/beefcake.htm>.

Morgan, Tracy. "Pages of Whiteness: Race, Physique Magazines, and the Emergence of Public Gay Culture." *Queer Studies: A Lesbian, Gay, Bisexual, and Transgender Anthology.* Eds. Brett Beemyn and Mickey Eliason. New York: NYU P, 1996.

Nealon, Christopher. "Invert-History: The Ambivalence of Lesbian Pulp Fiction." *New Literary History* 31 (2000): 745–64.

Nestle, Joan. *A Restricted Country.* New York: Firebrand, 1987.

Ramakers, Micah. *Dirty Pictures: Tom of Finland, Masculinity, and Homosexuality.* New York: St. Martin's, 2000.

Saslow, James M. *Pictures and Passions: A History of Homosexuality in the Visual Arts.* New York: Penguin/Putnam, 1999.

Stryker, Susan. *Queer Pulp: Perverted Passions from the Golden Age of the Paperback.* San Francisco: Chronicle Books, 2001.

Waldron, Gail. "Charles Atlas: A Brief Biography." *Charles Atlas.* 2000. Charles Atlas, Ltd. 3 April 2007 <www.sandowplus.co.uk/Competition/Atlas/atlasindex.htm>.

Walters, Suzanna Danuta. "As Her Hand Crept Slowly Up Her Thigh: Ann Bannon and the Politics of Pulp." *Social Text* 23 (1989): 83–101.

Webber, Jim. "Physique Magazines: Beefcake and the Origins of Gay Male Adult Magazines." *Lavendar Library.* N.d. 2 April 2006 <www.lavenderlibrary.org/pages/Physique.htm>.

Wheeler, Elizabeth. *Uncontained: Urban Fiction in Postwar America.* New Brunswick, NJ: Rutgers, 2001.

Young, Ian. "The Paperback Explosion: How Gay Paperbacks Changed America." N.d. 8 August 2008 <www.ianyoungbooks.com/GayPbks/Paperbacks.htm>.

Zaborowska, Magdalena J. "Giovanni's Room." *The Literary Encyclopedia* 13 June 2003. The Literary Dictionary Company. 8 August 2008 <http://www.litencyc.com/php/sworks.php?rec=true&UID=4964>.

Zimet, Jaye. *Strange Sisters: The Art of Lesbian Pulp Fiction, 1949–1969.* New York: Viking, 1999.

Zimmerman, Bonnie. *The Safe Sea of Women: Lesbian Fiction, 1969–1989.* Boston: Beacon, 1990.

READING

➢ **Ann Bannon**

From I Am a Woman *(1959)*

(1932–), United States

He didn't know, and she didn't want him to know. She was the one who cared about their relationship, who wanted love and trust and gentleness between them. Not her father. He didn't give a damn, as long as she minded him. "You said you had no daughter," she repeated bitterly.

"You wanted it that way, Laura."

She turned to stare at him, incredulous. "I?" she said. "*I* wanted it that way?"

"You denied my existence before I ever denied yours," he said. "You ran away from me."

"You *forced* me to."

"I did no such thing."

"You made life intolerable for me."

"I didn't mean to." It was an extraordinary admission, completely unexpected, and she looked at him speechless for a moment.

"Then why didn't you show me some kindness?" she said. "Just a very little would have gone a long way, Father."

He crushed out his cigarette in the heavy ashtray with an expression of contempt on his face. "You women are all alike, I swear to God," he said. "Give you a little and you demand a lot."

"What's wrong with a lot?" she said, trembling. "You're my father."

"Yes, exactly!" he said, so roughly that she ducked. "I'm your father!"

"Did you treat my mother this way?" she whispered. "Her life must have been hell."

He looked for a minute as if he would strangle her. She stood her ground, pale and frightened, until he relented suddenly and turned his profile to her, looking out the window. "Your mother," he said painfully, "was my wife. I adored her."

Laura was absolutely unable to answer him. She sat down weakly in the stuffed chair by the dresser and put her face in her hands. Her father—her enormous gruff harsh father—had never spoken such a tender word in her presence in all her life.

"I could never marry again, when she died," he said. Laura felt frightened as she always did when her mother's death was mentioned. She expected him to turn on her unreasonably as he had so often before. "I never struck her."

"Then why me?" she implored out of a dry throat.

He turned and looked at her, his mouth twisted a little, running a distraught hand through his hair. "You needed it," was all he would say.

"What for?"

"You *needed* it, that's what for!" And she was afraid to push him further. After some minutes he said, "Laura, you're coming back to Chicago with me."

"No Father, I can't. I won't."

"That's why I waited for you," he went on, as if she had said nothing.

"I won't go to Chicago or anywhere else with you. I'm through with you."

"You could look for work with a radiologist, if you like it so well. I won't insist on jour-nalism. You have a flair for it, it's a waste to leave the field, but I won't insist. You see, Laura, I can be human enough."

She stared at him. She had never heard him talk like this. He glanced at her, annoyed by the look on her face. "I've made reservations," he said, "for June first. That's Saturday. I could probably get earlier ones."

"Father." She stood up. "I can't come with you."

"Don't say that!" he commanded her, so sharply that she started.

"I can't," she whispered.

"You can, and you will. That's all I want to hear on the subject." As she started once again to protest he held his hands up for silence. "No more discipline, Laura. I promise you that. I was a fool. You were too, but never mind that now. I was too hard on you, it's true. I see that. Well, you're more or less grown up by this time. I guess we can dis-pense with spanking."

"Spanking! It was more than that and you know it!"

"Don't argue with me, Laura." He turned on her, his voice low and fierce. Then, making a visible effort to calm himself, he said, "Get your things together and I'll see about the reservations."

"No."

"Don't fight me, Laura."

"Father, there's something you don't know about me." *I have to tell him. I'll never be free from him till I tell him. Till he knows what he's made of his only child.* "There's some-thing you don't know about me," she whispered.

"I don't doubt it. Now hurry up, we've wasted enough time."

"Father . . . listen to me." It was almost too hard to say. Her legs were trembling and her heart was wild.

"Well, out with it, for God's sake! Jesus, Laura, you go through more agony . . . Well? What is it?" He frowned at her tense face.

"I—I'm a—homosexual."

His mouth dropped open and his whole body went rigid. Laura shut her eyes and prayed. She held her lower lip in her teeth, ready for the blow, and felt the humiliating tears begin to squeeze through her shut lids. She moaned a little.

He made up his mind fast and his voice cracked out like a lash. "Nonsense!" he snarled.

"It's true!" Her eyes flew open and she cried again, passionately, "It's true!" It was her bid for freedom; she had to show this courage, this awful truth to him, or she would never walk away from him. She would spend all her life in a panic of fear lest he find her out. "I'm in love with my roommate. I've made love—"

"All right, all right, all right!" he shouted. His voice was rough and his face contorted. He turned away from her and put his hands over his face. She watched him, every muscle tight and aching.

At last he let his hands drop and said quietly, "Did I do that to you, Laura?"

Without hesitating, without even certain knowledge, but only the huge need to hurt him, she said, "Yes."

He turned slowly around and faced her and she had never seen his face like that before. It was pained and full of gentleness. Perhaps it looked that way to her mother now and then. "I did that to you," he said again, to himself. "Oh, Laura. Oh, Laura." His heavy brow creased deeply over his eyes. He walked to her and put his hands on her shoulders and felt her jerk with fear. "Laura," he said, "have you ever loved a man?"

She shook her head, unable to speak.

"Have you ever wanted a man?"

Again she shook her head.

"Do you know what it's like to want a man?"

"No," she whispered.

"Do you want to know?" His eyes were wide and intense, his grip on her shoulders was very hard.

"I'm so afraid of them, Father. I don't want to know."

He seemed to be in another world. Laura was utterly mystified by his strange behavior, blindly grateful for his sudden warmth, and she let herself weep softly.

"Laura," he said, as if he derived some private pleasure from saying her name over and over. "Your mother—you look so much like your mother. You never looked like me at all. Every time I look at you I see her face. Her fragile delicate face. Her eyes, her hair." He put his arms around her. "Come back to Chicago with me," he said gently. "You don't have to love a man, Laura. I don't want you to. I don't want you to be like other girls, I don't want you to go off with some young ass and give him your youth and your beauty. I don't mind if you're different from the rest. I can take that if you are able to."

Laura clung to him, astonished, fearful, grateful, anxious, a whirlwind of confused feelings churning inside her.

"I want you to stay with me," he said. "I always did. I won't let you go."

"You made me go, Father. You punished me so."

"No, no Laura! Don't you see, it was myself." He was holding her so hard now, as if to make up for years of avoiding her, that she ached with it. She began to cry on his shoulder.

"Oh, Father, Father," she wept. "You never told me you wanted me to stay with you. You made me believe you hated me."

"No," he said. "I never hated you." He spoke in a rush, as if he couldn't help himself, as if it were suddenly forcing its way out of him after years of suppression. "Never, Laura, it was just that I was so lonely, so terribly lonely; I wanted her so much and she was gone. And there was only you, and you tormented me."

"I?" She tried to see his face, but he held her too close.

"You were so much like her, even when you were a child. Every time I looked at you, I—oh, Laura, it's myself I should have punished all this time. I *was* punished. I've suffered. Believe me. Laura, please believe me."

Laura was suddenly shocked rigid to feel his lips on her neck. He put his hand in her hair and kissed her full on the mouth with such agonized intensity that he electrified her. He released her just as suddenly and turned away with a kind of sob. "Ellie! Ellie!" he cried, his hands over his face.

Laura was shaking almost convulsively. At the sound of her mother's name she grabbed the thick and heavy glass ashtray from the dresser, picking it up with both hands. She rushed at him, unable to think or reason, and brought the ashtray down on the crown of his head with all the revolted force in her body. He slumped to the floor without a sound.

Laura gaped at him for a sick second and then she turned and fled. She left the door wide open and ran in a terrible panic to the elevators. She sobbed frantically for a few moments, and then she pushed the down button. She jabbed it over and over again hysterically, unable to stop until an elevator arrived and the doors opened. She stumbled in and pressed into a back corner, helpless in the grip of the sickness in her. The operator and his two other passengers stared at her, but she paid them no heed, even when one asked if he could help her. At the ground floor the operator had to tell her, "Everybody out."

She turned a wild flushed face to him and he said, "Are you all right, Miss?" And she glared at him, violently offended by his manner, his uniform, his question.

"Don't you know those pants won't make a man of you?" she exclaimed acidly. And rushed out, leaving him gaping open-mouthed after her.

Bannon, Ann. *I Am a Woman*. Tallahassee, FL: Naiad, 1986 [1959]. Reprinted by Cleis in 2002.

CHAPTER 11

Queer Transgressive Aesthetics

The work we will be considering in this chapter is work by artists, designers, and cultural producers who use transgression consciously as a mode of social or political critique and resistance. Such work is often edgy, sometimes even erotic—but it is also very much public, addressing many audiences and challenging their assumptions and values. Transgressive art and literature have played an increasingly important role in shaping the contemporary queer imagination, especially as such art figures and foregrounds the ways queers resist dominating, normalizing, and homophobic narratives about their lives and loves. The works of authors such as Kathy Acker, Dennis Cooper, Gary Indiana, and Jeanette Winterson often portray characters engaging in acts of transgressive resistance—acts that simultaneously work against the restrictive identities that we are called to adopt in a heteronormative world and that, through their resistance, transgress the dichotomies, binaries, and boundaries that attempt to order identity, culture, and social interaction along delimiting lines of patriarchal and heterosexist ideologies. These works provide much-needed imaginative models for carving queer spaces, identities, and lives out of an often hostile political and cultural matrix. But, as Winterson notes in a refrain repeated throughout her collection of experimental fiction, *The World and Other Places,* "What you risk reveals what you value." While acts of transgression are often deployed as acts of resistance, they are also acts of assertion, performances of the transgressors' investments, and values both against and within the social matrix they are transgressing. This chapter also presents some material that invites an analysis of sexuality that runs deeper than traditional distinctions among sexual preferences and affiliations. This is work that questions normalizing assumptions for both queers and straights.

Theoretical Transgressions: The Emergence of Queer Theory

In many ways, queer theory has been among the most transgressive movements within the academy. Growing out of feminism, gay and lesbian studies, and postmodern literary theory, queer theory asks that we take very seriously the representation—and construction—of sex and sexuality in a wide variety of cultural venues. Gay and lesbian studies began to take shape in the 1970s and 1980s, focused on identifying and analyzing representations of the homoerotic and the homosexual in the canons of literature. A queer approach, beginning with Eve Kosofsky Sedgwick's *Epistemology of the Closet* (1990), substantively shifted the question of representation to a radical reunderstanding of Western culture as principally preoccupied with the construction and control of identities based on sexual orientation. Sedgwick argues that "virtually any aspect of modern Western culture must be, not merely incomplete, but damaged in its central substance to the degree that it does not incorporate a critical analysis of modern homo/heterosexual definition" (1). Following the work of Michel Foucault, thinkers such as Sedgwick and Judith Butler wanted not just to "find" homosexuals but to analyze the power constructs that divide us in the modern and contemporary world, at least in the West, into two "categories": gay and straight. These theorists question and often even reject the binary construction of the species into gay/straight, even male/female, in such a way that one pole of the binary (straight, often male) is valorized, privileged, and normalized over the other (gay, often female).

Probing what had been assumed to be a given—our identification based on sexual orientation—is certainly a transgressive move, prompting scholars to reconsider basic assumptions about identity, community, and politics. If the way we understand sexual orientation isn't a natural given, then neither are heterosexuality, homophobia, or bias against those who engage in alternative or nonnormative intimate and filial practices. Such thinking called for a mode of critique and an activist politics that insisted that we question the "norm" or anything that is socially constructed as "natural" or "normal." As David Halperin put it in *Saint Foucault: Toward a Gay Hagiography,*

> Resistance to normativity is not purely negative or reactive or destructive; it is also positive and dynamic and creative. It is by resisting the discursive and

institutional practices which, in their scattered and diffuse functioning, contribute to the operation of heteronormativity that queer identities can open a social space for the construction of different identities, for the elaboration of various types of relationships, for the development of new cultural forms. (66–67)

"Resistance to normativity," encapsulated in embracing the term *queer,* is a transgressive move. It asks that we reconsider the desirability of the "normal," of being "normal," and that we transgress boundaries of taste, belief, and values to "open a social space" for considering and valuing different tastes, beliefs, and values. More recently, bisexual and transgender activists and scholars have been using the basic tenets of queer theory to challenge constructions of **monogamy** and gender.

Art and Consumerism

Queer artists have been producing work that challenges assumptions about sex, gender, sexuality, and identity. As we have seen in previous chapters, ACT UP's various kiss-ins and demonstrations in Catholic churches in New York were designed to be provocative and transgressive. The point was to insert queer into spaces where people either felt safe from queerness or were not expecting displays of sexuality [λ Chapter 4]. In transgressing social norms about when and where sexuality, particularly queer sexualities, can be performed, ACT UP hoped to remind a complacent, indifferent, and even hostile culture that queer people and their issues, such as the AIDS epidemic, are part of the larger social and political fabric. In an effort to be recognized as citizens demanding ethical treatment, queer activists transgressed some of the West's "sacred" spaces, such as churches and shopping malls.

A clearly discernible, public, and even somewhat queer transgressive aesthetic in American culture became apparent in the writings of those who identified with **Beat culture** in the 1950s. Authors such as Jack Kerouac, Gregory Corso, and Diane DiPrima urged their readers, through a variety of experimental forms and free-form genres, to question what they saw as an emerging culture dominated by consumerism, political complacency, and repressive norms, particularly around sex and sexuality. This work would eventually contribute to revolutionary youth cultures of the 1960s, particularly the so-called sexual revolution. A founding figure of the Beat movement and a lifelong proponent of sexual freedom was the gay poet Allen Ginsberg (1926–1997), whose work understood democracy as enabling a variety of expressions of intimate freedom [λ Chapter 9]. In one of his most famous poems, "Howl" (written in 1955), Ginsberg laments the devastation wreaked on creative youth by a cramped, uptight, repressive society:

> I saw the best minds of my generation destroyed by madness, starving hysterical naked,
>
> dragging themselves through the negro streets at dawn looking for an angry fix, angelheaded hipsters burning for the ancient heavenly connection to the starry
>
> dynamo in the machinery of night . . .

A bit later in the poem, Ginsberg speaks frankly of homosexuals as victims of a sexually repressive consumerist society, of those

> who let themselves be fucked in the ass by saintly
>
> motorcyclists, and screamed with joy,
>
> who blew and were blown by those human seraphim,
>
> the sailors, caresses of Atlantic and Caribbean
>
> love,
>
> [. . .]
>
> who lost their loveboys to the three old shrews of fate
>
> the one eyed shrew of the heterosexual dollar
>
> the one eyed shrew that winks out of the womb
>
> and the one eyed shrew that does nothing but
>
> sit on her ass and snip the intellectual golden
>
> threads of the craftsman's loom . . . (23)

"Howl" was so inflammatory that shortly after its publication, the poem was the subject of a censorship trial. Fellow poet and publisher, Lawrence Ferlinghetti, who published "Howl" as part of his City Lights series, noted that "[t]he 'Howl' that was heard around the world wasn't seized in San Francisco in 1956 just because it was judged obscene by cops, but because it attacked the bare roots of our dominant culture, the very Moloch heart of our consumer society" (qtd. in Ginsberg, xi). Ginsberg's transgression lay not only in depicting homosexuality but also in linking the repression of queerness and other forms of alternative, nonnormative behavior to the desires of a consumerist culture to squelch transgressive creativity and enforce conformity.

More recent lesbian, gay, bisexual, transgender (LGBT) and queer artists have used a comparable transgressive energy to enliven their work and offer cultural critiques within the consumer culture that the Beats sought to reject. Perhaps most famously in the late twentieth century, the artist Robert Mapplethorpe [λ Chapter 12] produced a series of photographs of queer sex acts—some frankly sadomasochistic—that simultaneously shocked and titillated a variety of viewers, both queer and straight. We discuss Mapplethorpe in more detail in the next chapter, but an obvious question one must ask about him is whether an artist whose work becomes familiar in the popular culture can still be considered transgressive; the same question could be asked of photographer Annie Leibovitz, who was named "America's Best-Known Photographer" by *Newsweek* in 2007. Leibovitz began her career shooting for the fledgling *Rolling Stone,* and among her most familiar photographs, shot for that magazine, is one of Yoko Ono and John Lennon taken only hours before Lennon's murder in 1981. In 1991, a Leibovitz photograph of Demi Moore seven months pregnant and nude appeared on the cover of the mainstream magazine *Vanity Fair.* Except in New York City, that issue of the magazine appeared on bookstore shelves wrapped in a white envelope, with only Moore's eyes showing above (Anderson). In *Pregnant Pictures,* Sandra Matthews and Laura Wexler argue that "Leibovitz crossed a boundary at a ripe cultural moment, and with her image of the pregnant woman, pregnant pictures crossed over into the public visual domain" (qtd. in Bartlett 3). Leibovitz's work also seems to find "ripe cultural moments" for transgressing normative sexual boundaries with photographs of "famous" lesbian and gay people such as Melissa Etheridge, Martina Navratilova, and Leibovitz's long-time partner, Susan Sontag.

Leibovitz has enjoyed great popularity, much of it in mainstream culture and, most recently, in advertising. This fact highlights some important questions about transgression: if, as often happens in capitalist societies, art is commodified and accepted as part of the popular culture, can it still be considered transgressive? Are there ways in which art popularized and commodified in a culture can transgress traditional boundaries by reaching an audience that would not necessarily seek exposure to that which is more clearly transgressive?

Desiring to collapse the boundaries between the public and the private, or perhaps to show the artificiality of such boundaries in a consumerist culture that uses sex to sell merchandise, some gay designers have created controversy with public advertisements depicting gays, lesbians, and bisexuals together, often holding hands or kissing. Italian photographer Oliviero Toscani has produced controversial advertising images that aim not only to sell products, such as clothing for Benetton, but also to level pointed social critiques at war, capital punishment, racism, and homophobia. One report chronicles Toscani's mixing of advertising and activism:

> In 1990, Toscani's "United Colors of Benetton" campaign launched a ten-year span [of] symbolic, poignant, jarring, and controversial ads that the man and the company became known for: a priest kissing a nun; a bloody baby fresh from the womb; a black stallion mounting a white mare; a colorful mix of condoms spread over a bright background; a white infant suckling a black woman's breast; the exposed pulsing hearts of three different races shown during surgery; the body of an AIDS victim moments before death; frightened refugees clawing for food at a ship's cargo net; and the bloody uniform of a dead Bosnian soldier. (Lyman)

Toscani's advertisements for the clothing company Ra-Re have stirred protest in some countries, particularly the photographer's home country of Italy. The advertisements are frank depictions of male-male intimacy; in one photo, an older man clutches a younger man's crotch, and in another photo, the pair embrace on a couch (McMahon). According to reports from Italy, some parents and conservative citizens have complained vociferously about such advertisements, saying that they do not know how to explain such flagrant displays of homosexuality to children. But creating such dilemmas may be the aim of Toscani's work: to provoke consideration and discussion of that which still, in much of the West, remains hidden, closeted, and out of the public view. Toscani's photos transgress those boundaries, forcing the queer into public consciousness.

From Pornography to Sadomasochism

While some LGBT and queer artists may transgress the norms and expectations of the larger cultures in which they work and live, other queer artists focus attention on troubling normative expectations within communities. These artists, writers, and designers often feel that queer people are too quick to assimilate into larger cultures unwilling to examine their sexual prejudices and repressions. Some of these artists also believe that queers have simply become another commodity market, full of consumers who are eager to buy the latest cars, don the latest fashions, and sport the latest "must-have" gadgets, knick-knacks, and art.

A number of books on "how to be gay" poke fun at normative constructions of LGBT identity. For instance, *So You Want to Be a Lesbian? A Guide for Amateurs and Professionals*, by Liz Tracey and Sydney Pokorny, covers a variety of topics from coming out, flirting, and the promises (and pitfalls) of monogamy to lesbian culture, lesbian cuisine, lesbian vehicles, and "dyke cult heroes." Full of humor and fun "facts," *So You Want to Be a Lesbian?*, much like its companion volume, *The Unofficial Gay Manual*, is largely a parody of a popular genre, the "self-help" book. But while these books are mostly tongue-in-cheek, the popularity of such "guides" suggests a relatively normative sense of what it means to be gay or lesbian. Recently, a comparable book has appeared for bisexuals, *The Bisexual's Guide to the Universe: Quips, Tips, and Lists for Those Who Go Both Ways*, by Nicole Kristal and Mike Szymanski. More seriously, books such as *Virtually Normal* by Andrew Sullivan and *A Place at the Table* by Bruce Bawer argue that gays and lesbians should strive to fit into the dominant culture, adopting its nonhomophobic norms, in an effort to increase tolerance for homosexuals.

British writer Mark Simpson's edited collection, provocatively titled *Anti-Gay*, soundly critiques such assimilationist moves and argues for valuing a more transgressive kind of queerness:

That many non-heterosexuals were already itching to escape from gay's clingy, cartoony embrace has already been demonstrated with queer. . . . [There was] initially at least a strong strain of punkish transgression running through queer which was quite liberating for many. Groups like Homocult, the situationist art collective in Manchester, who specialized in "negative" images of homosexuality; North American zinesters like *Bimbox* who arguably invented queer; the work of film directors like Bruce LaBruce, Tom Kalin, and Todd Haynes who, as Kalin put it, aimed to put the "homo" back in "homicide"; and Queercore, a bad-attitude trash sound attracting a younger generation of deviants who didn't want or weren't wanted by what they took to be heterosexuality but didn't want to sip cappuccino on Old Compton Street or Santa Monica Boulevard either. (xv)

Many "established" gay and queer artists, such as Ginsberg and Mapplethorpe, have exhibited just such "punkish" traits in their work, which troubles a gay and lesbian community hoping to fit into the mainstream Western culture. Ginsberg's pro-communist, pro-drug politics, for instance, were unsettling to many in the broader LGBT community. Moreover, not only certain sectors of the public but also some other queer authors and activists were disturbed by Mapplethorpe's work. In these cases, what is being transgressed is a sense of how a larger LGBT or queer community wants to represent itself to itself. As we grapple with our own values, with what is important to us in our diverse and often divergent communities, conflicts inevitably arise [λ Chapter 7].

Find Out More in "A Question of Class" in the readings at the end of this chapter.

Dorothy Allison (b. 1949), award-winning author of *Bastard out of Carolina*, has written provocatively about the importance of recognizing and honoring our sexual desires, particularly for lesbians. In her collection of essays, *Skin,* she writes about pornography, a touchy subject among those feminists who see porn as degrading to women. Allison maintains a sex-positive approach, arguing that "the word queer means much more than lesbian. Since I first used it in 1980 I have always meant it to imply that I am not only a lesbian but a transgressive lesbian—femme, masochistic, as sexually aggressive as the women I seek out, and as pornographic in my imagination and sexual activities as the heterosexual hegemony has ever believed" (23). Pat Califia, writing as a sex-positive lesbian long before he transitioned to a transman, wrote about recognizing the divergent sexual tastes of queer communities. Califia's erotic fiction often transgressed self-imposed norms of sexual behavior among gays and lesbians, particularly as it depicted intense sado-masochistic sex acts and bisexual intimacy. In the essays in *Public Sex: The Culture of Radical Sex,* Califia challenged conceptions of the place, role, and variety of sexuality within queer cultures. In "A Secret Side of Lesbian Sexuality" (1979), Califia argued that "[t]he sexual closet is bigger than you think" (157) and announced, "I identify more strongly as a sadomasochist than as a lesbian. I hang out in the gay community because that's where the sexual fringe starts to unravel" (158). What Califia most appreciates about "gay community" is that it can be a space in which boundaries of normative sex and sexuality are transgressed [λ Chapter 7].

One artist whose work challenges what he sees as a prudishness lurking within some parts of the larger LGBT/queer community is Dennis Cooper (b. 1953). A stylistic maverick, Cooper works in many forms, including the novel, poetry, and journalism. The content of his work, though, has disturbed a variety of audiences, queer and nonqueer alike. Cooper's themes and plots focus on homoerotic sadomasochism, and some elements of his work are reminiscent of **snuff** porn, in which people are killed for the erotic pleasure of others. Noted gay novelist Edmund White says that Cooper is "[a]s obsessive as Sade and as far from ordinary morality as George Bataille"; the work "meditates ceaselessly on violence and perversion [and seems] dedicated to drugs, kink, and a fragile sense of beauty fashioned out of the detritus of American suburbs" (282). One of Cooper's most famous novels is *Frisk,* the second book in a five-novel sequence depicting the underlife of young men engaging in a variety of sexual practices, taking drugs, and sometimes hustling their bodies to make money for food or the next quick fix. These young people are often used and abused by older men who pay them to perform sexual services. In this sense, the books are reminiscent of the works of authors such as John Rechy, whose 1963 novel, *The City of Night,* sympathetically chronicled the lives of street hustlers servicing men.

But Cooper's aim in writing is not just to chronicle a queer underlife; it is rather to explore the erotic imagination in its most transgressive and boundary-pushing dimensions. *Frisk,* for instance, is a bizarre coming-of-age story, tracing the sexual development of one young man, ironically named Dennis, and his interest in sexual torture and snuff. In one passage, Dennis reflects on his desires:

> It wasn't that I didn't fantasize murdering hustlers. It's just that I tend to be too scared or shy the first few times I sleep with someone to do what I actually want. The worst that could, and did, happen was I'd get a little too rough. But the hustler would stop me, or I'd stop myself, before things became more than conventionally kinky, as far as he knew. (36)

During a trip to Holland, Dennis begins sending to his friends back home letters that describe his sexual exploits in which he becomes more than a "little rough" and actually murders his tricks. For Dennis, such sexual murder is driven by his desire to know, to possess the objects of his attraction; meditating on the contradiction between loving and killing, he tells a friend of his, "I can actually imagine myself inside the skins I admire. I'm pretty sure if I tore some guy open I'd know him as well as anyone could, because I'd have what he consists of right there in my hands, mouth, wherever. [. . .] I want to know *everything* about you. But to really do that, I'd have to kill you, as bizarre as that sounds" (51, 67).

Novels such as *Frisk,* like most of Cooper's work, have been decried by numerous gay activists, who see artists like Cooper as validating a homophobic society's belief that queers are predatory, sick, and sinful. At the very least, such activists maintain, presenting a seedy underside of gay life makes it more difficult for LGBT people to assimilate into the dominant culture and to claim that queer people are, essentially, just like everyone else. But Cooper's goals in novels such as *Frisk* are precisely to trouble the desire to fit in, the desire to be normal. At the end of the book, we learn that Dennis has not in fact killed anyone; we've just been reading, like the friends who received his letters, about fantasies that he has no intention of fulfilling. Cooper draws our attention to how most people have fantasies that they will not enact and how the content of our imaginations is often far from normative. As he puts it in an interview, *Frisk* "is about the difference between what is possible in one's fantasy life, and what is possible in one's real life. . . . It tries, in various ways, to seduce the readers into believing a series of murders are real, then announces itself as a fiction, hopefully leaving readers responsible for whatever pleasure they took in believing the murders were real. [. . .] Murder is only erotic in the imagination, if at all" (Reitz). *Frisk,* then, points out that the transgressive lies, often latently, behind most any façade of normalcy and that ignoring it is to ignore part of what makes us complex and interesting. Cooper also insinuates that transgressive and normalizing impulses coexist, often uneasily, and that any ethical life will have to acknowledge their interrelationship and negotiate carefully between them. Novelists such as Cooper show us that the transgressive lies not just at the "fringes" of the mainstream; it is often at its center, critiquing the normative lives many of us build for ourselves.

Transgression and Politics

Throughout this chapter, we have outlined how many different LGBT and queer artists have used the transgressive to question the values, norms, and assumptions of both dominant cultures and LGBT communities. At this point, though, we must ask, what are the limits of transgression as a form of political agency? More broadly, to what political use can transgression be put, and is it a politically efficacious strategy? Certainly, artists such as Cooper, as well as other gay writers such as Bret Easton Ellis (*Less Than Zero* and *American Psycho*) and Jeannette Winterson (*Written on the Body* and *Oranges Are Not the Only Fruit*), challenge us with difficult topics, inviting us to identify with transgression and transgressive acts. In the process, these writers question our assumptions about what is normal and, through our periodic identifications with nonnormative characters, provoke us to reconsider our tendency to prejudge. At the same time, there are limits. Jeanette Winterson, at the end of her novel *Art and Lies,* depicts the relationship between a priest and a young boy whom the priest has gelded so that he can be a *castrato,* remaining boy-like and retaining his high-pitched singing voice. While Winterson's writing is beautiful and often moving, to what extent can we identify with the priest? Moreover, do we want to identify with such characters? What are our limits in questioning and stretching our own values?

Other questions about transgressive aesthetic practices and their ability to promote change have surfaced around drag performances and their exploration of gender. Judith Butler, in her groundbreaking book *Gender Trouble* (1990), which helped form the queer theoretical approach, argued that drag performances show us that gender isn't a given, that it is a "performance" to which people are called and that must be repeated again and again to pass as "normal." A drag queen can perform femininity, for instance, showing up femininity as a cultural construct. But does drag performance transgress gender norms and our understanding of gender as essential? Or does it reinforce normative notions of gender? Some critics believe that drag performances might actually disparage femininity and feminine behavior rather than celebrate them in their performances. In *The Drag King Book* (1999), Judith Halberstam argues that

> [t]he future of gender . . . remains uncertain. Gender rebellion seems to be standard fare in popular magazines, sitcoms, cartoons, mainstream film and it is in full display on many a college campus. But somehow the bending of gender has failed actually to shift the dominance of male and female as the binary poles of gender definitions. Gender play offers us, paradoxically, much room for trial and error, but also little prospect for momentous change. Girls and boys are still raised to be normal men and women, and gender experimentation is far from encouraged. (150)

In *The Sexual Citizen,* academics David Bell and Jon Binnie take up the issue of transgressive approaches, arguing ultimately that it is important, even imperative, that we question—and transgress—the boundaries that keep sex and sexuality a purely private affair. They ask, "How can we think about intimacy without reinstating the public/private divide; without keeping intimacy's link to privacy intact?

How do we think love in ways other than those hegemonically scripted by mainstream culture? What is it that we talk about when we talk about love?" (124).

One still wonders, though, if figuring queerness as "necessarily oppositional" (138), as transgressive, really *works.* Certainly, some will be alienated by such an approach. And it is important to keep in mind that understanding queerness as a mode of transgressive political agency is a very Western concept. In other cultures, in which queerness and the homoerotic are understood differently, opening up a space for transgressive politicking is difficult, if not impossible. Tom Boellstorff, for example, identifies how constructions of queerness in non-Western cultures problematize strategies for resistance. In Indonesia, he writes,

> *Gay* men and *lesbi* do not "come out of the closet" but speak of being "opened" . . . or "shut." . . . We find not an epistemology of the closet but an epistemology of life worlds, where healthy subjectivity depends not on integrating diverse domains of life and having a unified, unchanging identity in all situations but on separating domains of life and maintaining their borders against the threat of gossip and discovery. (228)

In Indonesia, then, queer transgression as we have described it might not register with the same amount of combined provocation and titillation. It might be rejected outright as simply an unhealthy management of identities, and thus the space for considering renegotiation of boundaries and values might not open up. More pointedly, in some countries, such as Iran, the appearance of open homosexuality may be considered transgressive enough to warrant the death penalty [λ Chapter 4]. A thorough understanding of a sociocultural and political context, including what boundaries can be pushed and how hard, is necessary if transgression is to help open up a space for reconsidering cultural values. Some boundaries pushed too hard may create backlash, counterresistance, and unintended consequences. And at many times, the pushing of boundaries around sex and sexuality, particularly homoerotic sexuality, has resulted in moral panics, even censorship—key subjects of the following chapter.

QUESTIONS FOR DISCUSSION

1. Transgressive tactics are dependent for their efficacy on particular contexts, and in some circumstances, transgression is an ineffective way to raise consciousness and spark debate. Interview an LGBT activist in your locale and ask him, her, or ze about the use of transgressive tactics in promoting awareness of LGBT/queer issues and concerns. You might easily find such an activist by calling an LGBT center in your area.

2.   What is the line between the pornographically and the transgressively erotic? Some would argue that certain kinds of pornography are in fact "trangressive" in that they force us to rethink attitudes about sex and sexuality and to consider new forms of sexual pleasure and desire. Write about this idea, highlighting the distinction between the pornographic and the transgressively erotic. As part of your thinking, you might consider the binary present in this question: Are there clear boundaries between the erotic and the pornographic?

3.   Sometimes we learn not just by reading and thinking about a subject but by *doing* and participating in it as well. Try your hand at creating some transgressive art. Create a collage in which you attempt to transgress a particular notion, idea, or norm. What norms would you choose to transgress? Gender norms? Sexual norms? Norms surrounding public and private behavior? Think of your collage as an advertisement that would be posted around your local community. How would that community respond? What kinds of transgressive collages would be particularly provocative in your community? That is, what kinds of transgressive tactics would be politically useful without so alienating community members that they simply ignore your message?

REFERENCES AND FURTHER READING

Allison, Dorothy. *Skin: Talking about Race, Sex and Class.* New York: Firebrand, 1994.

Anderson, Susan Heller. "Chronicle." *New York Times* 11 July 1991. 8 August 2008 <http://query.nytimes.com/gst/fullpage.html?res=9D0CE3D8173AF932A25754C0A967958260&sec=&spon=&partner=permalink&exprod=permalink>.

Bartlett, Alison. "Madonnas, Models, and Maternity: Icons of Breastfeeding in the Visual Arts." N.d. 8 August 2008 <www.usq.edu.au/resources/bartlettpaper.pdf>.

Bawer, Bruce. *A Place at the Table: The Gay Individual in American Society.* New York: Poseidon P, 1993.

Bell, David, and Jon Binnie. *The Sexual Citizen: Queer Politics and Beyond.* Malden, MA: Blackwell, 2000.

Boellstorff, Tom. "The Perfect Path: Gay Men, Marriage, Indonesia." In *Queer Studies: An Interdisciplinary Reader.* Ed. Robert J. Corber and Stephen Valocchi. Malden, MA: Blackwell, 2003. 218–36.

Bronski, Michael, ed. *Pulp Friction: Uncovering the Golden Age of Male Pulps.* New York: St. Martin's Griffin, 2003.

Butler, Judith. *Gender Trouble: Feminism and the Subversion of Identity.* New York: Routledge, 1990.

Califia, Pat. *Public Sex: The Culture of Radical Sex.* Pittsburgh, PA: Cleis, 1994.

Cooper, Dennis. *Frisk.* New York: Grove, 1991.

DiLallo, Kevin, and Jack Krumholtz. *The Unofficial Gay Manual.* New York: Main Street, 1994.

Ensler, Eve. "The Little Coochi Snorcher That Could." Deleted scene from *The Vagina Monologues.* 9 August 2008 <www.sacerdoti.com/jonathan/vaginas/coochie.html>.

Ginsberg, Allen. "Howl." *Howl on Trial.* Eds. Bill Morgan and Nancy J. Peters. San Francisco: City Lights, 2006. 16–30.

Halberstam, Judith. *The Drag King Book.* London: Serpent's Tail, 1999.

Halperin, David. *Saint Foucault: Toward a Gay Hagiography.* New York: Oxford UP, 1995.

Kristal, Nicole, and Mike Szymanski. *The Bisexual's Guide to the Universe: Quips, Tips, and Lists for Those Who Go Both Ways.* New York: Alyson, 2006.

Lyman, Eric J. "The True Colors of Oliviero Toscani." August 2001. 26 May 2007 <http://www.ericjlyman.com/adageglobal.html>.

McMahon, Barbara. "Italy Snaps over Gay Poster Excess." *The Observer.* 18 September 2005. 26 May 2007 <http://observer.guardian.co.uk/international/story/0,6903,1572822,00.html>.

Reitz, Daniel. "Dennis Cooper." *Salon.* 4 May 2000. 26 May 2007 <http://archive.salon.com/people/feature/2000/05/04/cooper/index.html>.

Sedgwick, Eve Kosofsky. *Epistemology of the Closet.* Berkeley: U California P, 1990.

Simpson, Mark. *Anti-Gay.* London: Freedom, 1996.

Sullivan, Andrew. *Virtually Normal: An Argument about Homosexuality.* New York: Knopf, 1995.

Tracey, Liz, and Sydney Pokorny. *So You Want to Be a Lesbian? A Guide for Amateurs and Professionals.* New York: St. Martin's Griffin, 1996.

Volcano, Del Lagrace, and Judith "Jack" Halberstam. *The Drag King Book.* London: Serpent's Tail, 1999.

White, Edmund. *The Burning Library: Essays.* New York: Random House 1994.

Winterson, Jeanette. *Art and Lies.* New York: Knopf, 1995.

———. *The World and Other Places.* New York: Knopf, 1999.

READING

> **Dorothy Allison**

From "A Question of Class"

(1949–), United States

[. . .]

When in the 1980s I ran into the concept of feminist sexuality, I genuinely did not know what it meant. Though I was, and am, a feminist, and committed to claiming the right to act on my sexual desires without tailoring my lust to a sex-fearing society, demands that I explain or justify my sexual fantasies have left me at a loss. How does anyone explain sexual need?

The Sex Wars are over, I've been told, and it always makes me want to ask who won. But my sense of humor may be a little obscure to women who have never felt threatened by the way most lesbians use and mean the words *pervert* and *queer.* I use the word queer to mean more than lesbian. Since I first used it in 1980 I have always meant it to imply that I am not only a lesbian but a transgressive lesbian—femme, masochistic, as sexually aggressive as the women I seek out, and as pornographic in my imagination and sexual activities as the heterosexual hegemony has ever believed.

My aunt Dot used to joke, "There are two or three things I know for sure, but never the same things and I'm never as sure as I'd like." What I know for sure is that class, gender, sexual preference, and prejudice—racial, ethnic, and religious—form an intricate lattice that restricts and shapes our lives, and that resistance to hatred is not a simple act. Claiming your identity in the cauldron of hatred and resistance to hatred is infinitely complicated, and worse, almost unexplainable.

I know that I have been hated as a lesbian both by "society" and by the intimate world of my extended family, but I have also been hated or held in contempt (which is in some ways more debilitating and slippery than hatred) by lesbians for behavior and sexual practices shaped in large part by class. My sexual identity is intimately constructed by my class and regional background, and much of the hatred directed at my sexual preferences is class hatred—however much people, feminists in particular, like to pretend this is not a factor. The kind of woman I am attracted to is invariably the kind of woman who embarrasses respectably middle-class, politically aware lesbian feminists. My sexual ideal is butch, exhibitionistic, physically aggressive, smarter than she wants you to know, and proud of being called a pervert. Most often she is working class, with an aura of danger and an ironic sense of humor. There is a lot of contemporary lip service paid to sexual tolerance, but the fact that my sexuality is constructed within, and by, a butch/femme and leather fetishism is widely viewed with distaste or outright hatred.

For most of my life I have been presumed to be misguided, damaged by incest and childhood physical abuse, or deliberately indulging in hateful and retrograde sexual practices out of a selfish concentration on my own sexual satisfaction. I have been expected to abandon my desires, to become the normalized woman who flirts with fetishization, who plays with gender roles and treats the historical categories of deviant desire with humor or gentle contempt but never takes any of it so seriously as to claim a sexual identity based on these categories. It was hard enough for me to shake off demands when they were made by straight society. It was appalling when I found the same demands made by other lesbians.

One of the strengths I derive from my class background is that I am accustomed to contempt. I know that I have no chance of becoming what my detractors expect of me, and I believe that even the attempt to please them will only further engage their contempt, and my own self-contempt as well. Nonetheless, the relationship between the life I have lived and the way that life is seen by strangers has constantly invited a kind of self-mythologizing fantasy. It has always been tempting for me to play off of the stereotypes and misconceptions of mainstream culture, rather than describe a difficult and sometimes painful reality.

[. . .]

By 1975 I was earning a meager living as a photographer's assistant in Tallahassee, Florida. But the real work of my life was my lesbian-feminist activism, the work I did with the local women's center and the committee to found a women's studies program at Florida State University. Part of my role, as I saw it, was to be a kind of evangelical lesbian feminist, and to help develop a political analysis of this woman-hating society. I did not talk about class, except to give lip service to how we all needed to think about it, the same way I thought we all needed to think about racism. I was a determined person, living in a lesbian collective—all of us young and white and serious—studying each new book that purported to address feminist issues, driven by what I saw as a need to revolutionize the world.

Years later it's difficult to convey just how reasonable my life seemed to me at that time. I was not flippant, not consciously condescending, not casual about how tough a struggle remaking social relations would be, but like so many women of my generation, I believed absolutely that I could make a difference with my life, and I was willing to give my life for the chance to make that difference. I expected hard times, long slow periods of self-sacrifice and grinding work, expected to be hated and attacked in public, to have to set aside personal desire, lovers, and family in order to be part of something greater and more important than my individual concerns. At the same time, I was working ferociously to take my desires, my sexuality, my needs as a woman and a lesbian more seriously. I believed I was making the personal political revolution with my life every moment, whether I was scrubbing the floor of the childcare center, setting up a new budget for the women's lecture series at the university, editing the local feminist magazine, or starting a women's bookstore. That I was constantly exhausted and had no health insurance, did hours of dreary unpaid work and still sneaked out of the collective to date butch women my housemates thought retrograde and sexist never interfered with my sense of total commitment to the feminist revolution. I was not living in a closet: I had compartmentalized my own mind to such an extent that I never questioned why I did what I did. And I never admitted what lay behind all my feminist convictions—a class-constructed distrust of change, a secret fear that someday I would be found out for who I really was, found out and thrown out. If I had not been raised to give my life away, would I have made such an effective, self-sacrificing revolutionary?

The narrowly focused concentration of a revolutionary shifted only when I began to write again. The idea of writing stories seemed frivolous when there was so much work to be done, but everything changed when I found myself confronting emotions and ideas that could not be explained away or postponed until after the revolution. The way it happened was simple and unexpected. One week I was asked to speak to two completely different groups: an Episcopalian Sunday school class and a juvenile detention center. The Episcopalians were all white, well-dressed, highly articulate, nominally polite, and obsessed with getting me to tell them (without their having to ask directly) just what it was that two women did together in bed. The delinquents were all women, 80 percent Black and Hispanic, wearing green uniform dresses or blue jeans and workshirts, profane, rude, fearless, witty, and just as determined to get me to talk about what it was that two women did together in bed.

I tried to have fun with the Episcopalians, teasing them about their fears and insecurities, and being as bluntly honest as I could about my sexual practices. The Sunday school teacher, a man who had assured me of his liberal inclinations, kept blushing and stammering as the questions about my growing up and coming out became more detailed. I stepped out into the sunshine when the meeting was over, angry at the contemptuous attitude implied by all their questioning, and though I did not know why, so deeply depressed I couldn't even cry.

The delinquents were another story. Shameless, they had me blushing within the first few minutes, yelling out questions that were part curiosity and partly a way of boasting about what they already knew. "You butch or femme?" "You ever fuck boys?" "You want to have children?" "What's your girlfriend like?" I finally broke up when one very tall, confident girl leaned way over and called out, "Hey, girlfriend! I'm getting out of here next weekend. What you doing that night?" I laughed so hard I almost choked. I laughed until we were all howling and giggling together. Even getting frisked as I left didn't ruin my mood. I was still grinning when I climbed into the waterbed with my lover that night, grinning right up to the moment when she wrapped her arms around me and I burst into tears.

That night I understood, suddenly, everything that had happened to my cousins and me, understood it from a wholly new and agonizing perspective, one that made clear how brutal I had been to both my family and myself. I grasped all over again how we had been robbed and dismissed, and why I had worked so hard not to think about it. I had learned as a child that what could not be changed had to go unspoken, and worse, that those who cannot change their own lives have every reason to be ashamed of that fact and to hide it. I had accepted that shame and believed in it, but why? What had I or my cousins done to deserve the contempt directed at us? Why had I always believed us contemptible by nature? I wanted to talk to someone about all the things I was thinking that night, but I could not. Among the women I knew there was no one who would have

understood what I was thinking, no other working-class woman in the women's collective where I was living. I began to suspect that we shared no common language to speak
those bitter truths.

In the days that followed I found myself remembering that afternoon long ago at the
county farm, that feeling of being the animal in the zoo, the thing looked at and laughed
at and used by the real people who watched us. For all his liberal convictions, that Sunday
school teacher had looked at me with the eyes of my cousin's long-ago guard. I felt
thrown back into my childhood, into all the fears I had tried to escape. Once again I felt
myself at the mercy of the important people who knew how to dress and talk, and would
always be given the benefit of the doubt, while my family and I would not.

I experienced an outrage so old I could not have traced all the ways it shaped my life.
I realized again that some are given no quarter, no chance, that all their courage, humor,
and love for each other is just a joke to the ones who make the rules, and I hated the
rule-makers. Finally, I recognized that part of my grief came from the fact that I no longer
knew who I was or where I belonged. I had run away from my family, refused to go home
to visit, and tried in every way to make myself a new person. How could I be working
class with a college degree? As a lesbian activist? I thought about the guards at the
detention center. They had not stared at me with the same picture-window emptiness
they turned on the girls who came to hear me, girls who were closer to the life I had been
meant to live than I could bear to examine. The contempt in their eyes was contempt for
me as a lesbian, different and the same, but still contempt.

While I raged, my girlfriend held me and comforted me and tried to get me to explain
what was hurting me so bad, but I could not. She had told me so often about her awkward relationship with her own family, the father who ran his own business and still sent
her checks every other month. She knew almost nothing about my family, only the jokes
and careful stories I had given her. I felt so alone and at risk lying in her arms that I could
not have explained anything at all. I thought about those girls in the detention center and
the stories they told in brutal shorthand about their sisters, brothers, cousins, and lovers.
I thought about their one-note references to those they had lost, never mentioning the
loss of their own hopes, their own futures, the bent and painful shape of their lives when
they would finally get free. Cried-out and dry-eyed, I lay watching my sleeping girlfriend
and thinking about what I had not been able to say to her. After a few hours I got up
and made some notes for a poem I wanted to write, a bare, painful litany of loss shaped
as a conversation between two women, one who cannot understand the other, and one
who cannot tell all she knows.

It took me a long time to take that poem from a raw lyric of outrage and grief to a
piece of fiction that explained to me something I had never let myself see up close
before—the whole process of running away, of closing up inside yourself, of hiding. It
has taken me most of my life to understand that, to see how and why those of us who
are born poor and different are so driven to give ourselves away or lose ourselves, but
most of all, simply to disappear as the people we really are. By the time the poem
became the story "River of Names," I had made the decision to reverse that process: to

claim my family, my true history, and to tell the truth not only about who I was but about the temptation to lie.

By the time I taught myself the basics of storytelling on the page, I knew there was only one story that would haunt me until I understood how to tell it—the complicated, painful story of how my mama had, and had not, saved me as a girl. Writing *Bastard out of Carolina* became, ultimately, the way to claim my family's pride and tragedy, and the embattled sexuality I had fashioned on a base of violence and abuse.

The compartmentalized life I had created burst open in the late 1970s after I began to write what I really thought about my family. I lost patience with my fear of what the women I worked with, mostly lesbians, thought of who I slept with and what we did together. When schisms developed within my community; when I was no longer able to hide within the regular dyke network; when I could not continue to justify my life by constant political activism or distract myself by sleeping around; when my sexual promiscuity, butch/femme orientation, and exploration of sadomasochistic sex became part of what was driving me out of my community of choice—I went home again. I went home to my mother and my sisters, to visit, talk, argue, and begin to understand.

Once home I saw that as far as my family was concerned, lesbians were lesbians whether they wore suitcoats or leather jackets. Moreover, in all that time when I had not made peace with myself, my family had managed to make a kind of peace with me. My girlfriends were treated like slightly odd versions of my sisters' husbands, while I was simply the daughter who had always been difficult but was still a part of their lives. The result was that I started trying to confront what had made me unable really to talk to my sisters for so many years. I discovered that they no longer knew who I was either, and it took time and lots of listening to each other to rediscover my sense of family, and my love for them.

It is only as the child of my class and my unique family background that I have been able to put together what is for me a meaningful politics, to regain a sense of why I believe in activism, why self-revelation is so important for lesbians. There is no all-purpose feminist analysis that explains the complicated ways our sexuality and core identity are shaped, the way we see ourselves as parts of both our birth families and the extended family of friends and lovers we invariably create within the lesbian community. For me, the bottom line has simply become the need to resist that omnipresent fear, that urge to hide and disappear, to disguise my life, my desires, and the truth about how little any of us understand—even as we try to make the world a more just and human place. Most of all, I have tried to understand the politics of *they,* why human beings fear and stigmatize the different while secretly dreading that they might be one of the different themselves. Class, race, sexuality, gender—and all the other categories by which we categorize and dismiss each other—need to be excavated from the inside.

The horror of class stratification, racism, and prejudice is that some people begin to believe that the security of their families and communities depends on the oppression of others, that for some to have good lives there must be others whose lives are truncated and brutal. It is a belief that dominates this culture. It is what makes the poor whites of the South so determinedly racist and the middle class so contemptuous of the poor. It is a myth that allows some to imagine that they build their lives on the ruin of others, a secret core of shame for the middle class, a goad and a spur to the marginal working class, and cause enough for the homeless and poor to feel no constraints on hatred or violence. The power of the myth is made even more apparent when we examine how, within the lesbian and feminist communities where we have addressed considerable attention to the politics of marginalization, there is still so much exclusion and fear, so many of us who do not feel safe.

I grew up poor, hated, the victim of physical, emotional, and sexual violence, and I know that suffering does not ennoble. It destroys. To resist destruction, self-hatred, or lifelong hopelessness, we have to throw off the conditioning of being despised, the fear of becoming the *they* that is talked about so dismissively, to refuse lying myths and easy moralities, to see ourselves as human, flawed, and extraordinary. All of us—extraordinary.

CHAPTER 12

Censorship and Moral Panic

In Chapter 10, we talked about the attempted censorship of the novel *Women's Barracks,* pointing out that the Canadian Crown's attorney identified the lesbian passages in Torres's book as obscene but ignored equally racy mention of heterosexual sex and sexuality. The public uproar that provided the context for the *Women's Barracks* trial had to do with a general sense in Canadian culture that obscene and sexually provocative material from the United States would corrupt Canadian youth [λ Chapter 10]. This impulse to focus on an offending object in order to encourage and perpetuate public outcry against transgressive behavior can create what Stan Cohen has termed *moral panic.* In a period of moral panic,

> [a] condition, episode, person or group of persons emerges to become defined as a threat to societal values and interests. . . . Sometimes the panic is passed over and forgotten, but at other times it has more serious and long term repercussions and it might produce changes in legal and social policy or even in the way in which societies conceive themselves. (9)

Not all censorship is the result of moral panic, but most censorship of homosexed art and literature occurs at cultural moments when the fear of corruption by sexually deviant material is framed as a pervasive social problem. It is tempting to equate censorship only with the banning of books or with historical attempts to eradicate what the Nazis called "degenerate art," but we will focus on campaigns or trials that fit Cohen's definition of moral panic in an attempt to elucidate the larger social and cultural complexities of the censoring impulse. Censorship often arises from a desire to protect the innocent, often women and children, from sexual values that certain queer art seems to propagate—sexual libertarianism, sexual freedom, and even transcendence or obliteration of sexual boundaries. We hope to show that attempts to censor queer art often represent contradictory motivations and constituencies. In this chapter, we focus attention on several high-profile moral panics triggered by homosexed art and literature.

Oscar Wilde

The three trials of Oscar Wilde in 1895 were among the most widely covered and discussed legal proceedings of their time. A large part of the public interest in them arose from the celebrities involved—primarily the author and playwright Oscar Wilde, who was enjoying great success in London's theater district with sold-out performances of *The Importance of Being Earnest,* and the hot-headed Marquess of Queensbury, father of Lord Alfred Douglas ("Bosie"), with whom Wilde had been in a multiyear relationship.

Already famous for his brilliant conversation, controversial writings, and flamboyant public behavior, Wilde paraded around London with Bosie, inciting Queensbury to call him a "Somdomite," a misspelling of "Sodomite." In response, Wilde injudiciously decided to bring a libel suit against Queensbury. Wilde's suit was dismissed; during the deliberations, however, Queensbury's lawyers unearthed evidence that Wilde had consorted with a variety of young working-class men. Wilde was arrested on charges of "gross indecency," pursuant to a relatively recent law that criminalized sexual conduct between men. Wilde's first trial with him as the defendant ended in a hung jury, but at the second trial, he was convicted and sentenced to the maximum punishment, two years of hard labor. Three years after being released from Reading Gaol, Wilde died in France a broken and impoverished man.

Figure 12.1 Oscar Wilde and Lord Alfred Douglas

Figure 12.2   Reading Gaol

During the trials, prosecutors focused on locating passages from Wilde's writings to corroborate other testimony supporting his supposed "gross indecency." Prosecutor Edward Carson read portions of the author's early poems and letters to Bosie where Wilde wrote romantically, even effusively, about their friendship. Carson also quoted from Wilde's novel, *The Picture of Dorian Gray,* in which the artist Basil Hallward accuses the increasingly corrupt Dorian of deleterious influences on his acquaintances. Hallward asks Dorian, "Why is your friendship so fatal to young men?[1] There was that wretched boy in the Guards who committed suicide. You were his great friend. There was Sir Henry Ashton, who had to leave England with a tarnished name" (Lawler, ed. 117). Carson pressed Wilde to name the "unnatural vice" alluded to in these passages, strongly insinuating that literature depicting immoral acts or feelings could contribute to the degradation of those reading it:

> C[arson]—Am I right in saying that you do not consider the effect [when writing] in creating morality or immorality?
>
> W[ilde]—Certainly, I do not.
>
> C—So far as your works are concerned, you pose as not being concerned about morality or immorality?
>
> [. . .]
>
> W—. . . I have no pose in this matter. In writing a play or a book, I am concerned entirely with literature—that is, with art. I aim not at doing good or evil, but in trying to make a thing that will have some quality of beauty. ("The Trials of Oscar Wilde")

Wilde's attempt to focus purely on aesthetic concerns proved an unfortunate strategy for his defense, making it appear that he had something to hide.

Carson's efforts to conflate the man and the work in order to damn them both led Wilde to defend his book, even implying that Dorian's demise at the end of the novel suggested that the story had a moral end. But the damage had already been done. In the famous Preface to *Dorian Gray,* Wilde had written that "[t]here is no such thing as a moral or an immoral book. Books are well written, or badly written. That is all" (3). By the time of the trial, many in the public were fully willing to believe that Wilde was not only writing about but also involved in a variety of immoral activities, particularly with other men, and that he was a potential danger to society. His writing and celebrity created nothing less than a moral panic, and some members of the public expressed relief when the author was sent off to prison. Author Eliza Lynn Linton, for example, remarked in late 1895, "Happily here the chief offender seems to have suddenly subsided—to have gone out like some noxious vapour which flared for a time over fetid marshes, luring the unwary into perils worse than death itself. The world is the cleaner by his absence—the cleaner and less ugly" (41).

Wilde's trials seem to presage future public debates and moral panics about homosexed art and literature; they helped position government agencies as protective of their citizens, safeguarding them against "unnatural" influences. In Carson's words, the public should be protected from books with "perverted moral views" (Lawler, ed. 355). As sexologists were developing categories that helped to create a visible homosexual identity [λ Chapter 2], legal structures began containing its expression, particularly its potential spread to the innocent.

Radclyffe Hall

Radclyffe Hall's novel, *The Well of Loneliness,* was the first to insist upon a literary space for the female sexual invert. The obscenity trials that resulted in the suppression of the book in England portrayed its subject as dangerous. Even more, the *Well of Loneliness* trials represented a moral panic in that an entire potential subject for literature—lesbianism—was prohibited for half a century afterward. First published by Jonathan Cape in late July 1928, *The Well of Loneliness* contained an introduction-cum-endorsement by sexologist Havelock Ellis [λ Chapter 2] and was generally recognized as a "long and very serious novel entirely upon the subject of sexual inversion" (Hall, qtd. in Doan 1). After a few weeks of thoughtful reviews in the press and relatively brisk sales at bookstores, the London *Sunday Express* printed a sensational editorial by journalist James Douglas. "I would rather give a healthy boy or a healthy girl a phial of prussic acid than this novel," wrote Douglas; "Poison kills the body, but moral poison kills the soul" (10). Suddenly the terms of the debate were altered, and many Britons took sides. Generally speaking, conservative traditionalists such as Home Secretary William Joynson-Hicks took the view that Hall's novel should be suppressed in order to protect the innocent "young generation" from so much as recognizing the existence of a potentially "polluting" practice such as lesbianism. Liberals, free-speech advocates, and literary figures, by contrast, supported the book as a "work of art finely conceived and finely written" ("Review" 13).

In the wake of Douglas's broadside, publisher Cape took a rash action: he sent a copy of the book to the Home Office, accompanied by a letter promising to withdraw it should it be found obscene. Presumably, Cape thought that Douglas's hypocritical "social purity" argument would fall flat with Joynson-Hicks. He could not anticipate that Joynson-Hicks would discuss the book with Sir Archibald Bodkin, the director of public prosecutions, and with Sir Chartres Biron, the Bow Street magistrate; all three men were members of what Laura Doan

Figure 12.3   Una Troubridge (top) and Radclyffe Hall (bottom)

calls "fringe organizations, with narrow interests in reviving religious values and policing public morality" (21). Joynson-Hicks, feeling that "there must be some limit to the freedom of what a man may write or speak in this great country of ours," especially when, in his opinion, "what is written or spoken makes one of the least of these little ones offend," ruled that *The Well of Loneliness* should be suppressed (qtd. in Souhami 208). This would have been the end of the matter had not the prescient Cape arranged to have *Well* reprinted and sold under a French imprint. The French edition began appearing in London bookstores, and the police were finally directed to impound all copies they could find. The book (not the author) was put on trial for obscenity.

In the two weeks between the announcement and the trial, battle lines were drawn. Although some appeared to fall in with the obscenity faction, many found the court's procedures and opinions repulsive. The *Daily Herald* made fun of Joynson-Hicks and Bodkin: "They, stifling their natural horror and disgust, plough through all the naughty books, heroically risking any possible shocks to their chaste minds in order to safeguard the innocent British public" ("Gadfly"). Publisher Geoffrey Faber complained that if the censors had their way, "the whole of the content of English literature is to be restricted in future to such stuff as Sir William thinks it safe to put in the hands of a schoolgirl" (qtd. in Souhami 208). Such protests were unavailing. In what Marc Vargo calls "arguably the most biased obscenity trial in the history of Great Britain" (63), in which Magistrate Biron refused to hear the testimony of expert witnesses, *Well* was found to be obscene and all copies were ordered destroyed. The appeal two weeks later was denied by the same court, and that was that. Interestingly, nothing in the book itself was actually found to be obscene (its sexiest line is probably "And that night they were not divided," referring to the hero Stephen Gordon and her lover Mary Llewellyn). It was the subject of lesbianism that was potentially corrupting; indeed, after the British trial in 1928, openly lesbian literature did not appear in England again for over fifty years.

Figure 12.4   Image of 1928 *The Well of Loneliness* cover by Radclyffe Hall, published by Jonathan Cape

In the United States, *Well* fared considerably better. It was challenged in late 1928, but the trial differed from its British predecessor in two important ways: (1) discussion of literary merit and testimony of expert witnesses were permitted, and (2) the justices assigned to decide the case made a point of reading the book before they passed judgment. They concluded that the accusation of obscenity was a matter of literary taste since *Well* did not violate any existing obscenity laws. Therefore, they found it not obscene and not subject to any limitation concerning sale or distribution.

It is worthwhile to consider the trials of *The Well of Loneliness* in the context of other widely publicized literary obscenity cases of the 1920s. In 1921, in a case brought by the New York Society for the Suppression of Vice, a trial court found

James Joyce's novel *Ulysses* obscene; it was also banned in England. D. H. Lawrence's novel *Lady Chatterley's Lover* was banned in 1928 (its year of publication) in both the United States and the United Kingdom; its classification as obscene was not overturned for thirty years. The *Well* American trial bears on the *Ulysses* case in that the finding that *Well* was not obscene rested on it being found not to be pornographic. The same legal logic obtained in 1933 when a U.S. court overturned the obscenity ruling against *Ulysses,* declaring it not pornographic and therefore not obscene. The U.S. *Lady Chatterley* and *Well* cases provide a point of fruitful comparison. The origins of the complaints against these texts are similar in that the complainants attempt to create a moral panic around sexual expression represented in art. However, the two trials highlight the contingent nature of the outcomes of the censoring impulse; different books, different judges, and slightly different times produce different results.

The suppression of *The Well of Loneliness* in the United Kingdom seems to have had a number of long-term negative effects. Radclyffe Hall herself was ill off and on for years after the trials; she attributed her bouts of poor health to residual stress from them. She also wrote no more lesbian novels after *Well.* Nor, it might be added, did anyone else; potential authors of books about love between women seemed to have been temporarily scared off by the hysteria around *Well.* Most seriously, writes Diana Souhami, "By this trial, the government stigmatized and criminalized a kind of love. Its idiocy echoed down the years, silencing writers, consigning people to concealment of their deepest feelings and to public scorn" (237). The obscenity ruling, like the Pirie-Woods libel suit from 1811 [λ Chapter 1] and the recasting of the lesbian plot of Lillian Hellman's *The Children's Hour* as a heterosexual love triangle in the 1930s [λ Chapter 9], contributed to the erasure of lesbian art and lesbian lives from the popular consciousness.

The conflation of literature and life that contributed to the gross indecency conviction of Oscar Wilde in 1895 and the Home Office's obscenity finding concerning *The Well of Loneliness* in 1928 represented legal milestones functioning to suppress lesbian, gay, bisexual, and transgender (LGBT) writing throughout much of the first half of the twentieth century in the United States and the United Kingdom. Some literature of the early to mid-century, to be sure, appeared despite the censors. Lesbian works such as Virginia Woolf's *Orlando* (1928), Djuna Barnes's *Ladies Almanack* (1928), and Gertrude Stein's *The Autobiography of Alice B. Toklas* (1936) avoided suppression through use of an intensely coded style that obscured the homosexed content. Certain gay male writers—Truman Capote (1924–1984) and Gore Vidal (b. 1925), for example—parlayed their maleness and their access to publishing venues into contracts with big-name companies. Still, even they were stymied by the McCarthy anticommunist, antihomosexual witch hunts of the early 1950s [λ Chapter 3], during which some books (*The Well of Loneliness*, Vidal's *The City and the Pillar* of 1948), previously available in handsome cloth bindings, vanished from upscale bookstores and reappeared in pulp editions at bus stations and drugstores [λ Chapter 10].

The fever broke in the 1960s, partly through new legislation that legalized a wider range of literary expression and partly through the rise of countercultural movements that established their own small presses. The 1959 Obscene Publications Act in the United Kingdom was found not to apply if the challenged work possessed so-called literary merit. In the United States, an obscenity ruling against the film version of *Lady Chatterley's Lover* was overturned by the Supreme Court in 1959, on the basis of the First Amendment guarantee of freedom of speech. The lifting of these restrictions led directly to the general availability of previously suppressed (heterosexual) works such as *Lady Chatterley* and Henry Miller's *Tropic of Cancer*. Soon thereafter, new presses specializing in LGBT subjects—Daughters, Gay Sunshine, Naiad, Crossing, and others—brought out hundreds of books, both originals and reprints, and helped build a body of homosexed literature in the 1970s and 1980s. In Chapter 4, we described the right-wing backlash against newly visible gay and lesbian movements that began with Anita Bryant in the late 1970s. Bryant, like journalist James Douglas nearly a century earlier, framed her "Save the Children" campaign as an effort to protect the innocent from the corrupting influence of homosexuality. By the end of the 1980s, this antigay impulse, now embodied in U.S. Senator Jesse Helms (R-NC), had gained sufficient momentum to challenge the principle of artistic freedom in Congress.

Mapplethorpe and Riggs

An example of a conservative, right-wing attempt to create a moral panic under the guise of protecting the American public from homosexed art was a resolution sponsored by Senator Helms in 1989. Helms's bill proposed prohibiting

> the use of funds by the National Endowment for the Arts or the National Endowment for the Humanities to promote, disseminate, or produce materials that may be considered obscene, including but not limited to, depictions of sadomasochism, homo-eroticism, the sexual exploitation of children, or individuals engaged in sex acts and which, when taken as a whole, do not have serious literary, artistic, political or scientific value. (HR 2788)

Defining such value required making highly contingent judgments. What might be considered devoid of literary value and merely obscene in one circumstance and by one group might be seen very differently in another circumstance or by another group.

Find Out More in Sapphire's "Wild Thing"—which Helms read on the House floor as an example of obscenity—in the readings at the end of this chapter.

One of Helms's targets was a posthumous exhibition of Robert Mapplethorpe's photography, titled *Robert Mapplethorpe: The Perfect Moment.* The exhibition had been slated to appear at art galleries across the nation over an eighteen-month period, beginning at the Institute of Contemporary Art in Philadelphia, which had organized it, and moving to Chicago; Washington, D.C.; Hartford, Connecticut; Berkeley, California; Cincinnati, Ohio; and Boston. The show met with positive response in Philadelphia and Chicago, but its appearance in Washington was canceled because Corcoran Art Gallery director Christina Orr-Cahall hoped to avoid giving Senator Helms ammunition for his battle against National Endowment for the Arts (NEA) funding for the work of controversial artists. So, by the time the exhibit moved to Cincinnati's Contemporary Arts Center (CAC) in 1989, much ado had been made of its contents, and local conservative forces, particularly those connected to Citizens for Community Values (the same organization that would later spearhead the successful effort to remove sexual orientation from the city's human rights ordinance [λ Chapter 4]), were prepared for a full-blown assault against the CAC.

On the day the Mapplethorpe exhibit opened in Cincinnati, according to one local newspaper, "Hundreds of people waited in the arcade outside the CAC while police closed the facility and videotaped the exhibit to use as evidence in criminal cases against [museum director Dennis] Barrie and the center. The crowd became agitated, chanting and booing the cops who remained stationed at the center's front doors" (Fox). Local prosecutors charged Barrie with obscenity, and while Barrie and the CAC were eventually acquitted in a jury trial, the fuss underscored Mapplethorpe's reputation as a provocative, boundary-pushing, transgressive artist.

Though these efforts to outlaw public exhibitions of Mapplethorpe's work have been at the forefront of recent debates about obscenity, it would be misleading to argue that conservative politicians and activists are alone in their objections to the work. Liberal and left-leaning critics, though usually not inclined to argue for censorship, have voiced their own objections to Mapplethorpe's photographs. For instance, gay African American author and poet Essex Hemphill was deeply disturbed by the apparent objectification of black male bodies in some of Mapplethorpe's photographs. Cultural critic Kobena Mercer also voiced concern about those Mapplethorpe photographs that feature African American men, saying that his first

Find Out More in Steven Dubin's "Art's Enemies" in the readings at the end of this chapter.

impulse when viewing the photos was to be "immediately disturbed by the racial dimension of the imagery and, above all, angered by the aesthetic objectification that reduced these individual black men to purely abstract 'things,' silenced in their own right as subjects and serving mainly as aesthetic trophies to enhance Mapplethorpe's privileged position as a white gay male artist in the New York avant-garde" (464).

Noting that the popular discussion of Mapplethorpe's work tended to be framed as a "straightforward opposition between censorship and freedom of artistic expression," Mercer warns against reducing that discussion to a "neat dichotomy between bigoted Philistines and enlightened cultural liberals" (472). In his essay, "Just Looking for Trouble," Mercer describes how cultural conservatives sometimes use seemingly progressive stances to forward their own agendas:

> In his original proposal to regulate public funding of art deemed "obscene and indecent," Jesse Helms went beyond the traditional remit of moral fundamentalism to add new grounds for legal intervention on the basis of discrimination against minorities. Helms wanted the state to intervene in instances where artistic and cultural materials "denigrate, debase or revile a person, group or class of citizens on the basis of race, creed, sex, handicap or national origin." By means of this rhetorical move, he sought to promote a climate of opinion favorable to new forms of coercive intervention. In making such a move, the strategy is not simply to win support from black people and ethnic minorities, nor simply to modernize the traditional "moral" discourse against obscenity, but to broaden and extend the threshold of illegitimacy to a wider range of cultural texts. (473)

The desire to protect the public from offensive material and the move to protect minorities from discrimination become conflated in censoring transgressive art. In other words, some cultural conservatives try to use politically progressive rhetoric to advance a conservative agenda. This move was not unprecedented; it had proved somewhat successful during the so-called sex wars of the 1980s, when feminists allied with conservative forces to create legislation that would allow women and other minorities to seek damages against producers and distributors of pornography.

The work of filmmaker Marlon Riggs (1957–1994) proved less easily manipulable for this kind of recasting. Riggs's *Tongues Untied,* a 1989 documentary about being both gay and black, provoked a firestorm of protest. Funded in part through federal grants, the film outraged conservatives who did not want taxpayers' money supporting explorations of homosexuality. In a powerful scene in the film, a Pride Day parade features a group of black men carrying a banner proclaiming, "Black Men Loving Black Men Is a Revolutionary Act." The film's boldness was simply too much for conservatives such as Pat Buchanan, who called *Tongues Untied* "pornographic art" (Smith). Riggs's counterclaim was both eloquent and pointed in its acknowledgment of how dominant cultures often elide any humane recognition of the diversity within them: "Implicit in the much overworked rhetoric of community standards is the assumption of only one central community (patriarchal, heterosexual and usually white) and only one overarching cultural standard (ditto)" (Riggs).

Queering Children's Books

Today it is possible to locate literally hundreds of queer-themed books for children, most aimed at young adult readers, that is, ages twelve and up. The problems arise around books aimed at elementary school-aged children. Diana Schemo writes, "According to a 2004 national poll by the Kaiser Family Foundation, Harvard University's Kennedy School of Government and National Public Radio, roughly three out of four parents say it is appropriate for high schools to teach about homosexuality, but about half say it is appropriate in middle school." Only tiny percentages approve of introducing LGBT subject matter to younger children. Lesbian author Lesléa Newman knows of no attempt to censor her young adult or adult writing, but her children's book, *Heather Has Two Mommies* (1989), has had quite a different history. When New York adopted the multicultural curriculum guide "Children of the Rainbow" in 1992, *Heather Has Two Mommies,* along with Michael Willhoite's *Daddy's Roommate* (1991), became flashpoints for angry discussions about making books with homosexual themes available in schools. New York City School Chancellor Joseph Fernandez suspended the school board of District 24, which had refused to endorse the new curriculum for fear of "promot[ing] a homosexual lifestyle" (Duberman 589). Eventually, Fernandez was forced out as chancellor over the controversy.

Even today, *Heather Has Two Mommies* and *Daddy's Roommate* regularly appear on lists of banned books; see, for instance, Wikipedia's "List of Most Commonly Challenged Books in the U.S." or Herbert Foerstel's *Banned in the USA: A Reference Guide to Book Censorship in Schools. Heather* and *Roommate* have come to stand in for claims that "gay agenda" advocates seek to corrupt children. Conservative organizations position themselves as protectors of the innocent, using Newman's and Willhoite's books as examples of the corrupting influence of homosexuality. For instance, Peter LaBarbera's articles, "How to Protect Your Children from Prohomosexuality Propaganda in Schools" and "When Silence Would Have Been Golden," cast curricula that promote tolerance or diversity as dangerously progay, even as "brainwashing kindergartners." Antigay demonizing of *Heather Has Two Mommies* and *Daddy's Roommate,* as well as of such more recent books as *King & King* (2002) and *Antonio's Card* (2005), seeks to initiate a moral panic, which can in turn invest received moral authorities with the responsibility—and, more to the point, with the power—to protect innocent, less powerful people from ideas they do not like.

Deepa Mehta

We can see the deployment of multiple protectionist rhetorics to censor queer art in the moral panic surrounding the release of Canadian Indian Deepa Mehta's 1996 film, *Fire.* The film tells the story of the evolving relationship between two sisters-in-law whose unhappiness in their marriages and growing attraction to one another take place in an oppressive environment where families live together in confined spaces and where women's lives are controlled by their social circumstances. Previous to the release of *Fire,* Daniel Lak of BBC Online, while clarifying that the film is "not meant to be about gay life," acknowledged that "one group of people in [India] is awaiting this film eagerly—the Indian lesbian community, which for years has maintained a silent, almost secret existence."

Find Out More in the excerpt from Gayatri Gopinath's "Local Sites/Global Contexts: The Transnational Trajectories of *Fire* and 'The Quilt'" in the readings at the end of this chapter.

Perhaps partly as an effort to maintain that silence, protesters reacted strongly to the film's 1998 release in India, claiming that it represented an affront not only to Indian sexual mores but to Indian culture and nationhood. Conservative Hindu activists called the film "un-Indian" and warned that portraying lesbianism will "spoil our women" ("Deepa").

This notion is reminiscent of the 1928 suppression of *The Well of Loneliness,* not on the grounds of obscenity but solely on account of its lesbian subject matter. Thus, the intersectional moral panic around *Fire* raised issues of nationalism, sexism, and heterosexism. As in other countries where homosexuality has been silenced until very recently, the Hindu protesters figure India as a land of heterosexuals, where gay men and lesbians present a

Figure 12.5 Deepa Mehta

powerful challenge to the national self-image. Moreover, as a danger to "our women," the film is seen as an "attack on the privileges of patriarchy" in India (Morris). *Fire*, however, gave voice to the "unhappiness of women in traditional families" ("Deepa") and thus exposed the pervasive sexism and misogyny of the culture. Finally, the vandalism and violence attending *Fire*'s release in Bombay revealed profound homophobia—disguised as a concern that the movie would "corrupt Indian women"—and unleashed a spate of gay bashing. This homophobic backlash occurred in the context of a general belief in the sanctity of marriage and related disapproval of pre- and extramarital sex.

The Indian Censor Board's decision to allow *Fire* to be shown may have led in the short term to right-wing protests and vandalism. But in the long term, it opens the door for other homosexed art in India. We note, for instance, that *Girlfriend*, a Bollywood film about a lesbian relationship, opened in 2004. The same right-wing protesters claimed that "such movies pollute the culture and should not be made" (Singh). However, Censor Board approval of *Girlfriend* and state protection of theaters showing it suggest that the moral panic around *Fire* did not completely squelch lesbian-themed filmmaking in India. We argue that this trajectory typically follows moral panics; the very rhetoric designed to muzzle transgressive art also tends to spur the creation of new work with similar themes. Even in the case of the *Well of Loneliness* trials, which resulted in the temporary erasure of lesbian-themed work from public view, the book itself has become a central lesbian text that has remained in print since its pulp version appeared in the 1950s. *The Picture of Dorian Gray* has also enjoyed enormous popularity and has been continuously available, and the hullabaloo over Mapplethorpe's work made him a popular, even an iconic, figure in the Western art world. As we will see in the final three chapters of this book, moral panics have failed to suppress the impulse to create queer community through transgressive artistic expression.

Note

1. In the version of *The Picture of Dorian Gray* that appeared in *Lippincott's Monthly Magazine* in July 1890, Hallward asks, "Why is your friendship so <u>fateful</u> to young men?" (258). Wilde changed the word to *fatal* for the revised, expanded version of the novel published by Ward, Lock and Company in 1891.

QUESTIONS FOR DISCUSSION

1. Consider the way this chapter has defined *censorship* and *moral panic*. Brainstorm a list of moral panics that have been initiated by or have resulted in the impulse to censor—instances in which books have been banned from libraries, in which there have been calls for the removal of advertisements or programming from television, or in which a media outlet has refused to publish specific kinds of

material. List several of these and try to identify the "players" involved in each situation. Identify each player's issues or concerns. If the issue was finally resolved in one way or another, write a short description of the resolution. Once you have compiled a list of notes about these moral panics, answer these questions: Who benefits if the material is censored? Who benefits from the panic around the issue? Who benefits from the resolution? Try to avoid easy answers. For instance, sometimes a moral panic seems to benefit only the person or group creating it, but try to consider the possibility that the moral panics you identified might have benefited the person or group whose work was initially censored. How does that work?

2.   As we discussed earlier in this chapter, some of the moral panic surrounding the public revelation of Oscar Wilde's homosexuality and his subsequent trials was fueled by discussion in newspapers and reviews of Wilde's novel, *The Picture of Dorian Gray.* Reviews of this novel are easily accessible on the World Wide Web. Find a few reviews and critically examine the language used either to condemn or to support this book. Does any of the rhetoric seem familiar? You might compare the language that circulated in response to Wilde's novel with language used in contemporary debates about homosexed art and literature. For instance, find an interview online in which Sapphire comments about Jesse Helms's condemnation in Congress of her poem "Wild Thing." How similar is the language in these two public debates, separated by nearly 100 years? How is it different? What might account for the similarities and differences?

3.   Censorship can take many forms other than suppression of works and themes in public art and entertainment. For example, current discussions of bullying in schools and of teen suicide typically elide mention of LGBT young people, who are disproportionately victimized by bullying and at risk for suicide. Do some research about one or both of these phenomena and try to locate the source of the censorship. Why are children and teens perceived to be LGBT not included in the discussion, and who stands to benefit from such censorship?

REFERENCES AND FURTHER READING

Cohen, Stan. *Folk Devils and Moral Panics.* London: MacGibbon and Kee, 1972.

"Deepa Mehta's *Fire* Creates Controversy and Protests in India." 19 August 1999. 8 August 2008 <http://www.sawnet.org/news/fire.html>.

de Haan, Linda, and Stern Nijlund. *King & King.* Berkeley, CA: Tricycle P, 2002.

Doan, Laura. *Fashioning Sapphism: The Origins of a Modern English Lesbian Culture.* New York: Columbia UP, 2001.

Douglas, James. "A Book That Must Be Suppressed." *Sunday Express* 19 August 1928: 10.

Duberman, Martin. Introduction to "Families, Values, and the Rainbow Curriculum: A Roundtable Discussion." *A Queer World: The Center for Lesbian and Gay Studies Reader.* Ed. Martin Duberman. New York: NYU P, 1997. 589.

Foerstel, Herbert N. *Banned in the USA: A Reference Guide to Book Censorship in Schools.* 2nd ed. Westport, CT: Greenwood, 2006.

Fox, John. "Then and Now: Mapplethorpe and the CAC." *CityBeat* 6.19 (2000). 9 August 2008 <http://citybeat.com/2000-03-30/cover.shtml>.

"Gadfly." *Daily Herald,* 7 March 1929: 7.

González, Rigoberto. *Antonio's Card.* San Francisco: Children's Book P, 2005.

Hall, Radclyffe. *The Well of Loneliness.* New York: Anchor, 1990.

Hemphill, Essex. *Ceremonies: Prose and Poetry.* New York: Penguin, 1992.

HR 2788. Summary as of 10/3/1989. 8 August 2008 <http://thomas.loc.gov/cgi-bin/bdquery/z?d101:HR02788:@@@D&summ2=m&>.

LaBarbera, Peter J. "How to Protect Your Children from Pro-homosexuality Propaganda in Schools." *The Fountain Gateway: The Christian Resource and Index Directory.* Family Research Council in Focus. 2 July 2006. 8 August 2008 <http://www.fountaingateway.com/SpecialsNMessages/messageindex/index.html>.

———. "When Silence Would Have Been Golden: Acts of Homosexual Promotion to Youth That We Wish Had Never Happened." *Concerned Women for America.* Culture and Family Issues. 10 April 2002. 8 August 2008 <http://www.cultureandfamily.org/articledisplay.asp?id=2580&department=CFI&categoryid=papers#propaganda>.

Lak, Daniel. "Lesbian Film Sets India on Fire." *BBC Online,* 13 November 1998. 8 August 2008 <http://news.bbc.co.uk/2/hi/south_asia/213417.stm>.

Lawler, Donald L., ed. *The Picture of Dorian Gray.* By Oscar Wilde. New York: W. W. Norton, 1988.

Linton, Eliza Lynn. "The Philistine's Coming Triumph." *National Review* (September 1895): 40–49.

"List of Most Commonly Challenged Books in the U.S." 11 July 2008. 8 August 2008 <http://en.wikipedia.org/wiki/List_of_most_commonly_challenged_books_in_the_U.S.>.

Mercer, Kobena. "Just Looking for Trouble: Robert Mapplethorpe and Fantasies of Race." *Feminism and Pornography.* Ed. Drucilla Cornell. Oxford, UK: Oxford UP, 2000. 460–76.

Morris, Gary. "Burning Love: Deepa Mehta's *Fire.*" *Bright Lights Film Journal.* 2000. 8 August 2008 <http://www.brightlightsfilm.com/30/fire.html>.

Newman, Lesléa. *Heather Has Two Mommies.* Los Angeles: Alyson, 1989.

Review of *The Well of Loneliness. The Daily Telegraph,* 17 August 1928: 13.

Riggs, Marlon. "Tongues Re-tied?" 15 April 1997. 8 August 2008 <http://www.current.org/prog/prog114g.html>.

Schemo, Diana Jean. "Lessons on Homosexuality Move into the Classroom." *New York Times,* 15 August 2007. 8 August 2008 <http://www.nytimes.com/2007/08/15/education/15education.html>.

Senate Report 105-086. "Arts & Humanities Amendments of 1997." 24 September 1997. 8 August 2008 <http://thomas.loc.gov/cgibin/cpquery/?&sid=cp105w2SuW&refer=&r_n=sr086.105&db_id=105&item=&sel=TOC_0&>.

Singh, Jupinderjit. "Protest in City against Screening of 'Girlfriend.'" 16 June 2004. 8 August 2008 <http://www.tribuneindia.com/2004/20040616/ldh1.htm>.

Smith, Justin. "Tongues Untied Screening and Panel Discussion." *GBMNews* 3 March 2008. 9 August 2008 <http://www.gbmnews.com/articles/3034/1/Tongues-UntiedScreening-and-Panel-Discussion/Page1.html>.

Souhami, Diana. *The Trials of Radclyffe Hall.* New York: Doubleday, 1999.

"The Trials of Oscar Wilde." N.d. 8 August 2008 <http://www.law.umkc.edu/faculty/projects/ftrials/wilde/wilde.htm>.

Vargo, Marc E. *Scandal: Infamous Gay Controversies of the Twentieth Century.* Binghamton, NY: Harrington Park/Haworth, 2003.

Willhoite, Michael. *Daddy's Roommate.* Los Angeles: Alyson, 1991.

READINGS

> ## Steven C. Dubin

Excerpt from "Art's Enemies: Censors to the Right of Me, Censors to the Left of Me"

(1994), United States

Those on the political right believe that many elements in contemporary culture are menacing, capable of contaminating pure minds. Reverend [James] Wildmon discovers these dangers everywhere, and expressions of his concern range from his fear that Mighty Mouse was giving youngsters lessons on how to snort cocaine to his authoritative appraisal of what he labels pornography: this stuff is so powerful you may be "hooked with one look." What he dreads most is imitation without reflection, without mediation.

From time to time, those on the left uncannily reflect the same sentiments. For *some* antipornography feminists, the motto is "Porn is the theory; rape the practice." In pragmatic terms this led prominent feminists to condemn Bret Easton Ellis's *American Psycho* (1991) as a guidebook on how to brutalize women. And gays similarly protested *Cruising* (1980), *Silence of the Lambs* (1991), and *Basic Instinct* (1992)—to the point of disrupting the shooting of these films on several occasions—fearing that each movie perpetuated negative stereotypes and could provoke actual violence toward gays.

These reactions are understandable but facile. They reflect a search for a "quick fix" to complex problems and disregard the historical and structural roots of discrimination and violence toward "the other." If eliminating violence were as uncomplicated as eradicating representations of it, a large part of the populace would undoubtedly support such a drive. Absolutists comfort themselves by seeking a magic-bullet-type solution. Yet their assumptions about society and the individual are simplistic and not very flattering. Humans are far more enigmatic than Pavlovian dogs.

Ideologues Possess a Sense of Apocalypse

Many of the issues ideologues struggle over may seem trivial. But to them, they are not. Absolutists clutch a *Weltanschauung* that perceives the forces of darkness and light coming to critical blows. Even minor skirmishes are part of escalating hostilities.

For those on the right, the threat is the cumulative effect of the changes that have come about since the 1960s, with various civil rights movements insisting on greater inclusion into society. The demands of these entitlement efforts have reshaped how we lead our lives and have shifted power from some groups to others to a certain degree. African-Americans, women, gays and lesbians, Hispanics, "secular humanists," and other constituencies have forced society to recognize their respective rights and talents, causing more established groups to feel left behind or left out. In a sample of writings from a variety of conservatives, an overarching theme uniting them is the sense that America has been steadily sliding into a moral sewer since the 1960s. "Decadent art," the way conservatives so often describe the expression of these newly enfranchised groups, puts additional nails in society's coffin.

The political left has been the beneficiary of many of the transformations the political right abhors. But where the right sees too much change, the left feels that there has not been enough. The left experiences a revolution of rising expectations: change has come, but accompanied by an impatience to speed the process along. Its goal, then, is to wipe out residual traces of prejudice and discrimination as quickly as possible. In the hands of absolutists, this means trying to enforce tolerance by eliminating or altering a wide range of offensive, archaic symbols.

Consider the humble crayon. Binney and Smith, manufacturers of Crayola, decided to "retire" eight traditional colors in 1990 and replace them with eight vibrant new ones. They did not anticipate the public uproar they would elicit by such meddling: scores of disgruntled people complained, and at least three grass-roots movements were initiated to symbolically restore order, the most telling being CRAYON: the Committee to Re-establish All Your Old Norms.

Binney and Smith quickly saw the error of its marketing ways, reviving the old colors in a 1991 commemorative tin. Chastened by this breach, they demonstrated that they are attuned to contemporary sensitivities by next issuing a multicultural "My World Colors" pack. These sixteen hues embody the skin, hair, and eye color of a broad sample of people, supplanting the antiquated, all-purpose "flesh" of the past. The smart shopper can now likewise find "adhesive bandages of color."

Ideologues Wish to Impose Their Own Sense of Morality onto the Entire Public

Senator Jesse Helms (R-N.C.) has distinguished himself as one of the most relentless crusaders against contemporary art. He declared in his book *Where Free Men Shall Stand,* "Our political problems are nothing but our psychological and moral problems writ large." When he views Robert Mapplethorpe's photograph *Embrace,* in which a white man and a black man tenderly hug one another, it is probably difficult for him to regard this type of affection in positive (or even neutral) terms. Rather than taking this as an alternative, legitimate relationship, he is likely to perceive a dual challenge to the bedrock of his own life: the norms of racial segregation and heterosexuality.

What's merely different can be quickly recast as immoral and unacceptable. Helms's counterparts on the progressive side are legion—Black aldermen in Chicago could not tolerate an extremely unflattering portrait of the late Mayor Harold Washington in a 1988 student show at the School of the Art Institute of Chicago. They had it "arrested" to foreclose the chance it might "spark a riot." African-Americans have similarly censored *The Adventures of Huckleberry Finn, Show Boat,* an outdoor sculpture by David Hammons ("How Ya Like Me Now?"), and a post–Civil War obelisk in downtown New Orleans. In 1991 the female director of the National Museum of American Art attempted to remove *Muybridge* 1 (1964) by Sol LeWitt from an exhibit because it suggested to her the voyeurism of a peep show, what she judged to be "a degrading pornographic experience." In 1988 AIDS activists demonstrated outside the Museum of Modern Art against the work of photographer Nicholas Nixon. They believed that his portraits of people with AIDS (PWAS) captured isolated and defeated individuals. They wished to substitute images of PWAS who are "vibrant, angry, loving, sexy, beautiful, acting up and fighting back."

In all these cases there was a rejection of the belief that viewers in a free society have a fundamental right to draw their own conclusions about what they see. At the very least, this requires that the public has access to a wide range of material. Yet this is a scary proposition for those engaged in a high-stakes battle for hearts and minds. Such preemptive, protective responses reveal deep insecurities about the strength of the moral stances certain advocates espouse, and stem from their urgent need to shore up their defenses lest people be lured away from "the right path."

The Result of Ideologues at Work: The Restraint of Expression and the Shredding of the Social Fabric

Intergroup relations in America are in a disturbingly fragmented state at present. Those on the extreme right wish to bury their heads in the sands of the past. If they could, they would force the genie of civil rights back into the bottle and restore the verities of yesteryear. But those on the extreme left insist on an "in your face" posture, guaranteeing that their demands must be addressed in some manner or another. Each side shares the sense of these being momentous times, with the very nature of their world at risk at virtually every turn.

Ideologues see everything in black and white. The nuance, contradiction, and complexity that characterize so much contemporary art are destined to trouble them. In fact, a basic property of most of the art that has generated controversy is the *mixture* of sacred and profane elements, blending ingredients that generally are kept apart.

This is evident in Andres Serrano's photograph *Piss Christ,* where a plastic crucifix was submerged in the artist's urine. It is manifest in Robert Mapplethorpe's photographs, and in the work of many other gay as well as feminist artists, where the attributes of "maleness" and "femaleness" may be deconstructed, merged, or reconfigured, and a heterosexual erotic preference cannot be taken for granted. And it is apparent in the work of performance artists who smudge the line between public and private, self and other, decency and morality.

Whereas some viewers enjoy the frisson created by these novel combinations (for them the thrill is in the sense of fresh possibilities), these same efforts may cause immense discomfort for the absolutist. What for one person signals a laudable burst of creativity at most, or silliness at the very least, for another sounds a warning about a world gone terribly awry. It is then that the absolutist frame of mind is activated, engendering the types of results I've enumerated in the examples I've cited.

➢ **Sir Chartres Biron, Chief Magistrate**

Judgment regarding The Well of Loneliness

(1928), United Kingdom

The magistrate: [. . .] I agree that this book has some literary merit, defamed, as I think everybody who has read it will admit, with certain deplorable lapses of taste; but the mere fact that a book is well written can be no answer to these proceedings, because otherwise we should be in this preposterous position, that because it is well written the most obscene book would be free from such proceedings. It is quite obvious to anybody of intelligence that the better an obscene book is written the greater the public to whom the book is likely to appeal. The more palatable the poison the more insidious.

[. . .]

There is one matter which I think should be cleared up, and that is that the mere fact that this book deals with unnatural offences between women would not in itself make it, in my view, an obscene libel. I can imagine a book written dealing with this subject presenting the whole matter as a tragedy, the tragedy being that there may be people so afflicted who try their best to fight against this horrible vice, find themselves impelled in that direction or unable to resist those tendencies, with the result of the moral and physical degradation which indulgence in these vices must necessarily involve; I can imagine a book dealing with the subject on those terms, presenting these women as the prisoners of circumstances which, however much they fight against them, they are unable to resist— I can imagine a book of that kind, whatever one's opinion may be as to whether it is or it is not desirable that these matters should form the subject of a novel for popular reading, having anything but an immoral influence; it might have a strong moral influence. But does that book do it? I am told here by Mr. Melville that the book is presented as a tragedy. It is true that in a sense that is so, but what is the tragedy of the book? It is not the tragedy which I have just indicated at all; it is not the tragedy of people fighting against horrible instincts and being unable to resist them; but, on the contrary, the tragedy as presented here is that people who indulge in these vices are not tolerated by decent people; they are not received in society and they are ostracized by decent people; and the whole note of the book is a passionate and almost hysterical plea for the toleration and recognition of these people who, in the view presented in this book, are people who ought to be tolerated and recognized, and their practices tolerated and recognized, in decent society. That is what is put forward in this book. It is a long book of some 500 pages dealing solely, or at any rate in the main, with unnatural offences. There is not a single word from beginning to end of this book which suggests that anyone with these horrible tendencies is in the least blameworthy or that they should in any way resist them. Everybody, all the characters in this book, who indulge in these horrible vices are presented to us as attractive people and put forward for our admiration; and those who object to these vices are sneered at in the book as prejudiced, foolish and cruel. Not merely that, but there is a much more serious matter, the actual physical acts of these women indulging in unnatural vices are described in the most alluring terms; their result is described as giving these women extraordinary rest, contentment and pleasure; and not merely that, but it is actually put forward that it improves their mental balance and capacity.

[. . .]

[The book] concludes with a very singular hysterical passage in which God is introduced. At the end the last sentence of the book is: "God" she gasped, "we believe; we have told You we believe. . . . We have not denied You, then rise up and defend us. Acknowledge us, oh God, before the whole world. Give us also the right to our existence." There are a good many other passages in which the name of the Deity is introduced in a way which is hardly appropriate. I do not know whether the word "reverence" is introduced in this discussion or whether it is necessary to introduce it, but I confess the way in which the Deity is introduced into this book seems to me singularly inappropriate and disgusting. There is a plea for existence at the end. That of course means a plea for existence in which the invert is to be recognized and tolerated, and not treated with condemnation, which they are at present, by all decent people.

This being the tenor of this book, I have no hesitation whatever in saying that it is an obscene libel, that it would tend to corrupt those into whose hands it should fall, and that the publication of this book is an offence against public decency, an obscene libel, and I shall order it to be destroyed.

Bow Street Police Court.

Friday, 16th November, 1928.

The National Archives, HO 144/22547.

➢ Sapphire

"Wild Thing"

(1996), United States

And I'm running,

running wild

running free,

like soldiers down

the beach,

like someone

just threw me

the ball.

My thighs pump

thru the air

like tires

rolling down
the highway
big & round
eating up the ground
of America
but I never been any
further than 42nd Street.
Below that is as
unfamiliar as my
father's face,
foreign as the smell of
white girls' pussy,
white girls on TV.
My whole world is
black & brown & closed,
till I open it
with a rock,
christen it with
blood.
BOP BOP
the music
pops thru me
like electric shocks,
my sweat is a
river running
thru my liver
green with hate,
my veins bulge out
like tomorrow,
my dick is
the Empire State Building,
I eat your fear
like a chimpanzee

ow ow

ow whee

ow!

My sneakers glide off

the cement like

white dreams

looking out at the world

thru a cage of cabbage

& my mother's fat,

hollering don't do this

& don't do that.

I scream against the restraint

of her big ass sitting on my face

drowning my dreams in sameness.

I'm scared to go

it hurts me to stay.

She sits cross-legged

in front the TV

telling me no

feeding me

clothing me

bathing me in her ugliness

high high in the sky

18th floor of the projects.

Her welfare check buys me $85 sneakers

but can't buy me a father.

She makes cornbread from Jiffy box mix

buys me a coat

$400, leather like everybody else's.

I wear the best, man!

14 karat gold chain

I take off before I go wildin'.

Fuck you nigger!

Nobody touches my gold!

My name is Leroy

L-E-R-O-Y

bold gold

I got the goods

that make the ladies

young & old

sign your name across my heart

I want you to be my baby

Rapper D

Rapper G

Rapper *I*

my name is lightning

across the sky

So what I can't read

you spozed to teach me

you the teacher

I'm the ape

black ape

in white sneakers

hah hah

I rape

rape

rape

I do the wild thing

I do the wild thing.

My teacher asks me

what would I do

if I had 6 months

to live.

I tell her I'd fuck her,

sell dope & do the wild thing.

My thighs are locomotives

hurling me thru the

underbrush of Central Park,

the jungle.

I either wanna be a cop

or the biggest dope dealer in Harlem

when I grow up.

I feel good!

It's a man's world,

my sound is king

I am the black man's sound.

Get off my face whining bitch!

No, I didn't go to school today

& I ain't goin' tomorrow!

I like how the sky looks

when I'm running,

my clothes are new & shiny,

my tooth gleams gold.

I'm fast as a wolf

I need a rabbit,

the sky is falling

calling my name

Leroy Leroy.

I look up

blood bust

in my throat

it's my homeboys

L.D., C.K. & Beanbutt!

Hey man what's up!

I got the moon

in my throat,

I remember when

Christ sucked my dick

behind the pulpit,

I was 6 years old
he made me promise
not to tell no one.
I eat cornbread &
collard greens.
I only wear Adidas
I'm my own man,
they can wear New Balance or Nike
I wear Adidas.
I'm L.D.
lover
mover
man with the money
all the girls know me.
I'm classified as mildly retarded
but I'm not
least I don't think
I am.
Special Education classes
eat up my brain
like last week's greens
rotting in plastic containers.
My mother never
throws away anything.
I could kill her
I could kill her
all those years
all those years
I sat
I sat in classes
for the mentally retarded
so she could get
the extra money welfare gives

for retarded kids.
So she could get
some money,
some motherfuckin' money.
That bitch
that bitch
I could kill her
all the years
I sat next to kids
who shitted on themselves,
dreaming amid
rooms of dull eyes
that one day
my rhymes
would break open
the sky
& my name would
be written
across the marquee
at the Apollo
in bold gold
me bigger
than Run DMC
Rapper G
Rapper O
Rapper *Me*
"Let's go!" I scream.
My dick is a locomotive
my sister eats like a 50¢ hot dog.
I scream, "I *said* let's go!"
It's 40 of us
a black wall of sin.
The god of our fathers

descends down & blesses us,

I say thank you Jesus.

Now let's do the

wild thing.

I pop off the cement

like toast outta toaster

hot hard crumbling

running

running

the park is green

combat operation

lost soul

looking for Lt. Calley

Jim Jones

anybody who could direct

this spurt of semen

rising to the sky.

Soldiers

flying thru

the rhythm

"Aw man!"

nigger please

nigger

nigger

nigger.

"I know

Who I am."

My soul sinks

to its knees &

howls under the

moon rising full,

"Let's get a female jogger!"

I shout into the twilight

looking at the
middle-class thighs
pumping past me,
cadres of bitches
who deserve to die
for thinking they're better
than me.
You ain't better than
nobody bitch.
The rock begs my hand
to hold it.
It says, "Come on man."
T.W., Pit Bull, J.D. & me
grab the bitch
ugly big nose white bitch
but she's beautiful cause she's white
she's beautiful cause she's skinny
she's beautiful cause she's gonna die
cause her daddy's gonna cry
Bitch!
I bring the rock down
on her head
sounds dull & flat
like the time I busted
the kitten's head.
The blood is real & red
my dick rises.
I tear off her bra
feel her perfect pink breasts
like Brooke Shields
like bitches in Playboy
Shit! I come all over myself!
I bring the rock down

the sound has rhythm

hip hop ain't gonna stop

till your face sees

what I see every day

walls of blood

walls of blood

she's wriggling like

a pig in the mud.

I never seen a pig

or a cow

'cept on TV.

Her nipples are like

hard strawberries

my mouth tastes

like pesticide.

I fart.

Yosef slams her

across the face with a pipe.

My dick won't get

hard no more.

I bring the rock down

removing what she

looks like forever

ugly bitch

ugly bitch

I get up

blood on my hands

semen in my jeans

the sky is black

the trees are green

I feel good baby

I just did

the *wild thing!*

In *American Dreams* by Sapphire, first published by Serpent's Tail in 1994.

> **Gayatri Gopinath**

From "Local Sites/Global Contexts: The Transnational Trajectories of Fire *and 'The Quilt'"*

(2005), United States

[. . .]

An analysis of *Fire*'s reception both within and outside India underscores the inadequacy of feminist analyses that seek to destabilize heterosexuality without adequately grappling with the significance of alternative sexualities in the constitution of communal and nationalist collectivities. The film and the controversy it engendered demand that we explore more fully the ways in which challenges to state-sanctioned sexual subjectivities are managed with hegemonic articulations of community and nation, and how they simultaneously threaten to interrupt the coherence of such entities. The violent hostility of religious nationalists in India toward a diasporic film like *Fire* highlights the urgent need for feminist scholarship both in India and in the diaspora to extend its scope of analysis in two directions: first, to view heterosexuality and contemporary nationalisms as overlapping structures of domination; and second, to move beyond the nation-state in order to account for the transnational circuits that both prop *and* challenge contemporary nationalisms.

[. . .]

Fire both adheres to and challenges a developmental narrative of gay and lesbian identity, which underlies dominant Euro-American discourses on non-Western sexualities. The film opens with a scene of the adult protagonist Radha's memory/fantasy of herself as a young girl, sitting beside her parents in an open field of yellow flowers. Her mother urges the young Radha to "see the ocean" lying just beyond the landlocked field: "What you can't see you can see, you just have to see without looking." This scene, with its exhortation to "see" without looking, to "see" differently, recurs and resonates throughout the film and suggests an analogy with the ways in which *Fire* interrogates the notion that the proper location of lesbianism is within a politics of visibility in the public sphere. However, the film's counterhegemonic representation of queer female desire is undercut and complicated by its own history of production, distribution, reception, and consumption. Funded largely with Canadian money, *Fire* had circulated from 1996 to 1998 mostly at international film festivals in India, Europe, and North America and had a lengthy art house release in major U.S. cities. Thus, prior to its general release in India in November 1998, it was available to a limited audience in India but gained a significant South Asian diasporic viewership as well as a mainstream lesbian and gay audience in the United States and Canada. Given the trajectory of the film's reception, it is worth asking how the film has become available and legible to its diasporic and international audiences.

Fire takes place in the middle-class neighborhood of Lajpat Nagar, in New Delhi, and tells the story of the burgeoning love and desire that emerges between Radha (Shabana Azmi) and her new sister-in-law Sita (Nandita Das), in a joint-family household. [Director Deepa] Mehta quickly establishes the familiar familial violences and compulsions that inhabit the household: the women do most of the labor for the family business while their husbands ignore or abuse them. Radha's husband, Ashok, is tender and attentive not to Radha but to his guru, with whom he spends all his free time and who preaches sexual abstinence, while Sita's husband, Jatin, is too preoccupied with his Westernized Chinese girlfriend to attend to Sita. The two women eventually turn to each other for sex and emotional sustenance. Mehta rather conventionally frames the dilemma of her heroines as one in which "modernity," with its promise of individual freedom and self-expression, pulls inevitably against "tradition," which demands that the women adhere to the roles prescribed for them as good Hindu wives and remain chaste, demure, and self-sacrificing. Indeed, their very names bespeak these roles. In Hindu mythology, Radha is the consort of the god Krishna, who is famous for his womanizing; together Radha and Krishna symbolize an idealized, transcendent heterosexual union. Sita, the heroine of the Hindu epic *Ramayana,* proves her chastity to her husband, Ram, by immersing herself in fire, and thus represents the ideal of wifely devotion and virtue. The image of Sita emerging unscathed from her *agni pariksha,* or trial by fire, is the inescapable motif around which the women's lives revolve throughout the film: for instance, the background noise in their daily lives is the popular serialization of the *Ramayana,* which plays incessantly on the television. Das's Sita, however, refuses to inhabit the overdetermined role of her legendary namesake: with her penchant for donning her husband's jeans instead of her heavy silk saris, and her willingness to pursue her attraction to Radha, she becomes the emblem of a "new India" and its promise of feminist self-fulfillment. Conversely, the stultifying effects of "tradition" are embodied in the character of Biji, the mute, paralytic grandmother who keeps a disapproving eye on the activities of her daughters-in-law.

The dichotomies through which the film is structured—between Biji and Sita, saris and jeans, silence and speech, self-denial and self-fulfillment, abstinence and desire, tradition and modernity—implicate it in a familiar teleological narrative of progress toward the individual freedom offered by the West, against which the "non-West" can only be read as premodern. In fact, a number of U.S. critics have used the film as an occasion to replay colonial constructions of India as a site of regressive gender oppression, against which the West stands for enlightened egalitarianism. Within the dominant discursive production of India as anterior to the West, lesbian or gay identity is explicitly articulated as the marker of full-fledged modernity. After Ashok spies the two women in bed together, Sita comments to Radha, "There is no word in our language to describe what we are to each other," to which Radha responds, "You're right; perhaps seeing is less complicated." Film critics in the United States, most notably Roger Ebert, have taken this exchange (as well as Mehta's own pronouncement in the press notes that "Indians don't talk about sex") as proof of the West's cultural superiority and advanced politicization: "Lesbianism is so outside the experience of these Hindus that their language even lacks a word for it." Indeed, almost all mainstream U.S. reviewers stress the failure of "these Hindus" to articulate lesbianism intelligibly, which in turn signifies the failure of the non-West to progress toward the organization of sexuality and gender prevalent in the West. To these critics, ironically, lesbian or gay identity becomes intelligible and indeed desirable when and where it can be incorporated into this developmental narrative of modernity.

Because *Fire* gains legibility within such narratives for at least some North American, non–South Asian viewers (both straight and gay), it is helpful to resituate it within other discourses of non-heteronormative sexuality that are available to South Asian and South Asian diasporic audiences. . . . *Fire* [can] be read as a diasporic appropriation and transformation of Ismat Chughtai's "The Quilt." Reading the film through the story provides an alternative to the tradition-modernity axis by foregrounding the complex model of queer female desire suggested by the film but foreclosed by its mainstream U.S. reception.

[. . .]

For Radha and Sita, then, like the women in Chughtai's story, queer desire becomes the means by which they are able to extricate themselves from the terms of patriarchal heteronormativity by creating their own circuits of pleasure, desire, and fantasy. While some critics have suggested that *Fire*'s depiction of lesbian sexuality capitulates to the familiar notion of lesbianism as merely a reaction to failed heterosexual marriages, I would argue that, at least in the middle-class urban Indian context that Mehta details, it is precisely within the cracks and fissures of rigidly heteronormative arrangements that queer female desire can emerge. As in Chughtai's text, where queer female desire is routed through and against heterosexuality, the attraction between Radha and Sita is enabled by those spaces of sanctioned female homosociality legislated by normative sexual and gender arrangements.

[. . .]

The reactions to *Fire* within and outside India force us to consider the function of cultural representation as a site of both "promise and peril," a site of both the subversion of nationalist ideologies and the reiteration of homophobic sentiments. *Fire* gains multiple and contradictory meanings as it circulates within India, within the South Asian diaspora, and within film festival circuits and theaters in Europe and North America. As the film circulates within India, it may pose a potent challenge to right-wing Hindu nationalism, yet it is simultaneously available for recuperation within a liberal humanist framework that subsumes sexuality under a human rights rubric. Similarly, as it travels outside India, the film both resists and plays into dominant developmental narratives of modernity. I have focused on *Fire* in particular since it is emblematic of the ways in which South Asian diasporic texts travel along increasingly complex trajectories of production and reception. In a Euro-American context, the film's strategy of disarticulation—where it refuses to collapse female homoerotic acts, desires, and practices into static identities—challenges dominant conceptions of what lesbian and gay identity looks like in the West; yet in an Indian context, this very strategy simultaneously allows for the elision of queer desire and the challenge it poses to dominant conceptions of community, home, and nation. The violent debates that have surrounded *Fire* demand that we develop frames of analysis supple enough to account for these transnational movements and the various discourses of gender and sexuality to which they give rise.

SECTION IV

Media

CHAPTER 13

Film and Television

In the early days of moviemaking, Magnus Hirschfeld [λ Chapters 2 and 5] introduced the film *Different from the Others* (1919), a German production by The Scientific Humanitarian Committee, which had been founded in 1897 to help bring about the abolition of Paragraph 175 [λ Chapter 2] by "eliminating false prejudices against homosexuals." Hirschfeld's introduction to the first showing of *Different* contained these lines:

> The matter to be put before your eyes and soul today is one of severe importance and difficulty. Difficult, because the degree of ignorance and prejudice to be disposed of is extremely high. Important, because we must free not only these people from undeserved disgrace but also the public from a judicial error that can be compared to such atrocities in history as the persecution of witches, atheists and heretics. . . . The film you are about to see for the first time today will help to terminate the lack of enlightenment, and soon the day will come when science will win a victory over error, justice a victory over injustice and human love a victory over human hatred and ignorance. (Russo 20)

Almost a century later, Hirschfeld's hopes for the film's impact have not been completely realized. What has happened, however, is that commentary about lesbian, gay, bisexual, and transgender (LGBT) presence in film has continued to use Hirschfeld's ideas; critics have repeatedly called for visibility and representation in

Figure 13.1   Still from *Different from the Others* (1919)

the same ways that Hirschfeld did when he introduced *Different from the Others.*

Film and television—two of the most important venues of contemporary mass media—serve as sites of intense cultural work. Through film and TV, larger cultures clarify their dominant values and ideological investments, while subcultures and minority groups negotiate their "place at the table" through positive representation or through critical interrogation of negative images. Much of the discourse around queers in film and television has focused on questions of visibility and representation. Do we see LGBT people in film and on TV? How often do we see them? Are these representations of LGBT people positive or negative? What do we mean when we use the terms *positive* and *negative?* Do those representations show LGBT people in realistic ways? In this chapter, we focus on a relatively small number of films and TV shows that feature LGBT characters to raise questions about the "cultural work" of film and television with LGBT content—explicit or not. We begin with some information about the way scholars and critics have talked about film, and then we offer several analyses of recent films, moving from reality-based subject matter to fiction to fantasy. From there we shift to television, analyzing significant moments when shows and characters appeared (or disappeared) and asking what these trends might mean. This chapter does not engage in exhaustive historical listing of LGBT characters in film and TV productions; rather, our focus will be on providing some specific analyses of the cultural work accomplished by a variety of representations of queers in mass media.

Visibility and Representation

V ito Russo's *The Celluloid Closet: Homosexuality in the Movies,* written in 1981 and revised in 1987, was in its time the most comprehensive discussion of gay characters in U.S. film. In 1990, it was made into a documentary film featuring interviews with people connected to Hollywood. Russo's book covers nearly a century of films with homosexual characters, asking whether they are presented in a positive or a negative light. Russo's account, written before the explosion of queer characters and issues in the mass media of the 1990s, depicts a startling and unsettling reality: when homosexuals were represented on film, they were often sad and suicidal or unstable and psychopathic. One prime example Russo cites is William Friedkin's controversial 1980 film *Cruising,* in which Al Pacino portrays an undercover cop assigned to infiltrate New York's gay leather underworld to catch a serial killer. By the end of the film, Pacino's character is seemingly seduced into becoming homosexual himself. Russo explains, "[T]he unavoidable conclusion is that Pacino . . . becomes a murderer of gays. . . . The audience is left with the message that homosexuality is not only contagious but inescapably brutal" (259). What's more, for Russo, "The fact that Pacino's girlfriend ends up in the last shot trying on his leather gear says that his lifestyle is seductive and contagious, threatening to what's good in the world" (261). Others agreed with Russo's analysis, and at the time of its original release, many gays picketed the film, which ultimately did poorly at the box office: "Usually, when gay people complain about this sort of thing their concerns are dismissed as partisan, but this time everyone complained because the evidence was too overwhelming to ignore" (261).

Certainly, *Cruising* created a stir, but we must remember that moviemakers' intentions only tell part of the story of how films and other mass media work in a culture. Stuart Hall's notions of "encoding" and "decoding" are useful here. For Hall, encoding refers to the messages deliberately included in cultural products by their makers; decoding refers to the messages cultural consumers glean from these products—not necessarily the encoded ones. Russo may be correct in ascribing

Figure 13.2   Al Pacino in *Cruising*

homophobic intent, or "encoding," to *Cruising*'s makers, and the gay picketers who protested the film read it in that way. But since the film's release, many gay video distribution companies, such as Theatre of the Living Arts (TLA), have marketed the film specifically to gay audiences. Many in the contemporary gay world find *Cruising* a rather sexy and provocative look at leathersex, despite the homophobic story that frames it. Different gay viewers thus "decode" the film in ways that make its message more interesting and complex to them as viewers or "readers."

In the revised 1987 version of *The Celluloid Closet,* Russo discusses the blockbuster film *The Color Purple* (Warner Bros. 1985, dir. Steven Spielberg). Russo, like many other LGBT reviewers, criticizes the film harshly for diluting the lesbian material that figured prominently in its inspiration, Alice Walker's 1982 book. The book had already been slammed by black male critics such as Mel Watkins, Courtland Milloy, Tony Brown, and Spike Lee for its unflattering portrayal of black men and for airing "dirty laundry" about domestic and sexual abuse in black households (Iverem, Bobo). Feminists criticized Spielberg's film for rehabilitating the principal abuser to the point where his smiling silhouette dominates the reunion between protagonist Celie and her long-lost sister Nettie. Moreover, as Russo observes, Spielberg "took a sexually explicit love affair in an existing work and, by his own admission, sanitized it into a series of chaste kisses to beg acceptance from a mass audience" (278). Andrea Weiss writes, "The joke in lesbian circles while the film was in production was that Steven Spielberg wasn't intimidated by creatures from outer space [in his 1982 movie *E.T: The Extra-Terrestrial*] but a lesbian relationship was more than he could handle" (79). Molly Hite goes still further, accusing Spielberg of erasing nonhegemonic behavior to the point where, unlike the book, the film insists on "restoring the patriarchal status quo" (141n).

Using Russo's terms, many LGBT viewers have criticized films such as *The Hunger, Bound,* and *Basic Instinct* for their lesbian characters who are portrayed as violent outsiders. Beginning in the late twentieth century, as attitudes toward LGBT people began to shift, some filmmakers worked to provide more sympathetic characters. *Longtime Companion, Philadelphia, Claire of the Moon,* and *The Incredibly True Adventures of Two Girls in Love* are probably the best known among these rehabilitative films. Russo himself acknowledged at the end of the revised version of *Celluloid Closet* that "[g]ay visibility has never really been an issue in the movies. Gays have always been visible. It's how they have been visible that has remained offensive for almost a century" (325). But even when such images become markedly less offensive, as in the dramatically increased gay and lesbian mass media visibility of the 1990s, critical questions remain. In our discussion of the following three films—*Monster, Unveiled,* and *Shrek 2*—we probe beyond the binary of "good representation"/"bad representation" to ask the following:

- How are representations of queer lives constructed?
- What complex realities do they depict?
- What biases or blind spots remain?

Varieties of Queerness in Contemporary Film

*M*onster (KW 2003, dir. Patty Jenkins) stars Charlize Theron, who won an Oscar for her portrayal of lesbian prostitute and serial killer Aileen (Lee) Wuornos. The film is "loosely based" on the two years of Wuornos's life during which she met and became involved with Tyria Moore (renamed Selby Wall in the film) and during which she murdered seven men (Kalwani). *Monster* depicts Wuornos as a psychologically unstable survivor of childhood sexual violence, who kills her first victim after being beaten and raped by him. The Selby Wall character is played by Christina Ricci as a doe-eyed and willfully blind young lesbian, who whines, "I just want a normal life" and feigns ignorance of Wuornos's murders. After Wuornos's arrest, Wall sells her out, engaging her in a telephone conversation in which Wuornos, realizing the phone is bugged, implicates herself and exonerates Wall. As Wuornos is sentenced to death in the film's final scene, we begin to see her life as a series of truly tragic circumstances.

As a film, *Monster* replays earlier representations of the man-hating lesbian and the psychopathic homosexual to provide psychological and social class context for the characters. Viewers see how lives can be tortured through a nexus of sexual abuse, devaluation of women, homophobia, and poverty. The film, then, is a complex intersectional portrait of social class, gender, and sexuality, which invites us to understand queer lives made desperate through interlocking oppressions. Regardless of the actual events upon which it is based, the film asks viewers not only to understand but also to *sympathize* with Wuornos. We begin to understand why she kills the men she does, and we come to see her relationship with Wall as an attempt to achieve intimacy and love. Wall's desire for a "normal life" seems abnormal, as it can only be achieved at Wuornos's expense. At the very least, Wall's return to normalcy is presented as a refusal to understand the systems that can immiserate queer lives, driving them to desperate acts. Ultimately, Wall's idea of normal and Wuornos's rage and violence are presented as equally pathological.

Attempts to negotiate a "normal life" are at the heart of the German film *Unveiled* (Wolfe 2005, dir. Angelina Maccarone), which tells the story of Fariba, an Iranian woman who flees to Germany to avoid punishment—imprisonment, rape, torture, possibly even death—after the discovery of her affair with a married woman. In Germany, Fariba takes on the identity of Siamak, a fellow (male)

Figure 13.3   Angelina Maccarone

Iranian refugee who has committed suicide. She becomes involved with Anne, a coworker at the sauerkraut factory where Siamak/Fariba is an undocumented employee. Germany turns out to be an unsatisfactory sanctuary for Fariba, as a toxic combination of government bureaucracy and threatening working-class men conspire to force her back to Iran. In *The Globalization of Sexuality*, Jon Binnie points out that "movement across national borders is restricted for some sexual dissidents because of heteronormative and homophobic migration policies" (99). *Unveiled* illustrates the impact of immigration policies that discriminate against LGBT people; it does not allow us simply to demonize the repressive country, in this case Iran, for Fariba is persecuted and ultimately denied asylum in "progressive" Germany as well. Fariba is suspended not only between two countries but also between two genders as she seeks her freedom. In fact, the film's intersectional analysis [λ Chapter 8] of sexuality, gender, and class—Fariba must pose as a man among working-class Germans and other immigrants to secure any possibility of sanctuary—depicts the multiple dangers that some queers must negotiate to find freedom from sexual-, gender-, and nation-based repression.

The German title of the film, *Fremde Haut* (*Strange Skin*), foregrounds at once the protagonist's fraught immigrant Iranian condition, her passing as a male, and her removal of the chador—a covering of the skin for women in conservative Islamic cultures. It also positions *Unveiled* as a contemporary link to the lurid sensational titles of 1950s pulp novels—*Strange Sisters, Veil of Torment, Three Strange Women, The Black Veil,* and so forth. Interestingly, the portrayal of Fariba as a dark-haired butch and Anne as a light-haired femme also recalls typical pulp covers [λ Chapter10]. We see this pattern in popular queer films as well; clear examples are the classic lesbian romance *Desert Hearts* (1986), the Brandon Teena bio-pic *Boys Don't Cry* (1999), and the "true-life" German film *Aimée and Jaguar*

(1999). The nod to pulp fiction and popular films underscores the apparently intentional derivativeness of *Unveiled;* many reviews of the film and even the publicity poster reproduced on the DVD box mention the similarities to *Boys Don't Cry,* for instance. And these are striking, beginning with the bleak, inhospitable landscapes in Germany and Nebraska but also including the perils of passing in a world populated by menacing, potentially murderous men and institutions.

Filmmakers sometimes treat oppression, even antiqueer intolerance, in subtle and even humorous ways. Right-wing conservative organizations such as the Traditional Values Coalition (TVC) have condemned *Shrek 2* (DreamWorks 2004, dir. Andrew Adamson, Kelly Asbury, Conrad Vernon) mostly because they see the film as attempting to "mainstream abnormal behaviors" ("A Gender Identity Disorder Goes Mainstream"). *Shrek 2,* they point out, "features a male-to-female transgender (in transition) as an evil bartender. The character has five o'clock shadow, wears a dress and has female breasts. It is clear that he is a she-male. His voice is that of talk show host Larry King" ("Parents Beware"). The film does indeed contain "subtle sexual messages," as the TVC suggests. But Larry King's MtF Ugly Stepsister bartender is merely a surface gag (and hardly subtle).

Shrek 2's central story revolves around newlyweds Shrek and Fiona seeking acceptance from the King and Queen, Fiona's parents. In the first *Shrek* movie (2001), Princess Fiona—doomed by a curse to live as a human by day and an ogre by night—"comes out" by choosing full-time ogre identity to be her true self and to marry Shrek. This film, however, mitigates its potential queer theme. For one thing, Fiona was attractively unconventional—athletic, powerful, eccentric—as a human but more conventionally "wifely" as a (married) ogre. For another, the "happily ever after" heterosexual marriage plot defuses and domesticates Fiona's potential queerness. *Shrek 2,* however, places the "coming out to parents" plot squarely in the middle of the filmic message. The King and Queen are confronted with a daughter who has chosen to live openly as an ogre and who brings her ogre husband home to meet the folks. We might observe that in this case, the ogre identities seem to stand in for race, not necessarily queerness; after all, green skin and bulky physique are clearly marked on the ogres' bodies. Still, as Eve Kosofsky Sedgwick points out in *Epistemology of the Closet* (1990), the tropes of the closet and coming out have become central metaphors in Western, particularly U.S., culture. Emerging from concealment into a true (even essential) identity symbolically characterizes any number of life trajectories: coming out as an alcoholic, as a Jew or a Muslim or a Christian, as the parent (or child) of a gay person, and so forth. *Shrek 2* finally places queerness at the center of its concerns, and it elaborates on the coming-out theme in ways that resonate powerfully for LGBT people. The Queen, for example, is more accepting of Fiona and Shrek than her husband the

King. This not only reflects the general tendency for straight women to be more open to sexual nonconformity than straight men (see, for example, Herek, Kite, Morin and Garfinkle), but it also highlights an interesting subplot in the movie. It turns out that the King is only human on sufferance of the scheming Fairy Godmother, who has threatened to turn him (back) into a frog if Fiona fails to marry her son, Prince Charming. The King's straight masculinity—even his humanity—is thus shown to be fragile and quickly revocable, and we are reminded of queer theorist Judith Butler's *Gender Trouble* (1990), where she observes that gender—particularly masculinity—is a precarious masquerade that can be reinforced only through performance and reperformance. *Shrek 2,* despite the TVC's focus on its transgender bartender, does far more than simply offer some possibly LGBT images. Rather, it is constructed around the central queer cultural trope of coming out to family, and its final message of acceptance (even of the King who is now a frog) is assumed to resonate with gay and straight people alike.

Small-Screen Queers

Partly because queers have always had some presence in Hollywood, films are frequently critiqued in terms of *type* of representation, while television is more often critiqued in terms of *number* of representations. Bucking this trend, in *All the Rage: The Story of Gay Visibility in America,* Suzanna Danuta Walters critiques the way gays were represented in television shows, films, and advertisements throughout the 1990s, the seeming "golden age" of gay representation, by discussing, for instance, *Ellen, Will & Grace,* and other shows. The sheer number of examples she is able to call upon is surprising: we are, apparently, everywhere. Walters identifies a pervasive "normalizing" trend in these representations: gays as good neighbors, gays placed in situations that highlight the liberal tolerance of straight friends and family, and gays as sick, dying, and alone (76). Lesbians and gay men are represented, but how—and what can be learned from this inclusion?

For decades, shows such as ABC's *The Corner Bar* (1972), *Hot L Baltimore* (1975), and *Soap* (1977–1981) had gay characters, but until the latter part of the twentieth century, queer representations on television were rare—so rare, in fact, that beginning around 1990, popular television shows such as *Roseanne* (1988–1997) and *Friends* (1994–2004) made news with episodes that not only featured gay characters but focused on queer behavior. In one episode of the sitcom *Mad about You* (1992–1999), Jamie Buchman observes the gay pride parade from her apartment window and ponders the difficulty of living in a world that proscribes public displays of affection between same-sex romantic partners. In 1993–1994, public broadcasting stations in the United Kingdom and the United

States screened *Tales of the City*, a miniseries based on Armistead Maupin's novels about gay (and straight) life in San Francisco. *Roseanne* introduced a minor recurring gay character, played mostly for comic relief by a swishy Martin Mull (1991), and followed up in 1994 with TV's first woman-to-woman kiss, between Roseanne and Mariel Hemingway. Hemingway had gained popularity among lesbians for her starring role in the now cult film *Personal Best* (1982). Also in 1994, MTV's hugely popular pseudo-reality show *The Real World* featured Pedro Zamora, an HIV+ man who shared a house with other young people for several months. The show offered the United States one of the first "real-life" views of how a gay person lived with HIV and negotiated relationships and intimacies with others. The popular graphic novel *Pedro and Me* (2000), written by *Real World* participant Judd Winick, chronicles the friendship between Zamora and Winick that lasted until Zamora's death and that inspired Winick to devote his energies to AIDS prevention.

The sitcom *Ellen* (1994–1998) is the first network television show to feature a main character who "comes out" as a lesbian. Noting that the lead character, Ellen Morgan, seemed uninterested in dating, one producer suggested she get a puppy. When that suggestion was cast aside in favor of Ellen's professing her love for a woman, the idea stuck and still today the coming-out episode is called "The Puppy Episode." Malinda Lo writes in "Back in the Day: Coming Out with Ellen" that

> [i]t wasn't until March 1997, after the first version of the coming-out script had been rejected, that Disney executives gave the official go-ahead to tape "The Puppy Episode." What followed was a media blitz: DeGeneres went on *The Oprah Winfrey Show*, was interviewed by Diane Sawyer, and was featured on the cover of *Time* with the headline "Yep, I'm Gay." At the same time, DeGeneres had just met Anne Heche, a heretofore heterosexual actress whose career was beginning to take off. DeGeneres and Heche also made the media rounds, even attending the White House Correspondents' Dinner together in late April.

Despite the enormous amount of attention paid to that episode, though, the show survived only one more season. Some claimed that the show lost momentum after "The Puppy Episode," and others said that the show's considerable attention to gay issues undermined it. Ron Miller of the *San Jose Mercury News*, for instance, argued that "DeGeneres is a funny and inventive woman, whose sexual orientation is only an important aspect of her life, not the sole purpose of it. Maybe the *Ellen* writers would have retained more viewers if they had let her gayness take over only when they really had some fresh and funny point to make" ("GLAAD"). Despite the cancellation, the impact of DeGeneres's real-life and fictional coming out prompted other producers to include a growing number of queer characters in

Figure 13.4   Ellen DeGeneres and wife, Portia di Rossi

their shows. Between 1997 and 2001, the number of recurring gay characters in television shows was consistently in the double digits (Walters 96–97). Such characters were no longer the simple buffoons or suicidal psychopaths depicted in earlier decades; they were, like Ellen in her show's last season, increasingly nuanced and complex characters, confronting discrimination and working on relationships. Seemingly, queers were beginning to achieve the kind of media visibility that critics such as Russo had longed for.

For instance, *Will & Grace*, about the friendship between a gay man and a straight woman, began on the heels of *Ellen*'s cancellation; its main characters were gay male Will and his zany, red-headed best (straight) female friend, Grace. The show also featured Jack, a flaming gay man, and Karen, who was wealthy and shallow but campy and served as Jack's foil. Interestingly, the show was touted as "gay," but the visual representations told a fairly heterosexualized story. Though Jack and Will were sometimes shown in scenes where they discussed their sexuality or their romantic exploits, more often Will and Grace appeared together, with Jack and Karen forming another platonic couple. Queer sexuality was often presented either as a kind of joke (as in the campy character, Jack) or erased altogether. For example, one slapstick episode focused on a sexual competition between Will and Grace, who were both attracted to a man who had just moved into their apartment building. The outcome of the competition was that the man in question, while never revealing his sexuality to either Will or Grace, proclaimed that he wanted friendship and not romance from them and scolded them for their shallowness. This is meant to be a lesson to Will *and* Grace to de-emphasize sexual attraction as a basis for relationships. A number of other episodes feature Will and Grace's friends, Rob and Ellen, a heterosexually married couple. In one episode, Will and Grace compete as a charades team against Rob and Ellen, a move that allows the writers to present Will and Grace as a heterosexualized couple, a dynamic that plays out in many episodes. *Will & Grace* was wildly popular (according to a blurb on the DVD cover, its final episode in 2006 is estimated to have drawn 18.1 million viewers), and the show kept sexual difference, camp, and interactions between professedly gay characters in the public consciousness. Queer responses to it, though, were not entirely positive. John Lyttle told *The Independent on Sunday* that, "[i]n a few years' time, we will look back on [*Queer Eye, Will & Grace* and a UK version of *Queer Eye* called *Fairy Godfathers*] in the same way we look

Figure 13.5   The cast of *Will & Grace*

back on [the book] *Uncle Tom's Cabin.* People will cringe. . . . The thing about camping it up [is that] it's gone from being very subversive—without it we wouldn't have had gay liberation—to being the norm on TV. Gay culture is not all about that stereotype. It's like gay men are only acceptable if they play the court jester" ("Edinburgh").

While complex and nuanced queer characters still continue to be rare on major American broadcast channels such as CBS, NBC, and ABC, cable channels have hosted a variety of long-running series with significant queer content, some focused primarily on lesbian and gay lives. Showtime's *Queer as Folk* (2000–2005), based on a short-lived British TV series, offered a sometimes explicit and frequently controversial look at the lives of several gay and lesbian friends in Pittsburgh. Featuring some of the most graphic same-sex erotic scenes in a television drama, *Queer as Folk* pushed boundaries and showed audiences some of the issues facing contemporary urban gay people, such as drug addiction, nonmonogamy, job discrimination, homophobic assaults, and difficulties encountered by same-sex parents attempting to raise children. A comparable show focusing on lesbian friendships and relationships, *The L Word* (2004–present), also on Showtime, focuses on a group of lesbian-identified friends living in Los Angeles. In 2006, Logo began airing the African American–themed *Noah's Arc,* which is described in promos in this way: "From new boyfriends to strained friendships to career changes, these men persevere and live their lives with grace and wit" ("*Noah's Arc*"). *Noah's Arc* foregrounds issues common to urban gay men, such as attraction to a man who is coy about revealing his sexuality, living together in a tiny apartment, and adjusting to a new lover's straight friends. The pay-for-TV location of these shows permits them to present queer lives in more depth and complexity than would be permitted on free channels, but it also limits the size and diversity of the audiences they reach and thus the conversations they can prompt about queer lives.

Walters maintains that such increased media visibility is a mixed blessing. On one hand, she argues that it is good because "cultural visibility can really push the envelope, bringing complicated and substantive gay identities into public view. And sometimes these cultural images slowly, almost imperceptibly, chip away around the edges of bigotry, never really getting to the core but perhaps revealing it all too clearly" (15). On the other hand, "We may be seen now, but I am not sure we are known" (10); "visibility does not erase stereotypes nor guarantee liberation" (13); and "[i]f gays are now a regular part of the visual landscape, then they too can be mocked and 'dissed'" (117). In fact, as Walters points out, the newfound media visibility might backfire: "Gay as chic can be used in ways that deflect attention away from more substantive concerns about lesbian and gay civil rights" (17). For instance, the media in general fail to represent homophobia as it moves through and even destroys some queer lives; this may be the most serious shortcoming of the new gay representation.

As we reflect on the films, television shows, and critical commentaries that we have discussed in this chapter, we see that filmic representations of queers, particularly in the past two decades, have been significant for a number of reasons: they provide LGBT people a set of images with which to relate and identify, they serve pedagogically to show the larger culture how to respond nonhomophobically to queers, and, as in the case of *Shrek 2* and its "queer" storyline, they offer metaphorical ways of thinking critically about culture and difference. While we view these as salutary uses of such images, we also wonder about their limitations. For instance, we find that many contemporary fictional representations of queerness in the movies and on television are freighted with what we might call the "imperative of the happy ending," that is, the insistence that plotlines featuring gay people, queer relationships, or LGBT romances end happily. While such endings serve the pedagogical purpose of showing straights and queers alike that LGBT people can—and should—be able to lead happy, healthy, and productive lives, the happy-ending imperative seems like merely the inverse of the negative representational patterns that Russo observed two decades ago. In the fictional film *Ma Vie En Rose* (1997), for example, the happy ending involves the "conversion" of adults and other children to the protagonist's point of view that "he" is a girl born into a boy's body as a result of the accidental loss of his second X chromosome.

In contrast, the "based on real life" movies, such as *Boys Don't Cry,* have room for less imperatively happy endings; in some cases, their grounding in reality can license a more complex rendering of queer lives and experiences. Finally, the widespread use of the "coming-out" narrative that we identified as a key thematic in

Shrek 2 allows viewers to build empathy with those who have secrets and are trying to negotiate their differences with the larger culture—a situation many LGBT people face today. At the same time, we wonder whether the extension of the metaphor of the closet to *all* differences dilutes a more specific consideration of the particular difficulties faced by queer people as they navigate sexist and homophobic systems, institutions, and ideologies.

QUESTIONS FOR DISCUSSION

1. Traditionally, the assumption has been that there is a clear relationship between visibility—in film, television, and so on—and movement toward equality. But is the path from visibility to equality really so direct? How might it proceed by fits and starts? And whose equality, specifically, are we talking about? Gays and lesbians? Bisexuals? The transgendered? *White* LGBT folk? *Middle-class* LGBT folk? And to complicate things even further, how do we define equality, and why do we assume that equality is a laudable goal? Think intersectionally about the visibility of LGBT people in the mass media to problematize and nuance your ideas about this issue.

2. We acknowledge that this chapter, by necessity, deals with a very small number of films and television shows. We note, for instance, that well-known feature films *The Adventures of Priscilla, Queen of the Desert; To Wong Foo, Thanks for Everything, Julie Newmar; Hedwig and the Angry Inch;* and *Transamerica* (all focused on transgender characters) did not make it into our narrative. How might you use the critique of representation and visibility that we present in this chapter to understand the cultural work around transgenderism in one or more of these films?

3. In this chapter, we have focused on major motion pictures and television series, ignoring a mixed genre: made-for-television movies. *Consenting Adults* (1985) depicted a mother trying to come to terms with her son's disclosure of his homosexuality, and *An Early Frost* (1985) showed a middle-class family dealing with a gay son's AIDS. Such movies served a pedagogical function in bringing some awareness of queer lives, however limited and sentimental, to the larger American (and Western) culture. Such movies taught the public about queerness by focusing primarily on family members' struggles to deal with homosexuality, as opposed to the individual lives of queers themselves. These movies are currently available on DVD. Locate one or more made-for-television movies, and contrast the cultural work they do with the cultural work done by recurring queer characters in sitcoms or ongoing TV dramas.

REFERENCES AND FURTHER READING

Binnie, Jon. *The Globalization of Sexuality.* London: Sage, 2004.

Bobo, Jacqueline. "Sifting through the Controversy: Reading *The Color Purple.*" *Callaloo* No. 39 (Spring 1989): 332–42.

Butler, Judith. *Gender Trouble: Feminism and the Subversion of Identity.* New York: Routledge, 1990.

Doty, Alexander. *Flaming Classics: Queering the Film Canon.* New York: Routledge, 2000.

———. *Making Things Perfectly Queer: Interpreting Mass Culture.* Minneapolis: U of Minnesota P, 1993.

Duralde, Alonso. "Gay Guide to the Oscars." *The Advocate* 1 March 2005. <http://findarticles.com/p/articles/mi_m1589/is_2005_March_1/ai_n12417610>.

"Edinburgh Festival: Gay Activists Attack TV over 'Poofs in Primetime.'" *The Independent on Sunday* 15 August 2004. <http://findarticles.com/p/articles/mi_qn4159/is_20040815/ai_n12759089>.

"A Gender Identity Disorder Goes Mainstream." Traditional Values Coalition *Special Report.* April 2005. 6 August 2008 <http://www.jesus-is-savior.com/Evils%20in%20America/Sodomy/homosexual_identity_disorder.pdf>.

"GLAAD Media Round-Up: *Ellen's* Gay, Gay World." 27 February 1998 <http://www.glaad.org/action/al_archive_detail.php?id=1883>.

Hall, Stuart. "Encoding/Decoding." *Media Studies: A Reader.* Eds. Paul Marris and Sue Thornham. New York: NYU P, 2000. 51–61.

Hanson, Ellis. *Out Takes: Essays on Queer Theory and Film.* Durham, NC: Duke UP, 1999.

Herek, G. M. "Assessing Heterosexuals' Attitudes toward Lesbians and Gay Men." *Psychological Perspectives on Lesbian and Gay Issues: Vol. 1. Lesbian and Gay Psychology: Theory, Research, and Clinical Applications.* Eds. B. Greene and G. M. Herek. Thousand Oaks, CA: Sage, 1994. 206–23.

Hite, Molly. "Writing—and Reading—the Body: Female Sexuality and Recent Feminist Fiction." *Feminist Studies* 14.1 (1988): 120–42.

Iverem, Esther. "An Interview with Alice Walker." 28 February 2002. 6 August 2008 <http://www.seeingblack.com/2003/x022803/walker.shtml>.

Kalwani, Dinesh. "Real-Life Beauty, Reel-Life 'Monster.'" Chicago GSB 26 January 2004. <http://media.www.chibus.com/media/storage/paper408/news/2004/01/26/ArtsEntertainment/RealLife.Beauty.ReelLife.monster-589672.shtml>.

Keeling, Kara. "'Joining the Lesbians': Cinematic Regimes of Black Lesbian Visibility." *Black Queer Studies: A Critical Anthology.* Eds. E. Patrick Johnson and Mae G. Henderson. Durham, NC: Duke UP, 2005. 213–27.

Kite, M. E. "Sex Differences in Attitudes toward Homosexuals: A Meta-Analytic Review." *Journal of Homosexuality* 10.1–2 (1984): 69–81.

Lo, Malinda. "Back in the Day: Coming Out with Ellen." In *After Ellen: News, Reviews & Commentary on Lesbian and Bisexual Women in Entertainment and the Media.* 9 April 2005. 6 August 2008 <http://www.afterellen.com/>.

Morin, S., and E. Garfinkle. "Male Homophobia." *Journal of Social Issues* 34.1 (1978): 29–47.

"*Noah's Arc*—Original Series from MTV's Logo Network Comes to DVD This Summer." 9 May 2006 <http://www.tvshowsondvd.com/newsitem.cfm?NewsID=5626>.

"Parents Beware: 'Shrek 2' Features Transgenderism and Crossdressing Themes." The Traditional Values Coalition. N.d. 6 August 2008 <http://www.traditionalvalues.org/modules.php?sid=1659>.

Russo, Vito. *The Celluloid Closet: Homosexuality in the Movies.* Rev. ed. New York: Harper & Row, 1987.

Sedgwick, Eve Kosofsky. *Epistemology of the Closet.* Berkeley: U of California P, 1990.

Walters, Suzanna Danuta. *All the Rage: The Story of Gay Visibility in America.* Chicago: U of Chicago P, 2001.

Weiss, Andrea. *Vampires and Violets: Lesbians in Film.* New York: Penguin, 1992.

Winick, Judd. *Pedro and Me.* New York: Henry Holt, 2000.

READINGS

➢ **Maria Pramaggiore**

"Fishing for Girls: Romancing Lesbians in New Queer Cinema"

(1997), United States

> *With the underground cinema gaining in strength, with all the publicity and all, the moneybags are beginning to see profitable possibilities in it. All the temptations and the commercial bustle is beginning to surround us. All kinds of clever commercial fishermen are beginning to tempt us with promises, contracts, sweet tongues. It's time to sound a warning.*
>
> Jonas Mekas, 1967

> *The 1990s have brought much less suspicion of the popular.*
>
> Cherry Smith, 1995

[. . .]

Little Movies That Could: Independent Cinema, New and Old

Although the contemporary film industry's search for lucrative independent film projects has created opportunities for the theatrical release of lesbian-themed films like Troche and Turner's *Go Fish* and Maggenti's *The Incredibly True Adventures of Two Girls in Love*, the premises and promise of New Queer Cinema as a radical formal and political weapon are part and parcel of the entertainment industry's commodification of queer identities. As gay "homocore" filmmaker Bruce La Bruce puts it: "The media will tolerate its bad children as long as they entertain and perform within the limitations it dictates; when it is no longer amused, or gets bored, you have to be savvy enough to transform yourself into something else or risk having your head chopped off" (188). When entertainment conglomerates and whiz-kid executives have exhausted the public's desire for a particular version of the "alternative"—"little movies that could" in *Time* film critic Richard Corliss's terms—will New (now Old?) Queer filmmaking face significant and all-too-familiar barriers to financing and distribution? And would that be a bad thing?

As [B. Ruby] Rich points out, New Queer cinema grew out of a particular tradition, whether it knows it or not: the marginal, alienated and avowedly resistant practices of Mekas's New American Cinema. Films associated with a tradition that self-reflexively thrives on its outsider status only reluctantly find bedfellows among the commercial successes of New Queer Cinema. Underground queer film lives on in spirit in the work of Bruce La Bruce and Sadie Benning, two filmmakers whose work is surprisingly widely distributed, given its raw pain, graphic sex and startling formal experimentation.

Increasingly, however, the hegemony of the feature-length 35 millimeter film and growing opportunities for mass distribution have lured a number of filmmakers out of the underground closet, enticed as much by the prospect of breaking even or having their films shown as by lucrative commercial deals.

The aesthetic and political ancestors of Rich's New Queer Cinema—the New American Cinema Group—met with a similar fate, although assimilation into Hollywood was carried out by the first generation of film-schooled "Hollywood Renaissance" directors in the late 1960s, not by the practitioners of New American Cinema themselves. Mekas and others championed a radical cinema defined by the improvisation of John Cassavetes and the hand-held camerawork of Robert Frank (techniques which interestingly but not surprisingly reappear with a vengeance in *Go Fish*). The New American Cinema Group rejected the production methods, distribution channels and aesthetic stranglehold of Hollywood, an economic and aesthetic monolith which, despite its dominance in the U.S. and abroad for thirty years, was literally disintegrating as a result of studio divestiture, the increasing competition from television, and the growing appeal of European art cinema.

Self-consciously subversive, New American Cinema distanced itself from the mainstream industry not only by money and miles (Hollywood versus New York and San Francisco) but also by a tangible, self-policed border that neatly divided commerce from art. That no man's land of anti-Establishment attitude spanned the irrecoverable distance between (to be intentionally perverse) Jack Smith's *Flaming Creatures* and Joseph Manckiewicz's *Cleopatra,* both released in 1963.

Today one might argue that *Flaming Creatures* and *Cleopatra* are somewhat aesthetically compatible, that they can be recovered and recycled as camp—and this is precisely the point. Postmodern understandings and practices of politics refuse to set art against commerce, to imagine, as Mekas and others did, an author-driven filmmaking practice unsullied by the society of the spectacle and its commercial encroachments. Today's entertainment corporations large and small are happy to promote films that uncritically embrace the power of the image and its accouterments, delighted to encourage mass audiences to consume a slice of an alternative "lifestyle" on-screen, recognizing queer subjects only when served up as delectable and exotic matinee fare. As a result, the energy behind contemporary independent cinema—itself rapidly becoming the fair-haired child of mainstream film culture—is increasingly directed toward features that look less like the thoughtful *The Return of the Secaucus Seven* (1981) and more like the unthinking *Pulp Fiction* (1993), to, once again perversely, compare films by two vastly different independent directors, John Sayles and Quentin Tarantino.

"Hollywood" is an increasingly problematic framework to use to describe an industry populated by a few voracious entertainment conglomerates, a growing number of small production companies, and the fashionable Indie circuit experiencing a feeding frenzy as a result of profitable (queer and non-queer) small films. Similarly, "New Queer Cinema" is an equally inadequate, if not vacuous, term to use to analyze the economic, political and aesthetic issues surrounding filmmaking by and about lesbians, gays, bisexuals, transsexuals, transvestites and other gender and sexual outlaws, particularly when the films and directors may or may not resist or oppose the genres, formal devices, production methods and distribution channels of traditional film culture.

Unlike the New American Cinema defined by Jonas Mekas, then, New Queer Cinema(s) must stake out its (their?) location(s) upon the heterogeneous map of post-classical, post-Renaissance filmmaking in a context in which "independent" has become a buzz-word for commercial viability rather than, or in addition to, an assertion of an anti-hegemonic aesthetic. Targeting queer markets has paid off, of course, as Gregory Woods writes of Great Britain: "Since the late 1980s it has become increasingly commonplace to speak, not only of the purchasing power of the so-called 'pink economy,' but also of the pink pound's extraordinary resilience during the recession of the early 1990s" (147). Bruce La Bruce's analysis is even more cynical and contradictory:

> [A friend] tells me I should direct the marketing for my new movie towards a "regular" audience and steer clear of the ghettoisation of the gay and lesbian film festival circuit. I'm at a bit of a loss to think how an explicit movie about a washed-up gay porno star who is shown sucking a lot of cocks and getting fucked up the ass could appeal to a heterosexual crowd, but I guess you can market anything these days. And you know, somehow, I think he's right. (191–92)

What puzzles La Bruce, momentarily at least, is the assertion that his film could be made palatable to a wide audience through marketing; the notion that a larger, general audience is preferable to a specialized gay market goes unquestioned. To read La Bruce's predicament in terms of both its economic and aesthetic implications requires not the rubric of New Queer Cinema, but instead, Eve Sedgwick's distinction between universalizing and minoritizing discourses surrounding sexuality. La Bruce's comments clearly show how that distinction operates in an environment of instantaneous and inescapable commodification. Minoritizing and universalizing "tendencies" differ according to whether they view sexuality as relevant for a subculture or for an entire culture, Sedgwick writes:

> I hypothesized in *Epistemology of the Closet* that modern homo/heterosexual definition has become so exacerbated a cultural site because of an enduring incoherence about whether it is to be thought of as an issue only for a minority of (distinctly lesbian or gay) individuals or, instead, as an issue that cuts across every locus of agency and subjectivity in the culture. ("Forward: T Times" xii)

As Sedgwick points out, it is one of the paradoxes of queernesses, Old and New, that minoritizing and universalizing impulses are interwoven and contained within them. It is no paradox at all that harnessing the universalizing tendency makes for good box office. In other words, the deceptively simple idea of "marketing" La Bruce refers to above encompasses not only blatant advertising ploys but also a film's textual strategies: both help to draw paying customers. Targeting gay and lesbian audiences as a specialized, minority market is one thing; successfully purveying queerness in a universalizing fashion [in the tradition of *The Wedding Banquet* (1993), *The Crying Game* (1992), and *To Wong Foo* (1995)] sends profitability ratios over the top.

Anxieties surrounding the greedy fishermen who calculate profit ratios—the sort Mekas describes in the epigram to this essay—underlie commentaries on authentically political queer film. In an article on the success *Go Fish* met with at the Sundance Film Festival, for example, Ruby Rich includes this disclaimer: "If this article has a hidden agenda, it's the attempt to head off the backlash and argue that this film is far more than any mainstream distributor's fishing expedition" ("Goings and Comings" 14). If Mekas's and Rich's fishermen have gone trolling for catch in New Queer Cinema, and if the resulting commercial success of small films like *Go Fish* no longer disqualifies them from functioning as political art, I would argue that textual analysis becomes an important tool with which to assess the political impact and aesthetic innovation of these films. If queer-made independent and straight-made studio-produced films become virtually indistinguishable in terms of production, marketing and distribution, then narrative and visual expression must carry the burden of the aesthetic-political project of queer, new and/or subversive cinema(s). At this point it is important to ask if the New Queer paradigm gives us greater access to these films in terms of textual address.

In my readings of *Go Fish* and *Two Girls,* aesthetic and political differences can be interpreted more usefully through Sedgwick's universalizing/minoritizing distinction than through the generality of New Queer Cinema because Sedgwick's terms anticipate the shifty politics of postmodern image-making apparatuses and address issues of audience appeal and political sensibilities without the circular logic implied by New Queerness: "we're here, we're queer, we're doing something with film that you will have to get used to." It seems fair to argue that the distinctive style of some recent queer films—like *Go Fish*—does pose challenges to dominant film aesthetics—in large part because they draw upon the legacy of an underground cinema that never quite stays underground. At the same time such New Queer films are already constructed in the dominant discourses of a mass culture of entertainment geared toward the continued repackaging of novelty for the sole purpose of generating box office receipts. It is not my intention to lambaste either *Go Fish* or *Two Girls*—two appealing and well-made films—as "selling out" to the amorphous specter of "Hollywood" or its fishermen-henchmen but, rather, to find a more productive way to interrogate the politics and aesthetics of and in films yoked together as New and Queer.

There is another shortcoming of the New Queer Cinema rubric which seriously hampers any analysis of the economics and aesthetics of lesbian films: it fails to address gender dynamics in independent and mainstream cinema. Analyzing lesbian films in terms of their history, generic patterns, and representational politics provides a perspective that a New Queer aesthetic vision cannot because the latter fails to explore the implications of the male-domination of the film industry for lesbian cinema.

"Decade of the Dyke": Girls, Genre and New Lesbian Cinema?

Rich alludes to the material realities affecting New Queer feature filmmaking (as opposed to videos and short films) in her 1992 *Sight and Sound* article, where she points out that gender still matters in the film industry:

> Surprise, all the new movies being snatched up by distributors, shown in mainstream festivals, booked into theatres, are by the boys. Surprise, the amazing new lesbian videos that are redefining the whole dyke relationship to popular culture remain hard to find. (32)

Videos, experimental short films such as those of Barbara Hammer, and the now-famous pixelvision of Sadie Benning are staples of lesbian cinema, new and old. The fact remains that gay men have made inroads into both mainstream and independent feature film-making with much greater and more visible success off and on-screen.

In 1994, with the long and torturous road to release of *Go Fish* in mind, Rich expresses hope that the time for lesbian cinema has come:

> Finally, critically, not incidentally, a lesbian feature cinema is emerging along-side lesbian video. After years of boys-only filmmaking, *Go Fish* is a dramatic lesbian film to cheer . . . if the papers are to be believed there are already more than a dozen mainstream lesbian films in production or pre-production in Hollywood. If this keeps up, then the 90s may just be the decade of the dyke after all. ("Goings and Comings" 16)

To confirm Rich's always prescient sense of film and culture, evidence for the critical mass necessary for a lesbian cinema is clear from the formidable increase in the number of lesbian features produced in the 1990s. By 1995, lesbian feature film production had nearly doubled that of the entire decade of the 1980s.

Specific industry practices of exclusion—in mainstream film production as well as independent film—and economic and power dynamics have effectively prevented lesbians from making films; thus identifying gendered imbalances further fractures the New Queer Cinema paradigm. Amy Taubin claims that, from the evidence available in 1992, "queer cinema is figured in terms of sexual desire and the desire it constructs is exclusively male . . . [i]ndeed, women are even more marginalised in 'queer' than in heterosexual film; at least in the latter, they function as objects of desire" (37). Because lesbians have had limited access to filmmaking and because lesbian image making is of critical importance to notions of gender, sexuality, queerness and cultural power, it is important to acknowledge that lesbian cinema participates in New Queer Cinema and to recognize that contemporary lesbian filmmaking is not characterized with enough precision or specificity by such a term.

With reference to the marginalization of women in queer and mainstream films alike, Guinevere Turner, who co-wrote, co-produced and acted in *Go Fish,* speaks with Holly

Willis about the personal and community empowerment associated with taking Sundance by storm and reaching a wide audience:

> We didn't imagine any crossover in terms of a heterosexual audience. We didn't think anyone would really pay attention; luckily we also didn't care about that. Also, lesbians are excited not only because it's a lesbian movie but also because it's getting so much attention. It's this affirmation for everyone. We are interesting. We are talented. We are real people. (20)

While an anecdotal statement cannot substitute for a systematic framework for analyzing questions of gender, power and queer film, Turner's comments suggest that for lesbian communities marginality is not a position of strength from which to express or enact resistance, a view which may differ in some ways from Turner's gay male counterparts. For Turner, producing lesbian images that affirm lesbian cultural production and materialize lesbian existence in the heterosexualist imagination is a powerful political act.

Lesbian cinema is, in fact, redefining itself in relation to ideas of community and affirmation, particularly in terms of narrative complexity, visual style, and genre, aspects of filmic form which the rubric of New Queer Cinema is unlikely to discern with appropriate specificity. For that matter, it is arguable whether "lesbian cinema" is nuanced enough to describe *Go Fish* and *Two Girls,* which are romantic comedies. The recurring adoption of the generic conventions of the romantic comedy in films by lesbians, however, suggests an interest—lesbian? queer? cinematic? all three and more?—in remapping romance. If, as Eve Sedgwick argues, heterosexuality "has been permitted to masquerade so fully as History itself—when it has not presented itself as the totality of Romance," it does so nowhere more seamlessly than in the darkened space of the movie theater ("Queer and Now" 11).

Recent lesbian romances go beyond the coming-out narrative to explore lesbian identities, communities and the relationship between lesbian culture and popular culture. One important facet of this increasing complexity is the transition from drama to comedy. *Go Fish* and *Two Girls,* for example, both complicate the coming-out narrative of "lesbian problem pictures" like *Desert Hearts* (1985) and *Claire of the Moon* (1993), partly because the comedies begin from the premise that out lesbians have interesting stories to tell that are not related to their coming out experiences. The origins and impetus for the transition from angst-ridden coming-out to playful outings are not entirely clear: Rich notes that "*Go Fish* is the daughter of [*A Comedy in Six Unnatural Acts* (Oxenberg, 1975)], the living proof that lesbian camp does exist and even has a lineage. Except that Troche and Turner have never seen it" ("Goings and Comings" 15). *Go Fish* and *Two Girls* do, however, speak directly to the fact that lesbians respond critically to the way that the romance genre, when it has represented lesbian characters, has almost exclusively constructed lesbian identity as not only a problem, but the problem.

The expansion and development of recent lesbian cinema in terms of narrative focus and complexity is not necessarily "generational," however, nor does it correlate with release dates. For example, Patricia Rozema's recent *When Night Is Falling* (1995) retells a familiar coming-out narrative, albeit with captivating and lyrical imagery, whereas her earlier *I've Heard the Mermaids Singing* (1987) explores lesbian image-making in a narrative that eschews the coming-out to coupledom scenario and instead situates lesbian desires in a variety of contexts: friendly, romantic, creative, and professional relationships.

Sedgwick's terminology of universalizing and minoritizing understandings of sexual difference (*Epistemology of the Closet* 9) is suited to addressing films that complicate queer identities and address multiplicitous sexual and racial identities. In fact, the tensions circulating among these impulses and lesbian image making are reflected in political and aesthetic differences between *Go Fish* and *Two Girls in Love,* not least because minoritizing and universalizing frames have implications for the use, abuse or transformation of a pre-existing genre. One of the most important distinctions between the films is that they treat the conventions of romantic comedy in very different ways.

It may be that the success of *Two Girls* and *Go Fish* is partly attributable to genre. After all, mass-produced film culture is nothing if not dedicated to the proposition that happily-ever-after is worth millions, expended at eight dollars a head. Mandy Merck places lesbian romance within the European art cinema tradition, a cinema which typically has eschewed Hollywood conventions but also has garnered a small but devoted audience. Merck claims that "lesbian romance is becoming a conventional—and highly conventionalized—narrative in the 'art' cinema of Europe and North America" and argues that, because art cinema emphasizes European cultural specificity and authorial expressivity, it translates into "adult," and, therefore, "sexy" film (377).

> [Art film] provides a sufficient degree of difference from dominant heterosexual conventions to be seen as "realistic," "courageous," "questioning"—all terms from British reviews of *Lianna* [Sayles, 1983]—but it does this by offering literally more of the same, more of the traditional cinematic use of the figure of the woman to signify sexual pleasure, sexual problems, sex itself. (378)

Merck contends that *Desert Hearts* was hailed as a remarkable achievement because it transformed lesbian distress into romance, while at the same time reinscribing traditional genre conventions. According to her analysis, lesbian romantic comedies generally rely upon the standard narrative involving the seduction of the reluctant woman and renew the popular romance genre by revitalizing the tired "boy meets girl, loses girl, gets girl back" formula (379). Furthermore,

> In order to succeed as a popular romance, *Desert Hearts* was divested of any social or political ramification or context that would restrict its generality. As Donna Deitch herself argues, "I didn't want to put it in seventies New York. It's not about lesbian custody or any particular issues, it's essentially a love story." This principle of universal applicability is conventionally seen as a mark of artistic success. (380)

Deitch's sentiments are echoed in statements by Maria Maggenti, director of *Two Girls,* who states that "My film is based on my experience falling in love for the first time. I cannot be more emphatic when I say that this has nothing to do with the commodification of lesbian experience nor the so-called current interest in our lives. I am interested in truth as a filmmaker not markets" ("[Transcript of] Conference" 4). While both *Go Fish* and *Two Girls* can be classified as romantic comedies, the former self-consciously interrogates the genre's terms and intervenes in them in minoritizing terms whereas *Two Girls* playfully adapts the classical romance narrative along the universalizing lines suggested by Merck's reading of *Desert Hearts.*

[. . .]

Terms of Enqueerment

If assessing the radical nature of a non-Hollywood film practice is difficult in postmodern culture, it is nevertheless the case that the terminology of New Queer Cinema poses a number of problems as a framework for economic and textual analysis. It may be the case that the marginal status of queer films is no longer an appropriate measure of political commitment; however, it does seem useful to address the politics of queer films in terms of universalizing or minoritizing understandings of sexual difference. In fact, these terms do have something to contribute in terms of a discussion of commodification—and not in the sense that films exhibiting a universalizing tendency will always be more marketable. Product differentiation in a heterogeneous industry may ensure that both styles of film will be produced and distributed; however, the current independent film scene does favor the production of universalizing queer films such as *Two Girls*. Changes in industrial structure may make the production of films like *Go Fish*—whose minoritizing lesbian politics intervene in heterosexual romance conventions and are embedded in its structure and style—less likely.

While the term "Queer" is useful in many contexts as a term that distinguishes the interests of a coalition of deviants—gay men, lesbians, bisexuals, transsexuals, transvestites, sexual and gender outlaws, non-narrow straights and others—from those who continue to press for discriminatory treatment of non-heterosexuals, the generality of "Queer" in terms of textual analysis poses significant drawbacks. To assess the political and aesthetic dimensions of recent films—lesbian, gay, queer or New Queer—specific attention to genre and gender history is required in order to analyze currents and undercurrents within queer and independent filmmaking.

Works Cited

Burston, Paul and Colin Richardson, eds. *A Queer Romance: Lesbians, Gays, and Popular Culture.* London: Routledge, 1995.

Corliss, Richard. "The Little Movies That Could." *Time* 12 Sept. 1994: np.

Gever, Martha, John Greyson, and Pratibha Parmar, eds. *Queer Looks.* New York: Routledge, 1993.

Interview 24.5 (1994): 22.

———. 24.6 (1994): 40.

La Bruce, Bruce. "The Wild, Wild World of Fanzines: Notes from a reluctant pornographer." In Burston. 186–95.

Mekas, Jonas. "On How the Underground Fooled Hollywood." *Village Voice* 21 Dec. 1967. Rpt. in *Movie Journal: The Rise of a New American Cinema 1959–71*. New York: Macmillan, 1972. 301–2.

———. "On the Commercial Temptations," *Village Voice* 11 May 1967. Rpt. in *Movie Journal: The Rise of a New American Cinema 1959–71*. New York: Macmillan, 1972. 278.

Merck, Mandy. "*Desert Hearts.*" In Gever 377–82.

Parmar, Pratibha. "That Moment of Emergence." In Gever 3–11.

Rich, B. Ruby, "New Queer Cinema." *Sight and Sound* 2.5 (1992): 32.

———. "Goings and Comings." *Sight and Sound* 4.7 (1994): 14–16.

Sedgwick, Eve Kosofsky. "Queer and Now." *Tendencies.* Durham: Duke UP, 1993. 1–20.

———. "Forward: T Times." *Tendencies.* Durham: Duke UP, 1993. xi–xvi.

———. *Epistemology of the Closet.* Berkeley: U of California P, 1990.

Taubin, Amy. "Beyond the Sons of Scorsese." *Sight and Sound* 2.5 (1992): 37.

"Transcript of Conference with Writer/Director Maria Maggenti." The *Two Girls* Homepage: http://www2.interpath.net/fineline/twogirls.htm. American Online. 28 June 1995.

Willis, Holly. "Fish Stories: Holly Willis on *Go Fish.*" *Filmmaker* 2.3 (1994): 18–20.

Woods, Gregory. "We're Here, We're Queer and We're not Going Catalogue Shopping." In Burston. 147–63.

"Fishing for Girls: Romancing Lesbians in New Queer Cinema," by Maria Pramaggiore, College Literature, West Chester State College.

➤ Kara Keeling

"'Joining the Lesbians': Cinematic Regimes of Black Lesbian Visibility"

(2005), United States

[. . .]

I offer the following examination of Cheryl Dunye's film *The Watermelon Woman* [First Run, 1996] as an example of a queer interpretative project that begins by interrogating the regime of visibility in which "black lesbian" appears and moves into a consideration of what that regime renders invisible in its efforts to produce the ethico-political subject "black lesbian."

[. . .]

Cheryl Dunye's *The Watermelon Woman* provides . . . insight into the nexus of "needs" and "interests" that a visible "black lesbian" currently serves. The film provides a fictional past for "black lesbian" that Cheryl (the film's main character) ultimately fashions into a past in which she finds "hope," "inspiration," "possibility," and "history." By so doing,

The Watermelon Woman provides insight into what must be rendered "invisible" in the image "black lesbian" in order for "black lesbian" to become "visible."

The Watermelon Woman has been received as a film in which the "typically invisible bodies" of "black lesbians" are "rendered visible in a number of ways."[i] The narrative of the film follows Cheryl (a character who identifies herself as "a black lesbian filmmaker" and who is played by Cheryl Dunye), in her efforts to excavate a story about a black actress who appeared in several "mammy" roles in Hollywood films and who is credited in those films as "the Watermelon Woman." While conducting research, Cheryl uncovers evidence of an erotic relationship between "the Watermelon Woman" (aka "Fae Richards" and "Faith Richardson") and a white female director, Martha Page. Based on the evidence she uncovers regarding Richardson's relationship with Page, Cheryl concludes, "I guess we have a thing or two in common, Miss Richards: the movies and women." The interracial relationship between Fae and Martha thus provides the initial context within which "the Watermelon Woman" becomes visible as "black lesbian."

During the course of her research, Cheryl talks to "Shirley Hamilton," a character who remembers Mae Richards as "quite a looker" who "used to sing for all us stone butches." Perhaps most significantly, however, Cheryl's research ultimately leads her to "June Walker," a character played by Cheryl Clarke, a writer whose theoretical and creative work during the late 1970s and early 1980s were part of a movement that provided a vocabulary through which a political articulation of "black lesbian" as a critique of "black," "lesbian," "woman," "patriarchy," and "capitalism" emerged. Clarke's character in the film, June, Fae's lover until her death, writes a letter to Cheryl in which June explains that she thinks that the mammy roles Fae played "troubled [Fae's] soul." In the letter, June implicates Martha Page in that vexed history. June's letter implores Cheryl to leave Page out of the movie on Fae's life. Speaking about Fae as part of a collective "we," June asserts, "She did so much, Cheryl. That's what you have to speak about. She paved the way for kids like you to run around making movies about the past and about how we lived then. Please, Cheryl, make our history before we are all dead and gone. But, if you are really in 'the family,' you better understand that our family will always only have each other."

June's comments draw attention to the way that "black lesbian" might be policed to keep some "in the family" and others out of "our family." Yet, the documentary that Cheryl makes about Fae Richards' life similarly reveals Cheryl's own choices about the value of the information she uncovers and, importantly, about the utility of that information to an enabling construction of "black lesbian." Cheryl tailors the documentary about "the Watermelon Woman" presented at the end of the film in order to provide, as Cheryl explains, "hope," "inspiration," "possibility," and a "history" that would rationalize and support the existence of Cheryl herself, as a "black lesbian filmmaker." Cheryl explains the choices she makes in crafting a historical narrative about Faith Richardson's life in the monologue, which introduces the film within a film. Cheryl explains that the historical narrative June provides of her life with Fae validates a different "world" than that which Cheryl inhabits as a "black lesbian filmmaker." In response to June's interrogation into Cheryl's interest in the relationship between Fae and Martha, Cheryl explains, "I know she meant the world to you, but she also meant the world to me, and those worlds are different."

Each world, Cheryl's and June's, is authorized via access to a different sheet of the past,[ii] and Cheryl makes it clear that the narrative she will tell is one that will validate and legitimate her existence, not June's: "What [Fae] means to me, a twenty-five-year-old black woman, means something else. It means hope. It means inspiration. It means possibility. It means history. And, most importantly, what I understand is that I'm gonna be the one who says, I am a black lesbian filmmaker who's just beginning. But I'm gonna say a lot more and have a lot more work to do."

The fictional "biography of the Watermelon Woman" that Cheryl presents at the end of *The Watermelon Woman* legitimates the "black lesbian filmmaker" as "the one" who will become visible as "black lesbian" by invoking a sheet of the past that supports Cheryl's needs and interests as they have been presented throughout *The Watermelon Woman,* a past wherein interracial lesbian desire is part and parcel of "black women's" participation in Hollywood and so continues to inform their entry into it. The world that Cheryl claims is hers, as "a twenty-five-year-old black woman," is one in which her professional aspirations demand that she articulate herself into the emergent market category of "black lesbian filmmaker" in a way that will register within the terms of that market.

With the character Cheryl, Dunye ruminates on the conditions for the success of her own film, *The Watermelon Woman.* The first feature-length "black lesbian film," *The Watermelon Woman* is a conjunction between the previously existing categories of "black film" and "lesbian film." The film's articulation into a category recognizable as "black lesbian film" proceeds according to the logic that currently governs post-70s Hollywood; on the film's promotional poster and video cover, the film is proclaimed to be "*Go Fish* Meets *She's Gotta Have It!*" Cheryl Dunye and Guinevere Turner (from the "lesbian film" *Go Fish*) are singled out in the promotional materials as the film's "stars" and they are named and featured prominently on the poster, both smiling.[iii] The choice to feature both Dunye and Turner in the promotional materials indicates that it is via the logic of an interracial "lesbian" relationship that the first "black lesbian feature film" to be picked up for distribution appears.

The marketing decision to feature Turner instead of Valarie Walker, the black actress who plays "Tamara," the other primary character in the film, is mirrored in the final account of "the Watermelon Woman's" life that Cheryl provides. That film-within-a-film begins with a shot of "Martha Page" and "Faith Richardson." While Fae's relationship with Martha Page, although not described explicitly as "lesbian," is granted an eroticism that provides the governing logic behind the film's embrace of Fae as a "black lesbian" foremother, June Walker's relationship with Fae is relegated via the voice-over narrative to the status of "special friend," a rhetorical move that un-self-consciously reproduces the homophobic discourse through which same-sex erotic attachments are obscured and rendered illegitimate within dominant conceptions of the world. Fae's relationship with June, the way she sang for the "stone butches" in the bar, etc., do not appear to be part of the past that enables Cheryl to find "hope," "inspiration," or her "history." Those who exist on a sheet of the past that might support a narrative that would challenge the construction of "black lesbian" that Cheryl provides are relegated by Cheryl's narrative to a "different" world, one that is incommensurate with that in which "black lesbian" can appear and circulate proudly in films.

Yet, because it re-creates the processes whereby Cheryl chooses what from the available past will support her own needs and interests as a "black lesbian filmmaker" and, hence, what will appear in the image that the film-within-a-film designates and puts into circulation as "black lesbian," *The Watermelon Woman* allows for a different possibility to be perceived in the image that Cheryl calls "black lesbian," one that remains hostile to the world Cheryl claims as hers because it is inassimilable into that world's logic. That possibility might collect the "stone butches," the "special friends," "the studs," "the femmes," "the woman-lovers," and "the queers" that were part of the working-class social milieu to which Fae Richards herself belonged and make those ambivalent, destabilizing, and unstable forces of desire and community cohere as a collective expression of a multifarious "we" that complicates any innocent notion of "the one" who says, "I am a black lesbian filmmaker." The multifarious "we" that challenges formulations of "the one . . . black lesbian" also drags "into the maelstrom of a continuously contingent, unguaranteed, political argument and debate,"[iv] even the conception of the world in which an "I" will be perceived to be writing as a "black queer film scholar" who authoritatively (even if passionately) cautions against "joining the lesbians" in favor of the (re)constitution of a multifarious "we."

Notes

i. Laura L. Sullivan, "Chasing Fae: *The Watermelon Woman* and Black Lesbian Possibility," *Callaloo* 23:1 (2000): 450. In another analysis of the film, Mark Winokur points out that Cheryl/Dunye (character/filmmaker) "creates a black lesbian body in order to recover her own" in an essay that focuses primarily on the way that Dunye's film "creates a representation of the negative oedipal stage of both identification and desire for the body of the black lesbian mother" (Winokur, "Body and Soul: Identifying (with) the Black Lesbian Body in Cheryl Dunye's *The Watermelon Woman*," in *Recovering the Black Female Body: Self-Representations by African American Women,* ed. Michael Bennett and Vanessa D. Dickerson [New Brunswick: Rutgers University Press, 2001], 244, 245).

ii. For an explanation of "sheets of the past" as they might be accessed through cinema, see Gilles Deleuze, *Cinema 2: The Time-Image,* trans. Hugh Tomlinson and Robert Galeta (Minneapolis: University of Minnesota Press, 1989), 98–125.

iii. Valarie Walker, the black actress who plays Tamara, Cheryl's best friend in the film, and a character that, arguably, is just as significant as Turner's Diana, is not mentioned and does not appear on the poster. Clearly, the promotional materials cannot feature every actress in the film. Yet, the choice not to feature Walker but rather Turner, recognizable from Rose Troche's film *Go Fish* as the "trendy, pretty, young Lesbian who is having trouble finding love," is indicative of, among other things, the extent to which *The Watermelon Woman*'s financial success was thought to reside in its ability to be recognizable as a "black lesbian film" according to the contours of existing categories.

iv. Stuart Hall, "New Ethnicities," in *Stuart Hall: Critical Dialogues in Cultural Studies,* ed. David Morley and Chen Kuan-Hsing (New York: Routledge, 1996), 444.

CHAPTER 14

Queers and the Internet

I n the previous chapter, we examined the cultural work done by filmic representations of queer identities and lives; these representations have been important to many lesbian, gay, bisexual, and transgender (LGBT) people. Nonetheless, they are still static; that is, viewers of films and television have to work with what they are given—not images that they themselves create. In this chapter, we examine the Internet, asking questions about the way it, as a space where viewers are transformed into participants, allows LGBT people the opportunity to exercise some control over their own self-representation at the same time that it uses many of the tools offered by other visual media. The Internet's "webbed" environment poses some unique challenges for writing about it in a textbook format, as issues consistently embed themselves in and complicate one another. What appears as a statement at one point reappears as a question, and what seems true when talking about one kind of site seems extraordinarily inaccurate when talking about others.

Some of the emerging scholarship about how LGBT people use the Internet focuses on the seemingly limitless opportunities for queers to connect with each other. Joanne Addison and Michelle Comstock, for instance, point out that many queers are "establishing cyberzines, discussion groups, and support services through the Internet" (371). While we share some of the general enthusiasm about the creation of what Nina Wakeford has called "cyberqueer spaces" (410), we also want to think critically about "queers on the Net." We examine some of the major myths about the Internet and its uses by sexual minorities, focusing on ongoing problems related to access and censorship, as well as the capitalist underpinnings of much queer-related Internet content. Taking a look at social networking and activist uses of the Internet allows us to consider not just how queers represent themselves but also how they form community and launch sites of political resistance and coalition. What's more, taking a global view of Internet usage provides us the richest context for understanding how queers have—and have not—connected via the Internet.

Access, Connection, and Identity

S ince its inception as a public communications tool in the mid-1990s, the Internet has garnered much attention as a means of disseminating information quickly and effectively. Many have hailed the Internet as a powerful source of information, but others have critiqued the inconsistent level of access that potential users have to it. While rates of use in the United States and other countries in the Global North are relatively high—165 to 210 million estimated users in the United States—that access still depends on users being able to afford both computer equipment and Internet Service Provider (ISP) charges necessary to use the Internet (Fallows). Fortunately for many, access is increasingly available in public places, such as libraries and community centers. However, the idea that the Internet provides interaction and information on a global scale and in an unequivocally egalitarian way is problematic; it does not take into account issues such as nationality, social class, and general access to resources—reliable electricity, for instance—needed to use the Internet. It also does not account for the fact that some governments prohibit access to specific sites and information or for the fact that in the United States, access can be limited for people whose primary Internet usage occurs in schools or libraries.

Find Out More in the articles by Heins and Cho, Gottschalk, and Anderson cited in this chapter's bibliography.

For those with access, the Internet, with its multiple venues for textually complex and visually rich expression, offers LGBT people some opportunity to articulate their concerns, interests, and desires. Given the highly interactive nature of the Internet, users can not only represent themselves but also exchange ideas, form a variety of communities, and meet others from around the world. Social networking sites are a significant way for queers to feel connected to a larger community of like-minded people. Working with basic templates that ask users to provide information on personal likes, dislikes, and identities, users can identify their romantic, emotional, and sexual interests and augment this information by uploading images and videos. Users can also create groups to affiliate with others of similar interests. Facebook, for instance, offers hundreds of queer and LGBT interest groups. LGBT affinity subgroups also function in less predictable online locations—within knitting websites such as Ravelry, for instance.

While social networking sites offer queers a potential sense of connection and community, they also unfortunately increase the ways in which one can encounter **homophobia**. For instance, when searching for "queer" groups on Facebook, we are just as likely to encounter homophobically tinged groups as LGBT-friendly communities. Users can create communities "for fun," such as "Jerry is SO Gay," to ridicule their friends and others. A surprisingly large number of groups use gay slurs. Moreover, self-identification on social networking sites may leave LGBT people vulnerable not only to virtual assault but also to attacks in physical space. In 2006, Jason Johnson was dismissed from the University of the Cumberlands in Williamsburg, Kentucky, when administrators learned that he had come out as gay on his MySpace page. Johnson wrote the following passage on his site: "I'm just starting out a wonderful dating adventure with a beautiful boy named Zac. I'm excited because I'll be moving close to him soon. Next semester, I'll be transferring to the University of Kentucky to finish my degree in theatre" (Bene).

Officials at the University of the Cumberlands, which is affiliated with the Southern Baptist Convention, told Johnson that he was being expelled because they did not approve of his "gay lifestyle," and even though Johnson had been on the dean's list, his grades were all converted to Fs. The university dismissed him on the basis of a 2005 revision of the student handbook indicating that students participating in premarital sex or promoting homosexuality would face expulsion. The handbook revision was not finalized, however, until after Johnson was already attending the university. Johnson eventually settled with Cumberland, which agreed to allow him to finish his in-progress coursework, reinstated his grades, and promised not to characterize his departure as an expulsion (Bene). This story highlights a reality about social networking sites: while they function as important venues for making connections among LGBT people, what appears on them can also be accessed and used maliciously—sometimes years later—to "punish" LGBT people and to control expressions of sexuality.

Beyond the facilitation of social interaction, the Internet can also provide LGBT people with an efficient way to find one another for sexual liaisons. Message boards, Yahoo! groups, craigslist, and a host of other sites enable people to locate others interested in a wide range of sexual practices. Much sexual activity also occurs *on* the Internet, as individuals use Internet technologies, such as chat and video chat, to engage in virtual sexual behavior. Shaka McGlotten notes that "[i]n video chat, the possibility for constructing alternate intimate scenarios [is] intensified." Furthermore, he argues that "[y]ou might do something a stranger asked you to do without question, an act that carried none of the delay or frustration that might come with having to explain to your partner [for instance] why spanking doesn't necessarily mean you want to be abused" (129). At a time when awareness of HIV and other sexually transmitted infections is heightened, particularly in the West, virtual sex can seem like a safe alternative to risky in-person encounters. And, as McGlotten's example illustrates, participants in virtual sex can explore a variety of nonnormative sexual practices and fantasies. Some queer and queer-friendly groups use the Internet to promote sex-positive practices; women-focused and queer-friendly Good Vibrations, for instance, uses its website to "enhance our customers' sex lives and to promote healthy attitudes about sex" (http://www.good-vibes.com/). At the same time, we should note that queer-identified people are not the only ones accessing queer porn and erotica on the Internet. Some lesbians observe that many so-called lesbian porn sites are merely "representations of all-female sexuality . . . so inaccurate, and so clearly geared toward a straight male audience, that very few could truly be considered lesbian" ("Pornographic"). More disturbingly, the Internet has been used by those seeking intergenerational sexual encounters to transmit erotica depicting sex with minors [λ Chapter 6].

Internet Censorship and Corporatization

Issues of access are often complicated by state-supported censorship, through which some governments and legal jurisdictions impose their ideologies. In China, for instance, "censorship, monitoring, rules, and enforcement make for a much more controlled Internet. Within China, maintaining this situation already requires tens of thousands of Internet police and many layers of accountability and potential punishment. (To give one relatively unpublicized example: ISPs convicted of hosting pornographic sites are in principle eligible for the death penalty)" (Fallows). We can catch a glimpse of how limited Internet use is in China when we consider that the Pew Internet Project reports that there are currently 137 million Internet users in that country—approximately one-tenth of their population (Fallows). The Iranian Queer Organization (IRQO) features on its website pictures of gay men who have been flogged for hosting queer gatherings in Iran, where sexual acts between men are punishable by death. In the words of its founders, the IRQO site exists "in the hope of building alliances and creating solidarity among Iranian homosexual, Bisexual and Transgender" people (http://www.pglo.net/). The site, however, is banned in Iran, limiting communication and connection among LGBT Iranians.

While such cases may seem extreme, it is important to keep in mind that censorship of queer content on Western ISP servers is not uncommon. Many public servers are programmed to prohibit access to information with LGBT content or to websites with streaming video. This is particularly important because public servers are often the only means of accessing the Internet for people who cannot afford to pay for high-speed lines in their homes. More and more Internet sites that contain information about and facilitate interaction among LGBT people require high-speed connections. Some governments censor the Internet by limiting the kinds of sites that can be offered by ISPs; in the United States, a similar kind of censorship occurs at the local level when public servers such as libraries and schools limit access to sites with LGBT content—ostensibly in the interest of "protecting children" from "sexually explicit" material.

While national governments or local boards of education can suppress some kinds of Internet content for ideological reasons, another form of control occurs when Internet content is shaped by market forces. In the West, the Internet, despite being figured by some as countercultural and even anarchical, betrays at every turn its capitalist underpinnings. It is fairly common knowledge, for instance, that twenty-something geeks Steven Chen and Chad Hurley sold their YouTube invention to Google in October 2006 for $1.65 billion. David Kushner, writing about the "Baby Billionaires of Silicon Valley," shows how popular applications, such as Facebook, Firefox, LicketyShip, and others, are inextricably tied to commercialism and commodity capitalism. Even craigslist, which offers "[l]ocal classifieds and forums for 450 cities worldwide" and claims to have a "service mission and non-corporate culture," has been incorporated as a for-profit company since 1999 ("craigslist").

Earlier in this book, we referred to Michel Foucault's *History of Sexuality* and John D'Emilio's "Capitalism and Gay Identity" as works that argue, in different ways, that contemporary gay identity could only develop within a capitalist economic framework that imposes social control through categorization [λ Chapter 2]. While categories allow queers to identify one another and thereby facilitate the creation of community, they also allow marketers to target potential consumers. Take, for example, the growing phenomenon of online "television" networks such as the lesbian- and gay-focused Logo TV site, which proclaims, "Watch Logo on TV. Or online. Or on your iPod. And that's only the beginning!" LGBT people might be excited to know that there is a network whose purpose is to offer "the LGBT world . . . a place all its own . . . [which] brings you the stories, shows and news you won't see anywhere else. From original series and films to groundbreaking documentaries to LGBT news and more" ("About Logo"). The issues of access addressed above come into play here; access to TV shows on the Internet requires high-speed connectivity and up-to-date software. Furthermore, the "free" access to the Logo site that most Internet users expect is supported by corporate sponsors. Again, LGBT people are the subjects of marketing, so the price we pay for virtual queer space is the price we pay for the services and equipment needed to access that space and for the products sold by those who underwrite it.

Even scholarly projects focused on the Internet can have corporate connections. The Annenberg Center for the Digital Future, one of the best-known organizations researching Internet usage worldwide, describes its work in this way: "In addition to its flagship surveys of America's involvement with the Internet and digital media, the Center administers the complementary World Internet Project in two dozen countries, manages the Annenberg School's On-line Communities Project, and is currently surveying Internet use by military personnel for the U.S. Department of Defense" ("Collaboration"). It is difficult to find LGBT-focused research on the Annenberg site, but LGBT and sexuality-related attitudes are part of what Annenberg surveys. Tellingly, Annenberg's research is at least partly funded by its "corporate partners," which include Coca-Cola, whose advertising on the Internet has become pervasive, and Microsoft, AT&T, and Time Warner, which have clear investments in encouraging Internet use. As is true of other mass media, then, what we know about and can access on the Internet is often influenced by corporations that stand to benefit from that information.

Internet Activism

As Jennifer Egan points out, Internet access is crucial for many seeking information, community, and contact with LGBT and queer people: "[F]or homosexual teenagers with computer access, the Internet has, quite simply, revolutionized the experience of growing up gay. Isolation and shame persist among gay teenagers, of course, but now, along with the inhospitable families and towns in which many find themselves marooned, there exists a parallel online community—real people like them in cyberspace with whom they can chat, exchange messages and even engage in (online) sex" (113). However, as Sandip Roy observes, "The very convenience of the Internet can lull people into a sense of 'keyboard activism,' forgetting that the real grassroots organizing still needs to be down on the ground" (189). The question becomes whether a one-to-one substitution can be made between the physical communities of family and town and the "parallel online community" described by Egan. We are inclined to believe that there is no easy equivalence between "real people" in physical communal space and "real people" online. If we also consider Roy's concerns about the possibility that the Internet can create illusions of social change rather than actual social change, then we must also ask about the impact on "inhospitable families and towns" when community is sought online rather than transformed in physical space.

In terms of LGBT activism, the Internet poses some interesting contradictions. As noted, much of what LGBT people have access to on the Internet is dependent on corporate support and is therefore controlled and normalized in some of the same ways as television and film. At the same time, the Internet provides LGBT people the opportunity to represent themselves in ways that are often creative, insightful, and political. What's more, on the Internet, LGBT people can learn about important sexuality-related activism throughout the world. For instance, Internet users can easily locate sites hosted by the National Gay and Lesbian Task Force (NGLTF), the International Lesbian and Gay Association (ILGA), and the Lambda Legal Defense and Education Fund. Especially in the United States, the proliferation of politically focused LGBT sites has undermined the notion that LGBT people represent a political monolith. While a fairly quick search can lead Internet users to sites like that of the Human Rights Campaign (HRC) or those of student LGBT organizations on high school and college campuses, it can also lead one to sites like that of the Log Cabin Republicans or the Pro-Life Alliance of Gays and Lesbians (PLAGAL). These organizations' websites facilitate membership as LGBT people look for others with similar interests. But they do something else as well: the presence of a carefully constructed site on the Internet can create a sense that an organization is cohesive and powerful, that there are "bodies" behind the name, and that, if need be, they might show up in force at physical locations to engage in loud, even disruptive, protest.

While some LGBT people see the Internet as a means of initiating political connections, others use it as a means of making those connections visible. Since the 1980s, one of the most controversial ways of doing that has been public "outing," that is, forcefully identifying the presence of queer people in a variety of social, cultural, and political spaces. The practice of media outing of LGBT celebrities and politicians was originally associated with gay anger at the slow and a half-hearted response to the AIDS crisis in mainstream American culture [λ Chapter 4]. Journalist Michelangelo Signorile admits that "ACT UP's rhetoric and shrill tactics fueled many of [his] early columns" in *OutWeek,* where he attacked columnist Liz Smith "for remaining closeted herself and for not reporting on the gay lives

Figure 14.1(a)   Michelangelo Signorile

Figure 14.1(b) Liz Smith

of some of the supposedly heterosexual celebrities mentioned in her column" (72). He also warned other closeted celebrities that if they refused to "[be] part of the solution instead of part of the problem, . . . we're coming through and nothing is going to stop us. And if that means we have to pull you down, well, then, have a nice fall" (73). This was shocking stuff, and *Time* magazine named it "outing." At that time, Signorile made clear that only those "queers who are closeted and harming others" should be outed. For him, outing was more than "mak[ing] the revelation of homosexuality into a punishment" (77). It was simply equalizing—treating homosexuality as equal to heterosexuality in the media.

The ease of posting on the Internet has added a digital dimension to outing. The advent of the Internet, as we have discussed, brought millions of people into what had previously been exclusively journalistic conversations, such as blogs and wikis. Not surprisingly, the Internet flexed to admit eager discussants who created sites specifically designed to produce knowledge through collaborative participation. Wikipedia is probably the best-known online collaborative site, describing itself as "a multilingual, web-based, free content encyclopedia project. Wikipedia is written collaboratively by volunteers from all around the world." As many Web searchers agree, Wikipedia entries tend to contain vastly more (and more interesting) content than typical encyclopedia entries. Still, some believe it susceptible to "vandalism," inaccuracy, or even incivility as contributors argue over content and interpretation ("Wikipedia: About"). For instance, Wikipedia has often served as an easy way to engage in homophobic false outings that assume that the label *gay* or *homosexual* is a slur. A recent example involved *The Sopranos* creator David Chase, whose Wikipedia entry was edited to read, "David Chase . . . is a homosexual American television

Find Out More in Julie Rak's "The Digital Queer" in the readings at the end of this chapter.

writer" (TMZ). The article describing this piece of Internet vandalism appeared in an online publication titled *A Critical Look at Wikipedia, the Online "Encyclopedia" That Anyone Can Edit,* and the assumption underlying the news item is that only a "wiki thug" would accuse someone of homosexuality. In the case of David Chase, the false outing seems to have been an expression of anger after the inconclusive ending of *The Sopranos*' last show in June 2007. Similarly, Tony O'Clery, a disgruntled former devotee of guru Sathya Sai Baba, used *QuickTopic* instant online discussion space to accuse the president of India, a follower of Sai, of being a "gay pedophile" ("Tony"). In these and other cases, the outing appears to have originated with presumably heterosexual accusers who construct homosexuality as obviously negating public credibility.

The Internet is also a venue for organized attacks on the very idea of queerness. The notorious "God Hates Fags" site, developed by the Reverend Fred Phelps of Westboro Baptist Church in Topeka, Kansas, is a prominent example of how some use the Web to garner support for their antigay sentiments. Phelps and his followers believe that what they perceive as "toleration" of homosexuality dooms the world to divine punishment, and their site features, among other hate propaganda, the "Perpetual Gospel Memorial to Matthew Shepard," which includes a counter indicating the number of days Shepard has been "burning in Hell" and a doctored photo of Shepard with animated flames beneath his face (http://www.godhatesfags.com).

Find Out More by reading Matthew Shepard's story in Chapter 4.

More generally, pundits, social critics, journalists, and newscasters seem to revel in frightening citizens with the many dangers of the Internet—not for queers, but for the public at large. It should come as no surprise that the national media often present the Internet as a danger zone. In part, of course, the hostile portrayal of the Internet by national video and print media results from their economic conflict with the Internet, which houses principal alternative news outlets—the Independent Media Center (IMC, or IndyMedia) or the Common Dreams News Center, for example. Both of these news outlets include LGBT issues among the progressive political causes they support. A search for the word *gay* on the IMC website produced 889 hits; the first ten article links displayed originated in eight different countries. Common Dreams includes the Gay and Lesbian Alliance Against Defamation (GLAAD), the HRC, the NGLTF, and Parents, Families and Friends of Lesbians and Gays (PFLAG) among their "Links to America's Progressive Community," as well as Planet Out, Gay Financial News, and Women's E-News among the news services from which they gather articles to republish on their websites. By treating LGBT-related stories as newsworthy, these sites underscore how readily the national media elide queer issues, concerns, and politics.

Globally, even in countries where officials censor the Internet to deny users access to LGBT-related sites, some are clearly receiving news of the political work and struggles of LGBT people in other parts of the world. Iranian activist Arsham Parsi, founder of the Persian Gay and Lesbian Organization (PGLO), says,

> We have been in existence for three years, and through this period we have become recognized by many gay and lesbian organizations throughout the world. We based most of our activities through Internet communication. We must communicate solely by Internet as we do not have the freedom to work in a public forum in our country. We do not have any sponsors locally in Iran as the religious extremists do not support gay rights, but would rather see all LGBT people silenced. (Parsi)

Parsi is now living in Canada, and he continues to speak on behalf of the PGLO. His gay advocacy illustrates the global reach of the Internet, in that alone or with a mere handful of like-minded associates living in exile from Iran, he could create an organization, give it a name, and put it into the global online conversation. To put this in context, Parsi's website gives his organization an import beyond its physical numbers, which it could not have had previous to the Internet; it facilitates identification among Iranian LGBT people "inside and outside of their homeland" and makes their existence visible (http://www.homanla.org). His tiny organization is then treated by others worldwide as a going concern and taken seriously as a player in queer activist circles.

Chinese LGBT people experience a similar silencing as their counterparts in Iran, and like them, Chinese activists have set up headquarters in exile. For example, the Institute for *Tongzhi* [Gay] Studies, located at the City University of New York, involves Chinese-speaking teachers and researchers in academic studies about LGBT people in China. But as China has gradually liberalized some attitudes toward gays over the past decade or so, more opportunities have arisen for Chinese gays and lesbians to connect with each other; Hong Kong's Court of Final Appeal, for instance, recently "rejected a ban . . . on public gay sex" (Hui). Still, gay and lesbian webmasters exercise extreme caution in openly discussing their online connections. Despite the fact that "there are now hundreds of gay websites in China and the number is growing all the time" (Chan), the November 2001 meeting of Chinese gay webmasters had to be held in secret. In a testament to the dangers associated with gay activism in China, Yuen Chan's article describing the Chinese webmasters' meeting provides no URLs for the websites it discusses.

While these Iranian and Chinese activists are using the Internet to organize politically, much as their counterparts in the United States do, they also struggle with whether to base their queer activism on a U.S. model. Roy asks important questions about what happens when one cultural model is imposed globally:

> Will the very speed of dissemination that the Internet provides create a borderless world where the American concept of a gay movement can spread like a virus and infect all cultures? Does it now just take a modem to start a movement? And once that movement gets off the ground, will it merely borrow from existing movements in the West? Will countries with fledgling GLBT movements risk losing the process of building a movement that is about them and their needs and end up assimilating into Western models because they are more accessible? What happens when the seeds of the movement are sown by members of their diaspora in the West? Is there a danger that the Internet will not only pull together people across oceans but at the same time offer them ready packaged visions of a GLBT movement that does not account for cultural differences? Or will cultural differences cease to matter in a well-homogenized "gay" world? (181)

Roy seems to be seeking a balance between the U.S.-centric notion of what Dennis Altman has called the "global gay" and the unique positioning of homosexuality in individual cultures worldwide. It is important to recognize how the Internet's enabling of communally constructed conversation across national and cultural borders depends on resisting global corporatization, which relies on constructing LGBT people as a monolithic economic market to maximize profit. Roy's questions highlight the need for a new way of thinking about the international LGBT community, one that imagines transnationality as transformational. The Internet's ability to facilitate the building of a diverse international LGBT community independent from corporate imperatives surely represents its most exciting potential.

QUESTIONS FOR DISCUSSION

1. If you have access to social networking sites such as Facebook or MySpace, keep notes on how queer-identified people represent themselves. How do gays and lesbians, for instance, use textual identifiers, images, and even video to mark their identities, their affiliations, their relationships, and their desires? Consider how bisexuality and transgenderism are comparably identified. Based on a number of observations, what might you assert about queer "self-fashioning" in online spaces, particularly on social networking sites?

2. Fact-check an ideologically pro- or antigay website of your choice. What do you learn from your research? Consider not only the content of the sites you examine but also their "layout" and design. How do different activists use the Web—textually, visually, aurally—to muster support for their positions?

3. Debate the value of LGBT pornography on the Internet. In particular, consider the position that the Internet, with its proliferation of millions of sex, erotica, porn, and fetish sites detailing a seemingly infinite diversity of sexual pleasures and possibilities, has done more to "queer" sex than nearly any other medium. Do you agree or disagree? What are the limits of this kind of "queering" of sex?

REFERENCES AND FURTHER READING

"About Logo: Welcome to Logo." *Logo Online.* 6 August 2008 <http://www.logoonline.com/about/>.

Addison, Joanne, and Michelle Comstock. "Virtually Out: The Emergence of a Lesbian, Bisexual and Gay Youth Cyberculture." *Generations of Youth: Youth and History in Twentieth-Century America.* Eds. Joe Austin and Michael Nevin Willard. New York: NYU P, 1998. 367–78.

Altman, Dennis. *Global Sex.* Chicago: U of Chicago P, 2001.

Anderson, Joseph. "CIPA and San Francisco, California: Why We Don't Filter." *Web Junction.* 6 August 2008 <http://www.webjunction.org/do/DisplayContent?id=996>.

Bene Diction (pseud.). "Gay Student Expelled from Baptist University." *Spero News.* 11 April 2006 <http://www.speroforum.com/site/print.asp?idarticle=3248>.

Bob Jones Univ. v. United States. Supreme Ct. of the US, 461 U.S. 574. 24 May 1983. <http://www.law.cornell.edu/supct/html/historics/USSC_CR_0461_0574_ZS.html>.

Chan, Yuen. "Out of the Closet in China." *BBC News, International Version.* 6 August 2008 <http://news.bbc.co.uk/2/hi/asia-pacific/3389767.stm>.

"Collaboration Will Deliver Leading-Edge Insights into the Impact of the Internet." *USC Annenberg School Center for the Digital Future.* 26 June 2006 <http://www.digitalcenter.org/pages/news_content.asp?intGlobalId=198>.

"craigslist fact sheet." *craigslist online community.* 6 August 2008 <http://www.craigslist.org/about/pr/factsheet.html>.

"Cyberbullying." *Stop Bullying Now!* 6 August 2008 <http://stopbullyingnow.hrsa.gov/adult/indexAdult.asp?Area=cyberbullying>.

"Dangers on the Internet." *Internet Evangelism Day: A Worldwide Awareness Resource for Christians.* 6 August 2008 <http://ied.gospelcom.net/dangers.php>.

Egan, Jennifer. "Lonely Gay Teen Seeking Same." *New York Times Magazine* 10 December 2000: 110–13.

Fallows, Deborah. "China's Online Population Explosion: What It May Mean for the Internet Globally . . . and for U.S. Users." *Pew Research Center Publications.* 12 July 2007. <http://pewresearch.org/pubs/537/china-online>.

"Fighting for Tomorrow: An Interview with Arsham Parsi." *Homan: The Iranian Gay, Lesbian, Bisexual, and Transgender Organization.* 6 August 2008 <http://www .homanla.org/New/Arsham_oct06.htm>.

Gottschalk, Lana. "Internet Filters in Public Libraries: Do They Belong?" *Library Student Journal* (Sept. 2006). <http://informatics.buffalo.edu/org/lsj/articles/gottschalk_2006_ 9_internet.php>.

Heins, Marjorie, and Christina Cho. "Internet Filters: A Public Policy Report." *National Coalition against Censorship.* 6 August 2008 <http://www.ncac.org/internet/filters.cfm>.

Hui, Sylvia. "Hong Kong Court Rejects Gay Sodomy Law." *Boston Globe* (17 July 2007). <http://www.boston.com/news/world/asia/articles/2007/07/17/hong_kong_court_ rejects_gay_sodomy_law/>.

"Interactive: Online Predators." *Cincinnati Enquirer.* 7 June 2007 <http://news.enquirer .com/apps/pbcs.dll/article?AID=/20070607/NEWS01/306060027>.

"Irish Boy, 14, Arranges Sex with Adult Men Using Gaydar." *Americans for Truth about Homosexuality.* 6 March 2007. 6 August 2008 <http://americansfortruth .com/news/irish-boy-14-arranges-sex-with-adult-men-using-gaydar.html>.

Karl, Irmi. "On-/Offline: Gender, Sexuality, and the Techno-politics of Everyday Life." *Queer Online: Media, Technology, and Sexuality.* Eds. Kate O'Riordan and David J. Phillips. New York: Peter Lang, 2007. 45–66.

Kushner, David. "The Baby Billionaires of Silicon Valley." *Rolling Stone* 1 November 2006. <http://www.rollingstone.com/news/story/12286036/the_baby_billionaires_of_ silicon_valley>.

Lee, Min. "Chinese Rules Limit Online Teen Gaming." *Cincinnati Enquirer* 18 July 2007: A8.

Leingang, Matt. "Data Theft Reaches 859,800: Number Rises on Device Stolen from State Intern." *Cincinnati Enquirer.* 12 July 2007 <http://news.enquirer.com/apps/pbcs .dll/article?AID=/20070712/NEWS01/707120341/-1/back01>.

McGlotten, Shaka. "Virtual Intimacies: Love, Addiction, and Identity @ The Matrix." *Queer Online: Media, Technology, and Sexuality.* Eds. Kate O'Riordan and David J. Phillips. New York: Peter Lang, 2007. 123–38.

"Nevada Couple Blame Internet for Neglect." *Yahoo! News.* 16 July 2007 <http://news.yahoo.com/s/ap/20070716/ap_on_re_us/neglect_Internet_addiction>.

"Nigerian Dating Scam (aka 419 scam)." *Dangers of Internet Dating.* 6 August 2008 <http://www.dangersofInternetdating.com/nigeriandatingscam.htm>.

Parsi, Arsham. Speech to Canadian Gay Groups, 13 June 2006. PGLO Advocacy Group. <http://www.homanla.org/New/pgloArsham.htm>.

"Pornographic Film and Video: Lesbian." *GLBTQ: An Encyclopedia of Gay, Lesbian, Bisexual, Transgender, & Queer Culture.* 2002. 6 August 2008 <http://www.glbtq .com/arts/porn_lesbian.html>.

Roy, Sandip. "From Khush List to Gay Bombay: Virtual Webs of Real People." *Mobile Cultures: New Media in Queer Asia.* Eds. Chris Berry, Fran Martin, and Audrey Yue. Durham, NC: Duke UP, 2003. 180–97.

Signorile, Michelangelo. *Queer in America: Sex, the Media, and the Closets of Power.* Rev. ed. Madison: U of Wisconsin P, 2003.

TMZ Staff. "*Sopranos* Fans Whack Creator's Wiki Entry." *Wikipedia: A Critical Look at Wikipedia, the Online "Encyclopedia" That Anyone Can Edit.* 6 August 2008 <http://wiki-problem-pedia.blogspot.com/>.

"Tony O'Clery Defames India's President." *Anthony Tony O'Clery Exposed.* 25 February 2007. 6 August 2008 <http://tony-oclery-exposed.blogspot.com/2007/02/tony-oclery-defames-indias-president.html>.

Wakeford, Nina. "Cyberqueer." *The Cybercultures Reader.* Eds. David Bell and Barbara M. Kennedy. London: Routledge, 2000. 403–15.

"Wikipedia: About." In *Wikipedia: The Free Encyclopedia.* 6 August 2008 <http://en .wikipedia.org/wiki/Wikipedia:About>.

READINGS

> **Julie Rak**

"The Digital Queer: Weblogs and Internet Identity"

(Winter 2005), Canada

It is clear that there is a developing body of scholarship devoted to a reading of a new and increasingly popular Internet phenomenon: weblogs—or blogs, as they are most commonly known. Thus far, most scholars who work in the area of life writing have chosen to see blogs as a development of the handwritten paper diary. This has created some problems, since even researchers themselves have found that weblogs seem to exceed the terms of diary writing as they use aspects of diary rhetoric. I suggest that there are parallels between the way that blogs are beginning to be "understood" as diary writing in scholarly discourse, and the relationship between the confession of deviant sexuality as part of one's identity and the growth of modern psychology. Like that confession of sexuality on which the developing area of psychology once depended, blogging relies on the conceit (however transparent) that the blogger is who s/he says s/he is, and that the events described actually happened to her/him personally. The performance of blogging is based on the assumption that experience congeals around a subject, and makes a subject who can be written and read, even when the discourse that seems to support this subject threatens to undermine it. This is also true of sexuality when it is talked about as identity. Therefore, the activity of blogging could be a potential site for thinking about queer identity, electronic identity, and liberal discourses of identity based on individual agency, unity, and the primacy of individual experiences important to many in the western world. What might "queer blogging" be, and how do bloggers who make queerness the focus of their blogs appeal to the "experience" of being queer as they construct queerness in discourse? How can this help us to understand what currency experience has in online environments?

[. . .]

Queer Blogging and Queer Theory

One way in which blog rhetoric works to create specific types of identities and communities with homogenous sets of values can be seen in the generation of queerness as an identity within blogs. The question of queer identity and genre, in the case of blogs, should be a difficult process, one that is akin to Lee Edelman's question of whether there can be a gay and lesbian literature that is not fetishized or commodified (3–5), or Eve Sedgwick's famous question about the problem of locating sexuality on the margins of western philosophy: has there ever been a gay Socrates? (52). The answer, for both these theorists, is that queerness cannot be quantified in this way, but that it is necessary to discuss queerness as more than merely strategic or discursive. At the same time, however, most queer theorists have regarded any thorough endorsement of essentialism suspiciously, since essentialist ideas about sex, sexual orientation, and sexual behavior have forced gays and lesbians into minority positions in society.

For an example in autobiography studies, Brian Loftus has written about how queer autobiography exists as a way to speak the love, and the identity, that cannot speak its name "properly" inside of autobiography as a genre. According to Loftus in the online version of his article, "what is at stake here, in generic terms, is to develop a dual technique that identifies the assumptions that the genre of autobiography makes in and about language and to subject these presumptions to their own logic in order to allow for a queer autobiography that cannot exist, properly speaking, except as silence." Loftus suggests that queer identity, and queer autobiography, surface as lack or abject within discourses that cannot accommodate them. But what I have found in my reading of blogs with queer content is what Margaretta Jolly mentions in her discussion of queer autobiography: popular notions of queer or gay/lesbian/bisexual/transgendered (that is, GLBT) identity treat that identity as if it were essential, particularly when these identities are placed under political pressure (475–76). To this, I will add that the rhetoric of blogging, with its focus on experience as the link between online and offline worlds and its tendency to demarcate a grey area between public events and private identity, works to produce gay identity and the scene of its writing as an experience of the absolute in everyday life.

So what happens when one looks for "queer blogs" on the internet? The answer is, perhaps surprisingly, homogeneity. In March 2004 I looked for blogs with queer content by searching for blogs as bloggers would—I searched for blogs on large sites where they are collected by the keywords "queer," "gay," "lesbian," "bisexual" and "transsexual." I also searched self-described collections of queer or GLBT blogs. I read forty blogs closely, and completed a more cursory reading of about one hundred more. I thought that I would get a lot of variety in terms of blog content this way, but I didn't. Although the ideology of blogging represents it as democratic, the blogs I read centered on a specific set of privileges, ideologies, and practices which would not be shared by most non-elites. For instance, all bloggers in the blogs I read live in the United States, write in English, and seem to be American. Most were from large urban areas known to have GLBT populations such as the San Francisco Bay Area or New York City. Without exception, all writers were relatively left-wing or liberal politically. Some writers in March 2004 were actively promoting Howard Dean's campaign for the Democratic presidential candidate nomination when Dean was still running, while others currently have open letters to Arnold Schwartzenegger or George W. Bush that oppose their conservative views about same-sex marriage and the US Constitution. Only one blogger, GeekSlut, a gay man whose identity is based on nonmonogamy, differed from the general position on same-sex marriage.

Moreover, the identities of all writers were based on relatively conservative ideas (for the GLBT communities) about sexual identity, even when the politics of the writers were more radical. This is related to the connection in blogging between identity, experience, and truthfulness. For all writers, identity is fixed in space and time, and it is related through narratives about location and the passage of time. Being gay, lesbian, or trangendered related to activities such as attending a gay pride parade or living in the Castro, as in MJ's blog

"Friday Fishwrap," where her biography freely says where she lives, and frequently documents her activities in San Francisco, or it is related to opinions about American politics and gay rights, as in comedian Margaret Cho's filter-style political blog. But being human (and not marked as queer) is related to everyday life that isn't related to place, such as child-rearing or what movies a blogger recommends. Although there is nothing to prevent them from doing this, no blogger whose work I read played with representation in a postmodern way. All represented their experiences (and their subject positions) as real and supported by documentation such as photographs of themselves, the use of their real first and last names, and references to the cities in which they live their offline lives. In fact, I found no blogs without these markers of documented experience, which suggests to me that experience as a category of knowledge is at the heart of blogging, and "queer" markers of experience all occur within this grammar of related links, other blogs, promotional "buttons" with gay pride slogans, rainbow designs, and so on.

Therefore, how are these blogs queer? How did I know how to find them?

My answer involves the centrality of classification to the circulation of blogs.

Whether or not the content of some of these blogs dealt with sexuality, these blogs show up on search engines as queer or GLBT because the bloggers placed these words in the subject headings for their blogs because the bloggers wanted them to be classified in this way. Blogs are collected in large clearinghouse sites which have searchable lists; these are organized by keyword and language group. Some large collections are based on area of interest, such as QueerFilter, which encourages GLBT bloggers to advertise their blogs on that list, or the general blog collection Blogwise, which has "queer" as a keyword to help users find queer content blogs. The need to have lists arranged in this way is explained by the tendency of blog communities to stress sameness at the expense of difference. Bloggers want to find similar people with similar interests. Clearly, even when these bloggers do not discuss sexuality, they decide that they want their blogs to be read as queer, within a community of other queer or queer-friendly bloggers. This occurs because blog rhetoric in general tends to produce subjects who, through their representation of themselves as real and honest, are meant to find other subjects like themselves.

Blog search engine rhetoric contributes to this when it categorizes blogs by key words in their subject lines, which bloggers understand represent their blogs and themselves—or their blogs as themselves—to the rest of the community. Although it could be argued that the representation of everyday life in these queer blogs as "ordinary" is a resistance to essentialist notions of queer identity that could be found in their subject lines, the untroubled way in which most of these bloggers discuss queer or GLBT identity in some entries says that ideas about universal humanity prevail. These bloggers do not have to present themselves as queer or GLBT in blog entries all the time, and they can present themselves that way some of the time, because they do not experience persecution on a daily basis. This is, therefore, a queer population with some privilege. The numerous incitements to bloggers to produce information about themselves also contribute to the production of a certain kind of queer identity based on a strategy of the real, where liberal ideas about the nature of the self and elaborate biographical documentation create an effect of the real online, to promote community and trust between bloggers. The rhetorical strategies in this segment of the blogging community do not differ much from those of other bloggers, because blogging as a genre tends to consolidate its own practices and subjects as one of its effects. And so, to conclude, is there such a thing as queer blogging? I would answer yes, in the sense that the activity of blogging itself, like offline activity, produces its own subjects, whose relationships to offline discourses of truth and reality are designed to create identity as its special effect.

Works Cited

Cho, Margaret. Weblog. "Margaret Cho." Sept. 2004. <http://www.margaretchocom/blog/blog.htm>.

Edelman, Lee. *Homographesis: Essays in Gay Literary and Cultural History.* NY: Routledge, 1994.

Jolly, Margaretta. "Coming Out of the Coming Out Story: Writing Queer Lives." *Sexualities* 4.4 (2001): 474–96.

Loftus, Brian. "Speaking Silence: The Strategies and Structures of Queer Autobiography." *College Literature* 24.1 (Feb. 1997): 28–44.

MJ. Weblog. "Friday Fishwrap." Aug. 2004. <http://www.fridayfishwrap.com/mt/aboutmj.html>.

Sedgwick, Eve Kosofsky. *Epistemology of the Closet.* Berkeley: U of California P, 1990.

"The Digital Queer: Weblogs and Internet Identity," by Julie Rak, University of Hawaii Press Journals.

> ## Andil Gosine

"Brown to Blond at Gay.com: Passing White in Queer Cyberspace"

(2007), Canada

> I am in love with the image and idea of white manhood, which is everything I am not and want to be, and if I cannot be that at least I can have that, if only for the night, if only for one week or the month. ([Reginald] Shepherd 1991)

> I would love to be white. Not forever, but perhaps a weekend. Don't you ever get sick of being a minority? . . . I have posed this question to other minority artists, and get stumped by answers like "No, not ever have I ever wanted to be white." And I just don't buy it. Why would you not want things to be easier? ([Margaret] Cho 2005)

So much social, economic, and cultural capital is invested in the idealization of white bodies (and in the devaluation and denigration of non-white ones) that neither Shepherd's confessional yearnings nor Cho's caustic daydream is surprising—nor are the disapproving reactions from those who find their declarations uncomfortable, even upsetting.

Fantasies and anxieties about the realization and loss of whiteness inform the configura-
tion of social relations and production of knowledge in much of the contemporary world.
Since at least the fifteenth century, white has connoted purity, virginity, beauty, and even
Godliness in European nations, and the accident of white skin has authorized its bearers
to claim, conquer, and colonize the lands and cultures of non-white peoples of Africa,
Asia, and the Americas. Whiteness, writes Kalpana Seshadri-Crooks, is a "master signifier
that establishes a structure of relations, a signifying chain that through a process of inclu-
sions and exclusions constitutes a pattern for organizing human difference" (2000:3–4).
Through the production of Orientalism, non-white subjects are characterized as a function of the white subject and are allowed no autonomy and purpose except as a means
of knowing the white self (Said 1978). Consequently, white people are systematically privileged and enjoy "unearned advantage and conferred dominance" in Western societies
(McIntosh 1992:74). They "create the dominant images of the world and don't quite see
that they construct the world in their own image," and "they set standards of humanity
by which they are bound to succeed and others bound to fail" (Dyer 1997:9). Frantz
Fanon concludes: "Sin is Negro as Virtue is white" (1967:138).

There are longstanding rituals through which white people are able to perform non-
white racialized ethnicities (e.g., casting white actors in Asian roles in films, donning
kimonos or turbans to play Japanese or Indian at costume parties) and for non-white
people to perform exaggerated expressions of racialized identities (e.g., American
Minstrel shows, representations in television and film), but not many choices exist for a
Korean-American comic like Cho or an African-American like Shepherd to assume white
racial identities. The advent of cyberspace provided a new venue for non-white people to
experience racial crossing into whiteness—an experience that was part of a parcel of
opportunities being trumpeted by queer, feminist, and cyberculture critics anticipating the
liberating potential of virtual worlds (Turkle 1995; Plant 1996; Sunden 2001; Gross 2004).

In November 1998, I engaged [in] "race" play in cyberspace as a way of examining
claims about its revolutionary promise, and of racial crossing. For five consecutive days, I
participated in conversations in the "Toronto" chat rooms at gay.com, and kept a journal
of my online interactions. Selecting a gay website feature to consider the operation of
"race" in cyberspace made sense for several reasons, including my own ties to and investments in queer culture, and the fact that queer scholars were among those leading the
celebration of this technological advance. Many of them, including Larry Gross, for
example, imagined that for queer men and women, the net would present more opportunities to inhabit sexual desires and identities, connect and create community, and refuse
gender and class restrictions that structured their offline, "real world" lives (2004). A
focus on chat rooms also seemed appropriate. As Lisa Nakamura observes, "cyberspace
is a place of wish fulfillments and myriad gratifications, material and otherwise and
nowhere is this more true than in chat spaces" (2002:32). Textual chat spaces, she says,
"encourage users to build different identities, to take on new identities . . . to describe
themselves in any way they wish to appear" (Nakamura 2002:32).

My chat room experiences did not prove to be as liberating an event as proclaimed in the cyberutopian rhetoric. Although opportunities to unfix and reconstitute meanings of identities and social markers were certainly available, processes of racialization were evident in and seemed to have an important structuring influence on the organization, flow of dialogues and relationships between users in the chat rooms. Returning to review the site seven years later, in 2005, I also found that whatever potential may have existed for dominant, colonial narratives of "race" to be displaced or undermined in cyberspace are fading (or have faded). Changes to gay.com's chat services since 1998 appear to have further reinforced racial categories and ensure the reproduction of "real life" racism. In this respect, the development of virtual worlds has been shown to be not unlike other technologies, merely mimicking dominant socioeconomic relations rather than challenging them.

What also emerged from this study of the chat rooms were compelling insights about desires for passing white. Very often, racial crossing from non-white to white is read as evidence of investments in racial imagery and symbolism. This presumption underlies the outrage expressed by Cho's friends about her wanting to be white for a weekend and the persistence of epithets to describe non-white people accused of "acting white" (e.g., "coconut" for South Asians, "banana" for East Asians). But analysis of the operation of "race"-racism in the gay.com chat rooms suggests that passing white is not simply the exercise of desires by non-white people to become white or fetishize whiteness, but, rather, to experience the privileges afforded to whiteness. Passing white expresses longing for the experience of racial disembodiment that cyberspace promises, but does not ultimately appear to fulfill.

[. . .]

Passing White: Resource Access and the Exercise of Agency

In one of her studies on white people engaging [in] racial passing in cyberspace, Nakamura observed that "many users masquerading as racial minorities in chat spaces tend to depict themselves in ways that simply repeat and reenact old racial stereotypes," including, for example, "users masquerading as samurai and geishas, complete with swords, kimonos, and other paraphernalia lifted from older media such as film and television" (2002:107). This type of play, she says, "reenacts an anachronistic version of 'Asian-ness' that reveals more about users' fantasies and desires than it does about what it 'feels like' to be Asian either on- or offline" (2002:107). Passing white, however, may serve a different purpose, not exclusively an exercise in fantasy or anxiety production but an opportunity to experience the material and cultural privileges afforded to white people. Unlike its reverse ritual, racial crossing from non-white to white may not be primarily motivated by fetishistic conscious or unconscious desire, but by struggles for access to resources and for experience of cultural and political agency.

Accessing Resources

One of the reasons queer scholars cheered the development of cyberspace was their expectation that virtual spaces would be better able than bars or clubs to provide affirmation for "many who do not find themselves welcomed or validated by the increasingly com-mercialized and mainstreamed institutions of the newly respectable GLBT communities, including marginalized sub-culture groups" (Gross 2004:xi). Keith Dorwick argues,

> One thing online communication has changed radically is that men can now speak to men they'd never speak to in the bars. The social barriers between races, between "hot men" and "dogs" or "trolls" and between younger and older men are much lower online. (Alexander et al. 2004)

But characterizations of chat rooms as more egalitarian spaces do not hold up on more attentive examination. Anxieties about race—held by both white and non-white men—may sometimes determine who is solicited for conversation, friendship or sex in bars, but they perform the same function in cyberspace as well, as evidenced by the shutting down of conversations after responses to the "background" question confirm non-white racial identity and, also, by the preferred status afforded to white men.

Of the many identities I adopted in the Toronto chat rooms at gay.com, blue-eyed and blond haired "Robbie" was easily the most fun to inhabit. Robbie fit my own physical description except, importantly, that he was blond and blue-eyed; I enjoyed the most attention from other online chatters than in any other representation of myself. I was over-whelmed with requests for private window conversations and many times I was chatting separately but simultaneously with five or six of the thirty users in the room. Changing only information about hair and eye color to indicate a white identity, I was invited to partici-pate [in] conversations with many more men and have an altogether different experience than when my descriptor indicated that I was non-white. Others engaged in similar projects have reported similar experiences. For example, one Taiwanese-born college student post-ing to a Bulletin Board System based in Orange County, California, also found that imme-diately after changing his ethnic identity from "Chinese" to "Caucasian," he received more queries and invitations to chat (Tsang 2000:435). Tsang also reports that consequent to their experiences of queer spaces on the Web, many non-white users refused to iden-tify themselves, or identified themselves as "Other" or "Mixed" when given a choice, "in the hopes that their chances [to interact with other men] would be improved" (2000:435). In the physical world, non-white men have often been refused entry to white-dominant gay bars and clubs; in cyberspace, self-identification as white often serves as a qualifier to access conversations with other users.

Exercising Agency

Interactions in the Toronto gay.com chat rooms make clear that the act of passing white is also an attempt to experience another kind of privilege of whiteness: the opportunity to be viewed as active, dynamic and complex agents. Dominant processes of racialization fix identities for non-white people in ways that generally do not apply to white people. Writing about gay bars and clubs in the real world, Mercer and Julien observe that representations of non-white men are "confined to a narrow repertoire of types—the supersexual stud and the sexual savage on the one hand, the delicate and exotic 'Oriental' on the other" ([Julien and Mercer] 1991:169). Choices placed to non-white men appear to oscillate between the two:

> Far too many of the white men I see in [. . .] clubs look at me as if to say, "I couldn't sleep with you. You're black." Or they desire me because I am black. (Shepherd 1991:54)

These representations, rooted in the experience of colonialism and empire, are circulated again in cyberspace. Toronto resident "Marshall," a twenty-six-year-old Asian male who regularly goes online, references a common experience among non-white men:

> I find that a lot of guys won't consider me because of my background . . . a lot of guys are not into Asians, or, if they are, are only into submissive Asians, but I'm a top. [. . .] I've had guys say to me . . . "if I were into Asians I'd totally get with you." I don't exactly consider those compliments, but they're part of my reality and so I deal. (Cited in Sanders 2005:83)

Similarly, "Big_Wolf" says of his experiences on IRC, "if they suspect or find out you are black MANY immediately go to the penis size thing" (Campbell 2004:79).

Byron Burkhalter makes the important point that racial identification occurs differently online. "Stereotyping in face-to-face interaction follows from an assumed racial identity," but online interaction, he says, "differs in that the imputation tends to go in the other direction—from stereotype to racial identity" (1999:73). In real-life situations, the complex, multidimensional realities of racialized peoples also serve to reveal race as a lie. Online, however, fixed stereotypes are the means through which users are received in interactions. "In online interactions," Burkhalter points out, "perspectives resist modification because participants confront an immutable text" (1999:73). There are of course occasions when the exploration of conversations in cyberspace might engage chatters in critical self-reflection—a user might be surprised about his interactions and be challenged to rethink race-based presumptions. But this happens in the real world bars as well, and I would even suggest that spontaneous acts leading to confrontations with and challenges to "race"-based expectations may be more likely to happen in bars than cyberspace. For example, suppose that I believe that I am not interested in forming friendships or relationships, or having sexual encounters with Japanese men. I might, however, walk into a bar and encounter a Japanese man whose gestures, body, or manner are attractive to me. Such a real-life meeting might challenge my imagination to be less fixed, resolve sub-/unconscious desires and undermine my investments in "race." If I come to a gay.com chat room with the same belief, I simply shut off the possibility of speaking to men identifying themselves as Japanese, allowing no opportunity for challenges to the same investments in "race" [which then] proceed, untroubled.

Insofar as racial identification is concerned, white men are generally not subject to this fixing gaze. As Dyer observes about his study of white representation:

> One cannot come up with a limited range of endlessly repeated images, because the privilege of being white in white culture is not to be subjected to stereotyping in relation to one's whiteness. White people are stereotyped in terms of gender, nation, class, sexuality, ability and so on, but the overt point of such typification is gender, nation, etc. Whiteness generally colonizes the stereotypical definition of all social categories other than those of race. To be normal, even to be normally deviant (queer, crippled), is to be white. White people in their whiteness, however, are imaged as individual and/or endlessly diverse, complex and changing. (1997:11–12)

When I represented myself as any kind of non-white man in the chat rooms, my "race" almost always figured into users' reactions. Whatever kind of non-white man I claimed to be, even opposed reactions referenced "race"; some respondents shut down conversations because I was non-white, others pursued me because I was Black/Indian/Chinese, etc. But as blond, blue-eyed Robbie, I was "normal," a complex human whose behavior and personality were not necessarily read through racial tropes. No longer trapped in my skin, I was neither repulsive nor alluring because of it. I was not a member of a group but an individual. I was not a "type" and I spoke for no community but myself. Raced white, I accomplished what Peggy McIntosh identifies as an ultimate achievement of whiteness: the belief that everything a white person does may be accounted for in his/her individuality (1992:70–81). I was imagined as white people were imagined to be: endlessly diverse, complex, and changing (Dyer 1997:12).

Conclusion/Epilogue

My experiences as "Robbie" seemed to achieve the kinds of experiences imagined by Shepherd and Cho, and revealed motivations for "passing white" and occupying white identities that were similar to their own. Passing white, whether in a chat room for a few hours, over the course of a trouble-free weekend, or, as Shepherd coyly suggests, for "just one night" if not all eternity, appears to be neither an idle expression of identity play, nor a pronouncement of faith in white supremacist mythologies. Those wishing to "pass white" may have no actual desires to inhabit or be with white bodies; I never imagined what "Robbie" might look like, nor was I motivated to undertake this project by conscious desires for white men in particular. Instead, as demonstrated in the analysis of the Toronto chat rooms at gay.com, this act more likely conveys a longing to experience the cultural, social and political privileges afforded to whiteness.

Although Shepherd introduces his "On Not Being White" essay as a reflection on his "obsessive attraction to white men" (1991:47), he provides no explanation other than a yearning to enjoy the same kinds of liberties enjoyed by them. Shepherd writes, "As a child I would go to sleep wishing that when I awoke I would be white" (1991:48). Yet, his imaginative energies are less spent on visualizing himself in a white body than in fleeing the restrictions placed on his movements because of the cultural meanings attached to blackness:

> The burden of my identity, one of the many burdens of my identity, has always been the burden of not being white. . . . I was the wrong one: wrong lips, wrong nose, wrong self. . . .
>
>   I've had notions, negative each one, images of what it is to *seem* black: to look black, to talk black, to walk black. . . . If one did not say those things, wear those things, if one didn't do things that way, then one would never, could never be branded with that word, that awful word; though of course one was. (1991:47–49)

Shepherd may want to sleep with white men, but says nothing about what he likes about their bodies. They are described as "beautiful" but [with] no details describing what exactly he likes about white bodies. No yearning is expressed to touch white skin, no allusions to phenotypes associated with white men.

   Sexual desires are the consequence of a complicated mess of personal experiences, social relations, and conscious and subconscious anxieties; for Shepherd, a yearning for political liberation is clearly part of that mix:

> If I am seen with a beautiful man, not only am I thus one who can acquire a valuable prize but I am by the same operation (as a man having it both ways) transformed into such a prize myself, sought after and acquired by the man I am with. . . . By being seen with him, I am made an honorary white man for so long as I am with him. Suddenly I am part of the community. So by being with him I manage almost to be him. (1991:54)

Writing two decades later than Shepherd, Cho gets right to the point about what motivates her daydreams of becoming white:

> What if I didn't have to bend anything? What if there really was a level playing field? I would love to see how far I could actually go. What if all I had to show off was my mad skills? Wouldn't I really be able to fly then? (margaretcho.com/blog, January 23, 2005)

Cho doesn't actually want to be white, just [to] enjoy access to the privileges it affords. Similarly, Shepherd concludes:

> My dream? Finally to be "myself," relieved of the baggage of my history both as an individual and as a member of an oppressed race and caste, relieved of my self-despisal in the shining warmth of the beloved's blond approbation. (1991:56)

Passing white in cyberspace makes a similar promise to Shepherd's beloved blond: temporary comfort from—but no absolution from—the inflictions of "race."

References

Alexander, J., Barrios, B., Blackmon, S., Crow, A., Dorwick, K., Rhodes, J., et al. 2004. "Queerness, Sexuality, Technology and Writing: How Do We Queers Write Ourselves When We Write in Cyberspace?" Retrieved January 20, 2005, from http://acadiana.arthmoor.com/cuppa

Burkhalter, B. 1999. "Reading Race Online: Discovering Racial Identity in USENET Discussions," in M.A. Smith and P. Kollock (Eds.), *Communities in Cyberspace* (pp. 60–75). London: Routledge.

Campbell, J.E. 2004. *Getting It On Online: Cyberspace, Gay Male Sexuality, and Embodied Identity.* London: Harrington Park Press.

Cho, M. 2005. "I Would Love to Be White." Retrieved January 23, 2005, from http://www.margaretcho.com/blog

Dyer, R. 1997. *White.* London: Routledge.

Fanon, F. 1967. *Black Skin, White Masks.* NY: Grove.

Gross, L. 2004. "Preface," in J.E. Campbell, *Getting It On Online: Cyberspace, Gay Male Sexuality, and Embodied Identity* (pp. ix–xii). London: Harrington Park Press.

Julien, I., and Mercer, K. 1991. "True Confessions," in E. Hemphill (Ed.), *Brother to Brother* (pp. 167–173). Boston: Alyson.

McIntosh, P. 1992. "White Privilege and Male Privilege: A Personal Account of Coming to See Correspondences through Work in Women's Studies," in Margaret L. Anderson and Patricia Hill Collins (Eds.), *Race, Class and Gender: An Anthology* (pp. 70–81). Belmont: Wadsworth.

Nakamura, L. 2002. *Cybertypes: Race, Ethnicity and Identity on the Internet.* NY: Routledge.

Plant, S. 1996. "On the Matrix: Cyberfeminist Simulations," in R. Shields (Ed.), *Cultures of the Internet: Virtual Spaces, Real Histories, Living Bodies* (pp. 170–183). London: Sage.

Said, E. 1978. *Orientalism.* London: Routledge.

Sanders, C. 2005. "M4M Online Chat Rooms: The Use of Gay Websites by Men Seeking Men." MA thesis, York University, York, UK.

Seshadri-Crooks, K. 2000. *Desiring White: A Lacanian Analysis of Race.* NY: Routledge.

Shepherd, R. 1991. "On Not Being White," in J. Beam (Ed.), *In the Life: A Black Gay Anthology* (pp. 46–57). Boston: Alyson.

Sunden, J. 2001. "What Happened to Difference in Cyberspace? The (Re)turn of the She-Cyborg." *Feminist Media Studies* 1(2), 215–232.

Tsang, D. 2000. "Notes on Queer 'n' Asian Virtual Sex," in D. Bell and B. Kennedy (Eds.), *The Cybercultures Reader* (pp. 432–438). NY: Routledge.

Turkle, S. 1995. *Life on the Screen: Identity in the Age of the Internet.* NY: Simon & Schuster.

Andil Gosine, "Brown to Blond at Gay.com: Passing White in Queer Cyberspace." *Queer Online: Media, Technology & Sexuality.* Ed. Kate O'Riordan and David J. Phillips. New York: Peter Lang.

CHAPTER 15

The Politics of Location

Alternative Media and the
Search for Queer Space

The experience of living queer has typically been located at the crossroads of embodiment and disembodiment. We are defined by our corporeal selves, our sexual desires and affectional preferences. As David Bell and Jon Binnie write, "[E]roticism is the basis of [our] community" (87). We tell each other to come out because we wish to be visible *as* queer; we wish to embody a real identity. Simultaneously, we are disembodied by our cultures. We are ordered to disappear, to inhabit a closet where we can't be seen by the straights, the young, and the innocent. We are told not to "speak its name," not to "flaunt it." Our experience of culture—our sexual citizenship, as it were—is fraught with this uncomfortable double consciousness. We often engage in commerce, in the arts, in political activism, precisely to find a visible viable place in our culture, a place where our embodied identities need not feel the erasure of a closeting hegemony. Jeffrey Weeks argues that the sexual citizen "makes a claim to transcend the limits of the personal sphere by going public, but the going public is, in a necessary but nevertheless paradoxical move, about protecting the possibilities of private life and private choice." This way of doing citizenship, Weeks goes on to say, is the only way that "difference can [ever] find a proper home" (37). Let us think about the concept of "home" as it relates to lesbian, gay, bisexual, and transgender (LGBT) people.

> Gays and lesbians do not have a "home" to return to, either in territorial/historical terms or in the sense of present-day enclaves; most gays and lesbians live amidst their heterosexual families and neighbors without the promise even of a local community center to find affirmation and support. Most grow up convinced that they are "the only one" in their communities. Urban centers ameliorate this situation for those with the resources and desire to relocate, but such relocation involves a separation from, and often a rejection of, their community of birth. Those who do not want to live in cities, or who cannot so choose, often live their lives in isolation. Even those who create a home or a common culture are in a situation drastically different from that faced by racial, ethnic, or national groups; such cultures and homes are created as adults, after the experience of isolation and rejection from one's family and community. (Phelan 30)

Queer "homes," then, are intensely sought after but, (for many) ephemeral spaces, purchased through the "pink economy," that mythical entity accessible only to rich entitled gay men and lesbians.

In this chapter, we consider how some types of alternative media—as opposed to the more mainstream media products discussed earlier in this book—are used by LGBT people to build community. We classify as "alternative" those media that have two characteristics: they aim to reach a particular (limited) audience, specifically a group that seeks knowledge and validation of a point of view, and they lie outside the realm of "mainstream" media, that is, high-budget, high-visibility productions that stand to gross millions of dollars at the box office, newsstand, or bookstore. Any of the media we discussed earlier—film, television, and the Internet—can have both "mainstream" and "alternative" manifestations. For instance, documentary films, unlike feature films, are typically shown in small-seating art theaters. They play to an educated, culturally elite audience, and studios spend little on advertising and promotion. Keeping this distinction between *mainstream* and *alternative* in mind, we begin with the assumption that cultural artifacts—such as comic strips, independent documentary films and music, LGBT newspapers and newsletters, and even festivals such as the Michigan Womyn's Music Festival—are produced and consumed to fulfill particular needs. One of the overriding needs seems to have to do with the search for community, a sense of home.

Documentary Films

The documentary *Flag Wars* (Zeitgeist 2003, dir. Linda Goode Bryant and Laura Poitras) was advertised as "a poignant account of the politics and pain of gentrification. Working-class black residents in Columbus, Ohio fight to hold on to their homes. Realtors and gay home-buyers see fixer-uppers. The clashes expose prejudice and self-interest on both sides, as well as the common dream to have a home to call your own" ("Flag Wars"). On one level, the opposition is direct: "We didn't have any problems till they moved in here," says a straight black resident. "If you don't want to renovate it, don't live in it," counters a white gay man. But *Flag Wars* is far more complex than this simple juxtaposition might suggest. It elucidates some traditional cultural divides: between rich and poor, gay and straight, black and white, even traditional and contemporary. These divides complicate what can be characterized as the search for community undertaken by many LGBT people. It's not uncommon to think of LGBT people as displaced and disenfranchised, and those characterizations are in many ways accurate, but this film asks what happens when the supposedly disenfranchised have access to the culture's resources—money and the legal system, for example—and use them to enfranchise themselves in new locations. The questions addressed in *Flag Wars* have to do with what happens when LGBT people begin establishing "homes" in locations where others are already living and with balancing the benefits to a community when property is materially "improved" at the cost of pricing out those who already live in it.

Jon Binnie reminds us that "[i]t is one of the touchstones of the geographies of sexualities that it is only possible to be queer in certain places and spaces. The search for fixity is one in which gay men and lesbians participate endlessly" (82). *Flag Wars* shows us both the need that gay gentrifiers have for habitable home space and community in an often hostile world, as well as the need current residents of urban neighborhoods have to hold onto the home spaces that sustain them. Both see themselves as the "rightful" inhabitants of the neighborhood—gentrifiers because their work "improves" the area's cultural capital and the current residents because they have built lives for themselves in the very homes others would "improve." Although the film seems at first to lay blame for the community conflict at the feet of gay white people—like a lesbian real estate agent whose attitude could be described as predatory—the filmmakers are finally careful to show "that villain and hero, victim and victimizer, good and bad are aspects of all of us" (Bryant). We see how both groups—black residents and gay gentrifiers—have been victimized by social, cultural, and legal forces. The real estate agent, referring to a string of muggings and robberies, justifies her presence in the neighborhood by saying, "We're all busting our ass out here trying to make a difference." A black community leader fighting to keep a colorful sign over his front door in defiance of housing codes remarks, "They've got a free right to occupy. It's our responsibility to keep our own identity."

In *Flag Wars*, then, the issue of identity for both groups is key to their understanding of home. In some of the same ways, the documentary film *Shinjuku Boys* (20th Century Vixen, 1995, dir. Kim Longinotto and Jano Williams) explores the connection between identity—in this case, a number of so-called

Onnabes described by the narrator as "women who have decided to live as men"—and the quest for place. The film is set in Japan and follows several Onnabes working in Tokyo's New Marilyn Club, whose clientele is "almost exclusively heterosexual women who have become disappointed with born men" ("Annabe"). The melancholy tone of the film results primarily from the exclusion experienced by the Onnabes—not only from tradition-bound patriarchal Japanese culture but also from their culture's normative identity categories. Although the women who visit the New Marilyn Club consider the Onnabes "ideal men" and compete for their attention, outside the club, the "boys" themselves, living as men but without the privilege of men-born-men, lack a "home" in the culture. Another documentary, *Dangerous Living: Coming Out in the Developing World* (After Stonewall Productions 2003, dir. John Scagliotti), offers narratives from lesbian, gay, and transgender-identified people in the Global South who are seeking both physical safety and a sense of home in often extremely hostile environments. Opening with the story of a Cairo resident, Ashraf Zanati, who was "tortured, humiliated, beaten and forced to spend 13 months in prison" ("Dangerous Living"), the film shows how queer visibility in some parts of the world can complicate the move to create community. The film characterizes the search for home in highly personal ways. Zanati powerfully declares, "My sexuality is my own sexuality. It doesn't belong to anybody. Not to my government, not to my brother, my sister, my family. No." Zanati sees the claiming of his sexuality as a move away from his family, perhaps even his country of origin. But the reality of sexuality lies in its embeddedness, not just in personal conceptions of self but in social, cultural, and even political matrices. The search for home, then, can rarely be an individual journey, as personal as it may seem; it is often a collective journey, as groups attempt to form new families, communities, and counterpublics.

Figure 15.1   Still from *Shinjuku Boys*

Film and Music Festivals

Film and music festivals have historically been configured as locations where LGBT people can meet to enjoy creative expressions of queer identification. These festivals are venues for viewing and distributing truly independent films whose makers lack the deep pockets for advertising that mainstream filmmakers enjoy. LGBT and queer film festivals are commonplace in many parts of the world. A quick Google search will provide links to advertisements for film festivals in many countries—Italy, Australia, the United States, the Canary Islands, Spain, and Canada, to name just a few. In fact, the PlanetOut website lists more than 150 lesbian and gay film festivals, many of which occur annually. This proliferation leads GLBTQ.com to ask whether these film festivals are "still necessary given the significant number of gay-themed films now seeing wider theatrical distribution" [λ Chapter 13]. In many ways, the answer is yes, they are, given that queers are a "complex people yearning for the experience of community—being together, sharing our different realities, exchanging ideas, cruising each other." LGBT film festivals are one of the "relatively few places where we get to experience community" ("Film Festivals").

Like film festivals, music festivals provide spaces for LGBT people to create community through creative expression. GALA (Gay & Lesbian Association)

Figure 15.2   MUSE, Cincinnati's women's choir

Choruses has as its mission "to support GLBT choruses as we change our world through song." Claiming the Philadelphia-based Anna Crusis Women's Choir, founded in 1975, as their "most-tenured" group, GALA boasts a membership of more than 100 choruses and 10,000 singers worldwide. The organization, which hosts periodic international and regional gatherings, holds concerts that attract not only queer participants but major musical and arts celebrities, such as Maya Angelou, Natalie Cole, Liza Minnelli, Holly Near, and Kate Clinton ("About GALA Choruses"). GALA festival performances are often profound experiences for participants, reflecting the diversity of queer life and community. Catherine Roma, founder of both Anna Crusis and MUSE, Cincinnati's Women's Choir, notes that "every movement for social change has been accompanied by strong singing." She goes on to say, "We in the gay and lesbian choral movement are really just in a long line of music for social change . . . the labor movement, the civil rights movement, the women's liberation movement" (Roma). A desire for such "social change" has found not just musical expression but also *political* expression in the work of many LGBT choruses in response to the AIDS crisis. Gay men's choruses in New York and San Francisco, for example, raised significant amounts of money and generated much volunteer time to address AIDS, even as their membership was being decimated by the epidemic ("Gay Men's Chorus").

Unlike film festivals and choral festivals, which inhabit different physical spaces year by year, the Michigan Womyn's Music Festival (MWMF) is tied to a particular place in central Michigan (called "The Land" by festiegoers). Boden Sandstrom writes, "The Festival was created as separate . . . 'womyn-only' space isolated from the hegemonic culture" (47). The MWMF first took place in 1976, a time when some lesbians were forming separatist groups [λ Chapter 4] on a communitarian model, based on "feminist political analysis which rejected the patriarchal and capitalist system" (77). The MWMF is the result of a conscious "process of building and creating an environment according to [women's] own vision" (111). Stressing this utopian feel, Bonnie Morris's book about women's music festivals, including Michigan, is titled *Eden Built by Eves*. After more than thirty years in existence, and despite weathering some intense ideological storms, Michigan still functions as a safe "home" for lesbian (and other) women born women [λ Chapter 6]. Sandstrom quotes a Michigan festiegoer talking about her experiences: "Coming into the total women's space of the festival was definitely a culture clash/shock initially. I felt a gradual relaxing of mind and muscle, and when I began to drink [at] this new well, my thirst was insatiable." She speaks of Michigan as "coming back home," contrasting its "warmth and support" with the "straight, patriarchal world [that] shakes and rattles and threatens" (283).

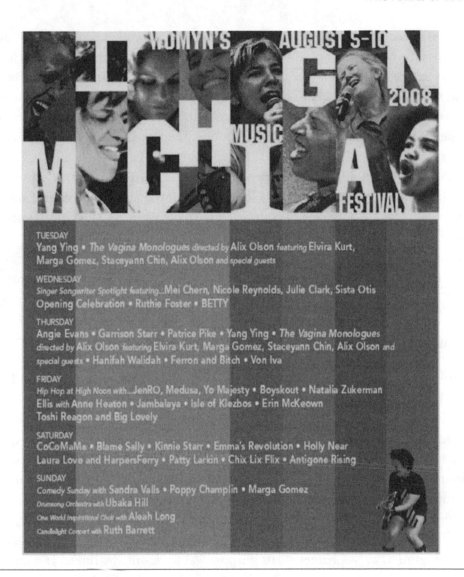

Figure 15.3   2008 MWMF poster

Queer Music

Certainly, queer music has its mainstream and commercial dimensions, and a number of openly lesbian, gay, and bisexual pop and rock artists have enriched the popular music industry and have served as role models for any number of young queer people. Elton John, Melissa Etheridge, and Michael Stipe of R.E.M, who identifies as a "queer artist," are among the most successful of such musicians. Still, not all of the "out" musicians address queer issues in their music, and if they do, they often do so in covert or subtle ways. At times, gay artists (George Michael, for example) are outed against their will, and other seemingly queer-friendly artists, such as Madonna, are accused of using homo- and bi-eroticism to be "edgy" and enhance their notoriety. So we are left with a crucial question: can we count on these artists to directly address the concerns and issues of queer people? To find the music that speaks—or sings—to this question, many look to alternative music and musical venues, which often eschew or limit ties to the corporate music industry in the hopes of maintaining a high degree of autonomy and freedom to pursue particular artistic visions.

Central to the MWMF experience is, of course, the music, a particular subgenre called Women's Music. To some extent a product of the lesbian-feminist generation but also appealing to younger women, the Women's Music phenomenon combines lesbian-feminist politics with intense emotional self-expression. Beginning in the early 1970s with the self-consciously feminist music and lyrics of Alix Dobkin, Maxine Feldman, Linda Tillery, and others, Women's Music crossed into the "mainstream" with k.d. lang, Ani DiFranco, Tracy Chapman, the Indigo Girls, and contemporary artists such as the Cliks. Composers including Kay Gardner and Therese Edell have used a contemporary classical style to celebrate spaces women have created, specifically the MWMF. Gardner's ritual music for Michigan and her Wiccan oratorio *Ouruboros* and Edell's Michigan festival anthem "Gather In" all express women's need for safe and empowering community.

The new women's music subgenre galvanized many lesbians into seeking and creating venues where all aspects of production—recording, mixing, sound quality, and so forth—were done by women. In 1972, Holly Near began bringing out albums on her Redwood label, and the next year, Alix Dobkin inaugurated Women's Wax Works. But "the most influential, most quintessential, most lesbionic label" was Olivia Records (Baumgardner). Cofounded in 1973 by Judy Dlugacz and other members of the Furies and Radicalesbians collectives in Washington, D.C. [λ Chapter 4], its purpose was to record, distribute, and market women's music. Olivia's first 45-rpm record featured Meg Christian on one side and Cris Williamson on the other; it brought in $12,000, enough to make Christian's first album, *Now You Know,* and then Williamson's blockbuster, *The Changer and the Changed. Changer* sold 60,000 to 80,000 copies in its first year and, as of 2007, had sold more than 300,000 copies. Its success allowed Olivia to outsource its distribution end, which became Goldenrod Music in 1975. In 1976, Laurie Fuchs established Ladyslipper, "a mail order catalog devoted to distributing women's music." Fuchs recalls, "When I first started the catalog, I thought I could cover everything recorded by women"—and ironically, in the mid-1970s, that was not outside the realm of possibility (Baumgardner). Olivia and the other labels established a powerful presence at Michigan and other music festivals in the United States, cementing the relationship between performance venues and alternative labels in the popularization of women's music.

Inspired by feminism and its musical offshoots, Mehn's music, written and performed by males, bills itself as antipatriarchal. According to Ron Romanovsky of the gay music group Romanovsky & Phillips, Mehn's music arises out of a "movement of gay and straight men who are [invested in] creating non-sexist music" ("Mehn's Music").

Believing that most Western music has been patriarchal, with male composers dominating music "his"tory, Romanovsky and others, such as Mark Weigle, Doug Stevens, and the group Pansy Division, promote music that

Figure 15.4 Romanovsky and Phillips just moments after receiving the Heritage Award from Outmusic, New York City, 2003

decries sexism and homophobia while celebrating male intimacy and homoerotic sexuality. Michael Callen (1955–1993), among the most famous of gay male songwriters, wrote poignantly about the need to revise normative conceptions of love, family, and community to create a space in which queer people could find respect. In his song "Redefine the Family," Callen composed an anthem in praise of alternative family constructions:

> My lover's name is Richard
>
> His lover's name is Pat
>
> We're one big happy family
>
> Is there a box for that?
>
> We live here with Pam and Lyn
>
> They're lesbians and lovers
>
> Together, we're raising three great kids
>
> Gertrude, and her two brothers. (Callen)

Recordings of Mehn's music are most readily available through distributors that specialize in women's and lesbian music, such as Ladyslipper.

LGBT Journalism: Magazines, Newspapers, and Comics

In *Unspeakable: The Rise of the Gay and Lesbian Press in America,* journalist Rodger Streitmatter contends,

> The most important single contribution lesbian and gay journalism has made—and will continue to make—may be one most straight people simply are not able to fathom. For half a century, reading gay publications has served as a first tenuous step for men and women embarking on the very personal, and often profoundly difficult, journey toward acknowledging their homosexuality to themselves and the world around them. (347)

Like the pulps and pictorials of the post–World War II period, early gay and lesbian newsletters let queers across the country know that they were not alone [λ Chapters 3 and 10]. But beyond providing touchstones for identifications and pleas for tolerance and understanding, gay and lesbian writers for newsletters, magazines, and other periodicals borrowed from the activist energies of the 1960s and 1970s to begin organizing queers communally and politically. Streitmatter notes that "America's alternative media have evolved because groups of people outside the mainstream of society—most notably African Americans and women—historically have been denied a voice in conventional media networks" (308). Gay and lesbian activists claimed journalistic spaces to promote increasingly politicized agendas, and magazines such as *The Advocate* provided journalistic coverage of social, cultural, and political issues of concern to gay and lesbian people. When *The Advocate* was still a local Los Angeles newspaper in the late 1960s, its writers attempted to mobilize queers to fight back against homophobic legal injustice. Writing about how L.A. police broke into a private residence to arrest two men on charges of "lewd conduct," *The Advocate* devoted its front page to urging gays to respond:

> We are bleeding now, and L.A. Gays sit in their big homes and fancy apartments planning their next garden party. Wake up! It isn't just the bar queer and the street walker who is in danger. Our fancy homes and apartments are no longer all that safe. Our lives and our freedom are on the line. (qtd. in Streitmatter 148)

While *The Advocate* continues today, offering U.S. LGBT people a prominent source of news about issues facing queer people, some short-lived publications from the 1960s and 1970s offered more radical advice. For instance, *Come Out!* "urged the annihilation of the nuclear family," and *Killer Dyke* "called for eliminating mental institutions, marriage, private property, and the state" and for all Americans to be given "free food, free housing, free clothing, free education, and free marijuana" (Streitmatter 150). The vision espoused by such publications was often one that agitated for an interrogation or reimagining of the idea of "home," at local and national levels. The advent of the AIDS crisis in the 1980s propelled a growing number of publications, such as *The Advocate* and *Outweek,* to address the homophobia that made the government largely silent about a disease dispropor-tionately affecting gay men [λ Chapter 4]. These publications were not beyond bickering among themselves, with *Outweek,* for instance, criticizing *The Advocate* for advertising porn videos depicting unsafe sex practices (Streitmatter 280–81).

Political journalism relating to LGBT issues continues with *The Washington Blade,* which claims to be the "oldest LGBT newspaper in the United States," hav-ing been founded in 1969. Situated in Washington, D.C., with versions in other major metropolitan areas, the *Blade* provides detailed coverage of issues such as gay marriage, gays in the military, and politicians who support (or not) a variety of LGBT concerns and issues. Comparable kinds of magazines and newspapers have sprung up throughout the world. Some originate in countries where LGBT organizing has been going on for decades: *Gay Times, QX Magazine, Diva,* and *Capital Gay* in England, for instance, or the *Sydney Star Observer, Bi the Way,* and *Brother Sister* in Australia. Other publications chronicle emerging LGBT consciousness in countries that are just beginning to articulate it: *Masok* from Hungary, *Lambda* from Turkey, *Gay News FILO* and *INACZEJ* from Poland, *O Pothos* from Greece, and *Kekec* from Slovenia represent a few examples. It is clear that throughout the world, LGBT magazines and newspapers constitute a lifeline, a neces-sary link and introduction to queer community for those already connected to it and for those seeking such community for the first time.

> **Find Out More:** Consider the claim in Michael Sibalis's article on Paris's Marais district at the end of this chapter: *"Consommer gay, c'est s'affirmer"* (To consume gay is to affirm oneself). Do you agree?

Today, a number of "lifestyle" magazines, such as *Out, Girlfriends, Genre* (for "smart, stylish, and tuned in" gay men), and *Gay Times,* among others, offer not only political commentary but social and cultural news, fashion advice, and con-sumer reports. Understanding the increasing buying power of queer markets, these magazines are often loaded with advertisements from corporations that seek a share of the "gay dollar." While such magazines may pander to a middle- and upper-class gay market, they still speak to attempts to create a sense of community, even on a national scale, for many queer people.

Important attractions included in many LGBT magazines and newspapers are gay-themed cartoons and comic strips. Over the past three decades, these publica-tions and, more recently, the Internet have enabled LGBT cartoonists to reach a wide audience with their pointed commentaries on queer life. Eric Orner's "play-fully self-reflexive . . . and surrealistic" strips narrating "The Mostly Unfabulous Social Life of Ethan Green" and Michael-Christopher's series "Living the Life" first became famous after appearing in gay-themed publications. According to Reyhan Harmanci, Orner's Ethan Green appeared in "more than a hundred newspapers

ANYWAY, THIS IS PRETTY FUCKING COOL! ONE MILLION QUEERS IN D.C. IS PROBABLY REALLY, REALLY PISSING A LOT OF PEOPLE OFF!

CAN'T HELP BUT NOTICE HOW PEACEFUL THE WHOLE THING IS!

Figure 15.5 Panel from DiMassa's "Hothead Paisan," *Dyke Strippers*

and alt-weeklies in America and Europe" before being made into a movie in 2006. "Living the Life" was aimed specifically at black gay men and ran in *WHASSUP!* and *CLIKQUE* magazines. In 1991, Diane DiMassa introduced "Hothead Paisan: Homicidal Lesbian Terrorist," which appeared in Robert Kirby's *Strange-Looking Exile, The Advocate,* and elsewhere. DiMassa describes Hothead Paisan as "comics for the fed-up, rage therapy for the marginalized. Way cheaper than a shrink." DiMassa's "lesbian terrorist" contrasts sharply with Alison Bechdel's "Dykes to Watch Out For" (DTWOF), whose early strips from the 1980s ran in such publications as *Chicago Gay Life, Hot Wire, Lesbian Contradiction,* and *Womanews.* DTWOF "documents the life, loves, and politics of a fairly diverse group of characters (most of them lesbians) . . . featuring both humorous soap-opera storylines and biting topical commentary" ("Dykes").

Set in several domestic locations—a women's bookstore, characters' homes, a commune where four of the characters live—Bechdel's DTWOF makes much of the daily interactions among characters Mo, Sparrow, Ginger, Tony, Sydney, Clarice, Jezanna, and others. Readers of the strip become intimately involved in the lives of these characters as they work their way through the books. When Tony and Clarice and their son Raffi move to the suburbs, we wonder how they will, as an interracial lesbian couple, be received by their new neighbors. And when Clarice locks horns with one of those neighbors over Raffi's insistence that he "can too marry Stone Cold Steve Austin" when he grows up, readers are invited to see the poignancy and humor of the moment when the neighbor child responds (much to his father's chagrin), "You can not, 'cause I'm gonna marry him, and we're gonna kick your butt" (*Post-Dykes* 77). Bechdel's work, like much lesbian and gay literature, also uses specific kinds of inside jokes, many of which have to do with romantic relationships and domestic issues. In one of her earliest collections, *Dykes to Watch Out For: Great Romances That Never Were,* Bechdel's "Guide to the First Sleepover" provides a number of dos and

Find Out More in Alison Bechdel's graphic novel *Fun Home,* which was a 2006 National Book Critics Circle award finalist for autobiography.

don'ts for the first date, one of which is "Don't Get Carried Away," a panel that shows one woman asking another, "So, when are you moving in?" This reference is picked up again on the cover of *Split-Level Dykes to Watch Out For*, where Clarice, Tony, and Raffi are shown moving into their suburban home with the aid of the strip's other characters and a truck from "Y'All Haul." These references are to one of the longest running lesbian inside jokes: what does a lesbian bring on the second date? A U-Haul.

The U-Haul joke reflects lesbians' (and, by extension, LGBT people's in general) desire to establish meaningful "home" spaces in a world that does not endorse nonnuclear, nonheterosexual families. Queer partners in DTWOF face rejection from their families of origin. Toni, for instance, refuses her father's request that she leave Clarice and "come home with us so Rafael can grow up in a real family" (*Hot Throbbing* 57). Sparrow's parents threaten, "If you expect to inherit a penny from us, we insist you marry this man" (*Carbon-Based* 153). In a real sense, much of DTWOF claims the right of queer people to form families of choice and establish "homesteads" in the face of a world that enforces compulsory heterosexuality [λ Chapter 5].

Many Journeys, Many Homes

Many of the alternative media and media venues we have been discussing in this chapter find homes for production and dissemination in what have come to be known as "gay ghettos"— urban areas that LGBT people have claimed as their own in some of the world's largest metropolitan areas. Locales such as the Castro in San Francisco, West Hollywood in Los Angeles, Greenwich Village in New York City, the Via San Giovanni in the Laterano district of Rome, or the Oxford Street area in Sydney, Australia, contain concentrations of queer-owned businesses, stores, entertainment complexes, sex shops, and housing. Often figured as refuges for LGBT people, gay ghettos serve as home for many queers who have migrated to large urban areas in search of greater

Figure 15.6　Street scene from Paris, Marais district.

freedom for self-expression; local and even national gay rights organizations often have headquarters and offices alongside the shops that queers frequent. These areas also support a variety of alternative media, including independent bookstores featuring books from gay and gay-friendly presses, movie theaters offering annual LGBT film festivals, and coffee shops providing access to numerous new weeklies, many of which are free. In these ways, the ghettos offer a sense of "home" that is often markedly different from that experienced by many queer people who grow up in households that are intolerant of their sexual and affectional desires. But they are more than just places of escape; they offer the opportunity to reinvent the idea of "home"—in often very queer, nonnormative, and unexpected ways.

In the United States, these neighborhoods arose in the decades following World War II, when many men and women found themselves shipped overseas or relocated to metropolitan areas after being drafted, into either the army or the wartime workforce. After the war, many lesbians and gays decided to stay in the metropolitan areas that served as their ports of embarkation. As urban areas underwent a variety of changes in the mid to late twentieth century, including the move of middle-class people into the suburbs, many queers moved into abandoned or decaying urban areas to revitalize them, claiming a home. In some ways, we might describe this movement of queers as a kind of diaspora—perhaps an *inverse* diaspora in which a group isn't forced to leave a homeland and disperse but rather exists as a dispersed people, journeying toward home and community. This search for home is not without cost; the gentrification described in *Flag Wars* can be one of the negative consequences of the development of gay neighborhoods, in that some queer people renovate and remodel existing communities into fashionable districts, pricing out previous residents. At the same time, commentator Richard Florida suggests that the presence of a strong and visible gay community is a sign of health in American cities; such communities speak to both a city's acceptance of diversity and its support of creative pursuits, such as alternative media.

One question that might arise concerning this chapter is how film and music festivals, as well as urban neighborhoods where LGBT people tend to live or visit, fit into a chapter about alternative media. Festivals and neighborhoods are, after all, locations rather than artifacts of creative expression. But if we look more closely, we recognize that alternative media depend on a kind of communal sharing, or "word of mouth" for their distribution and popularity. And more often than not, festivals and neighborhoods where LGBT people congregate are sites for exchange of information about new films, music, news, and ideas. Even this way of understanding festivals and neighborhoods, though, ignores what is perhaps a less obvious reality about these locations—namely, that their communal nature facilitates the exchange and development of creative work by bringing together diverse populations of people who share some similar interests. These places embody the "homing desire" that Anne-Marie Fortier says is "about *motions of attachment*":

> It is lived in motions: the motions of journeying between homes, the motions of hailing ghosts from the past, the motions of leaving or staying put, of "moving on" or "going back," the motions of cutting or adding, the motions of continual reprocessing of what home is/was/might have been. But "home" is also remembered by attaching it, even momentarily, to a place where we strive to *make* home and to bodies and relationships that touch us, have touched us, in meaningful ways. (130–31)

The locations where LGBT alternative creative expressions are nurtured and shared are thus "homes" in this dynamic sense, for they enable attachment to "bodies and relationships that touch us." For LGBT people, reinvented concepts of home and family through alternative spaces, activities, and artifacts can function as lifelines to community. These various aspects of communal experience have allowed many queer people—especially those in prosperous nations who have access to the resources available in large metropolitan centers—to construct a coherent identity-based subculture, a queer home.

QUESTIONS FOR DISCUSSION

1. The term *alternative media* is most often used to refer to media that fall outside the mainstream and are not corporately supported. In this chapter, we have defined it more broadly as a result of our sense that much media geared directly at an LGBT audience qualify as "alternative" in a world where many mainstream communications corporations are still hesitant to support work that deals with nonnormative sexuality. What do you think about the choices we have made? Write us a letter in which you make a cogent and well-developed case for your agreement or disagreement with our choices in this area. If you can find colleagues in your class with whom to discuss this issue, find out what they think and make your letter a community effort.

2. Throughout this chapter, we have evoked "the search for home" as a significant dimension of LGBT experience. This concept can be problematized in many ways: such a frame can be read as "normalizing" LGBT lives by making them fit a heteronormative model, the diversity of definitions of the word *home* can get lost if the term is used too generally, and the concept of home is often used in capitalist

societies to encourage uncritical participation in economic acquisition. What do you think about the way a journey toward a sense of home is used in this chapter? Do you accept it as related to alternative media and space? Why or why not?

3. Since this is the last chapter, we assume that you have now read all or most of the book. What have you learned? What has surprised you? What has disappointed you? What do you want to know more about? Write a short paper or journal entry in which you explore more fully through careful research an issue you have read about in *Finding Out*. Share the results by preparing a presentation or publication with a specific audience in mind.

REFERENCES AND FURTHER READING

"About GALA Choruses." 6 August 2008 <http://www.galachoruses.org/about/about_gala .html>.

"Annabe." In *Women in Suits—Eye Candy.* 6 August 2008 <http://www.dandeliondesign .ca/Ties/ties2.html>.

Baumgardner, Jennifer. "Women's Music 101." *Z Magazine.* 1 August 2007 <http://www .zmag.org/ZMag/articles/women%20music.htm>.

Bechdel, Alison. *Dykes and Sundry Other Carbon-Based Life-Forms to Watch Out For.* New York: Alyson, 2003.

———. *Dykes to Watch Out For: Great Romances That Never Were.* Ithaca, NY: Firebrand, 1986.

———. *Hot Throbbing Dykes to Watch Out For.* Ithaca, NY: Firebrand, 1997.

———. *The Indelible Alison Bechdel: Confessions, Comix, and Miscellaneous Dykes to Watch Out For.* Ithaca, NY: Firebrand, 1998.

———. *Post-Dykes to Watch Out For.* Ithaca, NY: Firebrand, 2000.

———. *Split-Level Dykes to Watch Out For.* Ithaca, NY: Firebrand, 1998: 79.

Bell, David, and Jon Binnie. *The Sexual Citizen: Queer Politics and Beyond.* Cambridge, UK: Polity, 2000.

Binnie, Jon. *The Globalization of Sexuality.* London: Sage, 2004.

Bryant, Linda Goode. "Filmmaker Interview." 6 August 2008 <http://www.pbs.org/pov/ pov2003/flagwars/behind_interview.html>.

Callen, Michael. "Redefine the Family." *Legacy Lyrics.* 6 August 2008 <http://hometown .aol.com/sigothinc/topdisc1.htm>.

"Dangerous Living." Al-Fatiha Foundation: The First-Ever Queer Muslim Film Festival Program Guide. 6 August 2008 <http://www.al-fatiha.org/docs/conference2004films.pdf>.

DiMassa, Diane. "Hothead Paisan: Homicidal Lesbian Terrorist." 6 August 2008 <http://hotheadpaisan.com/>.

"Dykes to Watch Out For." 6 August 2008 <http://en.wikipedia.org/wiki/Dykes_to_Watch _Out_For>.

Farley, Christopher John. "Michael Stipe and the Ageless Boys of R.E.M." *Time* 14 May 2001. 6 August 2008 <http://www.time.com/time/sampler/article/0,8599,109715,00.html>.

"Film Festivals." *GLBTQ: An Encyclopedia of Gay, Lesbian, Bisexual, Transgender, & Queer Culture.* 6 August 2008 <http://www.glbtq.com/arts/film_festivals.html>.

"Flag Wars." 6 August 2008 <http://www.pbs.org/pov/pov2003/flagwars/>.

Florida, Richard. *The Rise of the Creative Class.* New York: Basic Books, 2002.

Fortier, Anne-Marie. "Making Home: Queer Migrations and Motions of Attachment." *Uprootings/Regroundings: Questions of Home and Migration.* Eds. Sara Ahmed, Claudia Castaneda, and Anne-Marie Fortier. New York: Berg, 2003. 115–36.

"Gay Men's Chorus Carries on after Death of 257 Members." *A Cappella News.* 5 June 2006 <http://www.acappellanews.com/archive/001199.html>.

Halberstam, Judith. *In a Queer Time and Place: Transgender Bodies, Subcultural Lives.* New York: NYU P, 2005.

Harmanci, Reyhan. "Pioneer Gay Comic Strip Hero Ethan Green Finally Snags a Date with the Big Screen." *San Francisco Chronicle.* 29 June 2006 <http://sfgate.com/cgi-bin/article.cgi?file=/c/a/2006/06/29/DDG3FJLBDO1.DTL>.

"Mehn's Music." *Ladyslipper Music Online Catalogue.* 6 August 2008 <http://www.ladyslipper.org/rel/v2_home.php?storenr=53&deptnr=58>.

Michael-Christopher. *Living the Life.* 6 August 2008 <http://productionsfirehorse.com/ltl-gne.html>.

Morris, Bonnie. *Eden Built by Eves.* New York: Alyson, 1999.

Orner, Eric. "The Mostly Unfabulous Social Life of Ethan Green." 6 August 2008 <http://www.ethangreen.com/books.html>.

Phelan, Shane. *Sexual Strangers: Gays, Lesbians, and Dilemmas of Citizenship.* Philadelphia: Temple UP, 2001.

Roma, Catherine. "Interview: *Why We Sing.*" 6 August 2008 <http://www.cetconnect.org/msie_video.asp?id=1371>.

Sandstrom, Boden. "Performance, Ritual and Negotiation of Identity in the Michigan Womyn's Music Festival." Diss., Ethnomusicology, University of Maryland at College Park, 2002.

Streitmatter, Rodger. *Unspeakable: The Rise of the Gay and Lesbian Press in America.* Boston: Faber & Faber, 1995.

Weeks, Jeffrey. "The Sexual Citizen." *Love and Eroticism.* Ed. Mike Featherstone. London: Sage, 1999. 35–52.

READINGS

➢ **Michael Sibalis**

*"Urban Space and Homosexuality: The Example
of the Marais, Paris' 'Gay Ghetto'"*

(August 2004), Canada

[. . .]

Gay Men and Urban Space in Paris

Gay men have a special relationship to urban space. Only in cities are there enough homosexually inclined men to permit the emergence of a self-aware community with its own commercial venues, social and political organisations and distinctive sub-culture. In the words of the Danish sociologist Henning Bech, "being homosexual is a way of *being, a form of existence.*" Homosexuals belong to one of a number of social worlds (Bech does not identify the others) that are all essentially urban: they are largely worlds of strangers and not just of personal acquaintances; they depend in part upon the non-personal, urban free flow of signs and information, as well as upon the pool of strangers, for recruitment and reproduction; they occupy time-space slices of the city and need urban stages to be enacted on (Bech 153–156).

We know a great deal about the urban spaces used by Parisian homosexuals (generally called "sodomites" or "pederasts" before 1900) since the early 1700s, both outdoor ones (parks, gardens, riverbanks, quays and streets) and indoor ones (taverns, bars, clubs and restaurants). In the 18th and 19th centuries, these were spread across the city, but were usually situated on its margins, either literally (on its physical periphery) or figuratively (in poorer and seamier districts). Beginning in the 1880s, however, commercial venues catering to homosexuals clustered in the Montmartre quarter of northern Paris, known for bohemianism and illicit sexuality, including female prostitution. In the 1920s and 1930s, other districts, like the Rue de Lappe near the Bastille or Montparnasse in the south, also became important to Paris' homosexual sub-culture. After the Second World War, homosexuals frequented the bars, clubs and cafés of the Left Bank district of Saint-Germain-des-Prés, the centre of post-war intellectual life and non-conformity. In the 1970s, homosexual nightlife migrated across the Seine to the streets between the Palais-Royal and the Opera House and, most famously, to the Rue Sainte-Anne. In marked contrast to Montmartre and Saint-Germain, this was a quiet residential and business neighbourhood, almost deserted after the workday ended; the possibility of going out in relative secrecy is probably what attracted gay customers to its venues.

The popularity of the Rue Sainte-Anne lasted hardly more than a decade. In June 1983, a gay journalist observed that the homosexual geography of the capital has changed dramatically. Saint-Germain and the Rue Sainte-Anne are out. Les Halles and especially the Marais are in.

Several factors explain the shift. First of all, there was the accessibility of the Marais, which is centrally located and easily reached by public transport. A few hundred metres to the west lies Les Halles, former site of Paris' wholesale food market, which was transferred to the suburbs in 1969. In the 1970s, Les Halles underwent major commercial redevelopment, which included construction of an underground station (opened in December 1977) to link the subway system and the RER (Réseau Express Régional), a network of suburban trains that served 60 per cent of the population of the Paris region (Michel). The nearby Avenue Victoria, running between City Hall and Châtelet, is also the main terminus for the city's night buses, which operate from 1:30 AM to 5:30 AM.

Secondly, the renovated Marais had an undoubted aesthetic appeal. In the overblown rhetoric and rather stilted English of a recent bilingual guidebook:

> No other area of Paris has such a strong personality in spite of its [architectural] diversity. The same beauty of its dwellings can be seen in every street, the same refinement of the stones, the same warmth of the thoroughfares and everywhere the same poetic poetry [sic]. The Marais has a spirit, a soul, an immaterial existence beyond the mirror of life. (Auffray 8)

The attractiveness increased in the 1970s and 1980s, when the Marais was turned into an important cultural and artistic quarter. The Pompidou Centre (a new national museum of contemporary art) opened on its western edge in 1977 and the opening or refurbishing of other museums and the proliferation of commercial art galleries soon followed.

But there is a third factor that explains how and why the Marais became the centre of Parisian gay life. Gay businessmen recognised that the Marais, with its low rents and real-estate prices, was ripe for investment. In this respect, the gay Marais, like gay villages and ghettos in Britain and North America, developed spontaneously in response to favourable market conditions. But gay investors in Paris were concerned with more than the balance sheet. They consciously set out to create a new gay quarter as much because of their personal convictions as from their desire to benefit financially from an evident commercial opportunity.

[. . .]

The Marais and the Emergence of a Community

The Marais has thus become a clearly delineated gay space in the heart of Paris, where gay men and lesbians can stroll hand-in-hand or kiss in the street without embarrassment or risk of harassment. In the convoluted jargon of a geographer, such public displays of affection constitute an "appropriation and territorialisation [of a quarter] through the street behaviour of the clientele of gay establishments [who] challenge the hetero-centric character of public spaces and thus give the Marais a conspicuous territoriality" (Bordet 119).

The average homosexual would put it more simply. According to one gay man, "One feels more among family here [in the Marais] than anywhere else in Paris. Perhaps that's what we mean by the [gay] community" (Darne 8).

And for another, who recently moved from Lille to Paris, the Marais represents his community's financial clout: "I was glad to see that *les pédés* ['fags' or 'poofters'] had money and could open stylish establishments. I was glad to belong to something organized, which represented a certain economic power" (Laforgerie [1998] 20).

Their enthusiastic appreciation of the ghetto is a relatively recent attitude and even today is not shared by all gays and lesbians. As long ago as 1964, the monthly magazine *Arcadie,* organ of France's politically conservative "homophile" association, the Club Littéraire et Scientifique des Pays Latin (Literary and Scientific Club of the Latin Countries), warned French homosexuals against copying what was occurring in the US by creating

> a little artificial world, enclosed and suffocating, where everything would be homosexual: not only the bars, restaurants and movie theatres, but also the houses, the streets (in New York several streets are already almost entirely inhabited by homosexuals), the neighbourhoods. A world where one could live one's entire life without seeing anything other than homosexuals, without knowing anything other than homosexuality. In Europe that is called *ghettos.* We hate this false, harmful and grotesque conception of homosexuality. (Daniel 387)

Radical gay militants of the 1970s had little in common with their homophile elders, but they too denounced gay ghettos—both the "commercial ghetto," meaning the bars at Saint-Germain-des-Prés or on the Rue Sainte-Anne, and the "wild ghetto" constituted by the parks, gardens and public urinals where homosexual men hunted for sexual adventure (Martel 77).

Radicals believed that ghettos encouraged a separatist homosexual identity (J. Girard 132–133), whereas they wanted homosexuals to participate in the revolutionary transformation of society as a whole: "Instead of shutting everybody up in their own space, we need to change the world so that we find ourselves all mixed together" (Boyer 74).

Some gay radicals, however, eventually changed their minds and came to recognise the political potential of the gay ghetto. Guy Hocquenghem (1946–88), the emblematic radical militant of the 1970s, told an American interviewer in 1980:

> We don't have a gay community in France. That is, we have a gay movement—with several organisations actively working for political rights, as in all the Western countries—but people do not feel part of a *community,* nor do they live together in certain parts of the city, as they do here in New York City or in San Francisco—for example. And this is the most important difference and the most significant aspect of gay life in the U.S.: not only having a "movement," but having a sense of community—even if it takes the form of "ghettos"—because it is the basis for anything else. (Blasius 36)

The relationship evoked here by Hocquenghem—linking territory, collective identity and political activism—is a complex one. Veteran militant Jean Le Bitoux, for instance, has argued that the gay community appeared first and then produced the gay Marais:

> The homosexual community that was successfully emerging most likely wanted to complete this social emergence in the 1980s with a space "for expressing an identity" [*un espace "identitaire"*]. An emergent community needed a new geographical anchorage. (Le Bitoux 49)

Other analyses invert the equation, however, insisting that the Marais created a gay community and not the other way around. For example, Yves Roussel has noted that, whatever their political camp, homosexual activists of the 1950s–1970s rejected the formation of a distinct gay community (conservatives advocating assimilation into society, radicals wanting to overthrow it), but that by the 1990s a new generation had come to embrace "identity politics."

> Many are the men and women who see themselves as belonging to a minority group, which is the victim of a process of exclusion; this sentiment of exclusion has combined with the intense desire to constitute and to structure a homosexual community. (Roussel 85)

He has attributed this shift to several factors, including the need to mobilise against the AIDS epidemic, but one particularly significant determinant has been "the emergence of a vast ensemble of gay commercial enterprises [that] have allowed for the constitution of a community of homosexual consumers with characteristic lifestyles" (Roussel 107). Jan-Willem Duyvendak has similarly concluded that "in the middle of the 1980s, the concentration of gay clubs and bars, such as in the Marais in Paris, provided a certain 'infrastructure' for a community," although he minimises this community's political activism: "the militants took the occasion to go dancing rather than to demonstrate" (Duyvendak 79).

Gay businessmen share this view that their venues have contributed to the growing sense of community among French gays. In the mid 1980s, the gay entrepreneur David Girard (1959–90) responded to those activists who criticised him for his brazen capitalist spirit by declaring that "[t]he bar owner who, in the summer, opens an outdoor terrace where dozens of guys meet openly, is at least as militant as they are. I think that I have done more for gays than they ever have" (D. Girard [1986] 164).

He even told his customers: "This gay life that is ever more present and diversified in Paris, it is first of all you who create it by consuming" (D. Girard [1983]). This was precisely the message put out in an advertising campaign by the SNEG in 1996: "To consume gay is to affirm one's identity" ("*Consommer gay, c'est s'affirmer*"). The campaign's avowed purpose was to promote its members, but "it is equally a communitarian campaign, a way to bring home to people the visibility of gay establishments" (Primo).

Arguments like these are certainly self-interested on the part of the businessmen who advance them, but that does not mean that they are without merit. As Scott Gunther has recently pointed out,

The transformed Marais of the 80s provided a space for the development of a gay identity that had not existed before in France. As the community grew, gays themselves gained a reputation as respectable, resourceful, and affluent. Throughout the 80s, the emerging gay identity and geographical space of the Marais became increasingly inseparable and by the early 90s it seemed impossible to imagine the existence of one without the other. The resulting community, which may initially have been defined by a sexual orientation, became increasingly united by shared tastes, cultural preferences in music and food, and even by a distinct "Marais look" among the gay male inhabitants. (Gunther 34)

Not surprisingly, the proliferation and increasing visibility of gay establishments in the Marais and the concomitant development of a self-conscious gay community have resulted in conflict with some long-time residents who resent the on-going influx of gays and the dramatic changes that they have brought about in the quarter. There is also discord among homosexuals and lesbians themselves, many of whom disapprove of the Marais or feel excluded by its dominant cultural values.

Disputed Territory

Sudden change in a neighbourhood often alarms its residents, a problem that has by no means been unique to the Marais. In the Butte-aux-Cailles district in Paris' 13th *arrondissement,* the artists, writers and middle class who took over this once working-class neighbourhood in the 1980s now complain that it "has become one of the new meeting places for Parisian youth. All year long, music coming from the bars and noisy laughter invade the streets into the early hours of the morning. This nightlife has become a nightmare for certain inhabitants" (Chenay).

In the Popincourt district of the 11th *arrondissement,* it is the "Chinese invasion" by Chinese-born wholesalers in the clothing trades that upsets residents, who find the immigrants "discreet, kind, likeable," but insist that "they have killed the quarter" by taking over every shop that comes onto the market, with the result that there are fewer stores, bakeries and restaurants (Goudet). But nowhere in Paris has the changing character of a neighbourhood aroused more sustained animosity and acrimony than in the Marais.

Homosexuals have had relatively little trouble with the Marais' other significant minority, the orthodox Jews who live on and around the Rue des Rosiers on the very edge of the gay neighbourhood. When the only Jewish tobacconist's on the Rue Vieille-du-Temple became a gay bar in 1983, "[the Jews] were furious that we had taken over this sacred place on their territory," Maurice McGrath has recalled, but "very quickly, we fraternized." Gay businesses even lent their support to protect the quarter in 1986 during a wave of anti-Semitic terrorism (Chayet). In contrast, there has been a long-festering dispute with some of the Marais' middle-class residents who, unhappy with the gay influx, have sometimes expressed themselves in words that carry an explicit or implicit homophobic message.

The Association Aubriot-Guillemites has been at the forefront of the struggle against gay businesses. Residents founded the association, named for two small streets in the Marais, in 1978 to protect the area from damage to the architectural quality of buildings and to the environment, noise, especially at night, nuisances, various inconveniences, and generally anything that might trouble the peace and comfort of the inhabitants of the aforementioned area. (Association circular, c. 1996, reproduced in Méreaux)

By the mid 1990s, the association was denouncing "the major alteration in the atmosphere of the quarter brought about by the proliferation of homosexual businesses" and calling on its members to report "the multiple incidents that bear witness to the accelerated degradation of daily life in our quarter: noise pollution, solicitation of young boys, prostitution, sexual relations on the public street." (There is in fact little or no evidence for most of these charges.) The association warned that "a small group dreams of making this quarter the equivalent of the homosexual quarters of certain large American cities, which the inhabitants do not want at any price" (Razemon and Galceran, 1996a and 1996b; Rémès). In 1997, it went so far as to declare that

no normally constituted citizen, whether homosexual or heterosexual, can approve of the multiplication of these specialised bars the inevitable result of which is segregationist and discriminatory and the sole purpose of which is nothing other than the economic exploitation of homosexuality. (e-m@le magazine)

Under pressure from the Association Aubriot-Guillemites, the mayor of the 4th *arrondissement,* Pierre-Charles Krieg, told his constituents in 1996 that "a structured homosexual community has recently received coverage in the media that is disproportionate and dangerous to the harmony of local life." While deploring the "simplistic and racist ideas of thoroughgoing homophobes," he also criticised the "proselytism, ostentation or virulence" allegedly manifested by the neighbourhood's gay men (Krieg). Krieg was a conservative gaullist, but even a socialist municipal councillor declared herself "generally hostile to communitarianism, *a fortiori* if there is risk of [creating] a ghetto" (Pitte 51–52). The dispute crystallised in the "Affair of the Flags." In July 1995, Bernard Bousset, as president of SNEG, suggested that gay and gay-friendly businesses in the Marais display the "rainbow flag" (the internationally recognised symbol of gays) on their façades and some 15 businesses did so. The Association Aubriot-Guillemites objected and in April 1996 the police invoked an ordinance issued by the prefect of police in 1884 and ordered the removal of the flags (which Mayor Krieg contemptuously dismissed as "multicoloured rags") on the grounds that

the grouped and quasi-systematic display of overly large emblems risks arousing hostile reactions. And in these circumstances it is not necessary to wait for trouble to occur before imposing a ban. (Baverel; Berthemet; Razemon and Galceran 1996a)

The flags soon reappeared or were replaced with more discreet rainbow decals stuck on windows and doors, but the dispute was symbolic of deeper and more persistent concerns. In late 1990, a new police commissioner, determined to put an end to "ten years of laxness," began a crack-down on noise in the quarter which, bar owners claimed, amounted to "police harassment" of their establishments (Rouy; *Illico*). In 1995/96, gay bars in the Marais deplored another round of harassment by police, including reports for "disturbing the peace at night" actually drawn up in the late morning or early evening (Rémès). A series of meetings held in early 1997 by police, municipal officials and representatives of SNEG produced an agreement for concerted efforts "to diminish the nuisances for residents from 'nighttime' establishments" (*Paris Centre*). Another series of discussions followed in the spring of 1999, after renewed complaints about noisy bars and customers who gathered outside the doors of certain establishments, blocking the pavement and sometimes impeding the circulation of automobiles in the street. The Association of Co-owners in the Marais Quarter (Association des Copropriétaires du Quartier du Marais) even advocated closing bars at 11 PM (instead of 2 AM). One gay publication observed that "these problems raise the issue of a veritable redevelopment of the quarter by residents, businesspeople, police and administrators," but its proposed solution ("the creation of districts designated for partying, leisure and places for socializing") was probably unrealistic (Abal). In 2003, the municipality had to put metal rivets in the pavement to delimit the outdoor terraces of restaurants and cafés that were encroaching too far onto the pavement along the Rue des Archives (Laforgerie 2003, 31–32).

Although in the past decade or so the French press has been generally favourable to gay demands for equal rights, coverage of gay issues has rarely been free of unconscious prejudice, especially where the Marais is concerned. As David Caron has pointed out, the heading above one newspaper article about the Marais—"The gay flag hangs over the Rue Sainte-Croix-de-la-Bretonnerie"—typically used "a metaphor for foreign invasion" to describe the gay presence in the Marais (Caron 151). Newspapers tend to ignore lesbians, portray gay men as hedonistic and sex-obsessed revellers, equate homosexual "visibility" with "provocation" (of heterosexuals) and depict the Marais as a geographical and metaphorical "ghetto" and the headquarters of gay "corporatism," "communitarianism" or "militant *apartheid*" (Huyez). As these charges indicate, the conflict within the neighbourhood over the use of urban space has much broader ideological implications arising from the particular way that the French conceptualise their society.

References

Abal, O. (1999) Trop de bruits dans le Marais?. *CQFG* 3:(22 April), p. 12.

Auffray, M.-F. (2001) Le Marais: la légende des pierres, if stones could speak.—trans. by E. Powis. Paris: Hervas

Baverel, P. (1996) Le Drapeau gay flotte rue Sainte-Croix-de-la-Bretonnerie. *Le Monde* p. 11.—22 June

Bech, H. (1997) When Men Meet: Homosexuality and Modernity.—trans. by T. Mesquit and T. Davies. Chicago, IL: University of Chicago Press

Berthemet, T. (1996) Querelle de drapeau dans le Marais. *Le Figaro* p. 24.—25 April

Blasius, M. (1980) Interview: Guy Hocquenghem. *Christopher Street* 4:(8), p. 36.

Bordet, G. (2001) Homosexualité, altérité et territoire: les commerces gais sur le bas des pentes de la Croix-Rousse et dans le Marais.—Unpublished Mémoire de maîtrise de géographie, Université Lumière-Lyon 2

Boyer, J. (1979/80) Quand les homosexuels se lancent à la conquête de l'espace. *Masques* 3:(Winter), p. 73.

Caron, D. (2001) AIDS in French Culture: Social Ills, Literary Curses.—Madison, WI: University of Wisconsin Press

Chayet, S. (1996) Marais, le triangle rose. *Le Point* 1232:(27 April), p. 96.

Chenay, C. de (2003) A Paris, la Butte-aux-Cailles, des communards aux 'bobos'. *Le Monde* p. 9.—29 July

Daniel, M. (1964) Le plus grave danger. *Arcadie* 11:(129), p. 385.

Darne, R. (1995) Ghetto? Milieu? Communauté? Un débat ouvert. *Exit, le journal* p. 8.—21 July

Duyvendak, J.-W. (1993) Une 'communauté' homosexuelle en France et aux Pays-Bas? Blocs, tribus et liens. *Sociétés: Revue des Sciences Humaines et Sociales* 39, p. 75.

———. (1998) Pas de quartier pour les gays!. *e-m@le magazine* 23:(12 March) , p. 15.—e-m@le magazine

Girard, D. (1983) Édito. *5 sur 5* 1:(September), p. 1.

Girard, D. (1986) Cher David: les nuits de citizen gay.—Paris: Ramsey

Girard, J. (1981) Le Mouvement homosexuel en France 1945–1980.—Paris: Syros

Goudet, A. (2003) Pas de racisme, mais trop de Chinois dans le sape. *Marianne* 329:(11–17 August), p. 59.

Gunther, S. (1999) The indifferent ghetto. *Harvard Gay and Lesbian Review* 6:(1), p. 34.

Huyez, G. (2002) Dix ans de 'ghetto': le quartier gay dans les hebdomadaires français. *ProChoix* 22:(Autumn), p. 59.

———. (1991) Le Marais en alerte. p. 7.—Illico; 3 January

Krieg, P.-C. (1996) Éditorial. *Paris Centre: Le Journal du IVème* 93:(October/November), p. 3.

Laforgerie, J.-F. (1998) Dehors, dedans: mon ghetto. *Ex Aequo* 14:(January), p. 16.

Laforgerie, J.-F. (2003) Le Marais est-il en crise?. *Illico* 78:(6 June), p. 30.

Le Bitoux, J. (1997) Marcher dans le gai Marais. *Revue h* 1:(July), p. 47.

Martel, F. (1999) The Pink and the Black: Homosexuals in France since 1968.—Stanford, CA: Stanford University Press

Méreaux, J. (2001) Le "Marais": l'espace homosexuel comme métaphore du groupe: éléments pour une socio-anthropologie d'une culture territorialisée.—Unpublished Mémoire de Diplôme d'Études Approfondies, Université de Paris X-Nanterre

Michel, C. (1988) Les Halles: la renaissance d'un quartier 1966–1988.—Paris: Mason

———. (1997) 'Gays' dans le IVème. 95:(April/May), p. 7.—Paris Centre: Le Journal du IVème

Pitte, J.-R. (1997) L'avenir du Marais. *Cahiers du Centre de Recherches et d'Études sur Paris et l'Ile-de-France* 59, p. 49.

Primo, T. (1998) Bernard Bousset: de la mémoire avant toute chose. *e-m@le magazine* 17:(29 January), p. 18.

Razemon, O. and Galceran, S. (1996a) La bataille du Marais. *Ex Aequo* 2:(December), p. 16.

Razemon, O. and Galceran, S. (1996b) Marais: la guérilla. *Illico* 73:(December), p. 6.

Rémès, E. (1996) Les policiers harcèlent les bars gays du Marais. *Libération* p. 15.—18–19 May

Roussel, Y. (1995) Le mouvement homosexuel français face aux stratégies identitaires. *Les Temps Modernes* 50:(582), p. 85.

Rouy, P. (1990) Bars gais: nuisances policières. *Gai Pied Hebdo* 449/450:(20 December), p. 15.

Sibalis, Michael. "Urban Space and Homosexuality: The Example of the Marais, Paris' 'Gay Ghetto.'" *Urban Studies* 41.9 (2004): 1739–58.

➤ **Patricia Leigh Brown**

"Gay Enclaves Face Prospect of Being Passé"

(30 October 2007), United States

This Halloween, the Glindas, gladiators and harem boys of the Castro—along with untold numbers who plan to dress up as Senator Larry E. Craig, this year's camp celebrity—will be celebrating behind closed doors. The city's most popular Halloween party, in America's largest gay neighborhood, is canceled.

The once-exuberant street party, a symbol of sexual liberation since 1979 has in recent years become a Nightmare on Castro Street, drawing as many as 200,000 people, many of them costumeless outsiders, and there has been talk of moving it outside the district because of increasing violence. Last year, nine people were wounded when a gunman opened fire at the celebration.

For many in the Castro District, the cancellation is a blow that strikes at the heart of neighborhood identity, and it has brought soul-searching that goes beyond concerns about crime.

These are wrenching times for San Francisco's historic gay village, with population shifts, booming development, and a waning sense of belonging that is also being felt in gay enclaves across the nation, from Key West, Fla., to West Hollywood, as they struggle to maintain cultural relevance in the face of gentrification.

There has been a notable shift of gravity from the Castro, with young gay men and lesbians fanning out into less-expensive neighborhoods like Mission Dolores and the Outer Sunset, and farther away to Marin and Alameda Counties, "mirroring national trends where you are seeing same-sex couples becoming less urban, even as the population become slightly more urban," said Gary J. Gates, a demographer and senior research fellow at the University of California, Los Angeles.

At the same time, cities not widely considered gay meccas have seen a sharp increase in same-sex couples. Among them: Fort Worth; El Paso; Albuquerque; Louisville, Ky.; and Virginia Beach, according to census figures and extrapolations by Dr. Gates for The New York Times. "Twenty years ago, if you were gay and lived in rural Kansas, you went to San Francisco or New York," he said. "Now you can just go to Kansas City."

In the Castro, the Gay, Lesbian, Bisexual, Transgender Historical Society held public meetings earlier this year to grapple with such questions as "Are Gay Neighborhoods Worth Saving?"

With nine major developments planned for Market Street, including a splashy 113-unit condominium designed by Arquitectonica, anxiety about the future is swirling. Median home prices hover around $870,000. Local institutions like Cliff's Variety, a hardware store selling feathered boas (year-round) are not about to vanish from this storied homeland of the gay rights movement. But the prospect of half-million-dollar condos inhabited by many straight people underscores a demographic shift.

"The Castro, and to a lesser extent the West Village, was where you went to express yourself," said Don F. Reuter, a New York author who is researching a book on the rise and fall of gay neighborhoods, or "gayborhoods."

"Claiming physical territory was a powerful act," Mr. Reuter said. "But the gay neighborhood is becoming a past-tense idea."

In the Castro, the influx of baby strollers—some being pushed by straight parents, some by gay parents—is perhaps the most blatant sign of change. "The Castro has gone from a gay-ghetto mentality to a family mentality," said Wes Freas, a broker with Zephyr Real Estate. The arrival of a Pottery Barn down the street from the birthplaces of the AIDS quilt and the Rainbow Flag is a nod to change.

Sakura Ferris, a 28-year-old mother of a toddler, moved to the Castro because she liked its new eclecticism. At the Eureka Valley Recreation Center, a parent hot spot rife with Froggie pull-toys, Ms. Ferris's tot mingles with infants in onesies that read, "I Love My Daddies."

The Castro remains a top tourist destination for gay and lesbian visitors. But Joe D'Alessandro, president and C.E.O. of the San Francisco Convention and Visitors' Bureau, and a gay parent who lives in the Castro, predicted that eventually the neighborhood would go the way of North Beach, "still a historic Italian neighborhood though Italians don't necessarily live there anymore."

The Castro became a center for gay liberation in the late 1960s and early 1970s in a declining Irish Catholic and Scandinavian neighborhood. At its helm was Harvey Milk, the first openly gay city supervisor in San Francisco whose slaying in 1978 by a disgruntled former supervisor, Dan White, galvanized the community and set off riots when White was convicted of manslaughter instead of murder.

Decimated during the AIDS epidemic of 1990–1995, the neighborhood rebounded in the boom economy of the late 1990s. But the social forces that gave rise to the Castro and other gay neighborhoods like the West Village and West Hollywood may be becoming passé.

While the state's Eighth Congressional District, which includes the Castro, saw an increase of about 20 percent in the number of same-sex couples from 2002 to 2006, surrounding districts had a 38 percent increase in same-sex couples, according to Dr. Gates.

In West Hollywood, another traditional gay haven, the graying of the population and the high cost of real estate have resulted in once-gay watering holes like the Spike and the I Candy Lounge going hetero. A new kind of gentrification is under way in which young gay waiters and school teachers move instead to Hollywood and other surrounding neighborhoods. "We often clamored for equality where gay and straight could coexist," said Mayor John Duran of West Hollywood, who is gay. "But we weren't prepared to give up our subculture to negotiate that exchange."

While the Castro has been the center of a movement, it is also home to "an important political constituency," said Elizabeth A. Armstrong, an associate sociology professor at Indiana University and the author of "Forging Gay Identities: Organizing Sexuality in San Francisco 1950–1994."

"When people were angry about Dan White they were able to assemble quickly, spilling out of the bars," Professor Armstrong said. "Physical location mattered."

The Castro still has the city's largest progressive Democratic organization, the Harvey Milk Club. A survey of registered voters earlier this year by David Binder, a San Francisco political analyst, found that 33 percent of the Eighth District identified themselves as gay or lesbian, compared with 13 percent citywide.

The Castro's activist legacy continues to exert a strong emotional pull: the corner of 18th and Castro Streets, where Harvey Milk; Diana, Princess of Wales; and Matthew Shepard were mourned and where gay marriage was fleetingly celebrated, is for many a mythic homeland.

Amanda Rankin, a 40-year-old tourist from Hamilton, Ontario, was taking a "Cruisin' the Castro" walking tour with three lesbian friends the other day.

"In America there still seems to be a lot of sexual repression left over from Puritanism and the pilgrims," Ms. Rankin said. "Then there's San Francisco."

But its legacy has not prevented the neighborhood from harsh urban realities. As San Francisco real estate skyrocketed in the 1990s, the Castro had the city's highest concentration of evictions, as speculators "flipped" buildings, many of them housing people with disabilities and AIDS, to convert to market-rate apartments, said Brian Basinger, the founder of the AIDS Housing Alliance.

Even before Halloween, the Castro was grappling with violence and crime. Allegations of racial profiling at the Badlands, the neighborhood's most popular bar, led to a widespread boycott in 2005 and intervention by the city's Human Rights Commission.

The highly publicized rape of a man in the Castro in September 2006 led to the formation of Castro on Patrol, a whistle-wielding citizens' street brigade. In that attack, Mark Welch was raped five blocks from a store he managed on Castro Street. He said that he later learned there had been two previous similar rapes in the neighborhood, but they had not been widely reported.

He said it took months for it to surface on a sex-crimes Web site maintained by the authorities. There are signs that the dispersing of gay people beyond the Castro vortex and the rise of the Internet are also contributing to a declining sense of community. An annual survey by the San Francisco Gay Men's Community Initiative indicated that in 2007 only 36 percent of men under 29 said there was a gay community in the city with which they could identify.

Doug Sebesta, the group's executive director and a medical sociologist at the San Francisco Department of Public Health, said, "I've had therapists who have told me they are asking their clients to go back to bars as a way of social interaction."

The Internet is not a replacement for a neighborhood where people are involved in issues beyond themselves, said John Newsome, an African-American who co-founded the group And Castro For All after the Badlands incident. "There are a lot of really lonely gay people sitting in front of a computer," he said.

Which is why the cancellation of the Halloween party by the city has provoked such a sense of loss. Many residents say that their night has been taken away. "It's proof that whatever sense of safety we have is incredibly tenuous," Mr. Newsome said.

The city is shutting down public transportation to the Castro on Halloween and has begun a Web site, homeforhalloween.com, that lists "fun" alternatives, including a Halloween blood drive and a "Monster Bash"—in San Mateo.

On a recent Saturday, Sister Roma, a member of the Sisters of Perpetual Indulgence, an activist coterie of drag queens, sashayed down Castro Street in heavy eye shadow and a gold lamé top. Though she looked well prepared for Halloween, she said she planned to be in hiding that night.

She wasn't feeling too deprived, however.

"Sweetie," she said, "every day is Halloween in the Castro."

➢ **Alison Bechdel**

"Where's Mo?"

(1998), United States

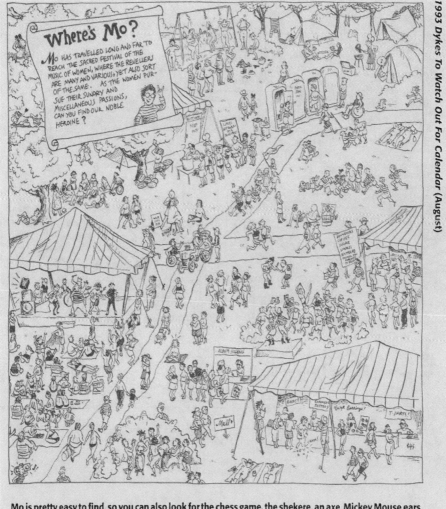

Mo is pretty easy to find, so you can also look for the chess game, the shekere, an axe, Mickey Mouse ears, a bucket, a raccoon, three cowboy hats, seven baseball caps, some alpha waves, and a T-bone steak.

"Where's Mo?" by Alison Bechdel, from *The Indelible Alison Bechdel,* Firebrand Books, Ann Arbor, Michigan. © Alison Bechdel 1998.

"The Game of Alternative Life"

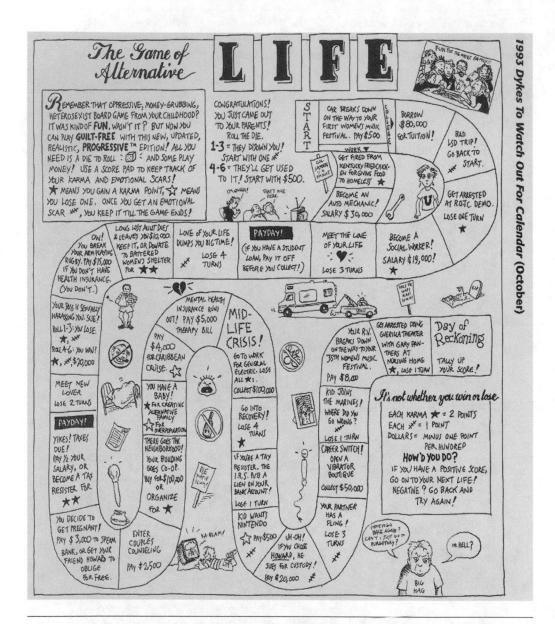

"The Game of Alternative Life," by Alison Bechdel, from *The Indelible Alison Bechdel*, Firebrand Books, Ann Arbor, Michigan. © Alison Bechdel 1998.

"Demographic Rift"

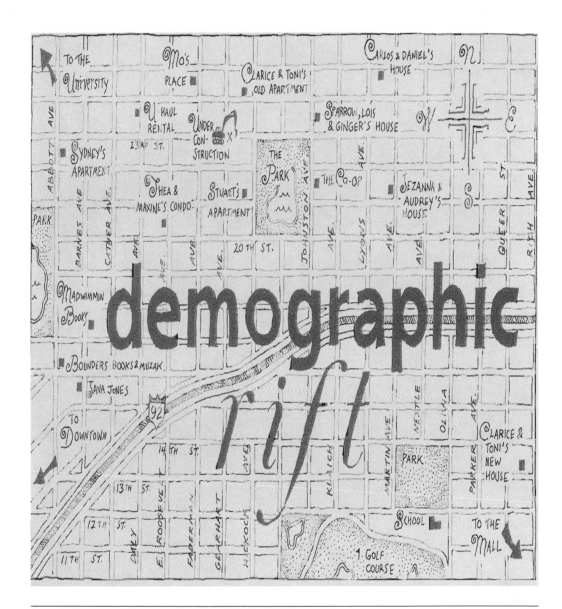

"Demographic Rift," by Alison Bechdel, from *Split-Level Dykes to Watch Out For,* Firebrand Books, Ann Arbor, Michigan. © Alison Bechdel 1998.

Glossary

Aesthete: a person who has an extreme appreciation for art and nature; a so-called fleshly poet.

Asexuality: lacking interest in or desire for sex.

Assimilationist: a lesbian, gay, bisexual, transgender (LGBT) activist who prioritizes civil rights, arguing the similarity of LGBT people to the heterosexual mainstream.

BCE (Before the Common Era): a synonym for BC (Before Christ) used in the fields of archaeology and anthropology.

BDSM: bondage, dominance, sado-masochism (see **Sadomasochist**).

Beat culture: a 1950s counterculture movement, including such writers as Jack Kerouac, Allen Ginsberg, and Diane DiPrima. The term *beat* describes both a sense of being "beaten down" by conservative forces and a desire to "march to the beat of a different drummer."

Belle Époque: French for "Beautiful Era." A period of relative peace and stability in Europe beginning in the late nineteenth century and lasting until World War I. This era saw advances in technology and the first "modern" art.

Bestiality: use of an animal for human sexual gratification.

Bildungsroman: a novel of personal development, describing the protagonist's journey from youth to maturity.

Biological determinism: the theory that a person's behavior is determined by inherited physical characteristics.

Bisexual: a person who is sexually attracted to people of both sexes.

Black Panthers: a progressive political organization formed by Huey Newton in the 1960s to fight for equality of all socially oppressed minorities. The Black Panthers differed from many black civil rights organizations in that they were armed and advocated the overthrow of the U.S. government.

Buggery: anal intercourse.

Butch: a lesbian gender characterized by performing stereotypical masculinity; also refers to gay men.

Congenital: inborn.

Cross-dressing: the wearing of clothing characteristic of a different gender; one who cross-dresses is sometimes referred to as being "in drag."

Culture wars: a term used primarily in the 1980s in the United States to describe the conflict between conservative or traditional views and those considered liberal or progressive.

Decadence: a period of perceived "decay" or decline, specifically within a generation or society; most often used to describe the European 1890s.

Diaspora: ancient Greek for "scattering." Refers to a group expelled from their homeland and scattered throughout the world, specifically Jews and Africans.

Dildo: a penis-shaped object used for sexual stimulation.

Drag king: a woman who dresses as a man and performs masculinity (see also Drag queen).

Drag queen: a man (usually gay) who dresses as a woman and performs femininity (see also Drag king).

Essentialism: a theory that a trait is innate rather than acquired.

Etiology: the study of origins and causes.

Eugenics: the study of how to improve a population through selective breeding.

Eunuch: a castrated male.

Femme: a lesbian gender characterized by performing stereotypical femininity; also refers to gay men.

Fetishism: sexual arousal using inanimate objects.

Fin de siècle: French for "end of the century." A term referring to the last decade of the nineteenth century.

FtM or F2M: a female-to-male transsexual.

Fundamentalism: a religious movement where followers adhere strictly to a literal interpretation of sacred texts.

Gender: learned behaviors and attitudes supposed to correspond with biological sex.

Gender dysphoria: another name for gender identity disorder.

Gender identity disorder (GID): a clinical psychological diagnosis marking a person who is strongly identified with the "other" sex.

Gender inversion: see Inversion.

Hegemony: influence of a dominant and normalized group over other groups.

Heteronormative: characterized by the presumed hegemony of heterosexuality over other forms of sexual expression.

Homophile movement: a movement in the mid-1900s in which gay men and lesbians refused to accept that homosexuality was a sickness. Through groups such as the Mattachine Society and the Daughters of Bilitis, they embraced their homosexuality and worked to gain acceptance from society.

Homophobia: the fear of homosexuals and/or homosexuality.

Hysteria: a vague and ill-defined mental disorder commonly diagnosed in women; its etymological association with the Greek word *hystera* ("womb") led to a tendency among nineteenth-century doctors to associate femaleness with illness.

Intersectionality: a theory that seeks to examine the ways in which socially and culturally constructed categories interact on multiple levels to manifest themselves as inequality in society. Intersectionality holds that the classical models of oppression within society, such as those based on race/ethnicity, gender, religion, nationality, sexual orientation, class, or disability, do not act independently of one another.

Intersex: born with genitalia that cannot be definitively classified as male or female; hermaphrodite.

Inversion: a term used by late nineteenth-century sexologists to describe performance of gender behavior or sexual desire thought to be appropriate only for the "other" sex.

Lilith: mythological demon believed to prey on newborn children. Jewish folklore believes her to be Adam's first wife, who ran away from him because he insisted on dominating her sexually.

Masochism: the derivation of pleasure from pain.

Miscegenation: sexual relations between a white person and a person of a different race.

Misogynist: a person who hates women.

Monogamy: having a single sexual partner during a period of time.

Monolithic: characterized by uniformity and resistance to change.

Monosexuality: identifying as a single (hetero- or homo-) sexuality, as opposed to more fluid constructions (bi-, pan-, etc.).

MtF or M2F: a male-to-female transsexual.

Paroxysm: obsolete term for a female orgasm.

Pederasty: a sexual relationship between an adult man and a boy.

Pedophile: an adult who is sexually attracted to children.

Progressive: favoring reform or change.

Queer: a word once used as a taunt against homosexuals, now reclaimed as an umbrella term to signify the diversity of LGBT identities and to assert the value of difference.

Sadism: the derivation of sexual gratification through the infliction of pain on others.

Sadomasochist: one who derives sexual gratification through inflicting or receiving pain; sadism and masochism combined.

Self-actualization: a psychological term for realizing one's full potential.

Separatism: separation from an established group, especially referring to groups of lesbians who wished to establish all-female communities.

Sexologist: a medical doctor specializing in the study of sexual behavior.

Sexology: the pseudo-scientific study of human sexual behavior and identity.

Sex-positive: embracing sexual openness without ethical distinction among sexual expressions or identities.

Sexual inversion: see Inversion.

Sexual libertarianism: the view that it is not wrong to engage in any noncoercive sexual conduct.

Snuff: pornography that depicts the killing of a human being.

Social constructionism: a theory that assumes that many personal identifications—homosexuality, for instance—develop through interaction with the surrounding environment.

Sodomy: oral or anal sexual intercourse.

Sodomy laws: laws criminalizing nonprocreative sexual acts, especially between members of the same sex.

Splice: to cut and manipulate DNA in order to insert genetic material.

Strategic essentialism: the conscious deployment of essentialism as an argument against discrimination; in terms of queer activism, using the assumption that homosexuality is innate to argue for gay rights.

Teleological: assuming that everything has an inherent purpose and a final cause.

Tommy: late nineteenth-century term for a boyish or passing woman.

Transgender: having a gender identity that does not align with physical sex; a willingness to challenge dominant gender norms in one's behavior or presentation.

Transman: a person who was born female but who identifies as male.

Transsexual: having a gender identity that does not align with physical sex; changing one's self-presentation or one's body in order to arrive at a more satisfactory gender expression.

Transvestite: an obsolete term for a cross-dresser; a person who derives erotic gratification from dressing in clothing presumed by the dominant culture to be that of the opposite sex.

Urnings: a term invented by Karl Heinrich Ulrichs to describe a third sex comprising homosexuals, whom he theorized displayed visible physical differences from heterosexuals.

Zap: a quick and unexpected direct action, designed to cause disruption or discomfort to make a political point.

Credits

Chapter 1

Figure 1.1 page 11 Illustration © Greg Reeder, 2008.

Figure 1.2 page 14 Artist unknown, seventeenth century, Reza Abbasi Museum.

Figure 1.3 page 15 Appeared in *The Zuñi Man-Woman*. Albuquerque: U of NMP, 1991.

Figure 1.4 page 17 Originally from the Monastery of St. Catherine on Mt. Sinai, now in Kiev Museum of Eastern and Western Art.

Figure 1.5 page 20 Lithograph by James Henry Lynch after Lady Leighton, 1887. (National Portrait Gallery, London)

Chapter 2

Figure 2.2 page 49 © Evening Standard/Hulton Archive/Getty.

Chapter 3

Figure 3.1 page 68 © Time, Inc.—*Time* Magazine, "Homosexual in America", 31 October 1969.

Figure 3.2 page 71 from Sachsenhausen Memorial Site, by Gen Baugher.

Chapter 4

Figure 4.1 page 91 © Bettmann/Corbis.

Figure 4.2 page 92 © Bettmann/Corbis.

Figure 4.3 page 92 © Bettmann/Corbis.

Figure 4.5 page 97 © Jeffrey Markowitz/ Sygma/Corbis.

Figure 4.6 page 101 © epa/Corbis.

Chapter 5

Figure 5.1 page 122 © The New Yorker Collection 1948 Peter Arno from cartoonbank.com. All rights reserved.

Figure 5.2 page 123 From Kinsey, Alfred C., Wardell B. Pomeroy, and Clyde E. Martin. *Sexual Behavior in the Human Male.* Philadelphia: W. B. Saunders, 1948.

Figure 5.3 page 124 © Michelle Gibson.

Chapter 6

Figure 6.1 page 156 © Mark Mainz/Getty.

Figure 6.2 page 156 U.S. Army/Associated Press.

Chapter 7

Figure 7.1 page 175 © Michelle Gibson.

Figure 7.2 page 176 © Michelle Gibson.

Chapter 8

Figure 8.1 page 205 © Bryan Bedder/Getty.

Figure 8.2 page 207 © Amy Sussman/Getty.

Figure 8.3 page 210 From Gibson, M., M. Marinara, and D. Meem. "Bi, Butch, and Bar Dyke: Pedagogical Performances of Class, Gender, and

Sexuality." *College Composition and Communication* 52.1 (2000): 69–95.

Figure 8.4 page 211 From Rubin, G. "Thinking Sex: Notes for a Radical Politics of the Politics of Sexuality." *The Lesbian and Gay Studies Reader.* Eds. H. Abelove, M. Barale, and D. Halperin. New York: Routledge, 1993.

Chapter 9

Figure 9.2 page 234 Amon Carter Museum, Fort Worth, Texas. Purchased by Friends of the Art, Fort Worth Art Association, 1925; acquired by the Amon Carter Museum, 1990, from the Modern Art Museum of Fort Worth through grants and donations from the Amon G. Carter Foundation, the Sid W. Richardson Foundation, the Anne Burnett and Charles Tandy Foundation, Capital Cities/ABC Foundation, Fort Worth Star-Telegram, The R. D. and Joan Dale Hubbard Foundation, and the people of Fort Worth.

Figure 9.3 page 235 1960 Oil on board 50 × 40, © David Hockney.

Figure 9.5 page 238 © 2008 Artists Rights Society (ARS), New York/ADAGP, Paris.

Figure 9.9 page 242 © Linda J. Russell.

Figure 9.11 page 245 Courtesy of Jersey Heritage Collections.

Chapter 10

Figure 10.1 page 270 © Time & Life Pictures/Getty.

Figure 10.2 page 271 © Bettmann/Corbis.

Figure 10.3 page 272 By Teresa Torres, copyright by Random House, Inc. Used by permission of Fawcett Books, a division of Random House, Inc.

Figure 10.5 page 276 By Vin Packer, copyright by Random House, Inc. Used by permission of Fawcett Books, a division of Random House, Inc.

Figure 10.6 page 277 Photo portrait of Ann Bannon by Tee Corinne.

Figure 10.7 page 277 © Sophie Bassouls/Sygma/Corbis.

Figure 10.8 page 278 Cover image by Marvin J. Taylor.

Figure 10.9 page 299 Photo: Harold Halma.

Figure 10.10 page 299 © Sophie Bassouls/Corbis Sygma.

Chapter 12

Figure 12.2 page 311 © Corbis.

Figure 12.3 page 313 © Hulton-Deutsch Collection/Corbis.

Figure 12.5 page 320 © Mike Cassese/Reuters/Corbis.

Chapter 13

Figure 13.1 page 346 © John Springer Collection/Corbis.

Figure 13.3 page 350 © Martial Trezzini/EPA/Corbis.

Figure 13.4 page 354 © Axel Koester/Corbis.

Figure 13.5 page 355 © Brad Barket/Getty.

Chapter 14

Figure 14.1a page 379 © Jodi Buren/Time & Life Pictures/Getty.
Figure 14.1b page 380 © Walter Weissman/Corbis.

Chapter 15

Figure 15.1 page 402 Image courtesy of Vixen Films.

Figure 15.2 page 403 By Dorothy Smith.

Figure 15.3 page 405 Designed by Cynthia Clabough.

Figure 15.5 page 410 By Roz Warren. Cleis, 1995, p. 59.

Figure 15.6 page 411 © Michelle Gibson.

Index

About the Authors

Deborah T. Meem is Professor and Interim Head of Women's Studies at the University of Cincinnati. Her academic specialties are Victorian literature, lesbian studies, and the nineteenth-century woman's novel. She earned a Ph.D. from Stony Brook University in 1985. Her work has appeared in *Journal of the History of Sexuality*, *Feminist Teacher*, *Studies in Popular Culture*, and elsewhere. Her edition of Eliza Lynn Linton's 1880 novel *The Rebel of the Family* was published in 2002 by Broadview Press, and she will edit Linton's 1851 novel *Realities* for Valancourt Press (2009). With Michelle Gibson, she has coedited *Femme/Butch: New Considerations of the Way We Want to Go* (2002) and *Lesbian Academic Couples* (2005), both published by Haworth Press. With Jonathan Alexander, she wrote "Dorian Gray, Tom Ripley, and the Queer Closet" for CLCWeb in 2003.

Michelle A. Gibson is the Director of Undergraduate Studies in the Department of Women's Studies at the University of Cincinnati. She received her Ph.D. in 1993 from Ohio University, where her areas of study were American literature, composition research and pedagogy, and creative writing. Her scholarship has continued in all three of these areas. Her most recent writing applies queer and postmodern identity theories to pedagogical practice and popular culture. She also continues to write and publish poetry. With Jonathan Alexander, she edited *QP: Queer Poetry*, an online poetry journal, and she and Alexander also edited a strain of *JAC: Journal of Advanced Composition* titled "Queer Composition(s)." With Deborah Meem, she coedited *Femme/Butch: New Considerations of the Way We Want to Go* and *Lesbian Academic Couples*.

Jonathan F. Alexander is Associate Professor of English and Campus Writing Coordinator at the University of California, Irvine. His work focuses primarily on the use of emerging communications technologies in the teaching of writing and in shifting conceptions of what writing, composing, and authoring mean. He also works at the intersection of the fields of writing studies and sexuality studies, where he explores what discursive theories of sexuality have to teach us about literacy and literate practice in pluralistic democracies. He is twice the recipient of the Ellen Nold Award for Best Articles in the field of computers and composition studies. His books include *Literacy, Sexuality, Pedagogy: Theory and Practice for Composition Studies* and *Digital Youth: Emerging Literacies on the World Wide Web;* the coedited collections *Bisexuality and Transgenderism: InterSEXions of the Others* and *Role Play: Distance Learning and the Teaching of Writing;* and the coauthored book *Argument Now: A Brief Rhetoric.* He is also the general editor for the *Journal of Bisexuality.*